T0398217

The Italian Yearbook of International Law

The Italian Yearbook of International Law

VOLUME 25

The titles published in this series are listed at *brill.com/iyil*

The Italian Yearbook of International Law
Volume XXV (2015)

BRILL

NIJHOFF

LEIDEN | BOSTON

Typeface for the Latin, Greek, and Cyrillic scripts: "Brill". See and download: brill.com/brill-typeface.

ISSN 0391-5107
E-ISSN 2211-6133
ISBN 978-90-04-33850-0 (hardback)

BOARD OF EDITORS

Editorial assistance for this volume has been provided by Anna Riddell. Manuscripts, books for review and correspondence may be sent to THE ITALIAN YEARBOOK OF INTERNATIONAL LAW - Prof. Riccardo Pavoni, Department of Law, University of Siena, Via Mattioli 10, 53100 Siena (Italy) and/or by e-mail pavoni@unisi.it.

Each article submitted with a view to publication in the IYIL is subject to peer-review by two anonymous referees.

CONTENTS

NOTES AND COMMENTS

PRACTICE OF INTERNATIONAL COURTS AND TRIBUNALS

ITALIAN PRACTICE RELATING TO INTERNATIONAL LAW

JUDICIAL DECISIONS
(edited by *Daniele Amoroso* and *Andrea Caligiuri*)

DIPLOMATIC AND PARLIAMENTARY PRACTICE
(edited by *Pietro Gargiulo* and *Marco Pertile*)

AGREEMENTS TO WHICH ITALY IS A PARTY AND AGREEMENTS AND UNDERSTANDINGS TO WHICH ITALIAN REGIONS AND AUTONOMOUS PROVINCES ARE PARTIES
(edited by *Chiara Altafin* and *Marina Mancini*)

I
AGREEMENTS TO WHICH ITALY IS A PARTY

A) AGREEMENTS SIGNED BY ITALY, PUBLISHED IN THE *GAZZETTA UFFICIALE* IN 2015

II
AGREEMENTS AND UNDERSTANDINGS TO WHICH ITALIAN REGIONS AND AUTONOMOUS PROVINCES ARE PARTIES

A)   AGREEMENTS SIGNED BY ITALIAN REGIONS AND AUTONOMOUS
    PROVINCES IN 2015

B)   UNDERSTANDINGS   SIGNED   BY   ITALIAN   REGIONS   AND
    AUTONOMOUS PROVINCES IN 2015

BIBLIOGRAPHIES

MARC WELLER (ed.), *The Oxford Handbook of the Use of Force in International Law*, Oxford, Oxford University Press, 2015 *(Natalino Ronzitti)*; ROBERTO VIRZO and IVAN INGRAVALLO (eds.), *Evolutions in the Law of International Organizations*, Leiden/Boston, Brill Nijhoff, 2015 *(Giulio Bartolini)*; ANDREA DE GUTTRY, FRANCESCA CAPONE and CHRISTOPHE PAULUSSEN (eds.), *Foreign Fighters under International Law and Beyond*, The Hague, Asser Press/Springer, 2016 *(Loris Marotti)*; SAVERIO DI BENEDETTO, *International Investment Law and the Environment*, Cheltenham/Northampton, Edward Elgar, 2013 *(Giovanni Zarra)*.

LIST OF ABBREVIATIONS

Periodicals[*]

AFDI	Annuaire Français de Droit International
AJIL	American Journal of International Law
ASIL	American Society of International Law Proceedings
AVR	Archiv des Völkerrecht
BISD	GATT – Basic Instruments and Selected Documents
BYIL	British Yearbook of International Law
CI	La Comunità Internazionale
CML Rep.	Common Market Law Reports
CML Rev.	Common Market Law Review
Columbia JTL	Columbia Journal of Transnational Law
Cornell ILJ	Cornell International Law Journal
CS	Comunicazioni e Studi
CYIL	Canadian Yearbook of International Law
DCI	Diritto del Commercio Internazionale
DCSI	Diritto Comunitario e degli Scambi Internazionali
DPCE	Diritto Pubblico Comparato ed Europeo
DUDI	Diritti Umani e Diritto Internazionale
DUE	Il Diritto dell'Unione Europea
EC Bull.	Bulletin of the European Communities
ECLR	European Competition Law Review
ECR	European Court Reports
EdD	Enciclopedia del Diritto
EG	Enciclopedia Giuridica (Treccani)
EHRR	European Human Rights Reports
EJIL	European Journal of International Law
EL Rev.	European Law Review
ETS	European Treaty Series
Foro It.	Foro Italiano
Giur. Cost.	Giurisprudenza Costituzionale
Giur. It.	Giurisprudenza Italiana
GU	Gazzetta Ufficiale della Repubblica Italiana
GYIL	German Yearbook of International Law

[*] The present list covers only the most frequently cited periodicals.

Harvard ILJ	Harvard International Law Journal
HRLJ	Human Rights Law Journal
ICJ Pleadings	International Court of Justice, Pleadings, Oral Arguments, Documents
ICJ Reports	International Court of Justice, Reports of Judgments, Advisory Opinions and Orders
ICLQ	International and Comparative Law Quarterly
IJCP	International Journal of Cultural Property
ILDC	International Law in Domestic Courts
ILM	International Legal Materials
ILR	International Law Reports
Int. Lawyer	International Lawyer
Int. Org.	International Organization
IRRC	International Review of the Red Cross
IYIL	Italian Yearbook of International Law
JDI	Journal du Droit International
JICJ	Journal of International Criminal Justice
JIEL	Journal of International Economic Law
JWT	Journal of World Trade
Leiden JIL	Leiden Journal of International Law
Max Planck UNYB	Max Planck Yearbook of United Nations Law
NILR	Netherlands International Law Review
NYIL	Netherlands Yearbook of International Law
OIDU	Ordine Internazionale e Diritti Umani
OJ EC	Official Journal of the European Communities
OJ EU	Official Journal of the European Union
PCIJ Series	Permanent Court of International Justice, Series
QIL	Questions of International Law
RBDI	Revue Belge de Droit International
RCADI	Recueil des Cours de l'Académie de Droit International de La Haye/Collected Courses of the Hague Academy of International Law
RCGI	Rivista della Cooperazione Giuridica Internazionale
RDI	Rivista di Diritto Internazionale
RDIPP	Rivista di Diritto Internazionale Privato e Processuale
RECIEL	Review of European Community and International Environmental Law
RGA	Rivista Giuridica dell'Ambiente
RGDIP	Revue Générale de Droit International Public
RIDPC	Rivista Italiana di Diritto Pubblico Comunitario
RMUE	Revue du Marché Unique Européen
RTDH	Revue Trimestrielle des Droits de l'Homme

Schw. ZIER	Schweizerische Zeitschrift für Internationales und Europäisches Recht
Texas ILJ	Texas International Law Journal
UNTS	United Nations Treaty Series
Yale JIL	Yale Journal of International Law
YEL	Yearbook of European Law
YIEL	Yearbook of International Environmental Law
YIHL	Yearbook of International Humanitarian Law
YILC/ACDI	Yearbook of the International Law Commission/ Annuaire de la Commission du droit international
ZAÖRV	Zeitschrift für Ausländisches Öffentliches Recht und Völkerrecht

Italian legal acts

Law	Legge (Act of Parliament)
DL	Decreto Legge (Decree-Law) (Decree adopted by the Government in case of extreme urgency which has the same, albeit provisional, effect of a Law, and which must be approved by the Parliament within 60 days. On the contrary, it looses its legal effect)
D.Lgs.	Decreto Legislativo (Legislative Decree) (Decree adopted by the Government upon delegation by the Parliament)
DPR	Decreto del Presidente della Repubblica (Decree of the President of the Republic)
DPCM	Decreto Presidente del Consiglio dei Ministri (Decree of the President of the Council of Ministers or Prime Minister)
DM	Decreto Ministeriale (Ministerial Decree)
Reg.	Regolamento (Administrative Regulation)

ITALIAN COURTS

Tribunale	Court of First Instance
Corte d'Appello	Court of Appeals
Corte di Cassazione	Court of Cassation
TAR	Regional Administrative Tribunal
Consiglio di Stato	Council of State (Supreme Administrative Court)
Corte Costituzionale	Constitutional Court

FOREWORD: ON MY WAY OUT

With this Volume I am leaving the job as General Editor of the Italian Yearbook of International Law. After more than sixteen years – yes, incredibly enough so much time has passed since I took up this responsibility in 1999 – this decision was over-due. The responsibility of co-ordinating the production and publication of the Yearbook is now falling into the able hands of Massimo Iovane, professor of international law at the University of Naples "Federico II" and already a member of the Editorial Committee of the Yearbook. This transition coincides also with the decision to refresh and expand the Board of Editors with the entry of new members, who represent a younger and vibrant generation of international lawyers (Giuseppe Cataldi, Marco Gestri, Giuseppe Nesi, and Riccardo Pavoni), and with the co-optation of two distinguished foreign colleagues: Pierre-Marie Dupuy and Nigel White. To all of them, and especially to Massimo in his new role as General Editor, go all my good wishes and personal support for a successful continuation of the Italian Yearbook.

Sadly, this moment of transition and renewal coincides with the loss of the two senior members of the Board: Professor Benedetto Conforti and Professor Luigi Ferrari Bravo, who both died at the beginning of 2016, at a distance of just a few weeks from each other. We all owe them a great debt of gratitude: not only because they had the vision of founding the Italian Yearbook in 1975, at a time in which international law scholarship was still rigidly cast into national languages; but also because they organized around this editorial project a diversified group of scholars of different generations and different cultural extraction united by the personal affection they poured on all of us. They are going to be sorely missed by the international law community. In this volume they are remembered by Massimo Iovane and Giorgio Sacerdoti.

FRANCESCO FRANCIONI

IN MEMORIAM

BENEDETTO CONFORTI

MASSIMO IOVANE[*]

1. It is a sad coincidence that my taking up the editorship of the *Italian Yearbook of International Law* coincides with the death of Benedetto Conforti, my mentor and one of the founders of the *Yearbook*. Professor Conforti died in Naples on 17 January 2016 and his loss leaves a great void in the international law community both at home and abroad. This is an irreparable loss for one who, like me, has had the privilege of sharing with him almost 40 years of experience as a student and the honour of inheriting his chair at the Law Department of the University of Naples "Federico II". So it is difficult for me to try to outline the life and work of Benedetto Conforti other than through the personal memories of this long acquaintance. My sense of loss is still too strong to allow me to concentrate fully and set out in every detail his extensive contribution to the evolution and systematisation of our discipline. This aspect will be analysed in depth at a special conference to be held at the Law Department where he taught international law for many years and concluded his career; and where above all he conceived and produced his famous textbook on international law, now translated into several languages. On this occasion, then, I would simply like to recall some significant moments from his life as a scholar and mentor to a great many pupils. Of course, I would also like to mention his role as co-founder and co-editor of the *Italian Yearbook* since the very first volume.

I met Professor Conforti – as I have always called him despite his frequent reminders that colleagues should be on first name terms – at the time when he was working on the 2nd edition of his textbook, which was in the process of becoming "Lectures"[1] rather than "Notions of International Law".[2] This was a very intensive and creative period for him, mostly spent in his office at the Naples Institute of International Law; a very thorough and methodical research among piles of books and journals filling his desk, a silent and hand-written operation, to then be typed up and sometimes sent directly to the publisher. Even then, the unmistakable features of this fundamental text began to take shape, namely the two interdependent aspects which would remain unchanged throughout the various later editions, namely the "model" chosen for the structure of the textbook and the "constant attention to describing international law from the point of view of its application within the State",[3] as he himself emphasised in the preface to the first edition. These two features would become a common thread making it possible to understand, from a

---

[*] Of the Board of Editors.
[1] CONFORTI, *Lezioni di diritto internazionale*, 2nd ed., Napoli, 1982.
[2] CONFORTI, *Appunti dalle lezioni di diritto internazionale*, 1st ed., Napoli, 1976.
[3] *Ibid.*, Preface (author's translation).

broader perspective, also the nature of his interests and the methodology he used throughout his vast scientific output.

First of all *the choice of model*, strictly connected to his conviction about the specific object of legal studies, namely identifying the exact rights and obligations of subjects. Unlike some modern trends, especially in non-Italian scholarship, Conforti constantly adhered to the notion of international law as a legal order with its own system of sources and guarantees in which the three distinct functions of law-making, law-ascertainment, and law-enforcement are clearly recognisable. Consequently, he always took a dim view of what he called "inconclusive studies" confusing legal analysis and political relations or those drifting towards ethical, philosophical, or sociological concepts. Even in the realm of public law, then, the task of a legal scholar should first and foremost be to organise the practice within well-defined legal categories, as well as establishing mutual logical relationships between the various parts of the legal order. The other branches of social sciences can only be auxiliary means to the interpretation of existing norms, especially useful in justifying normative and judicial innovations.

This passion for organisation is widely rendered in his inimitable clear and concise style thanks to which he was able to navigate among various opinions with his unique and acute legal insight, dismissing doctrinal diatribes and excessive quotations from the practice to focus on what he called "actual legal issue", namely what "States must effectively do and not do". And in relation to this "actual legal issue" he could always find a reasonable solution without forcing the practice, in a way that was realistically consistent with the limits of an order formally regulating relationships among sovereign States. Such solutions would appear so convincing that they seem to have always been there just waiting to be discovered. This is true of his monographs, articles and numerous commentaries that he produced to the very end, both in this *Yearbook* and other journals, in order to provide an insight, take a position regarding a controversy, or review previously expressed opinions.

This method and style of writing, when applied to his textbook of international law in particular, have greatly eased the study and understanding of international law by students who would become legal practitioners struggling with the application of international norms to concrete cases. This way of presenting the subject shows the essential similarity between problems of interpretation and textual analysis in *international* law and those already familiar to students from their studies of the different branches of *domestic* law. What is more, Conforti's entire oeuvre, and above all his textbook, are not only a model for understanding practice and presenting the results of scholarly research, but also a wealth of ideas to be developed, and original lines of thinking to reflect on.

2. This clarity and discipline not only concern the method of setting out the different functions of international law systematically, but also the criteria to illustrate the *content* of international rules. Specifically, he identifies a number of

substantive obligations all technically considered to be restrictions on a State's power of government, whose unhindered exercise within certain areas or over certain subjects traditionally represents the first and foremost legal interest protected by the entire international law system. I am of the opinion that this "guiding idea" has remained unaltered throughout the different editions of his textbook, although it has recently been defined as the idea whereby "the content of international law is made up of a set of restrictions on the domestic and international use of force by States".[4] By "the use of internal force" Conforti refers not only to coercive power over individuals, natural or legal persons, and their property, in a given State and wherever the latter exercises its power of government, but also mere law-making and judicial acts whenever "they are subject to enforcement".[5] Thus one may realize that international law seeks to condition the working of the organs of the State *both negatively*, by forcing them to abstain from certain acts, *and positively*, by requiring the concrete performance of acts necessary to enforce international obligations. Indeed, in the second part of his textbook he groups around this very idea, on the one hand, the traditional international obligations to abstain from exercising sovereign power (as is manifest, for example, in the area of jurisdictional immunities), and, on the other, obligations in the fields of human rights and the environment, which require positive intervention through legislation and judicial acts. This approach to systematising the content of international law also proved to be an excellent teaching instrument able to facilitate the study of our subject, as well as providing a solid framework for scholars and practitioners looking to understand where a new case fits into the system.

Those who really knew Professor Conforti may well confirm that this essential, immediate and penetrating approach went hand in hand with some aspects of his character. He knew just how to listen, to grasp the essence of a debate, and respond in an apposite and succinct manner. And this is how he was in both his personal and professional life. However, his simplicity, this reflective and measured nature should not be mistaken for coldness or excessive rigidity. I have always understood it as a sign of respect for his interlocutors and of intellectual honesty for his colleagues. In the same way, he always adopted a gentle tone in scientific debate, acknowledging the ideas of others, open to criticism and ready to change his mind regarding his opinions if he found the counterarguments convincing. If I may take a moral personal angle, I think he actually showed a sentimental side to his character, being a true Neapolitan, having built up a close-knit community that not only included his close family, but also longstanding and sincere friends and colleagues, not to mention his pupils and his pupils' pupils, whose works he would gladly supervise being curious about the new ways of looking at problems and solutions by younger generations.

---

[4] CONFORTI, *Diritto internazionale*, 10th ed., Napoli, 2015, p. 197 (author's translation).
[5] *Ibid.*, p. 200 (author's translation).

3. The second distinguishing feature of his work is, as mentioned, "*the constant wish to describe international law focusing on its application within the State*".[6] Compared with previous and contemporary Italian and international studies, this methodology was certainly something new. I once asked Professor Conforti what led him to centre his lectures and his textbook on this particular aspect. He explained that it all began with an argument with some colleagues from the University of Padua where he had been lecturing before returning to Naples. They considered international law to be a "cultural subject" like history or philosophy. However, a description of our subject seen from the point of view of its concrete application by domestic courts and its integration into domestic legal systems showed how international law could effectively influence the expectations of individuals and their demand for justice.

We must bear in mind that the problems that were prioritised in Italy up to then were completely different. The main interest of Italian academics had been pre-eminently theoretical. For example, they fiercely debated whether international law was binding because of some higher and hypothetical norm or the subjection of individual States to the power of the international community as a collective entity. Another general and heatedly argued topic was that of the international personality of the individual, and the inter-individual or interstate nature of the international community, not to mention the mutual accusations of falling into natural law, seen to be the lowest degeneration of legal studies. It should be noted that, most of the time, these works did not deal with the actual content of international norms, nor did they refer to State practice or to the existence of concrete disputes to which the practitioner would never have found a solution among the answers supplied by these theoreticians. Thus it comes as no surprise that scholars from other legal disciplines considered international law as a "cultural subject area". This was the climate to which Conforti's methodology brought a breath of fresh air in international law studies and a return to empirical analysis primarily based on the interpretation of the actual behaviour of States.

The "domestic" approach was farsighted, especially given the later developments of substantive international law, as a legal order increasingly focused on the protection of the interests of individuals. In particular, the increase in international conventions on the protection of human rights and the environment in turn determined an increase in claims brought before domestic courts in order to defend or strengthen individuals' rights. From this point of view, the clarification of the method of application of international law in domestic law, the hierarchy of international norms and their specificity within domestic legal orders, the resolution of conflicts between domestic and international norms on the balance between the principle of international co-operation and respect for the constitutional principles of the given legal order, has been of great importance to domestic courts since then. The same

---

[6] CONFORTI, *cit. supra* note 2, Preface (author's translation).

may be said of similar issues such as non self-executing treaties, the nullity of treaties concluded without parliamentary authorisation and therefore in violation of constitutional norms on the limitation of the powers of the Executive. The solution given to those concrete problems with the customary rational concision of both arguments and counterarguments was of enormous help to Italian courts. Indeed, over the years they have often called upon Conforti's theories as presented in his various articles and commentaries, but especially in his textbook of international law. We could mention in this regard the recent confirmation in the practice of his perennial idea that customary international norms should not be applied when in conflict with the liberal founding principles of a Constitution on the basis of the so-called theory of counter-limits. In its Judgment No. 238 of 22 October 2014, the Italian Constitutional Court found that the international customary norm on immunity of foreign States from civil jurisdiction may not be invoked in the Italian legal order if the responsible foreign State does not compensate Italians citizens who have been victims of war crimes and crimes against humanity.

4. In line with this way of thinking, Conforti never entered into doctrinal controversies, nor did he take a position on the monist/dualist question, simply stating that "whichever position you take makes no difference to the substance of the matter".[7] As for realists versus formalists, he used to repeat in our private conversations that it was better to concentrate on interpreting practice, because anyway the dividing line in public law between the concrete reality of facts and the authority of norms is always evanescent. Nor did he take a stance on the side of positivists and natural lawyers, although clearly for him the jurist's task should merely, as I have already mentioned, be that of discerning and interpreting norms arising from previously established and regulated law-making processes. Concerning international law, these processes are governed by the two sources *pacta sunt servanda* and *consuetudo est servanda*. The question concerning the international personality of the individual had long been "a purely theoretical controversy",[8] and he only changed his mind in recent years (only half-heartedly in my view), recognising private individuals as subjects of international law. Even in our informal discussions, he always avoided these subjects. Perhaps this was due to two contrasting influences in his formative years: one with formalist scholar Gaetano Morelli, who focused more on the relationship between categories of norms than their content, and then the later influence of Rolando Quadri's realist approach, centred mainly on the normative authority of effectiveness.

Taking his output as a whole, it serves no purpose today to establish whether he could be considered a supporter of one side or the other. One should however

---

[7] CONFORTI, *cit. supra* note 4, p. 336 (author's translation).
[8] *Ibid.*, p. 25 (author's translation).

underline how Conforti was far from insensitive to the ethical values and liberal ideas which often underlie some of these schools of thought on the nature of international law and public law. In this perspective, I feel we can appreciate even more Benedetto Conforti's contribution to the systematisation of our discipline, as well as showing all of us who loved and admired him how much his personality shone through in his writings.

Scholars who attempt to describe the way a legal order works as a whole, with its system of sources and enforcement procedures inevitably find themselves in a material world of values, power relations and competing forces. Writing and updating his highly successful textbook, Benedetto Conforti was of course fully aware of all this. He was a profoundly democratic man, with great respect for human dignity, imbued with Enlightenment values, caring strongly about social inequality and a stalwart supporter of the principles of the rule of law. An attentive reading reveals that he brought all of this to his interpretation of relevant practice and the review of some traditional concepts to a remarkable degree.

In keeping with his pragmatic mindset, Conforti believed, however, that in order to understand problems, criticise certain States' behaviour, and offer solutions in line with these principles, an international law scholar does not have to exclusively follow any one theoretical approach. What really mattered for him was to make the already existing norms, organs and interpretative devices function effectively.

Thus, there is no need to align oneself with natural lawyers and accept all their non-positivistic premises to endow international law with the function of defending certain values common to all humanity. For him, it is enough to interpret in this sense the general principles of law recognised by civilised nations as acknowledged by Article 38 of the Statute of the International Court of Justice. Furthermore, to explain the existence of a hierarchy of international norms, there is no need to artificially extend certain concepts such as Constitution and Constitutionalism to a community of sovereign States, as these are only suited to an inter-individual legal order. In reality, Article 103 of the United Nations Charter already provides for the priority of the norms promoting respect for fundamental values as set out in some of its provisions. Still further, in order to affirm international respect for the rule of law, it is not necessary to straightjacket the entire international law system within a formal hierarchy of norms, when it is sufficient to apply the normal instruments of supervision over international organs or unlawful acts of States. Lastly, Conforti reminds us that we are not bound to prove, as the most intransigent monists do, that individuals are international subjects in order to promote human dignity. Indeed, what is important is to effectively apply the norms on the protection of human rights established today by numerous international conventions.

In the same way, Conforti holds that is not acceptable to base the effectiveness of international law on positions of extreme legal realism, tantamount to equating the authority of international law with that of a group of States empowered to impose specific legal solutions. As a liberal, he moves away from the theory of "principles" developed by his mentor Rolando Quadri, who believed in a category of unwritten norms distinct from customary law in so far as they are the expression of the "direct and immediate will" of the prevailing social forces at work in the international community. Conforti rejects the notion that to discern the existence of a general international norm it is necessary to enquire what is the will of the "great powers" on a given matter. Although Quadri's notion of "prevailing social forces" is perhaps wider than that of "great powers", Conforti continues to democratically uphold the traditional concept of customary law to which the vast majority of States, as well as the various actors of the international community at a given moment in history, contribute.

Perhaps it is precisely this substantial respect for ethical values and his liberal vision of a society based on Enlightenment principles that is the key to understanding one of his much-debated articles.[9] The subject was the use of armed force in international law, which he presented in his last lecture at the University of Naples "Federico II". I distinctly recall that day, when the Professor addressed an audience consisting of relatives, pupils, friends, and colleagues. With a certain understated emotion, masked by the odd joke at his own expense, he stated that by now it is necessary for us all to acknowledge that international law has failed to rein in the *jus ad bellum* despite the enormous progress achieved by international cooperation in other fields such as commerce, human rights, and the law of the sea. Indeed, the existing conventional and customary norms, the United Nations, and regional regimes of collective security in force since the end of the Second World War have not been able to effectively halt the tendency of States to make use of armed force beyond the limits formally established by international law. If this is the current scenario, all the attempts by scholars to justify the recurrent violations of the prohibition of the use of force, creating new exceptions admitted by international law (preventive and subsequent self-defence, humanitarian intervention and so forth) serve little purpose. These new forms of legitimate violence ultimately make vain the norm on the prohibition of the use of force. Above all, these exceptions make a mockery of peace as a value, seen as the universal ethical principle behind the new international order envisaged in the aftermath of the Second World War and codified in the UN Charter. It is against this background that, in my opinion, Conforti wished to restore the natural law notion of the *bellum justum*, as a way to save at least the ethical identity of peace, if not its strict legal nature. From this perspective, the right to wage war would be limited by the respect on the part of States for a series of moral precepts stemming from a sort of universal conscience in the same way as mediaeval jurists and philosophers thought that the right of the sovereign to wage war was only limited by a concept of just war conceived in moral terms.

---

[9] CONFORTI, "The Doctrine of 'Just War' and Contemporary International Law", IYIL, 2002, p. 3 ff.

5. I believe that each of his pupils has formed a different tie with Conforti as mentor, depending on his or her own personality, and the time in the Professor's life and career when the relationship began. It cannot be denied that it was no easy task to gain, and keep, his esteem; he was a man of few words, with his own particular way of showing affection consisting in giving us his trust and support whenever necessary and constructive criticism of the work that we submitted to his judgment. He communicated above all through his sharp and expressive eyes. He loved us all enormously, but he showed it through the refinement of his sentiment, with natural discretion, always fearful of being intrusive, and respecting the individuality of each of us. He took pains to underline our true qualities, avoiding mere formality.

As for me, when discussing my work, he was always able to provide useful and insightful observations. He could get to the heart of the guiding idea, pruning the text of superfluous additions or repetitions, sometimes reordering chapters or sections so that the reader could better follow a line of thought without interruption. But if there was no originality, or the guiding idea was weak, he would say so and I would have to look again at my sources and rethink the outline, thus instilling a sense of self-criticism which has never left me.

I always understood that he had a deep knowledge of human nature and its weaknesses. It was pointless to hide things from him, and our human relationship, not only as pupil and mentor, was founded on this sincerity. His attitude to human weakness was always understanding and never censorious. I never heard him judge anyone for the way they lived their lives, and he always looked for the best in people. "You have to take people as a whole", was something I heard him say on many occasions. He always focused his humour on himself, never on others, often resorting to irony to put into perspective his personal problems as a way of finding hope after some personal or professional disappointment, as well as his health issues. He was always prepared to defend the scientific quality of his colleagues, even those whom he did not particularly esteem on the human level. This balance and wisdom in controlling his feelings with detachment and common sense were among his most characteristic traits, elevating him as a man, and earning him the devotion of those who knew him better.

6. I would like to complete this personal outline of Professor Conforti by recalling his fundamental role in setting up the *Italian Yearbook* in the 1970s and its renewal in the 1990s as a means of making Italian practice and scholarship known abroad. It is clear that Italy has never been peripheral in the field of international law studies. Italian international lawyers have widely contributed to the systematisation and development of the discipline, and the same holds true for Italian judicial practice. But the language barrier had become an insurmountable obstacle to making this contribution known by the growing academic community, especially because of the increasing number of topics governed by international law. Hence the idea of setting up a periodical in English presenting the Italian academic de-

bate and the wealth of its practice. Even after distancing himself from the active direction of the *Yearbook*, he continued to enrich the editorial committee meetings, encouraging the development of the original layout, selecting particularly meritorious articles and publishing his own articles on questions of current debate. He also played a fundamental role in raising the funds required to continue publication.

I am very much indebted to Professor Conforti for everything he taught me, and legal research is only a part of this, perhaps not the most important. He never lost his sense of irony even in the face of death, joking that we would soon forget him. But we will never forget Professor Conforti, whose absence will be felt deeply. My dialogue with him will not finish here, though of course it will go on in silence.

LUIGI FERRARI BRAVO

GIORGIO SACERDOTI[*]

The passing away of Luigi Ferrari Bravo on 7 February 2016 at the age of 82, just a few weeks after the sudden loss of Benedetto Conforti, has left the *Italian Yearbook of International Law* orphan of its two founding fathers almost at the same time. Age and illness had not prevented them to continue to be active in the Board. The meeting of 13 October 2015, convened to decide the basic content of the present Volume and the (timely!) admission of new members in the board, saw them active as usual. Destiny was instead that it would be their last appearance at the Board.

As to Luigi, Gigi for all his numerous friends and closer colleagues, the last opportunity to meet him was on 15 December 2015 in the historic premises of the Italian Society for International Organization (SIOI) at Piazza Venezia in Rome. His pupils and closest colleagues presented him the book with the contributions collected for the colloquium held in his honour in Trento on 28-29 November 2014, mostly dealing with the different subjects that had attracted his attention during his career. *Luigi Ferrari Bravo – Il diritto internazionale come professione*, published by Editoriale Scientifica, includes the contributions of Pietro Gargiulo, Giuseppe Nesi, Antonio Tizzano, Guido Raimondi, Tullio Treves, Mauro Politi, myself, Giuseppe Tesauro, Ugo Villani, Ennio Triggiani, Giandomenico Caggiano, Elena Sciso, Roberto Adam, Attila Tanzi, Paola Mori, Roberto Giuffrida, Ivan Ingravallo, Alfredo Rizzo, Antonello Tancredi, Francesco Maria di Majo, Benedetto Conforti, and Mario De Dominicis. This long list testifies the role of Professor Ferrari Bravo in inspiring jurists who have become prominent professors, judges, diplomats, and counsels, some of them having acted in several of these roles during their professional lives, as Luigi himself did.[1]

The title of the volume, *International Law as a Profession*, is perfect to characterize what Professor Ferrari Bravo has been since he left the students' rooms of the Law Faculty of the University of Naples, in the mid-fifties. He has held most if not all the different roles that an international lawyer can have the ambition to aim at and always at the highest level.

As one of the most brilliant graduates specializing in international law in Naples, he was immediately accepted among the group of pupils of Professor Rolando

---

[*] Of the Board of Editors.

[1] The book contains also a complete biography and a bibliography of Professor Ferrari Bravo and a recollection by me of his role in launching several initiatives aimed at projecting internationally the work of Italian scholars including this *Yearbook*, as is more briefly recalled in this contribution.

Quadri, a dominant personality among the Italian international law professors of the time, the founder of the "Neapolitan School" where many of amongst the most prominent and still active Italian international lawyers have grown.

After graduating in 1956, Luigi Ferrari Bravo, born in Naples in 1933 with roots in Rome and Venice, developed a brilliant and speedy academic career as an international law professor, first at *Istituto Orientale* in Naples, then at the University of Bari where he obtained the chair in 1968. In his years of teaching there, until 1974, at a time where Bari hosted prominent professors coming from Rome and Napoli, such as Francesco Capotorti, Gigi's predecessor at the chair, and Aldo Moro, just to name a couple, he engaged himself to develop research and teaching not just in international law but also in international relations and "new" subjects such as international trade law. He relied on young scholars, both graduates in Bari and from other universities. I myself was a beneficiary of his vision, having been invited by him to teach the new course in trade law a few years after I had met him for the first time at a conference at the *Collège d'Europe* in Bruges while I was working there at my graduation dissertation.

Professor Luigi Ferrari Bravo had the opportunity to develop his talent in Bari as a "cultural organizer", staging in what was until then a provincial university international conferences and events. I recall having met there at one of those occasions mythical personalities of our world whom he had invited, such as René Cassin and Eric Stein.

From Bari he went on to *La Sapienza* in Rome, where he would remain as a professor until retirement, a central location which allowed him to develop further his collaboration with *Servizio del Contenzioso*, the Legal Office of the Italian Foreign Ministry. He was first advisor for specific affairs, becoming thereafter its first permanent legal advisor at the United Nations in New York, where he represented Italy at various committees, chairing in 1978 the Sixth Committee of the General Assembly. Thanks to his presence, Italy was able to follow at a high level of competence and with continuity the manifold legal activities which take place within the UN. Thereafter he went to Geneva as legal advisor at the Permanent Mission of Italy to the international organisations there.

He went on to become the Head of *Servizio del Contenzioso* at the Ministry in Rome (1985-1994), that is the legal advisor of the Ministry. For a long time this key position had not been held by an international lawyer, so here too his competence and academic background, coupled with his diplomatic experience, allowed him to represent Italy with full know-how and prestige. In this position he involved younger academics to represent Italy in international committees and specialized bodies, thereby familiarizing them with the negotiating and diplomatic aspects of our profession, an experience that enabled several of us to later fill posts in international organizations and in the judiciary. It is a pity that currently the post has gone back to be held by diplomats who do not have by definition the qualification and international legal connections that enabled Ferrari Bravo to give effectiveness to Italian initiatives as to international legal affairs. I would just recall that he was instrumental in convening in Rome the international conference which negotiated and concluded the Convention for the Suppression of Unlawful Acts against the Safety of Maritime Navigation, that is against the hijacking of ships in the high seas, as a prompt institutional response to the hijacking of the *Achille Lauro* cruiser by Palestinian terrorists in the Eastern Mediterranean in 1985.

The participation to international legal affairs naturally projected Professor Ferrari Bravo to the world of international courts. After having been the agent for Italy in several cases and the coordinator of Italy's strategy, notably leading Italy to success in the *ELSI* dispute with the United States before the International Court of Justice in 1989, he was elected to complete the term of Roberto Ago at the Court when the latter passed away in 1995 (to 1997). He was later judge at the European Court of Human Rights from 1998 to 2001, while going on to contribute to the formation of international law, one of his preferred fields of thinking and action, as a member of the International Law Commission, succeeding to Professor Gaetano Arangio-Ruiz in 1997-1998, besides being a long time member of the *Institut de droit international*. He was also actively engaged for Italy in the diplomatic activity leading to the establishment of the Organization for Security and Co-operation in Europe and its dispute settlement mechanisms, a task he considered first of all a moral duty in order to overcome decades of division and distrust in our continent.

All along Professor Ferrari Bravo was a prolific writer in more than one field of international law, addressing initially issues of conflict of laws in his first course at the Hague Academy of International Law (RCADI, "Vol.146, 1975-III", p. 347 ff.) – as was the requirement and academic tradition in Italy – dealing thereafter with legal questions concerning international organizations and devoting remarkable studies to European law since the early beginnings of the process of European integration. I will only briefly recall as to general international law his first monograph on *La prova nel processo internazionale* (1958), his volume on *Diritto internazionale e diritto interno nella stipulazione dei trattati* (1964), a subject on which he offered further reflections in the volume *The Structure and Process of International Law* (McDonald and Johnston eds., 1983) and in the *Etudes* in honour of Professor Ago (1987). Charles Rousseau made a flattering review of his book of 1964: "L'ouvrage de M. Ferrari Bravo occupe dès maintenant une place de choix dans la littérature relative à la théorie générale des traités internationaux". His second course at the Hague Academy of International Law (RCADI, "Vol. 192, 1985-III", p. 233 ff.), "Méthodes de recherche de la coutume internationale dans la pratique des Etats", reflects not just his theoretical thinking but also the rich experience he had developed as a "legal diplomat" and his knowledge, indeed his passion, for diplomatic history as part of his rich cultural background and interests. In his writings he followed consistently an "inductive" approach: investigating international law as it results from practice, with special attention also to the influence of domestic systems on its evolution, in order to propose a systemic view well anchored in reality, rather than vice-versa starting with general theory.

The emerging European law system had attracted his attention from the outset, as for many international lawyers in his generation. This was not just an academic choice (thanks to which international lawyers have dominated the Italian scholarship of European law until recently) but also an ideological statement. A unified Europe, based on democratic legal institutions aiming at a federal continent, appeared to him as the strongest defence against totalitarianism, understood as fascism or Soviet-led communism. I recall his several contributions on the role of the European Court of Justice, especially with respect to the *renvoi préjudiciel* (starting with his contribution to the first Italian European law treatise edited by Quadri, Monaco and Trabucchi in 1965) by which the Court has been able to guide and "control" the application of European law in Member States through a direct channel with national courts. He has left his mark in the teaching and elaboration of EU law thanks to the several treatises, textbooks and EU law commented codes he authored and co-edited between 1983 and 2008.

I believe that Professor Ferrari Bravo should be especially noted and praised by his Italian colleagues and the younger generation of Italian international legal scholars as a tireless organizer of collective initiatives meant to make the voice of Italian scholars and Italian contributions to international law better known internationally, both as concerns practice, literature, and jurisprudence. The first barrier to be overcome in this respect has been in the second half of the XX century that of language. With the rise and then the practical monopoly of English as the international (legal) language, writing in Italian or even in French, as was common in Italy in the past, became useless for authors having the ambition to contribute to international debates, just as our masters of the previous generation (Ago, Arangio-Ruiz, Morelli, Capotorti and the like) had done, often in a leading position. Italian publications in English became necessary and the establishment of an international law grouping of Italian academics, cooperating on an equal footing with similar networks of other countries also became a must.

In helping Italian international lawyers to meet successfully these challenges Luigi had a decisive role. He was engaged, initially as a junior, in the truly gigantic effort to dig out in the archives, select, systematize, and finally publish the Italian diplomatic practice relevant to international law from the unification of Italy in 1861, a research and publishing activity sponsored and financed by the Italian Ministry of Foreign Affairs and *Consiglio Nazionale delle Ricerche*, similar to that undertaken in other major countries. Fourteen volumes in three series have been published from 1970 to 1995 covering the period up to 1929. Roberto Ago, as one of the editors in chief, paid a tribute to Professor Ferrari Bravo in the preface to the first volume of the second series (1979) writing: "Once more Luigi Ferrari Bravo has taken upon himself the principal responsibility for guiding and coordinating all the researchers. He has the principal merit for the carrying out of this work".

Luigi was the initiator with Francesco Capotorti and Benedetto Conforti of this *Yearbook*, whose first series appeared from 1975 to 1987 (eight volumes) and he was behind the successful efforts to restart it in 1999, never to stop since. It is not for us editors to stress the importance of having launched and carried on our *Yearbook*, as a showcase of Italian doctrine in English, focusing both on theory, practice and topical current issues, open also to non-Italian contributors, and intentionally published by a non-Italian major international publisher in the field. Professor Ferrari Bravo had all this clearly in mind when he signed the following introductory statement with his co-editors Francesco Capotorti and Benedetto Conforti in the very first volume:

> "The development of international legal studies has, in postwar years, been in direct proportion to the considerable increase in actual events both in the field of international relations and, in particular, in that of international organization [...]. No one can doubt the importance of a real and broadly-based dialogue between scholars beyond the confines of a single country".

They went on saying that since Italian is not the language in which these exchanges take place:

> "English has been chosen for the present Yearbook, whose main aims are: firstly, to spread Italian scholars' viewpoints as regards contemporary problems of international law to other countries; secondly, to make documentation pertaining to Italian international law practice more readily accessible, including the judicial decisions of major interest, diplomatic and parliamentary practice, relevant pieces of legislation, and treaties to which Italy is a party".

The editors continued:

> "It is important to stress that the present Yearbook is not the expression of any particular group, institution or school of legal thought. The editors belong to various schools, teach in different Italian universities and their concept of international law and of the most suitable research methods in this field are not necessarily the same. They intend to leave the Yearbook open to contributions from all Italian scholars and hope that in future volumes the presence of colleagues who are not members of the Board of Editors will considerably increase".

They concluded expressing their "proud conviction", which Ferrari Bravo has always shared, "that Italian doctrine has contributed significantly to international law studies and it is for this reason that the work being carried out in Italy in this field deserves even wider acknowledgment".

Finally, the last creature of Luigi and one of his dearest was the establishment of the *Società Italiana di Diritto Internazionale* (SIDI) in 1995 together with a small group of colleagues. The models were those of similar associations that were being created in those years in other European countries on the model of the venerable American Society. The aim was to have a specific organized body, distinct from the traditional, more "political-diplomatic" SIOI – although international jurists like Gigi, close to the Ministry of Foreign Affairs, had always been and remained active also in SIOI (he was the vice-president of SIOI when he passed away). SIDI has been a success in Italy and has established itself internationally through cooperation, such as joint colloquia with sister organizations. Through its yearly conferences, taking place each year in a different university, whose papers are duly published in individual volumes, and its specialized seminars, to which more recently website, blogs and alike – mostly in English – have been added, SIDI has managed to assemble practically all Italian experts in international and European law. A big success for Italy, where the tradition had been that of fragmentation of academics coming from different traditions or "schools", often in fierce competition among them at the expense of collective endeavours, a welcome necessity in today's global world.

For this we should also be grateful to Gigi, who had productively put at work in these efforts within Italy his precious, almost unique international experience. At this sad occasion his friends within the *Yearbook* wish to express their sorrow for his loss to his family: his daughters Federica and Laura and especially his wife Gabriella. We express to her also our gratitude for the support she gave him in his last years of illness, thanks to which our Friend was able to surmount crippling difficulties and go on contributing to the *Yearbook* until the very end.

Focus
THE MIGRATORY CRISIS:
CURRENT CHALLENGES FOR
INTERNATIONAL AND EUROPEAN LAW

EUNAVFOR MED: FIGHTING MIGRANT SMUGGLING UNDER UN SECURITY COUNCIL RESOLUTION 2240 (2015)

Marco Gestri*

Abstract

To face the extraordinary migration crisis and consequent human tragedy in the Mediterranean, the need has emerged to fight human smugglers and traffickers. The European Union (EU) has launched EUNAVFOR MED, a naval crisis management operation aiming to disrupt the business model of human smuggling in the Central Mediterranean. With Resolution 2240 of 9 October 2015, the UN Security Council, acting under Chapter VII of the Charter, authorised the EU operation to undertake "all measures commensurate to the circumstances" in order to visit, seize, and dispose of vessels used by smugglers. The EU operation is currently limited to the high seas, yet its expansion into Libyan waters and territory is envisaged. This article discusses some issues arising from Resolution 2240 and its implementation by the EU, notably from the viewpoint of the international law of the sea, the rules governing the use of force and human rights law. Problems have also emerged as to the prosecution in Italy of the smugglers apprehended on the high seas. It is submitted that a number of issues have not been clarified by the legal texts adopted and that the action of the EU in this field is still ineffective and rather opaque.

Keywords: UN Security Council; European Union; migrant smuggling; law of the sea; human rights; armed force; criminal law.

1. INTRODUCTION

In recent years, the Mediterranean Sea has been defined as the world's deadliest stretch of water, for thousands of migrants and asylum seekers have died since 2013, trying to reach Europe from Africa and the Middle East.[1] This unprecedented human tragedy has been addressed by the international community with a plurality of actions. Among other things, the need has emerged to fight the smuggling of migrants, addressing the conduct of individuals and organisations exploiting, for their personal profit, the situation of the thousands of people willing to cross

---

* Of the Board of Editors.
[1] See Council of the European Union, "Council Conclusions on Migrant Smuggling", Press release 120/16, 10 March 2016, para. 1.

the Mediterranean.[2] Of particular importance for human smuggling is the "Central Mediterranean Route", the migratory flow from North Africa to Italy and Malta through the Mediterranean Sea. In 2014, detections of illegal migrants in the Central Mediterranean area reached a record level, with more than 170,000 persons having arrived in Italy; in 2015 the Central Mediterranean Route was also under intense migratory pressure.[3] Smugglers have a traditional presence in Libya and, since the collapse of governmental structures, they have operated with impunity.[4] Fighting smugglers has been identified as a priority by the European Union (EU). On 20 April 2015, in the wake of one of the biggest tragedies to have occurred in Libyan waters, the EU Council presented a "ten point action plan on migration", outlining immediate actions to be taken. Among these, the Council included "a systematic effort to capture and destroy vessels used by the smugglers", noting that "the positive results obtained with the Atalanta operation should inspire us to similar operations against smugglers in the Mediterranean".[5] A few days later, the Heads of State and Government of the EU, at the special meeting of the European Council convened on 23 April 2015 to address the situation in the Mediterranean Sea, committed to fighting the traffickers and invited the High Representative of the Union for Foreign Affairs and Security Policy (HR) "to immediately begin preparations for a possible Common Security and Defence Policy (CSDP) operation to this effect".[6]

On 18 May 2015, the Council issued Decision (CFSP) 2015/778 on an EU military operation in the Southern Central Mediterranean (EUNAVFOR MED),[7] providing that "the Union shall conduct a military crisis management operation

---

[2] See, in general, RONZITTI, "Coastal State Jurisdiction over Refugees and Migrants at Sea", in ANDO et al. (eds.), *Liber Amicorum Judge Shigeru Oda*, The Hague, 2002, p. 1271 ff.; CAFFIO, "Immigraziome clandestina via mare", Rivista Marittima, Supplemento, October 2003; SCOVAZZI, "La lotta all'immigrazione clandestina alla luce del diritto internazionale del mare", Diritto, immigrazione e cittadinanza, 2003, p. 48 ff.; TREVISANUT, *Immigrazione irregolare via mare*, Napoli, 2012; and GALLAGHER and DAVID, *The International Law of Migrant Smuggling*, Cambridge, 2014.

[3] See Frontex, Central Mediterranean Route, available at: <http://frontex.europa.eu/trends-and-routes/central-mediterranean-route/>.

[4] See the Hearing of the Operation Commander of EUNAVFOR MED before the Italian Parliament, *Comitato parlamentare di controllo sull'attuazione dell'Accordo di Schengen*, 8 October 2015, available at: <http://webtv.camera.it/evento/8424>.

[5] Press release IP/15/4813, available at: <http://europa.eu/rapid/press-release_IP-15-4813_it.htm>.

[6] Final statement available at: <http://www.consilium.europa.eu/en/press/press-releases/2015/04/23-special-euco-statement/>. On 13 May 2015, the EU Commission published "A European Agenda on Migration" (COM (2015) 240 final) which singled out the fight against migrant smuggling as a priority, setting the objective "to transform smuggling networks from 'low risk, high return' operations for criminals into 'high risk, low return' ones" (pp. 3-4, 8).

[7] OJ EU, L 122, 19 May 2015, p. 31 ff. See FALEG and BLOCKMANS, "EU Naval Force EUNAVFOR MED Sets Sail in Troubled Waters", CEPS Commentary, 26 June 2015; and MATTIELLO, "Le operazioni militari navali nel Mediterraneo", Senato della Repubblica, I dossier di documentazione, Servizio affari internazionali, No. 2, 2015.

contributing to the disruption of the business model of human smuggling and trafficking networks in the Southern Central Mediterranean".[8] The Decision appointed an Italian Operation Commander (Rear Admiral Enrico Credendino)[9] and designated Rome as Operation Headquarters.[10] EUNAVFOR MED was conceived as an *operation structured into different phases*. In particular, under Article 2(2) of Decision 2015/778, it shall:

> "(a) in a first phase, support the detection and monitoring of migration networks through information gathering and patrolling on the high seas in accordance with international law; (b) in a second phase, (i) conduct boarding, search, seizure and diversion on the high seas of vessels suspected of being used for human smuggling or trafficking, under the conditions provided for by applicable international law, including UNCLOS and the Protocol against the Smuggling of Migrants; (ii) in accordance with any applicable UN Security Council Resolution or consent by the coastal State concerned, conduct boarding, search, seizure and diversion, on the high seas or in the territorial and internal waters of that State, of vessels suspected of being used for human smuggling or trafficking, under the conditions set out in that Resolution or consent; (c) in a third phase, in accordance with any applicable UN Security Council Resolution or consent by the coastal State concerned, take all necessary measures against a vessel and related assets, including through disposing of them or rendering them inoperable, which are suspected of being used for human smuggling or trafficking, in the territory of that State, under the conditions set out in that Resolution or consent".

The actual launch of the operation was conditional upon a decision of the EU Council, to be adopted upon the recommendation of the Operation Commander and following approval of the Operation Plan and of the Rules of Engagement.[11] The Council was also entrusted to assess the conditions necessary to move beyond the first phase of the operation, "taking into account any applicable UNSC Resolution and consent by the coastal States concerned",[12] whereas the transition between the different phases must be decided by the Political and Security Committee (PSC).[13] EUNAVFOR MED was launched on 22 June 2015, by Council Decision (CFSP)

---

[8] Art. 1(1).
[9] Art. 3.
[10] Art. 4.
[11] Decision 2015/778, *cit. supra* note 7, Art. 5.
[12] *Ibid.*, Art. 2(3).
[13] *Ibid.*, Art. 6(1).

2015/972, which also approved the Operational Plan and the Rules of Engagement.[14] Therefore, a second CSDP maritime operation is currently underway, along with the counter-piracy Operation Atalanta off Somalia.[15] On 14 September 2015, the Council adopted a positive assessment that the conditions to move "to the first step of phase two on the high seas" had been met. That assessment was followed by a force generation conference and the approval of new Rules of Engagement for phase 2 on the high seas. A formal Decision of the PSC was enacted to launch on 7 October 2015 the first step of phase 2 "as laid down in point (b)(i) of Article 2(2) of Decision (CFSP) 2015/778".[16] The PSC also agreed to rename the mission as "Operation Sophia", after the name given, in August 2015, to a baby born to a mother rescued by one of the ships assigned to the operation. At the time of writing (March 2016), the force consists of five naval units and six air assets.[17] Since its inception, 22 EU Member States have contributed, in different ways, to the operation.[18] As is the rule for CSDP military operations, Member States commitments to participate are decided at national level and on a voluntary basis.[19] On the other hand, Article 9 of Decision 2015/778 provides that third States may also be invited to participate in the operation.

2.   THE LEGAL BASIS OF EUNAVFOR MED UNDER EU LAW

The Council identified the legal basis for the establishment of EUNAVFOR MED, under EU law, in Articles 42 and 43 of the Treaty on European Union (TEU). Article 42(1) TEU states that a CSDP shall be an integral part of the Common Foreign and Security Policy (CFSP), providing the Union with an operational capacity drawing on civil and military assets; the EU may use these assets "on missions outside the Union for peace-keeping, conflict prevention and strengthening international security in accordance with the principles of the United Nations

---

[14] Council Decision (CFSP) 2015/972 of 22 June 2015 launching the European Union military operation in the Southern Central Mediterranean (EUNAVFOR MED), OJ EU L 157, 23 June 2015, p. 51.

[15] See TONELLI, "The EU Fight against Piracy in the Horn of Africa: The External Action at Stake", in ANDREONE et al. (eds.), *Insecurity at Sea: Piracy and Other Risks to Navigation*, Napoli, 2013, p. 53 ff.

[16] PSC Decision (CFSP) 2015/1772 of 28 September 2015, OJ EU L 258, 3 October 2015, p. 5.

[17] EUNAVFOR MED website, see at: <http://eeas.europa.eu/csdp/missions-and-operations/eunavfor-med/index_en.htm>.

[18] See the Hearing of the Operation Commander of EUNAVFOR MED before the Italian Parliament, *Commissione Difesa Senato e Camera*, 4 March 2016, available at: <http://webtv.senato.it/4194?video_evento=2346>.

[19] Under Art. 5 of the Protocol (No. 22) on the position of Denmark, the latter does not participate in the elaboration and implementations of decisions and actions of the Union which have defence implications.

Charter". Article 43 TEU specifies that the tasks pursued by these missions may include "joint disarmament operations, humanitarian and rescue tasks, military advice and assistance tasks, tasks of combat forces in crisis management, including peace-making and post-conflict stabilisation", and may all "contribute to fight against terrorism, including by supporting third countries in combating terrorism in their territories". EUNAVFOR MED is qualified by Article 1(1) of Decision 2015/778 as a "military crisis management operation", whose aim is to contribute to "the disruption of the business model of human smuggling and trafficking networks in the Southern Central Mediterranean"; that task is to be achieved "by undertaking systematic efforts to identify, capture and dispose of vessels and assets used or suspected of being used by smugglers and traffickers, in accordance with applicable international law, including UNCLOS and any UN Security Council Resolution".

Some scholars have criticised the choice of the legal basis for the Decision, arguing that the objective of countering human and migrant trafficking should have rather entailed the adoption of acts founded on the external dimension of the EU competence on *judicial and police cooperation in criminal matters* (Part III, Title V, of the Treaty on the Functioning of the European Union – TFEU). According to one commentator, the Council chose a legal basis under the CSDP "to avoid an intervention of the European Parliament, who is after Lisbon co-responsible for internal security and criminal justice matters".[20] These arguments seem however untenable, for the choice of the legal basis made by the Council must be regarded, in view of the *aim* and *content* of Decision 2015/778, as perfectly correct (at least from a legal viewpoint).[21] EUNAVFOR MED was conceived of by Decision 2015/778 as an operation of a *military nature*, to be conducted outside the territory of the Union, in order to identify, capture, and dispose of vessels and assets used by smugglers and traffickers. As will be seen, the mandate of the operation may involve the *use of armed force* against foreign private ships, in *international spaces* (the high seas) or, during phase 3 of the operation, even in *areas under the sovereignty of a third State* (territorial waters and territory). One could certainly say that some of Operation Sophia's assignments may share some features with police tasks. The Operation Commander spoke in this regard of a "new kind of operation", blending military with police tasks.[22] However, the planning of the operation was based on the as-

---

[20] MERCONE, "Some Notes on the Relations between UNSC Resolution 2240 (2015) Fighting Smugglers in Mediterranean and the EUNAVFOR MED 'Sophia' Operation", European Area of Freedom Security & Justice, FREE Group, 19 October 2015, available at: <http://free-group.eu/2015/10/19/some-notes-on-the-relations-between-unsc-resolution-2240-2015-fighting-smugglers-in-mediterranean-and-the-eunavfor-MED-sophia-operation/>.

[21] As to the choice of the legal basis for a measure of the EU, see, *ex multis*, Court of Justice of the European Union, Case C-658/11, *Parliament v. Council*, Judgment of 24 June 2014, para. 52.

[22] See Parliament Hearing of the Operation Commander, *cit. supra* note 18.

sumption, reaffirmed by its Commander, that in the present conditions of security these activities could not be carried out by mere police forces.[23]

As to the aims of EUNAVFOR MED, Decision 2015/778 focuses on the prevention of human tragedies resulting from the smuggling of people across the Mediterranean whereas, surprisingly enough, no reference is made to the undeniable threats to the security of the Union also deriving from that phenomenon. Yet, as previously seen, CSDP missions may carry out "humanitarian and rescue tasks" under Article 43 TEU. On the other hand, in the speech HR Mogherini delivered before the UN Security Council on 11 May 2015, in order to inform the latter of the decisions taken by the EU to fight migrant smuggling, she stressed that the Mediterranean crisis "is not only a humanitarian emergency, but also a security crisis, since smuggling networks are linked to, and in some cases finance, terrorist activities, which contributes to instability in a region that is already unstable enough".[24] In the light of all these considerations, one cannot deny that the main aims of the operation, at least as conceived in Decision 2015/778, fall within the CSDP, and more broadly within the CFSP. Besides, the competence of the EU in CFSP matters is in itself very wide, covering in accordance with Article 24(1) TEU, "all areas of foreign policy and all questions relating to the Union's security".

Two additional remarks are necessary. First, it is certainly possible to argue that a military operation such as EUNAVFOR MED *is not the most appropriate means, from a policy viewpoint, to tackle the current migration crisis*.[25] That has nothing to do with the assessment of the legality of Decision 2015/778 under the EU Treaties. Second, there is no denying that the fight against migrant smuggling and human trafficking by sea also requires actions which, under EU law, have to be adopted on the basis of the Treaty rules on judicial and police cooperation in criminal matters. The latter measures are however of a clearly distinct nature from the launching of a naval operation outside the EU. In effect, EU institutions have long since elaborated sets of legal rules dealing with migrant smuggling and human trafficking. As to migrant smuggling, on 28 November 2002 the EU Council adopted the so-called "Facilitators Package", composed of Directive 2002/90/EC defining the fa-

---

[23] *Ibid.* There have been cases in which the smugglers have threatened to use weapons against merchant or military ships carrying out rescue operations in order to regain possession of boats used for the traffic: "Immigrazione: minacciata motovedetta italiana", La Gazzetta del Mezzogiorno, 15 February 2015.

[24] See Security Council, UN Doc. S/PV.7439, 11 May 2015, p. 2 ff.

[25] See, for instance, "Remarks to the Press by the Vice-President of the International Federation of the Red Cross at United Nations Headquarters", 6 May 2015, available at: <http://www.ifrc.org/en/news-and-media/opinions-and-positions/speeches/2015/united-nations-head-quarters-new-york-6-may-2015-ifrc-vice-president-francesco-rocca---remarks-to-the-press/>; MEIJERS COMMITTEE, "Military Action against Human Smugglers: Legal Questions Concerning the EUNAVFOR MED Operation", 23 September 2015, available at: <http://www.statewatch.org/news/2015/sep/eu-meijers-cttee-eunavfor.pdf>.

cilitation of unauthorised entry, transit and residence,[26] and of Framework Decision 2002/946/JHA on the strengthening of the penal framework to prevent the facilitation of unauthorised entry, transit, and residence.[27] Both the Agenda on Migration[28] and the Agenda on Security[29] have identified the fight against the smuggling of migrants as a priority for the EU, and on 27 May 2015 the first EU Action Plan against migrant smuggling (2015-2020) was published.[30] The Action Plan sets forth a number of concrete actions to be undertaken by EU institutions over a five year period, among which is the revision and the amelioration of the legal framework *in subiecta materia*. As to human trafficking, the policy framework for action was outlined in 2012 by the Commission's Communication on the EU Strategy towards the Eradication of Trafficking in Human Beings 2012-2016,[31] whereas the main legislative instrument in force is Directive 2011/36/EU of 5 April 2011 on preventing and combatting trafficking in human beings and protecting its victims.[32]

At the operative level, a number of initiatives have been developed in order to strengthen the cooperation among Member States, EU institutions, and agencies in the investigation and prosecution of migrant smugglers and traffickers. As to police cooperation, in particular, in March 2015 Europol launched the Joint Operational Team Mare (JOT Mare): a specialised team of experts, combining national resources and Europol expertise, which specifically focuses on criminal organisations involved in migrant smuggling across the Mediterranean Sea. JOT Mare aims at identifying concrete investigative leads (e.g., lists of suspected vessels) and support its partners in initiating investigations. In February 2016, a European Migrant Smuggling Centre (EMSC) was launched within Europol, to act as the main information hub and coordinating entity on migrant smuggling within the agency.[33] As to cooperation between prosecuting authorities, of great interest is the creation, on

---

[26] OJ EC L 328, 5 December 2002, p. 17 ff.

[27] *Ibid.*, p. 1 ff. The Directive aims to approximate the legal provisions of Member States with regard to the precise definition of the infringement in question and the cases of exemption, whereas the Framework Decision sets out minimum rules for penalties, liability of legal persons and jurisdiction.

[28] See *supra* note 6.

[29] COM (2015) 185 final, 28 April 2015.

[30] "EU Action Plan against Migrant Smuggling (2015-2020)", COM (2015) 285 final.

[31] COM (2012) 286 final, 19 June 2012.

[32] OJ L 101, 15 April 2011, p. 1 ff. The Directive provides for minimum common rules for determining offences of trafficking in human beings and punishing the traffickers. It also includes measures for the prevention of the phenomenon and the protection of victims' rights. See also Council Directive 2004/81/EC of 29 April 2004 on the residence permit issued to third-country nationals who are victims of trafficking in human beings or who have been the subject of an action to facilitate illegal immigration, who cooperate with the competent authorities, OJ EU L 261, 6 August 2004, p. 19 ff.

[33] See EUROPOL, "Europol Launches the European Migrant Smuggling Centre", 22 February 2016, available at: <https://www.europol.europa.eu/content/EMSC_launch>.

29 September 2015, of a thematic group on migrant smuggling within Eurojust.[34] In accordance with Article 8 of Decision 2015/778, EUNAVFOR MED has concluded cooperation arrangements with Eurojust and Europol and established a structured cooperation with Frontex. Indeed, in the Central Mediterranean the Frontex led Joint Operation Triton is currently underway, whose main task is border surveillance and which is also carrying out activities in order to control irregular migration and to tackle cross-border crime. The two operations act in close coordination and have even established a division of responsibilities, EUNAVFOR MED operating immediately south of Triton's operational area.[35]

3. RESOLUTION 2240 (2015) OF THE UN SECURITY COUNCIL AND ITS LEGAL
    BASIS

In its preamble, Council Decision 2015/778 points out that on 11 May 2015 the HR "informed the UN Security Council about the crisis of migrants in the Mediterranean and on the ongoing preparation for a possible Union naval operation", and that she "expressed the need for the Union to work with the support of the UN Security Council".[36] Additionally, Articles 1 and 2 of the Decision make a number of references to the requirement to carry out the naval operation in accordance with any applicable UN Security Council resolution. In this case the EU followed a different line of conduct from that adopted with respect to Operation Atalanta, which was organized only *after the adoption* by the Security Council of umbrella resolutions. By any means, the *phased approach* envisaged for EUNAVFOR MED allowed the EU to launch a first phase of the operation, exclusively focused on *information gathering* and hence not raising any particular international law issue, while working at the UN for the adoption of a resolution authorising further, more problematic phases. The diplomatic action undertaken by the EU and its Member States, since early 2015, met however with a number of difficulties, due to the opposition of the Libyan Government (and other African countries) and, more importantly, of the Russian Federation, to some aspects of the proposals initially put forward.[37] These difficulties were overcome only after "lengthy negotiations", led by the United Kingdom, the initiator of the resolution.[38] On 9 October 2015, the Security Council adopted Resolution 2240 (2015), under the agenda item "Maintenance of

---

[34] On Eurojust, see Art. 85 TFEU.

[35] See Parliament Hearing of the Operation Commander, *cit. supra* note 18.

[36] *Supra* note 7. The intervention of the HR before the Security Council was the first application of Art. 34(2) TEU.

[37] See "Mediterranean Migrants: Libya Rejects EU Military Plans", BBC, 11 May 2015, available at: <http://www.bbc.com/news/world-africa-32686579>.

[38] See the statement of Chad to the UN Security Council, UN Doc. S./PV.7531, 9 October 2015, p. 3. A crucial role in the elaboration of the draft resolution was also played by Italy (currently not a member of the Security Council).

International Peace and Security".[39] According to the last paragraph of the preamble, the Security Council "acts under Chapter VII of the UN Charter", notably with specific regard to "the necessity to put an end to the recent proliferation of, and endangerment of lives by, the smuggling of migrants and trafficking of persons in the Mediterranean Sea off the coast of Libya". Resolution 2240 does not mention any of the three specific situations which, pursuant to Article 39 of the UN Charter, enable the Security Council to act under Chapter VII (threat to the peace, breach of the peace or act of aggression). This *modus operandi* is not uncommon in the practice of the Security Council,[40] and *in casu* it reflects a compromise. A draft initially presented by the United Kingdom had included references to the situation in Libya as being a "threat to the peace", in line with previous resolutions dealing with the North-African country.[41] That language was however deleted upon the insistence of the Libyan Government, which probably feared that any reference to the situation in the country as the *direct cause* of the migrant crisis could corroborate plans for international intervention in the Libyan territory.[42]

Some commentators, before the adoption of Resolution 2240, raised some doubts vis-à-vis *the qualification of migrant smuggling and human trafficking in the Mediterranean as a "threat to the peace"* under Article 39 or, more generally, as a situation justifying recourse to Chapter VII of the Charter.[43] These doubts do not seem, however, justified. As is known, the Security Council enjoys a wide political discretion in determining the existence of a situation allowing for the recourse to measures under Chapter VII of the Charter. Even if one shares the opinion

---

[39] Resolution 2240 received 14 votes in favour whereas one member (Venezuela) abstained. See WILSON, "The Mediterranean Migrant Crisis: Key Considerations for the UN Security Council", Harvard National Security Journal, 7 October 2015, available at: <http://harvardnsj. org/2015/10/mediterranean-migrant-crisis/>; BO, "Fighting Transnational Crimes at Sea under UNSC's Mandate: Piracy, Human Trafficking and Migrant Smuggling", *EJIL: Talk!*, 30 October 2015; ZICCARDI CAPALDO, "The EUNAVFOR MED Operation and the Use of Force", 18 December 2015, ASIL Insights, Vol. 19, issue 27, 18 December 2015, available at: <https:// www.asil.org/insights/volume/19/issue/27/eunavfor-med-operation-and-use-force>; CADIN, "La risoluzione 2240 (2015) sul traffico di migranti nel Mediterraneo: il Consiglio di sicurezza autorizza l'uso ... misurato della forza", OIDU, 2015, p. 696 ff.; and LICASTRO, "La seconda fase dell'operazione EUNAVFOR MED", DUE – Osservatorio europeo, 2015, available at: <http:// www.dirittounioneeuropea.eu/index.php/it/indice>.

[40] See LAVALLE, "The 'Acting under Chapter VII' Clause in Security Council Resolutions under Article 41 of the United Nations Charter: A Misconceived and Harmful Way of Invoking Authority", IYIL, 2009, p. 233 ff.; and RONZITTI, *Diritto internazionale dei conflitti armati*, 5th ed., Torino, 2014, pp. 58-59.

[41] See, among others, Resolution 2238 (2015) of 10 September 2015.

[42] In the statement issued after the adoption of the resolution, Libya recognized "the grave threat to international peace and security posed by the smuggling and trafficking of migrants" (UN Doc. S/PV.7531, *cit. supra* note 38, p. 10).

[43] See MEIJERS COMMITTEE, *supra* note 25; BO, *supra* note 39; and MANANASHVILI, "The Legal and Political Feasibility of the EU's Planned 'War on Smuggling' in Libya", *EJIL: Talk!*, 10 June 2015.

that such discretion is not unlimited,[44] Resolution 2240 does not seem to give rise to particular problems. It is true that the situation which the Security Council intends directly to confront is different from a conflict of military nature. However, it emerges from the text of the Resolution, as well as from the context, that the Security Council based its decision to act on the premise that the current crisis in the Mediterranean amounts to an exceptional "humanitarian tragedy", in view of the massive loss of lives which has occurred, a tragedy which is certainly worsened by the activities carried out by migrant smugglers and human traffickers.[45] That idea was reiterated in the interventions of many members of the Security Council after the adoption of the Resolution,[46] including Russia and African States, and is *widely shared in the international community*.[47] This is confirmed by the number of States having stressed, in the UN General Assembly, the magnitude of the migrant crisis in the Mediterranean, the fact that the latter is exacerbated by migrant smuggling and the consequent need to fight that criminal activity.[48] Resolution 2240 might be considered as yet another example of the trend to consider exceptional humanitarian emergencies as situations allowing the Security Council to act under Chapter VII of the Charter.[49]

Needless to say, the reference to *regional organisations* in the operative part of Resolution 2240 must be interpreted as concerning the EU (in the preamble of the Resolution the Security Council expressly takes note of the EU Decision establishing EUNAVFOR MED). In order to delimit the scope of the actions to be taken by Member States and regional organisations, in accordance with Resolution 2240, one must spell out the definitions of "smuggling of migrants" and "trafficking in persons" postulated by the Security Council. In Paragraph 4 of the Resolution, the Security Council reaffirms the UN Convention against Transnational Organized Crime (UNCTOC)[50] and its two supplementing Protocols against the Smuggling of

---

[44] Particularly convincing is the theory, put forward by CONFORTI AND FOCARELLI (*Le Nazioni Unite*, 10th ed., Padova, 2015, p. 246 ff.), according to which the Security Council should qualify as a threat to the peace only situations which are *effectively condemned by the majority of the international community*. The legal basis for this theory is found in Art. 24 of the UN Charter, under which the SC acts "on behalf of all Member States".

[45] In the first paragraph of the preamble of Resolution 2240 the Security Council recalls "its press statement of 21 April on the maritime tragedy in the Mediterranean Sea".

[46] See Russia, UN Doc. S/PV.7531, *cit. supra* note 38, p. 6; Nigeria, *ibid.*, p. 9; Libya, *ibid.*, p. 10.

[47] See also the Press statement of the African Union Peace and Security Council of 27 April 2015, African Union Doc. PSC/PR/COMM.1(D).

[48] See UN General Assembly, Meetings Coverage, 20 November 2015, GA/11729, available at: <http://www.un.org/press/en/2015/ga11729.doc.htm>.

[49] See RONZITTI, *Introduzione al diritto internazionale*, 5th ed., Torino, 2016, pp. 448-449. Cf., however, the statement of Venezuela before the Security Council, according to which the application of Chapter VII with respect to the humanitarian situation of migrants "is a serious mistake" (UN Doc. S/PV.7531, *cit. supra* note 38, p. 5).

[50] 15 November 2000, entered into force 29 September 2003.

Migrants by Land, Sea and Air[51] and to Prevent, Suppress and Punish Trafficking in Persons, Especially Women and Children[52] as the "primary legal instruments" to combat the activities in question. Paragraph 5 of the Resolution, with an unusual didactic language, underlines that "although the crime of smuggling of migrants may share, in some cases, some common features with the crime of trafficking in persons, Member States need to recognise that they are distinct crimes, as defined by UNCTOC and its Protocols, requiring differing legal, operational, and policy responses". On account of that language, States and the EU, when implementing Resolution 2240, will basically have to refer to the notions of "smuggling of migrants" and "trafficking in persons" as defined in the two supplementary Protocols to the UNCTOC. All EU Member States (with one exception)[53] are bound by both Protocols to the UNCTOC, of which the EU is also a party.

4.   THE RIGHT OF INSPECTION OF FLAGLESS VESSELS

The core of Resolution 2240 is represented by Paragraphs 5-11. Paragraph 5 calls upon Member States, acting nationally or through regional organisations that are engaged in the fight against migrant smuggling and human trafficking, to inspect on the high seas off the coast of Libya any unflagged vessels that they have reasonable grounds to believe have been, are being, or imminently will be used by organised criminal enterprises for migrant smuggling or human trafficking from Libya. The greater part of the illegal activities *in subiecta materia*, particularly in the Mediterranean, involve vessels without a flag or registration, notably "inflatable boats, rafts and dinghies", which are expressly mentioned in Resolution 2240 (2015).[54] The latter calls upon States *to inspect* the suspected vessels in question "as permitted under international law". Indeed, the conduct recommended by the Resolution vis-à-vis flagless vessels is in itself lawful under the international law of the sea. It must be recalled that Article 110(1)(d) of the UN Convention on the Law of the Sea (UNCLOS)[55] provides that a warship is entitled to exercise on the high seas the *right of visit* of any vessel when there is reasonable ground for suspecting that "the ship is without nationality". More particularly, the right of

---

[51] 15 November 2000, entered into force 28 January 2004 (hereinafter "Smuggling of Migrants Protocol").

[52] 15 November 2000, entered into force 25 December 2003.

[53] Ireland is not a party to the Smuggling of Migrants Protocol.

[54] See Frontex, *cit. supra* note 3; Parliament Hearing of the Operation Commander, *cit. supra* note 18. With respect to inflatable boats, rafts, dinghies, and the other boats being too little to be registered, it might even be questioned whether they can be considered "ships" under international law. See Council of the European Union, Doc. 9804/07, "Commission Staff Working Document, Study on the International Law Instruments in Relation to Illegal Immigration by Sea", 23 May 2007, p. 19.

[55] 10 December 1982, entered into force 16 November 1994.

visit under Article 110 UNCLOS involves a right to stop the vessel and to send a boat under the command of an officer to the suspected ship, in order to verify its nationality. If, after having checked the documents, there remains suspicion over the lack of nationality of the vessel, a "further examination" on board the ship (i.e. a search of the vessel) can be carried out, with all possible consideration. Such a right may be exercised also by any other duly authorised ship or aircraft clearly marked and identifiable as being on government service.[56] With special regard to the smuggling of migrants, the 2000 Protocol authorises States Parties "to board and search" vessels without a nationality suspected of being engaged in the activity in question.[57]

Considering that legal framework, EUNAVFOR MED ships are certainly allowed to stop, board, and search a ship without nationality suspected of migrant smuggling or human trafficking.[58] It might however be questioned whether *further rights* can be exercised, under Resolution 2240 and international law, in respect of a vessel carrying illegal migrants confirmed to be without nationality. In that regard, it must be noted that Paragraph 8 of Resolution 2240 (providing for an authorisation to *seize* suspected vessels and to *dispose* of them), surprisingly enough, does not expressly refer to Paragraph 5 (and, as a consequence, to flagless vessels). As to the international law of the sea, UNCLOS confines itself to setting forth the abovementioned right of visit. According to some scholars, flagless ships *do not enjoy any protection under international law* and can be subjected to the jurisdiction of any State. As a consequence, the boarding State would, *inter alia*, be empowered to escort the stateless ship to a port and subject it (and the persons on board) to law enforcement procedures under national law.[59] Other international lawyers, however, hold a more cautious approach, underlining that UNCLOS does not provide universal jurisdiction over a stateless vessel and confines itself to setting forth a right of visit in order to verify the flag. In the view of an important part of the doctrine, the boarding State could assert its adjudicative and enforcement jurisdiction on the stateless ship (and the persons on board) only in the presence of

---

[56] UNCLOS, Art. 110(5). See, in general, LOWE and TZANAKOPOULOS, "Ships, Visit and Search", in WOLFRUM (ed.), *The Max Planck Encyclopedia of Public International Law*, Oxford, 2012, para. 9.

[57] Smuggling of Migrants Protocol, Art. 8(7).

[58] With regard to Italian law, see Art. 12(9)-*quater* of the Legislative Decree No. 286 of 25 July 1998 (*Testo unico sull'immigrazione*), and Art. 7(3) of Decree of 14 July 2003 on the fight against illegal migration (GU No. 220 of 22 September 2003).

[59] This is the position under current US practice. See *Commander's Handbook on the Law of Naval Operations*, Doc. NWP 1-14M, 2007, para. 3.11.2.3; THOMAS and DUNCAN (eds.), *Annotated Supplement to the Commander's Handbook on the Law of Naval Operations*, *International Law Studies*, Vol. 73, 1999, p. 239. In the legal literature, see, among others, BROWNLIE, *Principles of Public International Law*, 7th ed., Oxford, 2008, p. 235; DE GUTTRY, *Lo status della nave da guerra in tempo di pace*, Milano, 1994, p. 183 ff.; and CAFFIO, *cit. supra* note 2, p. 53.

an appropriate nexus between the wrongful act, allegedly committed by the vessel, and its legal order.[60]

With specific regard to ships without nationality suspected of being used in the *smuggling of migrants*, Article 8(7) of the Smuggling of Migrants Protocol authorises States Parties not only to board and search the vessel but also, when evidence confirms the suspicion, "to take appropriate measures in accordance with relevant domestic and international law". Yet, many scholars argue that even that provision would not clarify the legal picture. On the one hand, it does not exactly spell out what kind of measures can be taken in respect of the ship; on the other hand, by referring to international law, it would leave the question, as to the need for an appropriate nexus between the wrongful act and the State asserting jurisdiction, open.[61]

In consideration of that unclear legal framework, *the lack of precision* of Resolution 2240 as to the exercise of adjudicative jurisdiction and enforcement actions vis-à-vis stateless ships is *unfortunate*. This is the more so, if one considers that, under the prevailing view in Italian case law, stateless ships are not *per se* subject to universal jurisdiction and the exercise of adjudicative and enforcement jurisdiction over the ships engaged in migrant trafficking would require *an appropriate link with the Italian legal order* (even if some recent judgments have identified that nexus on the basis of a "functional" interpretation of the legal norms concerning criminal jurisdiction).[62] The judgment of the Tribunal of Crotone on the *Cemil-Pamuk* case[63] is often quoted as an application of the theory that the statelessness of the vessel is sufficient for the exercise of criminal jurisdiction.[64] However, that reading of the judgment does not seem to be correct. The Tribunal asserted the Italian jurisdiction only in consideration of the fact that the stateless vessel had transferred, on the high seas, a number of illegal migrants into another ship and that the second ship had entered the Italian territorial waters. As a consequence, the Italian jurisdiction was established on the basis of the *territoriality principle*, for the event deriving from the conduct of the "mother ship" (illegal entry into the national territory) had taken place in Italian territorial waters (doctrine of constructive presence).

---

[60] CHURCILL and LOWE, *The Law of the Sea*, 3rd ed., Manchester, 1999, p. 214; TANAKA, *The International Law of the Sea*, Cambridge, 2012, p. 162; PAPASTAVRIDIS, *The Interception of Vessels on the High Seas*, Oxford/Portland, 2013, p. 265. See also GUILFOYLE, *Shipping Interdiction and the Law of the Sea*, Cambridge, 2009, pp. 16-17. According to O'CONNELL (*The International Law of the Sea*, ed. by SHEARER, Vol. II, Oxford, 1984) when a ship is not registered or loses its nationality "its status is then a question for the municipal law of the owners, and it is likely that this would then claim to regulate the ship, and, in that sense, to become a law of the ship's nationality" (pp. 755-757).

[61] See SCOVAZZI, *cit. supra* note 2, p. 51; GUILFOYLE, *cit. supra* note 60, p. 185.

[62] See *infra* section 10.

[63] *Tribunale di Crotone, Pamuk and Others*, 27 September 2001, RDI, 2001, p. 1155 ff; ANDREONE, IYIL, 2001, p. 273 ff.

[64] PAPASTAVRIDIS, *cit. supra* note 60, p. 265.

In any case, it is here argued that an *a contrario* interpretation of Paragraphs 5 and 8 of Resolution 2240, according to which Member States and regional organisations would not be allowed to carry out the enforcement actions envisaged by Paragraph 8 vis-à-vis flagless vessels, would lead to a result *clearly absurd* and *unreasonable*. As a consequence, one must conclude that the Security Council acted on the assumption that these kinds of measures can be taken in respect of ships without nationality *in accordance with customary international law* or at least that it left that issue open. Consequently, it is here submitted that in the course of operations directed at implementing Resolution 2240 the intervening State is allowed to take enforcement measures with respect to flagless ships (seizure of the vessel and apprehension of persons on board) and to assert adjudicative jurisdiction *when that is provided by its national law*.[65] That however does not solve all the problems. As previously seen, some legal orders set forth conditions or limitations as to the assertion of enforcement and adjudicative jurisdiction over flagless ships on the high seas and this in particular is the case with Italian law. Considering that all the suspected smugglers and traffickers apprehended at sea by EUNAVFOR MED are disembarked and prosecuted in Italy, this legal situation may determine problems as to the validation by Italian judges of the enforcement measures adopted with respect to flagless vessels and persons on board (seizure or destruction of the ship and arrest of suspected individuals). These issues will be dealt with in the following sections.[66]

5.   THE AUTHORISATION TO INSPECT AND SEIZE FLAGGED SHIPS AND ITS LIMITS *RATIONE TEMPORIS* AND *RATIONE LOCI*

As far as flagged vessels are concerned, in principle Paragraph 6 of Resolution 2240 (2015) calls upon Member States to inspect ships suspected of the activities at issue "with the consent of the flag State". Under the Smuggling of Migrants Protocol each State Party has an obligation to designate an authority having the competence to receive and respond requests from other Parties for confirmation of registry and for authorisation to take appropriate measures vis-à-vis national vessels.[67] Hopefully that should facilitate, among parties to the Protocol, the requests for flag-State consent. On the other hand, the Security Council also decides, in

---

[65] This interpretation of the international law of the sea seems to be followed by the Regulation (EU) 656/2014 of 15 May 2014 establishing rules for the surveillance of the external sea borders in the context of operational cooperation coordinated by the European Agency for the Management of Operational Cooperation at the External Borders of the Member States of the European Union, OJ EU L 189, 27 June 2014, p. 93 (Art. 7). The Regulation governs the maritime operations coordinated by Frontex, including Joint Operation Triton currently underway in the Central Mediterranean (see also *supra* note 35 and corresponding text).

[66] See *infra* sections 7 and 10.

[67] Art. 8(6).

Paragraph 7 of the Resolution, to authorise Member States, acting nationally or through regional organisations,

> "to inspect on the high seas off the coast of Libya vessels that they have reasonable grounds to suspect are being used for migrant smuggling and human trafficking from Libya, provided that such Member States and regional organisations make good faith efforts to obtain the consent of the vessel's flag State prior to using the authority outlined in this paragraph".

Furthermore, Paragraph 8 of the Resolution authorises Member States "to seize" vessels, inspected under the authority of the preceding paragraph, "that are confirmed as being used for migrant smuggling or human trafficking from Libya". These provisions authorise States to take measures (*inspection* and *seizure* of a foreign private vessel) that might go beyond what is currently allowed under the customary international law of the sea, in particular where action is undertaken *without the express consent of the flag State* (the cases in which that situation may arise will be discussed in the following paragraph). In accordance with the principle of the freedom of the high seas, any attempt at inspecting a ship without the consent of the flag State, and *a fortiori* any attempt at seizing it in principle entails a violation of the exclusivity of flag State jurisdiction and a breach of international law, unless that conduct may find an appropriate basis under international law.[68] Now, it is generally accepted that an authorisation by the Security Council, acting under Chapter VII of the UN Charter, may constitute such an appropriate legal justification.

The authorisations by the Security Council to inspect and seize the vessels in question are however limited (*ratione temporis, loci* and *materiae*) and are subjected to a precondition.[69] *Ratione temporis*, the authorisations have been granted by the Security Council for a period of one year since the date of adoption of Resolution 2240. Needless to say, a renewal of the authorisation will be possible, as acknowledged by Paragraph 19 of the Resolution. That would in any case require a *new resolution* of the Security Council. *Ratione loci*, inspections and seizures may be carried out only "on the high seas off the coast of Libya". Resolution 2240 does not authorise, for the time being, any enforcement action *within the Libyan territorial and internal waters*. That was "a step down" from the initial plans.[70] In effect, EU Council Decision 2015/778 envisages a second phase for EUNAVFOR MED, during which the European force should also conduct boarding, search, sei-

---

[68] See, in general, TREVES, "Codification du droit international et pratique des États dans le droit de la mer", RCADI, Vol. 223, 1990-IV, p. 218 ff.

[69] Para. 10 of Resolution 2240 points out that the authorisations in paras. 7 and 8 do not apply with respect to vessels entitled to sovereign immunity.

[70] See, for instance, Sengupta, "Europeans Seek to Use Force Against Smugglers at Sea", The New York Times, 10 September 2015.

zure, and diversion "in the territorial and internal waters" of Libya in accordance with "any applicable UN Security Council Resolution or consent of the coastal State concerned".[71] As to the *consent of the coastal State*, during the drafting of Resolution 2240 attempts at obtaining the authorisation of the then internationally recognised Government of Libya (based in Tobruk) met with considerable difficulties. In any case, the Tobruk Government did not control the whole Libyan territory and that would have complicated the conduct of the operation in areas under the authority of opposing factions, controlling in particular the region of Tripoli and its ports (where the majority of the smugglers operate). On the other hand, the Tobruk Government made it extremely clear that it would not have issued its consent if the EU had decided to negotiate with rival movements.

From a legal point of view, when acting under Chapter VII, the Security Council *could have authorised enforcement action in Libyan territorial waters or territory, even without the consent* of the territorial State. That would however represent an extraordinary action in the practice of the Security Council. In this case, that possibility looked immediately unrealistic due to the position of two permanent members of the Security Council (Russia and China) and of African States.[72] In practice, Resolution 2240 has only authorised *a first step* of the envisaged EUNAVFOR MED phase 2 ("phase 2 Alpha"). The full implementation of phase 2, with an expansion of the operation into the territorial and internal waters of Libya ("phase 2 Bravo") will be contingent upon the formation of a government of national unity in Libya, which could consent to that development, opening the way for a further Security Council resolution. In order to define the area covered by the abovementioned authorization, Resolution 2240 makes reference to "the high seas off the coasts of Libya". The precise identification of the maritime zones in which the operation can take place is not obvious. On the one hand, the legal regime governing the sea areas off the coasts of Libya is far from settled. On the other hand, it is not immediately clear whether the notion of "high seas" under the Resolution also includes areas over which Libya claims exclusive rights as to the regulation of economic activities. One has to take into account that in 1973 Libya declared that the Gulf of Sidra forms part of its internal waters: the Gulf was in particular enclosed by a line, of approximately 300 miles, along the 32°30' parallel of north latitude.[73] However, this claim was rejected by a good number of States, including major EU States (France, Germany, Italy, Spain, and the United Kingdom).[74]

---

[71] Decision 2015/778, *cit. supra* note 7, Art. 2.

[72] The need to fully respect the sovereignty and territorial integrity of Libya is affirmed in para. 2 of Resolution 2240 and was reasserted by some UN members after its adoption. See UN Doc. S/PV.7531 (*cit. supra* note 38), notably the statements of Chad (p. 3), Malaysia (p. 4), China (p. 6), Jordan (p. 7).

[73] UN Legislative Series, National Legislations and Treaties relating to the Law of the Sea (ST/LEG/SER.B/18), 1976, p. 26. See FRANCIONI, "The Gulf of Sidra Incident (United States v. Libya) and International Law", IYIL, 1980-81, p. 85 ff.

[74] See ROACH and SMITH, *Excessive Maritime Claims*, 3rd ed., Leiden, 2012, pp. 46-48.

In February 2005, Libya established a fisheries protection zone, in respect of the General People's Committee Decision No. 37 of 2005.[75] In order to delimit the exclusive fishery zone the Libyan General People's Committee issued a separate Decision (No. 105 of 2005).[76] The delimitation of the Libyan fishery zone met with the protests of a number of States and of the EU Presidency: considering that Libya claims the Gulf of Sidra as part of its internal waters, the new 62 mile fishery zone seemed to be measured from the external limit of a 12 mile territorial sea delimited from the closing line of the Gulf.[77] Additionally, in 2009 Libya declared an Exclusive Economic Zone (EEZ) "adjacent to and extending as far beyond its territorial waters as permitted under international law".[78] The outer limits of that zone have not been precisely delimited yet.

What conclusions can be drawn from such an intricate legal picture? First, EUNAVFOR MED is certainly not going to acknowledge the Libyan claim to the Gulf of Sidra and as a consequence will consider the Libyan territorial sea as not extending beyond a 12 mile belt from the coastline. Second, it seems safe to argue that the notion of "high seas off the coasts of Libya" also includes areas possibly claimed by Libya as part of its fisheries conservation zone or EEZ. It is true that according to Article 86 UNCLOS, which is expressly mentioned in Resolution 2240 as reflecting international law, the high seas provisions of the Convention "apply to all parts of the sea that are not included in the EEZ". Yet, UNCLOS attributes to the coastal State, in its EEZ, sovereign rights and jurisdiction linked to the economic exploitation of the zone, the protection of the marine environment and marine scientific research, reaffirming at the same time the freedom of navigation for all States in the EEZ. Considering that the authority given to EUNAVOR MED by Resolution 2240 concerns the control of navigation for the purpose of preventing unlawful migration, that authority should also extend to waters claimed by Libya as EEZ or fisheries conservation zones. That was indirectly confirmed by the Libyan delegate at the time of adoption of the Resolution. According to his statement, Libya does not object to the deployment of a European maritime force off its coasts, even if it invokes "coordination and cooperation" between the EU and the countries concerned, "particularly when it involves military operations in the EEZ of these countries".[79] That statement seems to allude to the claim, put forward by a number of coastal States, as to the control of the activities of foreign warships in their EEZs. More particularly, some coastal States require an authorisation with respect to the carrying out of military manoeuvres whereas others even claim to subject the navigation of warships in

---

[75] "Law of the Sea Bulletin", No. 58, 2005, p. 14 ff.
[76] *Ibid.*
[77] See ATTARD, "Mediterranean Maritime Jurisdictional Claims: A Review", in BASEDOW, MAGNUS and WOLFRUM (eds.), *The Hamburg Lectures on Maritime Affairs 2009 & 2010*, Berlin, 2012, p. 89 ff., p. 99.
[78] "Law of the Sea Bulletin", No. 72, 2010, p. 79.
[79] UN Doc. S/PV.7531, *cit. supra* note 38, pp. 10-11.

their EEZ to their consent. Apart from the dubious legality of these claims, one must underline that the authority, granted by Resolution 2240, to carry out the described activities on the high seas – which as noted above includes areas under the economic jurisdiction of the coastal States concerned – *is not subject to any specific condition concerning the coastal State's consent*.

6.   THE REQUIREMENT TO MAKE "GOOD FAITH EFFORTS" TO OBTAIN THE FLAG STATE'S CONSENT

Under Resolution 2240 (2015) the authorisation to inspect flagged ships is subject to some preconditions. First, the warship must have "reasonable grounds to suspect" that the vessels "are being used for migrant smuggling and human trafficking".[80] Second, before boarding a vessel suspected of the activities in question, the Member State or regional organisation must make good faith efforts to obtain the consent of the vessel's flag State. The model centred on the requirement to undertake "good faith efforts" is not completely new in UN practice. One may quote as a first precedent, also concerning the Libyan crisis, Resolution 2146 (2014). In Paragraph 5, the latter authorises States to inspect on the high seas a vessel suspected of illicitly exporting crude oil from Libya; in Paragraph 6 however it also requests that Member States "before taking the measures authorised in Paragraph 5, first seek the consent of the vessel's flag State". In this case the authorisation to carry out the inspections was confined to ships having previously been identified by a Security Council committee, as underlined by a number of States.[81] Another example is offered by Resolution 2182 (2014) on Somalia, with regard to the enforcement of the ban on charcoal export and of the arms embargo. Paragraph 15 of the Resolution authorises Member States to inspect, in Somali territorial waters and on the high seas off the coast of Somalia, vessels which they have reasonable grounds to believe are violating the ban or the embargo; yet the following paragraph requests States, prior to any inspection, "to make good-faith efforts to first seek the consent of the vessel's flag State". On both occasions, the formula was adopted in order to meet the preoccupations put forward by a number of Security Council members (notably, China, Russia, and some developing States) as to a possible erosion of the freedom of navigation and the principle of exclusive flag State jurisdiction.[82] These States

---

[80] The formula is identical to that of Art. 8(2) of the Smuggling of Migrants Protocol.

[81] UN Doc. S/PV.7142, 19 March 2014: see in particular the statements of Argentina, Russia, and China (pp. 2-3).

[82] As to Resolution 2146 (2014) see *supra* note 81. With regard to Resolution 2182 (2014) see UN Doc. S/PV.7286, 24 October 2014, notably the statements of China and Argentina (at 4-5). Jordan did not accept even that compromise and decided to abstain, arguing that the authorisation granted by the Security Council "may still be open to abuse and threaten the maritime trade on the high seas" (p. 3).

also stressed the need to scrupulously comply with the conditions and limitations set forth by the Security Council and that the authorisation should not be regarded as a precedent for establishing customary international law.

Going back to Resolution 2240 (2015), the text of Paragraph 7 clearly entails that, before carrying out the inspection, the warship *has to request the permission of the flag State*. On the other hand, the formula in question also implies that the inspection can take place in situations in which *the consent has not been expressly given by the flag State*, provided good faith efforts were made to get such a consent. The precise identification of these situations is however problematic.[83] Some of the aspects left open by Resolution 2240 (2015) should be clarified by the Operation Plan and Rules of Engagement of EUNAVFOR MED (both documents are classified "confidential").[84] Yet the imprecision of Resolution 2240 could open the way to disputes as to the lawfulness of more specific rules adopted by the EU. In any case, considering the text of the relevant paragraphs of Resolution 2240, as well as its context, it seems that an inspection (under the good faith efforts formula) can be carried out in case of *lack of response, on the part of the flag State*, to a request made by the intercepting State. One could speak in that regard of a sort of *tacit consent* on the part of the flag State.[85] However – in contrast to, for instance, some bilateral interdiction agreements concluded for fighting the proliferation of weapons of mass destruction, drug trafficking or illegal fishing – Resolution 2240 does not establish a precise time-limit within which a response has to come from the flag State.[86] In this regard, it must be noted that according to Paragraph 9 of Resolution 2240 flag States, having received requests under Paragraphs 7 and 8, are called upon "to review and respond to them in a rapid and timely manner". In the light of the above, one has to conclude that the intervening State, in order to comply with the good-faith efforts requirement, must transmit the request to the flag State and, before boarding the vessel, has to wait for a time *which it deems reasonable in the light of the concrete circumstances*. Among these, the existence of a danger to the human life of persons on board the vessel may naturally have a special weight.

Yet, *quid iuris* if the authorisation is *expressly denied* by the flag State? It is submitted that in that case an inspection could not be carried out and, if it had already started, should be immediately stopped. On the other hand, if the consent of the flag State is conditioned upon certain limitations, the inspection and possible

---

[83] WILSON, *supra* note 39, pp. 5 and 8.

[84] A request for access to these documents was refused, on 29 October 2015, by the General Secretariat of the Council. See at: <http://www.asktheeu.org/en/request/eunavfor_med_operation_sophia_op>.

[85] On this point Resolution 2240 clearly goes beyond the Smuggling of Migrants Protocol, which requires the *express authorisation* of the flag State in order to carry out any inspection of a suspected vessel.

[86] Resolution 2240 does not specify whether the request has to be in writing nor whether the flag State has to acknowledge receipt of the request. See also WILSON, *supra* note 39, pp. 5 and 8.

seizure of the vessel could take place only according to these limitations. These conclusions seem to be required by a reading of Resolution 2240 carried out in accordance with the criteria for the interpretation of Security Council resolutions outlined by the International Court of Justice.[87] In effect, in addition to the text of Resolution 2240, of great relevance are *in casu* the statements issued by a number of States, at the moment of its adoption, stressing the need to interpret the resolution in a strict manner and so as not to disrupt the principle of flag State jurisdiction.[88] Also the practice concerning previous references to the formula in question, or to analogous ones, confirms that, in the view of the majority of UN members, they do not intend to supersede the principle of the exclusive jurisdiction of the flag State. Overall, the "good faith efforts" formula clearly constitutes a compromise between the model characterised by the authorisation to inspect vessels *without flag State consent*, at times applied by the Security Council,[89] and the traditional rule under which *express flag State permission* has first to be obtained by the interdicting State (confirmed also by the Smuggling of Migrants Protocol). In any case, the Security Council has once again stated in Resolution 2240 that the authorisations there given shall not affect customary international law *in subiecta materia*.

7. THE "DISPOSAL" OF INSPECTED VESSELS CONFIRMED TO HAVE BEEN EMPLOYED BY THE TRAFFICKERS

Since its initial conception, the naval operation to be launched in the Mediterranean for fighting migrant smuggling was envisaged as necessarily including the authority to destroy, or at least render inoperable, vessels and other assets employed in order to commit this activity.[90] Council Decision 2015/778 delineates, in its Article 2(2), a third phase of the mission, in which EUNAVFOR MED shall

> "in accordance with any applicable UN Security Council Resolution or consent by the coastal State concerned, take all necessary measures against a vessel and related assets, including through disposing of them or rendering them inoperable, which are suspected of being used for human smuggling or trafficking, in the territory of that State, under the conditions set out in that Resolution or consent".

---

[87] *Accordance with International Law of the Unilateral Declaration of Independence in Respect of Kosovo*, Advisory Opinion, ICJ Reports, 2010, p. 403 ff., para. 94.

[88] See UN Doc. S/PV.7531 (*cit. supra* note 38), in particular the statements of Russia and Chile (pp. 6-7).

[89] See, for instance, Resolution 665 (1990) of 25 August 1990 on Iraq-Kuwait, para. 1; Resolution 787 (1992) of 16 November 1992 on Serbia and Montenegro; Resolution 1973 (2011) of 17 March 2011 on Libya, para. 13.

[90] European Council, special meeting of 23 April 2015, *cit. supra* note 6 and related text.

Under the EU Decision, the measures aimed at disposing of the vessels should take place in a third phase of the mission and "in the territory of the State concerned" whereas EUNAVFOR MED has only reached phase 2 on the high seas and the prospect of a resolution authorising the destruction of vessels in Libyan territory or territorial waters is still some way away.

Yet, in Paragraph 8 of Resolution 2240 the Security Council, after authorising Member States to seize the vessels that have been inspected and are confirmed as being used for human smuggling or trafficking, "underscores that further action with regard to [...] vessels inspected under the authority of Paragraph 7, including disposal, will be taken in accordance with applicable international law with due consideration of the interests of any third parties who have acted in good faith". The paragraph in question is obviously applicable only to foreign flagged vessels lawfully intercepted under the authority of the Resolution and, as previously argued, is also applicable to flagless ships.[91] It however displays a certain measure of ambiguity. First, one has to determine what is meant by "further action [...] including disposal". Second, one must clarify the proviso according to which such further action is allowed only "in accordance with applicable international law" and "with due consideration of the interests of any third parties who have acted in good faith".

As to the definition of further action, including disposal, considering that the first part of Paragraph 8 already authorises the seizure of the traffickers' vessel, it is clear that that notion refers to the *confiscation* of the vessels by the national courts of a Member State and also to the possible *destruction* of the ships, under the conditions spelled out below (the French version refers to "*leur destruction*"). That interpretation is confirmed by the reference to the EU Decision 2015/778, made in the preamble of the Resolution, and by a general assessment of the background circumstances of adoption of the resolution. More particularly, taking into account all these factors, it is submitted that Paragraph 8 of Resolution 2240 can safely be read by a Member State (and the EU) as giving it the power to take the following actions: (a) to *seize* the ship; (b) to *divert* it to a port and have it *adjudicated* upon by the national courts; (c) to *confiscate* or *destroy* it, in accordance with the decisions of national courts or of the commander of the intercepting ship. The proviso concerning due consideration of the interests of third parties having acted in good faith would seem to exclude in principle the confiscation or destruction of a flagged ship *without the consent of the flag State or a decision of a national court of the capturing State*. The latter would in particular be necessary in order to determine the owners of the seized vessel and their possible good faith.[92] It seems that this

---

[91] See *supra* section 4.

[92] In particular, if a legitimate owner is found and if it is also determined that the latter acted in good faith (e.g., having the ship being stolen) a court could decide to return the vessel to him. The adjudication of the vessel by the capturing State should in principle be subject to the existence of an appropriate title for the exercise of adjudicative and enforcement jurisdiction. See, in this regard, *infra* section 10.

rule should apply in principle even in respect of flagless ships, for it is generally considered that "a ship without nationality is not an ownerless movable because the lack of nationality does not affect the property of the ship".[93]

At the same time, one cannot exclude, under the broad formula employed by Resolution 2240, the *immediate destruction of a vessel*, confirmed as being used by traffickers, when the commander of the capturing ship *bona fide* determines that the vessel could not be escorted to a port, in particular considering its sea-unworthiness or on account of weather and sea conditions. It is worth noting that an official report submitted on 25 January 2016 by the Commander of EUNAVFOR MED, released by WikiLeaks in February 2016,[94] affirms that during the first six months of the operation 67 vessels (wooden and rubber) have been destroyed. In this regard, during a parliamentary hearing, Admiral Credendino has confirmed that the vessels intercepted by EUNAVFOR MED are destroyed at sea whenever it is not possible to divert them to a port, pointing out that abandoning them on the high seas would endanger international navigation.[95]

8. THE AUTHORISATION TO USE "ALL MEASURES COMMENSURATE TO THE SPECIFIC CIRCUMSTANCES" AND THE DUTY TO RESPECT HUMAN RIGHTS

In Paragraph 10 of Resolution 2240 the Security Council "decides" to authorise States and regional organisations to use all measures commensurate to the specific circumstances in confronting migrant smugglers or human traffickers. That clearly implies an authorisation to undertake *coercive measures* vis-à-vis those ships and individuals, suspected of being engaged in the smuggling of migrants, which resist boarding or any other activity covered by the resolution. This language is often used in resolutions adopted by the Security Council for authorising States or regional organisations to enforce compliance with international sanctions and is generally

---

[93] LAGONI, "Merchant Ships", in WOLFRUM (ED.), *The Max Planck Encyclopedia of Public International Law*, Oxford, 2012, para. 33.

[94] Council of the European Union, "EUNAVFOR MED Op. SOPHIA Six Monthly Report from 22 June to 31 December 2015", Doc. EEAS (2016) 126, 27 January 2016, pp. 11, 22.

[95] See Parliament Hearing of the Operation Commander, *cit. supra* note 18. Admiral Credendino has specified that disposal at sea would not contravene international conventions on environmental protection as it could be justified by the notion of *force majeure*. This practice seems to be followed also by Italian vessels operating within the national mission "Mare Sicuro" and by vessels assigned to Frontex Joint Operation Triton. In this regard, see the aggregate data on the activities carried out in the Central Mediterranean, from March to December 2015, by vessels from "Mare Sicuro", Frontex, EUNAVFOR MED, the Italian Coast Guard, and Guardia di Finanza published in the "Editorial", Rivista maritittma, January 2016: "Smugglers arrested: 502; ships seized: 1; total boats sunk: 768 rafts and boats (if we consider the total area of Mare Sicuro operation), 285 rafts and boats (if we consider only the boats destroyed by units operating within Mare Sicuro)".

interpreted as including a right to use armed force.[96] Indeed, after the adoption of Resolution 2240, France stressed that "the text precisely defines the circumstances in which the recourse to force would be authorised to combat resistance by traffickers".[97] The initial draft resolution circulated by the United Kingdom envisaged an authorisation to use "all necessary means" in confronting the smugglers.[98] Such formula was however regarded as too broad by some UN members, who wanted to prevent any possible "abusive" interpretation of the mandate granted.[99] As noted in the legal literature,[100] the language finally adopted in Paragraph 10 of Resolution 2240 on the one hand expressly refers to the criterion of *proportionality* in the use of coercion,[101] and, on the other hand, it seems also capable of including measures not amounting to an use of armed force properly so called (for instance, when activities are carried out with the flag State's authorisation). In effect, in the case in question force will be directed at private individuals, or vessels, for "law enforcement" objectives.[102] That also explains the requirement to carry out activities authorised by Resolution 2240 "in full compliance with international human rights law".[103] Furthermore, Member States and regional organisations are called upon "to provide for the safety of persons on board as an utmost priority and to avoid causing harm to the marine environment or to the safety of navigation". These require-

---

[96] See BLOKKER, "Outsourcing the Use of Force: Towards more Security Council Control of Authorized Operations?", in WELLER (ed.), *The Oxford Handbook of the Use of Force In International Law*, Oxford, 2015, pp. 213-214. For a recent example, see Resolution 1973 (2011), *cit. supra* note 89.

[97] UN Doc. S/PV.7531, *cit. supra* note 38, p. 6. Venezuela abstained from voting on Resolution 2240 (2015) precisely because the latter authorises "the use of military force to deal with the humanitarian situation of migrants" (p. 5).

[98] See also Art. 2 (2) of Decision 2015/778, *cit. supra* note 7.

[99] See FALEG and BLOCKMANS, *cit. supra* note 7, p. 3: "Russia insisted on a watertight mandate to prevent a repetition of what it considered to be an abuse by Western nations" of the 2011 Resolution on military intervention in Libya.

[100] See CADIN, *cit. supra* note 39, p. 700.

[101] See also the statement of the United Kingdom after the voting ("any action will be proportionate"): UN Doc. S/PV.7531, *cit. supra* note 38, p. 2.

[102] The issue whether one must conceptually distinguish between measures involving the use of armed force in international relations and mere "police actions" or "law enforcement activities" is beyond the scope of this article. See GUILFOYLE, *cit. supra* note 60, p. 272 ff.; and PAPASTAVRIDIS, *cit. supra* note 60, p. 68 ff.

[103] As to the applicability of the European Convention on Human Rights (ECHR) with respect to maritime interception activities carried out on the high seas see, *inter alia*, European Court of Human Rights, *Medvedyev v. France*, Application No. 3394/03, Judgment of 29 March 2010; *Hirsi Jamaa and Others v. Italy*, Application No. 27765/09, Judgment of 23 February 2012. See also TREVES, "Human Rights and the Law of the Sea", Berkeley Journal of International Law, 2010, p. 1 ff. available at: <http://scholarship.law.berkeley.edu/bjil/vol28/iss1/1>; PAPASTAVRIDIS, *cit. supra* note 60, p. 73 ff.; and LEHMANN, "The Use of Force Against People Smugglers: Conflicts with Refugee Law and Human Rights Law", *EJIL: Talk!*, 22 June 2015, available at: <http://www.ejiltalk.org/the-use-of-force-against-people-smugglers-conflicts-with-refugee-law-and-human-rights-law>.

ments reflect the safeguard clauses envisaged, in respect of maritime interception activities, by Article 9 of the Smuggling of Migrants Protocol.

It is generally accepted that the basic rules governing the use of force in boarding private vessels have been articulated in the international case law, notably by the International Tribunal for the Law of the Sea in its judgment on the *Saiga* case, where it is stated that international law "[r]equires that the use of force must be avoided as far as possible and, where force is unavoidable, it must not go beyond what is reasonable and necessary in the circumstances. Considerations of humanity must apply in the law of the sea, as they do in other areas of international law".[104]

One must keep in mind that in the case in issue coercion would be used against vessels generally having on board victims of trafficking and migrants (who can also be sometimes regarded as victims of the smugglers). Hence, taking into account the need to preserve as an the utmost priority the life of persons on board as well as the abovementioned *considerations of humanity* it is apparent that military force should be used only as a measure of last resort.[105] EUNAVFOR MED Rules of Engagement are classified as confidential.[106] However, from the remarks made before parliamentary bodies by the Operation Commander[107] and by Lieutenant General Wosolsobe,[108] it seems to emerge that current EUNAVFOR MED Rules of Engagement are very prudent as to the use of military force, basically confined to situations of *self-defence*.[109] In the Italian legal order, the rule currently governing the use of force in the framework of maritime activities directed at contrasting illegal immigration is also essentially based upon the principle of self-defence.[110]

Particular emphasis is placed by Resolution 2240 on the need to treat migrants with humanity and dignity and on the obligation of States and regional organisations to comply with *international human rights* and *refugee law*. In this regard,

---

[104] *The M/V "Saiga" (No. 2) Case (Saint Vincent and the Grenadines v. Guinea)*, Judgment of 1 July 1999, para. 155.

[105] According to PAPASTAVRIDIS (*cit. supra* note 60, pp. 301-302), the use of force in operations involving the "interception of human beings" would be allowed exclusively in self-defence.

[106] See *supra* note 84.

[107] See Parliament Hearing of the Operation Commander, *cit. supra* note 18.

[108] See House of Lords, EU External Affairs Sub-Committee, EU Naval Force – Mediterranean (Operation Sophia) Inquiry (available at: <https://www.parliament.uk>), Evidence Given by Lieutenant General Wolfgang Wosolsobe, Director General, European Union Military Staff, 3 March 2016.

[109] Under Resolution 2240 the use of force by EUNAVFOR MED vessels seems to be permitted also in order to carry out the basic task of the operation (contrasting human smugglers and traffickers), provided the abovementioned requirements of necessity, proportionality and humanity are fully respected.

[110] According to Art. 7 of the Ministerial Decree of 14 July 2003 (*cit. supra* note 58), when the use of force is necessary, the intensity, duration and scope of the response must be commensurate to the intensity of the offence, and to the imminence and effectiveness of the threat. See CAFFIO, *cit. supra* note 2, p. 44.

the Security Council expressly recognises that among the migrants "may be persons who meet the definition of a refugee under the 1951 Convention relating to the Status of Refugees and the 1967 Protocol thereto".[111] The same preoccupations were expressed, at the time of adoption of the Resolution, by many members of the Security Council.[112] As far as the EU is concerned, however, and notwithstanding the worries sometimes expressed,[113] there seems to be no reason to believe that the abovementioned obligations could be disregarded. The EU Decision establishing EUNAVFOR MED expressly states in its preamble that the operation will be conducted in accordance with international law and in particular with the 1951 Geneva Refugee Convention, "the principle of non-refoulement and international human rights law".[114] More importantly, the obligations stemming from international law with respect to the treatment of asylum seekers have been fully incorporated into the law of the EU, and of its Member States, and in many respects significantly expanded (notably, by the so called "subsidiary protection").[115] As to the basic principle of *non-refoulement*, envisaged by Article 33 of the 1951 Refugee Convention,[116] it is well established in EU primary law, particularly in Article 78 (1) TFEU and in Articles 18 and 19 of the EU Charter of Fundamental Rights (and implemented in relevant secondary legislation).[117] Last but not least, the case law of the Court of Justice of the EU[118] and of the European Court of Human Rights (ECtHR)[119] have certainly contributed to the full consolidation of the principle in the law and practice of the EU and its Member States.

---

[111] Resolution 2240, para. 7 of the preamble.

[112] See UN Doc. S/PV.7531 (*cit. supra* note 38), p. 3 (Chad), p. 4 (Malaysia), p. 6 (Russia and France), p. 7 (Chile and Jordan), p. 8 (USA), p. 9 (Nigeria).

[113] See, for instance, LEHMANN, *cit. supra* note 103.

[114] Para. 6.

[115] Under EU law, protection is also granted to a person who does not qualify as a refugee but in respect of whom substantial grounds have been shown for believing that the person concerned, if returned to his country of origin, would face a real risk of suffering "serious harm" as defined in Art. 15 of the "Qualifications Directive" (death penalty or execution; torture or inhuman or degrading treatment or punishment; serious and individual threat to a civilian's life or person by reason of indiscriminate violence in situations of international or internal armed conflict): see Directive 2011/95/EU of 13 December 2011 on standards for the qualification of third-country nationals or stateless persons as beneficiaries of international protection, for a uniform status for refugees or for persons eligible for subsidiary protection, and for the content of the protection granted, OJ EU L 337, 20 December 2011, p. 9 ff.

[116] See TREVISANUT, "The Principle of Non-Refoulement and the De-Territorialization of Border Control at Sea", Leiden JIL, 2014, p. 661 ff.

[117] See, in particular, Art. 4 of Regulation 656/2014, *cit. supra* note 65.

[118] See, among others, Joined Cases C-175/08, C-176/08, C-178/08, and C-179/08, *Salahadin Abdulla and Others* [2010] ECR I-1493, para. 53; Case C-31/09 *Bolbol* [2010] ECR I-5539, para. 38; and Joined Cases C-411/10 and C-493/10, *N. S. v. Secretary of State for the Home Department and M.E. and Others v. Refugee Applications Commissioner and Minister for Justice, Equality and Law Reform* [2011] ECR I-13905.

[119] *Hirsi Jamaa and Others v. Italy*, *cit. supra* note 103.

In practice, *all the migrants or asylum seekers* intercepted or rescued at sea by EUNAVFOR MED, in the framework of phases 1 and 2 Alpha, have been *disembarked in Italy* and entrusted to the Italian authorities for assessing their status. In effect, it seems that, in accordance with a PSC Decision, EUNAVFOR MED will comply with the procedures for the disembarkation of persons rescued at sea adopted for the Frontex Operation Triton.[120] In this regard, there has been no major incident reported as to violations of the international rules on refugees and other protected persons.[121]

Delicate issues could arise with respect to an eventual transition to the operation's "Phase 2 Bravo" in Libyan territorial waters. In that case one could suggest, as the most practical solution, the disembarkation in Libya of migrants rescued or intercepted in its territorial waters. Apart from the existence of an effective government of national unity in Libya, that solution would also require the adoption by the EU of adequate procedures or controls in order to exclude any possible violations of human rights and refugee law.

9.   THE ISSUE OF RESPONSIBILITY AND COMPENSATION

Resolution 2240(2015) does not include any reference to an obligation of the interdicting State (or regional organisation) to compensate a boarded vessel for the interference. On the other hand, Article 9(2) of the Smuggling of Migrants Protocol provides for an obligation to compensate the ship, for any loss or damage it may have sustained, where the grounds for the measures taken "prove to be unfounded" and the ship in question has not committed any act justifying them. A similar obligation is envisaged by Article 110(3) UNCLOS, with regard to ships suspected of being without nationality. How can this omission in the text of Resolution 2240 be explained?

One could argue that the compensation obligation, as envisaged by the abovementioned treaties, is nonetheless applicable by virtue of the references, in Resolution 2240, to the requirement to carry out inspections and other measures in accordance with international law and the express *renvoi* to the Smuggling of Migrants Protocol. However, the fact that Resolution 2240 does not refer to any rule on compensation could also suggest a different reading, which seems preferable. Particularly, it is suggested that *under Resolution 2240 a duty of compensation would arise for a boarding State, or regional organisation, only in the case of a breach of a requirement envisaged by the Resolution.* One may refer to the violation: (a) of the condition to carry out the inspection only in the presence of

---

[120] See Parliament Hearing of the Operation Commander, *cit. supra* note 18, and Council of the European Union, "EUNAVFOR MED Op. SOPHIA Six Monthly Report", *cit. supra* note 94, p. 11.
[121] See also European Parliament, Parliamentary Questions, 27 October 2015, Answer given by HR Mogherini on behalf of the Commission, E-012462/2015.

"reasonable grounds" to suspect involvement in the proscribed activities, notably where bad faith or negligence of the boarding State or organisation can be proved; (b) of any condition imposed by the flag State when delivering its authorisation; (c) of any other rule set forth by Resolution 2240 as to the manner in which the autho-rised activities have to be carried out, including those relating to the lawful use of force. In other words, it seems that an obligation to compensate should be limited to situations amounting to an unlawful act of the intercepting State or organisation, excluding *in casu* any reading in favour of forms of "strict liability" and *a for-tiori* any responsibility from lawful acts of the boarding State or organisation. That seems to be a logical consequence of the *lack of any reference to compensation obligations* in Resolution 2240 and, more importantly, of the fact that the boarding States, in the case in issue, carry out *functions of general interest*, in order to avert a humanitarian tragedy, under a specific mandate from the Security Council.

Another thorny issue, which is not tackled by the Security Council Resolution (which is obvious) nor by the EU Decision having established EUNAVFOR MED (which is less obvious), is that of the *attribution of a wrongful act* committed by a vessel assigned to the operation. It is not clear whether the responsibility should be attributed to the flag State of the vessel or to the EU, or to both.[122]

10. ARREST AND PROSECUTION OF SMUGGLERS AND TRAFFICKERS

Under Council Decision 2015/778, the mission of EUNAVFOR MED seems to be focused on the identification, capture, and disposal of the vessels and assets used by smugglers or traffickers. Unlike the legal acts adopted by the EU Council in order to establish the counter-piracy Operation Atalanta, Decision 2015/778 does not provide for a clear mandate of EUNAVFOR MED to ensure the arrest and pros-ecution of the individuals suspected of migrant smuggling or human trafficking. Possible action vis-à-vis suspected smugglers and traffickers is only referred to in the Decision's preamble. More particularly, in Paragraph 7 it is noted that States may intercept on the high seas vessels suspected of the activities in question, where there is flag State authorisation or where the vessel is without nationality, and that they "may take appropriate measures against the vessels, persons and cargo". Then, in Paragraph 9, the Council observes that "a State may take appropriate measures against persons present on its territory whom it suspects of smuggling or traffick-ing humans with a view to their possible arrest and prosecution, in accordance with international law and its domestic law".

As to Resolution 2240 (2015), its preamble includes a somewhat stronger lan-guage *in subiecta materia*, making reference to "the obligations of States under ap-

---

[122] On that issue, which is beyond the scope of this article, see, in general, EVANS and KOUTRAKOS, *The International Responsibility of the European Union*, Oxford, 2016.

plicable international law to exercise due diligence to prevent and combat migrant smuggling and human trafficking" and "to investigate and punish perpetrators". In addition, Paragraph 15 "calls upon all States with relevant jurisdiction under international law and national legislation, to investigate and prosecute persons responsible for acts of migrant smuggling and human trafficking at sea".[123]

That being the legal framework established at UN and EU level, one must underline that in practice a number of individuals suspected of the acts at issue have effectively been apprehended by ships participating in Operation Sophia. More particularly, they have all been entrusted to the Italian authorities, as acknowledged by the report submitted on 25 January 2016 by the Operation Commander,[124] and confirmed by HR Mogherini before the European Parliament. In answering, on 4 March 2016, to a parliamentary question, the HR stated:

> "[I]n the first part of the second phase of its mandate [...] EUNAVFOR MED Operation Sophia is authorised to conduct boarding, search, seizure and diversion on the high seas of vessels suspected of being used for human smuggling or trafficking. So far, 48 suspected smugglers/traffickers have been apprehended and are in the Italian judicial system; they have either been sentenced, awaiting trial or are under investigation".[125]

From a strictly legal perspective, this practice may give rise to a number of issues. First and foremost, *the existence of an appropriate basis under Italian law for asserting criminal jurisdiction over these individuals must be assessed*. Second, one must consider the possibility of legal actions challenging the legality, under human rights standards, of measures of arrest and detention of the suspected smugglers, carried out by EUNAVFOR MED ships in the course of their law enforcement operations. With regard to the first issue, it must be noted that under Italian legislation and jurisprudence the bases for asserting criminal jurisdiction vis-à-vis suspected smugglers and traffickers apprehended on the high seas are not so solidly established, at least in some cases. Indeed, the Italian criminal system is based upon the general *principle of the territoriality* of penal law (Articles 3 and 6 of the Criminal Code) and the exercise of national criminal jurisdiction in respect of a crime carried out by a foreigner on foreign territory (or on the high seas) has an

---

[123] At the time of adoption of Resolution 2240 the UK stated that all EU Member States contributing to EUNAVFOR MED now have the authority to interdict smugglers on the high seas and that "any smugglers stopped will be arrested and their boats seized" (UN Doc. S/PV.7531, *cit. supra* note 38, p. 2).

[124] See Council of the European Union, "EUNAVFOR MED Op. SOPHIA Six Monthly Report", *cit. supra* note 94, p. 11.

[125] European Parliament, Parliamentary Questions, 4 March 2016, Answer given by HR Mogherini on behalf of the Commission, E-015553/2015.

exceptional character. In accordance with Article 7 of the Criminal Code, foreigners can be prosecuted before Italian courts with regard to a set of specific offences affecting essential national interests, listed in numbers 1-4 and having nothing to do with the subject of the present discussion, or with respect to "any other offence for which special provisions of law or international conventions provide for the applicability of Italian law". Apart from these situations, under Article 10 of the Criminal Code a foreigner who commits a crime against a foreigner outside Italian territory can be prosecuted in Italy only when several conditions are met: (a) the alleged offender must be in Italy; (b) the offence must be one for which a minimum sentence of three years of imprisonment is established; (c) there must be a request from the Minister of Justice (or the complaint of the victim of the offence if required under Italian law); (d) no extradition may take place.

It goes without saying that the Italian jurisdiction is established when the ship boarded is of *Italian nationality*[126] or when the proscribed conduct is carried out *in Italian territorial or internal waters*. As far as *ships without nationality* are concerned, it has already been mentioned[127] that Italian case law does not seem to follow the theory according to which flagless ships *per se* can be subjected to the jurisdiction of any State. As a consequence, the assertion of Italian jurisdiction vis-à-vis suspected smugglers on board ships without nationality should be founded on one of the grounds envisaged by the Italian Criminal Code.

In this connection, one must underline a *trend in the Italian case law to broadly interpret the territoriality principle*, so as to establish the Italian jurisdiction vis-à-vis foreigners apprehended on the high seas (both on foreign flagged vessels and on flagless vessels). That is made possible by a broad construction of Article 6(2) of the Criminal Code which, in order to determine the *locus commissi delicti*, provides that a crime is considered to have been committed in the territory of the State when the act or the omission constituting the crime was at least "in part" perpetrated there, or the effects of the offence occurred there.[128] Indeed, Italian courts have declared their jurisdiction when the smugglers or traffickers are *part of a criminal network* and *at least a fraction of the conduct attributable to the network took place in Italian territory* (e.g. mother ship operating in connection with smaller vessels departing from the Italian coast or territorial waters,[129] or carried along with it and having penetrated into Italian waters;[130] and complicity in the crime by persons sit-

---

[126] See Art. 4 of the Italian Criminal Code.

[127] See *supra* section 4.

[128] See MASTROJENI, "I limiti spaziali di applicazione della legge penale e i rapporti con giurisdizioni straniere", in DE VERO (ed.), *La legge, penale, il reato, il reo, la persona offesa*, Torino, 2010, p. 101 ff.

[129] *Corte di Cassazione (Sez. I penale)*, 1 February 2013, No. 16653 (rubbed dinghy departed from Sicily).

[130] See the *Cemil-Pamuk* case, *cit. supra* note 63.

uated in Italy,[131] whose communications with the smugglers had for instance been intercepted). In these situations, the Italian jurisdiction is extended to all the participants in the crime, including the smugglers or traffickers operating on the high seas. A recent decision of the Court of Cassation has also affirmed Italian jurisdiction where a mother ship on the high seas transfers the migrants into smaller vessels, unfit for navigation, in order to deliberately provoke rescue interventions by other ships and the consequent transfer of the migrants into Italian territory. That, on the basis of a complex legal reasoning according to which the conduct of the rescuers, leading to the disembarkation of the migrants in Italy, should be considered as the action of an *autore mediato* (a person who is used in order to commit a crime, and who is not punishable for that crime); as a consequence *the conduct is attributed to the smugglers operating from the high sea* and the offence is regarded as committed in the Italian territory.[132] This interpretation, under which also the commander of a EUNAVFOR MED vessels could be regarded as an *autore mediato*, is however not generally accepted in the legal literature.[133]

Article 7 of the Italian Criminal Code has also been invoked in order to justify an extension of the Italian jurisdiction. On the one hand, according to some scholars, the assertion of the Italian criminal jurisdiction in respect of persons on board flagless ships could be justified under Article 7(5) of the Criminal Code if read in connection with Article 8(7) of the Smuggling of Migrants Protocol.[134] On the other hand, the Court of Cassation has extended the Italian jurisdiction in respect of the crime of participation in an organised criminal association (*associazione a delinquere*, Article 416 of the Criminal Code) on the basis of the joint application of Article 7(5) of the Criminal Code and Article 15(2)(c) UNCTOC.[135] Yet, both these interpretations may be disputed as not in line with the traditional reading of Article 7(5) of the Criminal Code. According to the latter, the applicability of Italian criminal law cannot simply derive from an international convention which provides for *a faculty* (or even *a generic obligation*) of the State to punish certain offences and which is implemented in the Italian legal system by a law including an *ordine di esecuzione* (order of execution); to that effect, the adoption, in the implementing

---

[131] *Corte di Cassazione (Sez. I penale)*, 23 June 2000, No. 4586; and *Corte di Cassazione (Sez. I penale)*, 20 August 2014, No. 36052.

[132] *Corte di Cassazione (Sez. I penale)*, 28 February-27 March 2014, No. 14510. See CATALDI, "Giurisdizione e intervento in alto mare su navi impegnate nel traffico di migranti", Giur. It., 2015, p. 1498 ff.

[133] See ANNONI, "L'esercizio dell'azione penale nei confronti dei trafficanti di migranti: le responsabilità dell'Italia... e quelle degli altri", *SIDI Blog*, 6 May 2015, available at: <http://www.sidiblog.org/author/alessandra-annoni/>; and LICASTRO, *supra* note 39, pp. 5-6.

[134] See LEANZA and GRAZIANI, "Poteri di *enforcement* e di *jurisdiction* in materia di traffico di migranti via mare: aspetti operativi nell'attività di contrasto", CI, 2014, p. 163 ff., p. 191.

[135] Under this provision a State Party may establish its jurisdiction when the offence is one of those established in accordance with Art. 5(1) UNCTOC and is committed outside its territory with a view to the commission of a serious crime within its territory.

legislation, of *a specific norm providing for the applicability of Italian criminal law to the offence in question* would also be necessary.[136]

In the light of that uncertain legal picture, one must share the opinion of a legal commentator who has advocated, for the sake of legal certainty, the introduction of *ad hoc* legislative rules governing the assertion of criminal jurisdiction over migrant smugglers or human traffickers apprehended at sea.[137] A laudable effort to clarify the legal regime, and systematise the Italian case law *in subiecta materia*, has been undertaken by the DNAA (*Direzione Nazionale Antimafia ed Antiterrorismo*). In particular, the *Procuratore nazionale* (National Prosecutor) issued on 9 January 2014 a document, addressed to the District Public Prosecutor Offices, including "operational proposals" for the solution of issues concerning the exercise of criminal jurisdiction and the adoption of other measures in respect of vessels engaged in the smuggling of migrants.[138] It is however apparent that these guidelines are far from settling all the issues. Besides, they confirm the existence of areas in which the possibility of exerting criminal jurisdiction is very much questionable (notably when it is not possible to establish that at least a fraction of the *iter criminis* occurred in Italian territory).

As mentioned above, in Resolution 2240 the Security Council calls upon all States with relevant jurisdiction to investigate and prosecute persons responsible for acts of migrant smuggling and human trafficking at sea; that action must however be "consistent with States' obligations under international law, including international human rights law and international refugee law, as applicable" (Paragraph 8). In this respect, regard being had to the case law of the ECtHR, one cannot exclude the possibility that the apprehension by ships assigned to EUNAVFOR MED (but also to Frontex Operation Triton) of individuals suspected of human smuggling and trafficking could give rise to legal actions, notably to individual applications lodged with the ECtHR, challenging the arrest and detention under Article 5 ECHR. Among other things, the ECtHR has stated that the Convention is applicable not only in respect of State conduct carried out on board a national vessel[139] but also when a foreign (and supposedly a flagless) private vessel is intercepted on the high seas by a State ship and then escorted into a port.[140] Even if the judgements issued by the ECtHR have thus far accepted that the special circumstances of an arrest during a maritime interception operation must be taken into account in interpreting Article 5 ECHR, intercepting States, as observed in the legal literature, would be wise to contemplate adequate measures to avoid any possible legal challenge, for

---

[136] ANNONI, *cit. supra* note 133. See also MANTOVANI, *Diritto penale. Parte Generale*, 7th ed., 2011, p. 905, note 15.

[137] See ANNONI, *cit. supra* note 133.

[138] "Proposte operative per la soluzione dei problemi di giurisdizione penale nazionale e possibilità di intervento", Diritto penale contemporaneo, with an introductory note of SPIEZIA, available at: <http://www.penalecontemporaneo.it>.

[139] See, in particular, *Hirsi Jamaa and Others v. Italy, cit. supra* note 103, paras. 81-82.

[140] See *Rigopoulos v. Spain*, Application No. 37388/97, Judgment of 12 January 1999; and *Medvedyev v. France, cit. supra* note 103, paras. 66 and 67.

"there are clearly many ECtHR judges who would apply the Strasbourg case law on point strictly, irrespective of the practical challenges that could present in many maritime law-enforcement operations".[141]

Considering that legal framework, it would also seem opportune to provide, at the European level, for a mechanism envisaging the exercise of criminal jurisdiction vis-à-vis the smugglers/traffickers also for other EU Member States, in order not to leave this onerous burden exclusively upon Italy.[142] Even if certainly complex, a mechanism of that kind would implement in the area under consideration the *principle of solidarity and fair sharing of responsibility*: expressly affirmed in EU primary law in respect of the policies of the Union in the field of border checks, asylum, and immigration (Article 80 TFEU), the latter also extends to measures adopted in order to combat illegal immigration and trafficking in human beings.[143] One could even contemplate the devolution to the new European Public's Prosecutor Office of competences *in subiecta materia*, although that possibility appears unlikely in practice.[144] For the time being, it is to be hoped that the "Hotspot Approach", developed by the EU Commission and recently triggered in Italy, will at least provide some operative support, notably by Europol and Eurojust, for the investigation and prosecution of the smugglers.[145]

11. SOME FINAL REMARKS ON THE IMPACT OF EUNAVFOR MED (PHASES 1 AND 2 ALPHA)

In the tenth paragraph of its preamble, Resolution 2240 recalls the International Convention for the Safety of Life at Sea (SOLAS) and the International Convention

---

[141] GUILFOYLE, "ECHR Rights at Sea: *Medvedyev and Others v. France*", *EJIL: Talk!*, 19 April 2010, available at: <http://www.ejiltalk.org/echr-rights-at-sea-medvedyev-and-others-v-france/>. Cf. PETRIG, "Arrest, Detention and Transfer of Piracy Suspects: A Critical Appraisal of the German *Courier* Case Decision", in ANDREONE et al. (eds.), *cit. supra* note 15, p. 153 ff. In answering a question before the House of Lords, Lieutenant General Wosolsobe stated that "much care has been taken to ensure a legally watertight process, using the Italian law enforcement authorities throughout" and that "to date, no prosecution has been dismissed due to a failure of process": House of Lords, EU Naval Force – Mediterranean, *cit. supra* note 108.

[142] See ANNONI, *cit. supra* note 133.

[143] On the principle of solidarity, see GESTRI, "La politica europea dell'immigrazione: solidarietà tra Stati membri e misure nazionali di regolarizzazione", in LIGUSTRO and SACERDOTI (eds.), *Problemi e tendenze del diritto internazionale dell'economia. Liber amicorum in onore di Paolo Picone*, Napoli, 2011, p. 895 ff.

[144] *Ex* Art. 86(4) TFEU the European Council may decide, by unanimous vote, "to extend the powers of the European Public Prosecutor's Office to include serious crime having a cross-border dimension".

[145] Cf. Explanatory Note on the "Hotspot" Approach, p. 8 (available at: <http://www.statewatch.org/news/2015/jul/eu-com-hotsposts.pdf>). See CASOLARI "The EU's Hotspot Approach to Managing the Migration Crisis: A Blind Spot for International Responsibility?", in this *Yearbook*.

on Maritime Search and Rescue (SAR). More specific in this regard is the preamble of the EU Decision establishing EUNAVFOR MED, which – after affirming that the operation shall be conducted in compliance with international law, including the UNCLOS, SOLAS and SAR treaties – points out that these conventions include "the obligation to assist people in distress at sea and to deliver the survivors to a place of safety; and to that end the vessels assigned to EUNAVFOR MED will be ready and equipped to perform the related duties under the coordination of the competent Rescue Coordination Centre".[146]

In practice, it seems that search and rescue tasks have so far absorbed a great part of the activities carried out by EUNAVFOR MED. According to the most recent data available (March 2016), vessels assigned to the operation have rescued nearly 9,000 migrants at sea, whereas the number of suspected smugglers apprehended is around 50 and the smuggling boats destroyed around 80.[147] These numbers have given rise to some doubts as to the effectiveness of EUNAVFOR MED in attaining its main declared objective. It was established as "a military crisis management operation contributing to the disruption of the business model of human smuggling and trafficking networks",[148] yet it has so far mainly operated as a search and rescue operation, not very different from the Frontex led Joint Operation Triton (whose main task is border control) or the Italian missions "Mare Nostrum" and "Mare Sicuro".[149]

There is no denying the extraordinary importance of the results obtained by EUNAVFOR MED with respect to the saving of lives. However, a number of analysts have argued that the assets assigned to the operation, combat vessels and aircraft with very sophisticated technology, are not the best resources, in terms of capability and costs, to be employed for rescue activities.[150] The Operation Commander and top EU officials have contrasted these arguments, by stressing that EUNAVFOR MED has attained important results in terms of intelligence gathering and, more importantly, would now constitute an effective deterrent to the smug-

---

[146] Decision 2015/778, *cit. supra* note 7, para. 6. For a recent overview of these issues, see DI FILIPPO, "Irregular Migration and Safeguard of Life at Sea", in DEL VECCHIO (ed.), *International Law of the Sea: Current Trends and Controversial Issues*, The Hague, 2014, p. 9 ff.

[147] See Parliament Hearing of the Operation Commander, *cit. supra* note 18; and House of Lords, EU Naval Force – Mediterranean (*cit. supra* note 108), Evidence Session, Witness: Richard Lindsay, Head of Security Policy Department, Defense and International Security Directorate, Foreign and Commonwealth Office, 17 March 2016.

[148] Decision 2015/778, *cit. supra* note 7, Art. 1.

[149] See, for instance, the testimony of Mr Kingsley before the House of Lords ("this is essentially a search and rescue operation by another name"): House of Lords, EU Naval Force – Mediterranean (*cit. supra* note 108), Evidence given by Mr Peter Roberts, Senior Research Fellow, Sea Power and Maritime Studies, Royal United Services Institute, and Mr Patrick Kingsley, Migration Correspondent, Guardian Media Group, 10 March 2016.

[150] See, e.g., the statement of Mr. Roberts in House of Lords, EU Naval Force – Mediterranean, *ibid.*

glers and traffickers.[151] These assertions are however difficult to assess and are far from being generally accepted.[152] As to the deterrence effect, it remains to be seen, for instance, whether the arrests and the prosecutions carried out in Italy will lead to the conviction of the suspected smugglers and to effective and dissuasive criminal penalties. Truly, a significant contribution to the disruption of the business model of human smuggling and trafficking networks may come from the confiscation or destruction of boats and rafts used by the traffickers. The smugglers have however adapted their practice; they are no longer using more expensive wooden or fiber-glass boats and prefer to place migrants on "rubber inflatable crafts, purchased in bulk in China".[153] In any case, it is clear that much more significant results could derive from the transition of EUNAVFOR MED to the Phases 2B and 3 and an expansion of the operation into Libyan territorial waters and territory.

More generally, the entire operation seems to suffer from a number of ambiguities. As previously noted, similarly to what happens with the Frontex Triton Operation, the disembarkation of all the apprehended smugglers, traffickers, migrants and asylum-seekers takes place in Italy (yet, the area of operation also covers the SAR zone of Malta). That, however, is not clearly stated in the Decision establishing EUNAVFOR MED nor, as far as is known, in other publicly available acts. The peoples of Europe deserve more transparency on the part of a Union in which decisions should be taken "as openly as possible and as closely as possible to the citizen" (Article 1 TEU).

As is well known, the present situation as to the management of migration flows through the Mediterranean Sea imposes an extraordinary burden upon Italy and some effective mechanism for the fair distribution of that burden among all Member States should be introduced. Apart from obvious policy considerations, such a solution would also be in line with the principle of solidarity and fair sharing of responsibility (Article 80 TFEU), as has already been mentioned.[154] We are however still a long way from that. As to the new "Hotspot Approach" launched by the EU Commission, although it might certainly represent an important operative support to frontline Member States, it seems more a palliative measure than a cure vis-à-vis such an unprecedented crisis.[155]

---

[151] See Parliament Hearing of the Operation Commander, *cit. supra* note 18, and the testimony of Lieutenant General Wosolsobe in House of Lords, EU Naval Force – Mediterranean, *cit. supra* note 108.

[152] See, for instance, the remarks of Lord Tugendhat (Chairman) in House of Lords, EU Naval Force – Mediterranean, *ibid.*

[153] See the testimony of Lieutenant General Wosolsobe in House of Lords, EU Naval Force – Mediterranean, *ibid.* Cf. also *supra* note 95.

[154] *Supra*, section 10.

[155] See *supra* note 145.

SIXTY-FIVE YEARS AND IT SHOWS THEM ALL: PROPOSALS FOR AMENDING THE 1951 CONVENTION RELATING TO THE STATUS OF REFUGEES

FEDERICO LENZERINI[*]

Abstract

The 1951 Convention Relating to the Status of Refugees was one of the major accomplishments of the post-Second-World-War international legal community. It became the cornerstone of the international regulation of the right of asylum and represented the spark that ignited subsequent developments of international law in the field of asylum and refugees. Even more notable is the fact that the Convention has continued to have considerable impact despite the passing of time. However, 65 years after its adoption the Convention is showing signs of ageing, because several of its provisions are inconsistent with the present state of evolution of international human rights law. These provisions would therefore need to be updated, taking into consideration contemporary human rights standards, so as to make the Convention a living instrument capable of effectively addressing the needs of the people to whose protection it is devoted. The provisions which most require amendment are Article 1(A)(2), providing the definition of "refugee", the exclusion clauses included in Article 1(F), and the exceptions to the prohibition of refoulement *contemplated by Article 33(2).*

Keywords: refugees; asylum-seekers; Convention Relating to the Status of Refugees; *non-refoulement*; human rights; exclusion clauses.

1. INTRODUCTION

The Convention Relating to the Status of Refugees[1] was certainly one of the major accomplishments of the post-Second-World-War international legal community. It was inspired by the "profound concern" felt by the United Nations (UN) for refugees and its determination to "assure [them] the widest possible exercise of [...] fundamental rights and freedoms".[2] It entered into force on 22 April 1954, although its scope of application was circumscribed to the protection of refugees produced

---

[*] Professor of International Law, University of Siena; Ph.D., International Law. The author wishes to express his gratitude to Professor Francesco Francioni, of the Board of Editors, for the very helpful comments to an earlier draft of this article.
[1] 28 July 1951, entered into force 22 April 1954 (hereinafter "Refugee Convention" or "the Convention").
[2] *Ibid.*, second sentence of the preamble.

by "events occurring before 1 January 1951".[3] In addition, the Convention allowed States Parties to further restrict its applicability in geographical terms, to events occurring before 1 January 1951 in Europe only.[4] However, both the temporal and geographic limitations were later removed by the 1967 Protocol Relating to the Status of Refugees,[5] making the Convention of universal and temporally-unlimited application.

Since the 1950s, the Refugee Convention has become the cornerstone of the international regulation of the right of asylum – already proclaimed by Article 13 of the Universal Declaration of Human Rights (UDHR) – although the term "asylum" never appears in the Convention text, with the only exception of the preamble.[6] In the following decades – up to the present – the Convention has found extensive application in many States Parties, especially during the recurring humanitarian crises which have produced vast flows of refugees throughout the 20th and 21st centuries. At the same time, the Refugee Convention has represented the spark for igniting subsequent developments of general international law in the field of asylum and refugees. In particular, it led to the transposition of the key principle of *non-refoulement* – provided for by its Article 33 – into a principle of customary international law, as recognised by the States Parties to the Convention themselves in a declaration released in 2001,[7] also welcomed by the UN General Assembly.[8] The Convention has also been the inspiration for the relevant (binding and non-binding) instruments elaborated at the regional level. For example, the Convention Governing the Specific Aspects of Refugee Problems in Africa[9] of the Organization of African Unity (now the African Union) recognizes that "the United Nations Convention of 28 July 1951, as modified by the Protocol of 31 January 1967, constitutes the basic and universal instrument relating to the status of refugees and reflects the deep concern of States for refugees and their desire to establish common standards for their treatment".[10] Similarly, the Cartagena Declaration on Refugees,[11] concerning the protection of refugees in Central America, Mexico, and

---

[3] *Ibid.*, Art. 1(A)(2).

[4] *Ibid.*, Art. 1(B)(1).

[5] 31 January 1967, entered into force 4 October 1967 (hereinafter "1967 Protocol").

[6] See the fourth recital of the preamble, stating that "the grant of asylum may place unduly heavy burdens on certain countries, and that a satisfactory solution of a problem of which the United Nations has recognized the international scope and nature cannot therefore be achieved without international co-operation".

[7] See Declaration of States Parties to the 1951 Convention and/or its 1967 Protocol Relating to the Status of Refugees, Ministerial Meeting of States Parties, Geneva, 12-13 December 2001, available at: <http://www.unhcr.org/419c74d64.pdf>, preamble, para. 4.

[8] See Resolution 57/187 of 18 December 2002, para. 3. For a more comprehensive assessment of the status of *non-refoulement* under customary international law see LENZERINI, *Asilo e diritti umani. L'evoluzione del diritto d'asilo nel diritto internazionale*, Milano, 2009, p. 378 ff.

[9] 10 September 1969, entered into force 20 June 1974.

[10] Ninth recital of the preamble.

[11] 22 November 1984.

Panama, emphasizes the need to "ensure that the countries of the region establish a minimum standard of treatment for refugees, on the basis of the provisions of [, *inter alia,*] the 1951 Convention and 1967 Protocol".[12] Furthermore, the Refugee Convention has constituted the foundational parameter of the whole corpus of asylum legislation of the European Union (EU). In fact, the European Council, at its special meeting of 15-16 October in Tampere, decided that a Common European Asylum System had to be established "based on the full and inclusive application of the Geneva Convention";[13] the pertinent EU legislation presently in force actually complies with this dictate.[14]

The foregoing clearly shows that the Refugee Convention has had an outstanding impact on the development of international law on asylum and refugees. Even more notable is the fact that the Convention has continued to have such an impact despite the passing of time.

In 2016, the Refugee Convention turns 65 and continues to represent the foundation of international refugee law, despite the text remaining unchanged since 1967 (when its only Protocol was adopted). However, it would be misleading to assert that, over six and half decades, the Convention has remained immune from the signs of ageing. Today several of its provisions are not consistent with the evolution which has characterized international human rights law since its adoption in 1951. Paradoxically, part of the success that the Refugee Convention continues to enjoy 65 years after its birth is precisely due to the fact that it offers States Parties opportunities to circumvent their legal obligations under contemporary international human rights law, and, consequently, to reject asylum-seekers to whom they would be bound to grant protection pursuant to other rules of human rights customary and conventional law. The clearest example of this reality is represented by the rules contemplated by Articles 1(F) and 33(2) of the Convention, which, as will be explained below, are evidently at odds with human rights standards; this notwithstanding, they are firmly defended by States Parties as the armour "ensuring the integrity of the asylum institution [...] in particular in light of new threats and challenges".[15]

---

[12] See para. 8.

[13] See "Presidency Conclusions", available at: <http://www.europarl.europa.eu/summits/tam_en.htm>, para. 13.

[14] See, in particular, Directive 2011/95/EU of 13 December 2011 on standards for the qualification of third-country nationals or stateless persons as beneficiaries of international protection, for a uniform status for refugees or for persons eligible for subsidiary protection, and for the content of the protection granted (hereinafter "revised Qualification Directive"), OJ EU L337, 20 December 2011, p. 9; Directive 2013/32/EU of 26 June 2013 on common procedures for granting and withdrawing international protection, OJ EU L180, 29 June 2013, p. 60; Directive 2013/33/EU of 26 June 2013 laying down standards for the reception of applicants for international protection, OJ EU L180, 29 June 2013, p. 96.

[15] See Declaration of States Parties, *cit. supra* note 7, para. 7.

Using the words of the European Court of Human Rights and the Human Rights Committee, human rights treaties must be interpreted "in the light of present-day conditions"[16] and needs. However, this may only be possible when the provisions included in the relevant treaty are flexible enough to be interpreted evolutionarily in light of the new challenges and human needs existing at the time of their concrete application. Some of the key provisions of the Refugee Convention lack this flexibility, and would therefore need to be updated taking into consideration contemporary human rights standards, so as to make the Convention a living instrument capable of effectively addressing the needs of the people to whose protection it is devoted. The articles of the Convention which require some "restyling" will be examined in the following sections.

2.   "RESTYLING" THE REFUGEE CONVENTION: A CRITICAL ASSESSMENT OF THE RELEVANT ARTICLES

The following assessment will focus on the provisions of the Refugee Convention which need to be updated in line with the current state of development of international human rights law. Only the provisions which this writer considers to require modification will be discussed, while those which are still fit for purpose will not. In particular, the provisions on which the following assessment will be concentrated are Article 1(A)(2) (definition of "refugee"), Article 1(F) (persons considered not to deserve international protection), Article 3 (non-discrimination), Article 9 (provisional measures), Article 31(2) (restrictions), Article 32 (expulsion), and Article 33(2) (derogations to the prohibition of *refoulement*).

2.1.   Article 1(A)(2): Definition of the Term "Refugee"

According to Article 1(A)(2) of the Refugee Convention, as modified by the 1967 Protocol, a refugee is a person who,

> "owing to well-founded fear of being persecuted for reasons of race, religion, nationality, membership of a particular social group or political opinion, is outside the country of his nationality and is unable or, owing to such fear, is unwilling to avail himself of the protection of that country; or who, not having a nationality and being outside the country of his former habitual residence as a result of such events, is

---

[16] See European Court of Human Rights, *Tyrer v. The United Kingdom*, Application No. 5856/72, Judgment of 25 April 1978, para. 31; Human Rights Committee, *Judge v. Canada*, Communication No. 829/1998, 5 August 2002, UN Doc. CCPR/C/78/D/829/1998, 20 October 2003, para. 10.3.

unable or, owing to such fear, is unwilling to return to it. In the case of a person who has more than one nationality, the term 'the country of his nationality' shall mean each of the countries of which he is a national, and a person shall not be deemed to be lacking the protection of the country of his nationality if, without any valid reason based on well-founded fear, he has not availed himself of the protection of one of the countries of which he is a national".

As emerges from its wording, this definition sets a number of conditions to be *contextually* satisfied in order for a person to be qualified as a refugee. First, the asylum-seeker must have a fear of being persecuted; second, this fear must be well-founded; third, it must exist due to one or more of the grounds listed by the definition (i.e. race, religion, nationality, membership of a particular social group or political opinion); fourth, the asylum-seeker must be outside of the country of nationality (or, for stateless persons, the country of former habitual residence); and fifth, he/she must be unable or unwilling to avail him/herself of the protection of that country.

Each of the elements listed by the provision trigger various interpretative problems, the assessment of which is outside the scope of this article.[17] What is important here is to extrapolate the critical elements which should be reconsidered and redesigned to modernize the Convention and align it with current human rights standards. In this respect, the key feature is represented by the need for the person seeking protection to run the risk of being subjected to some form of harmful treatment reaching the threshold of "persecution". According to the United Nations High Commissioner for Refugees (UNHCR), "it may be inferred that a threat to life or freedom on account of race, religion, nationality, political opinion, or membership of a particular social group is always persecution. Other serious violations of human rights – for the same reasons – would also constitute persecution".[18] This applies irrespective of the agents from which the threat emanates, whether governmental or non-governmental entities.[19] However, even in the event that one opts

---

[17] For a word-by-word assessment of the definition of refugee see LENZERINI, *cit. supra* note 8. p. 219 ff. See also UN High Commissioner for Refugees, *Handbook and Guidelines on Procedures and Criteria for Determining Refugee Status under the 1951 Convention and the 1967 Protocol relating to the Status of Refugees*, Reissued, Geneva, December 2011 ("UNHCR Handbook"), para. 35 ff.

[18] *Ibid.*, para. 51.

[19] The so-called "accountability theory" – according to which persecution could be considered as existing only when perpetrated by State organs – supported in the past by France, Germany, and Switzerland, has today been unanimously abandoned, thanks in particular to Directive 2004/83/EC of 29 April 2004 on minimum standards for the qualification and status of third country nationals or stateless persons as refugees or as persons who otherwise need international protection and the content of the protection granted (OJ EU L304, 30 September 2004, p. 12), which, at Article 6(c) included, among the actors of persecution, "non-State actors, if it can be demonstrated that [the

for the widest and most evolutionary possible interpretation – according to which "persecution" would coincide with the prospective violation of (all) internationally recognized human rights standards[20] – it would nevertheless require *active* behaviour by the agents of the persecution itself (again, whether State or non-State actors), aimed at harming the person concerned. This means that all human beings who are likely to suffer – or are actually suffering – violations of their internationally recognized human rights which are not due to the voluntary behaviour of somebody else, but arise from uncontrolled situations taking place irrespectively of the will of the relevant actors, are excluded from the concept of refugee and consequently deprived of international protection. This implies, in turn, that the international community reacts to human rights breaches with inaction and denial of protection – or, paraphrasing the Inter-American Court of Human Rights, that human rights protection is "render[ed] [...] illusory for millions of persons".[21] This is certainly inconsistent with the fundamental requirement that human rights are *effectively* enjoyed by all human beings.

This reasoning applies in particular to two categories of migrants, i.e. economic migrants and environmental refugees. In principle, the inclusion of these two categories within the scope of the Refugee Convention is, at the present state of the Refugee Convention, precluded precisely because they do not meet the requirement of the presence of a persecution established by Article 1(A)(2), although in the presence of certain conditions "[t]he distinction between an economic migrant and a refugee is [...] blurred in the same way as the distinction between economic and political measures in an applicant's country of origin is not always clear",[22] as noted in the UNHCR Handbook. In particular, when

---

State government or parties or organisations controlling the State or a substantial part of the territory of the State], including international organisations, are unable or unwilling to provide protection against persecution". The Directive 2004/83/EC has been replaced by the revised Qualification Directive (*cit. supra* note 14), which, however, has maintained this provision unchanged. See consistently, the UNHCR Handbook (*cit. supra* note 17), according to which, while "[p]ersecution is normally related to action by the authorities of a country [,] [i]t may also emanate from sections of the population that do not respect the standards established by the laws of the country concerned [...] [on the condition that the relevant acts] are knowingly tolerated by the authorities, or if the authorities refuse, or prove unable, to offer effective protection" (para. 65). On the accountability theory see, among others, CRAWFORD and HYNDMAN, "Three Heresies in the Application of the Refugee Convention", International Journal of Refugee Law, 1989, p. 155 ff., p. 171; ENDICOTT, "'International Meaning': Comity in Fundamental Rights Adjudication", International Journal of Refugee Law, 2001, p. 280 ff., p. 283 ff.; and WILSHER, "Non-State Actors and the Definition of a Refugee in the United Kingdom: Protection, Accountability or Culpability?", International Journal of Refugee Law, 2003, p. 68 ff.

[20] See LENZERINI, *cit. supra* note 8, p. 242 ff.

[21] See *Sawhoyamaxa Indigenous Community v. Paraguay*, Merits, Reparations and Costs, Judgment of 29 March 2006, Series C No. 146, para. 120.

[22] See UNHCR Handbook, *cit. supra* note 17, para. 63.

"[b]ehind economic measures affecting a person's livelihood there [are] racial, religious or political aims or intentions directed against a particular group [,] [w]here economic measures destroy the economic existence of a particular section of the population (e.g. withdrawal of trading rights from, or discriminatory or excessive taxation of, a specific ethnic or religious group), the victims may according to the circumstances become refugees on leaving the country".[23]

However, even outside the situation described in the UNHCR Handbook, people belonging to these categories are persons escaping situations where enjoyment of human rights is lacking to an extent similar to that characterizing victims of persecution.

Most economic refugees flee from awful living conditions, totally at odds with the idea of human dignity, characterised by starvation and lack of appropriate housing as well as of any opportunity of social and economic emancipation. It is undeniable that hunger, starvation, or lack of housing are inconsistent with human rights standards currently in force. Article 25 UDHR establishes that

"[e]veryone has the right to a standard of living adequate for the health and well-being of himself and of his family, including food, clothing, housing and medical care and necessary social services, and the right to security in the event of unemployment, sickness, disability, widowhood, old age or other lack of livelihood in circumstances beyond his control".

The same right is provided for by Article 11(1) of the International Covenant on Economic, Social and Cultural Rights (ICESCR),[24] which also contemplates the associated obligation of States Parties to "take appropriate steps to ensure the realization of this right". Furthermore, according to the Committee on Economic, Social and Cultural Rights, lack of access "to safe and potable water and adequate sanitation, [or to] an adequate supply of safe food, nutrition and housing, healthy occupational and environmental conditions" translates into a violation of the right to health contemplated by Article 12(1) ICESCR, as the latter extends "not only to timely and appropriate health care but also to the underlying determinants of health".[25] To a similar extent, the African Commission on Human and Peoples' Rights has interestingly held that the right to shelter and the right to food – although not explicitly contemplated by the African Charter on Human and Peoples' Rights

---

[23] *Ibid.*
[24] 16 December 1966, entered into force 3 January 1976.
[25] See General Comment No. 14 (2000), The Right to the Highest Attainable Standard of Health (Article 12 of the International Covenant on Economic, Social and Cultural Rights), UN Doc. E/C.12/2000/4, 11 August 2000.

(ACHPR)[26] – are part of the system of human rights protection established by the latter in the form of *implied rights*. These rights are determined by the combination of some of the provisions included in the Charter. Hence, the right to housing or shelter is

> "the corollary of the combination of the provisions protecting the right to enjoy the best attainable state of mental and physical health [...] [and] the right to property, and the protection accorded to the family forbids the wanton destruction of shelter because when housing is destroyed, property, health, and family life are adversely affected".[27]

Similarly, the right to food is the combination of the right to life, the right to health and the right to economic, social and cultural development; it is "inseparably linked to the dignity of human beings and is therefore essential for the enjoyment and fulfilment of such other rights as health, education, work and political participation".[28] One may easily note that, among the rights mentioned by the African Commission on Human and Peoples' Rights, the supreme right to life is included. Indeed, as emphasized by the Human Rights Committee, the content of such a right "cannot properly be understood in a restrictive manner, and [its] protection [...] requires that States adopt positive measures [...] [including] all possible measures to reduce infant mortality and to increase life expectancy, especially in adopting measures to eliminate malnutrition and epidemics".[29]

This author is aware that the extension of the concept of "refugee" to economic refugees would imply – besides an additional burden on States receiving asylum seekers – the problem of establishing the threshold to be reached for a person to be considered a refugee when he/she is a victim of violations of economic, social, and cultural rights. Indeed, with respect to the latter, it is inevitable that their level of realization and the quality with which they are enjoyed are heterogeneous in the different States, depending on the resources actually available in each of them. Access to healthcare – a prerogative naturally arising from the right to health – is a clear example of this reality. It is obvious that the said threshold cannot be intended as corresponding to the highest quality in the enjoyment of such rights available anywhere in the world. On the contrary, a person would be considered a refugee only if the conditions of life accessible in his/her home country are below a minimum level of decency, making his/her standards of living unacceptable, and,

---

[26] 27 June 1981, entered into force 21 October 1986.

[27] See Communication No. 155/96, The Social and Economic Rights Action Center and the Center for Economic and Social Rights v. Nigeria, 27 October 2011, para. 60, available at: <http://www1.umn.edu/humanrts/africa/comcases/155-96.html>.

[28] *Ibid.*, paras. 64-65.

[29] See General Comment No. 6, Article 6 (Right to life), 30 April 1982, para. 5, available at: <http://www.refworld.org/docid/45388400a.html>.

hence, inadequate to guarantee his/her dignity of human being. In this respect, it is unavoidable that a generous amount of judgement would be left to State authorities in determining the minimum level in each concrete case.

The considerations generally developed for economic refugees apply, *mutatis mutandis*, to environmental refugees,[30] i.e. persons displaced by natural events like tsunamis, desertification, or the disappearance of small islands due to sea level rise associated with climate change. The latter instance is especially illuminating as regards the point advanced by this author: how can a person whose homeland has been submerged by the sea enjoy internationally recognized human rights – including the right to an adequate standard of living, the right to health, and the right to life itself – without obtaining protection somewhere else?

Extending the scope of the Refugee Convention to economic migrants and environmental refugees would represent a decisive step towards allowing the Convention itself to achieve its main purpose, i.e. to "assure refugees the widest possible exercise of [...] fundamental rights and freedoms".[31] Certainly, one might assert that such a purpose is to assure the widest possible exercise of such rights and freedoms not to "human beings" *tout court*, but to "refugees" only, and that, consequently, its achievement is independent from the extension of the scope attributed to the concept of refugee. However, given that the Refugee Convention is a human rights instrument, restricting the possibility to enjoy such rights only to certain categories among those in need would clearly represent a contradiction in terms. Consequently, once it is established that the purpose of the Convention is to assure protection for people escaping (actual or potential) human rights breaches in their country of origin, such protection should be extended to *all* persons whose rights are threatened, irrespective of whether the threat arises from the conscious action of individuals or from events beyond human control.

This would be an epochal change in the text of the Refugee Convention. In terms of textual adjustments, maybe the most appropriate solution would be to leave the current text of Article 1(A)(2) unchanged with the addition of one sen-

---

[30] On environmental refugees see, among others, BLACK, "Environmental Refugees: Myth or Reality?", UNHCR, New Issues in Refugee Research, Working Paper No. 34, March 2001, available at: <http://www.unhcr.org/research/RESEARCH/3ae6a0d00.pdf>; McNAMARA, "Conceptualizing Discourses on Environmental Refugees at the United Nations", Population & Environment, 2007, p. 12 ff.; CHRISTIANSEN, *Environmental Refugees. A Legal Perspective*, Oisterwijk, 2010; HARTMANN, "Rethinking Climate Refugees and Climate Conflict: Rhetoric, Reality and the Politics of Policy Discourse", Journal of International Development, 2010, p. 233 ff.; ANAND, *Environmental Refugees: Recognition and Protection under International Refugee Law*, Saarbrücken, 2012; WESTRA, *Environmental Justice and the Rights of Ecological Refugees*, London, 2013; ALEKAJBAF, "The Legal Status and Causes of Environmental Refugees under International Law", Advances in Environmental Biology, 2014, p. 997 ff.; and ALBRECHT and PLEWA, "International Recognition of Environmental Refugees", Environmental Policy & Law, 2015, p. 78 ff.

[31] See *supra* note 2 and corresponding text.

tence. The resulting text of Article 1(A) of the Refugee Convention might be along the following lines:[32]

> "For the purposes of the present Convention, the term 'refugee' shall apply to any person who: (I) [...]; (II) Owing to well-founded fear of being persecuted for reasons of race, religion, nationality, membership of a particular social group or political opinion, is outside the country of his nationality and is unable or, owing to such fear, is unwilling to avail himself of the protection of that country; or who, not having a nationality and being outside the country of his former habitual residence as a result of such events, is unable or, owing to such fear, is unwilling to return to it; *or who in respect of whom significant grounds exist for believing that, if returned to his country of nationality, or, in the case of a person not having a nationality, to his country of former habitual residence, he would face a real risk of suffering serious harm, as he is at serious risk of, or has been the victim of, systematic, generalised or other serious violations of his human rights.* In the case of a person who has more than one nationality, the term 'the country of his nationality' shall mean each of the countries of which he is a national, and a person shall not be deemed to be lacking the protection of the country of his nationality if, without any valid reason based on well-founded fear, he has not availed himself of the protection of one of the countries of which he is a national".

In drafting such a proposed amendment, this author has been inspired by the text of Article 2(f) of the EU revised Qualification Directive,[33] as well as of Article 2 of Directive 2001/55 on temporary protection in the event of a mass influx of displaced persons.[34]

2.2. *Article 1(F): Persons Considered Not To Deserve International Protection*

Article 1(F) of the Refugee Convention reads as follows:

> "The provisions of this Convention shall not apply to any person with respect to whom there are serious reasons for considering that:

---

[32] The proposed addition is in italics.

[33] See *supra* note 14.

[34] Council Directive 2001/55/EC of 20 July 2001 on minimum standards for giving temporary protection in the event of a mass influx of displaced persons and on measures promoting a balance of efforts between Member States in receiving such persons and bearing the consequences thereof, OJ EC L/212, 7 August 2001, 12.

(a) he has committed a crime against peace, a war crime, or a crime against humanity, as defined in the international instruments drawn up to make provision in respect of such crimes; (b) he has committed a serious non-political crime outside the country of refuge prior to his admission to that country as a refugee; (c) he has been guilty of acts contrary to the purposes and principles of the United Nations".

The presence in the text of the Convention of these exclusion clauses was determined by the fact that,

"[a]t the time when the Convention was drafted, the memory of the trials of major war criminals was still very much alive, and there was agreement on the part of States that war criminals should not be protected. There was also a desire on the part of States to deny admission to their territories of criminals who would present a danger to security and public order".[35]

The parameter used by the Convention's negotiators for drafting the text of Article 1(F)(a) was the London Charter of the International Military Tribunal of 1945[36] for the trial and punishment of the major war criminals of the European Axis.[37] The *ratio* of the provision was to exclude from protection those with respect to whom there are serious reasons for considering that they have committed an "extremely serious" crime, "to the extent that there is no room for any weighing of the severity of potential persecution against the gravity of the conduct which amounts to a war crime, a crime against peace or a crime against humanity".[38] Article 1(F)(a) is "integral to the refugee definition", and, when it applies, "the claimant cannot be a Convention refugee, whatever the other merits of his or her claim".[39]

Differently, as regards perpetrators of serious non-political crimes, dealt with by Article 1(F)(b), the State from which protection is requested retains the possibility of granting asylum.[40] The decision taken by the competent authorities in this respect will usually be based on considerations of security, as "[t]he commission of a serious non-political crime may be sufficient reason for exclusion because it is indicative of some future danger to the community of the State of refuge".[41]

---

[35] See UNHCR Handbook, *cit. supra* note 17, para. 148.
[36] Agreement for the Prosecution and Punishment of the Major War Criminals of the European Axis, 8 August 1945, entered into force 8 August 1945.
[37] See GOODWIN-GILL and MCADAM, *The Refugee in International Law*, 3rd ed., Oxford, 2007, p. 165.
[38] *Ibid.*
[39] *Ibid.*
[40] See UNHCR Handbook, *cit. supra* note 17, paras. 160-161.
[41] See GOODWIN-GILL and MCADAM, *cit. supra* note 37, p. 176.

Finally, with respect to Article 1(F)(c), it overlaps in part with the clause established by Article 1(F)(a), "for it is evident that a crime against peace, a war crime or a crime against humanity is also an act contrary to the purposes and principles of the United Nations".[42] However, since it covers all acts against any purpose of the United Nations – as described in the preamble and Articles 1 and 2 of the UN Charter – its scope is undoubtedly wider. In practice, "it is intended to cover in a general way such acts against the purposes and principles of the United Nations that might not be fully covered by the two preceding exclusion clauses".[43]

Considered as a whole, Article 1(F) is grounded on the rationale that "that certain acts are so grave as to render their perpetrators undeserving of international protection as refugees".[44] It may be true that the impact of the exclusion clauses contemplated by the provision in point should be mitigated by the consideration that, "[c]onsidering the serious consequences of exclusion for the person concerned, […] [their] interpretation […] must be restrictive".[45] However, the fact remains that the article in point conditions the enjoyment of fundamental human rights upon the attitudes and behaviours of the asylum-seeker. In other words, the Convention's approach is that human rights are only for the good, while "bad people" do not deserve to enjoy them. Such an approach is clearly at odds with the rationale of human rights, conceived as "equal and *inalienable* rights of *all* members of the human family"[46] and deriving "from the dignity and worth *inherent* in the human person".[47] This said, since equivalent issues as raised by Article 1(F) also arise with respect to Articles 32 and 33(2) of the Refugee Convention, the issue will be discussed in relation to the three articles taken together, in section 2.7 below.

2.3. *Article 3: Non-Discrimination*

Article 3 of the Refugee Convention establishes that States Parties "shall apply the provisions of this Convention to refugees without discrimination as to race, religion or country of origin". Although it may appear a minor point, it is clear that in the present provision the list of the grounds on the basis of which discrimination is to be avoided is incomplete. In fact, taking a look at the main human rights instruments in force, it is quite surprising that such a list is limited to race, reli-

---

[42] See UNHCR Handbook, *cit. supra* note 17, para. 162.

[43] *Ibid.*

[44] See UNHCR, Guidelines on International Protection: Application of the Exclusion Clauses: Article 1F of the 1951 Convention Relating to the Status of Refugees, UN Doc. HCR/GIP/03/05, 4 September 2003, para. 2.

[45] See UNHCR Handbook, *cit. supra* note 17, para. 149.

[46] See UDHR, first recital of the preamble (emphasis added).

[47] See Vienna Declaration and Programme of Action, adopted by the World Conference on Human Rights, Vienna, 25 June 1993, UN Doc. A/CONF.157/23, 12 July 1993, second recital of the preamble (emphasis added).

gion, and country of origin. For instance, Article 2 UDHR affirms that everyone is entitled to human rights and freedoms "without distinction of any kind, such as race, colour, sex, language, religion, political or other opinion, national or social origin, property, birth or other status [...] [including] the political, jurisdictional or international status of the country or territory to which a person belongs". A nearly identical provision is included in Article 2 of the International Covenant on Civil and Political Rights (ICCPR),[48] which also establishes that derogations to the rights contemplated by the Covenant adopted in time of public emergency must "not involve discrimination solely on the ground of race, colour, sex, language, religion or social origin" (Article 4), as well as that "the law shall prohibit any discrimination and guarantee to all persons equal and effective protection against discrimination on any ground such as race, colour, sex, language, religion, political or other opinion, national or social origin, property, birth or other status" (Article 26). The same approach is adopted by the ICESCR, which declares that "[t]he States Parties to the present Covenant undertake to guarantee that the rights enunciated in the present Covenant will be exercised without discrimination of any kind as to race, colour, sex, language, religion, political or other opinion, national or social origin, property, birth or other status" (Article 2(2)). The same grounds of discrimination are also listed in Article 14 of the European Convention of Human Rights (ECHR),[49] which adds "association with a national minority", and Article 1 of the American Convention on Human Rights (ACHR),[50] which replaces "property" with "economic status" and "other status" with "any other social condition". Last but not least, the ACHPR establishes that "[e]very individual shall be entitled to the enjoyment of the rights and freedoms recognized and guaranteed in the present Charter without distinction of any kind such as race, ethnic group, color, sex, language, religion, political or any other opinion, national and social origin, fortune, birth or other status" (Article 2).

This brief (and incomplete) survey shows that, in the enjoyment of human rights under international law, discrimination is prohibited on any ground, and not only on the basis of race, religion, or country of origin. Article 3 of the Refugee Convention should be amended accordingly, replacing the original text with one phrased as follows: "[t]he Contracting States shall apply the provisions of this Convention to refugees without discrimination *of any kind, such* as race, religion, *national or social origin, sex, colour, ethnic group, language, political or other opinion, culture, economic condition, birth, association with a national minority, sexual orientation or other status*".[51]

---

[48] 16 December 1966, entered into force 23 March 1976.

[49] Convention for the Protection of Human Rights and Fundamental Freedoms, 4 November 1950, entered into force 3 September 1953.

[50] 22 November 1969, entered into force 18 July 1978.

[51] The proposed additions and replacements are in italics.

2.4. Article 9: Provisional Measures

Article 9 of the Refugee Convention provides for provisional measures, leaving States Parties free to adopt, "in time of war or other grave and exceptional circumstances", measures which they deem essential to the national security "in the case of a particular person, pending a determination by the Contracting State that that person is in fact a refugee and that the continuance of such measures is necessary in his case in the interests of national security". In principle, this provision is in line with the approach generally adopted by human rights instruments, which allow States Parties to take measures derogating from their obligations under the relevant treaty in time of public emergency threatening the life or security of the nation, to the extent required by the gravity of the situation. This approach, in particular, is followed by Article 4 ICCPR, Article 15 ECHR, and Article 27 ACHR. All these provisions, however, include a clause excluding the possibility of derogating from the most fundamental human rights standards, which are considered absolutely inalienable and, consequently, immune from any possible derogation even when the very life of the State is at stake. In this regard, Article 4(2) ICCPR excludes the possibility of making any derogation to the full enjoyment of the right to life, the right not to be subjected to torture or to cruel, inhuman or degrading treatment or punishment, the right not to be subjected to slavery, slave-trade or servitude, the right not to be imprisoned merely on the ground of inability to fulfil a contractual obligation, the right not to be held guilty of any criminal offence on account of any act or omission which did not constitute a criminal offence, under national or international law, at the time when it was committed, the right to recognition everywhere as a person before the law, as well as the right to freedom of thought, conscience and religion. A shorter list is included in Article 15(2) ECHR, according to which the rights with respect to which no derogation is possible even in time of emergency are the right to life ("except in respect of deaths resulting from lawful acts of war"), the right not to be subjected to torture or to inhuman or degrading treatment or punishment, the right not to be held in slavery or servitude, and the right to no punishment without law. A longer list is instead provided for by Article 27(2) ACHR, according to which no derogation is authorised with respect to the following rights: right to juridical personality, right to life, right to humane treatment, freedom from slavery, freedom from *ex post facto* laws, freedom of conscience and religion, rights of the family, right to a name, rights of the child, right to nationality, right to participate in government, and the judicial guarantees essential for the protection of such rights.

These clauses show that there are certain human rights standards which are considered by international law as being so fundamental that no measures may be taken, in whatever circumstances, which are capable of threatening the full enjoyment of such rights, including in time of war or any other situation endangering national security or even the very life of the State. The lack of a paragraph of this kind in the text of Article 9 of the Refugee Convention makes it inconsistent with international human rights standards, and, in order for this inconsistency to be removed, the provision in question should be amended through the inclusion of a clause similar to Article 4(2) ICCPR, Article 15(2) ECHR, or Article 27(2) ACHR. As for the "extension" of such a clause, it should include, *as a minimum*, the very fundamental standards common to all three articles, i.e. right to life, right not to be subjected to torture or to cruel, inhuman or degrading treatment or punishment, freedom from slavery or servitude, as well as freedom from *ex post facto* laws. However, other fundamental rights might be included among those with respect to which no derogation is possible even "in time of war or other grave and exceptional circumstances", in consideration of the fact that their derogation would in no way serve the purpose of pursuing the interests of national security "in the case of a particular person, pending a determination [...] that that person is in fact a refugee". This would apply, in particular, to the right not to be imprisoned merely on the ground of inability to fulfil a contractual obligation, the right to recognition as a person before the law, the right to freedom of thought, conscience and religion, the right to a name, and the right to access to a court for the protection of such rights. A second paragraph should therefore be added to Article 9 of the Refugee Convention, reading as follows:

> *"The provisional measures provided for in the previous paragraph will in no way result in measures threatening the full enjoyment by the person concerned of fundamental human rights, particularly the right to life, the right not to be subjected to torture or to cruel, inhuman or degrading treatment or punishment, the right to freedom from slavery or servitude, the right not to be held guilty of any criminal offence on account of any act or omission which did not constitute a criminal offence, under national or international law, at the time when it was committed, the right not to be imprisoned merely on the ground of inability to fulfil a contractual obligation, the right to recognition as a person before the law, the right to freedom of thought, conscience and religion, the right to a name, as well as the right to access to the judicial guarantees essential for the protection of such rights".*

2.5. *Article 31(2): Restrictions*

Article 31 of the Refugee Convention – dealing with refugees unlawfully in the country of refuge – reads as follows:

> "1. The Contracting States shall not impose penalties, on account of their illegal entry or presence, on refugees who, coming directly from a territory where their life or freedom was threatened in the sense of article 1, enter or are present in their territory without authoriza-

tion, provided they present themselves without delay to the authorities and show good cause for their illegal entry or presence. 2. The
Contracting States shall not apply to the movements of such refugees
restrictions other than those which are necessary and such restrictions
shall only be applied until their status in the country is regularized or
they obtain admission into another country. The Contracting States
shall allow such refugees a reasonable period and all the necessary
facilities to obtain admission into another country".

At first glance it could be considered that this provision is not inconsistent
with international human rights standards. A closer look, however, shows that its
second paragraph may be problematic given that it allows States Parties to apply
restrictions to the movements of refugees "which are necessary". The critical aspect of the textual construction of this provision does not lie in the fact of allowing
restrictions in itself. Restrictions to the exercise of rights – with the exception of the
fundamental standards listed in the previous sub-section – is common to all human
rights instruments, and is determined by the need to balance the rights of an individual or a collectivity with those of others or to guarantee the proper safeguarding
of the supreme values of society, particularly national security. The problem with
the provision in question is rather determined by the fact that it only requires, in
order for the restrictions to be legitimate, that they are necessary, without providing
any explanation of the meaning of "necessity". This leads to the conclusion that
the decision of whether or not a given restriction is necessary is left entirely to the
determination of the State concerned, without placing any limitation and/or condition on the judgement of State authorities. This obviously implies the possibility
that ability to apply restrictions to the movements of refugees within the national
territory will lead States to abuse their power in this respect. Therefore, while it is
true that no clause might prevent in absolute terms the possibility of practicing such
abuses, it is necessary to at least circumscribe to some measure the virtually unlimited discretional power of the State. This could be made through introducing a
more careful formulation of the conditions to be respected for applying restrictions
on movement in Article 31(2), following the example of virtually all human rights
treaties when limitations to the exercise of rights are contemplated.[52] The amended
text of Article 31(2) might read as follows:

"The Contracting States shall not apply to the movements of such
refugees restrictions other than those which are *prescribed by law
and are necessary in a democratic society in the interests of national
security, territorial integrity or public safety, for the prevention of*

---

[52] See, for example, Arts. 18, 19, 21, and 22 ICCPR, Arts. 8, 9, 10, and 11 ECHR, Arts. 12,
13, 15, and 16 ACHR, and Arts. 8, 9, 10, 11, and 12 ACHPR.

disorder or crime, for the protection of public order, health or mor-als, the economic wellbeing of the country, or for the protection of the rights and freedoms of others. Such restrictions shall only be applied until their status in the country is regularized or they obtain admission into another country. The Contracting States shall allow such refugees a reasonable period and all the necessary facilities to obtain admission into another country".[53]

Needless to say, the restrictions contemplated by this provision may in no way involve derogations from the fundamental rights listed in the previous sub-section with respect to the proposed amendment of Article 9 of the Refugee Convention.

2.6. Article 32: Expulsion

Article 32 of the Refugee Convention provides the possibility for States Parties to expel a refugee lawfully in their territory on grounds of national security or public order, "in pursuance of a decision reached in accordance with due process of law", and after allowing the refugee "to submit evidence to clear himself, and to appeal and to be represented for the purpose before competent authority or a person or persons specially designated by the competent authority", except "where compelling reasons of national security otherwise require". Similarly to what has been noted with respect to Article 1(F) of the Refugee Convention at section 2.2 above, this provision entails reflections similar to, and connected with, those to be developed regarding Article 33(2). These three articles will therefore be discussed jointly in the next sub-section.

2.7. Article 33(2): Non-Refoulement

As emphasized by the UNHCR, "[t]he principle of *non-refoulement* constitutes the cornerstone of international refugee protection".[54] It is a fundamental principle

---

[53] The proposed additions and replacements are in italics.

[54] See UNHCR, Advisory Opinion on the Extraterritorial Application of Non-Refoulement Obligations under the 1951 Convention relating to the Status of Refugees and its 1967 Protocol, Geneva, 26 January 2007, para. 5, available at: <http://www.unhcr.org/4d9486929.pdf>. The same principle is expressed by the 1984 Cartagena Declaration on Refugees (*cit. supra* note 11), part III, para. 5. Generally on *non-refoulement* see, *inter alia*, GOODWIN-GILL, "Non-Refoulement and the New Asylum Seekers", Virginia Journal of International Law, 1986, p. 899 ff.; STENBERG, *Non-Expulsion and Non-Refoulement: the Prohibition Against Removal of Refugees with Special Reference to Articles 32 and 33 of the 1951 Convention Relating to the Status of Refugees*, Uppsala, 1989; LAUTERPACHT and BETHLEHEM, "The Scope and Content of the Principle of Non-Refoulement: Opinion", in FELLER, TÜRKAND and NICHOLSON (eds.), *Refugee Protection*

of international human rights law which has attained the status of customary international law,[55] and, according to some sources, even of *jus cogens*.[56] It is expressed by the Refugee Convention in Article 33, which reads as follows:

> "1. No Contracting State shall expel or return (*'refouler'*) a refugee in any manner whatsoever to the frontiers of territories where his life or freedom would be threatened on account of his race, religion, nationality, membership of a particular social group or political opinion. 2. The benefit of the present provision may not, however, be claimed by a refugee whom there are reasonable grounds for regarding as a danger to the security of the country in which he is, or who, having been convicted by a final judgment of a particularly serious crime, constitutes a danger to the community of that country".

Article 33 cannot be the object of reservations, as explicitly specified by Article 42 of the Convention.

While the principle of *non-refoulement* does not, in itself, presuppose a right of the individual to be granted asylum, it implies that,

> "where States are not prepared to grant asylum to persons who are seeking international protection on their territory, they must adopt a course that does not result in their removal, directly or indirectly, to a place where their lives or freedom would be in danger on account of their race, religion, nationality, membership of a particular social group or political opinion".[57]

In practical terms, this means that the State from which protection is requested may choose from two options, i.e. granting protection to the asylum-seeker in its own territory or returning him/her to a *safe country*, that is, a country where the fundamental rights of the person concerned would not be threatened. The prohibition of *refoulement* extends to *indirect refoulement* – i.e. return of the asylum-seeker to a country which is safe in itself, but from where it is possible that he/she is returned to an unsafe third country – and applies *extraterritorially*, wherever a State "exercises effective jurisdiction".[58]

---

in International Law, Cambridge, 2003, p. 87 ff.; GOODWIN-GILL and MCADAM, *cit. supra* note 37, p. 201 ff.; and LENZERINI, *cit. supra* note 8, p. 335 ff.

[55] See *supra* notes 7-8 and corresponding text.

[56] See Cartagena Declaration on Refugees (*cit. supra* note 11), part III, para. 5. For a discussion of the status of the principle of *non-refoulement* as *jus cogens* see LENZERINI, *cit. supra* note 8, p. 384 ff.

[57] See UNHCR, *cit. supra* note 54, para. 8.

[58] *Ibid.*, para. 43. See also LENZERINI, "Il principio del *non-refoulement* dopo la sentenza *Hirsi* della Corte europea dei diritti dell'uomo", RDI, 2012, p. 721 ff.

Notwithstanding the fundamental character of the principle of *non-refoulement*, Article 33(2) contemplates certain exceptions to its application, pursuant to which it is legitimately possible to derogate from the prohibition to return a person to a country where his/her life or freedom would be threatened. In consideration of the seriousness of the threat faced by a refugee in the event of *refoulement*, such exceptions have to be "interpreted and implemented in a restrictive manner",[59] may only be applied for crimes of a very grave nature, and "should involve a careful examination of the question of proportionality between the danger to the security of the community or the gravity of the crime, and the persecution feared".[60]

However, in practice the evaluation of the danger which should exist to justify the application of Article 33(2) remains within the discretion of the State authorities, determining the impossibility of avoiding possible abuses. Even leaving this aside, and supposing that no abuses would take place, the application of Article 33(2) would lead to consequences which are unacceptable in light of contemporary human rights standards. Indeed – as noted with respect to Article 1(F) in section 2.2 above – the rationale of such provisions is that "bad people" – or even those who are presumed to be bad, as they are regarded as a danger to the security of the country in which they are located – do not deserve to enjoy human rights.

In principle this reasoning applies not only to Articles 1(F) and 33(2), but also to Article 32 of the Refugee Convention. In fact, all these provisions, in practice, allow a State Party to the Convention to return a human being to a country where his/her fundamental rights are under threat. However, with respect to Article 32 in particular, it is to be noted that its impact is in reality quite limited, because the power of States Parties to expel a refugee lawfully in their territory, pursuant to the conditions provided for by Article 32 itself, is constrained by the condition that expulsion does not result in *refoulement*. In other words, the power to expel under Article 32 does not include the power to return the individual concerned to a country where his life or freedom are threatened on account of his race, religion, nationality, membership of a particular social group or political opinion, unless – *according to the regime established by the Refugee Convention* – the conditions established by Article 33(2) are also satisfied.[61]

This said, the fact remains that, pursuant to the Refugee Convention, asylum-seekers and refugees may be lawfully deported to countries where their life, freedom, and other fundamental human rights are at risk, according to Articles 1(F) and 33(2). In this respect, it is worth reiterating that the reflections which need to be developed with respect to Article 33(2) may be extended to Article 1(F). In fact, the principle of *non-refoulement* "applies not only to recognized refugees, but also to those who have not had their status formally declared [...] [and] is applicable to

---

[59] See UNHCR, Note on the Principle of Non-Refoulement, November 1997, para. F, available at: <http://www.refworld.org/docid/438c6d972.html>.

[60] *Ibid.*

[61] See GOODWIN-GILL and MCADAM, *cit. supra* note 37, p. 263.

any form of forcible removal, including deportation, expulsion, extradition, informal transfer or 'renditions', and non-admission at the border".[62] This is consistent with the *declaratory* nature of the recognition of the status of refugee:

> "A person is a refugee within the meaning of the 1951 Convention as soon as he fulfils the criteria contained in the definition […]. Recognition of his refugee status does not […] make him a refugee but declares him to be one. He does not become a refugee because of recognition, but is recognized because he is a refugee".[63]

Therefore, the prohibition of *refoulement* is also violated when the person requesting protection is prevented from having access to the territory of the State and, obviously, no decision has been taken concerning his/her refugee status, provided that in the country where he/she is forced to return he/she is threatened by a risk of being persecuted. It follows that, since applying Article 1(F) implies that the asylum-seeker concerned is forced to go back to a country where he/she is subject to a threat of persecution, it concretely translates into a situation subsumed within the scope of the concept of *refoulement*.

As previously noted, the regulation provided by the articles in question is inconsistent with human rights standards in force. As stressed by the UNHCR, "[t]he provisions of Article 33(2) [and Article 1(F)] of the 1951 Convention do not affect the host State's *non-refoulement* obligations under international human rights law, which permit no exceptions".[64] In particular, pursuant to Article 3 of the Convention against Torture and Other Cruel, Inhuman or Degrading Treatment or Punishment,[65] "[n]o State Party shall expel, return ('refouler') or extradite a person to another State where there are substantial grounds for believing that he would be in danger of being subjected to torture". According to the Committee Against Torture, "the Convention's protections are absolute, even in the context of national security concerns", including with respect to the rule established by Article 3.[66] Similarly, as emphasized by the Human Rights Committee, the ICCPR presupposes an obligation for States Parties

> "not to extradite, deport, expel or otherwise remove a person from their territory, where there are substantial grounds for believing that there is a real risk of irreparable harm, such as that contemplated by Articles 6 [right to life] and 7 [right to be free from torture or

---

[62] See UNHCR, Advisory Opinion, *cit. supra* note 54, paras. 6-7.
[63] See UNHCR Handbook, *cit. supra* note 17, para. 28.
[64] See UNHCR, Advisory Opinion, *cit. supra* note 54, para. 11.
[65] 10 December 1984, entered into force 26 June 1987.
[66] See *Agiza v. Sweden*, Communication No. 233/2003, UN Doc. CAT/C/34/D/233/2003, 20 May 2005, para. 13.8.

other cruel, inhuman or degrading treatment or punishment] of the Covenant, either in the country to which removal is to be effected or in any country to which the person may subsequently be removed".[67]

With respect to Article 7 ICCPR in particular, the Committee also found that "States parties must not expose individuals to the danger of torture or cruel, inhuman or degrading treatment or punishment upon return to another country by way of their extradition, expulsion or refoulement".[68] The clear and unequivocal tone used by the Committee in expressing this concept indicates that no derogation is possible in this respect. This is also confirmed by the fact that, as previously noted, the provisions to which the Committee refers are included by Article 4 ICCPR among those of absolute character, which cannot be the object of derogation even in time of public emergency which threatens the life of the nation.

At the regional level, Article 22(8) ACHR is worth mentioning, according to which "[i]n no case may an alien be deported or returned to a country, regardless of whether or not it is his country of origin, if in that country his right to life or personal freedom is in danger of being violated because of his race, nationality, religion, social status, or political opinions". Similarly, Article 13 of the Inter-American Convention to Prevent and Punish Torture[69] establishes that

> "Extradition shall not be granted nor shall the person sought be returned when there are grounds to believe that his life is in danger, that he will be subjected to torture or to cruel, inhuman or degrading treatment, or that he will be tried by special or ad hoc courts in the requesting State".

Last but not least, the practice of the European Court of Human Rights concerning Article 3 ECHR[70] is particularly significant. With respect to this provision the Court has developed an extensive and unequivocal jurisprudence, affirming the extraterritorial application of the prohibition of torture and inhuman or degrading treatment or punishment. By virtue of this jurisprudence, any form of deportation – including expulsion, extradition, or *refoulement* – to a country where a person would face a threat of being subjected to a treatment contrary to Article 3 would produce a violation of the said provision.[71] Most notably, the Court has affirmed

---

[67] See General Comment No. 31, Nature of the General Legal Obligation on States Parties to the Covenant, UN Doc. CCPR/C/21/Rev.1/Add.13, 26 May 2004, para. 12.

[68] See General Comment No. 20, Article 7 (Prohibition of torture, or other cruel, inhuman or degrading treatment or punishment), UN Doc. HRI/GEN/1/Rev.7, 12 May 2004, para. 9.

[69] 9 December 1985, entered into force 28 February 1987.

[70] Article 3 ECHR reads as follows: "[n]o one shall be subjected to torture or to inhuman or degrading treatment or punishment".

[71] Among the many pertinent judgments see *Soering v. The United Kingdom*, Application No. 14038/88, Judgment of 7 July 1989; *Cruz Varas v. Sweden*, Application No. 15567/89,

that the *absolute character* of Article 3 applies also with respect to its extraterritorial characterization:

> "Article 3 [...] enshrines one of the fundamental values of democratic societies [...] prohibit[ing] in absolute terms torture or inhuman or degrading treatment or punishment, irrespective of the victim's conduct [...]. Accordingly, *the activities of the individual in question, however undesirable or dangerous, cannot be a material consideration*. The protection afforded by article 3 is thus *wider than that provided by article 33 of the United Nations 1951 Convention on the Status of Refugees*".[72]

This crucial aspect was better explained by the Court in the case of *Saadi v. Italy*,[73] concerning a Tunisian national who was a member of *Al-Qaeda* and who had expressly manifested his intention to take part in the "holy war" against the West. For this reason, Italy had decided to deport him to Tunisia. Intervening in the case, the United Kingdom Government asserted that the "rigidity" of the Court in establishing that,

> "in view of the absolute nature of the prohibition of treatment contrary to Article 3 of the Convention, the risk of such treatment could not be weighed against the reasons (including the protection of national security) put forward by the respondent State to justify expulsion [...] had caused many difficulties for the Contracting States by preventing them in practice from enforcing expulsion measures".[74]

As a consequence, the British Government tried to persuade the judges to accept that, "in cases concerning the threat created by international terrorism", States Parties to the ECHR would be allowed "to take into consideration all the particular circumstances of each case and weigh the rights secured to the applicant by Article 3 of the Convention against those secured to all other members of the community by Article 2". In other words, the United Kingdom was asking the Court to accept that States Parties were allowed to deport a terrorist in the event that the threat to

---

Judgment of 20 March 1991; *Vilvarajah and Others v. The United Kingdom*, Applications No. 13163/87, 13164/87, 13165/87, 13447/87, 13448/87, Judgment of 30 October 1991; *Chahal v. The United Kingdom*, Application No. 22414/93, Judgment of 15 November 1996; *Ahmed v. Austria*, Application No. 25964/94, Judgment of 17 December 1996; *Saadi v. Italy*, Application No. 37201/06, Judgment of 28 February 2008; *M.S.S. v. Belgium and Greece*, Application No. 30696/09, Judgment of 21 January 2011; and *Hirsi Jamaa and Others v. Italy*, Application No. 27765/09, Judgment of 23 February 2012.

[72] See, among others, *Ahmed v. Austria, ibid.*, para 40 ff. (emphasis added).

[73] *Cit. supra* note 71.

[74] *Ibid.*, para. 117.

national security determined by his presence in the State territory would take priority over his risk of being ill-treated in the receiving country.[75] The Court rejected this argument as follows:

> "[s]ince protection against the treatment prohibited by Article 3 is absolute, that provision imposes an obligation not to extradite or expel any person who, in the receiving country, would run the real risk of being subjected to such treatment. As the Court has repeatedly held, there can be no derogation from that rule [...]. It must therefore reaffirm the principle [...] that it is not possible to weigh the risk of ill-treatment against the reasons put forward for the expulsion in order to determine whether the responsibility of a State is engaged under Article 3, even where such treatment is inflicted by another State. In that connection, the conduct of the person concerned, however undesirable or dangerous, cannot be taken into account".[76]

Similar considerations to those developed with respect to Article 3 may be extended, *mutatis mutandis*, to other provisions of the ECHR, particularly Article 2 (right to life), Article 4 (prohibition of slavery and servitude), Article 6 (right to a fair trial), Article 8 (right to respect for private and family life), and Article 13 (right to an effective remedy).[77] Of course, the absolute non-derogability of the prohibition of *refoulement* is only valid when the threat faced by the person in the event of deportation involves the possible violation of those fundamental rights which cannot be the object of derogation in no circumstances. These include, in particular and in addition to the prohibition of torture or inhuman or degrading treatment or punishment, the right to life and the prohibition of slavery and servitude.

---

[75] *Ibid.*, para. 122.

[76] *Ibid.*, para. 138. It is opportune to note that voices also exist, especially at the domestic level, which dissent from the position shared by international monitoring bodies, as described in the text. In this respect, the view expressed by the Supreme Court of Canada in *Suresh v. Canada (Minister of Citizenship and Immigration)*, [2002] 1 SCR 3, is particularly renowned. In this case the Court held that "determining whether deportation to torture violates the principles of fundamental justice requires us to balance Canada's interest in combatting terrorism and the Convention refugee's interest in not being deported to torture. Canada has a legitimate and compelling interest in combatting terrorism. But it is also committed to fundamental justice. The notion of proportionality is fundamental to our constitutional system [...] generally to deport a refugee, where there are grounds to believe that this would subject the refugee to a substantial risk of torture, would unconstitutionally violate the [Canadian Charter of Rights and Freedoms]'s guarantee of life, liberty and security of the person. This said, we leave open the possibility that in an exceptional case such deportation might be justified [...] in the balancing approach [in accordance with the principles of fundamental justice] or [on the basis of the reasonable limits to the enjoyment of rights and freedoms prescribed by law as can be demonstrably justified in a free and democratic society]" (paras. 47 and 129).

[77] See LENZERINI, *cit. supra* note 8, p. 371 ff.

This practice unquestionably shows that, under contemporary international law, no derogation is allowed to the prohibition of *refoulement* when the latter would expose the person concerned to a threat to his/her life, liberty or personal integrity. In order to become consistent with international human rights law, the Refugee Convention should therefore be amended, through *deleting* Articles 1(F) and 33(2).

With respect to Article 32, for the sake of clarity it might be modified as follows:

> "1. The Contracting States shall not expel a refugee lawfully in their territory save on grounds of national security or public order. 2. The expulsion of such a refugee shall be only in pursuance of a decision reached in accordance with due process of law. Except where compelling reasons of national security otherwise require, the refugee shall be allowed to submit evidence to clear himself, and to appeal to and be represented for the purpose before competent authority or a person or persons specially designated by the competent authority. *In no case the expulsion of a refugee may result in the violation of the prohibition of* refoulement, *as established by Article 33*. 3. The Contracting States shall allow such a refugee a reasonable period within which to seek legal admission into another country. The Contracting States reserve the right to apply during that period such internal measures as they may deem necessary".[78]

3. OTHER POSSIBLE AMENDMENTS TO THE REFUGEE CONVENTION OF MORE GENERAL CHARACTER

3.1. *"Same Treatment as Nationals"*

A number of provisions of the Refugee Convention establish that, once a refugee has been granted protection by the authorities of a State Party, he/she has the right to be accorded a treatment at least as favourable as that accorded to the nationals of such a State. This is evident in particular in Articles 4 (freedom to practice one's own religion and freedom as regards the religious education of children), 14 (protection of industrial property, such as inventions, designs or models, trademarks, trade names, and of rights in literary, artistic, and scientific works), 16 (right to access to the courts, including legal assistance and exemption from *cautio judicatum solvi*), 20 (rationing systems applying to the population at large and regulating the general distribution of products in short supply), 22(1) (elementary

---

[78] The proposed additions are in italics.

education), 23 (public relief and assistance), 24 (labour legislation), 25(4) (fees for administrative assistance), and 29 (fiscal charges). Other articles, however, only attribute refugees the right to be granted a treatment not less favourable than that accorded to aliens generally in the same circumstances. While such a choice could be understandable when the Refugee Convention was negotiated, with respect to matters that at that time were considered by States as being particularly sensitive, in the present day it no longer seems reasonable. In fact, generally speaking the situation of refugees is drastically different from that of aliens in general, because, whereas the latter may enjoy the protection of their countries of nationality, the former are deprived of such a protection, and therefore need full assistance from the State of refuge. It would consequently be opportune to equate the treatment of refugees to that of the nationals of the country of refuge with respect to all issues addressed by the Refugee Convention, in order to favour the full integration of refugees within the society of that country, as well as the full enjoyment of their internationally recognized human rights. This would require the provisions of the Convention not equating the treatment of refugees to that of nationals of the State of refuge to be amended. The provisions in question are Articles 13, 15, 17, 18, 19, 21, 22(2), and 26, which, after incorporating the proposed amendments, should read as follows:[79]

> "Article 13 – Movable and Immovable Property: The Contracting States shall accord to a refugee treatment *not less favourable than that accorded to nationals in the same circumstances*, as regards the acquisition of movable and immovable property and other rights pertaining thereto, and to leases and other contracts relating to movable and immovable property.
> Article 15 – Right of Association: As regards non-political and non-profit-making associations and trade unions the Contracting States shall accord to refugees lawfully staying in their territory the most favourable treatment *accorded to nationals in the same circumstances*.
> Article 17 – Wage-Earning Employment: 1. The Contracting State shall accord to refugees lawfully staying in their territory the most favourable treatment *accorded to nationals in the same circumstances*, as regards the right to engage in wage-earning employment.[80]

---

[79] The proposed additions and amendments are in italics.

[80] The modification of paragraph 1 of Art. 17 would naturally lead to the deletion of paras. 2 and 3 of the same article, which read as follows: "2. In any case, restrictive measures imposed on aliens or the employment of aliens for the protection of the national labour market shall not be applied to a refugee who was already exempt from them at the date of entry into force of this Convention for the Contracting State concerned, or who fulfils one of the following conditions: (a) He has completed three years' residence in the country; (b) He has a spouse possessing the nationality of the country of residence. A refugee may not invoke the benefits of this provision if he has abandoned his spouse; (c) He has one or more children possessing the nationality of the country of residence. 3. The Contracting States shall give sympathetic consideration to assimilat-

Article 18 – Self-employment: The Contracting States shall accord to a refugee lawfully in their territory *the same treatment as that accorded to nationals in the same circumstances*, as regards the right to engage on his own account in agriculture, industry, handicrafts and commerce and to establish commercial and industrial companies.

Article 19 – Liberal professions: 1. Each Contracting State shall accord to refugees lawfully staying in their territory who hold diplomas recognized by the competent authorities of that State, and who are desirous of practicing a liberal profession, treatment *not less favourable than that accorded to nationals in the same circumstances*. 2. The Contracting States shall use their best endeavours consistently with their laws and constitutions to secure the settlement of such refugees in the territories, other than the metropolitan territory, for whose international relations they are responsible.

Article 21 – Housing: As regards housing, the Contracting States, in so far as the matter is regulated by laws or regulations or is subject to the control of public authorities, shall accord to refugees lawfully staying in their territory *the same treatment as accorded to nationals* in the same circumstances.

Article 22 – Public Education: [...] 2. The Contracting States shall accord to refugees treatment not less favourable *than that accorded to nationals* in the same circumstances, with respect to education other than elementary education and, in particular, as regards access to studies, the recognition of foreign school certificates, diplomas and degrees, the remission of fees and charges and the award of scholarships.

Article 26 – Freedom of Movement: Each Contracting State shall accord to refugees lawfully in its territory the right to choose their place of residence to move freely within its territory, *ensuring the same treatment as accorded to nationals* in the same circumstances".

3.2. *International Cooperation and Burden-Sharing*

The most critical aspect of asylum and refugee law is definitely represented by the burden it imposes on States. In some cases this burden may become unsustainable, especially when countries located at the (territorial or maritime) borders with areas upset by huge humanitarian crises have to face particularly large flows of asylum-seekers. The international community was already aware of this problem

---

ing the rights of all refugees with regard to wage-earning employment to those of nationals, and in particular of those refugees who have entered their territory pursuant to programmes of labour recruitment or under immigration schemes".

at the time the Refugee Convention was negotiated, as demonstrated by the fourth recital of the preamble, stressing that "the grant of asylum may place unduly heavy burdens on certain countries, and that a satisfactory solution of a problem of which the United Nations has recognized the international scope and nature cannot therefore be achieved without international co-operation". However, this statement of principle remained on paper, as no operational provision of the Convention regulated the issue of cooperation among States Parties. The only rule included in the text of the Convention dealing with cooperation is Article 35, which, however, concerns cooperation of States Parties with the UNHCR and other UN agencies.[81] To make the system established by the Convention more effective, as well as to ensure a more equitable distribution among States Parties of the burdens determined by the flows of refugees, the international community should imitate the example of the Convention Governing the Specific Aspects of Refugee Problems in Africa,[82] which at Article II(4) establishes that,

> "Where a Member State finds difficulty in continuing to grant asylum to refugees, such Member State may appeal directly to other Member States and through the [African Union], and such other Member States shall in the spirit of African solidarity and international co-operation take appropriate measures to lighten the burden of the Member State granting asylum".[83]

The inclusion of a provision of this kind in the Refugee Convention – and, especially, the accomplishment of the principle of burden-sharing in practice – would render its implementation more sustainable for all States Parties and, *a fortiori*, facilitate the proper execution of its provisions, as well as, eventually, the pursuit of its basic purpose, that is "to assure refugees the widest possible exercise of [...] fundamental rights and freedoms".[84]

4. CONCLUSION

A fundamental condition to be satisfied for ensuring the proper realization of human rights is the treatment of human rights instruments as "live instruments whose interpretation must adapt to the evolution of the times and, specifically, to

---

[81] The same rule is reproduced in Art. II of the 1967 Protocol.

[82] See *supra* note 9.

[83] On the implementation of this provision in the practice of African States see D'ORSI, *Asylum-Seeker and Refugee Protection in Sub-Saharan Africa. The Peregrination of a Persecuted Human Being in Search of a Safe Haven*, London/New York, 2016, p. 103 ff.

[84] See *supra* note 2 and corresponding text.

current living conditions".[85] However, as noted in section 1, for such an evolutionary interpretation to be possible in practice, it is necessary that the relevant treaties and provisions are characterized by some degree of flexibility. With respect to several provisions of the Refugee Convention such flexibility is lacking, and the operation of adapting them to the present needs of the international society is only possible through sophisticated interpretative acrobatics, when it is not altogether impossible. The Refugee Convention therefore needs to be appropriately amended, through redrafting some of its provisions, in order to make it responsive to the current characterization of international human rights law. This need is rendered even more urgent by the fact that in contemporary times flows of refugees are a problem the dimension of which is growing day after day.

The purpose of this article was to provide an opinion concerning the possible amendments which could be made to align the Refugee Convention with the state of advancement of human rights standards in contemporary international society. Each article which this author considers should be modified has been critically analysed and the necessary textual changes have been proposed. Of course, this writer is aware that, while proposing amendments to the Refugee Convention is relatively easy from a theoretical perspective, making such amendments acceptable to governments is a very different matter. In fact, given the present state of things, it is very unlikely that States would accept most of the changes proposed in this article. This certainly applies, for instance, to the proposal of broadening the definition of "refugee" to include the categories of economic migrants and environmental refugees, especially in a historical period like the present, when the burden on governments from immigration flows is greater than ever before, and certain States are even planning to fix quotas with respect to the number of refugees allowed to be admitted to their territory (in blatant violation of the Refugee Convention).[86] For many States, such an extension of the concept of "refugee" would probably lead to migratory burdens which would be unsustainable for their economy and/or social and cultural conditions. In a similar vein, it is implausible that governments would accept the elimination of Articles 1(F) and 33(2) from the Convention, which are perceived as the most effective shields for preventing the entry of dangerous persons into their territory (except when the operation of such clauses is barred by other treaty regimes in force, particularly the ECHR). Last but not least, it is unlikely that States would accept the introduction in the Convention's

---

[85] See Inter-American Court of Human Rights, *Mayagna (Sumo) Awas Tingni Community v. Nicaragua*, Judgment of 31 August 2001, Series C No. 79, para. 146.

[86] See, for instance, the decision of Austria to set daily limits on refugees entering and registering in the country, announced in January 2016. See Thomas and Pop, "Austria to Set Limit on Migrants Entering the Country", The Wall Street Journal, 20 January 2016, available at: <http://www.wsj.com/articles/dutch-leader-warns-europe-needs-urgent-fix-to-migrant-influx-1453285192>; and Huggler, "Austria to Reduce Its Cap on Refugees Entering the Country", The Telegraph, 20 January 2016, available at: <http://www.telegraph.co.uk/news/worldnews/europe/austria/12111426/Austria-to-reduce-its-cap-on-refugees-entering-the-country.html>.

text of a provision on burden-sharing, given their attempts to limit immigration flows as much as possible.

However, the purpose of this article is not to elaborate an apology of realism, but rather to try to describe how the Refugee Convention should be modified in order to become effectively consistent with human rights standards, keeping the evaluation of whether or not what is proposed is likely to be actually achieved as secondary thought. In other words, the reflections developed by this author are considerations *de jure condendo* aimed at illustrating what should be done to make the Refugee Convention responsive to the real needs of people in need of protection, which would represent the first step in improving the international regulation of asylum and refugee law. Then, of course, it would be necessary to make the achievement of this goal possible, through convincing governments to accept the proposed changes. In this author's opinion, this would only be possible through persuading governments that accepting the proposed changes would lead to the generation of benefits which, in the long term, would be enjoyed by international society as a whole, including States themselves.

There are strong arguments which could support this assertion. For instance, a more efficient international regime of refugee protection would ease international relations, to the benefit of all relevant actors. Also, through improving the conditions of people in distress a fairer international society might be promoted, which, in the long term, would bring benefits to all. Endorsing international cooperation in the field – not only with respect to reception of refugees, but especially in addressing the root causes leading to their production and in promoting efficient development programmes in the countries of origin[87] – would facilitate the task of States in the long run, as the burden determined by asylum-seekers would gradually decrease. To a related extent, accepting the insertion in the Refugee Convention of a rule on burden-sharing would also produce benefits which would be generally enjoyed. In fact, if it is true that, on the one hand, in certain periods some States should bear additional burdens determined by the duty of helping countries stretched by huge flows of refugees, on the other hand these efforts would be rewarded through allowing the same States to ease their own burdens when it is their turn to be hard-pressed by vast amounts of asylum-seekers.

In the end, governments should be able to adopt a position of foresight, to realise that updating the Refugee Convention in order to make it consistent with contemporary human rights standards would not only contribute to promoting a better international society, but would also bring benefits which would be enjoyed by States themselves, if not on an immediate basis, certainly in the long term.

---

[87] See LENZERINI, *cit. supra* note 8, p. 576 ff.

DETENTION AND EXPULSION OF MIGRANTS: THE *KHLAIFIA V. ITALY* CASE

MARIA ROSARIA MAURO[*]

Abstract

On 1 September 2015 the European Court of Human Rights adopted the judgment in Khlaifia and Others v. Italy, *concerning the detention and the ensuing repatriation to Tunisia of three irregular immigrants who had arrived in Italy in 2011 during the "Arab Spring". The Court found that the applicants had been unlawfully detained in Italy and that they were not provided information or the possibility to challenge their detention. Moreover, the conditions of detention amounted to inhuman and degrading treatment. Finally, according to the Court, the applicants had been subject to collective expulsion, as despite their individual identification by Italian authorities, the personal circumstances of each of them had not been evaluated prior to their removal to Tunisia. This note considers the Italian immigration policy in the light of the European Convention of Human Rights and of the examined decision, mainly in relation to the controversial aspects of the detention and expulsion of migrants.*

Keywords: detention; right to an effective remedy; inhuman or degrading treatment or punishment; individual identification; collective expulsion.

1. INTRODUCTION

In the last few years, political upheavals, human rights violations, and general deterioration of living conditions in some countries of Africa and the Middle East have significantly intensified flows of migrants and refugees towards Europe.[1] In

---

[*] Associate Professor of International Law, University of Molise.

[1] In 2015, about one million people reached Europe, according to estimates by the United Nations High Commissioner for Refugee (UNHCR) and the International Organization for Migration (IOM): UNHCR, "A Million Refugees and Migrants Flee to Europe in 2015", 22 December 2015, available at: <http://www.unhcr.org/news/press/2015/12/567918556/million-refugees-migrants-flee-europe-2015.html>. In the same year, about 1.3 million applications for asylum were received by the European Union (EU) States: Eurostat, "Asylum Statistics", data extracted on 2 March 2016 and on 20 April 2016, available at: <http://ec.europa.eu/eurostat/statistics-explained/index.php/Asylum_statistics#Decisions_on_asylum_applications>. The number of asylum seekers from non-EU countries in the EU Member States during the first quarter of 2016 reached 287,100, i.e. 97,500 persons more than in the same quarter of 2015: Eurostat, "Asylum Quarterly Report", 15 June 2016, available at: <http://ec.europa.eu/eurostat/statistics-explained/index.php/Asylum_quarterly_report>.

particular, in the aftermath of the so-called "Arab Spring" in 2011, Tunisians and Sub-Saharan Africans who had migrated to Libya began to arrive on the island of Lampedusa or move toward other parts of Europe. The phenomenon intensified following the overthrow of the Gaddafi regime. To date, European States have not been able to deal effectively with this serious humanitarian crisis and to respond with a uniform and coherent policy.[2]

In this context there are two opposing interests, which should be both safeguarded: on one hand, the necessity of the State to manage this massive and seemingly never-ending immigration flow; on the other hand, the need to protect human rights and to respect the dignity of all immigrants.[3] National authorities have to handle this massive illegal immigration flow, facing serious public order and security problems. To do this, host States can follow different paths, such as signing of international agreements with countries of origin providing for the return of migrants ineligible for asylum, establishing of preventive patrol operations, and the adoption of administrative and criminal law measures. But, simultaneously national authorities have the duty to act in conformity with international human rights

---

[2] See PARK, "Europe Migration's Crisis", CFR Backgrounders, 23 September 2015, available at: <http://www.cfr.org/migration/europes-migration-crisis/p32874>.

[3] On these topics, see among others: LILLICH, *The Human Rights of Aliens in Contemporary International Law*, Manchester, 1984; CHOLEWINSKI, *Migrant Workers in International Human Rights Law. Their Protection in Countries of Employment*, Oxford, 1997; GOODWIN-GILL, "Migration: International Law and Human Rights", in GHOSH (ed.), *Managing Migration: Time for a New International Regime?*, Oxford, 2000, p. 160 ff.; DENG, "The Global Challenge of Internal Displacement", Washington University Journal of Law & Policy, 2001, p. 141 ff.; TIBURCIO, *The Human Rights of Aliens Under International and Comparative Law*, The Hague, 2001; FELLER, TÜRK and NICHOLSON (eds.), *Refugee Protection in International Law, UNHCR's Global Consultations on International Protection*, Cambridge, 2003; FITZPATRICK, "The Human Rights of Migrants", in ALEINIKOFF and CHETAIL (eds.), *Migration and International Legal Norms*, The Hague, 2003, p. 169 ff.; BOGUSZ, CHOLEWINSKI, CYGAN and SZYSZCZAK (eds.), *Irregular Migration and Human Rights: Theoretical, European and International Perspectives*, Leiden, 2004; HATHAWAY, *The Rights of Refugees Under International Law*, Cambridge, 2005; SAROLÉA, *Droits de l'homme et migrations: de la protection du migrant aux droits de la personne migrante*, Bruxelles, 2006; CHETAIL (ed.), *Globalization, Migration and Human Rights: International Law Under Review*, Bruxelles, 2007; GOODWIN-GILL and MCADAM, *The Refugee in International Law*, 3rd edition, Oxford, 2007; WEISSBRODT, *The Human Rights of Non-Citizens*, Oxford, 2008; NASCIMBENE, "Le migrazioni tra sovranità dello Stato e tutela dei diritti della persona", in CARTA (ed.), *Immigrazione, frontiere esterne e diritti umani. Profili internazionali, europei ed interni*, Roma, 2009, p. 1 ff.; PALMISANO, "Trattamento dei migranti clandestini e rispetto degli obblighi internazionali sui diritti umani", DUDI, 2009, p. 509 ff.; HAILBRONNER, *EU Immigration and Asylum Law*, Munich, 2010; GAMMELTHOFT-HANSEN, *Access to Asylum: International Refugee Law and the Globalisation of Migration Control*, Cambridge, 2011; GOODWIN-GILL and WECKEL (eds.), *Migration and Refugee Protection in the 21st Century: International Legal Aspects*, Leiden/Boston, 2015; MITSILEGAS, *The Criminalisation of Migration in Europe: Challenges for Human Rights and the Rule of Law*, Cham, 2015; BURSON and CANTOR (eds.), *Human Rights and the Refugee Definition: Comparative Legal Practice and Theory*, Leiden/Boston, 2016.

law, notably the European Convention of Human Rights (ECHR).[4] In fact, regardless of whether States accept migrants, national authorities have to guarantee the basic human rights recognised by international law.

The ECHR does not actually include norms concerning extradition, expulsion, and asylum, therefore States Parties have the right "to control the entry, residence and expulsion of aliens".[5] However, in the past few decades, and particularly in the past few years, the European Court of Human Rights (ECtHR) has adopted some core decisions concerning these topics, which may have an impact on immigration national policies. In fact, by these decisions, the ECtHR has both contributed to the identification and development of the international human rights standards in this field and identified principles and guidelines on immigration for national authorities.

In this context, on 1 September 2015 the ECtHR adopted the judgment in *Khlaifia and Others v. Italy*,[6] affirming that the procedures followed by Italy in 2011 to repatriate three Tunisian nationals violated the ECHR, in particular Article 3, Article 5(1)(2), and (4), and Article 13 (concerning, respectively, the prohibition of inhuman or degrading treatment; the right to liberty and security, the right to be informed promptly of the reasons for deprivation of liberty and the right to an examination of the lawfulness of detention; the right to an effective remedy), and Article 4 of Protocol 4 of the ECHR (prohibition of collective expulsion of aliens).

The decision at hand has particular importance for its content and could have a significant impact on immigration and asylum law of European countries. The case deals with the detention, in a reception centre on Lampedusa and subsequently on ships anchored in Palermo harbour, and the following repatriation to Tunisia, of three irregular immigrants who had arrived in Italy in 2011, during the "Arab Spring".

The decision establishes three main points. First, detention of an individual not validated by a judge and without guaranteeing access to a lawyer is unlawful. Second, the poor conditions of detention in the *"Centro di soccorso e prima accoglienza"* (Centre for Rescue and initial Reception – CSPA) on Lampedusa represented inhuman and degrading treatment. Third, the expulsion of the applicants to Tunisia was illicit, since it occurred without considering the individual circumstances of each of them and without asking for validation by a judge; moreover, it was implemented merely on the basis of their nationality.

In order to face the migration crisis and to protect the right to life of migrants, on 18 October 2013, Italy decided to establish "Operation Mare Nostrum". In this context, the Italian Government took on the responsibility to improve maritime

---

[4] 4 November 1950, entered into force 3 September 1953.
[5] *Vilvarajah and Others v. The United Kingdom*, Applications No. 13163/87, 13164/87, 13165/87, 13447/87, and 13448/87, Judgment of 30 October 1991, para. 102.
[6] *Khlaifia and Others v. Italy*, Application No. 16483/12, Judgment of 1 September 2015. The Judgment was issued in French. On 1 February 2016 the case was referred to the Grand Chamber at the request of the Italian Government and a hearing was held on 22 June 2016.

security, patrol sea lanes, combat illegal activities, in particular human trafficking, and tackle the humanitarian emergency in the Mediterranean Sea.[7] Notwithstanding this worthy initiative, the Italian immigration policy and its implementation mechanisms present, at the moment, a number of flaws and deficiencies,[8] which have been condemned by the ECtHR on several occasions.

This note considers the Italian immigration policy in the light of the ECHR system and of the *Khlaifia* judgment, mainly in relation to some controversial aspects such as the adequacy of preventive action and the recourse to certain administrative security measures (push-backs/expulsions, administrative detention). In the last few years, Italy has made wide use of push-backs/expulsions and detention in the context of its immigration policy. This policy has been harshly criticized both at the international and domestic level, as it raises issues of compatibility with the Italian Constitution and international human rights obligations, as well as doubts about its effectiveness in relation to the objectives pursued.[9]

2.   THE *KHLAIFIA* CASE

In this case the applicants were three Tunisian nationals,[10] who left their home country with the aim of reaching Italy in September 2011. The Italian coastguard

---

[7] "Operation Mare Nostrum" concerned an area in the Straits of Sicily of about 70,000 sq. km. It lasted 364 days. During this period the Italian Navy engaged in 421 operations and rescued 150,810 migrants, 5 mother ships were seized, and 330 alleged smugglers were brought to justice. On 1 November 2014, "Operation Mare Nostrum" was replaced by Triton, a joint operation launched by Frontex (the European Agency for the Management of Operational Cooperation at the External Borders of the Member States of the European Union, set up by the Council Regulation (EC) 2007/2004 of 26 October 2004) following Italy's request determined by the high migratory pressure. Triton is carried out using resources and equipment of Schengen Member States.

[8] According to NICOSIA ("Massive Immigration Flows Management in Italy between the Fight Against Illegal Immigration and Human Rights Protection", QIL, Zoom-in 5, 2014, p. 25 ff., p. 39), these deficiencies "are most likely the result of a problematic mixture of many factors, including reactive action, caused by a lack of a long-term rational strategy and occasional endorsement of xenophobic pressures at the political level, with symbolic legislative amendments mainly aimed at gaining easy political and electoral consensus and at reassuring the public opinion". Furthermore, according to the author, "[i]t may also be down to issues of judicial inactivity, self-restraint and workload, administrative negligence and unlawful practices, limited human and financial resources, as well as objective factors, like the objective difficulties inherent in the task of managing a massive flow of thousands of poor and desperate people for a country which is particularly exposed to it as a result of its geographical position".

[9] See, e.g., CAVALIERE, "Diritto penale e politica dell'immigrazione", Critica del diritto, 2013, p. 17 ff.; and DI MARTINO, BIONDI DAL MONTE, BOIANO and RAFFAELLI, *The Criminalization of Irregular Immigration: Law and Practice in Italy*, Pisa, 2013.

[10] In particular: Saber Ben Mohamed Ben Ali Khlaifia, Fakhreddine Ben Brahim Ben Mustapha Tabal, and Mohamed Ben Habib Ben Jaber Sfar.

intercepted their boat and transferred the men to the island of Lampedusa, where they were led to a reception centre (CSPA) in Contrada Imbriacola, for registration. The centre proved to be overcrowded, with inadequate sanitation and limited space to sleep. Moreover, according to the applicants, any contact with the outside world was obstructed by the uninterrupted police surveillance.

Following an organised rebellion by immigrants, the CSPA was set on fire and partially destroyed. Then, the applicants fled and reached the village of Lampedusa, where they and about 1,800 other migrants began another protest. The three applicants were arrested by the police and transferred to a ship anchored in Palermo harbour, where they claimed to have been forced to stay in overcrowded areas with limited access to the sanitary services, with no information, and abused by police officers. Days later, they were finally taken to Palermo airport, where they were identified by the Tunisian consul and expelled to Tunisia in accordance with an informal bilateral agreement in force between the two countries.[11]

The decision takes into account three main legal issues related to Italian migration policy: arbitrary deprivation of freedom of migrants; reception conditions of migrants; and, collective expulsion of migrants. The ECtHR held unanimously that Italy's treatment of the migrants was in breach of Article 5(1) (right to liberty and security), Article 5(2) (right to be informed promptly of the charge against the applicants), and Article 5(4) (right to a speedy decision by a court on the lawfulness of detention) of the ECHR. On the contrary, the Court did not find any violation of Article 3 (prohibition of inhuman or degrading treatment) in respect of the conditions of detention on board the ships; even though, according to the majority of the judges, there had been a violation of Article 3 in respect of the conditions of detention in the CSPA in Lampedusa. Lastly, there had been a violation of Article 4 Protocol No. 4 (prohibition of collective expulsion of aliens) of the ECHR, and Article 13 (right to an effective remedy) taken in conjunction with Articles 3 ECHR and 4 Protocol No. 4. In particular, according to the Court, the applicants were deprived of their liberty in violation of Article 5(1) ECHR since under Italian law there was no basis for their detention;[12] therefore, the restriction of freedom was in conflict with the general principle of legal certainty and the duty to avoid arbitrary treatment. In fact, according to Italian law, irregular migrants can be detained ex-

---

[11] The text of the Italian-Tunisian agreement on cooperation to control the flow of irregular immigration of 5 April 2011 has not been made public.

[12] This aspect was confirmed by the Extraordinary Commission of the Italian Senate on Human Rights in its report "on the state of [respect for] human rights in penitentiary institutions and reception and detention centres for migrants in Italy", approved on 6 March 2012. The Court also makes reference to the report concerning "the mass arrival of irregular migrants, asylum seekers and refugees on the southern European coasts", published on 30 September 2011 by the *ad hoc* Sub-Commission of the Parliamentary Assembly of the Council of Europe (*Khlaifia, cit. supra* note 6, para. 70).

clusively in a *"Centro di identificazione ed espulsione"* (Centres for Identification and Expulsion – CIEs)[13] in accordance with the prescribed conditions.

Moreover, Italy violated Article 5(2) ECHR not providing the three men with any information as to the legal or factual basis of their detention. Furthermore, since the applicants had received the expulsion orders, stating that they had entered the country illegally and that their removal had been ordered, only at the time of execution of repatriation, the ECtHR considered the abovementioned acts incomplete as far as the content and additionally not being delivered in time. For this reason in the opinion of the Court the right of the three migrants to challenge their detention – according to Article 5(4) ECHR – was ineffective. Then, turning to the conditions of their detention, the Court observed that, although at that time Italy had to face an exceptional humanitarian crisis and a heavy situation of emergency determined by a flow of over 50,000 arrivals after the uprisings in Tunisia,[14] the State had the duty to guarantee the applicants conditions respecting their human dignity, due to the absolute and non-derogable nature of Article 3 ECHR. According to the majority of judges, the conditions of detention at the Contrada Imbriacola reception centre were not in accordance with Article 3, while there was no violation regarding conditions on board the ships in Palermo harbour.

Furthermore, the applicants complained they were victims of collective expulsion in breach of Article 4 Protocol No. 4 of the ECHR, affirming that they were summarily expelled due to their nationality without individual consideration of their personal situations.[15] In this regard, the Court concluded that the *refoulement* decisions did not specify the individual situation of each migrant and that a simple identification procedure was insufficient to disprove the existence of a collective expulsion. The Court also noted that, at the time, a great number of Tunisians were removed and repatriated under simplified procedures – namely identification by the Tunisian consular authorities – in accordance with the bilateral agreement between Italy and Tunisia. It therefore concluded that the Italian authorities had not taken

---

[13] Art. 14 of D.Lgs. No. 286 of 25 July 1998, *Testo unico delle disposizioni concernenti la disciplina dell'immigrazione e norme sulla condizione dello straniero* (GU No. 191 of 18 August 1998, Suppl. Ord. No. 139) (hereinafter "TU Immigrazione").

[14] The Court highlights the seriousness of the situation on Lampedusa, quoting the report published by the *ad hoc* Sub-Commission of the Parliamentary Assembly of the Council of Europe concerning "the mass arrival of irregular migrants, asylum seekers and refugees on the southern European coasts" (*Khlaifia, cit. supra* note 6, para. 124).

[15] Grounded on the cases *Čonka v. Belgium*, Application No. 51564/99, Judgment of 5 February 2002, and *Hirsi Jamaa and Others v. Italy*, Application No. 27765/09, Judgment of 23 February 2012, the applicants asserted that they had been subject to a collective expulsion, due to four factors: (i) the huge number of Tunisians affected by the measure; (ii) the announcement by the Italian Ministry of the Interior about collective expulsion operations in accordance with a bilateral agreement with Tunisia; (iii) the same wording of the expulsion orders; and (iv) the applicants' difficulty to access a lawyer. However, according to Italy, the orders were individually issued and translated into Arabic. Moreover, upon arrival on Lampedusa, the Italian police had individually interviewed each migrant (*Khlaifia, cit. supra* note 6, paras. 150, 151, and 152).

into account the personal circumstances of the involved people, violating Article 4 Protocol No. 4.

Lastly, the ECtHR also found a violation of Article 13 ECHR taken in conjunction with Articles 3 ECHR and 4 Protocol No. 4 since the applicants had not benefitted from any effective remedy in order to lodge a complaint and in any case an appeal to a magistrate could not have a suspensive effect on their removal to Tunisia.[16]

3. THE DETENTION OF MIGRANTS

According to customary international law, each State is free to exercise its territorial sovereignty, to protect its own borders, and to decide who to admit into its own territory, whether to detain migrants and to remove non-nationals.[17] Nevertheless, it has the duty to do so in conformity with its obligations under international human rights law. In particular, when the individual has entered the country, the territorial State is responsible for the protection of his or her rights. Therefore, some international law principles can limit the discretionary power of the State in migration control. Among these, the most important are the ban of arbitrary detention, the principle of *non-refoulement*, the right to family unity, and the prohibition of collective expulsion. These principles have not only been affirmed by several conventions but have also acquired the nature of customary international law rules.[18] In this context, the relevant role played by the ECtHR has to be highlighted, which by its case law has significantly contributed to clarifying and developing the principles concerning the human rights of migrants and refugees. Indeed, apart from a few provisions about the removal of aliens,[19] the ECHR and its protocols do not grant any special rights to aliens. Moreover, unlike the Charter of Fundamental Rights of the European Union,[20] the Convention system does not include any norm con-

---

[16] On the effectiveness of the remedies in case of collective expulsion, see *De Souza Ribeiro v. France*, Application No. 22689/07, Judgment of 13 December 2012, in particular para. 84 ff.

[17] *T.I. v. The United Kingdom*, Application No. 43844/98, Decision of 7 March 2000. On this aspect, see PISILLO MAZZESCHI, "Sui rapporti fra i diritti umani ed i diritti degli stranieri e dei migranti nell'ordinamento internazionale", in PISILLO MAZZESCHI, PUSTORINO and VIVIANI (eds.), *Diritti umani degli immigrati: tutela della famiglia e dei minori*, Napoli, 2010, p. 7 ff., pp. 10-11.

[18] See CHETAIL, "The Transnational Movement of Persons Under General International Law. Mapping the Customary Law Foundations of International Migration Law", in CHETAIL and BAULOZ (eds.), *Research Handbook on International Law and Migration*, Cheltenham, 2014, p. 1 ff.

[19] See Art. 1 of Protocol No. 7, adopted on 22 November 1984.

[20] The Charter was proclaimed on 7 December 2000 by the European Parliament, the Council of Ministers and the European Commission and became legally binding when the Treaty of Lisbon entered into force on 1 December 2009. According to its Art. 18, "[t]he right to asylum shall be guaranteed with due respect for the rules of the Geneva Convention of 28 July 1951

cerning the right of asylum. On the contrary, the ECtHR has recognised on many occasions that States are in principle free to control the entry, residence, and expulsion of foreigners.[21] Notwithstanding, the Court has also pointed out that without "call[ing] into question the right of the States to establish their own immigration policies [...] problems with managing migratory flows cannot justify a State's having recourse to practices which are not compatible with its obligations under the Convention".[22]

Therefore, starting from the interpretation of the main provisions of the ECHR, the Court has gradually developed a series of principles by which States Parties, and also the European Union (EU), have to abide in the management of migration flows and in the adoption and implementation of their migration policies.

In the *Khlaifia* judgment, the Court further defined States' obligations toward migrants, in particular in relation to their detention and to their collective expulsion. One of the most controversial aspects of the Italian immigration policy is the frequent recourse by national authorities to the administrative detention of immigrants in view of their removal. According to international law, detention measures towards migrants are not, *per se*, unlawful, unless these are arbitrary and/or in violation of human rights norms.[23] Migrants may be deprived of their freedom for different reasons. For example, detention of an immigrant is possible when he/she is refused entry to the country concerned; when he/she has entered the country illegally and has subsequently been identified by the authorities; when his/her authorisation to stay in the country has expired; or when asylum seekers' detention is considered necessary by the authorities.[24]

---

and the Protocol of 31 January 1967 relating to the status of refugees and in accordance with the Treaty establishing the European Community".

[21] See, for instance, the *Vilvarajah* case, *cit. supra* note 5, para. 102. On this topic, see KTISTAKIS, *Protecting Migrants Under the European Convention on Human Rights and the European Social Charter. A Handbook for Legal Practitioners*, Paris, 2013, pp. 17, 19, and 23, available at: <http://www.coe.int/t/democracy/migration/Source/migration/ProtectingMigrantsECHR_ESCWeb.pdf>.

[22] *Hirsi, cit. supra* note 15, para. 179.

[23] According to PISILLO MAZZESCHI (*cit. supra* note 17): "la detenzione deve essere adeguatamente motivata e giustificata, il migrante deve essere informato sui motivi della sua detenzione, deve poter rivolgersi ad un organo giudiziario per accertare la legittimità della medesima, ha diritto alla riparazione in caso di detenzione illegittima, la detenzione non deve avere una durata irragionevole, essa non deve impedire l'accesso a procedure per l'asilo e lo *status* di rifugiato, ecc" ("detention shall be adequately motivated and justified; the migrant shall be informed of the reasons for his detention; he shall be entitled to appeal to a judicial organ to verify the lawfulness of his detention; he shall have the right to compensation in case of unlawful detention; detention shall not last for an unreasonable period of time; detention shall not impede access to procedures for asylum or refugee status; etc") (p. 20).

[24] See European Committee for the Prevention of Torture and Inhuman or Degrading Treatment or Punishment (CPT), *CPT Standards*, Council of Europe Doc. CPT/Inf/E(2002)1 – Rev. 2011, December 2011, p. 64, available at: <www.cpt.coe.int/en/documents/eng-standards.doc>.

Italian immigration law foresees three different kinds of accommodation centres for migrants: CIEs, CSPAs, and CARAs (*"Centri di accoglienza per richiedenti asilo"* – Centres for Assistance of Asylum Seekers).[25] CIEs host migrants illegally in Italian territory who have received an expulsion order, if immediate execution of this order is not possible. CIEs are considered as places of detention, therefore migrants are guaranteed by all the relevant constitutional safeguards, in particular judicial control within strict time limits.[26] In this case, detention can last up to 18 months. On the contrary, CSPAs and CARAs are considered assistance structures, therefore immigrants resident in these centres are, in principle, free to leave at any time.

Actually, the system of administrative detention for irregular immigrants in view of their removal prescribed by Italian law, may constitute a deprivation of personal freedom and it may be incompatible not only with the Italian Constitution, but also with international human rights law. Firstly, CIEs could be considered not to be in accordance with the principle of equality nor in accordance with the principle of inviolability of personal freedom guaranteed by the Italian Constitution[27] due to the lack of a transparent and detailed legal regulation, causing arbitrariness and uncertainties, and significant differences in treatment from one CIE to another.[28] Moreover, CSPAs, notably the centre on Lampedusa, have been *de facto* converted into detention structures similar to CIEs, where migrants are detained for a long period, but without enjoying any right to a judicial review of their detention, nor any time limit.[29] Finally, it may be argued that inadequate and indecorous living conditions of the immigrants detained in CIEs and CSPAs – such as overcrowding, deficiency of hygiene and health care, bad quality of food, and generally degrading treatment – constitute in themselves a violation of fundamental human rights.[30]

Article 5(1) ECHR guarantees the fundamental right to liberty by protecting individuals against any form of arbitrary threat to their freedom by a State. It also includes an exhaustive list of reasons for which a person may be deprived of his/her own freedom. The ECHR does not expressly forbid administrative detention of aliens awaiting their expulsion; on the contrary, according to Article 5(1)(f), detention is one of the possible legitimate examples of restriction of the individual right

---

[25] On this subject, see NICOSIA, *cit. supra* note 8, pp. 32-33.

[26] See Art. 13 of the Italian Constitution.

[27] See Arts. 3 and 13 of the Italian Constitution. According to the Italian Constitutional Court, detention of immigrants represents a violation of their personal freedom; therefore, detention orders must be in accordance with the guarantees foreseen by Art. 13 of the Constitution, which cannot be lower in the case of immigrants in order to protect other public interests (see Judgment No. 105 of 10 April 2001, para. 4).

[28] On this topic, see DI MARTINO, BIONDI DAL MONTE, BOIANO and RAFFAELLI, *cit. supra* note 9, p. II ff. of the "Introduction".

[29] See MASERA, "Il 'caso Lampedusa': una violazione sistemica del diritto alla libertà personale", DUDI, 2014, p. 83 ff.

[30] *Ibid.*, p. 84.

to personal liberty, when it is prescribed by law. Indeed, in accordance with the case law of the ECtHR, on some occasions the territorial State has the right to limit an alien's liberty or freedom of movement: in fact, when a restrictive measure appears to be necessary, it does not constitute a violation of the ECHR. This is the case, for instance, of the so-called "reception" or "accommodation" centres, or points of entry to a country, such as international zones of airports. Nevertheless, even in these circumstances, a deprivation of liberty could occur, depending on the intensity, the length, the nature or the accumulation of the restrictions imposed.

Thus, in the decision *Guzzardi v. Italy*, the Court affirmed:

> "[…] In order to determine whether someone has been 'deprived of his liberty' within the meaning of Article 5, the starting point must be his concrete situation and account must be taken of a whole range of criteria such as the type, duration, effects and manner of implementation of the measure in question. The difference between deprivation of and restriction upon liberty is nonetheless merely one of degree or intensity, and not one of nature or substance. Although the process of classification into one or other of these categories sometimes proves to be no easy task in that some borderline cases are a matter of pure opinion, the Court cannot avoid making the selection upon which the applicability or inapplicability of Article 5 depends".[31]

Then, in the case *Amuur v. France*, the ECtHR observed that the confinement of aliens in holding centres in the international zones of an airport, under police surveillance for a period of 20 days, represented a deprivation of liberty.[32] Finally, in the decision *Abdolkhani and Karimnia v. Turkey*, the Court found that the applicants' placement in the police headquarters or in the Foreigners' Admission and Accommodation Centre constituted a deprivation of liberty due to the limits imposed on them by the administrative authorities, in spite of the qualification of the measure at issue under national law or by national authorities.[33]

---

[31] *Guzzardi v. Italy*, Application No. 7367/76, Judgment of 6 November 1980, paras. 92-93. As regards elements which permit the ascertainment of whether a restriction on liberty represents a deprivation of liberty, see also *Engel and Others v. The Netherlands*, Applications No. 5100/71, 5101/71, 5102/71, 5354/72, and 5370/72, Judgment of 8 June 1976, para. 59: "account should be taken of a whole range of factors such as the nature, duration, effects and manner of execution of the penalty or measure in question".

[32] *Amuur v. France*, Application No. 19776/92, Judgment of 25 June 1996, para. 45.

[33] *Abdolkhani and Karimnia v. Turkey*, Application No. 30471/08, Judgment of 22 September 2009, para. 127: "The Court further observes that the applicants have not been free to leave the Hasköy police headquarters or the Kırklareli Foreigners' Admission and Accommodation Centre. Besides, they are only able to meet a lawyer if the latter can present to the authorities a notarised power of attorney. Furthermore, access by the UNHCR to the applicants is subject to the authorisation of the Ministry of the Interior. In the light of these elements, the Court cannot accept the

However, Article 5(1)(f) does not render legitimate any kind of administrative detention of aliens, for instance, when national legislation does not specify the maximum duration of detention of a person expecting his/her expulsion.[34] Furthermore, administrative detention must always be implemented in accordance with all other principles provided by the ECHR and, in particular, in conformity with the prohibition of inhuman or degrading treatment imposed by Article 3 ECHR. What this consideration means is that adequate conditions have to be granted to those migrants who are deprived of their liberty pending their removal procedure. Furthermore, the ECtHR has extensively interpreted Article 3, as this provision would imply a positive obligation to prevent exposure to banned treatment, to effectively investigate alleged violations and, where appropriate, to punish those responsible, whether they are State agents or private actors.[35] Finally, migrants must have the possibility to challenge the legitimacy of their detention, as laid down in Article 13 ECHR.

In any case, according to the case law of the Court, detention is lawful only if a removal procedure is pending; otherwise, if removal appears to be impossible, the detention is no longer justified.

To conclude, if the legal conditions prescribed by Article 5 ECHR have been complied with, the individual involved has the possibility of a judicial review of deprivation of freedom and, above all, the concrete situation does not represent inhuman or degrading treatment, administrative detention of irregular migrants should not be considered, in principle, as prohibited by the ECHR nor condemned by the ECtHR. Indeed, administrative detention in Italian CIEs does not appear in itself incompatible with Articles 5 and 13 ECHR. In fact, this kind of detention is provided for by national law, according to which it lasts maximum 18 months. Furthermore, the possibility of judicial review regarding the legitimacy of the measure is guaranteed, since detention has to be authorised by a judicial organ, the Justice of the Peace. However, it must also be stressed that the compatibility of CIEs with Articles 5 and 13 ECHR is often more formal than substantial due to several factors: for instance, their legal basis has no well-defined content; judicial validation of the detention order by the Justice of the Peace is impaired by deficiencies, such as failure to respect the strict term, the difficulty for migrants to commu-

---

definition of 'detention' submitted by the Government, which in fact is the definition of pre-trial detention in the context of criminal proceedings. In the Court's view, the applicants' placement in the aforementioned facilities amounted to a 'deprivation of liberty' given the restrictions imposed on them by the administrative authorities despite the nature of the classification under national law. It therefore concludes that the applicants have been deprived of their liberty". See also CPT, *cit. supra* note 24, p. 64.

[34] See *Mathloom v. Greece*, Application No. 48883/07, Judgment of 24 April 2012, paras. 65-71, concerning an Iraqi national who was kept in detention for over two years pending his deportation, despite the adoption of an order for his conditional release.

[35] On this topic, see ERDAL and BAKIRCI, *Article 3 of the European Convention on Human Rights: A Practitioner's Handbook*, Geneva, 2006, p. 211 ff. See also BESTAGNO, *Diritti umani e impunità. Obblighi positivi degli Stati in materia penale*, Milano, 2003.

nicate with translators and *ex officio* lawyers, and inadequacy of the legal reasoning included in judicial decisions.[36]

However, *de facto* detentions in some CSPAs, such as on Lampedusa, bring about even further controversy. As observed above, this is one of the issues claimed by the three applicants in the *Khlaifia* case, who alleged violation of Articles 5 and 13 ECHR, as there was no legal basis according to Italian law for their detention in this CSPA on Lampedusa, nor was their detention subject to judicial review.[37] In accordance with its previous case law, the ECtHR recognised the abovementioned violation.

Indeed, there are some core principles that apply to any deprivation of liberty under Article 5 ECHR, in particular: the principle of the rule of law, as well as the principle of legal certainty, which refer to the legal basis of the detention; the principle of due diligence, concerning the procedure of detention; the principle of proportionality, related to the measure at issue; and, the principle of protection against arbitrariness, which is linked to all the legal conditions prescribed by Article 5. This signifies that the detention of any individual must have a precise and foreseeable legal basis. Furthermore, even though domestic law provides for the establishment of reception centres, this does not mean that the aliens are not deprived of their liberty unlawfully. In fact, the detention in these centres must follow a formal decision, and must be subject to a judicial review. On the contrary, in *Khlaifia*, the "reception" of irregular migrants was not founded on a domestic legal basis, nor was a formal decision adopted: therefore, it represented a *de facto* detention and an unlawful deprivation of liberty, which proved to be incompatible with Article 5 ECHR.[38] Moreover, the reasons for the detention were not clearly explained to the detainees and they had no means through which they could challenge their detention.

Furthermore, even though inappropriate concrete conditions of detention are quite probable, when there is an emergency situation (like the one which has been ongoing in Italy over the last few years as a result of the significant immigration pressure), the seriousness of the circumstances does not constitute a justification for the territorial State.[39] In fact, guaranteeing basic living conditions to people who are stripped of their freedom is a core standard for the protection of their human dignity.

4.   COLLECTIVE EXPULSIONS

The second fundamental problem considered by the Court in *Khlaifia* regards collective expulsions. The expression "collective expulsion [...] is to be understood

---

[36] DI MARTINO, BIONDI DAL MONTE, BOIANO, RAFFAELLI, *cit. supra* note 9, p. 58 ff.

[37] On this aspect, see MASERA, *cit. supra* note 29, p. 91 ff.

[38] *Khlaifia, cit. supra* note 6, para. 170.

[39] *Ibid.*, paras. 124-128.

as any measure compelling aliens, as a group, to leave a country, except where such a measure is taken on the basis of a reasonable and objective examination of the particular case of each individual alien of the group".[40] According to Italian immigration law, migrants without valid documents for entry or the right to stay in the national territory may be expelled by the border police.[41] In this context, there are different kinds of expulsion that can be applied to aliens. The first is administrative expulsion, which is ordered by the *Prefetto* (the most important local home affairs administrative authority), in the case of irregular entry or residence or threat to public security.[42] Second, there is judicial expulsion, which constitutes a criminal law security measure and is decided by the judicial authority together with or alternatively to usual criminal sanctions (detention and/or fine), when aliens have committed a crime.[43] In the last few years, the Italian authorities have increasingly resorted to tools of push-backs and expulsions of migrants, especially following the legislative amendments adopted in 2008-2009: the so-called "Security Packages".[44]

The abovementioned practice has been strongly contested, mainly because this approach proves itself in violation of international law, EU law, and the Italian Constitution, particularly Article 10,[45] but also because it is considered excessively focused on the protection of public order/security concerns instead of following a model of integration.

However, it should be underlined that removal of aliens in itself does not violate international law. In fact, it is universally recognised that a State has the right to expel aliens in case of illegal entry or residence on the national territory. On the contrary, the absolute prohibition of collective expulsions is prescribed by both customary and treaty international law.[46] At the European level too, collective expulsions are banned. In particular, in the EU legal order, these measures may be incompatible with Article 78(1) of the Treaty on the Functioning of the European Union (TFEU), according to which the asylum policy has to be in ac-

---

[40] *Čonka, cit. supra* note 15, para. 59.

[41] See Art. 10 TU Immigrazione.

[42] See Art. 13 TU Immigrazione.

[43] See Arts. 235 and 312 of the Italian Criminal Code, as well as Arts. 15 and 16 TU Immigrazione.

[44] On this subject, see NICOSIA, *cit. supra* note 8, pp. 29-30.

[45] See DI MARTINO, BIONDI DAL MONTE, BOIANO, RAFFAELLI, *cit. supra* note 9, p. 21. According to the authors: "Pushbacks, both at the border and delayed, involve limitations to personal freedom and a large margin of discretional evaluation. This does not seem to comply with either the principle that 'the legal status of foreigners is regulated by law' (article 10 (2) of Italian Constitution) nor the principles established by article 13 of the Italian Constitution, according to which all limitations to personal freedom shall be established by law (so called *riserva di legge*) and be subjected to jurisdictional control (so called *riserva di giurisdizione*). In fact in many cases, push-back orders have been adopted some days after the immigrant had been identified" (p. 23).

[46] See CHETAIL, *cit. supra* note 18, p. 55.

cordance with "other relevant treaties",[47] and are explicitly forbidden by Article 19 of the EU Charter of Fundamental Rights.[48] The European Social Charter (ESC) also makes reference to expulsions. In fact, its Article 19(8) provides that the Contracting Parties undertake to ensure that migrant workers lawfully residing within the territory of the Parties are not expelled. With regard to this provision, for example, the European Committee of Social Rights (ECSR) observed, in *European Roma and Travellers Forum v. France*, that the administrative decisions which provided for the expulsion of Roma of Romanian and Bulgarian origins from French territory (in which they were resident) were not in accordance with the ESC. In particular, since these decisions were not founded on an analysis of the personal situation of the Roma, they were incompatible with the proportionality principle; furthermore, by targeting the Romany community, the decisions were also discriminatory. Consequently, the Committee concluded that there had been a breach of Article E on non-discrimination read in conjunction with Article 19(8) ESC.[49] However, it must be also stressed that, in order to encourage the number of ratifications, the ESC permits States to select a minimum of articles which they have to commit themselves to applying, and that Article 19 is included in this category.

In the context of the Council of Europe, as has been pointed out, the ban on collective expulsions is also contained in Article 4 Protocol No. 4 ECHR.[50] Furthermore, it is restated under Guideline 3 of the "Twenty Guidelines on Forced Return", according to which a "removal order shall only be issued on the basis of a reasonable and objective examination of the particular case of each individual person concerned, and it shall take into account the circumstances specific to each case. The collective expulsion of aliens is prohibited".[51]

The *Khlaifia* case represents the fifth case in which the ECtHR has found a violation of the collective expulsion prohibition provided for in Article 4 Protocol No.

---

[47] According to Art. 78(1): "The Union shall develop a common policy on asylum, subsidiary protection and temporary protection with a view to offering appropriate status to any third-country national requiring international protection and ensuring compliance with the principle of *non-refoulement*. This policy must be in accordance with the Geneva Convention of 28 July 1951 and the Protocol of 31 January 1967 relating to the status of refugees, and other relevant treaties".

[48] According to Art. 19: "1. Collective expulsions are prohibited. 2. No one may be removed, expelled or extradited to a State where there is a serious risk that he or she would be subjected to the death penalty, torture or other inhuman or degrading treatment or punishment".

[49] *European Roma and Travellers Forum v. France*, Complaint No. 64/2011, Decision on the merits of 24 January 2012, paras. 51-67, available at: <https://wcd.coe.int/ViewDoc.jsp?id=1902187&Site=CM>.

[50] Adopted on 16 November 1963.

[51] Committee of Ministers, *Twenty Guidelines on Forced Return*, adopted on 4 May 2005 at the 925th meeting of the Ministers' Deputies.

4.[52] In *Čonka v. Belgium*,[53] the Court held that the removal of a group of Romany asylum seekers decided by the Belgian authorities violated Article 4 Protocol No. 4 of the ECHR. In particular, according to the Court, the expulsion procedure failed to guarantee the evaluation of each claim by analysing the personal circumstances of every applicant seeking asylum before they were expelled to their home country, Slovakia. In fact, they were summoned, with other Slovakian Romany families, at a police station in Ghent, allegedly to complete their asylum applications. There, all of the members of the group received expulsion orders which were expressed in identical terms. Furthermore, according to the Court, contacting a lawyer turned out to be very complex for the applicants and the asylum procedure was not completed.[54]

Then, in the decision *Hirsi Jamaa and Others v. Italy*,[55] the Court pondered for the first time whether Article 4 Protocol 4 applies extraterritorially and, in particular, to migrants intercepted at sea. In this case the Court considered international law and EU law norms concerning sea interventions and the duties of coast guards and flag ships in international waters where the State still has jurisdiction within the meaning of Article 1 ECHR[56] and it asserted that the ban on expulsion also concerned measures taken on the high seas. Effectively, Article 4 merely states that "collective expulsion of aliens is prohibited", without any specific reference to territory. Also the *travaux preparatoires* do not clarify the issue of territoriality, however an extraterritorial application of Article 4 is not explicitly excluded. In particular, the ECtHR affirmed that Italy, by applying a push-back of a boat intercepted at sea full of Somali and Eritrean migrants towards Libya without considering their personal conditions, violated Article 4 Protocol No. 4. Moreover, the Court found that Article 3 ECHR was also violated, as the applicants had been exposed to the direct risk of ill-treatment in Libya, where, furthermore, there was also the danger of a secondary *refoulement* to Somalia or Eritrea, which were facing "serious problems of insecurity". Finally, there was a breach of Article 13, since

---

[52] The other cases in which the ECtHR found a violation of the article at issue are: *Čonka, cit. supra* note 15; *Hirsi, cit. supra* note 15; *Georgia v. Russia (I)*, Application No. 13255/07, Judgment of 3 July 2014; *Sharifi and Others v. Italy and Greece*, Application No. 16643/09, Judgment of 21 October 2014. See RAMJI-NOGALES, "Prohibiting Collective Expulsion of Aliens at the European Court of Human Rights", ASIL Insight, 4 January 2016, available at: <https://www.asil.org/insights/volume/20/issue/1/prohibiting-collective-expulsion-aliens-european-court-human-rights>.

[53] *Čonka, cit. supra* note 15.

[54] *Ibid.*, paras. 59-63.

[55] *Hirsi, cit. supra* note 15. On this case, see LENZERINI, "Il principio del 'non-refoulment' dopo la sentenza Hirsi della Corte europea dei diritti dell'uomo", RDI, 2012, p. 721 ff.; LIGUORI, La Corte europea dei diritti dell'uomo condanna l'Italia per i respingimenti verso la Libia del 2009: il caso 'Hirsi'", RDI, 2012, p. 415 ff.; and DEN HEIJER, "Reflections on 'Refoulement' and Collective Expulsion in the 'Hirsi' Case", International Journal of Refugee Law, 2013, p. 265 ff.

[56] According to Art. 1: "The High Contracting Parties shall secure to everyone within their jurisdiction the rights and freedoms defined in Section I of this Convention".

the aliens affected had not been given the chance to lodge an effective complaint against their expulsion.[57]

Since the decision in *Hirsi*, the ECtHR has gradually begun to pay attention to this previously less prominent provision of the European human rights protection system.[58] Thus, in *Georgia v. Russia*, it held again that Article 4 Protocol 4 was violated.[59] In this case, concerning a Russian administrative practice of arresting, detaining, and collectively expelling Georgian nationals, the ECtHR affirmed that the prohibition of collective expulsion covers all individuals, even if their residence is unlawful. Moreover, the Court concluded that, due to the limited duration of the process and the quantity of expulsion orders (4,600), it was not plausible that the applicants' cases had really been examined individually. Finally, in citing *Hirsi*, the Court restated that even though States Parties have the right to decide their own immigration policies, nevertheless problems with managing migratory flows cannot justify the adoption of national measures which are in violation of obligations of the ECHR.[60]

Shortly afterwards, in *Sharifi v. Italy and Greece* the Court found that Italy had once again violated Article 4 Protocol 4.[61] In this case thirty-two Afghani nationals, two Sudanese nationals and one Eritrean national, who entered Italy without authorisation from Greece, challenged the Italian authorities' decision to push them back immediately to Greece; in fact, from there they had to return to their home countries, where they alleged they were at risk of death or torture. According to the Court, Italy had the duty to provide the applicants with access to the asylum process or to any other immigration remedy at the port of arrival, without returning the migrants to Greece. It concluded that Italy violated Article 4 Protocol 4 because the applicants were collectively and indiscriminately expelled. Furthermore, in breach of the right to an effective remedy and the prohibition of inhuman or degrading treatment, Italy failed to guarantee access to the asylum process for the applicants. Italy invoked the application of the "Dublin norms". At the European level common rules have been adopted in order to individuate the Member State who is responsible for examining an asylum application lodged in one of the Member States by a third-country national. These rules constitute the so-called "Dublin system". The cornerstone of this system is the principle according to which the first Member State where finger prints are stored or an asylum claim is lodged is in charge of the person's asylum claim. The regime was initially prescribed by the Dublin

---

[57] *Hirsi, cit. supra* note 15, in particular paras. 151, 166-182, 185, 205, and 211.

[58] However, it must be pointed out that the ECtHR has not always adjudicated in favour of the applicant. For instance, in July 2013 it found that the detention and deportation of a Syrian Kurd as part of a group of individuals by Cypriot authorities did not violate Art. 4 Protocol No. 4 because his asylum application had been considered individually. See *M.A. v. Cyprus*, Application No. 41872/10, Judgment of 23 July 2013, paras 252-255.

[59] *Georgia v. Russia (I), cit. supra* note 52, para. 178.

[60] *Ibid.*, para. 170-177.

[61] *Sharifi, cit. supra* note 52, paras. 214-225.

Convention.[62] Subsequently, Regulation 343/2003 ("Dublin II")[63] was adopted in order to replace the Dublin Convention in all EU Member States, originally with the exception of Denmark, which concluded an agreement in 2006 accepting the application of the Regulation. Finally, Regulation 604/2013 ("Dublin III")[64] replaced the Dublin II Regulation, and it applies to all Member States, except Denmark. However, in the case at issue, Italy's argument that under the EU Dublin Regulation the asylum process is started in the first European country reached by applicants (in this circumstance, Greece) was rejected. The Court affirmed that, although States have the sovereign right to control immigration and the duty to respect obligations resulting from their EU membership, the hardship deriving from managing huge migration flows does not justify breaching the ECHR or its Protocols. In particular, according to the ECtHR, the Dublin system had to be enforced in a compatible way with the ECHR and no form of collective expulsion could be admitted with reference to that system.[65]

On the contrary, in *Sultani v. France*, the ECtHR concluded that the principle was not violated, as both the global situation and the personal circumstances of the applicant were genuinely and individually examined.[66] In this case the applicant, who had been refused asylum in France, denounced the way in which he was to be expelled to Afghanistan, affirming that sending him back on a "grouped flight" constituted a collective expulsion. The ECtHR restated that collective expulsions represented measures compelling aliens, as a group, to leave a country, unless the expulsion at issue is decided on a reasonable and an objective evaluation of the individual case of each alien in the group. Therefore, if each individual affected had the chance to allege arguments against expulsion to the competent authorities on a personal basis, as was the case with the applicant, then, although several aliens were submitted to similar decisions or moved in a group for practical reasons, it did not necessarily imply a measure of collective expulsion.

The *Khlaifia* case differs from the aforementioned cases as it involved a limited number of persons, who were not asylum seekers and whose identities were

---

[62] Convention Determining the State Responsible for Examining Applications for Asylum Lodged in One of the Member States of the European Communities, 15 June 1990, entered into force 1 September 1997.

[63] Council Regulation (EC) 343/2003 of 18 February 2003 establishing the criteria and mechanisms for determining the Member State responsible for examining an asylum application lodged in one of the Member States by a third-country national.

[64] Regulation (EU) 604/2013 of 26 June 2013 establishing the criteria and mechanisms for determining the Member State responsible for examining an application for international protection lodged in one of the Member States by a third-country national or a stateless person (recast).

[65] *Sharifi*, *cit. supra* note 52, paras. 223-224.

[66] *Sultani v. France*, Application No. 45223/05, Judgment 20 September 2007, paras. 77-81. The other case in which the Court found no violation of Art. 4 Protocol No. 4 is *M.A.*, *cit. supra* note 58, paras. 245-255.

duly registered by the authorities. First, the ECtHR noted that expulsion procedures must evaluate the personal situation of the individuals concerned. Then, in order to verify if there was a collective expulsion, the Court kept in mind some specific elements, among which: the existence of deportation orders with equal terms; the absence of individual interviews; obstacles for the aliens to contact a lawyer; and, the fact that the expulsion order covered a large number of persons having the same nationality and receiving the same treatment simultaneously. In this case, the ECtHR admitted that, unlike *Hirsi*, the Tunisian applicants had been subjected to individual identification by Italian authorities. Nevertheless, the Court asserted that an identification procedure alone was not sufficient, since it did not demonstrate the lack of a collective expulsion.[67] In fact, the prohibition of collective expulsion originates from the necessity that each claim be considered on an individual basis, evaluating objective conditions. Therefore, according to the ECtHR, if the personal circumstances of each person, subject to expulsion, are not taken into account in a genuine and a specific way, the procedure may represent a violation of Article 4 Protocol No. 4. Accordingly, when the particular circumstances regarding the expulsion of each asylum seeker belonging to a group of aliens in a similar condition are not taken into consideration, or when the members of this group have simultaneously undergone the same procedure of expulsion, as per the ECtHR case law, it qualifies as collective expulsion in violation of the ECHR.

On the contrary, in their dissenting opinions, Judges Sajó and Vučinić upheld a stricter interpretation of the requirements to satisfy the ban of collective expulsion, affirming that the identification procedure was sufficient to distinguish the case at hand from *Čonka* and *Hirsi*. In particular, according to the two judges the case at issue did not represent a collective expulsion as the prior case law individuated only two methods of collective expulsion, neither of which applied: first, when individuals are identified for expulsion based on their group membership, as occurred with the minority groups in *Čonka* and *Georgia v. Russia*; and second, when a group is individuated for expulsion without any specific evaluation of individual claims of the group members, as happened in *Hirsi* and *Sharifi*. Furthermore, Judges Sajó and Vučinić quoted *M.A. v. Cyprus* to attenuate the relevance of the identical wording

---

[67] *Khlaifia, cit. supra* note 6, para. 156: "La Cour est cependant d'avis que la simple mise en place d'une procédure d'identification ne suffit pas à exclure l'existence d'une expulsion collective. Elle estime de surcroît que plusieurs éléments amènent à estimer qu'en l'espèce l'expulsion critiquée avait bien un caractère collectif. En particulier, les décrets de refoulement ne contiennent aucune référence à la situation personnelle des intéressés; le Gouvernement n'a produit aucun document susceptible de prouver que des entretiens individuels portant sur la situation spécifique de chaque requérant auraient eu lieu avant l'adoption de ces décrets; un grand nombre de personnes de même origine a connu, à l'époque des faits incriminés, le même sort des requérants; les accords bilatéraux avec la Tunisie (paragraphes 28-30 ci-dessus) n'ont pas été rendus publics et prévoyaient le rapatriement des migrants irréguliers tunisiens par le biais de procédures simplifiées, sur la base de la simple identification de la personne concernée de la part des autorités consulaires tunisiennes".

of the expulsion orders. In this case, the ECtHR found that the stereotypical wording of the detention orders was not by itself sufficient to prove the existence of a collective expulsion, since Cyprus had evaluated the asylum applications individually and considered the personal situation of the group members before expulsion.[68] The two judges concluded that, in *Khlaifia*, the applicants were not expelled due to membership of an "ethnic, religious or national group", that they were sent back to a safe country and that they were not asylum seekers and, thus, there was no problem of *non-refoulement*. Therefore, opting for a restrictive reading of the ban on collective expulsions, they asserted that "the majority do a grave disservice to an intentionally focused and narrow concept in international law which is meant to apply only in the most severe of circumstances".[69]

The Court preferred an extensive interpretation of the prohibition of collective expulsion of aliens. Indeed, the thesis adopted in the dissenting opinion seems too strict in relation to the developments of the ECtHR case law. The dissenting judges followed the traditional approach to the issue, according to which there is a collective expulsion when the aim is to remove from the territory a group of individuals who have some specific characteristics. In such hypothesis, the ban of collective expulsions is connected with the prevention of practices related to discrimination on ethnic or racial grounds, or even genocide. On the contrary, according to the ECtHR case law, in accordance with the principles of effectiveness of guaranteed rights and of evolutionary interpretation,[70] an expulsion can be considered as collective even though it is not "target oriented" and personal characteristics are not taken into consideration. According to this approach, the prohibition of collective expulsion impedes automatic decisions, which may result in violations of the human rights of the expellees. In fact, only an analysis of the personal situation permits the verification of the absence of a collective expulsion, the mere identification of the expellees not being sufficient, because only an individual evaluation can highlight factors which could preclude the possibility of expelling a person.

Also the circumstance that the applicants were not asylum seekers is not enough to hinder the collective nature of the measure, as the Italian authorities did not even assess this possibility; in any case the ban applies even in the absence of a request for asylum. Furthermore, even when applicants are not asylum seekers, they may have other rights that should be safeguarded and other factors should be taken into account before adopting an expulsion decision, for example, the risk of torture, inhuman or degrading treatment in the country of origin, their health and physical condition, and their right to family unity.

---

[68] *M.A.*, cit. *supra* note 58, paras. 252-255.

[69] *Khlaifia*, cit. *supra* note 6, partly dissenting opinion of Judges Sajó and Vučinić, paras. 12-18.

[70] See DEL VECCHIO, *I Tribunali internazionali tra globalizzazione e localismi*, 2nd ed., Bari, 2015, p. 172.

Finally, as *Conka* proves, the number of persons involved does not affect the qualification of the measure at hand. Therefore, the worth of the *Khlaifia* judgment is the adoption of a wide concept of "collective expulsions", which is in accordance with the main aim of the ban at issue, i.e. preventing the violations of migrants' human rights by deciding on their expulsion without evaluating their personal situation. Furthermore, by limiting the applicable factors, the analysed decision gives guidelines both to applicants and to national authorities so that possible expulsions occur in accordance with the ECHR and its Protocols. Prior to the *Khlaifia* judgment, all cases examined by the Court had concerned facts which had happened before the recent considerable flows of migrants to Europe. In fact, though the *Hirsi* decision was adopted post the "Arab Spring", while mass fluxes of North African migrants were escaping political instability, the facts at issue occurred in May 2009. For this reason, *Khlaifia* sets the precedent as the first decision being rendered by the Court directly concerning the huge migration flows determined by the political instability linked to the "Arab Spring".

In conclusion, in the ECHR system any measure of removal of aliens as a group is forbidden, unless such a measure is decided on the basis of a reasonable and objective evaluation of the particular situation of each person of the group.[71] Moreover, individual push-backs or expulsions must be always enforced in accordance with all ECHR articles.[72] For instance, in conformity with Article 2 and Article 3 ECHR, expelling or deporting a person to a State where he/she could be at risk of death or ill-treatment is banned.[73] At the same time, in accordance with Article 8 ECHR, when an order of removal or expulsion affects the private or family life of an alien, it cannot be enforced, if it appears unjustified and unnecessary in order to reach one of the legitimate aims indicated in the same provision.[74] Instead, removal from the territory of a State should be permitted if it follows an evaluation of the individual circumstances of the alien.

Thus, it may be argued that the prohibition of removal under the ECHR is broader than the *non-refoulement* principle in the Convention Relating to the Status of Refugees.[75] In fact, this latter principle is not absolute, as a refugee may excep-

---

[71] See *Čonka, cit. supra* note 15.

[72] It must be emphasised that Art. 1 Protocol No. 7 (Procedural safeguards relating to expulsion of aliens) refers only to "lawfully resident" aliens, therefore it cannot be enforced in the context of massive illegal immigration.

[73] On this aspect, see *Soering v. The United Kingdom*, Application No. 14038/88, Judgment of 7 July 1989; and *Chahal v. The United Kingdom*, Application No. 22414/93, Judgment of 15 November 1996. Italian immigration law also prescribes a similar prohibition: see Art. 19(1) TU Immigrazione.

[74] On this issue, see *Boultif v. Switzerland*, Application No. 54273/00, Judgment of 2 August 2001; *Benhebba v. France*, Application No. 53441/99, Judgment of 10 July 2003; and *Maslov v. Austria*, Application No. 1638/03, Judgment of 23 June 2008.

[75] 28 July 1951, entered into force 22 April 1954. See also the Protocol Relating to the Status of Refugees, 31 January 1967, entered into force 4 October 1967.

tionally be expelled from a country if he constitutes "a danger to the security of the country in which he is, or who, having been convicted by a final judgement of a particularly serious crime, constitutes a danger to the community of that country".[76] On the contrary, according to the ECtHR case law, there is an absolute prohibition of the removal of an individual who could be at risk of ill-treatment or torture in the destination country. In effect, in the opinion of the Court, the possibility that an individual may represent a threat to the community if not expelled does not reduce his/her risk of ill-treatment in the destination country.[77] Moreover, the absolute prohibition of expulsion applies not only to refugees and asylum seekers, but also to persons who have not even been able to apply for such status.[78] Then, as *Hirsi* proves, the ban applies also to migrants intercepted at sea. Finally, *Khlaifia* indicates that all expulsions have to be preceded by an individual evaluation of the personal situation. Therefore, the Court has boosted the protection accorded by the 1951 Refugee Convention.

5. CONCLUSION

Europe is currently in a situation of deep crisis determined both by economic factors and a strong migration pressure, which have caused serious violations of human rights and conflicts among European countries, putting at risk not only the principles of democracy and rule of law but also the EU itself. The human rights of migrants are recognised and protected by international law. However, the main challenge is often their implementation at the domestic level.[79]

Nevertheless, through the last few years, a growing awareness of migrants' vulnerability and the correlated urgency to guarantee their rights has developed. As a consequence, numerous initiatives have been implemented at international level and several instruments have been adopted by States and international organisations.[80] Notwithstanding, much remains to be done by European countries and the EU to manage these mass flows of migrants in accordance with the safeguard of human rights and the respect of principles of democracy and rule of law.

---

[76] See Art. 33.

[77] *Saadi v. Italy*, Application No. 37201/06, Judgment 28 February 2008, para. 139.

[78] For instance, in the *Sharifi* case (*cit. supra* note 52, paras. 166-181), regarding automatic returns from Adriatic ports, the Court considered the existence of a context of general violence or armed conflict sufficient in itself to prevent a person's push-back. See also *Sufi and Elmi v. The United Kingdom*, Applications No. 8319/07 and 11449/07, Judgment of 28 June 2011, paras. 241-250, and 293, concerning the indiscriminate violence in Somalia.

[79] CHOLEWINSKI, *cit. supra* note 3, p. 180.

[80] On this topic, see CHOLEWINSKI, "Human Rights of Migrants: The Dawn of a New Era?", Georgetown Immigration Law Journal, 2010, p. 585 ff., pp. 614-615; and CHETAIL, "The Human Rights of Migrants in General International Law: From Minimum Standards to Fundamental Rights", Georgetown Immigration Law Journal, 2013, p. 225 ff., p. 254.

The ECtHR pointed out the deficiencies of the EU policy on immigration and asylum and the related necessity of improvements well before the present migration crisis, for example, accentuating the necessity of changing the Dublin system. This system imposes a heavy burden on States that are on the frontline when asylum seekers arrive, even if it includes the "sovereignty clause", which enables States to derogate from the foreseen rules and to assume responsibility themselves for an asylum application.[81] For example, the ECtHR challenged the "automaticity" deep-rooted in the Dublin system in order to guarantee other important interests safeguarded by the ECHR.[82] Undoubtedly, the ECtHR case law, denouncing and sanctioning human rights violations towards migrants, may constitute an efficient input for national authorities and the EU in order to facilitate a progressive improvement of their immigration policies in accordance with human rights.

As far as Italy is concerned, the most sensitive and problematic issue is whether the deficiencies of its immigration policy are determined by structural or merely occasional factors. Indeed, it can be argued that the Italian immigration legal system is not *in itself* incompatible with the ECHR, although it could be incompatible with other norms of international law, EU law, or the Italian Constitution. Nevertheless, what represents normally a violation of the ECHR norms is a practical enforcement of national law.

In the *Khlaifia* judgment the Court analysed, in particular, two aspects: the lawfulness of detention of migrants in the CSPA on Lampedusa and their collective expulsion. As regards the first issue, it derives from the examined decision that the exceptional character of the present crisis cannot serve as a justification for European States to establish informal detention practices for migrants in reception centres, in violation of their obligations under the ECHR and of human dignity. In particular,

---

[81] See Art. 17 of Regulation (EU) 604/2013, and also Art. 3(2) of Regulation (EC) 343/2003 which has the same content.

[82] See, for example, *M.S.S. v. Belgium and Greece*, Application No. 30696/09, Judgment of 21 January 2011, in particular, paras. 350-360. In this case, the ECtHR recognised the existence of "structural deficiencies" in the asylum procedure in Greece (para. 300). The term "systemic deficiencies" has since then been used by the European Court of Justice in Joined Cases C-411/10 and C-493/10, *N.S. v. Secretary of State for the Home Department and M.E. and Others v. Refugee Applications Commissioner and Minister for Justice, Equality and Law Reform* ([2011] ECR I-13905, Judgment of 21 December 2011), in which the Court affirmed: "It follows from the foregoing that in situations such as that at issue in the cases in the main proceedings, to ensure compliance by the European Union and its Member States with their obligations concerning the protection of the fundamental rights of asylum seekers, the Member States, including the national courts, may not transfer an asylum seeker to the 'Member State responsible' within the meaning of Regulation 343/2003 where they cannot be unaware that systemic deficiencies in the asylum procedure and in the reception conditions of asylum seekers in that Member State amount to substantial grounds for believing that the asylum seeker would face a real risk of being subjected to inhuman or degrading treatment within the meaning of Article 4 of the Charter" (para. 94). See also ECtHR, *Tarakhel v. Switzerland*, Application No. 29217/12, Judgment 4 November 2014, paras. 118-120.

according to the Court, the detention of the three applicants was illegal since it had no legal basis in Italian law, its reasons were not clearly explained to the migrants and they were not provided with means to challenge their detention. Therefore, in the case at hand the ECtHR has clarified the protection that States have to grant to aliens entering their territory, independently of their status and whether they are irregular migrants, asylum seekers, or refugees. In particular, recalling the concept of human dignity, the Court seems to underline that migrants are, first of all, human beings and not simply aliens subject to State control.[83] The underlying idea is that the existence of an extraordinary situation imposes on States to give *more* and not less weight to human rights of migrants.

Also in relation to the issue of collective expulsions, the Court opted for a broad concept of the ban in order to guarantee a wider protection of human rights, according to which expulsions have to be preceded by an individual analysis of the specific situation of the expelled person. In any case, even when there is a previous identification of each of the members of the group, an automatic expulsion may amount to a collective expulsion if the authorities do not take into account their personal story. However, if it is demonstrated that the individual situation of each migrant was evaluated, then the use of a standardised document does not constitute, *per se*, sufficient proof that the expulsions were collective. Therefore, the general thesis, which comes to light from the *Khlaifia* judgment, is that the level of protection guaranteed by the ECHR does not decrease in times of crisis.

This decision should serve as a further admonishment for the EU and its Member States in the process of modifying their policy toward refugees and migrants reaching Europe.[84] After all, if Europe is unable to give a common and constructive answer to the migration crisis, some EU Members may decide to revive border controls in the free-movement Schengen zone.[85] However, the settlement of this serious crisis implies not only a reform of Schengen but also a comprehensive reevaluation of the EU aims and its foreign policy.

---

[83] See DEMBOUR, *When Humans Become Migrants, Study of the European Court with an Inter-American Counterpoint*, Oxford, 2015, p. 5.

[84] See Human Rights Watch, "Europe's Refugee Crisis. An Agenda for Action", 16 November 2015, available at: <https://www.hrw.org/report/2015/11/16/europes-refugee-crisis/agenda-action>.

[85] The Schengen Agreements were signed on 14 June 1985 by France, Germany, Belgium, the Netherlands, and Luxembourg, for the gradual abolition of border checks at the signatories' borders. On 19 June 1990 the Agreements were supplemented by the Schengen Convention (entered into force on 26 march 1995), aimed at the abolition of internal border controls and the establishment of a common visa policy. The Amsterdam Treaty of 1997 incorporated the Schengen system into the EU law, allowing the chance to be outside of the area through opt-outs clauses. At the present, the Schengen zone is comprised of 26 European countries: 22 EU Member States (Bulgaria, Croatia, Cyprus, Romania, Ireland, and the United Kingdom are outside the Area) and 4 non-EU countries (Iceland, Liechtenstein, Norway, and Switzerland). On this topic, see FIJNAUT, "The Refugee Crisis: The End of Schengen?", European Journal of Crime, Criminal Law and Criminal Justice, 2015, p. 313 ff.

THE EU'S HOTSPOT APPROACH TO MANAGING THE MIGRATION CRISIS: A BLIND SPOT FOR INTERNATIONAL RESPONSIBILITY?

FEDERICO CASOLARI[*]

Abstract

Announced by the European Commission in its 2015 European Agenda on Migration as one of the EU's priority tools to face the "unprecedented" migration crisis the Union was experiencing, the "hotspot" approach consists of a common platform for EU agencies (namely, the European Asylum Support Office, Frontex, Eurojust, and Europol) to intervene, rapidly and in an integrated manner, in frontline Member States when there is a crisis due to specific and disproportionate migratory pressure at their external borders. The goal was to reduce the pressure at the borders of the most affected Member States to "normal" levels while ensuring the proper reception, identification, and processing of arrivals. The present contribution makes some introductory remarks on issues of international responsibility under international law emerging from the implementation – by State and EU actors – of the hotspot approach. In particular, the analysis will focus on problems related to the attribution of conduct, in light of the large number of subjects involved in the relevant activities. In this respect, this contribution will highlight first the function of hotspots. Then, the discussion will analyze the position of different actors involved in the hotspot approach in light of the international law framework on international responsibility. An assessment of what has been discussed in the preceding sections is contained in the final part.

Keywords: European Union; EU agencies; refugee crisis; hotspot approach; relocation mechanism; shared responsibility; Draft Articles on Responsibility of States for Internationally Wrongful Acts; Draft Articles on the Responsibility of International Organizations.

[*] Associate Professor of European Union Law, Alma Mater Studiorum – University of Bologna (federico.casolari@unibo.it). Unless otherwise indicated, this contribution takes into account the development of practice and legislation until 31 March 2016. All Web pages were last visited on 4 April 2016. The author wishes to thank Carlo Tovo for his valuable comments on previous drafts. The usual disclaimer applies.

1. INTRODUCTION

Announced by the European Commission in its 2015 European Agenda on Migration as one of the EU's priority tools to face the "unprecedented" migration crisis the European Union (EU) was experiencing,[1] the "hotspot" approach, which was set up in the second part of the same year, consists of a common platform for EU agencies (namely, the European Asylum Support Office, Frontex, Eurojust, and Europol) to intervene, rapidly and in an integrated manner, in frontline Member States when there is a crisis due to specific and disproportionate migratory pressure at their external borders.

The rationale behind this approach can easily be appreciated. As recalled by the European Commission itself in its report on the implementation of the priority actions identified by the European Agenda on Migration,

> "Well-functioning and effective migration management at the external borders which are under most pressure is key to restoring confidence in the overall system, and in particular in the Schengen area of free movement without internal border controls. Central to the EU's strategy and credibility is to demonstrate that the migration system can be restored to proper functioning [...]".[2]

The goal was thus to reduce the pressure at the borders of the most affected Member States to "normal" levels while ensuring the proper reception, identification and processing of arrivals. This also explains why it was envisioned that the hotspot approach would decisively contribute to facilitating the implementation of the emergency relocation mechanism, which has been established in parallel by the Council on the basis of Article 78(3) of the Treaty on the Functioning of the European Union (TFEU) to allow the transfer of people in clear need of international protection from Italy, Greece, and other Member States directly affected by the refugee crisis to the territory of other EU countries.[3]

Both tools – the hotspots and the relocation scheme – bespeak a clearly pragmatic and customized approach, an approach heavily reliant on flexibility as the

---

[1] EU Commission, A European Agenda on Migration, COM (2015) 240 final, 13 May 2015, p. 6.

[2] EU Commission, Managing the Refugee Crisis: State of Play of the Implementation of the Priority Actions under the European Agenda on Migration, COM (2015) 510 final, 14 October 2015, p. 3.

[3] Council Decision 2015/1523 of 14 September 2015 establishing provisional measures in the area of international protection for the benefit of Italy and of Greece (OJ 2015 L 239/146), and Council Decision 2015/1601 of 22 September 2015 establishing provisional measures in the area of international protection for the benefit of Italy and of Greece (OJ 2015 L 248/80).

best way to face the challenges posed by the massive influx of migrants without delay. In particular, according to the hotspot mechanisms, the support offered at the request of the Member State concerned and the duration of assistance to that Member State would only depend on its needs and the development of the situation.

However, all too regrettably, the situation that developed on the ground immediately after these two tools were triggered took a dramatic turn away from the expected scenario. On the one hand, the relocation scheme has largely failed to materialize. As of now, indeed, only a mere fraction of the 160,000 people the EU Member States are supposed to accommodate under the relocation mechanism have been moved.[4] Moreover, Slovakia and Hungary, citing various concerns and indicating a clear preference for Christian, over Muslim, refugees from Syria, decided to challenge the validity of the relocation scheme before the EU Court of Justice.[5]

Like the relocation scheme, the hotspot approach also suffered significant delays in its set-up.[6] But, most importantly for present purposes, it attracted several criticisms from NGOs[7] and international actors[8] due to concerns about the protection of migrants' fundamental rights. More precisely, major concerns deal with:

---

[4] As of 22 March 2016, 22 countries had made 7,015 places available for asylum seekers to be relocated under the programme and a total of 953 asylum seekers had been relocated (384 out of Italy and 569 out of Greece). EU Commission, Member States' Support to Emergency Relocation Mechanism (communicated as of 22 March 2016), available at: <http://ec.europa. eu/dgs/home-affairs/what-we-do/policies/european-agenda-migration/press-material/docs/state_ of_play_-_relocation_en.pdf>.

[5] Case C-643/15, *Slovak Republic v. Council of the European Union* (OJ 2015 L 248/80); and Case C-647/15, *Hungary v. Council of the European Union* (*ibidem*). Both cases are still pending. For a critical analysis of Hungary's action for annulment see VARJU and CZINA, "Hitting Where It Hurts the Most: Hungary's Legal Challenge against the EU's Refugee Quota System", *Verfassungsblog*, 17 February 2016, available at: <http://verfassungsblog.de/hitting-where-it-hurts-the-most-hungarys-legal-challenge-against-the-eus-refugee-quota-system/>.

[6] As of mid-January 2016, of the 11 planned hotspot facilities, just 3 were operational: in Lampedusa and Trapani (Italy), and Lesvos (Greece). UNHCR, Building on the Lessons Learned to Make the Relocation Schemes Work Effectively – UNHCR's Recommendations, January 2016, p. 2, available at: <http://www.unhcr.org/569fad556.pdf>.

[7] Cf., for instance, Amnesty International, "Report 2015/16 – The State of the World's Human Rights", where concerns about the possibility that migrants may be subject to arbitrary detention, dire reception conditions, and forced fingerprinting in both the Italian and Greek hotspots have been clearly expressed (pp. 169, 205).

[8] Concerns on the possibility that hotspots are detention centres in disguise have been expressed by the UN High Commissioner for Human Rights: Office of the UN High Commissioner for Human Rights, EU Migration Policy Will Fail Unless Comprehensive and Grounded in Human Rights – Zeid, 6 October 2015, available at: <http://www.ohchr.org/EN/NewsEvents/Pages/DisplayNews.aspx?NewsID=16570&LangID=E>.

(i) the reception/detention conditions of migrants in the hotspots; (ii) the personal safeguards during fingerprinting and photographic registration; (iii) the lack of information provided to migrants on their arrival about the possibility of requesting international protection; and (iv) the limits of access to the asylum procedure based solely on nationality, without any personal investigations.[9] Interestingly enough, the deficiencies in the function of the hotspot approach have also been stressed by the European Council.[10]

The situation at the hotspots is arguably destined to get even worse due to measures recently agreed upon by the EU and Turkey to tackle the large-scale arrival of refugees and migrants in Greece and beyond into Europe, measures that include the transfer back to Turkey of all migrants not in need of international protection crossing from Turkey into Greece.[11] The first signs that the new deal with Turkey is likely to worsen the situation appeared immediately. On 22 March

---

[9] As for the Italian situation, see the "Letter to the Italian Minister of Interior from the National Asylum Committee", available at: <http://www.cir-onlus.org/en/home/1903-hotspot-approach-concerned-national-asylum-committee-has-requested-a-meeting-with-minister-alfano>. Recently, the disappearance of young West African women hosted in the hotspots in Sicily was denounced by the Fundamental Rights Agency (FRA) of the Union: see FRA, "EU Agencies Meet to Coordinate Work with EU Anti-Trafficking Coordinator", 9 March 2016, available at: <http://fra.europa.eu/en/news/2016/eu-agencies-meet-coordinate-work-eu-anti-trafficking-coordinator>. Perhaps even more worrying is the situation in Greek hotpots: NGOs on the ground have indeed depicted the conditions in the first Greek hotspot (established on the island of Lesvos) as "life-threatening". Cf. Médecins Sans Frontières Sea, "The rain has stopped in #Lesvos but the inadequate reception conditions are still life-threatening", 25 October 2015, available at: <https://twitter.com/MSF_Sea/status/658334514012409856>; European Council of Refugees and Exiles, "'Hotspot' Opens in Lesvos, but Reports of Conditions on the Island Remain Worrying", 29 October 2015, available at: <http://www.ecre.org/component/content/article/70-weekly-bulletin-articles/1239-hotspot-opens-in-lesvos-but-reports-of-conditions-on-the-island-remain-worrying.html>. In some cases, the criticisms are also related to the working conditions of the officers deployed in the hotspots: Frontex, "Frontex temporarily suspends registration activities on Chios due to concerns over asbestos contamination", 18 December 2015, available at: <http://frontex.europa.eu/news/frontex-temporarily-suspends-registration-activities-on-chios-due-to-concerns-over-asbestos-contamination-gqMedB>.

[10] The first explicit admissions on the malfunction of the hotspots were made in December 2015: General Secretariat to the Council, European Council meeting (17 and 18 December 2015), Conclusions, EUCO 28/15, 18 December 2015, para. I.1(b). In February 2016, the Heads of State and Government acknowledged that "much remains to be done": General Secretariat to the Council, European Council meeting (18 and 19 February 2016), Conclusions, EUCO 1/16, 19 February 2016, para. II.8(f).

[11] The text of the EU-Turkey Statement of 18 March 2016 is available at: <http://www.consilium.europa.eu/en/press/press-releases/2016/03/18-eu-turkey-statement/>. For a first comment on the document see PEERS, "The Final EU/Turkey Refugee Deal: A Legal Assessment", EU Law Analysis, 18 March 2016, available at: <http://eulawanalysis.blogspot.it/2016/03/the-final-eu-turkey-refugee-deal-legal.html>; ROMAN, "L'accordo UE-Turchia: le criticità di un accordo a tutti i costi", *SIDIBlog*, 21 March 2016, available at: <http://www.sidi-isil.org/sidiblog/?p=1736>; CANNIZZARO, "Disintegration Through Law?", European Papers, 2016, p. 3 ff.; and GATTI, "The EU-Turkey Statement: A Treaty That Violates Democracy", *EJIL: Talk!*, 18-19 April 2016, avail-

2016, only three days after the adoption of the EU-Turkey Statement on migrant crisis, the UNHCR, which had supported the national authorities in the hotspots on the Greek islands up to that point, announced the suspension of some of its activities at the centers.[12] In particular, the UN agency denounced the fact that, pursuant to the new EU-Turkey deal, these sites have become detention facilities, a circumstance which is not in line with the agency's policy of opposing mandatory detention. Some days later, the UNHCR further stigmatized the reception conditions in the Greek hotspots. The UNHCR's description of the situation on-site could not be clearer:

> "On Lesvos, conditions have been deteriorating at the Moria 'hotspot' facility, which since 20 March has been used to detain people pending a decision on deportation. There are now some 2,300 people there. This is above its stated capacity of 2,000. People are sleeping in the open, and food supply is insufficient. Anxiety and frustration is widespread. Making matters worse, many families have become separated, with family members now scattered across Greece – and presenting an additional worry should returns begin.
> On Samos, at the Vathy hotspot, reception conditions have also been worsening. Sanitation is poor, there is little help available for persons with special needs, and food distributions are chaotic. There are currently up to 1,700 people staying at the Vial hotspot on Chios, which has a maximum capacity of 1,100. We are very worried about the situation there. Rioting last night left three people with stab injuries".[13]

Moreover, the concrete risk that the implementation of the EU-Turkey deal may develop into collective expulsions has been stressed by the UN High Commissioner for Human Rights, even if the text of the Statement clearly recognizes that all migrants will be protected in full accordance with EU and international law, thus theoretically excluding any kind of collective expulsion.[14]

---

able at: <http://www.ejiltalk.org/the-eu-turkey-statement-a-treaty-that-violates-democracy-part-1-of-2/>.

[12] Cf. UNHCR, UNHCR Redefines Role in Greece as EU-Turkey Deal Comes into Effect, Briefing Notes, 22 March 2016, available at: <http://www.unhcr.org/56f10d049.html>.

[13] UNHCR, UNHCR Urges Immediate Safeguards to Be in Place before Any Returns Begin under EU-Turkey Deal, 1 April 2016, available at: <http://www.unhcr.org/56fe31ca9.html>.

[14] The High Commissioner pointed out that there is "a contradiction at the heart of the agreement. […] The declared aim to return all refugees and migrants contrasts with the assurances about individual assessments". Office of the UN High Commissioner for Human Rights, UN Rights Chief Expresses Serious Concerns over EU-Turkey Agreement, 24 March 2016, available at: <http://www.ohchr.org/EN/NewsEvents/Pages/DisplayNews.aspx?NewsID=18531&LangID=E>.

Against this background, the present contribution makes some introductory remarks on issues of international responsibility under international law emerging from the implementation – by State and EU actors – of the hotspot approach. In particular, the analysis will focus on problems related to the attribution of conduct, in light of the large number of subjects involved in the relevant activities.

A note on the rules of international law on international responsibility which will be considered in this contribution is needed. The legal analysis will be conducted in light of the solutions suggested by the UN International Law Commission (ILC), both in the Draft Articles on Responsibility of States for Internationally Wrongful Acts (DARS)[15] as well as in its Draft Articles on the Responsibility of International Organizations (DARIO).[16] Notoriously, the two documents are not binding *per se*. However, it should be recalled that several provisions contained in the DARS have already been considered by the International Court of Justice (ICJ) as a codification of general international law.[17] On the other hand, even if some authors have questioned the possibility that the DARIO may usefully be invoked to shape the responsibility of the EU,[18] due to the specific traits characterizing the Organization, and even though the EU repeatedly called for the drafting of special rules of attribution of conduct before the ILC,[19] the present analysis is based on the

---

[15] The text of the Draft Articles, as it appears in the annex to General Assembly Resolution 56/83 of 12 December 2001, and corrected by Doc. A/56/49 (Vol. I)/Corr.4, is available at: <http://legal.un.org/ilc/texts/instruments/english/draft_articles/9_6_2001.pdf>.

[16] The text of the Draft Articles is available at <http://legal.un.org/ilc/texts/instruments/english/draft_articles/9_11_2011.pdf>.

[17] See CRAWFORD, "The International Court of Justice and the Law of State Responsibility", in TAMS and SLOAN (eds.), *The Development of International Law by the International Court of Justice*, Oxford, 2013, p. 71 ff., p. 81 ff.

[18] Cf., for instance, HOFFMEISTER, "Litigating against the European Union and Its Member States. Who Responds under the ILC's Draft Articles on International Responsibility of International Organizations?", EJIL, 2010, p. 723 ff.; KUIJPER and PAASIVIRTA, "EU International Responsibility and Its Attribution: From the Inside Looking Out", in EVANS and KOUTRAKOS (eds.), *The International Responsibility of the European Union. European and International Perspectives*, Oxford, 2013, p. 35 ff., esp. p. 69. The (possible) EU "exceptionalism" vis-à-vis the general rules on the responsibility of international organizations is also considered by CORTÉS MARTÍN, "European Exceptionalism in International Law? The European Union and the System of International Responsibility", in RAGAZZI (ed.), *Responsibility of International Organizations. Essays in Memory of Sir Ian Brownlie*, Leiden/Boston, 2013, p. 189 ff.; D'ASPREMONT, "A European Law of International Responsibility? The Articles on the Responsibility of International Organizations and the European Union", SHARES Research Paper 22 (2013), ACIL 2013-04, p. 8, available at: <http://www.sharesproject.nl/wp-content/uploads/2013/04/SHARES-RP-22-final.pdf>; and, more recently, by SPAGNOLO, *L'attribuzione delle condotte illecite nelle operazioni militari dell'Unione europea*, Torino, 2016.

[19] See the comments by the European Commission, in UN Doc. A/CN.4/545 (2004), p. 18, and UN Doc. A/CN.4/637 (2011), p. 7. As it is well-known, the ILC changed its position on the matter and decided to explicitly recognizing the possibility of special rules of attribution. The *lex specialis* rule is today enshrined in Article 64 DARIO: "These draft articles do not apply where

assumption that the 2011 Draft Articles still represent the most authoritative contribution to shed light on the responsibility of international organizations, whatever their institutional features look like, provided that no special rules of international responsibility may be found in the rules of the organization in question. Any attempt to deal with this topic shall thus stem from the ILC's work.[20]

As a matter of methodology, it shall also be noted that triggering the hotspot mechanism may also engender forms of responsibility under EU law – starting from possible breaches of Articles 1, 2, 4, and 19(1) of the EU Charter of Fundamental Rights, dealing with the human dignity, the right to life, the prohibition of torture and inhuman or degrading treatment or punishment, and the prohibition of collective expulsion, respectively. However, some elements deserve to be mentioned in this respect.

First, in light of the celebrated passages in *Commission v. Luxembourg and Belgium* ("the basic concept of the [EU] Treaty requires that Member States shall not fail to carry out their obligations and shall not take the law into their own hands")[21] and in *Mutton and Lamb* ("A Member State cannot under any circumstances unilaterally adopt, on its own authority, corrective measures or measures to protect trade designed to prevent any failure on the part of another Member State to comply with the rules laid down by the Treaty"),[22] it is today generally recognized that EU law has developed its own system of State responsibility: when a Member State breaches obligations under EU law, the enforcement procedure under Articles 258-259 TFEU should be triggered. Secondly, specific mechanisms have been put in place – at national and EU levels – to invoke the non-contractual liability of either

---

and to the extent that the conditions for the existence of an internationally wrongful act or the content or implementation of the international responsibility of an international organization, or of a State in connection with the conduct of an international organization, are governed by special rules of international law [...]".

[20] Cf. BARROS, RYNGAERT and WOUTERS, "Member States, International Organizations and International Responsibility. Exploring a Legal Triangle", International Organizations Law Review, 2015, p. 285 ff., p. 286; PUSTORINO, "The Control Criterion between Responsibility of States and Responsibility of International Organizations", in VIRZO and INGRAVALLO (eds.), *Evolutions in the Law of International Organizations*, Leiden/Boston, 2015, p. 406 ff., p. 407; NOLLKAEMPER, "Introduction", in NOLLKAEMPER and PLAKOKEFALOS (eds.), *Principles of Shared Responsibility in International Law. An Appraisal of the State of the Art*, Cambridge, 2014, p.1 ff., p. 3. See also D'ASPREMONT, *cit. supra* note 18, p. 8, maintaining that "[...] the EU regime does not contain express provisions that put in place special rules of international responsibility of the EU and/or the MS. According to this position, there are no express rules of international responsibility found under EU law which constitute a *lex specialis* for the sake of the international responsibility of the EU and/or the MS".

[21] Joined Cases 90/63 and 91/63, *Commission v. Luxemburg and Belgium*, ECLI:EU:C:1964:80, p. 631.

[22] Case 232/78, *Mutton and Lamb*, ECLI:EU:C:1979:215, para. 9.

the Member States[23] or the Union.[24] In sum, even if, arguably, public international law still has a potential application as a last resort, in the event of a failure of the EU's own rules, breaches of EU law are normally subject to special rules enshrined in EU Treaties or developed via the case law of the Court of Justice.[25] Thus, for the purposes of this analysis, it is not considered necessary to examine the role the EU enforcement/liability mechanisms may play in managing the hotspot approach.

On the other hand, it is also evident that the implementation of the hotspot approach may call into question the individual responsibility of natural persons involved in the related activities. Like the responsibility issues under EU law, also this profile will be not discussed here, unless deemed relevant for the purposes of the rules of attribution of conduct.

In light of these introductory considerations, this contribution will highlight first the function of hotspots (section 2). Then, the discussion will analyze the position of different actors involved in the hotspot approach in light of the international law framework on international responsibility (section 3). An assessment of what has been discussed in the preceding sections is contained in the final part (section 4).

2.   SETTING THE SCENE: HOW THE HOTSPOTS (SHOULD) WORK

Describing the function of the hotspot approach is not an easy task. Unlike the relocation tool, the hotspot approach has not been established by means of EU secondary law.[26] By itself, this is no surprise; the tool was conceived by EU institutions

---

[23] Reference has to be made in this respect to the *Brasserie du Pêcheur* doctrine dealing with the principle of Member States' liability for damage caused to individuals by breaches of Community law: Joined Cases C-46/93 and C-48/93, *Brasserie du Pêcheur SA v. Bundesrepublik Deutschland and The Queen v Secretary of State for Transport, ex parte: Factortame Ltd and Others*, ECLI:EU:C:1996:79.

[24] The obvious starting point for responsibility issues under EU law is Article 340 TFEU. Specific references to the liability of the EU agencies are present in the founding instruments of these organs. Cf., in particular: Article 19 of the Council Regulation (EC) 2007/2004 of 26 October 2004 establishing a European Agency for the Management of Operational Cooperation at the External Borders of the Member States of the European Union (OJ 2004 L 349/1) and subsequent amendments; Article 45 of the Regulation (EU) 439/2010 of the European Parliament and of the Council of 19 May 2010 establishing a European Asylum Support Office (OJ 2010 L 132/11); Article 53 of the Council Decision 2009/371/JHA of 6 April 2009 establishing the European Police Office (Europol) (OJ 2009 L 121/37); and Article 27(c) of the Council Decision 2002/187/JHA of 28 February 2002 setting up Eurojust with a view to reinforcing the fight against serious crime (OJ 2002 L 63/1) and subsequent amendments.

[25] See CONWAY, "Breaches of EC Law and the International Responsibility of Member States", EJIL, 2002, p. 679 ff.; SIMMA and PULKOWSKI, "Of Planets and the Universe", EJIL, 2006, p. 483 ff.; and GRADONI, Regime Failure *nel diritto internazionale*, Padova, 2009.

[26] That circumstance is also stressed by Moreno-Lax, who, however, maintains that the hotspot approach has been based on Articles 78(3) and 80 TFEU: MORENO-LAX, "Europe in Crisis: Facilitating Access to Protection, (Discarding) Offshore Processing and Mapping

as an *approach*, and, as such, it only implies a reshaping of existing legal instruments (namely, the founding instruments of the EU agencies involved).[27] Having said this, however, the fact remains that the absence of a specific piece of legislation makes a proper understanding of the tool more difficult, starting with the roles and responsibilities of the different actors involved in its implementation.

The European Agenda on Migration, which contains the commitment to set up the hotspot approach, does not provide a definition of what a hotspot is. Such a definition may be reconstructed from other documents drafted by the European Commission, where it is defined as an external border section of a Member State characterized by specific and disproportionate migratory pressure, consisting of mixed migratory flows, which are largely linked to the smuggling of migrants, and where the Member State concerned might request support and assistance to better cope with the migratory pressure.[28] It follows from that definition that, in principle, hotspots should be activated for a limited period of time in the event of an emergency or crisis situation during which the support of the hotspot approach is necessary. Moreover, the decision to trigger the hotspot approach lies only with the affected Member State, which must submit a request outlining its needs to the Commission and the relevant EU agencies. Should the State concerned decide to make a recourse to "ordinary" means (i.e. support and assistance programs run by EU agencies in accordance with their funding instruments), the Commission might propose that the Member State request the triggering of the hotspot approach. To date, hotspot areas have only been identified in Italy[29] and Greece.[30]

The European Agenda on Migration contains an articulated description of how the hotspot approach should be applied:

> "The European Asylum Support Office, Frontex and Europol will work on the ground with frontline Member States to swiftly identify,

---

Alternatives for the Way Forward", Red Cross EU Office, December 2015, p. 11, available at: <http://www.redcross.eu/en/upload/documents/2016international_development/Europe%20 in%20Crisis_Dr%20Moreno-Lax_final.pdf>.

[27] Cf. Council Regulation (EC) 2007/2004, *cit. supra* note 24; Regulation (EU) 439/2010, *cit. supra* note 24; Council Decision 2009/371/JHA, *cit. supra* note 24; Council Decision 2002/187/ JHA, *cit. supra* note 24.

[28] See in this respect the Explanatory Note on the "Hotspot" Approach, drafted by the EU Commission in close cooperation with the EU agencies involved and the host Member States concerned (namely, Italy and Greece), and sent by Commissioner Dimitris Avramopoulos to Justice and Home Affairs Ministers (available at: <http://www.statewatch.org/news/2015/jul/eu-com-hotsposts.pdf>).

[29] Italy designated six hotspot areas: Lampedusa, Pozzallo, Porto Empedocle/Villa Sikania, Trapani, Augusta, and Taranto. Cf. European Commission, Progress Report on the Implementation of the Hotspots in Italy, COM (2015) 679, 15 December 2015.

[30] Five hotspots areas have been identified by the Greek authorities in Lesvos, Leros, Kos, Chios, and Samos. Cf. European Commission, Progress Report on the Implementation of the Hotspots in Greece, COM (2015) 678, 15 December 2015.

register and fingerprint incoming migrants. The work of the agencies will be complementary to one another. Those claiming asylum will be immediately channelled into an asylum procedure where EASO support teams will help to process asylum cases as quickly as possible. For those not in need of protection, Frontex will help Member States by coordinating the return of irregular migrants. Europol and Eurojust will assist the host Member State with investigations to dismantle the smuggling and trafficking networks".[31]

This description makes it clear that the hotspot approach requires strong integration and operational coordination among all subjects involved in its implementation. The overall coordination of the different teams of experts involved in the hotspot approach and the information exchange among these teams is ensured through a joint operational headquarters called EU Regional Task Force (EURTF). According to the Commission's arrangements,[32] the EURTF is conceived as the organizational entity to implement the hotspot approach in administrative and operational terms. Officers from all agencies directly concerned, as well as from national authorities of the host State, are present in the EURTF. Moreover, representatives from other Member States' authorities could be temporarily deployed to the EURTF upon previous agreement with the host Member State only for purposes related to a relocation scheme. The operational support and assistance provided by closer interaction among national and EU actors can be further enhanced by liaising with international actors such as Interpol, the International Organization for Migration ("IOM"), UNHCR, and relevant NGOs. Depending on whether the major challenge is pressure at the external borders, processing asylum applications or investigating criminal networks, the relevant EU agency would need to take up the role of coordinator in the EURTF. The coordinating EU agency will take care of the administrative and logistical arrangements in cooperation with the appropriate authority of the host Member State.[33]

On the spot, the EURTF must liaise, through its different components, with the teams of experts involved in the hotspot approach.[34] As will be apparent in the following, the notion of "expert" is understood in the relevant documents in a broad sense, so as to include not only private individuals involved in the relevant activities (e.g. interpreters, cultural mediators) but also (*rectius*, especially) State officers. The teams' composition and expertise are tailored to the specific situation

---

[31] *Cit. supra* note 1, p. 6.

[32] Explanatory Note on the "Hotspot" Approach, *cit. supra* note 28, p. 3.

[33] In Italy the EURTF is based in Catania, while in Greece it has been set up in Piraeus. In both cases, Frontex was assigned as the service provider and took the lead in the EURTF, and all related operating costs are being covered by the extended agency's budget.

[34] Explanatory Note on the "Hotspot" Approach, *cit. supra* note 28, p. 3.

and needs at the hotspot where they operate to support the authorities of the host Member State.[35]

Further specifications on the functioning of hotspots have been adopted by the competent authorities of the States concerned. In particular, in February 2016, the Italian Ministry of the Interior, with support from the EU Commission, Frontex, Europol, the European Asylum Support Office, the International Organization for Migration, and the UNHCR, has drafted Standard Operating Procedures outlining the activities and their logical sequence in the hotspots.[36] A similar document should be adopted by Greece as a consequence of the amendment to Law 3907/2011 on the establishment of an Asylum Service and a First Reception Service.[37]

3. EU STATES' AND THE EU'S RESPONSIBILITY IN IMPLEMENTING THE HOTSPOT APPROACH

In light of the preceding section, it should be clear that possible unlawful acts in the implementation of the hotspot approach may call into question – theoretically, at least – the international responsibility of different subjects.

The possible responsibility of the host State is obviously undisputed. All relevant documents framing the hotspot approach stress, indeed, that both the EU's and the other Member States' intervention is intended to *support* and *assist* the actions put in place by the authorities of the host State, thus making it clear that the latter has the primary responsibility to ensure the respect of all relevant instruments of international law in facing migration flows to its territory. This is hardly surprising, considering the fact that the ultimate responsibility of the Member States with regard to the maintenance of law and order and the safeguarding of internal security is expressly recognized by EU primary law – namely, by Articles 4(2) TEU and 72 TFEU. According to this understanding, the Explanatory Note on the "Hotspot"

---

[35] For the last update of the existing hotspots' capacity, see EU Commission, State of Play of Hotspot Capacity, 22 March 2016, available at: <http://ec.europa.eu/dgs/home-affairs/what-we-do/policies/european-agenda-migration/press-material/docs/state_of_play_-_hotspots_en.pdf>. Key figures show that the requests opened so far by EU agencies for personnel to be deployed in the hotspots have not been successful. See also MAIANI, "Hotspots and Relocation Schemes: The Right Therapy for the Common European Asylum System?", EU Immigration and Asylum Law and Policy, 3 February 2016, available at: <http://eumigrationlawblog.eu/hotspots-and-relocation-schemes-the-right-therapy-for-the-common-european-asylum-system/>.

[36] EU Commission, Annex 3 to the Communication from the Commission to the European Parliament and the Council on the State of Play of Implementation of the Priority Actions under the European Agenda on Migration. Italy – State of Play Report, COM (2016) 85 final, 10 February 2016, p. 2.

[37] EU Commission, Annex 2 to the Communication from the Commission to the European Parliament and the Council on the State of Play of Implementation of the Priority Actions under the European Agenda on Migration. Greece – State of Play Report, COM (2016) 85 final, 10 February 2016, p. 2.

Approach specified that such an approach does not provide reception facilities to the host Member State.[38] Rather, it builds (*rectius*, it should build) on their existence and (proper) functioning. It follows thus that the legality and conditions of migrants' reception largely depends on the measures adopted by the host States' authorities.[39]

In this respect, a relevant role may be played by the European Convention on Human Rights (ECHR) control mechanism based on the judicial scrutiny of the European Court of Human Rights (ECtHR). Indeed, besides the so-called "Dublin Cases",[40] focusing on the condition of asylum seekers in Italy and Greece, there already exists an abundant case law of the Strasbourg Court where both the Italian and Greek migration policies have been scrutinized through the prism of the ECHR. Such cases concern, *inter alia*, the respect of the principle of *non-refoulement*,[41] the measures adopted to face the massive influx of migrants during the events linked to the "Arab Spring",[42] and the detention conditions of third-country nationals.[43]

Moreover, there would seem to be no reason why the migration-related ECtHR's jurisprudence concerning other Contracting Parties could not represent a viable paradigm to assess whether or not the responsibility of Italy and Greece may arise in cases concerning the reception of migrants in their hotspots, although that jurisprudence has to be weighed against the notorious casuistic approach characterizing the legal reasoning of the Strasbourg Court. Due to space constraints, it is not possible here to enter into an in-depth analysis of the relevant ECtHR's case law.[44] Suffice it here to mention two specific (and rather paradigmatic) precedents.

---

[38] *Cit. supra* note 28, p. 5.

[39] See also PICHOU, "Reception or Detention Centres? The Detention of Migrants and the New EU 'Hotspot' Approach in Light of the European Convention on Human Rights", 10 February 2016, p. 14, available at: <http://papers.ssrn.com/sol3/papers.cfm?abstract_id=2730654>.

[40] See, *inter alia*, *M.S.S. v. Belgium and Greece*, Application No. 30696/09, Judgment (Grand Chamber) of 21 January 2011; *Mohammed Hussein v. The Netherlands and Italy*, Application No. 27725/10, Decision of 2 April 2013; *Sharifi v. Austria*, Application No. 60104/08, Judgment of 5 December 2013; *Sharifi and Others v. Italy and Greece*, Application No. 16643/09, Judgment of 21 October 2014; *Tarakhel v. Switzerland*, Application No. 29217/12, Judgment (Grand Chamber) of 4 November 2014; *A.S. v. Switzerland*, Application No. 39350/13, Judgement of 30 June 2015.

[41] *Hirsi Jamaa and Others v. Italy*, Application No. 27765/09, Judgment (Grand Chamber) of 23 February 2012.

[42] *Khlaifia and Others v. Italy*, Application No. 16483/12, Judgment of 1 September 2015. The case was referred to the Grand Chamber in February 2016 at the request of the Italian Government.

[43] Cf., *inter alia*, *Rahimi v. Greece*, Application No. 8687/08, Judgment of 5 April 2011; *A.A. v. Greece*, Application No. 12186/08, Judgment of 22 July 2010; *R.U. v. Greece*, Application No. 2237/08, Judgment of 7 June 2011; *Mahmundi and Others v. Greece*, Application No. 14902/10, Judgment of 31 July 2012; *A.F. v. Greece*, Application No. 53709/11, Judgment of 13 June 2013; *Mohamad v. Greece*, Application No. 70586/11, Judgment of 11 December 2014; *Mahammad and Others v. Greece*, Application No. 48352/12, Judgment of 15 January 2015.

[44] A detailed analysis is present in PICHOU, *cit. supra* note 39.

The first is represented by a passage of the ECtHR's judgment in *Louled Massoud v. Malta*, where the Court observed that:

> "It [is] hard to conceive that in a small island like Malta, where escape by sea without endangering one's life is unlikely and fleeing by air is subject to strict control, the authorities could not have had at their disposal measures other than the applicant's protracted detention to secure an eventual removal in the absence of any immediate prospect of his expulsion".[45]

It is clear that such a statement may be easily applied to the management of Greek hotspots located in its islands, as well as to the Italian centers in Sicily and Lampedusa.

The second case which deserves to be mentioned is *Saadi v. The United Kingdom*, where the Grand Chamber found a breach of the right to be promptly informed under Article 5(2) ECHR, when the applicant's detention was the result of administrative convenience for processing fast-track claims of asylum.[46] Arguably, the same legal reasoning could be invoked to assess the validity of the screening process carried out in the hotspots if one considers that it has been set up to facilitate speedy decision-making on requests submitted by claimants "hosted" in the centers.[47]

Having said this, and even if the responsibility of host States concerned cannot be brought into question, it does not seem possible to exclude *a priori* that the responsibility of other Member States, and that of the EU, may arise in the implementation of the hotspot approach. The specific situations of these further actors are discussed below.

3.1. *The Position of States Other Than the Host Country...*

The possible involvement of other Member States in the implementation of the hotspot approach may follow two different schemes, depending in particular on the degree to which Member States retain control over the exercise of powers related to the hotspot management. In both cases, Member States' role shall be assessed within the legal framework of the relevant EU agencies in charge of developing that approach, together with the host State and the European Commission. It is

---

[45] *Louled Massoud v. Malta*, Application No. 24340/08, Judgment of 22 July 2010, para. 68.

[46] *Saadi v. The United Kingdom*, Application No. 13229/03, Judgment of 29 January 2008.

[47] Cf. WEBBER, "'Hotspots' for Asylum Applications: Some Things We Urgently Need to Know", EU Law Analysis, 2 September 2015, available at: <http://eulawanalysis.blogspot.it/2015/09/hotspots-for-asylum-applications-some.html>.

worth mentioning that those schemes are also applicable to third-party countries, in so far as they are integrated into the activities carried out in the hotspots.[48]

The first scheme which shall be mentioned for present purposes is the possibility of seconding national officers to the EU agencies. The secondment of national officers is expressly provided for in Articles 3b and 17 of the Regulation 2007/2004 establishing Frontex, in Article 38(1) of the Regulation 439/2010 on the European Asylum Support Office, in Articles 9, 39, 42, and 51 of the Council Decision 2009/371/JHA establishing Europol, and in Articles 2, 30, and 34 of the Council Decision 2002/187/JHA setting up Eurojust. As will be better explained below,[49] there are significant elements that make it arguable in this case that, with the exception of border guards seconded to Frontex and national members seconded to joint investigation teams,[50] the conduct of seconded national experts may be considered – in light of Article 6 DARIO – as an act of the EU. For this reason, the legal implications of that scheme will be further explored in the next sub-section, categorized under the attribution of conduct to the Union.

The second scheme arises in cases where the EU agencies decide to establish joint teams composed of national experts made available by Member States. Such a possibility is expressly provided by the founding instruments of all the EU agencies involved in the hotspot approach.

Concerning Frontex, Article 3(1) of the founding Regulation establishes joint activities at the external borders especially in cases of "specific and disproportionate pressures". Also, Frontex may form a pool of border guards called European Border Guard Teams for possible deployment during joint operations (Articles 2(1) (ea) and 3(1b) of the Frontex Regulation). The border guard teams are mainly composed of national pools (Article 3b(1) and (2)), but Frontex shall also contribute to the teams with competent border guards seconded by Member States as national experts (Article 3b(3)). Moreover, the possibility of activating Rapid Border Intervention Teams (RABIT) to assist Member States facing a situation of urgent and exceptional pressure, especially the arrival at points of the external borders of large numbers of third-country nationals trying to enter the territory of the Member State illegally, is expressly recognized.[51] Significantly, the establishment of joint

---

[48] It is the case, for instance, that Switzerland, following the entry into force of the Agreement on the Modalities of the Participation of the Swiss Federation in the Work of EASO (OJ 2016 L 65/22), will be entitled to participate in the agency's activities. Moreover, Swiss national experts may be engaged by EASO, and deployed in EASO operations, including those in the hotspots in Italy and Greece. Cf. EASO, "EASO-Swiss Working Arrangement Enters into Force, Enabling Switzerland to Further Participate in the Work of EASO and Make Use of Its Tools", Press Release PR 05/2006, 1 March 2016, available at: <https://easo.europa.eu/wp-content/uploads/EASO-Switzerland_PR05.pdf>.

[49] See *infra* section 3.2.

[50] See *infra*.

[51] Regulation (EC) 863/2007 establishing a mechanism for the creation of Rapid Border Intervention Teams and amending Council Regulation (EC) 2007/2004 with regard to that mech-

activities of Frontex experts situated at EU border hotspots in Greece and Italy is expressly mentioned in the Explanatory Note on the "Hotspot" Approach,[52] as well as in a document attached to the Explanatory Note which explains the support provided by Frontex to frontline Member States.[53] On 28 December 2015, the Rapid Intervention Team (Poseidon) in the Aegean islands was actually launched.[54] As of 4 March 2016, there were 775 guest officers deployed under that operation: 243 crew members, 248 fingerprinters, 53 screening experts, 30 advanced documents experts, 75 interpreters, 16 debriefing experts, 8 Frontex support officers, 31 team leaders, and 71 coordinating staff.[55]

Joint expert teams may also be deployed under the EASO Regulation. In particular, pursuant to Article 13, asylum support teams may be deployed on a temporary basis in the territory of a Member State that is subject to particular pressure. Like the Frontex expert teams, the asylum support teams are composed of national experts corresponding to the required profiles. The above-mentioned Explanatory Note on the "Hotspot" Approach makes it clear that asylum support teams are also an essential component of the hotspot machinery, destined to be deployed to assist with the registration of asylum seekers and the subsequent preparation of cases.[56]

Moreover, in accordance with Article 1(12) of the Council Framework Decision 2002/465/JHA on joint investigations teams,[57] as well as Article 13 of the 2000 Convention on Mutual Assistance in Criminal Matters between the Member States of the European Union,[58] Eurojust and Europol can participate in joint investigation teams either separately or jointly.

Finally, it is important to recall that joint activities developed under the hotspot approach shall be understood as strictly intertwined with pre-existing joint operations, such as the EUNAVFOR MED, the Joint Operation Triton, and the Joint Operational Team Mare.[59]

---

anism and regulating the tasks and powers of guest officers (OJ 2007 L 199/30).

[52] Cit. supra note 28, pp. 8, 10. The document refers to screening and debriefing teams of experts, as well as to joint return operations.

[53] Cf. "Information Note on the Support to be Provided by Frontex to Frontline Member States on the Return of Irregular Migrants", available at: <http://www.statewatch.org/news/2015/jul/eu-com-frontex-role.pdf>.

[54] EU Commission, Progress Report on the Implementation of the Hotspot Approach in Greece, COM (2016) 141 final, 4 March 2016.

[55] Ibid., p. 15.

[56] Explanatory Note on the "Hotspot" Approach, cit. supra note 28, p. 8.

[57] OJ 2002 L 162/1.

[58] OJ 2000 C 197/1.

[59] Explanatory Note on the "Hotspot" Approach, cit. supra note 28. The profiles related to harmful activities developed under those further operations will be not discussed here. For a legal analysis of some relevant aspects related to such initiatives see GESTRI, "EUNAVFOR MED: Fighting Migrant Smuggling under UN Security Council Resolution 2240 (2015)", in this Yearbook.

At first glance, one could be tempted to maintain that national experts made available by Member States for joint activities shall be qualified as organs of the sending State under Article 4 DARS ("Conduct of organs of State"), leading thus to the attribution of their conduct to the latter. The requirements that shall be met to invoke the application of Article 4 are well-known: the person whose conduct is in question shall have the status of an organ of the State in accordance with the relevant internal law provisions. It is also important to recall that, as clarified by the ILC in its commentary to Article 4, the notion of "State organ" shall be intended in the most general sense, "[i]t extends to organs of government of whatever functions, and at whatever level in the hierarchy, including those at provincial or even local level. No distinction is made for this purpose between legislative, executive or judicial organs".[60] According to those clarifications, it is not difficult to conclude that the great majority of national experts involved in the joint activities of EU agencies are organs of the sending State. Indeed, the majority of experts are likely to be civil servants of the Member States' Interior Ministries.[61] But having said this, other scenarios should be explored.

First of all, the possibility of recognizing a transfer of attribution between the sending States and the host State should be noted. In this respect, the legal framework on the status of "guest officers" that is contained in the Frontex Regulation is particularly illustrative. The Regulation defines "guest officers" as the officers of border guard services of Member States other than the host Member State participating in joint activities (Article 1a(6)). Quite significantly, such a definition includes not only the national pool made available for deployment at the request of the agency (Article 3b(2)), but also border guards seconded to the agency as national experts (Articles 3b(3) and 17(5)). According to the Frontex Regulation, guest officers "may only perform their tasks and exercise powers *under instructions from and, as a general rule, in the presence of border guards of the host Member State*".[62] Moreover, the use of force by guest officers shall only be authorized with the consent of the home Member State and the host Member State, in the presence of border guards of the host Member State and in accordance with its national law (Article 10(6)). The liability regime established for guest officers is also relevant. Pursuant to Article 10b of the Regulation, the host Member State shall be liable, in accordance with its national law, for any damage caused by guest officers during their operations.[63] Article 10c establishes that, during the deployment on a joint operation, guest officers shall be treated in the same way as officials of the host

---

[60] ILC, Report of the International Law Commission on the Work of its Fifty-Third Session, UN Doc. A/56/10, YILC, 2001, Vol. II, Part Two, p. 40.

[61] WEBBER, *cit. supra* note 47.

[62] Article 10(3) (emphasis added).

[63] In the event of a damage caused by gross negligence or wilful conduct, the host Member State may request the home State to have any sums paid to the victims (Article 10b(2)).

Member State with regard to any criminal offences that might be committed against them or by them.

In light of the previous description, the argument could be made that the deployment of guest officers in Frontex joint operations may trigger the transfer of attribution of conduct provided for by Article 6 DARS, which states that the "conduct of an organ placed at the disposal of a State by another State shall be considered an act of the former State under international law if the organ is acting in the exercise of elements of the governmental authority of the State at whose disposal it is placed".

The mechanism enshrined in Article 6 DARS is based on three fundamental requirements. First, the organ in question shall have the status of an organ of the home State. In the case of border guest officers, this criterion appears to be automatically met: they are, indeed, officers of the border guard services of the Member States. Worthy of mention, in this respect, is the first paragraph of Article 7 of the Regulation on Rapid Borders Intervention Teams, stating that "[m]embers of the teams shall remain national border guards of their home Member States". Second, organs placed at the disposal of the host State must be acting in the exercise of elements of the governmental authority of that State. Arguably, activities carried out by guest officers in Frontex operations may easily be covered by this definition, since they aim at ensuring the maintenance of law and order in the host State, as well as safeguarding its internal security. Third, and most importantly, Article 6 DARS requires that the organs concerned are "placed at [the] disposal" of the host State. This is the most complex condition to be met, to be sure. According to the ILC's commentary to Article 6, this condition implies that "the organ must [...] act in conjunction with the machinery of that State and under its *exclusive direction and control*, rather than on instructions from the sending State".[64] It is a fact that the definition concerning the status of guest officers deployed in Frontex joint operations does not completely set aside the role of the home State. As it has been rightly recalled in the literature,[65] guest officers shall wear their own uniforms while performing their tasks (Article 10(4) of the Frontex Regulation). They may carry weapons, ammunition, and equipment as authorized according to the home Member State's national law (Article 10(5)), and the use of force, as already highlighted, shall be authorized by the host State with the consent of the home State (Article 10(6)). Also, the home Member State shall provide for appropriate disciplinary measures in case of violations of fundamental rights or international protection obligations in the course of a joint operation (Article 3(1a)).

These elements have been considered by some scholars as evidence of the fact that the home State is supposed to retain, under the Frontex Regulation, significant

---

[64] ILC Report, *cit. supra* note 60 (emphasis added).

[65] LIGUORI and RICCIUTI, "Frontex ed il rispetto dei diritti umani nelle operazioni congiunte alle frontiere esterne dell'Unione", DUDI, 2012, p. 539 ff., pp. 555-556.

control over its officers, so as to exclude the invocation of Article 6 DARS.[66] Rather, in this case, Article 17 DARS ("direction and control exercised over the commission of an internationally wrongful act") could be applied.[67] To the present author, however, it seems that, in the case under consideration, the link established with the host State prevails. In particular, what is deemed decisive in this regard is the Regulation provision that dictates that guest officers may only perform their tasks and exercise powers under instructions from the host State. That provision, in fact, excludes any possibility that the home State may instruct its officers, thus restricting the role the sending State may play in joint operations quite significantly. Also, it should be stressed that, even in cases where the Frontex Regulation expressly acknowledges a role for the home State, such a role may be limited by the host State. This is the case, for instance, in the provision regulating the use of force by guest officers. According to that provision, the host State may prohibit the carrying of certain weapons, ammunition, and equipment by guest officers, provided that its own legislation applies the same prohibition to its own border guards (Article 10(5) of the Frontex Regulation). It follows that the possibility of a transfer of attribution in light of Article 6 DARS still preserves its relevance, even if the effectiveness of such a transfer shall be assessed on a case-by-case basis.[68] This does not exclude, obviously, the possibility to invoke the responsibility of the sending State for failing to fulfill its due diligence obligations to prevent human rights violations.[69]

A similar reasoning may be applied to assess the status of national members of the joint investigation teams established under the Council Framework Decision 2002/465/JHA. According to the Framework Decision, the members of the joint investigation team (JIT) from Member States other than the Member State in which

---

[66] *Ibid.*

[67] *Ibid.*

[68] See, in general terms, BARTOLINI, "Attribution of Conduct and Liability Issues Arising from International Disaster Relief Missions", Vanderbilt Journal of Transnational Law, 2015, p. 1029 ff., p. 1041, arguing that "[...] without additional elements to clarify that [...] teams are [...] acting autonomously 'on instructions from the sending State,' it seems difficult to deny the relevance of Art. 6 ARS". The position expressed in the present contribution was also highlighted by the Standing Committee of experts on international immigration, refugee and criminal law in its Comment on the proposal for a Regulation establishing a mechanism for the creation of Rapid Border Intervention Teams and amending Council Regulation (EC) 2007/2004 with regard to that mechanism. In that Comment, the Committee, after mentioning Article 6 DARS, expressed the view that "[s]ince the proposed regulation envisages that guest officers will operate under the direct command of the host State and shall only take instructions from the host Member State, it is appropriate to confer responsibility for actions of these guest officers to the host Member State" (*ibid.*, p. 4; available at: <http://www.statewatch.org/news/2006/oct/meijers-cttee-rabits.pdf>). See also SPAGNOLO, *cit. supra* note 18, p. 205, according to whom guest officers involved in Frontex joint operations are under the command of the host State.

[69] See *Application of the Convention on the Prevention and Punishment of the Crime of Genocide (Bosnia and Herzegovina v. Serbia and Montenegro)*, Judgment of 26 February 2007, ICJ Reports, 2007, p. 43 ff.

the team operates shall be considered "seconded" to the team itself (Article 1(4)).[70] However, unlike the first scheme mentioned, where national officers are fully seconded to the EU agencies and are thus requested to carry out duties solely with the interests of the agency concerned in mind, the secondment to the team implies here, similarly to what happens for the border guards seconded to Frontex as national experts, that the members from other States shall carry out their tasks under the *leadership* of a representative of the Member State in which the team operates (Article 1(3b)). Furthermore, the legal regimes related to both the criminal and civil liability of officials from a Member State other than the Member State of operation (Articles 2-3 of the Framework Decision) coincide with those applied to guest officers under the Frontex Regulation and show thus a strict linkage to the latter State.

Having said this, like in the case of Frontex joint operations, only a case-by-case analysis may allow the proper assessment of the attribution of conduct of the JITs. In this respect, the written agreement upon which each JIT is based undoubtedly represents a useful tool. These agreements, indeed, integrate the provisions of relevant EU legal instruments, thus helping shed light on attribution issues. Unfortunately, JIT agreements are confidential, and the Model Agreement adopted at the EU level does not contain significant elements thereof.[71]

Other situations related to the implementation of the hotspot approach are more ambiguous. This is the case, in particular, of national pools of experts employed in the EASO joint operations. The EASO Regulation does not define the status of such individuals. It limits itself to specifying, on the one hand, that the composition of the teams, as well as their tasks and instructions, are included in the operational plan set up between the Executive Director of the agency and the requesting Member State (Article 18(1)(d) and (e)). On the other hand, the Regulation replicates the same liability regimes contained in the Frontex founding instrument. In particular, Article 21(1) establishes that the host Member State is liable for any damage caused by members of an asylum support team operating in its territory, while Article 22 states that, for criminal liability purposes, the members of an asylum support team shall be treated in the same way as officials of the host Member State. Neither of the available support plans agreed upon with Italy[72] and Greece[73] shed light on the status of experts. Those documents only state that experts "are expected to meet obligations imposed upon them by the provision of the EASO

---

[70] See also Council of the European Union, Joint Investigation Teams Manual, 15790/1/11 REV 1, 4 November 2011, para. 5.3.

[71] Cf. Council Resolution on a Model Agreement for Setting Up a Joint Investigation Team (JIT), OJ 2010 C 70/1.

[72] Cf. EASO Special Support Plan to Italy – Phase 2, Valletta Harbour and Rome, 11 March 2015, available at: <https://easo.europa.eu/wp-content/uploads/20150311-SSP-PHASE-2-Italy-DEF.pdf>.

[73] Cf. EASO Special Support Plan to Greece, Valletta Harbour and Athens, 13 May 2015, available at: <https://easo.europa.eu/wp-content/uploads/EASO_SPECIAL-SUPPORT-PLAN-TO-GREECE_MAY_2015.pdf>.

Special Support Plan [...] and shall comply with the rules of their mandates".[74] Against this background, it seems difficult to advocate a transfer of attribution of conduct in light of Article 6 DARS. But again, only a case-by-case analysis could allow the assessment of whether the criteria defined by the ILC for that purpose may be met. This said, it should also be highlighted that relevant elements of practice seem to indicate that experts deployed by EASO to provide assistance in the hotspots will be mainly seconded to the EASO itself. In the September 2015 issue of its newsletter, EASO announced a call for 374 experts to participate in its operations in the hotspots in Italy and Greece,[75] representing the largest call that has ever been made by EASO. According to the agency, under this call, national "officers [...] need to be seconded from EU Member States". This point leads to the questions of attribution of conduct to the EU emerging from the implementation of the hotspot approach.

3.2.   ... and that of the European Union

Nollkaemper and Jacobs have posed the question of the distribution of responsibility among the Member States and organizational actors involved in the implementation and management of a Frontex joint operation.[76] The authors maintain that the responsibility of the EU Member States concerned, together with that of the EU, may give rise to a *shared responsibility*, that is, a situation where "the responsibility of two or more actors for their contribution to a particular [harmful] outcome is distributed to them separately, rather than resting on them collectively", provided that individual causal contributions cannot be determined.[77]

Actually, the possibility that the EU may incur responsibility in contributing to the implementation of Frontex joint operations is stressed by several authors.[78] On the other hand, concerns and criticisms about the consistency of Frontex activities with the need to ensure a strict respect of fundamental rights have been expressed on several occasions in recent years. In 2012, the European Ombudsman decided to undertake an inquiry on her own initiative concerning Frontex's implementation of its fundamental rights obligations. In the course of the inquiry, the European Ombudsman recommended clarifying "the legal framework applicable to the con-

---

[74] Cf. Article 1(3) of the EASO Special Support Plan to Italy, and Article 1(3) of the EASO Special Support Plan to Greece.

[75] Cf. EASO, EASO Newsletter September 2015, p. 4, available at: <https://easo.europa.eu/wp-content/uploads/EASO-Newsletter-September-2015_final1.pdf>.

[76] NOLLKAEMPER and JACOBS, "Shared Responsibility in International Law: A Conceptual Framework", Michigan Journal of International Law, 2013, p. 359 ff., p. 362.

[77] *Ibid.*, p. 368.

[78] See also LIGUORI and RICCIUTI, *cit. supra* note 65, p. 556; SPAGNOLO, *cit. supra* note 18, p. 206; and GALLAGHER and DAVID, *The International Law of Migrant Smuggling*, Cambridge, 2014, p. 348.

duct of all participants in Frontex operations".[79] Similar concerns were expressed by the European Ombudsman on the occasion of a new inquiry opened in 2014 on the means through which Frontex ensures respect for fundamental rights in joint return operations.[80] At the European level, it is also worth noting the position taken by the Parliamentary Assembly of the Council of Europe in its Resolution 1932 (2013), significantly titled "Frontex: Human rights Responsibilities". Here, the Parliamentary Assembly notes that "[n]otable in this respect is the lack of clarity over Frontex's responsibility in co-ordinating and implementing joint land, air, sea and return operations with member States and regarding liabilities for human rights violations or other breaches of international law resulting from the Agency's actions".[81]

The position taken by Frontex vis-à-vis those criticisms is perfectly illustrated by a clear-cut statement its former Executive Director, Ilkka Laitinen, gave in 2010 on the occasion of the Interparliamentary Committee Meeting of the LIBE Committee on "Democratic Accountability in the Area of Freedom, Security and Justice, Evaluating Frontex": "As regards fundamental rights, Frontex is not responsible for decisions in that area", he said.[82] The rationale behind this position is also crystal-clear: according to the Frontex Regulation "[...] responsibility for the control and surveillance of external borders lies with the Member States" (Article 1(2)). From this perspective, thus, Frontex would only support actions carried out by Member States, who should be considered the only subjects responsible for an alleged violation of international law.[83]

It is true that the agency has developed significant tools to strengthen the fundamental rights protection in its activities.[84] However, several observers and institutional actors remain concerned about whether these changes alone may effectively address all the human rights issues at stake.[85] On the other hand, as the implementation of the hotspot approach clearly illustrates, the strategies developed to face

---

[79] Draft Recommendation A, Decision of the European Ombudsman closing the own-initiative inquiry OI/5/2012/BEH-MHZ concerning the European Agency for the Management of Operational Cooperation at the External Borders of the Member States of the European Union (Frontex), available at: <http://www.ombudsman.europa.eu/en/cases/decision.faces/en/52477/html.bookmark>.

[80] Case OI/9/2014/MHZ, available at: <http://www.ombudsman.europa.eu/en/cases/correspondence.faces/en/58135/html.bookmark>.

[81] Para. 3 of the Resolution, available at: <http://assembly.coe.int/nw/xml/XRef/Xref-XML2HTML-EN.asp?fileid=19719&lang=en>.

[82] Cited in GALLAGHER and DAVID, cit. supra note 78, p. 342.

[83] See also SPAGNOLO, cit. supra note 18, p. 218; European Parliament, Directorate-General for Internal Policies, "The Proposal for a European Border and Coast Guard: Evolution or Revolution in External Border Management?", Study for the LIBE Committee by Dr. Jorrit Rijpma, 2016, p. 29, available at: <http://www.europarl.europa.eu/RegData/etudes/STUD/2016/556934/IPOL_STU(2016)556934_EN.pdf>.

[84] European Parliament, Directorate-General for Internal Policies, ibid., p. 30.

[85] Cf. Council of Europe Parliamentary Assembly Resolution 1932 (2013), para. 5.

the actual migration crisis have strengthened criticisms of Frontex activities (also in light of the role played by the agency as EU Regional Task Force) and extended these criticisms to the other EU agencies concerned.[86]

Before taking into consideration the provisions of the DARIO which could be arguably invoked in the hotspot scenario, two preliminary features deserve to be considered. The first feature deals with the position of EU agencies vis-à-vis the European Union. More precisely, the question arises as to whether the EU agencies involved in hotspot management may be considered autonomous international entities, thus leading to a responsibility distinct from that of the EU. This argument is mainly based on some provisions contained in the founding instruments allowing EU agencies to interact with third countries or other international organizations. Space limitations here do not allow the analysis of such provisions and the related practice.[87] It seems, however, that the (limited) external action of EU agencies, which often leads to the conclusion of administrative agreements, cannot be considered a decisive element in recognizing that they possess a separate international legal personality distinct from that of the Union, which still represents, therefore, the sole legal entity acting as the bearer of relevant rights and duties under international law.[88] A relevant confirmation of this argument may be seen in the Draft Agreement on the Accession of the European Union to the European Convention for the Protection of Human Rights and Fundamental Freedoms. The Draft Agreement, indeed, expressly established that the ECHR could "impose on the European Union obligations with regard only to acts, measures or omissions of its institutions, bodies, offices, *agencies*, or of persons acting on their behalf".[89]

---

[86] On the accountability gap the EU home affairs agencies show in the field of fundamental rights' protection, see European Parliament, Directorate-General for Internal Policies, "Implementation of the EU Charter of Fundamental Rights and its Impact on EU Home Affairs Agencies – Frontex, Europol and the European Asylum Support Office", Study for the LIBE Committee by Prof. Elspeth Guild et al., 2011, available at: <http://www.europarl.europa.eu/meetdocs/2009_2014/documents/libe/dv/02_study_fundamental_rights_/02_study_fundamental_rights_en.pdf>.

[87] A very detailed analysis is present in OTT, VOS and COMAN-KUND, "EU Agencies and Their International Mandate: A New Category of Global Actors", CLEER Working Paper 2013/7, available at: <http://www.asser.nl/media/1642/cleer_13-7_web.pdf>.

[88] Cf. also, in this respect, TOVO, *Le agenzie decentrate dell'Unione europea*, Napoli, 2016, pp. 39-47; and KUIJPER and PAASIVIRTA, *cit. supra* note 18, p. 50, arguing that "the internal EU rules show that there exist 'institutions' and a variety of other 'bodies, offices and agencies', all of which can be considered organs of the EU for international law purposes". A different view is expressed by OTT, VOS and COMAN-KUND, *cit. supra* note 87, p. 38, maintaining "[n]ot only that agencies result from a hybrid legal system of supranational nature which is neither national nor international law but also [that] such agencies participate in networks of international administrative unions and national bodies".

[89] Article 1(3) (emphasis added). Cf. Fifth negotiation meeting between the CDDH *ad hoc* negotiation group and the European Commission on the accession of the EU to the European Convention on Human Rights, Final Report to the CDDH, 47+1(2013)008rev2, Strasbourg, 10

The second preliminary feature regards the interaction between the DARS and the DARIO in cases of "shared attribution" among international organizations and States. Such a relationship has been depicted in the literature in problematic terms. To some authors, indeed, not only does "the law of international responsibility as construed by the ILC [...] provide little or no guidance for solving problems of shared responsibility", but, in some respects, that law "complicates or even impedes such solutions".[90] Even though the ILC's work has shown its limits, especially as far as the DARIO are concerned, the present author believes that it may still give some guidance in defining scenarios of shared responsibility. In fact, as Giorgio Gaja, former special rapporteur for the responsibility of international organizations, has rightly pointed out, it is true that the DARIO only consider issues of attribution related to international organizations. However, and quite significantly, "they do not exclude the possibility that conduct may also be attributed to another subject of international law".[91] Obviously, in the case of States, questions of attributions should be solved in light of the general rules set out by the DARS.

If one applies this formula to the activities related to the management of hotspots, it is possible to maintain that the EU could be held responsible, under international law, in all cases where it breaches its international law obligations related to the protection of migrants.[92] Particularly relevant for present purposes is the situation concerning the obligation to prevent the relevant wrongful act of a Member State, or at least not to contribute to it. As is well-known, the ICJ has made it clear, with regard to the position of States vis-à-vis the 1948 Genocide Convention, that the due diligence obligation to prevent genocide implies the State's "capacity to influence effectively the action of persons likely to commit, or already committing, genocide".[93] By way of analogy, it could be said, thus, that the international responsibility of the EU may be invoked in the hotspot framework when it has the capacity to "influence effectively" the action of the host Member State but fails to prevent the breaches of that State. More precisely, borrowing again from the ICJ,

---

June 2013, available at: <http://www.coe.int/t/dghl/standardsetting/hrpolicy/Accession/Meeting_reports/47_1(2013)008rev2_EN.pdf>.

[90] NOLLKAEMPER, cit. supra note 20. See also BARROS, RYNGAERT and WOUTERS, cit. supra note 20, p. 286, maintaining that the difficulties encountered by the DARIO in this respect are "largely explained by taking the traditional concept of the law of international responsibility and applying it to the independent conduct of States and international organizations, rather than by considering the cooperative or joint conduct involving both an international organization and a member State".

[91] GAJA, "The Relations between the European Union and Its States from the Perspective of the ILC Articles on Responsibility of International Organizations", SHARES Research Paper 25 (2013), p. 2, available at: <http://www.sharesproject.nl/wp-content/uploads/2013/06/SHARES-RP-25-final.pdf>.

[92] These obligations mainly arise from general international law, due to the (extremely) limited participation of the EU to human rights' treaties.

[93] Application of the Convention on the Prevention and Punishment of the Crime of Genocide (Bosnia and Herzegovina v. Serbia and Montenegro), cit. supra note 69, para. 430.

"responsibility is [...] incurred if the [EU] [...] manifestly failed to take all measures to prevent [the violation] [...] which were within its power, and which might
have contributed to preventing the [violation] [...]".[94]

If one considers the role the EU may play in joint activities implemented under the hotspot scenario, there is no doubt that the conditions requested by the test
elaborated by the ICJ are met. More precisely, in the cases of both Frontex and
EASO joint operations, the agencies are fully involved in the definition of relevant
operations.[95] Moreover, and most significantly for present purposes, Article 3(1a)
of the Frontex Regulation expressly provides that the Executive Director shall suspend or terminate, in whole or in part, joint operations if violations of fundamental
rights or international protection obligations are registered and he/she considers
that such violations are of serious nature or are likely to persist. Also relevant is the
role played by the EURTF, which, being in charge of implementing the hotspot approach in administrative and operational terms, is vested of the necessary authority
to exercise an effective influence on the host State.[96] Finally, the role played by the
European Commission, which is expected to exercise an "overall coordination" of
the assessment carried out by EU Agencies on the requests submitted by the affected Member State[97] must also be mentioned.

As already pointed out, the attribution of the relevant conduct to the EU results
from the application of the general rules enshrined in the DARIO. In this respect,
reference has to be made to Article 6(1) DARIO ("Conduct of organs or agents of
an international organization").[98] Pursuant to this provision, "[t]he conduct of an
organ or agent of an international organization in the performance of functions of
that organ or agent shall be considered an act of that organization under international law [...]".

---

[94] *Ibid.*

[95] See Article 3 of the Frontex Regulation and Articles 13(2) and 15-18 of EASO Regulation,
respectively.

[96] The role played by hotspot teams is so relevant that, in the literature, the argument has
been made that they are "increasingly perceived by [...] Member States as a variant of the *troika*
in the context of the EFSM/EFSF/ESM and therefore as unduly interfering with their national
sovereignty". Cf. Editorial Comments, "From Eurocrisis to Asylum and Migration Crisis: Some
Legal and Institutional Considerations about the EU's Current Struggles", CML Review, 2015,
p. 1437 ff., pp. 1443-1444.

[97] Explanatory Note on the "Hotspot" Approach, *cit. supra* note 28, p. 3.

[98] See also GALLAGHER and DAVID, *cit. supra* note 78, pp. 347-348. For a different view,
see LIGUORI and RICCIUTI, *cit. supra* note 65, p. 556, maintaining the possibility of a transfer of responsibility according to Article 14 DARIO ("Aid or assistance in the commission of
an internationally wrongful act"). It should be however recalled that such provision requests a
full awareness by the aiding or assisting international organization that the aid supplied would
be used to violate international law (see, in this respect, *Application of the Convention on the
Prevention and Punishment of the Crime of Genocide*, *cit. supra* note 69, para. 423, where the ICJ
analyses the corresponding provision contained in the DARS). Its scope seems thus quite strict.
Cf. GAJA, *cit. supra* note 91, p. 6.

It is self-evident that the staff of EU agencies involved in the implementation of the hotspot approach may be easily included in the notion of "organ" covered by Article 6 DARIO. Moreover, it must also be noted that, as made clear in the ILC's commentary, the provision also covers situations where an organ of a State is *fully* seconded to an international organization.[99] It follows, thus, that the general rule set out in Article 6 would also apply in cases of secondment of national officers to EU agencies within the framework of the hotspot strategy.[100] Indeed, pursuant to the rules adopted by EU agencies on secondment of national experts, the latter are requested to carry out duties solely with the interests of the agency concerned in mind, without taking instructions from any government, authority, organization, or person outside that agency.[101]

4. CONCLUDING REMARKS

This article has tried to contribute to the legal analysis of issues of attribution of conduct related to the framing and implementation of the hotspot approach by both the EU and its Member States. As has been shown, that approach depicts a rather obscure scenario without clearly specifying the mandates and roles of relevant actors. Particularly illustrative of that trend is the circumstance that the approach has been elaborated so far in the absence of a proper piece of EU legislation.

Notwithstanding this fact, as this analysis tried to demonstrate, a possible reconstruction of the relevant attribution schemes is still possible even if, in some cases, a confirmation of their soundness should come from elements of practice which are either confidential or missing.

Quite significantly, the schemes elaborated are largely based on the ILC's Draft Articles on international responsibility, thus confirming the guidance role that the ILC's work still plays *in subiecta materia*. In particular, the Draft Articles have been here understood to cover not only cases of Member States' responsibility, but also cases of shared responsibility between Member States and the EU emerging from the hotspot approach.

---

[99] ILC, Report of the International Law Commission on the Work of its Sixty-Third Session, UN Doc. A/66/10, p. 87.

[100] Such cases are illustrated *supra* section 3.1.

[101] Cf. Article 7(1)(a) of the Management Board Decision No. 22/2009 laying down rules on the secondment of national experts (SNE) to Frontex; Article 7(1)(a) of the Decision No. 1 of the Management Board laying down rules on the secondment of national experts (SNE) to the European Asylum Support Office; Article 8(1)(a) of the Decision laying down rules on the secondment of national experts to Europol; and Article 9(1)(a) of the College Decision 2013-6 on implementing arrangements for the secondment to Eurojust of national experts. On the particular status of border guards seconded to Frontex and national members seconded to JITs, see *supra* section 3.1.

In this respect, it is interesting to note that, in the recent proposal for a regulation on the European Border and Coast Guard elaborated by the European Commission,[102] a proposal which confirms the recourse to the hotspot approach (thus strengthening the concerns related to the absence of a proper piece of legislation framing that tool), the EU institution makes explicit reference to the notion of "shared responsibility". To the Commission, indeed, "[t]he challenges which have arisen from the migratory crisis cannot be adequately dealt with by Member States acting in an uncoordinated manner. Integrated border management is a shared responsibility of the European Border and Costal Guard Agency".[103] More precisely, the proposal clarifies that, while Member States retain the primary responsibility for the management of their section of the external borders, the European Border and Cost Guard Agency should ensure the application of EU measures relating to the management of the external borders by reinforcing, assessing, and coordinating the actions of the Member States which implement those measures. The European Border and Cost Guard Agency, which should succeed to Frontex, thus presents a strengthened mandate.[104]

All too regrettably, however, the proposal reproduces, in essence, the relevant text of provisions on joint operations contained in the Frontex Regulation,[105] giving the impression that the reference made by the Commission to the notion of "shared responsibility" is here understood in general terms, only to clarify that both Member States and the EU agencies shall act in a spirit of loyal cooperation to ensure a proper management of EU borders. In so doing, the proposal is therefore unable to support the enhancement of the accountability of the new agency, and thus the international responsibility of the EU. On the other hand, such an approach risks replicating in turn the arguments made by Frontex to dismiss its accountability with regard to the joint activities deployed to face the migrant crisis. Arguments which could be also made by other EU actors involved in the management of hotspots. In sum, should this trend be confirmed, only the recourse to the general rules set out in the ILC's Draft Articles on international responsibility could prevent transforming the hotspot approach in a blind spot for international responsibility.

---

[102] COM (2015) 671 final, 15 December 2015. For a detailed analysis of the Proposal, see European Parliament, Directorate-General for Internal Policies, *cit. supra* note 83.

[103] COM (2015) 671 final, *cit. supra* note 102, p. 3.

[104] See Article 5 of the Proposal.

[105] See *supra* section 3.1.

SOME OBSERVATIONS ON THE LEGAL RESPONSIBILITY OF STATES AND INTERNATIONAL ORGANIZATIONS IN THE EXTRATERRITORIAL PROCESSING OF ASYLUM CLAIMS

ANNA LIGUORI*

Abstract

The idea of establishing centres for the "external processing" of asylum claims – already supported by some European Union (EU) Member States, and actually realized in the Caribbean by the United States and in the Pacific area by Australia – has recently come to the fore again in European debates. The recent proposals – which tend to create offshore centres in Turkey and probably in African countries too – envisage various levels of involvement of EU Member States and of the EU itself. The present contribution aims to analyse, in particular, which of the various actors implicated would be responsible, and to what extent, in cases of violation of asylum seekers' human rights. The scenario that could be envisaged is extremely complex. Disentangling the web of action/attribution/responsibility is very difficult and the risk of "blame shifting" or "passing the buck" among the various actors is high. The possibility of the extraterritorial application of the European Convention on Human Rights will also be explored, in order to assess to what extent individuals would have access to a remedy before the European Court of Human Rights.

Keywords: asylum; extraterritorial jurisdiction; responsibility of international organizations; European Convention on Human Rights.

1. INTRODUCTION

The idea of establishing centres for the "external processing" of asylum claims – already supported by some European Union (EU) Member States, and actually realized in the Caribbean by the United States (US)[1] and in the Pacific

* Researcher and Lecturer, University of Naples "L'Orientale"; Member of the Steering Committee of the Jean Monnet Centre of Excellence on Migrants' Rights in the Mediterranean (http://www.jmcemigrants.eu/team). The author is grateful to the anonymous referees for their helpful suggestions. This article takes into account developments up to 27 May 2016.

[1] US management of migration flows has varied between *refoulement* (endorsed by the Supreme Court in the *Sale* judgment) and pre-screening in the Naval Base of Guantanamo, in Jamaica, and Turks and Caicos, violating human rights for conditions of detention, and giving rise to difficulties in accessing fair procedures and the risk of *refoulement* to unsafe countries. See FLYNN, "There and Back Again: On the Diffusion of Immigration Detention", Journal on Migration and Human Security, 2014, p. 165 ff.; LEGOMSKY, "The USA and the Caribbean

area by Australia[2] – has recently come to the fore again in European debates. Those who support such a proposal think that it could reduce the dramatic death toll in the Mediterranean (a death toll which has increased since the transition from *Mare Nostrum* to *Triton*);[3] moreover, they argue that it would contribute to lasting solutions for those refugees who are not able to leave their own region and help to put an end to smuggling at its very source. On the other hand, several concerns have been raised about this idea[4] since some States tend to consider offshore cen-

---

Interdiction Program", International Journal of Refugee Law, 2006, p. 680 ff.; and KOH, "The 'Haiti Paradigm' in United States Human Rights Policy", Yale Law Journal, 1994, p. 2391 ff. On the *Sale* judgment see in particular GOODWIN-GILL, "YLS Sale Symposium: The Globalization of High Seas Interdiction. Sale's Legacy and Beyond", 16 March 2014, available at: <http://opiniojuris.org/2014/03/16/yale-sale-symposium-globalization-high-seas-interdiction-sales-legacy-beyond>.

[2] Australia has experimented with extraterritorial processing twice, from 2001 to 2008 and again from 2012 onward, outsourcing to Nauru and Papua New Guinea the examination of the asylum claims of individuals, intercepting them before they reach Australia or sending them to offshore centres after initial identity and health screening in Australia. See, *ex multis*, KNEEBONE, "The Pacific Plan: The Provision of 'Effective Protection'", International Journal of Refugee Law, 2006, p. 696 ff. For an analysis of human rights' violations (arbitrary or inhuman detention, risk of *refoulement* to unsafe countries, lack of access to effective remedies etc.), see *infra* section 4 and, in particular, the reports quoted *infra* at note 65. On the influence of the Australian practice on Europe see in particular MCADAM, "Migrating Laws? The 'Plagiaristic Dialogue' between Europe and Australia", in LAMBERT, MCADAM and FULLERTON (eds.), *The Global Reach of European Refugee Law*, Cambridge, 2013, p. 25 ff.

[3] On 18 October 2013, the *Mare Nostrum* operation was launched by the Italian Navy, following a very high number of deaths in the Mediterranean (over 300 people died). In one year of activity, more than 150,000 people were rescued. Nevertheless, on 31 October 2014 the *Mare Nostrum* operation came to an end because it was very costly for the Italian Government (and the EU provided no financial support). In addition, the operation had received harsh criticism, both at home and abroad. For instance, an Italian politician called it a "taxi service", while a British politician accused it of becoming "a pull factor" for immigration into Europe. On 1 November 2014, operation *Triton* was launched, under the umbrella of the EU Agency Frontex, with a much lower operational cost and a much more limited geographical scope (no further than 30 nautical miles from Italy's coastlines). See CARRERA and DEN HERTOG, "Whose Mare? Rule of Law Challenges in the Field of European Border Surveillance in the Mediterranean", CEPS Paper, January 2015, available at: <https://www.ceps.eu/publications/whose-mare-rule-law-challenges-field-european-border-surveillance-mediterranean>. Only as a consequence of another very serious death toll in April 2015, was it finally decided to "expand both the capability and the geographical scope" of the operation. See European Commission, European Agenda on Migration, COM (2015) 240 final, p. 4.

[4] See MCADAM, "Policy Brief 1. Extraterritorial Processing in Europe: Is 'Regional Protection' the Answer, and If Not, What Is?", April 2015, p. 2, available at: <http://www.kaldorcentre.unsw.edu.au/publication/policy-brief-1-extraterritorial-processing-europe-regional-protection-answer-and-if-not>. See also GUILD, COSTELLO, GARLICK and MORENO-LAX, "Enhancing the Common European Asylum System and Alternatives to Dublin", CEPS Paper, September 2015, available at: <https://www.ceps.eu/publications/enhancing-common-european-asylum-system-and-alternatives-dublin>, which concludes that the "idea of establishing EU asy-

tres as "rights-free zones"[5] where it is not clear whether domestic or international legal obligations apply and human rights violations are extremely likely,[6] as the US and Australian experiences demonstrate.[7] As observed, "the Australian and US governments put in place asylum procedures at their Extraterritorial Processing Centres that were of a lower standard than those offered within Australia and the US respectively", thus leading, *inter alia*, "to an increased risk of *refoulement* by denying due process and access to tribunals and courts that scrutinize asylum decision-making".[8] Finally – and in the opinion of the author a crucial issue – it is not clear where responsibility lies in the event of a violation of human rights or what remedies would be available for individuals.

On 29 November 2015, the EU and Turkey signed a Joint Action Plan for Ankara to stem the influx of migrants into Europe.[9] As we shall see in the following section, the proposal of the EU Commission for a "voluntary humanitarian admission scheme with Turkey", launched in a Recommendation of 15 December 2015[10] as part of this Joint Action Plan, should be monitored with particular attention. Indeed, the proposed scheme – "a hybrid between a normal resettlement plan (managed by the UNHCR) and a full-fledged offshore processing programme"[11] – is ambiguous on many crucial issues, such as the applicable law and the exact role of the various actors involved: the State hosting the centre ("the host State"), the EU Member States that will participate on a voluntary basis, the European Asylum Support Office (EASO), and the UN High Commissioner for Refugees (UNHCR). However, since the EU-Turkey Statement of 18 March 2016, which will be analyzed in the next section, the activation of this scheme has been indefinitely postponed and, through the notion of "safe third country",[12] a form of externalization

---

lum reception centres outside the EU is unrealistic, unworkable and highly questionable from a human rights perspective" (p. 29).

[5] See DEN HEIJER, *Europe and Extraterritorial Asylum*, Oxford, 2012, p. 274; and NOLL, "Visions of the Exceptional: Legal and Theoretical Issues Raised by Transit Processing Centres and Protection Zones", European Journal of Migration and Law, 2003, p. 338 ff.

[6] On the possible violations of human rights see NOLL, *cit supra* note 5; and FRANCIS, "Bringing Protection Home: Healing the Schism Between International Obligations and National Safeguards Created by Extraterritorial Processing", International Journal of Refugee Law, 2008, p. 273 ff.

[7] For an analysis of US practice in the Caribbean see *supra* note 1. For Australia, see *supra* note 2 and *infra* para. 4.

[8] See FRANCIS, *cit. supra* note 6, pp. 292 and 298.

[9] In return the EU is to provide money, visa facilitation measures and help with the EU accession process.

[10] C (2015) 9490.

[11] See MORENO-LAX, "Europe in Crisis: Facilitating Access to Protection, (Discarding) Offshore Processing and Mapping Alternatives for the Way Forward", December 2015, p. 20, available at: <http://www.migrantsrights.org.uk/files/news/Europe_in_Crisis_Dr_Moreno-Lax_final.pdf>.

[12] See the following section. The notion of *safe country* can be defined as "a procedural mechanism for shuttling asylum seekers to other States said to have primary responsibility for them, thereby avoiding the necessity to make a decision on the merits because another coun-

of asylum processing has been put into place in Turkey. Moreover, a number of EU Member States[13] have proposed agreements with some African countries similar to that concluded with Turkey. The European Commission has announced that it will issue a communication on these matters[14] in June 2016.

After a brief history of the proposals launched at European level,[15] this contribution will analyse in particular – among the multiple legal issues involved in the establishment of offshore centres – which of the various actors involved would be responsible, and to what extent, in the event of violations of asylum seekers' human rights. In fact, the scenario that could be envisaged is extremely complex. Disentangling the web of action/attribution/responsibility is very difficult and the risk of "blame shifting" or "passing the buck" among the various actors is high. Finally, the possibility of the extraterritorial application of the European Convention on Human Rights (ECHR) will also be explored, in order to assess the extent to which individual victims would have access to a remedy before the European Court of Human Rights (ECtHR).

2.   THE EUROPEAN DEBATE ABOUT EXTRATERRITORIAL PROCESSING

One of the first countries to suggest establishing offshore processing centres was Denmark, which in 1986 prepared a draft resolution[16] for the UN General

---

try is deemed or imagined to be secure": see GOODWIN-GILL AND MCADAM, *The Refugee In International Law,* Oxford, 2010, p. 392. For a critical analysis of this notion, see KNEEBONE, "The Legal and Ethical Implications of Extra-territorial Processing of Asylum Seekers: The Safe Third Country Concept", in MCADAM (ed.), *Moving on: Forced Migration, Human Rights and Security,* Oxford, 2008; and MORENO-LAX, "The Legality of the 'Safe Third Country' Notion Contested: Insights from the Law of Treaties", in GOODWIN-GILL AND WECKEL (eds.), *Migration & Refugee Protection in the 21st Century: Legal Aspects,* Leiden, 2015, p. 665 ff.

[13] See Italy's "Migration Compact" proposal of 15 April 2016 (available at: <http://www. governo.it/sites/governo.it/files/immigrazione_0.pdf>), which provides, *inter alia*, for a system of reception and management of migratory flows in third countries "which should foresee careful on-site screening of refugees and economic migrants, coupled with resettlement measures to Europe for those in need of international protection and returns for irregular migrants".

[14] See the Note from Presidency to Strategic Committee on Immigration, Frontiers and Asylum: Central Mediterranean Route, No 8624/16 of 3 May 2016, para. 1, p. 1, available at: <http://www.statewatch.org/news/2016/may/eu-council-central-mediterranean-route-8624-16. pdf>. The Note, at pp. 1 and 2, makes explicit references to Italy's "Migration Compact" proposal, *cit. supra* note 13.

[15] For non-European cases of offshore processing see, with reference to the Comprehensive Plan of Action for Indochinese Refugees (1988/1996), the observations of GOODWIN-GILL, "Refugees and Migrants at Sea: Duties of Care and Protection in the Mediterranean and the Need for International Action", available at: <http://www.jmcemigrants.eu/category/working-papers>.

[16] UNGA, International Procedures for the Protection of Refugees (draft resolution), UN Doc A/C.3/41/L.51, 12 November 1986.

Assembly, recommending the institution of centres administered by the UN. However, this draft resolution did not receive the necessary support. Later on it was the turn of the Netherlands, which proposed the setting up of processing centres managed by a coalition of different actors.

In 2003, the Government of the United Kingdom (UK) launched its "New Vision for Refugees", proposing "Regional Protection Zones" and "Transit Processing Centres" (where asylum seekers arriving in participating Member States would be transferred) and pursuing an explicit aim of deterrence.[17] The proposal of establishing centres outside EU territory, which would be managed by the International Organization for Migration (IOM) and financed by participating Member States, received the support of the Netherlands, Denmark (already favourable to this kind of proposal), Spain, and Italy, but was strongly opposed by Sweden, Germany,[18] and France, partly because it was not clear who would be responsible for the protection in such centres.

The UNHCR, on the other hand, opposed to the idea of setting up "Transit Processing Centres" outside the EU, and launched a counter-initiative,[19] including, *inter alia*, the establishment of closed processing centres within the EU, so that "[u]pon arrival anywhere within the territory of EU Member States or at their borders, all asylum seekers from designated countries of origin would be transferred to these centres immediately", with the exception of persons unable to travel or stay in closed reception centres for medical reasons, as well as unaccompanied and separated children; the people to be transferred to such centres were therefore to be "populations who consist primarily of economic migrants, that is, persons from specific countries of origin whose asylum applications are likely to be manifestly unfounded". In December 2003 this proposal was modified, the UNHCR suggesting the setting up of "a comprehensive EU system", including EU reception cen-

---

[17] See "New International Approaches to Asylum and Protection", 10 March 2003, p. 5, available at: <http://www.statewatch.org/news/2003/apr/blair-simitis-asile.pdf>.

[18] After the Cap Anamur episode (see on this point GARLICK, "The EU Discussions on Extraterritorial Processing: Solution or Conundrum?", International Journal of Refugee Law, 2006, pp. 615-616), Germany changed its position. The German Interior Minister, Otto Schily, suggested joint interception at sea and pushbacks to extraterritorial processing centres in North Africa. See "Effective Protection for Refugees, Effective Measures against Illegal Migration", available at: <http://www.proasyl.de/fileadmin/proasyl/fm_redakteure/Archiv/presseerl/Schily_ueberlegungen.pdf>.

[19] See UNHCR, Three-Pronged Proposal, June 2003, available at: <http://www.ref-world.org/docid/3efc4b834.html>. On the Convention Plus initiative see <http://www.un-hcr.org/pages/4a2792106.html>. For a critical assessment of the UNHCR position see BETTS, "The International Relations of the 'New' Extraterritorial Approaches to Refugee Protection: Explaining the Policy Initiatives of the UK Government and UNHCR", Refuge, 2004, p. 58 ff., available at: <http://refuge.journals.yorku.ca/index.php/refuge/article/view/21318>.

tres, an EU Asylum Agency, and an EU Asylum Review Board for Appeals – and, remarkably, reception centres would no longer be closed.[20]

What was the response of the EU? In 2003, the EU Commission issued a Communication "Towards More Accessible, Equitable and Managed Asylum Systems",[21] without supporting either the UK or the UNHCR proposals, but instead inviting Member States to consider the introduction of "Protected Entry Procedures".[22] The Commission was then urged, in the Hague Programme, to prepare two studies, one to "look into the merits, appropriateness and feasibility of joint processing of asylum applications outside the EU territory, in complementarity with the [Common European Asylum System] and in compliance with the relevant international standards", and another "on the appropriateness, the possibilities and the difficulties, as well as the legal and practical implications of joint processing of asylum applications within the Union". At the time of writing, only the second study has been completed (in February 2013).[23]

In 2009, the Stockholm Programme, "in rather cryptic terms",[24] urged "the Commission to explore [...] new approaches concerning access to asylum procedures targeting main transit countries, such as protection programmes for particular groups or certain procedures for examination of applications for asylum, in

---

[20] Recently, however, the UNHCR seems to have assumed a different position. In fact, it has cautiously affirmed that "[u]nder certain circumstances, such processing could be envisaged through a multilateral cooperative arrangement". See the UNHCR, UNHCR Proposals to Address Current and Future Arrivals of Asylum-Seekers, Refugees and Migrants by Sea to Europe, March 2015, available at: <http://www.refworld.org/pdfid/55016ba14.pdf>, in which the UNHCR reports having "been informally approached by a number of EU Member States inquiring as to whether it would be ready to participate in arrangements that may be set up in some transit and first asylum countries in Africa and the Middle East to assess the claims of third country nationals for international protection *in situ*" (p. 5). The UNHCR has also stated that, when asylum claims are examined in extraterritorial processing centres, "[r]esponsibility for the identification and implementation of solutions for those in need of international protection and resolution for others would remain with all States involved in the regional processing arrangement". See UNHCR, Protection Policy Paper. Maritime Interception Operations and the Processing of International Protection Claims: Legal Standards and Policy Considerations with respect to Extraterritorial Processing, November 2010, available at: <http://www.refworld.org/docid/4cd12d3a2.html>. The UNHCR is indeed ready to cooperate in the "voluntary humanitarian admission scheme with Turkey", provided for in the Recommendation of the European Commission of 15 December 2015 (*cit. supra* note 10).

[21] COM (2003) 315 final.

[22] NOLL, *cit. supra* note 4, p. 308.

[23] See URTH et al, "Study on the feasibility and legal and practical implications of establishing a mechanism for the joint processing of asylum applications on the territory of the EU", HOME/2011/ERFX/FW/04, February 2013, available at: <http://ec.europa.eu/dgs/home-affairs/e-library/documents/policies/asylum/common-procedures/docs/jp_final_report_final >.

[24] See MORENO-LAX, "External Dimension", in PEERS, MORENO-LAX, GARLICK and GUILD (eds.), *EU Immigration and Asylum Law (Text and Commentary)*, 2nd ed., Leiden/Boston, 2015, p. 653.

which Member States could participate on a voluntary basis".[25] In the same period, while Italy's policy of pushing migrants and asylum seekers back to Libya was at its height,[26] the former Justice and Home Affairs (JHA) Commissioner, Jacques Barrot, launched[27] the proposal that Libya should open *points d'accueil* for asylum seekers in its territory. This was notwithstanding several reports from international organizations (IOs) and NGOs, which showed the risk of violations of human rights in Libya[28] (as the ECtHR recognised in the judgment *Hirsi v. Italy*).[29] In

---

[25] The Stockholm Programme, p. 73.

[26] In accordance with bilateral agreements concluded between Italy and Libya in the years 2007-2009, including the Treaty on Friendship, Partnership and Cooperation signed in August 2008. For further details see ECtHR, *Hirsi Jamaa and Others v. Italy*, Application No. 27765/09, Judgment of 23 February 2012, paras. 19-20.

[27] See at: <http://www.migreurop.org/article1470.html?lang=fr>.

[28] As early as 2009 and even before, several governmental and non-governmental bodies reported the inhuman conditions of the Libyan detention centres and the risk of human rights' violations. See Human Rights Watch, "Stemming the Flow: Abuses against Migrants, Asylum Seekers and Refugees", September 2006; UN Human Rights Committee, Concluding Observations: Libyan Arab Jamahiriya, 15 November 2007; Amnesty International Report 2008 - Libya, 28 May 2008; Human Rights Watch, "Libya Rights at Risk", 2 September 2008; UNHCR Press release, "UNHCR Deeply Concerned Over Returns from Italy to Libya", 7 May 2009; Letter of 15 July 2009 from Jacques Barrot, Vice-President of the European Commission, to Lopez Aguilar, President of the European Parliament Committee on Civil Liberties, Justice and Home Affairs, Brussels; Report by Thomas Hammarberg, Commissioner for Human Rights of the Council of Europe, following his visit to Italy on 13-15 January 2009, CommDH (2009)16, Strasbourg, 16 Apr 2009. For further reports on the respect of human rights in Libya see United States Department of State, "2010 Human Rights Report: Libya", 4 April 2010; and Report of the Council of Europe's Committee for the Prevention of Torture and Inhuman or Degrading Treatment or Punishment (CPT) of 28 April 2010.

[29] The *Hirsi* judgment (*cit. supra* note 26) concerned the interception at sea and push back to Libya of 11 Somalians and 13 Eritreans by the Italian authorities in May 2009. With this judgment the ECtHR condemned Italy for the violation of Art. 3 ECHR (prohibition of torture and inhuman and degrading treatment), Art. 4 of Protocol No. 4 (prohibition of collective expulsions), and Art. 13 (right to an effective remedy) taken in conjunction with Arts. 3 and 4 of Protocol No. 4. On the *Hirsi* judgment see DEN HEIJER, "Reflections on *Refoulement* and Collective Expulsion in the Hirsi Case", International Journal of Refugee Law, 2013, p. 265 ff.; GIUFFRÉ, "Watered-Down Rights on the High Seas: Hirsi Jamaa and Others v. Italy", ICLQ, 2012, p. 728 ff.; LIGUORI, "La Corte europea dei diritti dell'uomo condanna l'Italia per i respingimenti verso la Libia del 2009: il caso *Hirsi*", RDI, 2012, p. 415 ff.; MESSINEO, "Yet Another *Mala Figura*: Italy Breached *Non-Refoulement* Obligations by Intercepting Migrants' Boats at Sea, Says ECtHR", available at: <http://www.ejiltalk.org/yet-another-mala-figura-italy-breached-non-refoulement-obligations-by-intercepting-migrants-boats-at-sea-says-ecthr>; MORENO-LAX, "*Hirsi v. Italy* or the Strasbourg Court v. Extraterritorial Migration Control?", Human Rights Law Review, 2012, p. 574 ff.; NAPOLETANO, "La condanna dei 'respingimenti' operati dall'Italia verso la Libia da parte della Corte europea dei diritti umani: molte luci e qualche ombra", DUDI, 2012, p. 436 ff.; RYAN, "Hirsi: Upholding the Human Rights of Migrants at Sea", available at: <www.kent.ac.uk>; and TONDINI, "The Legality of Intercepting Boat People Under Search and Rescue and Border Control Operations with Reference to Recent Italian Interventions in the Mediterranean Sea and the ECtHR Decision in the Hirsi Case", Journal of International Maritime Law, 2012, p. 59 ff.

the same year, the French delegates proposed a "partnership with migrants' countries of origin and of transit" with the aim of "finding innovative solutions for access to asylum procedures".[30] The plan suggested "joint maritime operations at the EU's external borders"[31] and that people intercepted would be taken to Libya for processing,[32] with the cooperation of the UNHCR and the IOM (and the financial aid of the EU). The plan received not only the support of the Italian Government, as one could expect in the light of the Italian push-back campaign, but also of the European Council[33] and of the JHA Council.[34] Only the outbreak of the civil war in Libya put a stop to this initiative.

In 2014, the idea of establishing offshore centres resurfaced in the EU Commission's Communication "An Open and Secure Europe: Making It Happen"[35] and some EU Member States re-proposed the idea of establishing refugee centres in Libya.[36]

An explicit reference to the setting up of offshore centres appears also in the Khartoum process, launched on 28 November 2014. This gathered Ministers of the 28 EU countries, plus Eritrea, Ethiopia, Somalia, South Sudan, Sudan, Djibouti, Kenya, Egypt, and Tunisia, the European and African Union Commissioners in charge of migration and development, and the EU High Representative. They agreed, among other things, to, "[w]here appropriate, on a voluntary basis and upon individual request of a country in the region, assisting the participating countries in establishing and managing reception centres, providing access to asylum processes in line with the international law, if needed, improving camp services and security, screening mixed migratory flows and counselling migrants". [37]

---

[30] Council of the European Union, Migration Situation in the Mediterranean: Establishing a Partnership with Migrants' Countries of Origin and of Transit, Enhancing Member States' Joint Maritime Operations and Finding Innovative Solutions for Access to Asylum Procedures, Doc. 13205/09, 11 September 2009.

[31] *Ibid.*, p. 4.

[32] The plan also suggested, as an alternative, the presenting of applications at Member States' embassies.

[33] See Council of the European Union, Presidency Conclusions, European Council 29-30 October 2009, Doc. 15265/09, 30 October 2009, para. 40.

[34] See Council of the European Union, 29 Measures for Reinforcing the Protection of the External Borders and Combating Illegal Immigration, Conclusions, JHA Council, Brussels 25-26 February 2010.

[35] COM (2014) 154 final.

[36] "Italian Premier Renzi Calls for UN Refugee Camps in Libya", ANSAMed News, 20 May 2014, available at: <http://www.ansamed.info/ansamed/en/news/nations/italy/2014/05/20/italian-premier-renzi-calls-for-un-refugee-camps-in-libya_49bd97fb-61c7-4e9a-8d03-beb9124b02b3.html>.

[37] See Declaration of the Ministerial Conference of the Khartoum Process, p. 4, available at <http://www.esteri.it/mae/approfondimenti/2014/20141128_political_declaration.pdf>.

After the deaths of 18 April 2015, the idea gained new momentum.[38] However, in the documents adopted as a consequence of the new crisis,[39] there is only a reference to the necessity of enhancing cooperation with the countries of origin and transit of migration flows. In particular in the EU Commission Agenda for Migration,[40] launched by the Commission on 13 May 2015, the suggestion of putting "in place concrete measures to process migrants before they reach the EU's borders", provided for in a leaked draft of the Commission communication,[41] was substituted for the more vague proposal of putting "in place concrete measures to prevent hazardous journeys". The Agenda also proposes setting up, by the end of the year, a *pilot multi-purpose centre* in Niger, which, "working with the International Organization for Migration (IOM), the UNHCR and the Niger authorities [...], will combine the provision of information, local protection and resettlement opportunities for those in need". Even if "it is unclear precisely what its function would be",[42] it "could imply the extraterritorial assessment of asylum and other protection claims", as the European Parliament Research Centre suggests.[43] It certainly cannot be excluded that – in a more or less transparent way – it might become an intermediate step towards the establishment of transit processing centres.

The Action Plan agreed by the EU and African leaders present at the 2015 Valletta Summit on Migration[44] also made no explicit reference to EU extrater-

---

[38] See McADAM (*cit. supra* note 4), which reports the Australian media questioning whether "the Pacific Solution" could be the solution for the Mediterranean as well. See Wroe, "Refugee Crisis: Europe Looks to Australia for Answers", Sydney Morning Herald, 24 April 2015, available at: <http://www.smh.com.au/national/refugee-crisis-europe-looks-to-australia-for-answers-20150424-1ms804.html>; "Australia's Refugee Policy: Should Europe Emulate It?", DW, 22 April 2015 <http://www.dw.de/australias-refugee-policy-should-europe-emulate-it/a-18399274>; and Pearlman, "How Australia's Migrant Policy Works – And Is It Transferable to the Mediterranean?", The Telegraph, 22 April 2015, available at: <http://www.telegraph.co.uk/news/worldnews/australiaandthepacific/australia/11554161/How-Australias-migrant-policy-works-and-is-it-transferable-to-the-Mediterranean.html>.

[39] See EU Commission, Joint Foreign and Home Affairs Council: Ten Point Action Plan on Migration, 20 April 2015, available at: <http://europa.eu/rapid/press-release_IP-15-4813_en.htm>; European Council, Special Meeting of the European Council, 23 April 2015, available at: <http://www.consilium.europa.eu/en/press/press-releases/2015/04/23-special-euco-statement>; European Parliament, Resolution of April 2015 on the Latest Tragedies in the Mediterranean and EU Migration and Asylum Policies (2015/2660(RSP)), available at: <http://www.europarl.europa.eu/sides/getDoc.do?pubRef=-//EP//TEXT+TA+P8-TA-2015-0176+0+DOC+XML+V0//EN>.

[40] COM (2015) 240 final.

[41] Available at: <http://eulawanalysis.blogspot.it/2015/05/commission-strategy-on-eu-immigration.html>.

[42] See McADAM, *cit. supra* note 4, p. 16. According to this author, it is "something very different from an extraterritorial processing centre for the EU".

[43] See at: <http://epthinktank.eu/2015/06/10/extraterritorial-processing-of-asylum-claims>.

[44] Valletta Summit on Migration, 11-12 November 2015, see at: <http://www.consilium.europa.eu/en/meetings/international-summit/2015/11/11-12>.

ritorial processing centres,[45] but it envisaged jointly exploring "the concept of enhanced capacities in priority regions along the main migratory routes, with a view to developing possible *pilot projects*, in cooperation with UNHCR".[46]

As mentioned in the introduction, on 15 December 2015 the EU Commission proposed – as a "flanked measure"[47] of the EU-Turkey Joint Action Plan of 29 November 2015 – establishing "an expedited process whereby the participating States, based on a recommendation of the UNHCR following referral by Turkey, admit persons in need of international protection, displaced by the conflict in Syria". Only asylum seekers registered by the Turkish authorities prior to 29 November 2015 are eligible; once admitted, they should be granted subsidiary protection as defined in Directive 2011/95/EU or an equivalent temporary status. The admission procedure should consist of seven steps: (i) identification; (ii) confirmation of the fact that the person is displaced from Syria and was registered by the Turkish authorities prior to 29 November 2015; (iii) preliminary assessment of the reasons for fleeing from Syria (and, where relevant, assessment of reasons for exclusion from international protection); (iv) security checks; (v) medical checks; (vi) assessment of vulnerability criteria according to UNHCR standards; and (vii) assessment of possible family links in the participating States.

This sort of pre-screening should be "a collaborative effort of the participating States, Turkey, UNHCR and EASO",[48] although the "final decision on the admission of a person should rest with the participating States". In this regard, the Commission added:

> "In order to facilitate the process, the authorities of the participating States should cooperate through *common processing centres* and/or mobile teams, where staff of one participating State is authorised to represent another participating State for the purpose of conducting whole or part of the selection process on behalf of that other State. This could include the assessment of documentation and conducting of interviews, which could take place either at the representation or in the province where the admission candidate is registered".[49]

---

[45] The explicit idea of establishing "centres for potential asylum seekers where, after pre-screening, they could benefit from safe and legal ways to the EU for further asylum procedure or adequate information and assistance for their return to their respective countries of origin in compliance with relevant national legislation, international refugee and human rights law" was provided for in a previous draft of the Action Plan (Doc. 12560/1/15 REV 1, available at: <http://www.statewatch.org/news/2015/oct/eu-council-valletta-WD2-12560-rev-1-15.pdf>).

[46] Action Plan, p. 10 (emphasis added).

[47] See Recommendation of 15 December 2015, *cit. supra* note 10 and related text, p. 2.

[48] *Ibid.*, para. 8, p. 5.

[49] Para. 9, p. 5 (emphasis added).

The Commission does not specify, however, on what basis the participating State might deny admission and what remedies would be at the asylum seekers' disposal. Moreover, the recommendation does not provide for information on crucial aspects, such as the roles of the different actors involved and "common criteria and procedures related to the admission procedure and the status to be granted to the persons admitted", affirming that these aspects should be defined at a later stage.[50] In addition, in Paragraph 15, it provides that "a joint committee consisting of Turkey, the European Union, represented by the Commission, and participating states" should meet at regular intervals to monitor the implementation of the scheme (the UNHCR and IOM should take part "as and when necessary"). As observed, however, monitoring mechanisms "whereby the parties involved in the scheme also judge their own performance, do not meet the requirements of independence and impartiality to be credible".[51] Finally, it is not specified if those "common centres" might work as "reception centres" too, and if detention measures could be adopted.

On 18 March 2016 an agreement was reached between the EU and Turkey,[52] establishing that:

> "All new irregular migrants crossing from Turkey into Greek islands as from 20 March 2016 will be returned to Turkey. [...] Migrants arriving in the Greek islands will be duly registered and any application for asylum will be processed individually by the Greek authorities in accordance with the Asylum Procedures Directive, in cooperation with UNHCR. Migrants not applying for asylum or whose application has been found unfounded or inadmissible in accordance with the said directive will be returned to Turkey. [...] For every Syrian being returned to Turkey from Greek islands, another Syrian will be resettled from Turkey to the EU [...]".

To this end, a mechanism has been established, with the assistance of the Commission, EU agencies and other Member States, as well as the UNHCR: "[T]he system would envisage the initial referral by Turkey to UNHCR of a list of candidates to be resettled and the involvement of UNHCR in identifying the Syrians willing to be resettled, assessing their vulnerability and referring them to the specific Member States",[53] who will make the final decision. In addition, it has been

---

[50] Para. 1.5.2, p. 9.

[51] See MORENO-LAX, *cit. supra* note 11, p. 24.

[52] See EU-Turkey Statement, 18 March 2016, available at: <http://www.consilium.europa.eu/en/press/press-releases/2016/03/18-eu-turkey-statement>.

[53] See the First Report on the progress made in the implementation of the EU-Turkey Statement of 20 April 2016, COM(2016) 231 final, p. 7. The Report adds that "[i]n order to fast-track the implementation of the resettlement leg of the 1:1 scheme, Standard Operating Procedures were

established that the Voluntary Humanitarian Admission Scheme examined above will be activated only "once irregular crossings between Turkey and the EU are ending or at least have been substantially and sustainably reduced".[54]

As observed by the Commission,[55] there are two legal possibilities that can be used to declare asylum applications inadmissible, i.e. considering Turkey: 1) a "first country of asylum", according to Article 35 of the Asylum Procedures Directive[56] (if the persons already enjoyed sufficient protection in Turkey), or 2) a "safe third country", according to Article 38 of the Asylum Procedures Directive.[57]

Several concerns have been raised about this agreement both in literature[58] and by NGOs[59] and international institutions,[60] especially because it is difficult to consider Turkey a "safe third country", "as Turkey does not provide [the asylum seekers] with protection in accordance with the 1951 Convention relating to the Status of Refugees, non-Syrians do not have effective access to the asylum procedure and there have been reports of onward *refoulement* of both Syrians and non-Syrians".[61]

Moreover, since the Mediterranean Sea is re-emerging as the primary route to enter Europe, a number of Member States have proposed the conclusion of similar

---

developed in close cooperation between the Commission, Member States, EASO, UNHCR and Turkey and will be finalized shortly".

[54] See EU-Turkey Statement of 18 March 2016, *cit. supra.*

[55] See the Communication "Next Operational Steps in EU-Turkey cooperation in the field of Migration" of 16 March 2016, COM(2016) 166 final, p. 3.

[56] "Where the person (a) has been recognized in that country as a refugee and he or she can still avail himself/herself of that protection; or (b) he or she otherwise enjoys sufficient protection in that country, including benefiting from the principle of *non-refoulement*".

[57] "Where the person will be treated in accordance with the following principles in the third country concerned: (a) life and liberty are not threatened on account of race, religion, nationality, membership of a particular social group or political opinion; (b) there is no risk of serious harm as defined in Directive 2011/95/EU; (c) the principle of *non-refoulement* in accordance with the Geneva Convention is respected; (d) the prohibition of removal, in violation of the right to freedom from torture and cruel, inhuman or degrading treatment as laid down in international law, is respected; and (e) the possibility exists to request refugee status and, if found to be a refugee, to receive protection in accordance with the Geneva Convention".

[58] See PEERS, "The Final EU/Turkey Refugee Deal: A Legal Assessment", available at: <http://eulawanalysis.blogspot.it/2016/03/the-final-euturkey-refugee-deal-legal.html>; ROMAN, "L'accordo UE-Turchia: le criticità di un accordo a tutti i costi", available at: <http://www.sidiblog.org/2016/03/21/laccordo-ue-turchia-le-criticita-di-un-accordo-a-tutti-i-costi>.

[59] See Amnesty International Report, "Europe's Gatekeeper", 16 December 2015, available at: <https://www.amnesty.org/en/documents/eur44/3022/2015/en>. This report shows that the "European Union is in danger of being complicit in serious human rights violations" because hundreds of refugees and asylum-seekers have been held incommunicado in prolonged detention and in some cases even sent back to Syria and Iraq.

[60] See Resolution 2109 (2016), "The Situation of Refugees and Migrants under the EU-Turkey Agreement of 18 March 2016", adopted by the Parliamentary Assembly of the Council of Europe on 20 April 2016.

[61] *Ibid.*, para. 2.5.

agreements also with some African States (countries of origin or transit of mixed migration flows) and, at the time of writing, the European Commission has announced a Communication on these matters. However, as has been observed, the EU-Turkey Agreement – "highly problematic in itself, as described above – cannot be replicated for other countries even less capable of protecting refugees and migrants".[62] Moreover, while Turkey might be called to respond directly before the ECtHR in cases of asylum seekers' human rights violations, this possibility vis-à-vis potential African partners is excluded, since they are not members of the European Convention on Human Rights.

In any case, it cannot be excluded that in offshore centres violations of human rights could occur (with reference to the principle of *refoulement*, the prohibition of inhuman or degrading treatment, the right to effective remedies, the right to family unity and to the special protection of vulnerable persons). An investigation into the legal responsibility of outsourcing States and IOs therefore appears to be particularly urgent.

3. WHO WOULD BE RESPONSIBLE FOR CONDUCT AFFECTING ASYLUM SEEKERS AND REFUGEES IN OFFSHORE CENTRES?

It is uncontroversial that States have often had recourse to extraterritorial practice in an attempt to deal with asylum claims "outside the law". But, as Professor Goodwin-Gill has observed, "like many measures which a State may take in the grey, apparently unregulated areas of international law, offshore processing is in fact subject to law, and subject to the rule of law".[63] It has also been pointed out that "European proposals to date have left many unanswered questions".[64] One of them is that of responsibility for the centres in cases of violations of asylum seekers' human rights, which, as borne out by Australian practice,[65] are highly probable.

---

[62] See Doc. 14028, 19 April 2016, "The situation of refugees and migrants under the EU-Turkey Agreement of 18 March 2016", Report by T. Strik for the Parliamentary Assembly, Committee on Migration, Refugees and Displaced Persons, para. 33, p. 12.

[63] GOODWIN-GILL, "The Extraterritorial Processing of Claims to Asylum or Protection: The Legal Responsibilities of States and International Organisations", UTS Law Review, 2007, p. 27 ff. See also RIJPMA and CREMONA, "The Extra-Territorialisation of EU Migration Policies and the Rule of Law", EUI Working Papers LAW, 2007.

[64] See MCADAM, *cit. supra* note 4, p. 8.

[65] Report of the Special Rapporteur on Torture and Other Cruel, Inhuman or Degrading Treatment or Punishment, 28th sess., Agenda item 3, UN Doc. A/HRC/28/68/Add.1, 6 March 2015, 7-9; Amnesty International, Report 2014/15, "The State of the World's Human Rights 2015", pp. 63-64; Legal and Constitutional Affairs References Committee, Parliament of Australia, "Incident at the Manus Island Detention Centre from 16 February 2014 to 18 February 2014", 2014, available at: <http://www.aph.gov.au/Parliamentary_Business/Committees/Senate/Legal_and_Constitutional_Affairs/Manus_Island/Report>; Australian Human Rights Commission, "The Forgotten Children: National Inquiry into Children in Immigration Detention

The possible scenarios might in effect involve multiple actors: the EU and/or EU agencies directly involved (such as Frontex and/or EASO), EU Member States, the third State hosting the centre, IOs (such as the UNHCR and IOM), NGOs and/ or private actors possibly concerned with the processing (to whom the EU and/or EU Member States or the territorial State might outsource the processing). In the opinion of this author there might be a shared responsibility[66] between the hosting State, the outsourcing State and/or the IO involved and the IOs which may be co-operating in the processing.

The present contribution aims in particular to identify the possible legal basis for considering the outsourcing State and/or IO responsible in case of human rights breaches, according to the rules on the international responsibility of States, and on the international responsibility of IOs, as codified by the International Law Commission (ILC).[67] Indeed, it must be stressed that offshore processing is at risk of triggering *refoulement*, arbitrary and inhuman detention and a lack of effective remedies, and that both the EU and EU Member States are obliged not to commit these violations (under, e.g., the EU Charter of Fundamental Rights, the ECHR, Geneva Conventions, and the Convention on the Rights of the Child).[68]

3.1. The Legal Responsibility of States

Regarding the responsibility of States, there are multiple legal bases for affirming direct or at least indirect responsibility. According to general international law, a State is directly responsible for the conduct of its organs and agents (the organ or agent exercising elements of government authority acts for the State, even when it exceeds its authority or acts contrary to instructions):[69] this might entail direct responsibility on the part of the State either if it adopts a decision of transfer for those who have already arrived on its territory, or if it intercepts a vessel carrying asylum seekers and diverts it to the State eventually hosting the extraterritorial processing

---

(2014)"; and Moss, "Review into Recent Allegation Relating to Conditions and Circumstances at the Regional Processing Centre in Nauru", 6 February 2015.

[66] By the expression "shared responsibility" we mean "responsibility of multiple actors for their contribution to a single harmful outcome". See NOLLKAEMPER and JACOBS, "Shared Responsibility in International Law: A Conceptual Framework", Michigan Journal of International Law, 2013, p. 359 ff., p. 367 ff.

[67] See, respectively, Draft Articles on Responsibility of States for Internationally Wrongful Acts with Commentaries, 2011 (ASR), and Draft Articles on Responsibility of International Organizations for Internationally Wrongful Acts with Commentaries, 2011 (ARIO).

[68] For a detailed analysis of relevant obligations under International and EU law for the EU and EU Member States in the various possible processing schemes see Advisory Committee on Migration Affairs, "External Processing Conditions Applying to the Processing of Asylum Applications Outside the European Union", The Hague, 2010, p. 26 ff.

[69] See Articles 4-11 of ASR.

centre. This is now uncontested at the European level, following the famous *Hirsi* judgment,[70] in which the ECtHR affirmed that there might be a responsibility not only as a consequence of the violation of the principle of *non-refoulement* (a direct violation, if the conditions in the centres in the host State prove to be inhuman or arbitrary, or indirect, if from that centre there is a risk for the asylum seeker of being sent back to the country of origin) but also of the prohibition of collective expulsion and of the right to an effective remedy (if there is no individual examination of each specific situation, nor the possibility of appealing before an independent body).[71]

The responsibility for the conduct of its organs and agents might entail the responsibility of the outsourcing State also if its agents are directly involved in the processing in the hosting country. In addition, the outsourcing State could be held responsible for the conduct of persons or entities exercising elements of government authority[72] (in the case for instance of outsourcing to private actors) and for the conduct of an organ placed at its disposal by another State[73] (if it is proved that the organ of the territorial State is at the disposal of the outsourcing State). Where the organ of one State acts on the joint instructions of its own and another State (for instance the State hosting the centre), or where a single entity is a joint organ of several States, the conduct in question is attributable to each State (Article 47 ASR).

The outsourcing State can also be indirectly responsible if it aids or assists (Article 16 ASR) or directs and controls (Article 17 ASR) another State in the commission of an internationally wrongful act by the latter, if it does so with knowledge of the circumstances of the internationally wrongful act and the act would be internationally wrongful if committed by that State. While the latter is probably unlikely in practice,[74] the former could be very useful as a legal basis for establish-

---

[70] On this judgment see the literature *cit. supra* note 29.

[71] See MORENO-LAX, *cit. supra* note 24, p. 661 ff. It has been argued, however, that international obligations such as *non-refoulement* do not apply extraterritorially. As has been observed, "the discord is highlighted by the divergent opinions of domestic courts and treaty monitoring bodies": DEN HEIJER, *cit. supra* note 29, p. 265, which recalls the following decisions: US Supreme Court, *Chris Sale, Acting Commissioner, Immigration and Naturalization Service, et al. v. Haitian Centers Council Inc et al.*, 21 June 1993, 509 US 155; Inter-American Commission on Human Rights, *The Haitian Centre for Human Rights et al. v. United States*, 13 March 1997; Federal Court of Australia, *Victorian Council for Civil Liberties Inc. v. Minister for Immigration & Multicultural Affairs (& Summary)* [2001] FCA 1297, 11 September 2001 ("Tampa Decision"); Federal Court of Australia, *Minister for Immigration and Multicultural Affairs & Others v. Vadarlis*, [2001] FCA 1329, 17 September 2001 ("Tampa Appeal"); UN Committee Against Torture (CAT), *JHA v. Spain*, CAT/C/41/D/323/2007, 21 November 2008 (case *Marine I*); *Audiencia Nacional* (Spain), 12 December 2007, No. 3/2007; *Tribunal Supremo* (Spain), 17 February 2010, No. 548/2008 (case *Marine I*).

[72] Art. 5 ASR.

[73] Art. 6 ASR.

[74] The ASR Commentary of Art. 17 (para. 7) says "[i]n the formulation of article 17, the term 'controls' refers to cases of domination over the commission of wrongful conduct and not simply

ing the responsibility of the outsourcing State in those cases where the State does not participate in the processing, but only finances the centres.

3.2. The Legal Responsibility of IOs

When we discuss the legal responsibility of IOs, we think both of the EU (in the case of EU-sponsored processing centres), and also of the IOs which may be directly involved in the processing (for instance the UNHCR and/or the IOM). What might the legal basis for such responsibility be? ARIO, in addressing the issue of the responsibility of IOs, follows the same approach adopted with regard to State responsibility and so provides for direct responsibility of an IO for conduct of their organs or agents and for the conduct of organs of a State placed at its disposal.

The ARIO Commentary also envisages the possibility of *dual attribution* of the same conduct to both a State and an IO. In this respect, Paragraph 4 of the Introduction to Commentary of Chapter II ARIO states:

> "[A]lthough it may not frequently occur in practice, dual or even multiple attribution of conduct cannot be excluded. Thus, attribution of a certain conduct to an international organization does not imply that the same conduct cannot be attributed to a State; nor does attribution of conduct to a State rule out attribution of the same conduct to an international organization".[75]

Finally, ARIO envisages the responsibility (without attribution) of an IO in connection with the acts of a State or of another organization (which would cover, among other things, those cases in which an IO aids or assists and directs and controls a State or another organization), and of responsibility of a State in connection with the conduct of an IO, which covers, among other things, the cases in which a State aids or assists and directs and controls an IO.

---

the exercise of oversight, still less mere influence or concern".

[75] The European Court has implicitly acknowledged the possibility of dual attribution: see *Al-Jedda v. United Kingdom*, Application No. 27021/08, Judgment of 7 July 2011, para. 80. On this point see MILANOVIC, "*Al-Skeini* and *Al-Jedda* in Strasbourg", EJIL, 2012, p. 134 ff.; PAPA, "Le autorizzazioni del Consiglio di sicurezza davanti alla Corte europea dei diritti umani: dalla decisione sui casi *Behrami e Saramati* alla sentenza *Al-Jedda*", DUDI, 2012, p. 229 ff.; LIGUORI, "*Shared responsibility* nel corso di *peacekeeping operations* delle Nazioni Unite: quale ruolo per la Corte europea dei diritti umani?", RDI, 2015, p. 517 ff. The admissibility of *dual attribution* has been affirmed also in some domestic judgments delivered by Dutch courts with respect to the massacre in Srebrenica: Supreme Court (Hoge Raad), *State of the Netherlands v. Mustafić et al.*, *State of the Netherlands v. Nuhanović* (Judgments of 6 September 2013), and District Court, *Mothers of Srebrenica v. State of the Netherlands* (Judgment of 16 July 2014).

In this author's opinion the last rule could be useful particularly in the case of the involvement of Frontex in intercepting and diverting boats. The question of the allocation of responsibility among Member States and Frontex in cases of violations of human rights during joint operations at sea is a particularly complex one.[76] Despite the fourth recital of Frontex Regulation which says that the "responsibility for the control and surveillance of external borders lies with the Member States", it is the author's opinion that Frontex also bears responsibility – and therefore also the EU[77] – at least for aiding and abetting.[78]

Most interestingly, ARIO also provide for the possibility of responsibility if the IO circumvents an international obligation through decisions and authorizations addressed to member States or IOs.[79] As was noted by the Austrian delegate during the preparatory works of ARIO,[80] "an international organization should not be allowed to escape responsibility by 'outsourcing' its actors". One may wonder if this rule could be a valid basis for preventing the EU from escaping its obligations, for instance, by authorizing an IO (such as the UNHCR) to process the asylum claims in a third country. In parallel, Article 61 ARIO provides for the possibility of a responsibility of the State that, by taking advantage of the fact that the organization has competence in relation to the subject-matter of one of the State's international obligations, circumvents that obligation by causing the organization to commit an act that, if committed by the State, would have constituted a breach of the obligation. This might imply that no State may circumvent its own obligations, for instance, by contracting out to an IO (the UNHCR or IOM) the screening, the determination of status and/or the reception of asylum seekers. Of course, in this case, the responsibility of the Member States of the IO would add to the responsibility attaching directly to the organization as a subject of international law.[81]

---

[76] As has been observed, "[i]f two states contribute to joint Frontex missions to control the external borders of the EU, and the rights of persons seeking asylum are violated, the question will arise whether the EU, and/or one or both of the states involved are responsible and, if so, how responsibility is distributed among them". See NOLLKAEMPER and JACOBS, *cit. supra* note 66.

[77] Accepting as a premise that Frontex involves the responsibility of the EU, based on the thesis which does not recognize a separate and independent international personality of EU agencies. On this point see FINK, "Frontex Working Arrangements: Legitimacy and Human Rights Concerns Regarding 'Technical Relationships'", Utrecht Journal of International and European Law, 2012, p. 26 ff. For the opposite thesis see SCHUSTERSCHITZ, "European Agencies as Subjects of International Law", International Organizations Law Review, 2004, p. 169.

[78] On this point see LIGUORI and RICCIUTI, "Frontex ed il rispetto dei diritti umani nelle operazioni congiunte alle frontiere esterne dell'Unione Europea", DUDI, 2012, p. 554 ff., at 556.

[79] Article 17. It is, however, doubtful whether this provision reflects customary law. On this point see NEDESKI and NOLLKAEMPER, "Responsibility of International Organizations 'in Connection with Acts of States'", International Organizations Law Review, 2012, p. 33 ff.

[80] ARIO Commentary, Art. 17, para. 1.

[81] With reference to offshore centres managed directly by the EU or an EU Agency, in order to establish the responsibility not only of the EU, but also of the EU Member States, see the re-

This brief outline shows that a shared responsibility – between the territorial State and the EU and/or the Member States and the IOs which may be involved in the processing – is highly probable (direct responsibility for some of the actors, indirect for others, according to the circumstances), whatever form potential cooperation agreement(s) between the EU and the Third State may take.

The advantages of envisaging shared responsibility are that this limits the risk of "blame shifting" or "passing the buck" among the various actors and that it might multiply the possibilities of recourse available to victims and therefore better facilitate the realization of the right to a remedy.[82]

4. REMEDIES – THE ACHILLES' HEEL

In this last section of the article it shall be analysed whether claims could be brought against the outsourcing States before international human rights bodies, and in particular before the ECtHR, in the light of the effectiveness of this kind of recourse (thanks, among other things, to the jurisprudence of the Strasbourg Court, which has been able in various cases to adopt a creative approach in responding to the new challenges in asylum and migration issues)[83] and to the binding nature of the decisions delivered by this court.

A State that is party to a human rights treaty is bound to respect and uphold the rights contained in that treaty only for persons within its "jurisdiction".[84] Traditionally a State's jurisdiction, for the purposes of its human rights obligations, was assumed to be limited mainly, if not exclusively, to its territory. As international human rights law has evolved, it is now accepted that a State's jurisdiction for human rights purposes can extend to persons outside its territorial limits, whenever the State has a certain degree of "power, authority or 'effective control'" over them, or over the territory in which they are located.

---

port "External Processing Conditions Applying to the Processing of Asylum Applications", *cit. supra* note 68, pp. 24-26.

[82] See, *mutatis mutandis*, DANNENBAUM, "Translating the Standard of Effective Control into a System of Effective Accountability: How Liability Should Be Apportioned for Violations of Human Rights by Member State Troop Contingents Serving as United Nations Peacekeepers", Harvard ILJ, 2010, p. 170 ff. (with reference to another hypothesis considered in literature as "shared responsibility").

[83] See, in particular, *M.S.S. v. Belgium and Greece* (regarding Dublin transfers), and *Hirsi v. Italy* (on interception in high seas). See also COSTELLO, "Courting Access to Asylum in Europe: Recent Supranational Jurisprudence Explored", Human Rights Law Review, 2012, p. 287 ff.

[84] Among the human rights treaties which specify that the obligations they contain extend to the protection of persons within the State's jurisdiction see the International Covenant on Civil and Political Rights, Art. 2(1); the Convention Against Torture, Art. 2(1); the Convention on the Rights of the Child, Art. 2(1); and the ECHR, Art. 1.

In order to give a concrete example of the questions at issue, the case of Australia will be briefly discussed (although the scenario in the case of EU off-shore processing centres would likely be more complex).[85] Australia experimented with extraterritorial processing during two time periods, from 2001 to 2008 and again from 2012 onward, by outsourcing to Nauru and Papua New Guinea the ex-amination of asylum claims of individuals, intercepting them before they reached Australia or sending them to offshore centres after initial identity and health screen-ing in Australia. Did Australia acknowledge its jurisdiction? In most public inter-views, Australian Government representatives denied any responsibility, affirming that "[the] regional processing centres are a matter for the Nauru and Papua New Guinea governments as these centres are located in their sovereign territory",[86] and arguing that Australia "does not have the 'very high level' of effective control nec-essary to establish its jurisdiction over asylum seekers and refugees offshore".[87] A very interesting reply on this point was given by the Committee against Torture (CAT) in its Concluding Observations on the fourth and fifth periodic reports of Australia, adopted on 26 November 2014, which stated that:

> "The Committee is concerned at the State party's policy of trans-ferring asylum seekers to the regional processing centres located in Papua New Guinea (Manus Island) and Nauru for the processing of their claims, despite reports on the harsh conditions prevailing in these centres, including mandatory detention, also for children; overcrowding, inadequate health care; and even allegations of sexual abuse and ill-treatment. The combination of these harsh conditions, the protracted periods of closed detention and the uncertainty about the future reportedly creates serious physical and mental pain and suffering. All persons who are under the *effective control* of the State party, because inter alia they were transferred by the State party to centres run with its financial aid and with the involvement of private contractors of its choice, enjoy the same protection from torture and ill-treatment under the Convention (arts. 2, 3, 16)".[88]

In other words, according to the CAT, Australian jurisdiction was triggered in those centres. However, it is not clear, whether, according to the CAT, this may hap-pen only in the presence of the three criteria enumerated – having transferred the

---

[85] Because in this case the responsibility of the EU and/or EU Member States would also be at stake (see *supra* para. 3.2).

[86] See GLEESON, "Factsheet: Offshore Processing and Australia's Responsibility for Asylum Seekers and Refugees in Nauru and Papua New Guinea", April 2015, p. 8, which reports various interviews and statements delivered by Australian Government representatives.

[87] *Ibid.*

[88] Para. 17 (emphasis added).

asylum seekers there, chosen the private contractor and financed the centres – or whether jurisdiction may be established also in the presence of just one of them. The CAT concluded by urging Australia

> "to adopt the necessary measures to guarantee that all asylum seekers or persons in need of international protection who are under its effective control are afforded the same standards of protection against violations of the Convention regardless of their mode and/or date of arrival. The transfers to the regional processing centres in Papua New Guinea (Manus Island) and Nauru, [...] does not relieve the State party from its obligations under the Convention".[89]

Further confirmation of Australia's jurisdiction in offshore centres came in December 2014, when an Australian Senate Committee inquiry[90] concerning a riot in the Manus Island detention centre in February 2014, expressly acknowledged that Australia was at that time, and still is, exercising *effective control* over the Manus Island centre and over the individuals held there and that "the degree of involvement by the Australian Government in the establishment, use, operation, and provision of total funding for the centre clearly satisfies the test of effective control in international law". The Australian Committee founded its conclusions on evidence provided by experts in international human rights law, in particular on the following elements:

> "[T]he only reason asylum seekers are in detention and at risk of human rights violations in Nauru or PNG is because Australia forcibly sent them there; certain decisions made by Australian authorities have created or exacerbated the risks of harm in offshore detention centres, for example the decision to start sending asylum seekers to Nauru and PNG before construction of the centres was complete, or in such numbers as to cause overcrowding; Australian authorities exercise a considerable degree of control and enjoy substantial decision-making

---

[89] See also the *Marine I* case (*cit. supra* note 71), concerning the recovery of 369 migrants of Asian and African origin by the Spanish authorities off the coast of Mauritania, within the framework of an agreement between Spain and Mauritania. The CAT Committee affirmed that the applicants were subject to Spanish jurisdiction "from the time the vessel was rescued and throughout the identification and repatriation process that took place at Nouadhibou", confirming what was already stated in General Comment No. 2, i.e. "the scope of territory" under Art. 2 must also include situations where a State Party exercises, directly or indirectly, *de facto* or *de jure* control over persons in detention". For more on this case (which was however declared inadmissible on *locus standi* grounds), see WOUTERS and DEN HEIJER, "The Marine I Case: a Comment", International Journal of Refugee Law, 2010, p. 1 ff.

[90] See at: <http://www.aph.gov.au/Parliamentary_Business/Committees/Senate/Legal_and_Constitutional_Affairs/Manus_Island>.

powers in relation to asylum seekers detained offshore, and therefore have a significant and direct impact on their enjoyment of rights [...]; and Australian DIBP officers have either conducted or closely supervised the refugee status determination processes in both offshore processing countries".[91]

5. OFFSHORE CENTRES AND THE ECHR

Could Member States be brought before the ECtHR and held accountable for alleged violations of human rights in offshore centres? Currently, and before it accedes to the ECHR, the EU cannot be brought before the Strasbourg Court.[92]

The case law on jurisdiction before the Strasbourg Court is very complex.[93] The leading case is *Al-Skeini*,[94] where the Court, after reiterating that "[a] State's jurisdictional competence under Article 1 is primarily territorial", affirmed the existence of jurisdiction "whenever the State, through its agents, exercises control and authority over an individual" (personal model), and "when, as a consequence of lawful or unlawful military action, a Contracting State exercises effective control of an area outside that national territory" (spatial model). According to this case law, extraterritorial jurisdiction will most probably be established where offshore migration controls entail the detention of those intercepted in the high seas or removed from Europe, while it is uncertain whether simply carrying out immigration interviews or just financing the creation of a centre (without intercepting or taking an expulsion decision) might trigger the jurisdiction of a State,[95] unless a more functional approach to extraterritorial jurisdiction is affirmed.

---

[91] See GLEESON, *cit. supra* note 86, p. 8.

[92] On 18 December 2014, the ECJ ruled that the Draft Agreement of 5 April 2013 was not compatible with EU law. See Opinion 2/13, available at: <http://curia.europa.eu/juris/document/document.jsf?docid=160882&doclang=EN>.

[93] See, *ex multis*, GAJA, "Art. 1", in BARTOLE, CONFORTI and RAIMONDI (eds.), *Commentario alla Convenzione europea per la salvaguardia dei diritti dell'uomo*, Padova, 2001, p. 28 ff.; DE SENA, *La nozione di giurisdizione statale nei trattati sui diritti dell'uomo*, Torino, 2002; O'BOYLE, "The European Convention on Human Rights and Extraterritorial Jurisdiction: A Comment on 'Life after Bankovic'", in COOMANS and KAMMINGA (eds.), *Extraterritorial Application of Human Rights Treaties*, Antwerpen, 2004; LAGRANGE, "L'application de la Convention de Rome à des actes accomplis par les Etats parties en dehors du territoire national", RGDIP, 2008, p. 521 ff.; NIGRO, "The Notion of 'Contracting Parties' Jurisdiction' in Art. 1 of the ECHR", IYIL, 2010, p. 11 ff.; DE SENA, "The Notion of 'Contracting Parties' Jurisdiction' in Art. 1 of the ECHR: Some Marginal Remarks on Nigro's Paper", *ibid.*, p. 75 ff.; SAPIENZA, "Art. 1", in BARTOLE, DE SENA and ZAGREBELSKY (eds.), *Commentario breve alla Convenzione europea*, Padova, 2012, p. 13 ff.; and MILANOVIC, *cit. supra* note 75.

[94] *Al-Skeini v. United Kingdom*, Application No. 55721/07, Judgment of 7 July 2011.

[95] See GAMMELTOFT-HANSEN, *Access to Asylum: International Refugee Law and the Globalization of Migration Control*, Cambridge, 2011, p. 133.

ECHR jurisprudence on jurisdiction is in effect quite puzzling. One might ask if the *Bankovic*[96] case – where the Court held that the text of "Article 1 does not accommodate" an approach to a "cause-and-effect" notion of jurisdiction (vigorously denying a functional approach) – has been overruled by *Al-Skeini*. In the *Hirsi* case the Court recalls both judgments, and also the *Medvedyev* case, which considered that *de facto* control over a ship suffices to establish the State party's jurisdiction (even if the people on board were not transported on the French warship).[97] Moreover, in a few cases, the Court seems to have applied a more "functional test". In the *Xhavara* case,[98] in effect, the Court seems to have adopted a "cause-and-effect" approach[99] since, within the framework of a collision which took place on the high seas, it admitted implicitly the existence of Italian jurisdiction (and excluded that of Albania)[100] apparently because an Italian warship *caused* the sinking of a vessel carrying Albanian migrants: "La Cour note d'emblée que le naufrage du Kater I Rades a été directement *provoqué* par le navire de guerre italien Sibilla. Par conséquent, toute doléance sur ce point doit être considérée comme étant dirigée

---

[96] *Bankovic v. Belgium*, Application No. 52207/99, Decision of 12 December 2001, para. 75.

[97] In *Medvedyev and Others v. France* (Application No. 3394/03, Judgment of 29 March 2010), the events in question took place on board the *Winner*, a vessel flying the flag of a third State. "[W]hen they boarded the Winner, the French commando team were obliged to use their weapons to defend themselves, and subsequently kept the crew members under their exclusive guard and confined them to their cabins during the journey to France, where they arrived on 26 June 2002. The rerouting of the Winner to France, by a decision of the French authorities, was made possible by sending a tug out of Brest harbour to tow the ship back to the French port" (para. 66). This is the reason why the Court concluded that France exercised "full and exclusive control over the Winner and its crew, at least *de facto*, from the time of its interception, in a continuous and uninterrupted manner until they were tried in France" (para. 67). The *Hirsi* case was easier, because the events took place entirely on board Italian military ships. Nonetheless, the Court affirmed that "the applicants were under the continuous and exclusive *de jure* and *de facto* control of the Italian authorities" (para. 81). As observed, "by stressing that Italy exercised not only *de jure* control (because it enjoys under the flag ship principle exclusive jurisdiction over its vessels) but also *de facto* control (because the migrants were within the factual power of the Italian authorities) over the migrants between the boarding and their transfer to Libya, the Court sends out the message that scenarios, such as in the *Marine I* and *Tampa* cases, where migrants remain on their own vessel but are subjected to the complete control of the authorities, are also to be brought within the ambit of the Convention". See Den Heijer, *cit. supra* note 29, p. 269; see also Liguori, *cit. supra* note 29, pp. 424 e 434.

[98] *Xhavara v. Albania and Italy*, Application No. 39473/98, Decision of 11 January 2001.

[99] See also Brouwer, "Extraterritorial Migration Control and Human Rights: Preserving the Responsibility of the EU and Its Member States", in Ryan and Mitsilegas (eds.), *Extraterritorial Immigration Control. Legal Challenges*, Leiden-Boston, 2010, p. 216.

[100] The collision took place during a border surveillance operation, deployed within the framework of an agreement between Albania and Italy, authorising the latter to board Albanian boats.

exclusivement contre l'Italie".[101] The same approach emerges in *PAD v. Turkey*,[102] concerning the killing of Iranian citizens by a Turkish helicopter, where the Court affirmed that "it is not required to determine the exact location of the impugned events, given that the Government had already admitted that the fire discharged from the helicopters *had caused the killing* of the applicants' relatives".[103] Similarly, in the judgment *Andreou v. Turkey*,[104] concerning Turkish authorities positioned behind the border killing a demonstrator inside the UN-controlled area, the Court stated that "even though the applicant had sustained her injuries in territory over which Turkey exercised no control, the opening of fire on the crowd from close range, which was the direct and immediate cause of those injuries, had been such that the applicant should be regarded as 'within [the] jurisdiction' of Turkey". To quote the most recent developments, the *Jaloud v. The Netherlands* judgment[105] is remarkable: here the Court declared that Jaloud fell within the jurisdiction of the Netherlands because he passed through a checkpoint "manned by personnel under the command and direct supervision of a Netherlands Royal Army officer". However, this case too shows that the Court is probably not yet ready for a notion of "cause and effect" jurisdiction; otherwise, as observed,[106] "[a]ll the talk [in Jaloud] about occupation, exercise of public authority and manning checkpoints would have been quite unnecessary". In any case, given the significant progress made in this field so far, further developments in Strasbourg case law are not to be excluded.

6. CONCLUSIONS

To sum up, as Professor Goodwin-Gill has written, "no State can avoid responsibility by outsourcing or contracting out its obligations, either to another State, or to an international organization".[107] Therefore the outsourcing of migration control, and in particular of the processing of asylum claims, cannot imply a shift of responsibility. As we have seen, according to the rules of general international law, an outsourcing State and/or an IO is likely to be responsible in most circumstances, at least for complicity.

---

[101] The case was however declared inadmissible for non-exhaustion of domestic remedies.

[102] *PAD and Others v. Turkey*, Application No. 60167/00, Decision of 28 June 2007.

[103] Para. 54 (emphasis added).

[104] *Andreou v. Turkey*, Application No. 45653/99, Judgment of 27 October 2009, para. 25.

[105] *Jaloud v. The Netherlands*, Application No. 47708/08, Judgment of 20 November 2014.

[106] See the response by SARI to LEHMANN ("The Use of Force against People Smugglers: Conflicts with Refugee Law and Human Rights Law") at: <http://www.ejiltalk.org/the-use-of-force-against-people-smugglers-conflicts-with-refugee-law-and-human-rights-law/>. See also the judgment of the High Court of Justice (Queen Bench Division Administrative Court), *Al-Saadoon & Others v. Secretary of State for Defence*, 15 March 2015.

[107] GOODWIN-GILL, *cit. supra* note 63, p. 34.

The Achilles' heel is, however, whether it is or will be possible to bring the responsible IOs and States before an international human rights body given, on the one hand, that IOs cannot yet be brought before international courts[108] and, on the other, that it might be difficult in some cases to demonstrate the existence of a jurisdictional link between the individuals concerned and the outsourcing State.

Indeed, one of the most problematic hypotheses – and also one of the most likely to occur – concerns the case in which a European State is financing a third State to stop the influx of irregular migrants and process asylum seekers *before* they reach Europe. In this case, since the asylum seekers are stopped before coming into contact with the European State, it would be difficult to affirm, in the light of current ECHR case law, the existence of the jurisdiction of the financing State.

---

[108] After the accession of the EU to the ECHR, it will be possible to bring a claim against the EU before the Strasbourg Court. This possibility is however quite remote given ECJ Opinion 2/13 (see *supra* note 92).

THE PROTECTION OF EUROPEAN UNION CITIZENS VICTIMS
OF HUMAN TRAFFICKING IN EUROPE

FULVIA STAIANO*

Abstract

On February 2015, Eurostat issued a report highlighting that 65% of registered victims of human trafficking in Europe between 2010 and 2012 were citizens of the European Union (EU). Despite the seriousness of this phenomenon, EU citizens who are victims of trafficking are afforded little protection in the European legal space. First, the multi-level legal framework against trafficking applicable on the Union territory does not recognise clear residence rights to this group. Second, the general freedom of movement granted to all EU citizens under Directive 2004/38 might be precluded to victims of trafficking due to the economic prerequisites required by this instrument. It follows that the granting of refugee status to EU citizens who are victims of trafficking becomes a crucial source of protection. The safe country presumption in force between EU Member States under the so-called Aznar Protocol, however, precludes access to international protection for this group. This article critically reviews the Common European Asylum System, in search of normative and judicial interpretations capable of ensuring a stronger protection of EU citizens who are victims of trafficking. In this context, a special focus is devoted to the jurisprudence of the European Court of Human Rights and of the Court of Justice of the European Union.

Keywords: human trafficking; right to asylum; Aznar Protocol; safe country of origin; nationality discrimination.

1. INTRODUCTION

In its EU Strategy towards the Eradication of Trafficking in Human Beings for 2012-2016,[1] the European Commission defined this phenomenon as "the slavery of our times" as well as a serious infringement of individual freedom and dignity. Recognising the transnational dimension of trafficking, the Commission noted that the number of citizens of the European Union (EU) trafficked within their own or

---

* Irish Research Council Postdoctoral Researcher, School of Law, University College Cork. E-mail: fulvia.staiano@ucc.ie.
[1] Communication from the Commission to the European Parliament, the Council, the European Economic and Social Committee, and the Committee of the Regions, EU Strategy towards the Eradication of Trafficking in Human Beings 2012-2016, COM (2012) 286.

another Member State was on the rise. In fact, a more recent report by Eurostat has shown that the majority of registered victims of trafficking (65%) between 2010 and 2012 were citizens of EU Member States.[2] In this context, freedom of movement is a facilitating factor for trafficking, due to the related low risk of identification and detection.[3] With the exception of the Netherlands, the top five countries of citizenship of EU victims of trafficking are States of relatively recent access to the Union, i.e. Bulgaria, Romania, Hungary, and Poland.

Despite the dimension and seriousness of this phenomenon, citizens of EU Member States who are victims of trafficking enjoy very little protection under EU law. While EU citizens in general enjoy freedom of movement within the Union, the latter is subjected to compliance with economic prerequisites that might be hard to satisfy for victims of trafficking. Beyond this realm, residence rights for EU citizens who are victims of trafficking are severely restricted. The albeit limited residence rights envisaged for trafficking victims by the Convention on Action against Trafficking in Human Beings of the Council of Europe (CoE)[4] are precluded to EU citizens through application of the disconnection clause enshrined in its Article 40(3). The EU anti-trafficking regime, indeed, reserves the right to access residence permits exclusively to third-country national victims.

As a result, EU citizens who are victims of trafficking might resort to international protection in another Member State in order to be authorised to reside there. The route of pursuing international protection, however, is equally precluded to EU citizens. The Common European Asylum System (CEAS) relies on the premise that Member States constitute safe countries of origin in respect of each other. By virtue of this principle, the 1997 Protocol on Asylum for Nationals of Member States of the EU[5] already clarified that asylum applications submitted by Union citizens should be presumed as manifestly unfounded by Member States.

Against this background, this article will critically examine the main legal barriers to an effective protection of asylum seekers who are EU citizens and enquire on possible solutions. In doing so, it will engage with doctrinal critiques of the safe country of origin assumption between EU Member States, discussing their possible limitations and offering an alternative solution that draws from Canadian jurisprudence.

---

[2] Eurostat, Trafficking in Human Beings, 2015, p. 11, available at: <https://ec.europa.eu/anti-trafficking/publications/trafficking-human-beings-eurostat-2015-edition_en>.

[3] Europol, EU Serious and Organised Crime Threat Assessment (2013), p. 24, available at: <https://www.europol.europa.eu/content/eu-serious-and-organised-crime-threat-assessment-socta>.

[4] 16 May 2005, entered into force 1 February 2008 (hereinafter "CoE Convention against Trafficking").

[5] Protocol (No 29) on asylum for nationals of Member States of the European Union (1997), OJ C 340 of 10 November 1997.

2. PROTECTION GAPS IN THE EUROPEAN LEGAL SPACE IN RELATION TO EU CITIZENS

The eradication of trafficking in human beings is a well-established aim of the EU. Article 5(3) of the EU Charter of Fundamental Rights includes a specific prohibition of trafficking in human beings within the scope of the prohibition of slavery and forced labour. In addition to the abovementioned EU Strategy, the EU anti-trafficking framework rests on two main sources of secondary law. Directive 2004/81/EC[6] clarifies the conditions for the granting of residence permits to victims of trafficking, while Directive 2011/36/EU[7] establishes minimum standards in relation to Member States' criminal law response to trafficking in human beings. Only the latter, however, includes Union citizens within its scope of application. Directive 2004/81 explicitly restricts residence rights to third-country nationals who are victims of trafficking and "who cooperate in the fight against trafficking in human beings or against action to facilitate illegal immigration".[8] The exclusion of Union citizen victims from the scope of application of Directive 2004/81 appears to be motivated by the conviction that a sufficient level of protection for this group is already ensured by Directive 2004/38/EC on freedom of movement.[9] The preamble of Directive 2011/36 points in this direction. In clarifying that the directive does not deal with residence conditions of victims of trafficking on the EU territory, paragraph 17 of the preamble refers to Directive 2004/81 and Directive 2004/38 as normative sources in this field for third-country nationals and Union citizens respectively. The latter directive, however, grants EU citizens a right to reside in another Member State for more than three months only provided that certain economic preconditions are fulfilled (i.e., provided that they are employed or self-employed, or have sufficient resources to support themselves and their family members, as well as comprehensive health insurance). Arguably, such requirements might be particularly difficult to satisfy for victims of trafficking due to financial and personal hardship.

Furthermore, all EU Member States are parties of the Protocol to Prevent, Suppress and Punish Trafficking in Persons, Especially Women and Children, sup-

---

[6] Directive 2004/81/EC of 29 April 2004 on the residence permit issued to third-country nationals who are victims of trafficking in human beings or who have been the subject of an action to facilitate illegal immigration, who cooperate with the competent authorities, OJ L 261 of 6 August 2004.

[7] Directive 2011/36/EU of 5 April 2011 on preventing and combating trafficking in human beings and protecting its victims, and replacing Council Framework Decision 2002/629/JHA, OJ L 101/1 of 15 April 2011.

[8] Art. 1 of Directive 2004/81.

[9] Directive 2004/38/EC of 29 April 2004 on the right of citizens of the Union and their family members to move and reside freely within the territory of the Member States amending Regulation (EEC) 1612/68 and repealing Directives 64/221/EEC, 68/360/EEC, 72/194/EEC, 73/148/EEC, 75/34/EEC, 75/35/EEC, 90/364/EEC, 90/365/EEC, and 93/96/EEC.

plementing the UN Convention against Transnational Organized Crime.[10] The provisions of the 2000 Protocol include the recognition of victims' right to receive assistance and protection within and beyond judicial proceedings (Article 6), the obligation for States Parties to consider allowing victims to reside temporarily or permanently on their territory (Article 7), as well as the obligation for a State Party of which a victim of trafficking is a citizen to facilitate and accept the return of that person without undue or unreasonable delay (Article 8).[11]

Lastly, all EU Member States – with the exception of the Czech Republic – have ratified the CoE Convention against Trafficking. This Convention – whose broad scope is defined by Article 2 as encompassing "all forms of trafficking in human beings, whether national or transnational, whether or not connected with organised crime" – applies to any natural person subject to trafficking, regardless of nationality.[12] Moreover, its Article 14(1) envisages a specific right of victims to receive residence permits whenever their stay is considered necessary by the competent authorities, either due to their personal situation or for the purpose of their cooperation in investigations or criminal proceedings. Pursuant to Article 14(5), said residence permits will not undermine the right of victims to seek and enjoy asylum.

The CoE Convention against Trafficking, however, does not entirely compensate for the lack of recognition in EU law of residence rights to Union citizens victims of trafficking. Article 40(3) of the Convention, indeed, includes a disconnection clause whereby "Parties which are members of the European Union shall, in their mutual relations, apply Community and European Union rules in so far as there are Community or European Union rules governing the particular subject concerned and applicable to the specific case". As it emerges from the Explanatory Report to the Convention,[13] the European Community and EU Member States justified the need for such a clause by referring to the objective of taking into account the institutional structure of the Union when acceding international conventions. The ultimate aim of the clause was to prevent EU Member States from invoking the Convention directly among themselves or in their relationships with EU.[14]

The inclusion of disconnection clauses at the request of the EU and its Member States is not exclusive to the CoE Convention against Trafficking. This practice also marked the negotiation and adoption of the CoE Convention on the Prevention of Terrorism[15] (where it sparked controversies between the EU and the CoE),[16] and the

---

[10] 15 November 2000, entered into force 25 December 2003.

[11] Art. 8 includes within the scope of application of this obligation also State Parties where victims of trafficking enjoy the right of permanent residence.

[12] See Art. 4(e) of the Convention.

[13] Explanatory Report to the Council of Europe Convention on Action against Trafficking in Human Beings, 16 May 2005.

[14] *Ibid.*, para. 375.

[15] 16 May 2005, entered into force 1 June 2007.

[16] KOLB, *The European Union and the Council of Europe*, Basingstoke, 2013, p. 100 ff.

CoE Convention on Laundering, Search, Seizure and Confiscation of the Proceeds from Crime and on the Financing of Terrorism.[17] In the specific context of the CoE Convention against Trafficking, the main issue related to the disconnection clause under Article 40(3) concerns its detrimental effects for EU citizen victims. This provision excludes this category of individuals from the legal guarantees available in the European legal space. Access to residence rights for EU citizen victims of trafficking in a Member State other than their own – in theory recognised by Article 14(1) of the CoE Convention against Trafficking – will indeed be precluded due to the prevalence of the more restrictive Directive 2011/36.

In this light, an alternative route to obtaining residence rights for EU citizens who are victims of trafficking can consist in applying for international protection or asylum. On a general level, victims of trafficking are entitled to pursue the recognition of refugee status. Article 40(4) of the CoE Convention against Trafficking itself is careful to clarify that the Convention does not affect State obligations under international humanitarian law and international human rights law, particularly in relation to the Convention Relating to the Status of Refugees[18] and its 1967 Protocol.[19] The Explanatory Report emphasized that "the fact of being a victim of trafficking in human beings cannot preclude the right to seek and enjoy asylum and Parties shall ensure that victims of trafficking have appropriate access to fair and efficient asylum procedures".[20] Moreover, EU asylum law includes victims of trafficking among the categories of refugees or persons eligible for international protection identified as particularly vulnerable persons and therefore in need of special consideration by Member States. This provision, in particular, is established by Article 20(3) of Directive 2011/95/EU (the so-called "Qualification Directive"),[21] and Article 21 of Directive 2013/33/EU (the so-called "Reception Conditions Directive").[22]

Even in the realm of international protection and asylum, however, EU law fails to grant an effective protection to EU citizens. Since its inception, CEAS has rested on the assumption that EU Member States are safe countries of origin. This was already clear in Protocol No. 24 on Asylum for Nationals of Member States of the European Union (the so-called Aznar Protocol, from the Spanish President who

---

[17] 16 May 2005, entered into force 1 May 2008.

[18] 28 July 1951, entered into force 22 April 1954.

[19] Protocol Relating to the Status of Refugees, 31 January 1967, entered into force 4 October 1967.

[20] Explanatory Report, *cit. supra* note 13, para. 377.

[21] Directive 2011/95/EU of 13 December 2011 on standards for the qualification of third-country nationals or stateless persons as beneficiaries of international protection, for a uniform status for refugees or for persons eligible for subsidiary protection, and for the content of the protection granted, OJ L 337/9 of 20 December 2011.

[22] Directive 2013/33/EU of 26 June 2013 laying down standards for the reception of applicants for international protection, OJ L 180 of 29 June 2013.

was its main promoter),[23] initially annexed to the Amsterdam Treaty.[24] Pursuant to the sole article of the Protocol, "Member States shall be regarded as constituting safe countries of origin in respect of each other for all legal and practical purposes in relation to asylum matters". Asylum applications submitted by citizens of a Member State may be declared admissible or examined by another Member State only in four exceptional circumstances. The first occurs when the Member State of which the asylum seeker is a national takes measures derogating from its obligations under the European Convention of Human Rights (ECHR) in time of war or other public emergency, pursuant to Article 15 ECHR.[25] The second and third respectively relate to the initiation of the procedure established by Article 7(1) and (2) of the Treaty on European Union (TEU) and to the adoption of a final decision in this context. As is known, Article 7(1) TEU grants the Council with the power to determine, under certain conditions, the existence of a clear risk of a serious breach by a Member State of the values of the Union as defined by Article 2 TEU (respect for human dignity, freedom, democracy, equality, the rule of law and respect for human rights, including the rights of persons belonging to minorities). Under Article 7(2), the European Council may determine the existence of a serious and persistent breach by a Member State of such values. It may consequently suspend certain of the rights deriving from EU treaties, such as the voting rights of their representatives in the Council. Lastly, the fourth case relates to a unilateral decision by a Member State to examine an asylum application of a national of another Member State, provided that the application is dealt with on the basis of the assumption of its manifestly unfounded character.

The presumption that EU Member States are safe countries of origin is reflected in the exclusion of EU citizens from the personal scope of secondary legislation making up the CEAS. Both the Qualification Directive and the Reception Conditions Directive indeed exclusively apply to third-country nationals. The same holds for the so-called Asylum Procedures Directive,[26] and Regulation 604/2013

---

[23] For a brief history of the Protocol, see GUILD, "Between Persecution and Protection: Refugees and the New European Asylum Policy", Cambridge Yearbook of European Legal Studies, 2000, p. 169 ff., pp. 175-176.

[24] Treaty of Amsterdam amending the Treaty on European Union, 2 October 1997, entered into force 1 May 1999.

[25] This provision appears quite questionable in the light of the existence of internal guarantees envisaged in the ECHR system, not least the exclusion from the scope of Art. 15 of certain ECHR rights (including those enshrined in Art. 3) which cannot be derogated even in time of emergency. In this respect, see PEERS, MORENO-LAX, GARLICK and GUILD, EU Immigration and Asylum Law (Text and Commentary), Volume 3, EU Asylum Law, 2nd ed., Beaverton, 2015, p. 44; and COSTELLO, The Human Rights of Migrants and Refugees in European Law, Oxford, 2015, p. 190.

[26] Directive 2013/32/EU of 26 June 2013 on common procedures for granting and withdrawing international protection, OJ L 180 of 29 June 2013.

concerning the competence of EU Member States for the examination of applications for international protection (also known as the "Dublin III Regulation").[27]

3. CRITIQUES TO THE SAFE COUNTRY PRESUMPTION WITHIN THE CEAS

The safe country presumption between EU Member States has been vastly criticised by legal scholars who have highlighted the virtually non-existent possibilities for asylum seekers who are citizens of an EU Member State to obtain protection against persecution by another Member State. Such criticism follows two main routes. On the one hand, some academics have attempted to counter the safe country assumption by referring to the existence of EU citizens who are recognised as refugees outside of the territory of the Union.[28] Other scholars[29] rely on the jurisprudence of the European Court of Human Rights (ECtHR) and of the Court of Justice of the European Union (CJEU) concerning the expulsion of third-country national asylum seekers to another EU Member State.

As to the first theoretical strand, such critiques refer to the case of EU citizens of Roma origin. They highlight the contrast between the extensive and widespread breaches of the Roma's human and fundamental rights in Europe, and their exclusion from the scope of the CEAS for those who are EU citizens. Particular reference is made to the fluxes of Hungarian asylum seekers – many of which of Roma origin – to Canada between 2008 and 2012.

It is undeniable that the Roma have historically experienced – and continue to experience – severe human rights violations in Europe. The ECtHR, for instance, has repeatedly identified breaches of the prohibition of inhuman or degrading treatment as well as of the right to family life (*ex* Articles 3 and 8 ECHR respectively) in instances of involuntary sterilisation of Roma women.[30] In other cases, it identified breaches of Roma children's right to education under Article 2 of Protocol No. 1 to the ECHR due to State practice of placing these children in schools for children

---

[27] Regulation (EU) 604/2013 of 26 June 2013 establishing the criteria and mechanisms for determining the Member State responsible for examining an application for international protection lodged in one of the Member States by a third-country national or a stateless person, OJ L 180 of 29 June 2013.

[28] CAPARINI, "State Protection of the Czech Roma and the Canadian Refugee System", in BIGO, GUILD and CARRERA (eds.), *Foreigners, Refugees, or Minorities? Rethinking People in the Context of Border Controls and Visas*, Burlington, 2013; GUILD and GARLICK, "Refugee Protection, Counter-Terrorism, and Exclusion in the European Union", Refugee Survey Quarterly, 2010, p. 63 ff., pp. 69-70.

[29] O'NIONS, *Asylum – A Right Denied: A Critical Analysis of European Asylum Policy*, Burlington, 2014, p. 103; STERN, "At a Crossroads? Reflections on the Right to Asylum for European Union Citizens", Refugee Survey Quarterly, 2014, p. 54 ff., p. 66 ff.

[30] *V.C. v. Slovakia*, Application No. 18968/07, Judgment of 8 November 2011; *I.G. and Others v. Slovakia*, Application No. 15966/04, Judgment of 13 November 2012; *N.B. and Others v. Slovakia*, Application No. 29518/10, Judgment of 12 June 2012.

with mental, social or learning disabilities.[31] Violations of Article 3 ECHR have also been found in cases concerning police brutality and States Parties' failure to offer Roma people effective protection and redress.[32]

However, an exclusive focus on this issue presents some theoretical limitations. First, it should not be taken for granted that all forms of discrimination against the Roma amount to persecution. In fact, even cumulative discrimination – i.e., the combination of multiple forms of discrimination not amounting to persecution if taken alone – is not consistently accepted as a form of persecution in State practice.[33] Second, these fluxes were ultimately characterised by the Canadian Government as made up by bogus asylum seekers, which led to restrictions within Canadian asylum law. Such restrictions included the borrowing of the notion of safe country of origin from European asylum law, with the aim of curbing the acceptance of asylum seekers from European countries.[34] Specifically, Section 58 of the Protecting Canada's Immigration System Act[35] reformed Section 109(1) of the Balanced Refugee Reform Act[36] so as to grant the Minister of Citizenship and Immigration the power to designate safe countries of origin. The assessment process of asylum applications brought by citizens of these countries is more expedite. Applicants are ineligible for work permits pending the application and enjoy very limited access to health care.[37] As a result, both claims of Hungarian asylum seekers in Canada and their overall acceptance rate have dropped dramatically.[38]

---

[31] *D.H. and Others v. The Czech Republic*, Application No. 57325/00, Judgment of 13 November 2007; *Sampanis and Others v. Greece*, Application No. 32526/05, Judgment of 5 June 2008; *Oršuš and Others v. Croatia*, Application No. 15766/03, Judgment of 16 March 2010; *Horváth és Vadászi v. Hungary*, Application No. 45407/05, Judgment of 17 May 2011; *Sampani and Others v. Greece*, Application No. 59608/09, Judgment of 11 December 2012; *Horváth and Kiss v. Hungary*, Application No. 11146/11, Judgment of 29 January 2013; and *Lavida and Others v. Greece*, Application No. 7973/10, Judgment of 30 May 2013.

[32] For example, see *Bekos and Koutropoulos v. Greece*, Application No. 15250/02, Judgment of 13 December 2005; *Cobzaru v. Romania*, Application No. 48254/99, Judgment of 26 July 2007; *Stoica v. Romania*, Application No. 42722/02, Judgment of 4 March 2008; and *Stefanou v. Greece*, Application No. 2954/07, Judgment of 22 April 2010.

[33] GUILD and ZWAAN, "Does Europe Still Create Refugees? Examining the Situation of the Roma", Queen's Law Journal, 2014, p. 141 ff., p. 161 ff.

[34] MACKLIN, "A Safe Country to Emulate? Canada and the European Refugee", in LAMBERT, MCADAM and FULLERTON (eds.), *The Global Reach of European Refugee Law*, Cambridge, 2013, p. 99 ff.

[35] Protecting Canada's Immigration System Act, S.C. 2012, c. 17, assented to on 28 June 2012.

[36] Balanced Refugee Reform Act, S.C. 2010, c. 8, assented to on 29 June 2010.

[37] For a thorough and critical account of the Canadian Designated Countries of Origin scheme, see STEFANOVA, "The 'Safe' Need Not Apply: The Effects of the Canadian and EU 'Safe Country of Origin' Mechanisms on Roma Asylum Claims", Texas ILJ, 2014, p. 121 ff.

[38] LEVINE-RASKY, BEAUDOIN and ST CLAIR, "The Exclusion of Roma Claimants in Canadian Refugee Policy", Patterns of Prejudice, 2014, p. 67 ff.

A more extensive and widespread practice of acceptance by non-EU Member States of asylum claims submitted by EU citizens could have grounded an argumentation against the safe country presumption underlying the CEAS. Whenever certain groups of EU citizens are consistently recognised as refugees only outside of the Union, one may argue that a rigid enforcement of this presumption within the EU undermines their enjoyment of the substance of the rights connected to Union citizenship itself. EU citizens' victims of trafficking or more broadly of persecution would indeed be forced to leave the territory of the Union to obtain effective protection. In the present circumstances, however, it is doubtful that the isolated and short-lived Canadian practice towards EU asylum seekers before the described legal reform could offer a solid legal argument in this sense.

The second group of critiques recall that both the ECtHR and the CJEU have established a prohibition to expel asylum seekers to EU Member States where there is a substantial risk they will be subjected to torture or inhuman or degrading treatment. This jurisprudence on third-country national asylum seekers would prove that the principle of mutual trust between EU Member States implied in the CEAS' safe country presumption is no longer defensible. However, a closer look at these judgments reveals that neither the ECtHR nor the CJEU have ever fundamentally questioned such a presumption on the grounds of human or fundamental rights law.

As to the ECtHR, its landmark judgment of *M.S.S. v. Belgium and Greece*[39] established key principles with respect to the transfer of asylum seekers to the EU Member State of first entry under the so-called Dublin Regulation.[40] Among other violations, the ECtHR found that Belgium had breached the prohibition of inhuman or degrading treatment under Article 3 ECHR by transferring an Afghan asylum seeker (Mr. M.S.S.) to Greece under Article 10(1) – now Article 13(1)[41] of the Dublin Regulation. The transfer, indeed, had exposed Mr. M.S.S. to detention and living conditions amounting to degrading treatment (the existence and diffusion of which among asylum seekers in Greece was well known to the Belgian

---

[39] *M.S.S. v. Belgium and Greece*, Application No. 30696/09, Judgment of 21 January 2011.

[40] At the time of the judgment, the Dublin Regulation in force was the Council Regulation (EC) 343/2003 of 18 February 2003 establishing the criteria and mechanisms for determining the Member State responsible for examining an asylum application lodged in one of the Member States by a third-country national (OJ L50/01 of 25 February 2003). This source was amended by Regulation (EU) 604/2013 of 26 June 2013 establishing the criteria and mechanisms for determining the Member State responsible for examining an application for international protection lodged in one of the Member States by a third-country national or a stateless person (OJ L 180 of 29 June 2013).

[41] Pursuant to Art. 13(2) of Regulation 604/2013, "where it is established, on the basis of proof or circumstantial evidence as described in the two lists mentioned in Article 22(3) of this Regulation, including the data referred to in Regulation (EU) 603/2013, that an applicant has irregularly crossed the border into a Member State by land, sea or air having come from a third country, the Member State thus entered shall be responsible for examining the application for international protection [...]".

authorities).[42] The *M.S.S.* judgment has been referred to in some instances as a blow to the safe country presumption in force between EU Member States. This case concerned necessary safeguards with respect to the transfer of third-country national asylum seekers to the Member State of first entry, and did not delve into the different question of State obligations towards EU citizens applying for asylum in another Member State. However, it has been argued that the reasoning of the ECtHR in *M.S.S.* – by contesting the presumption of safety for third-country national asylum seekers – offers "an opening of possibilities for those who seek, or could seek, protection in one EU country from persecution […] they claim to have been subjected to in another EU country".[43] This judgment, therefore, would suggest that "there can no longer be a 'conclusive presumption' that all EU states are safe".[44]

Such views also lean on the influence of the *M.S.S.* judgment on an almost contemporary decision of the CJEU in the same field. In the joined cases *N.S. v. Secretary of State for the Home Department* and *M.E. et al. v. Refugee Applications Commissioners, Minister for Justice, Equality and Law Reform*,[45] the CJEU established an obligation for Member States to refrain from Dublin transfers whenever the responsible Member State fails to comply with EU fundamental rights. On the one hand, it recognised that the CEAS is based on a "principle of mutual confidence" whereby it is possible "to assume that all the participating States, whether Member States or third States, observe fundamental rights, including the rights based on the Geneva Convention and the 1967 Protocol, and on the ECHR".[46] On the other, it stated that "European Union law precludes the application of a conclusive presumption that the Member State which Article 3(1) of Regulation No 343/2003 indicates as responsible observes the fundamental rights of the European Union".[47] Nonetheless, the CJEU was extremely careful to delimit this principle to the specific circumstances of the case. Its reasoning was strictly focused on Member States' asylum procedures and reception conditions, and on asylum seekers' fundamental rights in these contexts. In rebutting the conclusive character of the principle of mutual confidence, the CJEU noted how "it is not […] inconceivable that [the CEAS] may, in practice, experience major operational problems in a given Member State, meaning that there is a substantial risk that asylum seekers may, when transferred to that Member State, be treated in a manner incompatible with their fundamental rights".[48] Moreover, in clarifying the meaning of such "ma-

---

[42] *Ibid.*, paras. 362-368.

[43] STERN, *cit. supra* note 29, p. 76.

[44] O'NIONS, *cit. supra* note 29, p. 104.

[45] Joined Cases C-411/10 and C-493/10, *N. S. v. Secretary of State for the Home Department* and *M.E. and Others v. Refugee Applications Commissioner and Minister for Justice, Equality and Law Reform* [2011] ECR I-13905.

[46] *Ibid.*, paras. 78-79.

[47] *Ibid.*, para. 105.

[48] *Ibid.*, para. 81

jor operational problems", the CJEU distinguished between minor infringements of secondary EU law sources making up the CEAS (irrelevant in this context) and "systemic flaws in the asylum procedure and reception conditions [...] resulting in inhuman or degrading treatment, within the meaning of Art. 4 of the Charter".[49]

The specifications elaborated in *N.S.* and *M.E* suggest the difficulty of reading a willingness of the CJEU to fundamentally question the safe country presumption between EU Member States. The recognition of a State obligation not to transfer asylum seekers in Member States where systemic deficiencies of the domestic reception system might give rise to inhuman and degrading treatment does not equate to an acknowledgement that EU Member States might also *create* refugees. The question of whether and in which cases EU citizens might be victims of persecution in their Member State remains addressed exclusively by the restrictive norms of the Aznar Protocol.

4. THE NOTION OF SAFE COUNTRIES OF ORIGIN AND ITS INFLUENCE ON PROCEDURAL SAFEGUARDS

It follows from the foregoing analysis that, arguably, the case law of the CJEU on EU asylum law does not coincide with the ECtHR case law. With respect to safe third countries, the ECtHR has clarified that being a party to international conventions and agreements in the field of asylum and refugee protection is not sufficient to qualify a State as such. Thus, Article 3 ECHR prevents States Parties to transfer asylum seekers to a third country whenever they are (or should have been) aware of situations of systematic human rights violations in respect of this group taking place therein.[50] These principles have been affirmed regardless of whether said third country belonged or not to the EU, as for the well-established prohibition to expel asylum seekers towards countries were they would face a real risk of treatment contrary to Article 3 ECHR.[51] For this purpose, it is irrelevant whether the danger emanates from State or non-State actors – as long as the involved State is incapable or unwilling to offer appropriate protection.

EU asylum law envisages different rules and procedures for asylum seekers originating from safe countries, depending on whether these are third countries or EU Member States. In the latter case, as we have seen, the rules of the Aznar

---

[49] *Ibid.*, para. 86.

[50] In addition to the *M.S.S.* case (*cit. supra* note 39), see *Hirsi Jamaa v. Italy*, Application No. 27765/09, Judgment of 23 February 2012, paras. 127-138; and *Mohammadi v. Austria*, Application No. 71932/12, Judgment of 3 July 2014, paras. 57-70.

[51] *Saadi v. Italy*, Application No. 37201/06, Judgment of 28 February 2008; *N.A. v. The United Kingdom*, Application No. 25904/07, Judgment of 17 July 2008; *Abdolkhani and Karimnia v. Turkey*, Application No. 30471/08, Judgment of 22 September 2009; and *Sufi and Elmi v. The United Kingdom*, Applications Nos. 8319/07 and 11449/07, Judgment of 28 June 2011.

Protocol apply. In the former case, the applicable regime is much more sophisticated. Articles 36-38 of the Asylum Procedures Directive regulate the designation of a safe country of origin. Article 36(2) leaves the establishment of rules and modalities for the application of this concept to the domestic legislation of Member States. Pursuant to Article 37, the designation must be based on information provided by other Member States as well as international organisations such the CoE or agencies such as the European Asylum Support Office (EASO) and the United Nations High Commissioner for Refugees (UNHCR). Member States are under an obligation to periodically review the domestic situation of countries designated as safe, and may only provide this designation when they are satisfied the concerned country will respect key principles in relation to a person seeking international protection. Article 38(1) includes among these principles the lack of threats to life and liberty "on account of race, religion, nationality, membership of a particular social group or political opinion", the lack of risk of serious harm within the meaning of the Qualification Directive, the principle of *non-refoulement*, freedom from torture and cruel, inhuman or degrading treatment and the possibility to obtain refugee status. Article 39 also envisages the possibility to designate a State that is not a member of the EU as a "European safe third country". For this purpose, a State must have ratified and observe the 1951 Refugee Convention as well as the ECHR, and have in place asylum procedures prescribed by law.

The notion of safe country of origin – already envisaged in respect to third countries by Directive 2005/85/EC,[52] which the current Asylum Procedures Directive subsequently repealed – is quite controversial within legal scholarship. Doubts have been raised as to its compatibility with the prohibition of discrimination on the grounds of race, religion, or country of origin enshrined in Article 3 of the Refugee Convention, as well as to its procedural consequences.[53] The CJEU faced the key issue of procedural guarantees in a 2013 preliminary ruling concerning two Nigerian asylum seekers in Ireland.[54] The applicants complained that the designation of Nigeria as a safe country had meant that less time and resources had been devoted to their application, and that they had had fewer opportunities to supply additional information. They argued that this procedural disadvantage constituted discrimination on the grounds of nationality. The referring court thus asked the CJEU to determine, among other things, whether EU law prevented Member

---

[52] Council Directive 2005/85/EC of 1 December 2005 on minimum standards on procedures in Member States for granting and withdrawing refugee status, OJ L326/13 of 13 December 2003.

[53] COSTELLO, "The Asylum Procedures Directive and the Proliferation of Safe Country Practices: Deterrence, Deflection and the Dismantling of International Protection?", European Journal of Migration and Law, 2005, p. 35 ff.; and GARLICK, "Asylum Procedures", in PEERS, MORENO-LAX, GARLICK and GUILD (eds.), *cit. supra* note 25, p. 211 ff.

[54] C-175/11, *H.I.D., B.A. v. Refugee Applications Commissioner, Refugee Appeals Tribunal, Minister for Justice, Equality and Law Reform, Ireland, Attorney General*, Judgment of 31 January 2013.

States from examining determining asylum applications submitted by nationals of certain countries through accelerated or prioritised procedures. The CJEU answered this question by upholding the rules established by Directive 2005/85 on safe country designation.[55] First, it observed that nationality plays a key role in the matter of asylum, since the country of origin of asylum seekers must be taken into consideration in the assessment of the need for international protection. Second, the possibility to assess applications submitted by asylum seekers from countries considered safe through accelerated procedures is not discriminatory if the rights and procedural guarantees envisaged by Chapter II of the Directive are respected. The CJEU referred in particular to the need to ensure that asylum seekers "enjoy a sufficient period of time within which to gather and present the necessary material in support of their application".[56]

The issue of procedural safeguards is key in respect to the perspectives of protection available for asylum seekers who are citizens of EU Member States. The Aznar Protocol merely establishes a presumption of inadmissibility of asylum applications submitted by this category of citizens. The strict and limited exceptions to this principle depend on the initiative of either Member States or EU institutions. The Protocol remains silent on the possibility for asylum seekers to reverse such a presumption, as well as on their rights and procedural guarantees throughout the eventual assessment of their application. These aspects remain completely entrusted to the discretion of each Member State, allowing for an uneven legal regime of this matter within the EU. The Asylum Procedures Directive, on the other hand, grants third-country national asylum seekers with the right to contrast a safe country presumption. Pursuant to Article 36(1), it is possible for them to submit "serious grounds for considering the country not to be a safe country of origin in [their] particular circumstances and in terms of [their] qualification as a beneficiary of international protection". The currently pending proposal for a regulation on an EU common list of safe countries[57] has further clarified this principle. Although the chances for its ultimate adoption are quite low,[58] it is worth noting how its recital 5 states that "the circumstance that a third country will be on the EU common list of safe countries of origin cannot establish an absolute guarantee of safety for nationals of that country and will not dispense therefore with the need to conduct an appropriate individual examination of their applications for international protection".

---

[55] While the judgment refers to the now repealed Directive 2005/85, the principles established therein are still relevant. Indeed, the norms examined by the CJEU that are of interest for our purposes have been left substantially unmodified by Directive 2013/32.

[56] *H.I.D.*, *cit. supra* note 54, p. 75.

[57] Proposal for a Regulation of the European Parliament and of the Council establishing an EU common list of safe countries of origin for the purposes of Directive 2013/32/EU on common procedures for granting and withdrawing international protection, and amending Directive 2013/32/EU, COM/2015/0452.

[58] Pascouau, "The October 2015 European Council and Migration: No News, Good News", Migration Policy Centre, 19 October 2015.

According to the same provisions, the designation of a country as safe will not apply to a specific applicant whenever he or she "shows that there are serious reasons to consider the country not to be safe in his or her particular circumstances".

As shown above, the existence of a safe country presumption among EU Member States can hardly be rebutted by referring to instances of recognition of refugee status for EU citizens outside of the Union territory. Similarly, the examined jurisprudential principles concerning the safety assumption in respect to EU Member States are strictly focused on issues related to asylum procedures and reception conditions. The observed disparity in available EU standards as to procedural guarantees, on the other hand, constitutes a possible instance of discrimination on the grounds of nationality in the field of asylum. While it may be difficult to argue against the safe country presumption among EU Member States in its entirety, the lack of procedural guarantees raises the issue of proportionality of such a presumption to the aim pursued. The next paragraph will examine this issue more closely.

5. STEREOTYPING AND LACK OF PROPORTIONALITY AS INDICATORS OF NATIONALITY DISCRIMINATION IN THE AZNAR PROTOCOL

Legal presumptions concerning safe countries of origin of asylum seekers arguably constitute one of the few areas of EU law where third-country nationals enjoy a more favourable legal treatment than EU citizens. The complete lack of standards at supranational level as to the possibility for EU asylum seekers to reverse the safe country presumption is particularly questionable in this context.

In the field of nationality discrimination, both the ECtHR and the CJEU have produced a substantial jurisprudence.[59] The vast majority of cases, however, concern third country nationals who submitted claims of discrimination against preferential treatment granted to EU citizens. The latter arguably enjoy stronger legal protections within European human and fundamental rights law. On the one hand, the ECtHR has interpreted the principle of non-discrimination enshrined in Article 14 ECHR as allowing preferential treatment of nationals of EU Member States. This reasoning rests on the notion of the EU as a special legal order, and thus on the

---

[59] BROUWER and DE VRIES, "Third-Country Nationals and Discrimination on the Ground of Nationality: Article 18 TFEU in the Context of Article 14 ECHR and EU Migration Law: Time for a New Approach", in VAN DEN BRINK, BURRI and GOLDSCHMIDT (eds.), *Equality and Human Rights: Nothing But Trouble?*, Utrecht, 2015, p. 123 ff. From the specific angle of access to social security benefits, see PENNINGS, "The Approaches of the EU Court of Justice and the European Court of Human Rights vis-à-vis Discrimination on the Grounds of Nationality in Social Security", in PENNINGS and VONK (eds.), *Research Handbook on European Social Security Law*, Cheltenham, 2015, p. 121 ff.

objective and reasonable justification for such differential treatment.[60] On the other hand, the prohibition of nationality discrimination under Article 18 of the Treaty on the Functioning of the European Union (TFEU) – whose text is mirrored by Article 21(2) of the EU Charter – has been interpreted by the CJEU as only applicable to EU citizens.[61]

Against this background, the question of the possibly discriminatory character of the different legal treatment of asylum seekers who are EU citizens (in respect to those who are third-country nationals) becomes central. While neither the ECtHR nor the CJEU have established useful principles on this specific matter, the Canadian Federal Court has offered an interesting example of judicial assessment of the proportionality of safe country of origin presumptions. In the case of *Y.Z., G.S. and C.S.*,[62] the Ontario Federal Court assessed the constitutionality of paragraph 110(2) (d.1) of the Immigration and Refugee Protection Act (IRPA).[63] This norm establishes a prohibition for asylum seekers who are citizens of countries considered as safe under the Canadian designated country of origin (DCO) system to appeal against a negative decision concerning their application. Interestingly, this case originated from the application of three citizens of EU Member States seeking asylum in Canada. Their applications, deemed credible by the Refugee Protection Division of the Immigration and Refugee Board, were nonetheless rejected on the grounds that adequate State protection was available for them in Croatia and Hungary.

The Federal Court found that paragraph 110(2)(d.1) was incompatible with the right to equality and non-discrimination under Section 15(1) of the Canadian Charter. From the outset, the Court noted that the distinction between DCO and non-DCO claimants in respect of the right to appeal was "discriminatory on its face". Its effects were to "further marginalize, prejudice, and stereotype refugee claimants from DCO countries which are generally considered safe" because it perpetuated "a stereotype that refugee claimants from DCO countries are somehow queue-jumpers or 'bogus' claimants who only come here to take advantage of Canada's refugee system and its generosity".[64] Such a normative presumption

---

[60] *Moustaquim v. Belgium*, Application No. 12312/86, Judgment of 18 February 1991; and *Ponomaryovi v. Bulgaria*, Application No. 5335/05, Judgment of 21 June 2011.

[61] See C-22/08, *Athanasios Vatsouras and Josif Koupatantze v. Arbeitgemeinschaft (ARGE) Nürnberg 900*, Jugdment of 4 June 2009; C-45/12, *Office national d'allocations familiales pour travailleurs salariés (ONAFTS) v. Radia Hadj Ahmed*, Judgment of 13 June 2013. It is uncertain whether in the latter case the CJEU has partially opened to the possibility of extending the personal scope of Art. 18 TFEU as also including third-country nationals, at least in situations coming within the scope of EU law. For a commentary on this matter, see BROUWER and DE VRIES, *cit. supra* note 59, pp. 140-141.

[62] Ontario Federal Court, Joined Cases *Y.Z. and the Canadian Association of Refugee Lawyers v. The Minister of Citizenship and Immigration and the Minister of Public Safety and Emergency Preparedness*, and *G.S. and C.S. v. The Minister of Citizenship and Integration*, Judgment of 23 July 2015, 2015 FC 892.

[63] Immigration and Refugee Protection Act, SC 2011, c 27.

[64] Joined Cases *Y.Z., G.S. and C.S.*, *cit. supra* note 62, para. 124.

prevents an individual assessment of claims, undermining the substantive equality of asylum seekers from designated countries of origin and discriminating them by "expressly imposing a disadvantage on the basis of national origin alone".[65] Moreover, the Court deemed that the denial of an appeal to all asylum seekers from designated countries was "not proportional to the government's objectives" and "an inequality that is disproportionate and overbroad"[66] – thus breaching Section 1 of the Charter. Indeed, the objective of making asylum assessment procedures swifter and of providing a disincentive for fraudulent claims could not justify the exclusion of certain claimants from the right to appeal.[67] This matter, together with the lack of an automatic stay of removal pending the assessment procedure, prompted the Court to conclude that not all asylum seekers in Canada could have their claims "fairly and thoroughly assessed under the DCO regime".[68]

This judgment, albeit isolated, raises important points that can be fruitfully applied to the European context. It must be noted from the outset that the Canadian DCO system was adopted with the declared aim of reducing the financial burden of the domestic immigration and asylum seekers.[69] This system also constitutes a response to the increasing fluxes of Hungarian refugees to Canada, and more broadly to the need to prevent abuse of the institution of asylum by "bogus" claims.[70] Such a motivation echoes the Preamble of the Aznar Protocol, which refers to the aim to "prevent the institution of asylum being resorted to for purposes alien to those for which it is intended". In respect to the Aznar Protocol, however, the DCO system appears more flexible. The former establishes a blanket presumption of safety covering all EU Member States, and thus a presumption of inadmissibility of asylum claims from EU citizens. Even when an EU Member State unilaterally decides to exercise its discretional power to examine such claims, it will do so on the grounds of the presumption of its manifest inadmissibility. The DCO system, on the other hand, envisages a separate procedure for refugee claims made by nationals of a designated country. The latter still enjoy the right to a full hearing before the Refugee Protection Division, but they will have less time to prepare due to the accelerated character of the procedure and – as clarified before – they may not appeal its final decision.

Against this background, two main points appear of particular interest for the issue of the compatibility of the Aznar Protocol to European human rights standards. The first relates to the characterisation as stereotypical and discriminatory of the denial of basic procedural rights to asylum seekers from countries considered safe. The ECtHR too has traced links between normative stereotyping and discrimi-

---

[65] *Ibid.*, para. 128.
[66] *Ibid.*, para. 170.
[67] *Ibid.*, para. 162.
[68] *Ibid.*, para. 169.
[69] STEFANOVA, *cit. supra* note 37, p. 139.
[70] *Ibid.*

nation for quite some time. This court has repeatedly established that State Parties may not restrict certain groups' fundamental rights on the grounds of classifications that reinforce and perpetuate stereotypical notions concerning those groups, finding domestic laws that did so in breach of Article 14 ECHR.[71] The ECtHR takes issue with the fact that such normative stereotyping prevents an individualised assessment of each individual's capacities and needs.[72] This judicial interpretation stemmed from the identification of a very narrow margin of appreciation for States Parties in relation to certain groups who have been subjected historically to discrimination and prejudice (such as HIV-positive persons, Roma people, or individuals affected by mental health issues).[73] In the case *M.S.S. v. Belgium and Greece*, the ECtHR included asylum seekers within the definition of vulnerable groups in need of special protection.[74] Arguably, EU citizens who are asylum seekers – including those who have been victims of trafficking – may be considered as also part of this category.

The blanket qualification of all EU Member States as safe countries of origin within the Aznar Protocol appears to be at odds with the standards elaborated by the ECtHR in this field. The obligation for Member States to consider inadmissible or at the very best manifestly unfounded any asylum application submitted by citizens of another EU Member States does in fact impose a stereotypical view of EU citizens as "bogus" asylum seekers.

A second observation relates more strictly to the proportionality of the safe country presumption underlying the Aznar Protocol. Both the ECtHR and the CJEU refer to proportionality as a criterion to examine possible instances of nationality discrimination. For the ECtHR, the proportionality test is essential. According to its established case law, any difference in treatment is discriminatory if it has no objective or reasonable justification, that is, if it does not pursue a legitimate aim

---

[71] *D.H. and Others v. The Czech Republic*, Application No. 57325/00, Judgment of 13 November 2007; *Kiyutin v. Russia*, Application No. 2700/10, Judgment of 10 March 2011; and *Alajos Kiss v. Hungary*, Application No. 38832/06, Judgment of 20 May 2010. An early formulation of this principle can already be found in *Abdulaziz, Cabales and Balkandali v. The United Kingdom*, Applications No. 9214/80, 9473/81, 9474/81, Judgment of 28 May 1985. On this jurisprudence, see TIMMER, "Judging Stereotypes: What the European Court of Human Rights Can Borrow from American and Canadian Equal Protection Law", American Journal of Comparative Law, 2015, p. 239 ff.; and ARNADÓTTIR, "The Differences that Make a Difference: Recent Developments on the Discrimination Grounds and the Margin of Appreciation under Article 14 of the European Convention on Human Rights", Human Rights Law Review, 2014, p. 647 ff.

[72] See for instance *Alajos Kiss, ibid.*, para. 42; and *Kiyutin, ibid.*, para. 63.

[73] PERONI and TIMMER, "Vulnerable Groups: The Promise of an Emerging Concept in European Human Rights Convention Law", International Journal of Constitutional Law, 2013, p. 1056 ff.

[74] *M.S.S.* case, *cit. supra* note 39, para. 251. Judge Sajó contested this qualification in his partly concurring and partly dissenting opinion.

or if it is not possible to identify a relationship of proportionality between the aim pursued and the means envisaged to fulfil it.[75]

It is also possible to find references to proportionality in the CJEU's jurisprudence on nationality discrimination.[76] As a general principle of EU law, proportionality embodies an obligation for Member States to transpose secondary legislation in their domestic order through measures that do not go beyond what is necessary to attain the objectives of that legislation. At the same time, the CJEU understands proportionality as a precondition for the compatibility of Member States' domestic legislation with EU law. In *Förster*,[77] for instance, the CJEU examined a Dutch norm that required five years of continuous legal residence as a precondition to grant students from other Member States a maintenance grant. In this context, it established that such a requirement "must also be proportionate to the legitimate objective pursued by the national law in order to be justified in the light of Community law".[78] The CJEU reaffirmed this principle on multiple occasions, in respect to differences in treatment between EU citizens within domestic laws of Member States that gave preferential treatment to their own nationals or residents.[79] The principle of proportionality also extends to acts of EU institutions, which must not go beyond what is appropriate and necessary to achieve the legitimate objectives pursued by EU law.[80]

---

[75] The ECtHR has relied on this tenet from the very beginning of its judicial activity, starting from the *Case "Relating to Certain Aspects of the Laws on the Use of Languages in Education in Belgium" v. Belgium*, Applications No. 1474/62, 1677/62, 1691/62, 1769/63, 1994/63, 2126/64, Judgment of 23 July 1968. In the field of nationality discrimination, see for instance *Gaygusuz v. Austria*, Application No. 1731/90, Judgment of 16 September 1996; *Ponomaryovi v. Bulgaria*, Application No. 5335/05, Judgment of 21 June 2011; and *Dhahbi v. Italy*, Application No. 17120/09, Judgment of 8 April 2014.

[76] GALETTA, "General Principles of EU Law as Evidence of the Development of a Common European Legal Thinking: The Example of the Proportionality Principles (from the Italian Perspective)", in ZILLER, WEBER, KLEIN, BLANKE and CRUZ VILLALON (eds.), *Common European Legal Thinking: Essays in Honour of Albrecht Weber*, New York, 2015, p. 221 ff.

[77] C-158/07, *Jacqueline Förster v. Hoofddirectie van de Informatie Beheer Groep*, Judgment of 18 November 2008.

[78] *Ibid.*, para. 53.

[79] See for instance C-221/07, *Krystyna Zablocka-Weyhermüller v. Land Baden-Württemberg*, Judgment of 4 December 2008, para. 37; C-544/07, *Uwe Rüffler v. Dyrektor Izby Skarbowej we Wrocławiu Ośrodek Zamiejscowy w Wałbrzychu*, Judgment of 23 April 2009, para. 74; and C-589/10, *Janina Wencel v. Zakład Ubezpieczeń Społecznych w Białymstoku*, Judgment of 16 May 2013, para. 71.

[80] Case C-343/09, *Afton Chemical v. Secretary of State for Transport*, Judgment of 8 July 2010, para. 45; Cases C-9209 and C-93/09, *Volker und Markus Schecke and Eifert v. Land Hessen*, Judgment of 9 November 2010, para. 74; Cases C-581/10 and C-629/10, *Nelson and Others v. Deutsche Lufthansa AG* and *TUI Travel plc and Others v. Civil Aviation Authority*, Judgment of 23 October 2010, para. 71; Case C-283/11, *Sky Österreich v. Österreichischer Rundfunk*, Judgment of 22 January 2013, para. 50; and Case C-101/12, *Schaible v. Land Baden-Württemberg*, Judgment of 23 May 2013, para. 29.

The compatibility with the principle of proportionality not only of eventual domestic norms implementing the Aznar Protocol, but of this source itself, is doubtful to say the least. The Protocol does not explicitly bar Member States from allowing asylum seekers to submit evidence capable of reversing the safe country of origin presumption in their specific situation, or to grant them the possibility to appeal a decision on their application. Nonetheless, the lack of any kind of standards on these matters, together with the obligation for Member States who unilaterally decide to examine asylum claims in this context to presume them as manifestly unfounded, suggests the disproportionate character of the norms of the Protocol in respect to its aim. The CJEU has clarified that the lack of clear and precise rules within secondary legislation governing the extent of their interference with fundamental rights enshrined in the EU Charter breaches said principle of proportionality.[81] Being a source of EU primary law, it is unsure whether the Aznar Protocol could be subjected to a similar judicial control. As an act of EU institutions, however, it is still bound to respect the principle of proportionality. As the Canadian Federal Court rightly observed in relation to its much less restrictive domestic regime, the aim of preventing abuse of the right to asylum can hardly justify a blanket exclusion from key procedural rights on the sole ground of nationality. For the reasons stated above, it is doubtful that the Aznar Protocol could pass a proportionality test in respect to the differential legal regime it establishes for citizens of Member States who seek asylum within the territory of the Union.

6. CONCLUDING REMARKS

The creation of a common area of freedom, security and justice, where the free movement of EU citizens as well as respect of fundamental rights are ensured, is one of the key objectives of the EU set forth in Article 3(2) TEU. It would be contradictory to pursue this objective to the detriment of EU citizens themselves. Yet, at present EU law offers extremely low guarantees of protection for the citizens of EU Member States in the context of trafficking. Their exclusion from residence rights under the EU anti-trafficking regime and the safe country assumption underlying the Aznar Protocol combine to create a situation of complete unresponsiveness by EU Member States to this numerically relevant phenomenon.

This purposeful normative void constitutes an utterly disproportionate solution to the legitimate aim of preventing abuses of the European asylum system. On the one hand, this aim is of crucial importance for the EU, which is increasingly burdened by asylum claims. According to the latest Eurostat data, in the third quarter of 2015 the number of first time asylum applicants increased by 150% in

---

[81] Joined Cases C-293/12 and C-594/12, *Digital Rights Ireland Ltd v. Minister for Communications, Marine and Natural Resources et al.* and *Irish Human Rights Commission and Kärntner Landesregierung*, Judgment of 8 April 2014, paras. 63-69.

comparison to the same quarter of 2014 and doubled compared with the second quarter of 2015.[82] On the other hand, *de facto* nullifying the chances for citizens of EU Member States to be recognised as refugees by another Member State appears excessive and discriminatory.

The Canadian practice offers an interesting example on how to reconcile these competing needs. First, the restrictions introduced with the adoption of the DCO system did not entirely rule out the possibility for any asylum seeker to obtain an individualised assessment of their situation by competent authorities, regardless of their nationality. Second, the extensive interpretation by the Federal Court established important guarantees against nationality discrimination in respect to procedural rights. An effective enjoyment of the latter is particularly crucial for asylum seekers. Being able to play an active part in the assessment process of their application can make the difference between the denial or the enjoyment of basic human rights such as the right to life and the right not to be subjected to torture or inhuman and degrading treatment.

---

[82] Eurostat, *First Time Asylum Applicants, EU-28*, January 2014-September 2015, and *First Time Asylum Applicants by Citizenship, EU-28, Absolute Change between Q3 2014 and Q3 2015*, available at: http://ec.europa.eu/eurostat/statistics-explained/index.php/Asylum_quarterly_report.

NOTES AND COMMENTS

THE LEGAL REGIME OF WRECKS OF WARSHIPS AND OTHER STATE-OWNED SHIPS IN INTERNATIONAL LAW: THE 2015 RESOLUTION OF THE *INSTITUT DE DROIT INTERNATIONAL*

SARAH DROMGOOLE[*]

Abstract

The status in international law of operational warships and other ships used only on governmental non-commercial service has been long established. In contrast, the status of such vessels after they have sunk has been, and remains, a matter of considerable uncertainty. The uncertainty arises in no small part from the absence of any provision in the 1982 UN Convention on the Law of the Sea relating to sunken State vessels or, indeed, to wrecks more generally. Over the last 30 years, technological advances have led to the discovery of many new wreck sites, fuelling international interest in the status of sunken State wrecks. At its Santiago Session in 2007, the Institut de droit international *established its 9th Scientific Commission to look into the matter. A Preliminary Report, drafted by the Commission's Rapporteur, Professor Natalino Ronzitti, was discussed at the Rhodes Session in 2011 and, after further deliberations, a Resolution entitled "The Legal Regime of Wrecks of Warships and Other State-Owned Ships in International Law" was adopted by the Tallinn Session in August 2015. This contribution sets out the background to the work of the 9th Commission, outlines the substance of the Resolution, and offers some observations thereon.*

Keywords: *Institut de droit international*; sunken State vessels; warships; wrecks; sovereign immunity.

1. INTRODUCTION

On 29 August 2015, at its 77th Session held in Tallinn, Estonia, the *Institut de droit international* (IDI) adopted a Resolution on "The Legal Regime of Wrecks of Warships and Other State-Owned Ships in International Law". The Resolution arose out of the work of the 9th Scientific Commission of the IDI, which produced

[*] Professor of Maritime Law, University of Nottingham. The author would like to thank Professor Natalino Ronzitti, of the Board of Editors, for his helpful comments on a draft of this article. Any views expressed and errors are, of course, those of the author alone.

a Preliminary Report on the topic for consideration at the Institute's 75th Session, in Rhodes, in 2011.[1]

The IDI's purpose is to promote the progress of international law through, among other things, clarifying and highlighting the characteristics of the law as it exists (*lex lata*), in order to encourage respect for that law, and opining on what the law ought to be (*de lege ferenda*).[2] One way that it does this is through the adoption, and promulgation, of resolutions of a "normative character".[3]

It is certainly the case that the international legal regime appertaining to the wrecks of warships and other State owned ships is in serious need of clarification, as well as progressive development. While the status in international law of *operational* warships and other ships operated on governmental non-commercial service has been long established, there has been considerable uncertainty over the status of those vessels once they are sunk. At the root of that uncertainty is political sensitivity. A number of international treaties are of relevance but their objectives are not always compatible and their application to sunken State vessels is piecemeal. There is also a considerable body of State practice but the exact bounds of customary law are hard to determine. The result is a legal regime that is deeply complex, fractured and misunderstood. For a range of reasons, not least the fact that advances in marine technology over the last 30 years have led to the discovery of numerous wrecks of all kinds, the need for greater certainty in this field is becoming ever more urgent.

2. BACKGROUND

Articles 95 and 96 of the UN Convention on the Law of the Sea (UNCLOS)[4] enshrine the long-standing rule of international law that warships and other ships "owned or operated by a state and used only on government non-commercial service"[5] have "complete immunity from the jurisdiction of any state other than the flag state"[6] when sailing on the high seas. With limited provisos, this principle also extends to such vessels sailing in the exclusive economic zone (EEZ) and territorial sea of another State. The principle also applies to State aircraft and spacecraft. A notable omission, however, from the so-called "Constitution of the Oceans" is

---

[1] The Preliminary Report, prepared by the Rapporteur, Professor Natalino Ronzitti, and the plenary discussion on the topic that took place at the Rhodes Session were published in the *Annuaire de l'Institut de droit international*, Vol. 74, 2011, pp. 131-177. Preparatory works for the Tallinn Session, including an Addendum to the Report prepared by Professor Ronzitti, comments of IDI members, and the text of a Draft Resolution, are available on the IDI website.

[2] See at: <http://justitiaetpace.org/historique.php>. See also the IDI Statutes, Art. 1(2).

[3] See at: <http://justitiaetpace.org/historique.php>.

[4] 10 December 1982, entered into force 16 November 1994.

[5] UNCLOS, Art. 96.

[6] UNCLOS, Arts. 95 and 96.

any specific provision relating to the status of *sunken* State vessels[7] or, indeed, of wrecks more generally. As a result, there has been ongoing academic debate about whether or not the principle of sovereign immunity applies to a State vessel after it has sunk and, if it does, the basis for extending the principle to a vessel that no longer retains its essential function.[8] The issue is clouded by the fact that a separate but closely related question also arises concerning the *ownership* of a sunken State vessel and, in particular, the extent to which ownership rights are retained over the passage of time. However, using the premise of immunity, or the premise of ownership (or both), maritime States – including the United States (US), United Kingdom (UK), Russia, Japan, France, Germany, and Spain – assert that the recovery of sunken State vessels is subject to a different set of rules from those applying to private vessels and take the firm stance that such vessels cannot be interfered with without the express permission of the flag State.

In today's world, more than 30 years on since the adoption of UNCLOS, the question of the legal regime relating to wrecks and the recovery of material from wrecks is of increasing international interest and the legal status of sunken warships and other State vessels is an important facet of that regime and has significant ramifications. The increasing accessibility of the seabed, and of wrecks lying on the seabed, beyond coastal fringes has led to burgeoning interest in cultural and environmental aspects of wrecks and in such questions as: the treatment of wrecks where they are regarded as constituting cultural heritage; the treatment of human remains to be found on wreck sites and of the sites themselves where they are significant gravesites; the need to deal with wrecks that cause hazards of one kind or another (e.g. obstacles to navigation or to commercial development, or threats to the marine environment); and the relative rights of coastal States and flag States.

While UNCLOS makes no specific mention of wrecks, it does include two provisions – Articles 149 and 303 – relating to "objects of an archaeological and historical nature" found at sea and designed to afford such objects with a degree of protection. Such objects may, of course, include wrecks; and it is the case that the wrecks of warships and other types of State vessel may have particular historical significance for one reason or another. However, even in the years immediately following the adoption of UNCLOS, Articles 149 and 303 were regarded as woefully inadequate as a framework for protection of heritage values. In light of this inadequacy, UNESCO promulgated its controversial Convention on the Protection of the Underwater Cultural Heritage.[9] This instrument is designed to create a comprehensive regime for "underwater cultural heritage", as defined by the Convention,

---

[7] In the wake of the *Glomar Explorer* incident, informal proposals to include provision for the recovery of such vessels were tabled by the Soviet bloc but rejected: see Preliminary Report, *cit. supra* note 1, p. 146.

[8] For details, see Preliminary Report, *ibid.*, pp. 142-143.

[9] 2 November 2001, entered into force 2 January 2009. As at 1 April 2016 it had 55 States Parties.

and it makes special provision for "State vessels and aircraft". It also makes some, albeit limited, provision with respect to the treatment of human remains and maritime gravesites. Another treaty of some significance is the Nairobi International Convention on the Removal of Wrecks, promulgated by the International Maritime Organisation.[10] This is designed to provide a scheme for intervention where wrecks pose a hazard, but its application is relatively limited: although it does have potential to apply in the territorial sea, it is designed to apply primarily in the EEZ; its application to wrecks that sank before its coming into force is doubtful;[11] and it generally excludes warships and other State vessels. A number of other treaties also have relevance to some degree, including the UN Convention on Jurisdictional Immunities of States and their Property,[12] and the Salvage Convention.[13]

A complicating factor is that the objectives of the conventional and other international legal regimes impacting on wrecks are sometimes far from compatible: most notably, the central archaeological principle underlying the 2001 UNESCO Convention – that underwater cultural heritage should be preserved *in situ* – is in direct conflict with the notion that troublesome wrecks should be "removed" and that commercially valuable property should be rescued from peril and returned to its owner (or, in the absence of an owner, to the "stream of commerce"). The fractured way in which international law in this field has developed has been aggravated by the special but uncertain status of State vessels. This means that the treaties dealing with salient matters have either excluded State vessels from their scope of application, or differentiate between State vessels and commercial vessels in ways that add complexity.

Over recent years, there has been a growing body of State practice on the part of the major maritime States with regard to sunken warships. Virtually all of that practice has been designed to reinforce the notion that interference with such wrecks, wherever they lie, is impermissible under international law without the express consent of the flag State. The political contentiousness of that notion, however, became manifest during the difficult negotiations leading up to the adoption of the 2001 UNESCO Convention. Tensions on this matter, and also on the question of the compatibility of the treaty with UNCLOS in relation to coastal State jurisdiction over the continental shelf, threatened to derail the whole process. Ultimately, a

---

[10] 18 May 2007, entered into force 14 April 2015. As at 8 March 2016 it had 27 States Parties.

[11] On this point, see DROMGOOLE and FORREST, "The 2007 Nairobi Wreck Removal Convention and Hazardous Historic Shipwrecks", Lloyd's Maritime and Commercial Law Quarterly, 2011, pp. 92 ff., p. 94.

[12] 2 December 2004, not yet in force. As at 1 April 2016, 21 instruments of ratification, acceptance, approval, or accession had been deposited. Thirty are required for the Convention to enter into force.

[13] 28 April 1989, entered into force 14 July 1996. As at 8 March 2016 it had 69 States Parties. Like the 2007 Nairobi Convention, and many other maritime treaties, it generally excludes warships and other State vessels from its scope of application.

bloc of maritime States rejected the final text because of the way it dealt with these issues.[14] It is noteworthy, however, that several maritime States are now parties to the 2001 Convention, including Italy, Spain, Portugal, and France. The position of France is particularly significant: having initially abstained from voting for the Convention on grounds that included its treatment of sunken warships, France later changed its view after concluding that the Convention provided the only effective means of controlling commercial treasure hunting in its offshore waters.

3.   SUBSTANCE OF THE RESOLUTION

The 2015 IDI Resolution comprises 15 substantive articles covering a panoply of issues to which sunken State vessels give rise. These are preceded by eight pre-ambular clauses. The preamble makes it clear that the purpose of the Resolution is to "contribute to the clarification of international law" in this field and draws attention to the relevance of a number of treaties. The following comments are not intended to provide a comprehensive discussion and analysis of the Resolution, but rather to highlight some of its core features and make some observations thereon.

3.1. Definitions

Article 1 defines two key terms for the purposes of the Resolution. By doing so, it identifies the material scope of the Resolution. First of all, the article defines "wreck" as meaning "[a] sunken State ship which is no longer operational, or any part thereof, including any sunken object that is or has been on board such ship".[15] It then goes on to define "a sunken State ship" in the following terms:

> "[A] warship, naval auxiliary or other ship owned by a State and used at the time of sinking solely for governmental non-commercial pur-poses. It includes all or part of any cargo or other object connected with such a ship regardless of whether such cargo or object is owned by the State or privately. This definition does not include stranded ships, ships in the process of sinking, or oil platforms".

These two definitions taken together make it clear that the provisions of the Resolution are intended to apply to any ship that has actually sunk, along with any object connected with the ship, in circumstances where the ship was owned by a

---

[14] Russia and Norway voted against the 2001 UNESCO Convention; France, Germany, the Netherlands, and the UK abstained. The US did not have a vote as it was not a member of UNESCO at the time, but it expressed serious reservations.

[15] Art. 1(1).

State and used at the time of sinking solely for governmental non-commercial purposes. These definitional criteria are generally consistent with definitions employed in relevant treaties.[16] In accordance with the restrictive theory of sovereign immunity, government-owned ships that were operating wholly or partly for commercial purposes are not encompassed. In light of the close relationship between the notion of immunity and the ownership of the State, the definition of a sunken State ship covers only those ships *owned* by a State and not those merely operated by a State, for example those under charter, or requisitioned in wartime.

The inclusion of the cargo or other objects connected with the ship, regardless of the ownership of those objects, accords with general principles of international maritime law which tend to treat the components of a wreck as a single unit.[17] The significance of this point in the context of a sunken warship was shown in recent US litigation with respect to the Spanish frigate, the *Nuestra Señora de las Mercedes*.[18] While the ownership of the cargo of *specie* on board the vessel was the subject of dispute and remained undetermined, the US Court of Appeals confirmed the decision of the District Court that the cargo was effectively "cloaked" in the immunity of the vessel, given it was a Spanish warship, and as a consequence a salvage company was not entitled to recover the cargo without the express authorisation of Spain as the flag State.[19]

One notable aspect of the definitions set out in Article 1 of the Resolution is that they do not explicitly encompass sunken State *aircraft*. Given the many thousands of warplanes that have been lost at sea, especially during the First and Second World Wars, this seems surprising.[20] However, the principles enshrined in the Resolution presumably would apply by analogy to aircraft (and spacecraft).[21]

3.2. Cultural Heritage

The Resolution gives due prominence to the fact that, in today's world, the question of sunken State vessels is inextricably entwined with the question of the

---

[16] See UNCLOS, Art. 32; 1989 Salvage Convention, Art. 4(1); 2001 UNESCO Convention, Art. 1(8); 2007 Nairobi Wreck Removal Convention, Art. 4(2).

[17] See, e.g., 2007 Nairobi Convention, Art. 1(4); 2001 UNESCO Convention, Art. 1(1)(a) (ii).

[18] *Odyssey Marine Exploration, Inc., v. Unidentified, Shipwrecked Vessel*, 675 F. Supp. 2d 1126 (MD Fla. Dec. 22, 2009); *aff'd*, 657 F.3d 1159 (11th Cir. (Fla.) 21 September 2011); *cert. denied*, 132 S. Ct. 2379 (US 14 May 2010). The *Mercedes* was lost in battle in 1804 off the coast of Portugal and discovered by the American shipwreck recovery company, Odyssey Marine Exploration, in 2007.

[19] See DROMGOOLE, *Underwater Cultural Heritage and International Law*, Cambridge, 2013, pp. 151-152.

[20] Cf. the definition used in the 2001 UNESCO Convention, Art. 1(8).

[21] See, e.g., Preliminary Report, *cit. supra* note 1, p. 135.

protection of cultural heritage. A substantial proportion of the global stock of underwater cultural heritage comprises sunken State craft of one sort or another and the Resolution emphasises the importance of the need to protect the heritage value of such craft by choosing to deal with this matter in its first substantive article and also in its first preambular clause.

Article 2, headed "Cultural heritage", draws (implicitly rather than explicitly) on the provisions in UNCLOS relating to "objects of an archaeological and historical nature", as well as the provisions of the 2001 UNESCO Convention, and attempts to distil some of their essence. Article 2(1) provides: "A wreck of an archaeological and historical nature is part of cultural heritage when it has been submerged for at least 100 years". The words "of an archaeological and historical nature" derive from Articles 149 and 303 UNCLOS. It is questionable, however, whether they add anything in the context of Article 2(1) of the Resolution since, presumably, the provision is intended to indicate that *any* wreck (as defined by the Resolution) is part of cultural heritage provided it has been submerged for at least 100 years. The 100 year "cut-off" employed here to define when a wreck qualifies as cultural heritage derives from the 2001 UNESCO Convention.

Article 2(1) of the Resolution appears to assume that 100 years should now be taken as the accepted time limit for application of the UNCLOS provisions, as well as the more detailed protective framework in the 2001 Convention.[22] However, while the regime in the 2001 Convention does not cover younger material, this does not mean that the international community does not regard younger material as having potential cultural value warranting protective measures. While it is not entirely clear, it is likely to have been pragmatic reasons – including the need to draw a clear distinction between material to which the law of salvage applies and material to which the regulatory framework in the 2001 Convention applies – that led the negotiators of the 2001 Convention to adopt a temporal criterion of 100 years to determine the scope of application of the treaty regime. As the 2001 Convention to all intents and purposes excludes the application of salvage law, it was politically expedient to avoid treading on too many toes within the commercial salvage industry.[23] However, there is little doubt that the term "objects of an archaeological and historical nature" employed by Articles 149 and 303 of UNCLOS is widely interpreted in State practice as covering objects *younger* than 100 years.[24] The international agreement to protect the site of the *Titanic* is a prominent example of State practice that supports this view. This agreement was negotiated by the US, France, Canada, and the UK more than a decade before the centenary of the liner's

---

[22] See Preliminary Report, *ibid.*, pp. 136 and 166.

[23] 2001 UNESCO Convention, Art. 4. By contrast, Art. 303(3) UNCLOS specifically preserves the law of salvage.

[24] For a detailed discussion of the issue, and examples of State practice, see DROMGOOLE, *cit. supra* note 19, pp. 73-76, esp. p. 75.

sinking.[25] The reference in its preamble to Article 303 of UNCLOS indicates that the negotiating parties regarded the agreement as an implementation of the duty to cooperate to protect objects of an archaeological and historical nature set out in paragraph (1) of that article. In the UK, in 2001 seven vessels of the German High Seas Fleet, scuttled at Scapa Flow in 1919, were afforded protected status under heritage legislation,[26] well before the centenary of their sinking, and in other parts of the world wrecks from the Second World War have been singled out for protection on grounds of their historical significance, including the USS *Arizona*, listed on the US National Register of Historic Places, and the Japanese submarine *I-124*, the very first vessel to be declared as "historic" under the Australian Historic Shipwrecks Act 1976. There is a risk that the wording of Article 2(1) of the Resolution could lead to a widespread assumption that material underwater for less than 100 years does not fall within the scope of Articles 303 and 149 UNCLOS. In the view of the present author, such a development would be a serious setback for the cause of cultural heritage protection in the marine sphere.

Article 303(1) UNCLOS requires States to protect objects of an archaeological and historical nature found at sea and to cooperate for that purpose. That duty, reiterated in the 2001 UNESCO Convention,[27] is reflected in Article 2(2) of the Resolution. This provides: "All States are required to take the necessary measures to ensure the protection of wrecks which are part of cultural heritage". The first preambular clause also emphasises the fact that States are under a duty to cooperate for the preservation and protection of cultural heritage. The IDI therefore appears to be confirming that Article 303(1) UNCLOS has evolved into a rule of customary international law.

The provisions of Article 2(3)-(5) of the Resolution draw attention to three of the cardinal principles of the 2001 Convention: that preservation *in situ* should be the first option to be considered in the management of material falling within the Convention's application;[28] that, where recovery is permitted, that recovery should be undertaken in accordance with internationally accepted archaeological standards and practices;[29] and that commercial exploitation and "pillage" is prohibited.[30]

The 2001 UNESCO Convention is undoubtedly a politically controversial instrument. However, it should not be thought that the controversy extends to its fundamental principles. A vital component of the Convention is its Annex. This reiterates and expounds upon the cardinal principles and contains Rules enshrining

---

[25] 2000 Agreement Concerning the Shipwrecked Vessel RMS *Titanic*.

[26] The wrecks were scheduled under the Ancient Monuments and Archaeological Areas Act 1979.

[27] See 2001 Convention, Art. 2(2) and (3).

[28] 2001 UNESCO Convention, Art. 2(5).

[29] See the Rules set out in the Annex to the 2001 Convention, which according to Article 33 are an integral part of the Convention itself.

[30] 2001 UNESCO Convention, Art. 2(7). See also Rule 2 of the Annex, which elucidates on the meaning of commercial exploitation.

benchmark standards for deliberate interference with underwater cultural heritage. Significantly, despite the lack of consensus on the text of the Convention itself, none of the States participating in the final vote on the Convention objected to the content of the Annex and, in fact, it was widely praised at the end of the negotiations, including in the statements by maritime States outlining their reservations about specific technical aspects of the text.[31] In the 16 years since the adoption of the Convention, it could be argued that the Annex has gained the status of "soft law". The UK Government, for example, though not currently minded to ratify the 2001 Convention, has adopted the principles set out in the Annex as "best practice" with respect to the management of historical and archaeological sites[32] and, in official guidance, explicitly states that it applies the Annex as best practice to "historic" British military wrecks.[33] It is worth observing that these wrecks are not defined by the 100-year temporal criterion in the 2001 Convention, but instead simply as wrecks that "are valuable to this and future generations because of their heritage interest".[34]

3.3. Legal Status of Sunken State Ships

Five articles of the Resolution address the legal status of sunken State ships in terms of the two related questions of immunity and ownership. These are Articles 3-6 and 11. Arguably, the most valuable provision in the entire Resolution is Article 3. This provides: "Without prejudice to other provisions of this Resolution, sunken State ships are immune from the jurisdiction of any State other than the flag State".

As demonstrated all too well during the UNESCO negotiations, uncertainty as to the status of sunken State vessels presents a serious impediment to creating an effective international legal framework to cater for such wrecks. Unfortunately, while Article 16 of the UN Convention on Jurisdictional Immunities of States and Their Property confirms the immunity from jurisdiction of a foreign State of operational warships and other vessels owned or operated by a State and used only on government non-commercial purposes, it does not plug the gap left by UNCLOS by explicitly addressing the question of the immunity of such vessels after they have sunk. By indicating that the eminent jurists of the IDI consider that there is suffi-

---

[31] See, e.g., statements by France, Norway, Russia, UK, and US, reprinted in CAMARDA and SCOVAZZI (eds.), *The Protection of the Underwater Cultural Heritage: Legal Aspects*, Milano, 2002, pp. 426-434.

[32] Hansard, House of Commons, Written Answers for 24 January 2005, Col. 46W.

[33] Department for Culture Media and Sport/Ministry of Defence, "Protection and Management of Historic Military Wrecks Outside UK Territorial Waters: Guidance on How Existing Policies and Legislation Apply to Historic Military Wreck Sites", April 2014, para. 1.

[34] *Ibid.* The guidance goes on to say that the significance of the wrecks "can be defined in terms of their archaeological, artistic, and/or historic interest".

cient consistent State practice, motivated by a sense of legal obligation, to amount to customary international law with respect to the immunity of sunken State ships,[35] the categorical statement in Article 3 of the Resolution should be extremely helpful in putting to rest doubts on the matter.

Exactly what immunity entails in the context of a sunken State vessel depends on the precise circumstances pertaining to the wreck. The saving clause at the start of Article 3 is a reference, *inter alia*, to provisions in the Resolution relating to the circumstances where a sunken State wreck is located in waters within the jurisdiction of a State other than the flag State. The relevant articles – Articles 7, 8 and 9 – are discussed in section 3.4 below.

Article 4 of the Resolution states: "Sunken State ships remain the *property* of the flag State, unless the flag State has clearly stated that it has abandoned the wreck or relinquished or transferred title to it".[36] The principle enshrined in this article goes hand-in-hand with the principle set out in Article 3. The fact that a chattel sinks to the bottom of the sea does not mean that the owner loses its property rights. Instead, generally speaking, for the owner to lose its rights it must be shown that it has either transferred those rights or abandoned them. In the case of abandonment, physical abandonment is not sufficient; there must also be a positive *intention* on the part of the owner to relinquish its property rights. In the case of private ownership rights, it may be possible to infer such intention from the circumstances. However, in the case of sunken State vessels, the maritime powers have taken the firm position that *express* relinquishment is required.[37] Article 4 confirms that there is sufficient State practice on the matter to support a rule of customary law.[38] Again, this is very helpful.

Article 4 needs to be read alongside Article 5. This addresses the legal status of cargo. It makes it clear that cargo owned by the flag State remains the property of that State,[39] that cargo owned by *other* States remains the property of those States,[40] and that the sinking of the ship has no effect on property rights relating to cargo.[41] While the Resolution does not explicitly address the question of the persistence of ownership rights after sinking in cargo belonging to *private* owners or, indeed,

---

[35] For reviews of State practice in this regard, see Preliminary Report, *cit. supra* note 1, pp. 145-151; and DROMGOOLE, *cit. supra* note 19, pp. 139-152.

[36] Emphasis added.

[37] See, e.g., the formal statements to this effect in the US Federal Register, Vol. 69, No. 24, 5 February 2004. See also the terms of the US Sunken Military Craft Act of 2004. This position was affirmed by the Fourth Circuit Court of Appeals in 2000 in the landmark *Sea Hunt* case, which related to the question of whether Spain had abandoned its ownership rights in two galleons *Juno* and *La Galga* (221 F.3d 634 (4th Cir. 2000)).

[38] Arguably, the degree of *consistency* in the practice on this question is in fact greater than that in respect of the question of immunity: see DROMGOOLE, *cit. supra* note 19, at p. 153.

[39] Art. 5(2).

[40] Art. 5(3).

[41] Art. 5(4).

in the personal possessions of crew and other individuals on board, such property must surely be treated *pari passu*. Article 5 also confirms that the principle set out in Article 3 that immunity continues after sinking applies not just to the vessel and its fixtures and fittings, but also the cargo (and, again, presumably other objects on board), regardless of in whom the ownership is vested, and that the consent of the flag State is required before it is disturbed or removed.[42] This is all consonant with the notion applied in the *Mercedes* case that the cargo and ship are to be treated as a single unit and that the cargo and other items on board are thus, in effect, "cloaked" in the ship's immunity even where their ownership is vested in someone other than the flag State.

Articles 6 and 11 address two quite specific issues that may affect the ownership of a sunken State ship. Article 6 reiterates the well-established principle that "[w]recks of captured State ships are the property of the captor State if the capture occurred in accordance with the applicable rules of international law".[43] Article 11 highlights the fact that the principles and rules of international law regarding State succession have the potential to impact upon the question of ownership; in light of this, the provisions of the Resolution must be taken to be without prejudice to those principles and rules.[44]

One question the Resolution does not explicitly clarify is the theoretical basis for immunity persisting after a warship or other State vessel has sunk. While there has been much academic rumination on this issue, it is not of mere academic interest. In particular, it would be very helpful if the question of whether immunity is *predicated* on the ownership of the flag State could be conclusively answered. The definition of "[a] sunken State ship" set out in Article 1(2) of the Resolution means that this question is neatly side-stepped because the Resolution does not encompass ships *operated*, but not owned, by a State. The fact that this is the case may be an indication that such vessels, once sunk, should *not* be regarded as subject to immunity.[45] In other words, that immunity *is* predicated on ownership. If that is the case, other questions then arise: does a wreck's immunity continue for as long as

---

[42] Art. 5(4).

[43] See Preliminary Report, *cit. supra* note 1, pp. 151-152 and 173, where reference is made to the famous *Admiral Nakhimov* incident involving the capture of a Russian warship by the Japanese navy during the Japanese-Russian war of 1904-1905. In the case of the capture of warships and auxiliary ships (as opposed to merchant ships) there is no need for prior prize adjudication before property is transferred to the capturing State. The property is transferred immediately upon capture. Presumably the same is also the case in the event of the surrender of a vessel before sinking. An interesting question is whether the deliberate scuttling of a vessel to avoid its capture by the enemy amounts to abandonment of title. An abandonment of the vessel does not necessarily amount to an abandonment of the property interest.

[44] Interestingly, the question of State succession arose, but was not determined, in the case of the *Mercedes* with respect to the dispute between Spain and Peru as the ownership of the *specie* on the wreck.

[45] At least some of the maritime States, including France, Germany, and the UK, claim immunity for such vessels: see DROMGOOLE, *cit. supra* note 19, pp. 138 and 146.

the wreck remains in the ownership of the flag State? And is immunity lost if a State sells a wreck, for example for scrap? The answer to this latter question is probably yes. Interestingly, the point arose quite recently in a case involving the wreck of a British warship. It was unclear whether the UK Government could prohibit interference with the site on the grounds of immunity given that there was some evidence that the wreck may have been sold to scrap merchants many years previously.

3.4. *Zonal Provisions*

Articles 7-10 of the Resolution address some of the implications of the geographical location of a sunken State ship with reference to the maritime zone in which it is situated. Articles 7-9 deal with the thorny question of the rights of the coastal State in circumstances where the sunken State ship of one State is located in a maritime space within the national jurisdiction of another. Article 10 addresses the situation where a sunken State ship is located in the international seabed Area.

When the wreck of a sunken State vessel of one State is found in the territorial sea of another State, or in other maritime spaces under coastal State sovereignty, a direct tension arises between the sovereignty of the coastal State and the notion that the wreck is immune from the jurisdiction of any State other than the flag State. It is in this context that political sensitivities are at their most acute.[46] Article 7 of the Resolution provides: "The coastal State, in the exercise of its sovereignty, has the exclusive right to regulate activities on wrecks in its internal waters, archipelagic waters, and territorial sea without prejudice to Article 3 of this Resolution".

The saving clause in Article 7, together with that in Article 3, create a circularity that reflects the fact that a delicate balancing act needs to be struck between the rights and jurisdiction of the coastal State and those of the flag State. At least on the face of it, there appears to be an irreconcilable conflict between two apparently exclusive jurisdictional rights. While disinclined to admit it, flag States ultimately do appear to concede that the coastal State has the right to control access to the site of a sunken State wreck.[47] Difficult questions then arise regarding the extent to which the flag State has a right to be advised, or consulted, in advance of any interference and, even more crucially, to *prohibit* interference. This is reflected in the wording of Article 7 of the 2001 UNESCO Convention. Paragraph 1 of that article provides that, in the exercise of their sovereignty, States Parties have the exclusive right to regulate and authorise activities directed at underwater cultural heritage in their internal waters, archipelagic waters and territorial sea. Paragraph 3 of the same article provides that States Parties should inform the flag State Party of the discovery of an identifiable State vessel or aircraft in their territorial sea or archipelagic waters. Aspects of this provision that proved

---

[46] See *ibid.*, at p. 139 ff.

[47] See, e.g., ROACH and SMITH, *United States Responses to Excessive Maritime Claims*, The Hague, 3rd ed., 2012, p. 546.

contentious during the negotiations were the use of the hortatory word "should" rather than "shall" and the rather curious exclusion of explicit reference to internal waters in paragraph 3. This exclusion, it was felt, "creates a negative implication that flag states have no rights at all over their vessels in [internal waters]".[48]

Article 8 of the Resolution provides: "In accordance with Article 303 of the United Nations Convention on the Law of the Sea, the coastal State may regulate the removal of sunken State ships from its contiguous zone". The reference here to Article 303 UNCLOS is one of only two references to specific treaty provisions in the Resolution. The paragraph of Article 303 which is relevant is paragraph 2. Through the device of a legal fiction, this affords the coastal State the authority to regulate the removal of objects of an archaeological and historical nature found in the contiguous zone. In light of this provision, the position with respect to sunken State vessels located in this zone, *assuming* they qualify as an object of an archaeo-logical and historical nature, will not be so very different from that in relation to the territorial sea. Again, maritime States appear to accept that, ultimately, the coastal State does have the right to control access.[49]

Article 9 of the Resolution addresses the situation where a sunken State ship is located in the EEZ or on the continental shelf of a State other than the flag State. It can be broken down into three parts. The first sentence of Article 9 provides: "Any activity of the flag State on a sunken ship in the exclusive economic zone or on the continental shelf of a foreign State should be carried out with due regard to the sovereign rights and jurisdiction of the coastal State". This provision reflects the principle enshrined in Article 58(3) UNCLOS that a foreign State must have "due regard" to the rights and duties of the coastal State in its EEZ when exercis-ing its own rights in that maritime space. The first sentence of Article 9 of the Resolution suggests that this principle should apply to circumstances where the flag State undertakes activities on its own wreck, or authorises such activities. In so far as a wreck located on the *outer* continental shelf beyond 200 nautical miles is concerned, i.e. where there is no overlying EEZ, the legal basis for application of the "due regard" principle in the circumstances envisaged in Article 9 is, it must be said, less apparent.[50] In light of this, it may be that Article 9 is intended to address only the situation of a wreck lying *within* 200 nautical miles.

---

[48] BLUMBERG, "International Protection of Underwater Cultural Heritage", in NORDQUIST et al. (eds.), *Recent Developments in the Law of the Sea and China*, The Hague, 2006, p. 506, footnote 22. The concerns about Article 7 were not allayed by the terms of Art. 2(8) of the 2001 Convention which suggest that nothing in the treaty modifies: "the rules of international law and State practice pertaining to sovereign immunities, nor any State's rights with respect to its State vessels and aircraft".

[49] ROACH and SMITH, *cit. supra* note 47. Article 8 of the 2001 UNESCO Convention makes provision for the contiguous zone based on Art. 303(2) UNCLOS. Unlike its provision for the other maritime zones, it does not include any specific reference to sunken State vessels.

[50] No equivalent of the "due regard" principle in Art. 58(3) UNCLOS is to be found in Part VI of the treaty, which sets out the regime for the continental shelf. Indeed, according to

The second sentence of Article 9 provides: "In accordance with applicable treaties, the flag State should notify the coastal State of any activity on the wreck which it intends to carry out". At first sight, it has to be said that this sentence is rather perplexing. Some relevant treaties, for example the 2001 UNESCO Convention and the 2007 Nairobi Wreck Removal Convention, provide for notification in the *opposite* direction, in other words that in certain circumstances the coastal State must notify the flag State of activities it intends to carry out, or sanction.[51] However, the Preliminary Report indicates that a number of other treaties and instruments dealing with marine environmental matters and human rights are in contemplation here,[52] and that, from these, it is possible to construe a duty of information on the part of the flag State in circumstances where its activity on a wreck represents a threat to the environment or to human life, directly or indirectly.[53]

The third and final sentence of Article 9 provides: "The coastal State has the right to remove a wreck interfering with the exercise of its sovereign rights if the flag State does not take any action after having been requested to co-operate with the coastal State for the removal of the wreck". This sentence appears to have in contemplation circumstances where a wreck poses a hazard in broad terms, in other words where its presence prejudices the legitimate interests of the coastal State. For example, it may pose an obstacle to activities relating to the economic exploration and exploitation of the zone, such as the installation of an oil platform or a wind turbine. In such circumstances, the IDI appears to construe (again primarily from relevant treaty texts) that the flag State is obliged to take measures to remove the hazard; if it does not do so, the coastal State then has the right to deal with the threat.[54]

The final zonal provision in the Resolution is Article 10. This provides: "Without prejudice to Article 149 of the United Nations Convention on the Law of the Sea, wrecks of sunken State ships in the Area are under the exclusive jurisdiction of the flag State". Article 10 includes the second reference in the Resolution to a specific treaty provision, in this case Article 149 UNCLOS. This provides for objects of an archaeological and historical nature located in the international seabed Area, i.e. on

---

Art. 78(2) of that Part, "the exercise of the rights of the coastal State over the continental shelf must not infringe or result in any unjustifiable interference with navigation and other rights and freedoms of other States as provided for in this Convention". There is therefore a presumption that, in the event of a conflict between the activity of a flag State on its sunken wreck (which would amount to an exercise of high seas freedoms) and the exercise of the rights of the coastal State over the continental shelf, the flag State's interests would prevail.

[51] See 2001 UNESCO Convention, Arts. 10(3) and 10(7), which go beyond notification to consultation and agreement (although, controversially, not in every instance). See also 2007 Nairobi Wreck Removal Convention, Art. 9 (1)-(6)(b) and (c). The latter treaty does not apply to State vessels unless the flag State decides otherwise.

[52] Preliminary Report, *cit. supra* note 1, pp. 163-165.

[53] *Ibid.*, pp. 164-165.

[54] *Ibid.*, p. 164. In practice what is required is removal of the threat, rather than necessarily removal of the wreck itself. The question of hazardous wrecks is dealt with more generally in Art. 14, on which see *infra* section 3.7.

the seabed beyond the limits of national jurisdiction.[55] Article 149 is a notoriously unhelpful provision as it essentially sets out an aspiration with respect to the treatment of such objects without giving any indication as to how that aspiration can or should be fulfilled. Article 10 of the Resolution makes it clear that, in so far as a sunken State ship qualifies as an object of an archaeological and historical nature, the flag State must take cognizance of Article 149 in determining the fate of the wreck site and of any material recovered from the site. It is worth noting that the provisions of the 2001 UNESCO Convention that relate to the Area, Articles 11 and 12, provide that States Parties have a responsibility to protect underwater cultural heritage in conformity with Article 149 UNCLOS,[56] and specify that "[n]o State Party shall undertake or authorize activities directed at State vessels and aircraft in the Area without the consent of the flag State".[57] In the Area, at least, there is no doubt about the "exclusivity" of the jurisdiction of the flag State.

3.5. War Graves

With the possible exception of security concerns relating to sensitive information that may be gleaned from a wreck site (which generally are likely to arise only in relation to recent casualties), for flag States a matter that is accorded the highest priority when the wreck of a warship or other State vessel is under consideration is the question of whether lives were lost when the vessel met its fate and, if so, whether there are – or may be – human remains still present at the site. As a result, there is a wealth of State practice indicating a general acceptance that human remains found on State wrecks should be treated with appropriate respect and that sites that represent substantial gravesites should be treated as places of sanctity. The exact bounds of this practice are hard to gauge, however, although it does seem to extend beyond the confines of lives lost in direct wartime combat. With the exception of international agreements relating to specific wreck sites, the 2001 UNESCO Convention is the only treaty that makes direct reference to human remains and gravesites found at sea. It provides that "States Parties shall ensure that proper respect is given to all human remains located in maritime waters",[58] and that "[a]ctivities directed at underwater cultural heritage shall avoid the unnecessary disturbance of human remains or venerated sites".[59] Equal treatment is therefore ac-

---

[55] UNCLOS, Art. 1(1)(1).
[56] 2001 UNESCO Convention, Art. 11(1).
[57] 2001 UNESCO Convention, Art. 12(7).
[58] 2001 UNESCO Convention, Art. 2(9).
[59] 2001 UNESCO Convention, Annex, Rule 5. Archaeologists are used to dealing with sites containing human remains, both on land and at sea, and have well-developed codes of practice in this respect, for example the Vermillion Accord on Human Remains, adopted at the World Archaeology Congress, 1989 Inter-Congress.

corded to human remains and maritime gravesites, civil and military, and whatever the circumstances of the loss.[60]

Article 12 of the Resolution, headed "War graves", provides:

> "Due respect shall be shown for the remains of any person in a sunken State ship. This obligation may be implemented through the establishment of the wreck as a war cemetery or other proper treatment of the remains of deceased persons and their burial when the wreck is recovered. States concerned should provide for the establishment of war cemeteries for wrecks".

Despite the heading of Article 12 and the content of the second two sentences, the first sentence appears to be confirmation that there is a customary rule of international law that appropriate respect must be shown for human remains present in any sunken State ship, whatever the context of its loss. This accords with two key domestic legislative instruments, the US Sunken Military Craft Act of 2004 and the UK Protection of Military Remains Act 1986, both of which afford protection to sites where military personnel lost their lives whether or not in the context of war. The second sentence indicates that the duty to show due respect may be implemented by the establishment of a wreck as a "war cemetery" and the third sentence exhorts States to establish such cemeteries. Where there has been mass loss of life through the sinking of a State vessel, in all likelihood this will have occurred in the course of a war and many mass maritime gravesites are, indeed, *de facto* war graves. Presumably what is envisaged is legal protection of specific sites. Domestic legislation, such as that referred to above, is a mechanism that can be used to effect such protection. However, depending on the maritime zone in which a wreck is situated, an international agreement may be required to ensure that controls on interference are enforceable. Interestingly, the two most notable international agreements creating maritime memorials relate to civil vessels lost in peacetime: the *Titanic*[61] and the passenger ferry M/S *Estonia*.[62]

---

[60] The question of whether or not military gravesites should be accorded a special status was the subject of lively debate. A proposal for specific reference to military maritime graves was rejected: see GARABELLO, "Sunken Warships in the Mediterranean: Reflections on Some Relevant Examples in State Practice Relating to the Mediterranean Sea", in SCOVAZZI (ed.), *La Protezione del Patrimonio Culturale Sottomarino nel Mare Mediterraneo*, Milano, 2004, p. 171 ff., p. 187.

[61] See *supra* note 25 and related text.

[62] 1995 Agreement between the Republic of Estonia, the Republic of Finland, and the Kingdom of Sweden Regarding the M/S *Estonia* (with additional Protocol of 1996 allowing for accession of other parties).

3.6. Salvage

Article 13 of the Resolution provides: "The salvage of sunken State ships is subject to the applicable rules of international law, the provisions of this Resolution, and appropriate archaeological practices". It must be assumed that the reference here to "salvage" means the recovery of material from wrecks. The prevailing international salvage law regime is to be found in the 1989 International Salvage Convention but this does not apply to warships or other non-commercial State vessels unless the flag State "opts-in".[63] There is some debate, too, as to its application in any circumstances to *sunken* vessels.[64] The applicable rules of international law referred to are therefore presumably principally the rules of immunity, which mean that recovery of material from a State wreck is prohibited without the express authorisation of the flag State, and – to the extent that the material qualifies – the rules designed to protect cultural value laid down in Articles 149 and 303 UNCLOS and in the 2001 UNESCO Convention. The reference to "appropriate archaeological practices" is a helpful reminder that many sunken State wrecks *will* be regarded as historical and archaeological sites and that any interference with such sites must take account of internationally accepted archaeological standards, now enshrined in the Annex to the 2001 Convention.

3.7. Hazardous Sunken State Ships

Many sunken State vessels present a hazard of one sort or another. They may constitute an obstacle to shipping or to marine development activities such as the laying of a new pipeline; they may contain unexploded ordnance that constitutes a threat to human life; and they may pose a pollution risk if they have oil or other noxious materials on board. The issue of hazardous wrecks is addressed by the 2007 Nairobi Wreck Removal Convention. This allows a coastal State to remove, or have removed, a wreck that poses a hazard to the environment, to navigation or to the broader economic interests of the State. Designed to apply primarily in the EEZ, the 2007 Convention clarifies the powers of intervention of coastal States with regard to pollution hazards and also extends existing powers to cover navigation hazards. Like the Salvage Convention and other treaties relating to marine pollution and maritime casualties, it does not apply to warships or other non-commercial State vessels unless the flag State decides otherwise.[65]

Article 14 of the Resolution addresses the situation of a State wreck posing a hazard. To some degree it echoes the third sentence of Article 9. However, unlike Article 9, it applies to all maritime zones, not just the EEZ. It provides: "1. Subject to

---

[63] 1989 Salvage Convention, Art. 4(1).
[64] See DROMGOOLE, *cit. supra* note 19, p. 178.
[65] 2007 Nairobi Convention, Art. 4(2).

Article 7 of this Resolution, the flag State shall remove wrecks constituting a hazard to navigation or a source of, or threat to, marine pollution. 2. The coastal State may take the measures necessary to eliminate or mitigate an imminent danger".

Paragraph 1 indicates that, in the view of the IDI, it is possible to construe – once again primarily from relevant treaty law – a duty on flag States to remove sunken State wrecks that pose a hazard with respect to navigation, or are a source of marine pollution or threaten to become so. Presumably, the duty extends by analogy to other hazards too. The Nairobi Convention, for example, defines hazard quite widely to include "any condition or threat [...] that may reasonably be expected to result in major harmful consequences to the marine environment, or damage to the coastline or related interests of one or more States", the key restriction being that "major harmful consequences" must be expected if the threat is not dealt with.[66] The reference to the notion of removal in paragraph 1 should probably be interpreted in line with the definition of "removal" in the Nairobi Convention, which makes it clear that what must be removed is the hazard and, depending on the circumstances, action short of removal of the wreck may suffice.[67] The fact that the duty on flag States is subject to Article 7 suggests that the flag State may be under a procedural obligation to consult with the coastal State and perhaps even obtain its consent before taking action with respect to a wreck posing a hazard in the territorial sea or other maritime space under coastal State sovereignty. Given that it is in the coastal State's interests that the hazard is dealt with, it seems unlikely that the coastal State would preclude the flag State from taking action, although it might well have a view about the nature of the action to be taken.

In practice, in any waters over which a coastal State has national jurisdiction, including the EEZ, in all likelihood the coastal State will be the party that generally initiates action by requesting that the flag State intervene to deal with a wreck posing a hazard. Despite the immunity of wrecks falling within the scope of the Resolution, Article 14(2) indicates that where a wreck in such waters poses an "imminent danger", the coastal State should itself be able to take the necessary measures to eliminate or mitigate the danger and to do so *without* the consent of the flag State. For example, this might be necessary if the flag State is tardy in taking action itself. The Preliminary Report cites the doctrine of necessity to support coastal State intervention in these sorts of circumstances.[68] Drawing on the Nairobi Convention, it seems likely that the measures should only be taken where "immediate action" is required; they should be "proportionate to the hazard"; should "not go beyond what is reasonably necessary", and should not "unnecessarily interfere with the rights and interests" of the flag State.[69]

---

[66] 2007 Nairobi Convention, Art. 1(5).

[67] See Art. 1(7) of the Nairobi Convention, which defines removal as meaning "any form of prevention, mitigation or elimination of the hazard created by a wreck".

[68] Preliminary Report, *cit. supra* note 1, p. 164.

[69] Nairobi Convention, Arts. 2(2)-(3) and 9(8).

Article 14 and the related provisions in Article 9 are important in showing that, although relevant treaties tend to exempt State vessels from their scope of application, the flag State is not *legibus solutus* but instead should abide by the treaty principles as far as it is reasonable and practicable to do so.[70]

3.8. Duty of Cooperation

The final provision of the Resolution, Article 15 provides:

> "All States should co-operate to protect and preserve wrecks which are part of cultural heritage, to remove wrecks which are a hazard to navigation, and to ensure that wrecks do not cause or threaten pollution of the marine environment. In particular, States bordering an enclosed or semi-enclosed sea should co-operate in the performance of their duties set out in this Resolution in a manner consistent with the rights and duties of other States".

From the discussion above, it is clear that certain issues relating to sunken State wrecks can only be satisfactorily addressed if there is cooperation between the flag State and an affected coastal State, such cooperation entailing at the least the sharing of information, consultation, and the seeking and giving of consent. Given the uncertainties that exist concerning the precise respective rights and jurisdiction of flag States and coastal States in maritime zones within national jurisdiction, Article 15(1) may well be designed, at least in part, to exhort States to cooperate with one another in the circumstances outlined *whatever* the precise legal niceties may be.

In practice cooperative action may take many forms and may also extend beyond the immediate coastal State and the flag State. Article 15(2) is evidently designed to encourage cooperation on a regional basis. In the context of cultural heritage protection, regional cooperation is often necessary in order to tackle deliberate unwarranted interference with shipwrecks.[71] In the context of potentially hazardous wrecks, the impact of any potential incident, for example an oil spill, clearly may be felt by the whole region.

---

[70] See Preliminary Report, *cit. supra* note 1, at p. 162.

[71] The 2001 UNESCO Convention explicitly encourages States Parties to enter into regional agreements that are in conformity with the Convention, envisaging that they may be utilised in order to afford "better" protection than that provided by the Convention itself (Art. 6(1)). There have been discussions with respect to a potential regional agreement to protect underwater cultural heritage in the Mediterranean Sea: see GARABELLO, *cit. supra* note 60, pp. 197-199.

4. CONCLUDING REMARKS

The IDI's initiative on sunken State vessels is extremely timely. The centenary period of the First World War has focused the attention of the international community on the fate of the vast number of sunken wrecks and other material remains associated with the war and highlighted the practical relevance and importance of many of the issues and questions discussed above. The Resolution, and the report that preceded it, contribute significantly to the crucial task of teasing out and clarifying international law in this field.

While some consideration was given to the possibility that the Resolution could call for an international treaty to deal with the subject, in the end it holds back from doing so. Given the surfeit of treaties in the field already and the complexities of their interaction with each other and with customary international law, this is probably wise. Among other things, it is far from clear which international organisation would be prepared to sponsor a treaty that cuts across so many different issues and the difficulties encountered by the UNESCO initiative, focusing as it did on just one of those issues, makes it clear that the negotiation of a new treaty would be a hugely formidable task.

Inevitably, the IDI Resolution leaves lots of unanswered questions. For example, is there, and should there be, a distinction in the legal status of sunken warships lost in war and those lost in other circumstances? What, if any, legal distinctions are to be drawn between sunken warships and other State-owned ships engaged, at the time of sinking, on non-commercial service? For the purposes of the Resolution, these two categories are assimilated, but are they necessarily assimilated for all purposes? What is the status of the wrecks of ships operated, but not owned, by a State and in use on non-commercial service when they sank and what duties are incumbent on both the operating State and the flag State in those circumstances? In what circumstances, if at all, should the flag State be held responsible for damage caused by wrecks? What *exactly* are the respective rights and jurisdiction of the coastal State and the flag State when a State wreck is located in waters within national jurisdiction, especially within the limit of the territorial sea? Further questions arise in relation to wrecks more generally. Does the flag State retain jurisdiction after a civil ship has sunk?[72] How should a wreck that is hazardous *and* of historical value be managed?[73]

It is to be hoped that the work of the IDI will be taken up and built upon by another international body. As Natalino Ronzitti pointed out in the Addendum to his Preliminary Report, the topic of wrecks has been on the long-term work programme of the International Law Commission since 2001. The time may now be ripe for this item to be activated.

---

[72] See Preliminary Report, *cit. supra* note 1, p. 149.
[73] The 2001 UNESCO Convention makes no provision in this regard.

STRENGTHENING COMPLIANCE WITH INTERNATIONAL HUMANITARIAN LAW: THE FAILED PROPOSAL FOR A "MEETING OF STATES ON INTERNATIONAL HUMANITARIAN LAW"

GIULIO BARTOLINI[*]

Abstract

Within current debates on international humanitarian law (IHL) attempts to strengthen compliance are a key issue. Several existing mechanisms provided by IHL treaties have proved to be unsuccessful, mainly due to States' unwillingness to activate them and to their limited field of application, that is, such mechanisms are principally restricted to international armed conflicts. Conversely, instruments pertaining to other branches of international law have progressively come to play a significant role in this area, emphasizing a series of challenges and opportunities. Against this background this contribution explores attempts to identify further options, such as the proposal submitted to the 32nd International Conference of the Red Cross and Red Crescent held in December 2015. Its aim was to facilitate the creation of a new compliance mechanism for IHL, the so-called "Meeting of States on International Humanitarian Law": a regular, voluntary, yet institutionalized forum for dialogue on IHL among States Parties to the Geneva Conventions, to be provided with a series of functions intended to improve the implementation of IHL. However, due to disagreements among States during the Conference, delegations were ultimately unable to reach a consensus on this new mechanism, thus emphasizing serious difficulties in bringing about effective improvements with regard to IHL compliance mechanisms.

Keywords: compliance with international humanitarian law; International Committee of the Red Cross; armed conflicts; human rights law.

1. INTRODUCTION

One of the major current challenges for international humanitarian law (IHL) concerns compliance. Considering that this term is currently understood "as respect for all relevant obligations under IHL"[1] or as "ensuring that belligerents act in con-

---

[*] Associate Professor of International Law, Department of Law, University of Roma Tre, e-mail: giulio.bartolini@uniroma3.it.

[1] ICRC/Swiss Federal Department of Foreign Affairs, Strengthening Compliance with International Humanitarian Law, Concluding Report, June 2015, p. 12, footnote 25: "The goal of the IHL compliance system discussed within the Swiss-ICRC facilitated consultation process is to strengthen respect for IHL. The term 'compliance' may be understood in the present context as respect for all relevant obligations under IHL". The Concluding Report, as well as documents

formity with IHL",[2] it is clear that compliance represents one of the hardest tests for IHL. Better compliance with IHL rules is however of paramount importance, as it would not only permit the proper application of international obligations, but would also provide enhanced protection for victims of armed conflicts.

It is therefore no surprise that growing attention has been paid to the assessment of existing mechanisms related to the application of this branch of law, also in the light of internal and external challenges to the IHL compliance system, as explored in section 2. Shared scepticism about the current framework has fostered discussions regarding both potential reforms to the existing system and possible new mechanisms to favour the implementation of IHL.[3]

In this regard activities carried out under the aegis of the International Conference of the Red Cross and Red Crescent (IC) – a unique institutional forum, gathering delegations from States Parties to the Geneva Conventions (GCs), National Red Cross and Red Crescent Societies, the International Committee of Red Cross (ICRC) and the International Federation of Red Cross and Red Crescent Societies[4] – have assumed a pivotal role. The ICs have represented periodic opportunities for debate on the possibility of strengthening IHL compliance mechanisms, as testified by Resolution 1 adopted at the 31st IC in 2011.[5] This Resolution led to the development of the so-called "compliance track", requiring the ICRC and Switzerland to pursue consultations with the aim of identifying solutions to enhance the effectiveness of IHL compliance mechanisms and submit potential proposals in this regard to the 32nd IC, held in Geneva on 8-10th December 2015 (see section 4).

---

related to this initiative managed by the ICRC and Switzerland, such as Chairs' conclusions and background reports, are available at: <https://www.icrc.org/en/document/strengthening-compliance-international-humanitarian-law-ihl-work-icrc-and-swiss-government>.

[2] BOUTRUCHE, "Good Offices, Conciliation and Enquiry", in CLAPHAM, GAETA and SASSÒLI (eds.), *The 1949 Geneva Conventions. A Commentary*, Oxford, 2015, p. 661 ff., p. 661: "Unlike the complementary notion of enforcement of IHL that focuses on the ways to restore observance with IHL when it has been violated, compliance pertains to ensuring that belligerents act in conformity with IHL".

[3] SASSÒLI, "The Implementation of International Humanitarian Law: Current and Inherent Challenges", YIHL, 2007, p. 45 ff.; PFANNER, "Various Mechanisms and Approaches for Implementing International Humanitarian Law and Protecting and Assisting War Victims", IRRC, 2009, p. 307 ff.; and BENVENUTI and BARTOLINI, "Is There a Need for New International Humanitarian Law Implementation Mechanisms?", in KOLB and GAGGIOLI (eds.), *Research Handbook on Human Rights and Humanitarian Law*, Cheltenham, 2013, p. 590 ff.

[4] On the institutional features of the IC see BUGNION, "The International Conference of the Red Cross and Red Crescent: Challenges, Key Issues and Achievements", IRRC, 2009, p. 675 ff.

[5] See 31st IC, Resolution 1: Strengthening Legal Protection for Victims of Armed Conflicts, 2011, available at: <https://www.icrc.org/eng/resources/documents/resolution/31-international-conference-resolution-1-2011.htm>.

On this basis, in October 2015 the facilitators submitted a draft resolution on "Strengthening Compliance with International Humanitarian Law" in view of the 32nd IC.[6] The significant novelty of this draft resolution was self-evident: the document contained a comprehensive proposal recommending that States create a new compliance mechanism for IHL, the so-called "Meeting of States on International Humanitarian Law" (hereinafter "Meeting of States"). This would mainly be a regular, voluntary, but institutionalized forum to favour dialogue on IHL among States party to the GCs; the operative paragraphs of the draft resolution identified the Meeting's key features, on the basis of the main elements apparently agreed upon by participants during the consultation process. This new mechanism was to be vested with a series of functions intended to be beneficial in improving the implementation of IHL, even if a series of potential shortcomings risked significantly limiting its efficacy (see section 4).

However, due to the fierce debate that took place during the 32nd IC, when clear divisions among States became apparent, the delegations were unable to reach a consensus on this new mechanism and the final Resolution 2[7] merely recommends the continuation of consultations in this area, to be informed by a series of guiding principles. As a result the 32nd IC, rather than being the expected turning point in the longstanding debate on potential reforms to the IHL compliance system, represented a fiasco among the law/policy-making activities related to this body of law and raised doubts about the real willingness of stakeholders (mainly States) to introduce significant improvements. This article will explore the debate surrounding potential reforms to the IHL compliance mechanisms, focusing in particular on the failed proposal to create the Meeting of States, the latter being the touchstone for any future discussions in this area.

2. A REVIEW OF EXISTING MECHANISMS FOR THE IMPLEMENTATION OF IHL: INTERNAL AND EXTERNAL CHALLENGES FOR THE IHL COMPLIANCE SYSTEM

An analysis of the abovementioned proposal to establish a Meeting of States must necessarily be based on a review of the current compliance mechanisms provided by IHL, as well as instruments pertaining to other branches of international law that have progressively assumed a role in this area. In both cases a series of challenges and opportunities can be highlighted in order to facilitate understanding of the legal framework behind current proposals.

---

[6] For the Draft Resolution 2 circulated among delegations see at: <https://perma.cc/X3K2-G3AD>.

[7] See 32nd IC, Resolution 2: Strengthening Compliance with International Humanitarian Law, 32IC/15/R2, available at: <http://rcrcconference.org/wp-content/uploads/sites/3/2015/04/32IC-AR-Compliance_EN.pdf>.

2.1. The "Internal" Mechanisms for Compliance with IHL

Taking into account the internal dimension of the IHL compliance system, i.e. the mechanisms in force and factors that might prompt the development of additional instruments within the realm of this body of law, various elements highlight the shortcomings of the current system. In particular, attention should be paid to: (a) the unsuccessful nature of several IHL mechanisms, also due to States' unwillingness to activate them; (b) the absence of an institutional forum devoted to supervising compliance with IHL obligations; and (c) the limited field of application of several treaty-based mechanisms, which are mainly restricted to international armed conflicts (IACs).

(a) First, several compliance mechanisms provided by IHL rules have proven to be largely ineffective, mainly due to States lacking the political/legal will to trigger their application.[8] As many mechanisms rely on the consent of States involved in armed conflicts in order to be operative, this reluctance has implied their progressive irrelevance.

The role of Protecting Powers, i.e. neutral States called upon to ensure the implementation of IHL[9] (following the consent of the States involved), has been progressively neglected. Indeed, Protecting Powers have been appointed in only five IACs since the adoption of the 1949 GCs. This decline can be attributed to several concurrent causes. In particular, very few States are perceived as properly neutral and either able or willing to carry such a burden, which might expose them to foreign policy difficulties. Furthermore the ICRC's *de facto* substitution of Protecting Powers when the latter mechanism does not function has made it possible to partly overcome the difficulties related to the non-application of this mechanism.[10] However, as recently recognised in the 2016 ICRC's Commentary, "[t]he obstacles do not appear to result from the inadequacy of the procedures nor from the financial burden, but are more likely to be related to political considerations".[11] Also in this regard the lack of will by the States concerned is the driving factor for the inactivity of these mechanisms.

Similarly, the enquiry procedures provided for by the 1949 Conventions[12] have not worked at all. As they are intended to resolve disputes between States Parties to

---

[8] SASSÒLI, *cit. supra* note 3, p. 52.

[9] Arts. 8 and 9 of the 1949 GCs, and Art. 5 of the 1977 AP I. See BUGNION, "Article 8. Protecting Powers", in ICRC, *Convention (I) for the Amelioration of the Condition of the Wounded and Sick in Armed Forces, Commentary of 2016* (on-line edition); and KOLB, "Protecting Powers", in CLAPHAM, GAETA and SASSÒLI (eds.), *cit. supra* note 2, p. 549 ff.

[10] ICRC, "Improving Compliance with International Humanitarian Law. ICRC Expert Seminars", October 2003, pp. 10-12, available at: <http://www.icrc.org/eng/assets/files/other/improving_compliance_with_ihl-oct_2003.pdf>.

[11] BUGNION, *cit. supra* note 9, para. 116.

[12] GC I, Art. 52; GC II, Art. 53; GC III, Art. 132; GC IV, Art. 149. See VITÉ, "Article 52. Enquiry Procedure", in ICRC, *cit. supra* note 9, para. 1 ff.

an IAC regarding alleged violations of the GCs, and request the wrongful State to repress such violations, it is not surprising that these procedures have not engaged the interest of States. Attempts to establish enquiry procedures have failed in the past due to a lack of consent on the part of the States involved in conflicts, this being a fundamental prerequisite for their activation.[13] Also in this case, the new Commentary to the GCs recognises that "the ineffectiveness of the enquiry mechanism established under the 1949 GCs is due mainly to lack of political will" and its absence of institutionalization.[14]

A similar unhappy fate has been met by the complex machinery of the International Humanitarian Fact-Finding Commission (IHFFC), provided for by Article 90 of the 1977 Additional Protocol I (AP I)[15] and primarily intended to enquire into any facts alleged to constitute a grave breach or other serious violation of the GCs and AP I, through a confidential procedure. Notwithstanding the potential of such a mechanism, to date the Commission has not been used, despite more than 70 States having made a general declaration accepting the competence of the IHFFC. Likewise, the longstanding willingness expressed by the IHFFC to extend its activities to non-international armed conflicts, as long as all parties to the conflict agree, has come to nothing.[16] Even recent events, such as the 2015 attack on a *Médecins sans frontières* hospital in Afghanistan,[17] have demonstrated how appeals by humanitarian actors to permit the Commission to operate cannot have any effect when the States involved do not request its services.

Another additional mechanism that has not yet been tested is the meeting of the High Contracting Parties, as provided for by Article 7 AP I.[18] This mechanism, as well as similar meetings of States Parties mentioned below, is of particular interest taking into account the 2015 proposal to create a Meeting of States. Under Article 7 AP I, at the request of one or more of the States Parties and upon the approval of the majority of the parties to AP I, Switzerland shall convene a meeting to con-

---

[13] Regarding the failed attempts by the ICRC to facilitate the creation of an enquiry procedure related to the 1973 Israeli-Arab countries' conflict see BUGNION, *Le Comité International de la Croix-Rouge et la protection des victimes de la guerre*, Geneva, 1994, p. 1099.

[14] VITÉ, *cit. supra* note 12, para. 34.

[15] DE PREUX, "Article 90", in SANDOZ, SWINARSKI and ZIMMERMANN (eds.), *Commentary on the Additional Protocols of 8 June 1977 to the Geneva Conventions of 12 August 1949*, Geneva, 1987, p. 1039 ff.; and CONDORELLI, "The International Humanitarian-Fact Finding Commission: An Obsolete Tool or a Useful Measure to Implement International Humanitarian Law?", IRRC, 2001, p. 393 ff.

[16] KALSHOVEN, "The International Humanitarian Fact-Finding Commission: A Sleeping Beauty?", Humanitäres Völkerrecht, 2002, p. 213 ff., p. 214.

[17] HARWOOD, "Will the 'Sleeping Beauty' Awaken? The Kunduz Hospital Attack and the International Humanitarian Fact-Finding Commission", EJIL: Talk!, 15 October 2015, available at: <http://www.ejiltalk.org/will-the-sleeping-beauty-awaken-the-kunduz-hospital-attack-and-the-international-humanitarian-fact-finding-commission>.

[18] ZIMMERMANN, "Article 7", in SANDOZ, SWINARSKI and ZIMMERMANN (eds.), *cit. supra* note 15, p. 104 ff.

sider "general problems concerning the application of the Conventions and of the Protocol". This kind of mechanism could therefore provide a sort of institutional framework for debates concerning IHL, but no meeting has ever been convened, partly due to certain inherent limitations. First, taking into account the ratification of AP I by 174 States, this mechanism can only operate on the basis of a common request by a significant number of parties. Second, it is not envisaged as a regular conference of States Parties, also because it lacks any of the proper institutional and bureaucratic machinery required to manage such meetings in a fruitful manner. Third, the broad reference to the possibility of debating "general problems" regarding the application of the Geneva Conventions limits its functions. This expression has mainly been interpreted as having a negative character, aiming "to exclude the discussion of specific situations"[19] from its area of operation. On this basis, for instance, preliminary requests to convene urgent meetings in relation to ongoing armed conflicts involving alleged violations of IHL, such as the 2006 Lebanon conflict, have been refused by Switzerland as being outside the scope of application of Article 7 AP I.[20]

Until now, only a sort of substitute meeting of States Parties has been realised in exceptional circumstances. Its basis can be found in Resolution 1[21] adopted by the 26th IC held in 1995, which endorsed the recommendation of a group of intergovernmental experts[22] to request "the Depositary to organize periodical meetings of the States Parties to the 1949 Geneva Conventions to consider general problems regarding the application of IHL". So far, Switzerland has only managed to organize one meeting in 1998, following consultations with States, which aimed to discuss both armed conflicts in relation to the disintegration of State structures, and respect for and the security of the personnel of humanitarian organizations.[23] This initiative, had it been replicated in a periodic manner as originally suggested by the 26th International Conference, could have helped create a forum for discussion on the current challenges for IHL, even if its non-institutionalized nature as well as uncertainties concerning the management of key issues (e.g. the selection of topics,

---

[19] *Ibid*, p. 104.

[20] The request had been made by twenty States parties. See "Federal Department of Foreign Affairs, Notification to the Governments of the State Parties to the Geneva Conventions of 12 August 1949 for the Protection of War Victims", 12 September 2006, available at: <https://www.eda.admin.ch/content/dam/eda/fr/documents/aussenpolitik/voelkerrecht/geneve/060912-GENEVE_e.pdf>. See also DISTEFANO and HENRY, "Final Provisions, Including the Martens Clause", in CLAPHAM, GAETA and SASSÒLI (eds.), *cit. supra* note 2, p. 155 ff., p. 172.

[21] "Resolution 1 of the 26th International Conference of the International Red Cross and Red Crescent (Geneva, Switzerland, 3-7 December 1995)", IRRC, 1996, p. 58 ff.

[22] "Meeting of the Intergovernmental Group of Experts for the Protection of War Victims: Recommendations", IRRC, 1995, p. 37 ff.

[23] BURCI, "The First Periodic Meeting of the States Parties to the 1949 Geneva Conventions", CI, 1998, p. 116 ff.; and CAFLISCH, "First Periodical Meeting on International Humanitarian Law", IRRC, 1998, p. 366 ff.

outcomes of the meetings, etc.) would have represented major challenges. Hence evaluations similar to those above in relation to Article 7 AP I can be reiterated in this regard.

Nonetheless, conferences involving States Parties to the GCs have occasionally been organized on a different basis. In particular, through certain resolutions the UN General Assembly has recommended that the High Contracting Parties to the Fourth GC, or specifically the government of Switzerland as depositary of this Treaty, organize conferences related to the application of this Convention in the occupied Palestinian Territories.[24] The departure from the model envisaged above is clear. In this case the focus is on the arrangement of conflict-specific meetings of High Contracting Parties to the Fourth GC, the occurrence of which Switzerland has subordinated to a sufficient consensus being achieved by States Parties. The main legal basis for these meetings has been their qualification as a concrete expression of the measures that States can adopt on the basis of Common Article 1.[25] So far, Switzerland has convened three conferences dealing with this conflict, in 1999, 2001, and 2014.

The main aim of the above meetings has therefore been to reaffirm the relevance of basic IHL rules and the need for their full respect in such a scenario, as expressed in brief statements or more detailed documents adopted at the end of such conferences. However, being closely connected to a clearly-defined conflict scenario, these experiences have emphasized a series of difficulties. First, the highly sensitive nature of the situation addressed has made it necessary to develop a delicate balance between different exigencies and legal perceptions, as carefully enshrined in the final documents. Second, the need to identify a minimum level of consent among States to set up such meetings has implied lengthy negotiations, which have not favoured the timely examination of the situations in hand. For instance, the multilateral process initiated in 2009 on the basis of Resolution 64/10 of the UN General Assembly only ended in 2014, when it was partly favoured by an additional military escalation affecting the area. Similarly, relevant States, including those directly involved in the situations under examination, have opposed

---

[24] See UN Doc. A/RES/64/10 (2009); UN Doc. A/RES/ES-10/7 (2000); UN Doc. A/RES/ES-10/6 (1999); and UN Doc. A/RES/ES-10/3 (1997). See HAPPOLD, "The Conference of High Contracting Parties to the Fourth Geneva Convention", YIHL, 2001, p. 389 ff.; and LANZ, MAX and HOEHNE, "The Conference of High Contracting Parties to the Fourth Geneva Convention of 17 December 2014 and the Duty to Ensure Respect for International Humanitarian Law", IRRC, 2015, p. 1116 ff.

[25] LANZ, MAX and HOEHNE, *cit. supra* note 24, p. 1116. The 2016 Commentary mentions these meetings as practice confirming an obligation to ensure respect for IHL under Common Article 1: HENCKAERTS, "Article 1. Respect and Ensure Respect", in ICRC, *cit supra* note 9, para. 39. On Common Art. 1 see: DÖRMANN and SERRALVO, "Common Article 1 to the Geneva Conventions and the Obligation to Prevent International Humanitarian Law Violations", IRRC, 2015, p. 707 ff.; and GEISS, "The Obligation to Respect and Ensure Respect for the Conventions", in CLAPHAM, GAETA and SASSÒLI (eds.), *cit. supra* note 2, p. 111 ff.

to such conferences, thus raising doubts about their efficacy.[26] The difficulties of replicating this kind of conflict-specific conference in other contexts are easy to perceive. At the same time, they could have some merits, especially if repeated in other situations to avoid the perception of selectivity, as they may help to raise awareness about the humanitarian consequences of certain situations, and to exercise diplomatic pressure on parties.

The above survey of the compliance mechanisms provided by IHL treaty provisions emphasizes their limited role, even if other more effective tools also exist. Reference could be made to the multifaceted activities of the ICRC, which are of paramount importance in this area.[27] Similarly, even if mainly related to the enforcement phase, individual criminal responsibility for war crimes could also be mentioned, especially in light of its deterrent effect, aimed at favouring compliance with IHL.[28] However, criminal responsibility for war crimes can only be a part of the overall mechanisms for strengthening compliance with IHL.

(b) A second shortcoming of the current IHL compliance mechanisms is the lack of a proper institutional framework aimed at favouring the application of this body of law and verifying its fulfilment. This could be provided by monitoring bodies or, to a lesser extent, by periodic meetings of States Parties, intended to facilitate general dialogue on the application of relevant provisions. As it is known, conferences of States Parties have also been experienced in areas closely related to IHL, such as in international criminal law,[29] or weapons treaties,[30] where States are required (for instance) to report to Meetings of States Parties, and on occasion to the UN Secretary-General, on measures adopted at the national level to implement treaty obligations, even if such mechanisms have largely acted on a bureaucratic manner.

An institutional framework could have some positive effects in this area, also taking into account that IHL pays significant attention to obligations to be fulfilled by States in view of potential armed conflicts, as maintained in Common Article

---

[26] HAPPOLD, cit. supra note 24, pp. 391-393; LANZ, MAX and HOEHNE, cit. supra note 24, p. 1125.

[27] See for instance GILADI and RATNER, "The Role of the International Committee of the Red Cross", in CLAPHAM, GAETA and SASSÒLI (eds.), cit. supra note 2, p. 525 ff.

[28] For different views compare JENKS and ACQUAVIVA, "Debate: The Role of International Criminal Justice in Fostering Compliance with International Humanitarian Law", IRRC, 2015, p. 775 ff.

[29] ICC Statute, Art. 112. See SCHABAS, The International Criminal Court: A Commentary on the Rome Statute, Oxford, 2010, pp. 1115-1134.

[30] E.g., Art. 8 of the Convention Prohibiting Certain Conventional Weapons (10 October 1980, entered into force 2 December 1983); Art. 11 of the Convention on Anti-Personnel Mines (1997, entered into force 1 March 1999); Art. 11 of the Convention on Cluster Munitions (2008, entered into force 1 August 2010).

2 to the 1949 GCs and detailed elsewhere in the Conventions and APs.[31] For instance, a series of provisions require States to enact legislation and provide effective criminal sanctions for persons responsible for acts contrary to treaty obligations. Similarly, obligations to preventively disseminate IHL among the civilian population and the armed forces are also imposed upon States. Failing the acceptance of the ICRC proposals to oblige States to periodically report to the Depositary and to the ICRC on measures taken with regard to dissemination,[32] the implementation of IHL is basically delegated to State discretion.[33] Such preventive measures should allow States to create a sound legal framework and help relevant actors to apply IHL rules, through appropriate legislative and practical measures for that purpose. Especially in this regard, the possibility for States to benefit from an institutional framework supporting the fulfilment of such activities, for instance through the sharing of best practices and the development of fruitful discussion, would represent an added value regarding proper compliance with IHL.

Currently the only regular momentum in institutional dialogue among relevant stakeholders is represented by the ICs, held every four years. However, the ICs have a more diplomatic and policy-making nature than a monitoring approach, as delegations avoid turning this meeting into a possible site of scrutiny.[34] Furthermore, its busy agenda and long periods of inactivity impede any regular dialogue.

Similarly, at the national level the existence of an institutional framework capable of fostering a legal and policy environment that favours the implementation of IHL cannot be taken for granted. In several areas of international law the positive feature of such bodies can be seen in the development of national platforms and focal points aimed at permitting the better application of treaties[35] as well as nonbinding international standards.[36] Notwithstanding recommendations in this regard by ICs,[37] in the IHL system the creation of similar institutions depends on the willingness of States, which may create national committees on IHL, usually made up of representatives of government departments, academics, and the National Red

---

[31] For required activities see ZIEGLER and WEHRENBERG, "Domestic Implementation", in CLAPHAM, GAETA and SASSÒLI (eds.), cit. supra note 2, p. 647 ff.

[32] On such proposal submitted by the ICRC at the 1974-1977 Diplomatic Conference see DE PREUX, "Article 83", in SANDOZ, SWINARSKI and ZIMMERMANN (eds.), cit. supra note 15, p. 959 ff., p. 963.

[33] GC I, Art. 47; GC II, Art. 48; GC III, Art. 127(1); GC IV, Art. 144(1); AP I, Art. 83(1); AP II, Art.19. See MÜLLER, "Article 47. Dissemination", in ICRC, cit. supra note 9, para. 1 ff.; and MIKOS-SKUZA, "Dissemination of the Conventions, Including in Times of Armed Conflicts", in CLAPHAM, GAETA and SASSÒLI (eds.), cit. supra note 2, p. 597 ff.

[34] PFANNER, cit. supra note 3, p. 307.

[35] See for instance the activities of focal points in relation to several multilateral environmental agreements or as provided by the WHO International Health Regulations.

[36] See for instance requests to create national focal points in relation to disaster risk reduction, as already envisaged in the Hyogo Framework for Action (2005-2015) and reaffirmed in the Sendai Framework for Disaster Risk Reduction (2015-2030).

[37] See in particular para. 4 of the Resolution 1 of the 26th IC, cit. supra note 21.

Cross / Red Crescent Societies.[38] However, these bodies are present in only about half of the States Parties to the GCs[39] and the significant differences in their effectiveness are notorious, in many cases due to sporadic action and lack of capacity to significantly address challenges.

The detrimental effects of the absence of IHL institutional frameworks at the international and national level can be exemplified with regard to Italy. For instance, Italy has yet to translate into appropriate criminal provisions some of the offences that the GCs and AP I required be introduced into domestic legal orders.[40] Equally, the inter-ministerial Committee on IHL, originally established in 1998 and formally still in force, is not operative. Hence it is clear that other legislative priorities, budget concerns, and the allocation of insufficient human resources devoted to addressing IHL issues can render the proper fulfilment of IHL provisions even more complex. Conversely, the availability of appropriate institutional fora in which to debate and support activities in this area would be beneficial.

(c) Finally, a major shortcoming of several IHL compliance mechanisms lies in their field of application, which is essentially circumscribed to IACs. They are thus inapplicable in relation to the most common scenario for the application of IHL, namely non-international armed conflicts (NIACs).[41] Furthermore, challenges posed by organized armed groups are almost entirely neglected in IHL provisions dealing with compliance, thus enhancing a perception of legal asymmetry which hardly favours their observance of IHL rules.

2.2. Mechanisms "External" to the IHL System

Awareness of the limits faced by the IHL compliance mechanisms has progressively favoured the resort to a multifaceted series of instruments outside this body of law, borrowing mechanisms external to it when potentially advantageous to IHL: the measures provided by human rights law (HRL) and the law of international organisations are of particular relevance here. The increasing use of such mechanisms has implied both positive aspects – as they enrich the catalogue of tools available

---

[38] PELLANDINI, "Ensuring National Compliance with IHL: The Role and Impact of National IHL Committees", IRRC, 2015, p. 1043 ff.

[39] Currently, 108 national IHL committees or commissions are formally in force. For relevant data see at: <https://www.icrc.org/en/document/table-national-committees-and-other-national-bodies-international-humanitarian-law>.

[40] BARTOLINI, "Le modifiche al codice penale militare di guerra a seguito della missione italiana in Afghanistan", CI, 2002, p. 179 ff.; and BENVENUTI, "Il ritardo della legislazione italiana nell'adeguamento al diritto internazionale umanitario", in LAMBERTI ZANARDI and VENTURINI (eds.), Crimini di guerra e competenza delle giurisdizioni nazionali, Milano, 1998, p. 107 ff. Similar concerns apply to the implementation of the ICC Statute.

[41] ICRC, cit. supra note 10, pp. 20-24.

to favour the implementation of IHL – and challenges: they are perceived as being driven by politics and selective in their agenda, as lacking specific expertise in relation to the inherent dynamics of IHL, or, equally, as being ineffective.

In particular, a series of mechanisms provided by HRL at the universal and regional levels are increasingly used to deal with armed conflicts – primarily, but not exclusively, from the perspective of human rights violations that may have occurred in such scenarios. Various instruments can be cited in this regard.

First, the increased involvement of judicial or quasi-judicial HRL bodies in IHL matters has primarily occurred in the case of individual claims, and has partly compensated for the lack of similar mechanisms in the IHL system.[42] However, such a trend is far from being unproblematic, due to the legal tensions between HRL and IHL and the different approaches adopted by monitoring bodies.[43] The examination of periodic reports has similarly permitted monitoring bodies to make general references to States regarding respect for IHL or certain specific provisions of the specific HR treaty under exam.[44] However, such references do not follow a uniform approach, since only a small number of States involved in armed conflicts have been affected by these requests and not all human rights bodies have followed such a pattern.

At the universal level an added contribution could be provided via the universal periodic review (UPR) activities of the Human Rights Council (HRC). Specifically, the UPR system expressly mandates the HRC to examine States regarding their IHL-related obligations.[45] This has led to increasing practice in this regard,[46] although it remains cursory, also on account of some States' express criticism of such a possibility.[47] Furthermore, the system's diplomatic-political nature could affect the possibility of such issues being examined substantively. This element is reflected in the rather general character of observations proposed by other States during the examination process when dealing with IHL. Concerns for compli-

---

[42] KLEFFNER, "Improving Compliance with International Humanitarian Law through the Establishment of an Individual Complaints Mechanisms", Leiden JIL, 2002, p. 237 ff.

[43] See for instance JINKS, MAOGOTO and SOLOMON (eds.), *International Humanitarian Law in Judicial and Quasi-Judicial Bodies. International and Domestic Aspects*, The Hague, 2014; KOLB and GAGGIOLI (eds.), *cit. supra* note 3, 2013; and BEN-NAFTALI (ed.), *International Humanitarian Law and International Human Rights Law: pas de deux*, Oxford, 2011.

[44] See for instance Human Rights Committee, Concluding Observations (Central African Republic), UN Doc. CCPR/C/CAF/CO/2 (2006), para. 8; Committee on the Rights of the Child, Concluding Observations (Canada), UN Doc. CRC/C/OPAC/CAN/CO/1 (2007), para. 12. On such practice see OBERLEITNER, *Human Rights in Armed Conflict. Law, Practice, Policy*, Cambridge, 2015, pp. 262-270.

[45] Human Rights Council, Institution-Building of the United Nations, UN Doc. A/HRC/RES/5/1 (2007).

[46] ZHU, "International Humanitarian Law in the Universal Periodic Review of the UN Human Rights Council", Journal of International Humanitarian Legal Studies, 2014, p. 186 ff.

[47] E.g., Report of the Working Group on the Universal Periodic Review. The United Kingdom of Great Britain and Northern Ireland, UN Doc. A/HRC/8/25 (2008), para. 36.

ance with IHL have also prompted a significant increase in special sessions of the HRC devoted to situations involving armed conflicts: during these meetings IHL issues have been addressed,[48] with focuses on activities carried out by organized armed groups in NIACs. Resolutions condemning violations of IHL could also be mentioned,[49] which might help increase the diplomatic pressure on parties to the conflict to comply with IHL.

A very significant novelty has been the establishment of independent commissions of inquiry and fact-finding missions related to armed conflicts, managed by the HRC,[50] other UN bodies,[51] and regional international organizations.[52] These activities are particularly relevant as they have progressively shifted the focus of fact-finding activities – originally envisaged as part of the IHL compliance system – toward external mechanisms. In fact, apart from providing analysis under HRL, such commissions usually possess the faculty to review events from an IHL perspective. They also share the advantage of considering conduct carried out by organized armed groups involved in NIACs. Significantly, acting on a mandate provided by an international organisation means that such commissions need not rely on the consent of parties to the conflict to perform their activities, i.e. an element that has prevented similar IHL compliance mechanisms from acting.

Such bodies have nonetheless been characterized by approaches that broadly differ from the IHL mechanisms. For instance, one of the aims of the abovementioned bodies is to provide public scrutiny of the events, whereas the IHFFC would be required to conduct its activities according to the principle of confidentiality, unless otherwise determined by the parties. Similarly, such commissions have hardly limited themselves to mere fact-finding activities. They have also displayed ele-

---

[48] Out of the 23 special sessions of the HRC, eighteen have been devoted to situations involving an armed conflict, where IHL issues were consequently discussed (Iraq, Central African Republic, Sri Lanka, Democratic Republic of Congo, Sudan, Israel, Syria, and Libya). See recently Twenty-third special session on activities carried out by the terrorist group Boko Haram (2015).

[49] See for instance UN Doc. A/HRC/RES/S-23/1(2015) in relation to Boko Haram; UN Doc. A/HRC/RES/S-8/1 (2008), Democratic Republic of Congo.

[50] See commissions of inquiry of fact-finding missions related to: Lebanon, 2006 (UN Doc. A/HRC/S-2/1); Gaza Conflict, 2009 (UN Doc. A/HRC/RES/S-9/1); Freedom Flotilla, 2010 (UN Doc. A/HRC/RES/14/1); Libya, 2011 (UN Doc. A/HRC/RES/S-15/1); Ivory Coast, 2011 (UN Doc. A/HRC/RES/16/25); and Syria, 2011 (UN Doc. A/HRC/RES/S-17/1).

[51] For commissions, fact-finding missions or panel of experts established by the UN Secretary-General or by the Security Council see: Darfur, 2004 (UN Doc. S/RES/1564); Guinea, 2009 (UN Doc. S/2009/556); Sri Lanka, 2010 (UN Doc. SG/SM/12967); Central African Republic, 2013 (UN Doc. S/RES/2127).

[52] See EU Council Decision 2008/901/CFSP creating an independent fact-finding mission on the conflict in Georgia; Report of the African Commission on Human and Peoples' Rights' Fact-Finding Mission to the Republic of Sudan in the Darfur Region, EX.CL/364 (XI), Annex III, 2004; Inter-American Commission on Human Rights, Third report on the human rights situation in Colombia, OEA/Ser.L/V/II.102, Doc. 9 rev. 1, 1999.

ments of an adjudicative nature, making broad use of legal assessments to evaluate alleged violations of IHL and provide legal opinions regarding events at issue. Furthermore some of such bodies have also been requested to identify individual responsible for violations of HRL and IHL in view of subsequent prosecutions, prompting a debate on legal standards related to such evaluations.[53]

Attention has also been paid to IHL by some Special Procedures managed by the HRC, such as thematic[54] or country[55] mandates, also regarding activities carried out by non-State actors. Similar functions are identifiable in the activities of the Special Representative of the Secretary-General for Children and Armed Conflict,[56] or the periodic reports of the Secretary-General on the Protection of Civilians in Armed Conflicts.[57] The UN Security Council has also recurrently made use of its broad powers to adopt a complex set of measures regarding the enforcement of IHL.[58] Finally, other institutions have gradually focused on activities aimed at favouring the application of IHL or monitoring its application, such as the UN General Assembly,[59] the Office of the High Commissioner for Human Rights,[60] and other international organisations.[61]

The abovementioned measures developed outside the realm of the IHL system reveal quite a fragmented scenario. Though hardly conclusive when considered individually, these mechanisms can nonetheless contribute to improving compliance

---

[53] See HENDERSON, "Commissions of Inquiry: Flexible Temporariness or Permanent Predictability?", NYIL, 2014, 287 ff.; VEZZANI, "Fact-Finding by International Human Rights Institutions and Criminal Prosecution", in POCAR, PEDRAZZI and FRULLI (eds.), *War Crimes and the Conduct of Hostilities: Challenges to Adjudication and Investigation*, Cheltenham, 2013, p. 349 ff.

[54] See special procedures dealing with: extrajudicial, summary or arbitrary executions; torture; arbitrary detentions, etc.

[55] See for instance reports of the Independent Experts on Sudan (UN Doc. A/HRC/14/41, 2010, paras. 52-58), and Somalia (UN Doc. A/HRC/15/48, 2010, paras. 12-18).

[56] As for its mandate see UN Doc. A/Res/51/77 (1997). See KLOSTERMANN, "The UN Security Council's Special Compliance System – The Regime of Children and Armed Conflict", in KRIEGER (ed.), *Inducing Compliance with International Humanitarian Law*, Cambridge, 2015, p. 313 ff.

[57] For the latest report see UN Doc. S/2015/453 (2015).

[58] ROSCINI, "The United Nations Security Council and the Enforcement of International Humanitarian Law", Israel Law Review, 2010, p. 330 ff. See for instance resolutions aimed to: deplore violations of IHL; create fact-finding commissions; focus on thematic issues dealing with armed conflict. Serious violations of IHL are also relevant criteria for the sanction mechanism. See, e.g., Côte d'Ivoire, UN Doc. S/RES/1572, 2004, para. 9.

[59] See resolutions devoted to general IHL topics (for an early example see UN General Assembly Resolution 2444 (XXIII) on respect for human rights in armed conflict of 1968) or condemning IHL violations (e.g., UN Doc. A/RES/64/10 (2009), and UN Doc. A/RES/64/254 (2010), on Israel).

[60] BELLAL, "Building Respect for the Rule of Law in Violent Contexts: The Office of the High Commissioner for Human Right's Experience and Approach", IRRC, 2015, p. 881 ff.

[61] NAERT, *International Law Aspects of the EU's Security and Defence Policy, with a particular Focus on the Law of Armed Conflict and Human Rights*, Antwerpen, 2010.

with and the enforcement of IHL, thus complementing measures provided by the IHL system itself. In some cases, external measures have *de facto* substituted ineffective mechanisms originally envisaged by IHL treaty-provisions, as in the case of fact-finding activities, even if such external mechanisms have ultimately been developed according to their own distinctive features. Likewise, several external mechanisms share the advantage of avoiding the need to obtain the consent of parties to the conflict to be operative, a limit which has contributed to determining the ineffectiveness of some IHL mechanisms. Furthermore, external mechanisms have also made it possible to focus in particular on NIACs: an area in which the IHL compliance mechanisms are much less developed. At the same time some tensions related to the development of such external mechanisms can be identified. For instance, the attention to IHL issues has been cursory or focused on specific topics, and controversial legal evaluations provided by such bodies have sometimes fuelled diplomatic debates. Furthermore, political limits may be in place, implying selectiveness in the decision of which conflicts or issues are addressed.

The development of such external mechanisms is consequently far from being unproblematic for States. Indeed, States' discomfort in relation to the increasing proliferation of such mechanisms expressly emerged during the consultation process for the "compliance track". The politicized agenda and inappropriate expertise on IHL issues of external fora were specifically underlined in the Concluding Report to the 32nd IC, which maintained:

> "While IHL is being increasingly referenced in international political fora and in specialized bodies overseeing the implementation of other branches of international law, such attention is of a sporadic and therefore insufficient nature. Focus on IHL is often the result of real or perceived emergencies, in which political considerations prevail over the need to expertly assess the specific content and implementation of this body of rules".[62]

Hence, alongside the inherent shortcomings of IHL treaty provisions devoted to such issues, the current trend of referring to mechanisms external to the IHL system has represented a significant prompt for the exploration of potential solutions, within this body of law, to strengthen compliance with IHL.

---

[62] Concluding Report, *cit. supra* note 1, p. 19. See, furthermore, the Chairs' conclusions to the Informal Meeting held on 13 July 2012, p. 3 (*cit. supra* note 1): "The positive contributions of these mechanisms and bodies of law to enhancing the protection of victims of armed conflict are beyond doubt. Yet the discussion showed that the specificities of IHL, which reflect the extraordinary situation it regulates, suggest a need for further thinking on how best to conceptualize specific IHL compliance".

3. THE PATH TOWARD THE PROPOSAL FOR THE MEETING OF STATES

Against this background we can turn our focus to the longstanding debate on improvements to the IHL compliance system. A comprehensive analysis of the possibility of establishing a permanent body charged with the implementation of IHL – either within the UN framework or by States Parties to the GCs – was already included in the seminal 1970 UN Secretary-General's Report on Respect for Human Rights in Armed Conflicts.[63] Similarly, in the mid-1990s the ICRC made a proposal to develop, through a committee of experts, a mechanism "to examine reports and advise States on any matters regarding the implementation of IHL".[64] This mechanism would have reflected the monitoring bodies' characteristic of HRL, but it was not supported by States, as they were clearly concerned about the scrutiny to be carried out by autonomous IHL experts. Equally, in relation to the UN Millennium Summit, the proposal by Kofi Annan to establish "a mechanism to monitor compliance by all parties with existing provisions of international humanitarian law"[65] was not endorsed and subsequent reforms linked to the HRC have only addressed IHL issues to a limited extent.

The ICs have consequently represented periodic opportunities for debate on the possibility of strengthening IHL compliance mechanisms. For instance, in view of the 28th IC held in 2003 the ICRC organized a consultation process, the results of which were submitted to the IC for consideration.[66] However, the ensuing debate was not reflected in Resolution 1 adopted at the 28th IC, which merely called upon States to use and to ensure the effective functioning of existing IHL mechanisms.[67]

Nonetheless, following additional consultations on the occasion of the 60th anniversary of the GCs,[68] a consensus regarding the development of concrete activities in this area was finally reached at the 31st IC held in 2011. In particular, Resolution 1 adopted by the IC entrusted the ICRC (later joined by Switzerland) with the pursuit of "further research, consultation and discussion in cooperation

---

[63] Report of the UN Secretary-General, Respect for Human Rights in Armed Conflicts, UN Doc. A/8052 (1970), paras. 75-79.

[64] "Proposals by the International Committee of the Red Cross, Special Rapporteur at the International Conference for the Protection of War Victims (Geneva, 1993)", IRRC, 1995, p. 25 ff.

[65] ANNAN, We the Peoples. The Role of the United Nations in the 21st Century, New York, 2000, p. 46.

[66] 28th IC, ICRC's Report on "IHL and the Challenges of Contemporary Armed Conflicts", pp. 20-25 and 45-70, available at: <https://www.icrc.org/eng/assets/files/other/ihlcontemp_armedconflicts_final_ang.pdf>.

[67] 28th IC, Resolution 1: Adoption of the Declaration and Agenda for Humanitarian Action, 2003, available at: <https://www.icrc.org/eng/resources/documents/resolution/28-international-conference-resolution-1-2003.htm>.

[68] See 60 Years of the Geneva Conventions and the Decades Ahead, 2010, pp. 34-43, available at: <https://www.eda.admin.ch/content/dam/eda/en/documents/publications/Voelkerrecht/Konferenzpapier-60-Jahre-Genfer-Konventionen_en.pdf>.

with States [...] to: [...] ii) enhance and ensure the effectiveness of mechanisms of compliance with international humanitarian law [...] and to submit a report [...], with a range of options, to the 32nd International Conference".[69] The 2011 Resolution was therefore the starting point for the current proposals. It triggered the development of a consultation process among the facilitators, mainly through nine meetings held between 2012 and 2015 and involving around 140 States.[70] Consultations with National Red Cross and Red Crescent Societies were also arranged, although their role was overshadowed by the debates among States, which brought to light elements expressed in draft Resolution 2.

According to the reports prepared by the facilitators, States emphasized their limited interest in further enhancing the existing IHL compliance mechanisms. The inherent limits characterizing such mechanisms were reiterated, and a shared scepticism was expressed about the possibility of introducing modifications.[71] An interest in revitalizing the IHFFC was expressed, but the facilitators did not suggest any further action due to a lack of specific proposals by States. Hence the latter consultation process also failed to help this mechanism change its image as a "sleeping beauty".[72]

Conversely, a shared interest among States did seem to emerge concerning the creation of an institutional structure devoted to GC and AP-related compliance activities[73] in order to deal with a detrimental characteristic of the IHL system: the absence of regular meetings of States Parties to enhance compliance with this body of law. Consultations therefore aimed to clarify the content of such a proposal and identify the key institutional elements and functions of the suggested Meeting of States. Discussions were particularly intense from mid-2015, when draft elements for Resolution 2 were circulated, providing delegations with the opportunity to engage with the process of refining its content. On this basis the final text of draft Resolution 2 was openly circulated in October 2015 in view of its potential adoption by the 32nd IC.

4. THE PROPOSAL SUBMITTED TO THE 32ND INTERNATIONAL CONFERENCE OF THE RED CROSS AND RED CRESCENT: A CRITICAL ANALYSIS

Draft Resolution 2 provided a comprehensive proposal for the creation of an innovative Meeting of States on IHL, although the settlement of several issues was

---

[69] See 31st IC, Resolution 1, *cit. supra* note 5.

[70] For relevant documents see *supra* note 1.

[71] See the Chairs' conclusions on the second (June 2013) and third (June 2014) Meeting of States (*cit. supra* note 1).

[72] KALSHOVEN, *cit. supra* note 16, p. 213 ff.

[73] As for early references see the Chairs' conclusion to the Informal Meeting of 13 July 2012, p. 2, see. *supra* note 1.

deferred to future decisions by the States involved, to be adopted within the framework of the planned body.

The first relevant point to be addressed is the way in which the Meeting of States was intended to be created. According to draft Resolution 2 the IC was only to be entrusted with recommending "the establishment, by States, of a regular Meeting of States on International Humanitarian Law, with the functions and features described above, at the first Meeting of States, which the government of Switzerland is invited to convene within one year".[74] During the consultation process alternative proposals were rejected. The idea of amending the GCs or adopting a new AP was not endorsed, due to the States' wish to preserve the non-binding nature of the Meeting. Similarly, the possibility of the 32nd IC directly setting up the Meeting was ruled out, partly due to the difficulty of reconciling the multipolar nature of the IC's components with the strictly inter-State character of the planned mechanism. As a result, draft Resolution 2 merely aimed to facilitate the subsequent step to be taken by States, deferring the formal establishment of this body to its initial sessions.

Furthermore, through a series of operative paragraphs, draft Resolution 2 was also intended to act as a blueprint for the identification of the Meeting of States' core elements; it encapsulated the elements considered as acceptable for States and to be endorsed by other participants in the IC.

Firstly, draft Resolution 2 recommended that the forum should convene annually,[75] which would have finally guaranteed a set venue for regular dialogue among States on IHL issues. The difficult relationship with mechanisms external to the IHL system also influenced this solution: this was emphasized in the Concluding Report, where a yearly timeframe was qualified as necessary "given the important challenges to IHL observance on the ground, which are being dealt with on an almost continuous basis in other international *fora not specifically dedicated to IHL*".[76]

Another significant characteristic of the Meeting of States was to be its voluntary nature, being potentially open to participation by all the 196 States Parties to the 1949 GCs.[77] This would have represented a challenge for the effectiveness of the mechanism, as the concrete involvement of key political and military States would have been entirely uncertain. Only confidence in the mechanism and States' willingness to engage in fruitful cooperation would have permitted it to gain importance. Furthermore, taking into account its voluntary nature, the proposed Meeting of States would not have represented a proper conference of States Parties, with the need to tailor its activities to this specific feature in order to avoid tensions among States not taking part in the mechanism.

---

[74] Draft Resolution 2, *cit. supra* note 6, operative para. 17. See, furthermore, the Concluding Report, *cit. supra* note 1, pp. 31-33.

[75] Draft Resolution 2, *cit. supra* note 6, operative para. 9.

[76] Concluding Report, *cit. supra* note 1, p. 25 (italics in the original).

[77] Draft Resolution 2, *cit. supra* note 6, operative paras. 4-5.

Resolution 2 also provided for the participation of other stakeholders as observers, due to their role in strengthening compliance with IHL. In this regard mention was made of international organizations, civil society actors, and components of the Red Cross Movement.[78] Hence, the Meeting of States would have largely differed from the IC in order to emphasize its State-driven character. In this latter forum membership is granted to States Parties, the ICRC, IFRC, and National Red Cross and Red Crescent Societies, with each of these delegations having equal rights, including voting rights.[79] Resolution 2 failed to detail the modalities of attendance as observers for National Societies. Various options were discussed, ranging from their representation under the umbrella of the IFRC, regional groups or as members of the Governmental delegations,[80] hence not providing them with an autonomous standing. On the contrary a specific role was expected for the ICRC, able to contribute to the Meeting "in an expert or other capacity",[81] for instance supporting its management.

However, the modalities of observers' participation were deferred to further deliberations as this sensitive issue deserved additional attention, also taking into account different models concerning the participation of observers in similar forums. Their involvement could take various forms along a spectrum of options, including the possibility to: circulate documents, directly or via the support of States; attend public sessions; take the floor during debates; and organize side events.[82] Different solutions could have had a significant impact on the characteristics of the Meeting of States.

The possibility for representatives of civil society to attend the planned Meeting was in line with current trend of aiming to emphasize the positive role that such non-State actors can play regarding compliance with international provisions, also in the area of IHL where "implementation is seen less and less as the sole prerogative of state or of state-driven actors".[83] Mention could be made, for instance, of activities performed by NGOs such as Geneva Call,[84] or to institutions devoted to IHL training, such as the Sanremo International Institute of Humanitarian Law.

---

[78] Draft Resolution 2, *cit. supra* note 6, operative paras. 11-12.

[79] See Art. 9 of the Statutes of the International Red Cross Red Crescent Movement adopted by the 25th IC held in 1986 and amended in 1995 and 2006, available at: <https://www.icrc.org/eng/assets/files/other/statutes-en-a5.pdf>.

[80] See Concluding Report, *cit. supra* note 1, pp. 25-26.

[81] Draft Resolution 2, *cit. supra* note 6, operative para. 13.

[82] VABULAS, "Consultative and Observer Status of NGOs in Intergovernmental Organizations", in REINALDA (ed.), *Routledge Handbook of International Organization*, London, 2013, 189 ff.; and GARCIA, *Les observateurs auprès des organisations intergouvernamentales: contribution à l'étude du pouvoir en droit international*, Bruxelles, 2012.

[83] MÉGRET, "Universality of the Geneva Convention", in CLAPHAM, GAETA and SASSÒLI (eds.), *cit. supra* note 2, p. 669 ff., p. 685.

[84] BONGARD and SOMER, "Monitoring Armed Non-State Actor Compliance with Humanitarian Norms: A Look at International Mechanisms and the Geneva Call Deed of Commitment", IRRC, 2011, p. 673 ff.

Likewise, in areas close to IHL, such as weapons conventions, the participation of "relevant non-governmental organisations" in review conferences or regular meetings of States Parties is expressly provided for in treaty provisions, thus recognizing their supportive role and expertise in dealing with challenges arising from the implementation of such conventions.[85]

Similarly, the draft resolution deferred to further negotiations among States the settlement of issues related to the creation of an institutional structure to support the Meeting of States. Taking into account its permanent character, draft Resolution 2 made a broad reference to the need to establish a chair, bureau, and secretariat[86] for the management of Meetings. Budget issues were also not settled in the draft document, although the Concluding Report explored several alternatives to guarantee the predictability of funds, an essential element for the efficacy of the planned mechanism.[87]

Concerning its key substantive elements, draft Resolution 2 defined the Meeting's areas of activity, maintaining the need "to find appropriate ways to ensure that all types of armed conflicts, as defined in the Geneva Conventions of 1949 and their Additional Protocols (for the latter as may be applicable), and the parties to them are included".[88] This reference rightly required that the Meeting of States' activities encompass both IACs and NIACs, even if, as emphasized below, its concrete relevance to NIACs may be questioned.

With regard to the relevant legal framework, not a single line of draft Resolution 2 was devoted to this fundamental element. Such a shortcoming is difficult to justify, except by States' uncertainty regarding the proper legal boundaries for this new compliance mechanism due to the difficulties of balancing the need to guarantee its efficacy against the desire to preserve State sovereignty and the voluntary character of this body. In this regard only the Concluding Report provided some insights on the potential alternatives evaluated by States.

In particular, as a starting point the report maintained that "the Meeting of States [...] should focus on the 1949 Geneva Conventions and their Additional Protocols".[89] This approach was clearly understandable, also to avoid overlapping

---

[85] E.g., Arts. 11(3) and 12(3) of the Convention on Cluster Munitions (30 May 2008, entered into force 1 August 2010), and Arts. 11(4) and 12(3) of the Convention on Anti-Personnel Landmines (18 September 1997, entered into force 1 March 1999). See CASEY-MASLEN, "Article 11. Meeting of States Parties", in NYSTUEN and CASEY-MASLEN (eds.), *The Convention on Cluster Munitions. A Commentary*, Oxford, 2010, p. 496 ff., pp. 504-506.

[86] Draft Resolution 2, *cit. supra* note 6, operative para. 10. For further references see Concluding Report, *cit. supra* note 1, pp. 28-30.

[87] Draft Resolution 2, *cit. supra* note 6, operative para. 15, and Concluding Report, *cit. supra* note 1, pp. 30-31.

[88] Draft Resolution 2, *cit. supra* note 6, operative para. 4, and Concluding Report, *cit. supra* note 1, pp. 13-14.

[89] Concluding Report, *cit. supra* note 1, p. 19.

with other treaties of relevance for IHL which have already established conferences of States Parties.[90]

At the same time, to expand the efficacy of the Meeting of States, the Concluding Report emphasized that "States not party to the Additional Protocols should be able to invoke them if they so wish". The same general view was expressed with respect to IHL customary rules.[91] This stance aimed to avoid an approach strictly limited to the 1949 GCs' for States not party to the APs, also by making reference to the substantive role of customary provisions in the IHL system. This potential expansion of the relevant legal framework should have been welcomed. The 1949 GCs mainly focus on the protection of persons not taking or no longer taking part in armed conflicts, while rules pertaining to the conduct of hostilities have largely been codified in the 1977 APs. Similarly, the Concluding Report was correct in reaffirming the potential complementary role of customary IHL, especially in NIACs. It goes without saying that in NIACs reference needs to be made to general rules to achieve a comprehensive analysis of pertinent legal obligations. Furthermore, references made by States to customary rules during the Meeting's activities would have implied an additional effect, making it possible to gather evidence of States' *opinio juris* related to customary provisions of IHL.

However, the abovementioned additional possibilities were inherently limited by their reliance on a proactive attitude on the part of the States involved. If a State participating in the Meeting wished to maintain an approach strictly limited to the 1949 GCs it would be free to do so: this implies an ability to avoid sensitive topics, for instance those related to the conduct of hostilities or NIACs, as common Article 3 can hardly provide a comprehensive picture of current challenges in such scenarios. Furthermore the solution envisaged, primarily focusing on the 1949 GCs and APs, appears to be a departure from past attempts by the 26th IC to establish regular meetings of States competent to discuss "general problems regarding the application of IHL": such wording expressly aimed at enlarging their sphere of competence in comparison to the reference made by Article 7 AP I to meetings of the High Contracting Parties focusing on "the application of the Conventions and of the Protocol".[92]

One key element addressed by draft Resolution 2 was which potential functions should be attributed to the proposed Meeting of States. The consultation process was of crucial relevance as States were able to evaluate different options. In particular, the second consultative meeting of States held in Geneva on June 2013 could be identified as a turning point. On that occasion States dealt with a series

---

[90] Apart from examples related to weapons treaties, as provided *supra* note 30, see Art. 27 of the Convention for the Protection of Cultural Property in the Event of Armed Conflict (14 May 1954, entered into force 7 August 1956).

[91] Concluding Report, *cit. supra* note 1, p. 14.

[92] LANZ, MAX and HOEHNE, *cit. supra* note 24, pp. 1117-1118.

of proposals submitted by the ICRC and Switzerland in a background document.[93] These proposals were based on existing compliance functions operating in other areas of international law, such as: examinations of individual and inter-State complaints; dispute settlement functions; country visits; early warnings; urgent appeals; good offices; fact-finding activities; periodic reports; and thematic discussions. The set of proposal therefore permitted States to evaluate several options, which could have attributed particularly far-reaching powers to the Meeting of States if accepted. However, it almost goes without saying that States favoured only the minimal options, i.e. periodic reports and thematic discussions, while the possibility of attributing to the Meeting of States a role in fact-finding activities was deferred to further discussions during future sessions of the proposed body.

The attribution of extensive functions to the Meeting of States was therefore excluded from the very outset, and this minimal approach fitted with the overall non-legally binding character of the mechanism. As for the Meeting of States' tasks, the draft resolution emphasized that "among the possible functions [...] two were deemed by the consultation process to be particularly relevant [...]: thematic discussions on issues of IHL and periodic reporting on national compliance with IHL [...]. [T]hese voluntary functions should be organized so as to be non-contextual and non-politicized". As further indications were lacking from the draft resolution, additional references were provided in the Concluding Report.[94]

Concerning State reports, the proposal was to develop an initial "basic report" aimed at highlighting how States generally implement IHL in their domestic legal systems. This report was to focus mainly on an overall assessment of the implementation measures related to IHL obligations to be fulfilled preventively in relation to an armed conflict. These would include, for instance, dissemination activities, the appointment of legal advisers, and procedures for investigating violations of IHL, also in order to identify best practices and lessons learned to be shared. Furthermore, the possibility of preparing "subsequent reports", intended both to update the "basic report" and focus on issues linked to the thematic discussions, was also mentioned. In such a case the mixed nature of the "subsequent reports" would have also made it possible to establish a fruitful link with the additional function of the Meeting, i.e. thematic discussions. In particular through these documents States would have been able to analyse issues related to thematic discussions in depth and highlight relevant practice in these areas, thus compensating for the limited time expected to be devoted to such discussions during plenary sessions.

In any case the review of reports would not have represented a significant form of legal scrutiny for States. Being informed by a non-contextual and non-politicized evaluation, thus implying a "no naming, no shaming" approach, an individ-

---

[93] Second Meeting of States on Strengthening Compliance with International Humanitarian Law. Background Document, May 2013 (*cit. supra* note 1).
[94] Draft Resolution 2, *cit. supra* note 6, operative para. 8. See also the Concluding Report, *cit. supra* note 1, pp. 12-24.

ual review of reports was excluded, while a preference was expressed for a single follow-up document intended to include best practices, common challenges, and/or general recommendations, while not directly pinpointing single States.[95] Therefore not even the mild control represented by specific concluding observations relevant to the States under exam, as experienced in HRL, could have been expected from the proposed mechanism. The effectiveness of such a review function would also have been unlikely due to States' notorious "reporting fatigue", implying delays and shortcomings in periodic reports.[96] Furthermore, taking into account the non-contentious nature of this function, neither the Concluding Report nor the previous Chairs' conclusions addressed techniques to avoid obstacles due non-collaborative States, as the preparation of "shadow reports", or how to deal with situations involving non-reporting States. It was quite clear, therefore, that this function was entirely dependent on a positive attitude on the part of the States involved.

The additional function attributed to the Meeting of States was the possibility to devote sections of the plenary sessions to thematic discussions among States on IHL issues.[97] Such sections were intended to facilitate exchanges of views on States' legal and policy positions regarding existing challenges, also in order to share best practices and technical expertise. In this latter regard the possibility of benefitting from external input, as expert presentations or background documents, was mentioned. However, the establishment of subsidiary bodies, such as a committee of independent experts, was rejected, thus further confirming the State-driven nature of the Meeting. The latter function would have permitted States to discuss IHL topics on a peer-to-peer basis at regular intervals, thus facilitating frank debates on sensitive issues. Nonetheless, to appease States' concerns, thematic discussions were to be non-politicized, non-selective and voluntary, and the same characteristics were to influence the possible follow-up of debates: the proposal made was for an outcome document to summarize discussions. Also in this regard the diplomatic and non-adversative nature of the Meeting was confirmed, being aimed at fostering dialogue among States, rather than highlighting misapplications of IHL.

5. THE OUTCOME OF THE 32ND INTERNATIONAL CONFERENCE: RESOLUTION 2
    AND THE WAY FORWARD

Draft Resolution 2 was therefore an attempt to synthesize States' positions as expressed during consultations. The proposal had several merits, favouring the creation of a regular forum for the discussion of IHL issues, with the inherent hope

---

[95] Concluding Report, *cit. supra* note 1, pp. 19-20.
[96] On proposals to address "reporting fatigue" see MORIJN, "Reforming United Nations Human Rights Treaty Monitoring Reform", NILR, 2011, p. 295 ff.
[97] Concluding Report, *cit. supra* note 1, pp. 20-22.

that this mechanism could gradually help increase mutual confidence among States in this area.

At the same time, it had potential shortcomings, which were mainly attributable to States' self-restricting approach and resulted in minimal options being supported during the consultation phase, as subsequently translated into draft Resolution 2. Being of a voluntary nature, the proposed Meeting of States would have been unlikely to attract key military-political States, especially in the event that this body's practice ever departed from its original features in order to assume a more incisive character. Similarly, it would have been hard to maintain its non-contextual and non-politicized nature when faced with the recurring political-diplomatic crises related to armed conflicts. The poor record of the IC's past efforts to create partially similar meetings of States Parties, as required in particular by Resolution 1 adopted in 1995, represents a warning in this regard. Similarly, the likelihood of the (quite limited) functions to be attributed to the Meeting of States actually enhancing compliance with IHL could be queried, also because their effectiveness would have been highly dependent upon a proactive attitude by participating States.

The development of a State-driven process in order to create "a venue [...] for dialogue and cooperation on IHL issues *among* States"[98] also implied the total irrelevance of organized armed groups in the planned new compliance mechanism. Such a solution was obvious due to political concerns, but represented a missed opportunity as limiting discussions on NIACs to States' views alone can hardly provide a comprehensive perspective on the legal and practical challenges related to compliance in such contexts. In particular, as NIACs represent the most complex scenario for the application of IHL, the abovementioned process dedicated to strengthening compliance with IHL could have been expected to identify this as a priority area and recognize the need to accommodate non-State actors' perspectives, as already emphasized in the past.[99]

Past experiences at the 1974-1977 Diplomatic Conference, where national liberation movements acted as observers, emphasized the potentialities of their involvement in activities aimed at strengthening IHL.[100] Similarly, recent practice has emphasised how such armed groups, or at least some of them, could be involved in initiatives aiming to generate respect for IHL.[101] Perhaps certain compromises could have been adopted in the Meeting of States' future activities, as extending participation in thematic discussions among panels of experts to include, with the

---

[98] Concluding Report, *cit. supra* note 1, p. 16 (italics in the original).

[99] ICRC's Report, *cit. supra* note 66, pp. 24-25 and 64-68.

[100] PICTET, "General Introduction", in SANDOZ, SWINARSKI and ZIMMERMANN (eds.), *cit. supra* note 15, p. xxix ff., p. xxxiii; and SASSÒLI, "Involving Organized Armed Groups in the Development of Law?", in ODELLO and BERUTO (eds.), *Non-State Actors and International Humanitarian Law*, Milano, 2010, p. 213 ff., p. 217.

[101] Reference could be made to activities managed by the Geneva Call, see *supra* note 84, as well as the ICRC with regard to non-State actors.

consent of concerned States, former members of organized armed groups involved in peace processes, thus permitting them to share their experiences and perspectives. Likewise, from an abstract viewpoint, other possibilities for the involvement of non-State actors could have been explored, in order to make it effective in favouring compliance with IHL in NIACs.[102] It was, however, clear from debates during the consultation process that States were not interested in such additional possibilities.

Draft Resolution 2 submitted to delegations at the 32nd IC therefore reflected the current minimal law-making agenda of many States regarding IHL issues. This attitude was also apparent during negotiations at the Conference where, as disappointedly stressed by ICRC President Maurer,[103] States were unable to reach a consensus on the proposed mechanism, despite it being crafted according to the main elements that emerged during the consultation process. It is clear that the current political tensions characterizing international relations, as well as potential concerns about a new compliance mechanism, which might be perceived as implying additional possibilities of scrutiny over armed conflicts and the parties involved in them, did not favour a positive outcome of the negotiation process. As a result it was not entirely surprising that delegations were unable to reach an agreement on the recommendation to create the Meeting of States as proposed in draft Resolution 2.

Conversely, as finally adopted, Resolution 2 merely recommends the continuation of State consultations "to find agreement on features and functions of a potential forum of States and to find ways to enhance the implementation of IHL"[104] in view of the 33rd IC. Furthermore, its operative paragraph 1 underlines a series of principles required to inform future consultations, as:

> "the State-driven and consensus-based character of the process; [...] the importance to avoid politicization [...]; the need to [...] address all types or armed conflicts [...]; [...] the voluntary, i.e. non-legally binding, nature of the consultation process, as well as its eventual outcome; the need for the process and the mechanism to be non-contextualized".

The divergence of the final text of Resolution 2 from the original draft version is clear, as it mainly provides for an additional round of consultations among States with the hope of reaching an agreement on the features and functions of a potential forum devoted to IHL issues. It is hard to grasp what any potential future compromise may look like, as the current proposal was already a minimal option

---

[102] BENVENUTI and BARTOLINI, *cit. supra* note 3, pp. 617-620.

[103] See the press statement of 10 December 2015 by the ICRC President Peter Mauer, available at: <https://www.icrc.org/en/document/no-agreement-states-mechanism-strengthen-compliance-rules-war>.

[104] 32nd IC, Resolution 2, *cit. supra* note 7, operative para. 2.

for strengthening compliance with IHL. Nonetheless it would have had the merit of planting a tiny seed in the IHL system, with a view to one day reaping its ripening fruits, as experienced by IHL in other contexts.[105]

---

[105] KALSHOVEN, "The Undertaking to Respect and Ensure Respect in All Circumstances: From Tiny Seed to Ripening Fruit", YIHL, 1999, p. 3 ff.

COUNTERING "FOREIGN TERRORIST FIGHTERS": A CRITICAL APPRAISAL OF THE FRAMEWORK ESTABLISHED BY THE UN SECURITY COUNCIL RESOLUTIONS

FRANCESCA CAPONE*

Abstract

Terrorism constitutes one of the most serious threats to international peace and security. The newest challenge posed by this threat is represented by the phenomenon of "foreign terrorist fighters". Current estimates place the number of foreigners who have joined the ongoing armed conflicts in the Middle East between 20,000 and 30,000. How many of these foreign fighters also fall within the definition of foreign terrorist fighters (i.e. those travelling abroad with a "terrorist" intent) provided by UN Security Council Resolution 2178 (2014) is very difficult to assess. In primis because the resolution refers to "terrorists", "terrorist acts", and "terrorist training" without actually defining "terrorism" and thus leaving to each Member State the task to determine the breadth and the contours of this concept. Secondly because the text lacks legal certainty with regard to many other crucial aspects, e.g., the relationship between counter-terrorism and international humanitarian law, the interpretation of the term "State of residence", and the risk of abuse of refugee status. These shortcomings not only jeopardize the ability to implement a uniform approach, but they also increase the likelihood of fostering abusive responses. This article argues that Resolution 2178 has not been adopted in a legal vacuum, on the contrary it extensively builds on the anti-terrorism framework established by previous Security Council resolutions and thus it inherits and exacerbates many old and unresolved issues. Ultimately, the present article seeks to determine to what degree the new set of binding obligations placed upon Member States to thwart the phenomenon of foreign terrorist fighters is effective and it discusses the extent to which it could enhance or hinder counter-terrorism's compliance with international human rights law, international humanitarian law and international refugee law.

Keywords: foreign terrorist fighters; foreign fighters; UN Security Council Resolution 2178 (2014); counter-terrorism.

* Research Fellow in Public International Law and Didactic Coordinator of the Master in Human Rights and Conflict Management, Scuola Superiore Sant'Anna, Pisa, Italy. E-mail: f.capone@sssup.it. The author wishes to express her gratitude to Professor Massimo Iovane, Dr. Daniele Amoroso, and the anonymous referee for their valuable comments.

1. Introduction

The crisis in the Middle East has attracted many foreigners, eager to join one of the parties involved in the current armed conflicts taking place in Syria and Iraq.[1] Today, both conflicts are closely connected, especially since the rise of the group called Islamic State of Iraq and the Levant (ISIL), which spans the Syrian and Iraqi territories and proclaimed the establishment of a Caliphate in the summer of 2014.[2] This unprecedented flock of foreigners to a war zone is increasingly worrying the international community,[3] concerned not so much by the contribution that these individuals may make to the conflicts that they join abroad, nor by the violations that they may commit while there, but rather due to the fact that they may engage in terrorist activities in their home countries upon their return.[4]

The terms "foreign fighters" and "foreign terrorist fighters" may generate confusion and are often used in the wrong way.[5] In this regard, an important clarifica-

---

[1] Due to the number of different forces involved, the increasing interventions by external actors and the recurring spillovers, both conflicts are difficult to label as simply internal or international. Consistently with this statement, the Independent International Commission of Inquiry on the Syrian Arab Republic has stressed that "the conflict has devolved into a multisided proxy war steered from abroad by an intricate network of alliances". Human Rights Council, Report of the Independent International Commission of Inquiry on the Syrian Arab Republic, A/HRC/31/68, para. 17. On the armed conflicts in Syria and Iraq see generally PAULUSSEN, DORSEY and KOULEN, "Year in Review 2013", YIHL, 2013, p. 147 ff. On the armed conflict in Syria see CASEY-MASLEN, "Armed Conflicts in Syria in 2013", in CASEY-MASLEN (ed.), *The War Report Armed Conflict in 2013*, Oxford, 2014, p. 207 ff. On the armed conflict in Iraq see TURNS, "The International Humanitarian Law Classification of Armed Conflicts in Iraq since 2003", in PEDROZZO (ed.), *The War in Iraq: A Legal Analysis, International Law Studies*, Newport, 2010, p. 97 ff., p. 109.

[2] "Isis Rebels Declare 'Islamic State' in Iraq and Syria", BBC News, 30 June 2014, available at: <http://www.bbc.com/news/world-middle-east-28082962>. See NEUMANN, "Foreign Fighter Total in Syria/Iraq Now Exceeds 20,000; Surpasses Afghanistan Conflict in the 1980s", International Centre for the Study of Radicalization and Political Violence, 21 January 2015, available at: <http://icsr.info/2015/01/foreign-fighter-total-syriairaq-now-exceeds-20000-surpasses-afghanistan-conflict-1980s/>.

[3] See generally MALET, *Foreign Fighters Transnational Identity in Civil Conflicts*, Oxford, 2013; ID. "Why Foreign Fighters? Historical Perspectives and Solutions", Orbis Journal of Foreign Affairs, 2010, p. 97 ff., pp. 97-99. See also HEGGHAMMER, "The Rise of Muslim Foreign Fighters. Islam and the Globalization of Jihad", International Security, 2011, p. 53 ff., pp. 53-60.

[4] The Rand Corporation has reported that 300-400 of the Sunni extremists from Europe, who joined terrorist/jihadist groups from January 2012 to July 2014, appeared to have now left the Middle East. JONES, "Jihadist Sanctuaries in Syria and Iraq: Implications for the United States", Rand Testimony, 24 July 2014, available at: <http://www.rand.org/content/dam/rand/pubs/testimonies/CT400/CT414/RAND_CT414.pdf>.

[5] KRÄHENMANN, "Foreign Fighters under International Law", Academy Briefing No. 7, Geneva Academy of International Humanitarian Law and Human Rights, Geneva, October 2014.

tion is needed from the outset as the present article will focus on the issues raised while dealing with "foreign terrorist fighters", not to be mistaken with the broader phenomenon of "foreign fighters". The latter have been defined as "individuals, driven mainly by ideology, religion and/or kinship, who leave their country of origin or their country of habitual residence to join a party engaged in an armed conflict".[6] Thus the accent is placed on the individuals' departure from their State of origin in order to support one of the actors, an armed group or the State's armed forces, engaged in an armed conflict of international or internal character.[7] Instead, the term foreign terrorist fighters, according to United Nation Security Council (UN SC) Resolution 2178 (2014), refers to "individuals who travel to a State other than their States of residence or nationality for the purpose of the perpetration, planning, or preparation of, or participation in, *terrorist acts* or the providing or receiving of *terrorist training*, including in connection with armed conflict".[8] Therefore, Resolution 2178 calls on Member States to deal specifically with those who travel abroad with a "terrorist intent", i.e. not simply to support a government or a non-State armed group. Moreover, since the resolution expressly refers to foreign terrorist fighters recruited by ISIL, the Al-Nusra Front (ANF), and other Al-Qaida associates listed under the UN SC's Resolution 1267 sanctions regime, the scope of application of Resolution 2178 is further limited as it encompasses exclusively non-State actors which are recognised as "terrorist groups", either through the 1267 sanctions regime or in light of a State's own understanding of terrorism. Therefore, for example, an Italian citizen who travels to Syria to fight with Bashar al-Assad's troops will not be considered as a foreign terrorist fighter, but as a foreign fighter.[9] However his/her fellow countrymen who join ISIL or any other terrorist group will be subject to the newly adopted Italian legislation on terrorism,[10] which prohibits the recruitment (both active and passive) of potential terrorists; the organisation, planning and financing of trips abroad for the purposes of committing terrorist conduct; as well as the training (including self-training and online training) to acquire

---

[6] See DE GUTTRY, CAPONE and PAULUSSEN, "Introduction", in DE GUTTRY, CAPONE and PAULUSSEN (eds.), *Foreign Fighters under International Law and Beyond*, Den Haag, 2015, p. 1 ff., p. 2.

[7] On the difference between international armed conflicts and non-international armed conflicts see generally SIVAKUMARAN, "Re-Envisaging the International Law of Internal Armed Conflict", EJIL, 2011, p. 219 ff., p. 221. See also FLECK, "The Law of Non-International Armed Conflict", in FLECK (ed.) *The Handbook of International Humanitarian Law*, 3rd ed., Cambridge, 2013, p. 581 ff., p. 603.

[8] UN SC Res. 2178 (2014), para. 8 of the preamble.

[9] In most countries fighting abroad does not automatically amount to an offence. Foreigners may face criminal charges for participating in a non-international armed conflict because they do not enjoy combatant status; or they can be charged if a national law makes it illegal to enlist in a foreign army at war with a State at peace with their country of origin, e.g., the UK Foreign Enlistment Act 1870; or, the most relevant scenario for our analysis, under national counter-terrorism laws when foreigners join or attempt to join an armed terrorist group.

[10] Law No. 43 of 17 Avril 2015, GU No. 91 of 20 Avril 2015.

knowledge and skills to commit terrorist acts.[11] This approach is consistent with the traditional understanding that acts of terrorism are conducted against a State, rather than by it,[12] and also with the scope of Resolution 2178, which was not to outlaw *tout court* foreigners' participation in an armed conflict abroad, a practice which under international law is not forbidden in absolute terms,[13] but to thwart their association with terrorist groups.

Even though the distinction between foreign fighters and foreign terrorist fighters seems, in principle, easy to draw, in practice it is very difficult to establish whether a foreigner travelling abroad to join a party to an armed conflict is also a terrorist or not. In the case of the armed conflicts occurring in the Middle East, for instance, it is very challenging to determine who sides with which party and foreign fighters from all over the world are flocking there to support either the governments' forces or the insurgents.[14]

Then, when exactly do we speak of foreign terrorist fighters? Is it strictly dependant on whether the insurgents that the foreign fighters join are identified as a terrorist group in accordance with the existing legal framework, regardless of the actual preparation or commission of terrorist offences?[15] Given the current lack of a universally binding instrument defining the exact meaning of "terrorism", the definition of foreign terrorist fighters enshrined in Resolution 2178 fails to provide Member States with sufficient guidance as to whom, exactly, falls within this category.[16] The absence of legal certainty infers that the term foreign terrorist fighters may also cover those who travel abroad *only* to "fight", i.e. suggesting their direct participation in hostilities, which is in principle "unlawful" in a non-international armed conflict,[17] whereas in an international armed conflict it is a lawful activity,

---

[11] *Ibid.*, Arts. 1-2.

[12] HOFFMAN, *Inside Terrorism*, 2nd ed., New York, 2006, pp. 34-35.

[13] Whenever foreign fighters are taking part in an armed conflict, the State on whose territory the conflict occurs, and (if applicable) its State allies, may call on the States of nationality of foreign fighters, and transit States, to take measures to prevent them from joining the battlefield. This is a corollary of the law of neutrality and of the customary international law principle of non-intervention. KRÄHENMANN, *cit. supra* note 5, pp. 49-51.

[14] See International Crisis Group, "New Approach in Southern Syria", Middle East Report No.163, 2 September 2015.

[15] UN Doc. S/2015/358, p. 3.

[16] Mercenaries, as defined by Art. 47 of Additional Protocol I to the Geneva Conventions, do not belong to the category of foreign fighters, because the former fight by definition for private gain, while a foreign fighter mostly pursues an ideological or religious motivation. Protocol Additional to the Geneva Conventions of 12 August 1949, and relating to the Protection of Victims of International Armed Conflicts (Protocol I), 8 June 1977, entered into force 7 December 1978. On the definition of mercenaries under IHL see IPSEN, "Combatants and Non-Combatants", in FLECK *cit. supra* note 7, p. 79 ff., p. 84.

[17] Ultimately the lawfulness, or lack thereof, of direct participation in hostilities in non-international armed conflicts is governed by national law. As a result any individuals, including foreign fighters, may be punished for the mere fact of fighting or for acts that are potentially lawful under IHL. See KRÄHENMANN, *cit. supra* note 5, p. 20.

regardless of the combatant's nationality or permanent residency status,[18] although without the purpose of committing a terrorist offence. Similarly, girls and women who usually do not perform military tasks may fall within the category of foreign terrorist fighters because conducts like the preparation of terrorist activities and the provision of training are not duly defined. As a result of this it is likely that States will implement different, and in some cases even abusive, responses, thus jeopardising the chances to counter in an effective and legitimate way the phenomenon of foreign terrorist fighters and the threat that they may pose to the maintenance of international peace and security.

The present article moves from two basic assumptions. *In primis* it is important to note that Resolution 2178 is not a stand-alone document, on the contrary, it extensively relies on the existing skeleton of anti-terrorism norms developed by the international community and as such it inherits, and even amplifies, a number of problems. Secondly an adequate and effective response to the widespread phenomenon of foreign terrorist fighters must necessarily comply with human rights law (IHRL), international humanitarian law (IHL), and refugee law, as stressed in the preamble of Resolution 2178, because overbroad, and in some cases even unlawful, counter measures risk significantly exacerbating the current threat. The scope of this article is twofold: (i) to provide a general overview of the most controversial issues raised by this new legislative effort of the UN SC;[19] and (ii) to discuss the shortcomings of the legal framework which predated the adoption of Resolution 2178, focusing mainly on the other anti-terrorism resolutions that have created uniform legally binding obligations for all UN Member States, rather than

---

[18] On the definition of "direct participation in hostilities" see MELZER, *Interpretive Guidance on the Notion of Direct Participation in Hostilities under International Humanitarian Law*, Geneva, 2009, p. 43. See also DOSWALD-BECK, *Human Rights in Times of Armed Conflict and Terrorism*, Oxford, 2011, p. 526; and SANDOZ, SWINARSKI and ZIMMERMANN (eds.), *Commentary to the Additional Protocols to the Geneva Conventions*, Den Haag, 1987, para. 3185. On the "combatant status" and the irrelevance of nationality see VIERUCCI, "Prisoners of War or Protected Persons qua Unlawful Combatants? The Judicial Safeguards to which Guantanamo Bay Detainees are Entitled", JICJ, 2003, p. 284 ff., p. 298.

[19] The controversial aspects of UN SC Resolution 2178 (2014) were immediately commented upon by several distinguished authors: AMBOS, "Our Terrorists, Your Terrorists? The United Nations Security Council Urges States to Combat 'Foreign Terrorist Fighters', but Does Not Define 'Terrorism'", EJIL: Talk!, 2 October 2014, available at: <http://www.ejiltalk.org/our-terrorists-your-terrorists-the-united-nations-security-council-urges-states-to-combat-foreign-terrorist-fighters-but-does-not-define-terrorism/>; SCHEININ, "Back to Post-9/11 Panic? Security Council Resolution on Foreign Terrorist Fighters", Just Security, 23 September 2014, available at: <https://www.justsecurity.org/15407/post-911-panic-security-council-resolution-foreign-terrorist-fighters-scheinin/>; PETERS, "Security Council Resolution 2178 (2014): The 'Foreign Terrorist Fighter' as an International Legal Person, Part I-II", EJIL: Talk!, 21 November 2014, available at: <http://www.ejiltalk.org/security-council-resolution-2178-2014-the-foreign-terrorist-fighter-as-an-international-legal-person-part-ii/>; and DE GUTTRY, "The Role Played by the UN in Countering the Phenomenon of Foreign Terrorist Fighters", in DE GUTTRY, CAPONE and PAULUSSEN (eds.), *cit. supra* note 6, p. 259 ff., pp. 270-277.

on the counter-terrorism treaties which only bind States that have ratified them. The approach adopted aims at shedding light on the most problematic features of the implementation of Resolution 2178, tying them up with those stemming from the existing anti-terrorism framework established under the aegis of the UN SC. The present work thus highlights how the controvertible aspects of Resolution 2178 represent a continuum in the recent struggle against international terrorism, ushered in after identifying Al-Qaida and its affiliates as the top terrorist threat against the international community. In the concluding paragraph the article reflects on the degree to which the existing legal framework, as reinforced and expanded by UN SC Resolution 2178, is able to adequately thwart the threat posed by foreign terrorist fighters in compliance with all the relevant spheres of international law.

2. THE UN SECURITY COUNCIL'S RESPONSE TO THE PHENOMENON OF FOREIGN TERRORIST FIGHTERS: AN OVERVIEW OF THE MAIN ISSUES AT STAKE

Resolution 2170 (2014) condemned the "terrorist acts of ISIL […] and its violent extremist ideology, and its continued gross, systematic and widespread abuses of human rights and violations of international humanitarian law",[20] and placed three main obligations upon Member States. First, it reiterated the obligation set out in Resolution 1373 (2001) on the duty to prevent and suppress the financing of terrorism. Second, it confirmed the applicability of the 1267 (1999) sanctions regime. Third, it reprehended the recruitment of foreign terrorist fighters by ISIL, ANF, and other entities associated with Al-Qaida.[21] Resolution 2170 in a nutshell represented the international community's comprehensive rejection of certain terrorist groups and expressed its determination to respond, promptly and effectively to the phenomenon of foreign terrorist fighters. However, besides openly condemning the recruitment of foreign terrorist fighters, adding six individuals associated with ISIL and ANF to the 1267 sanctions list and expressing the SC's readiness to consider further designations of individuals involved in financing or facilitating the travel of foreign terrorist fighters, Resolution 2170 did not enhance or expand the existing anti-terrorism framework.

With regard to foreign terrorist fighters the true legislative exercise carried out by the UN SC is represented by Resolution 2178, adopted on 24 September 2014 during a summit presided over by President Barack Obama, opened by UN Secretary-General Ban Ki-moon and addressed by scores of national leaders.[22] The

---

[20] UN SC Res. 2170 (2014) of 15 August 2014, para. 1.

[21] KRÄHENMANN, *cit. supra* note 5, p. 41.

[22] UN SC, "Security Council Unanimously Adopts Resolution Condemning Violent Extremism, Underscoring Need to Prevent Travel, Support for Foreign Terrorist Fighters", Meetings Coverage, 24 September 2014, available at: <http://www.un.org/press/en/2014/sc11580.doc.htm>.

composition of the meeting *per se* gives an idea of the political and strategic importance of this resolution, which has imposed new anti-terrorism obligations upon the UN Member States.

After providing the definition of foreign terrorist fighters reported above, the UN SC, acting under Chapter VII of the Charter of the United Nations, demanded that "all foreign terrorist fighters disarm and cease all terrorist acts and participation in an armed conflict".[23] Moreover, in accordance with their obligations under IHRL, IHL, and international refugee law, States shall suppress and prevent the recruitment, organization, transport and equipment of such foreign terrorist fighters, including by precluding their departure, entry and transit.[24]

Besides being extremely ambitious as it set a significant number of new obligations which must be enforced by Member States, the resolution poses several unprecedented challenges, many of which – i.e. those connected to "who" (individuals leaving their countries of residence or nationality), "why" (the purpose of their departure), and "the context" (including in connection with armed conflict) – emerge already when reflecting on the definition of foreign terrorist fighters enshrined in the preamble and unfolded in the operative paragraphs, as the following analysis will show.

Foreign terrorist fighters are described as individuals who travel to a State other than their States of residence or nationality, the former concept, i.e. State of residence, is not commonly defined under international law and each State has adopted and applied its own definition of residency, thus making it difficult to ascertain the Member States' obligation to prosecute and penalize "their nationals who travel or attempt to travel to a State other than their States of residence or nationality, and any other individuals who travel or attempt to travel from their territories to a State other than their States of residence or nationality".[25] States of residence or nationality shall, thus, prevent and punish the recruitment, organization, transport and equipment of foreign terrorist fighters, including by averting not only their departure, but also their entry and transit. As a result of this obligation States of nationality may abuse their powers and resort to the denationalization of potential terrorists as a policy instrument.

It goes without saying that the right to a nationality[26] is paramount to the realization of many other fundamental human rights and that IHRL limits the right

---

[23] UN SC Res. 2178 (2014), para. 1.

[24] *Ibid.*, para. 6(a)-(c).

[25] UN SC Res. 2178 (2014), para. 6(a). See KRÄHENMANN, "The Obligations Under International Law of the Foreign Fighter's State of Nationality or Habitual Residence, State of Transit and State of Destination", in DE GUTTRY, CAPONE and PAULUSSEN (eds.), *cit. supra* note 6, p. 229 ff., pp. 235-236.

[26] See Art. 15 of the Universal Declaration of Human Rights, 10 December 1948; Art. 24(3) International Covenant on Civil and Political Rights, 16 December 1966, entered into force 23 March 1976; Arts. 7 and 8 of the Convention on the Rights of the Child, 20 November 1989, entered into force 2 September 1990; Art. 29 of International Convention on the Protection of the

of States to decide "who" their nationals are as the granting and loss of nationality cannot be arbitrary and must comply with States' human rights obligations. Yet, within a period of just over a year since the adoption of Resolution 2178, many States, including the United Kingdom (UK), Canada and Austria, have passed amendments to their domestic laws to expand the powers of deprivation of nationality by including new grounds which, as emerged from the public debate in these countries, were triggered by the foreign terrorist fighters problem.[27] Remarkably under the laws introduced in the UK and in Austria the procedures that lead to the deprivation of nationality are largely discretionary and based on broad security considerations. Only under the Canadian law is a criminal conviction for terrorism offence an explicit requirement for deprivation of nationality,[28] whereas under the UK and the Austrian laws the accent is placed on the urge to promote security by protecting a nation from its own citizens, thus inferring the preventive, rather than punitive, nature of these measures. This approach is worse than that of Canada because the deprivation stems from a discretionary exercise of sovereignty rather than from the achievement of legal certainty and the implementation of due process guarantees.[29]

The second aspect to consider in order to analyze the potential impact of the current framework is the goal that, according to Resolution 2178, triggers individuals' decision to leave their country of origin, i.e. the purpose of the perpetration, planning, or preparation of, or participation in, terrorist acts or the providing or receiving of terrorist training. With regard to this element in the first place it is important to stress that Resolution 2178 has not even tried to outline, or at least to contextualize, the concept of terrorism, which in any case, as will be explained in the coming paragraphs, is not embedded in a universally binding instrument.[30] On the contrary it has left this task to the Member States operating almost freely within the framework outlined by the previous anti-terrorism resolutions. The paradoxical, but not preposterous, outcome is that States, which label as "terrorist" groups

---

Rights of All Migrant Workers and Members of their Families, 18 December 1990, entered into force 1 July 2003.

[27] VAN WAAS, "Foreign Fighters and the Deprivation of Nationality: National Practices and International Law Implications", in DE GUTTRY, CAPONE and PAULUSSEN (eds.), *cit. supra* note 6, p. 469 ff., pp. 472-473.

[28] *Ibid.*

[29] In any case, even if the deprivation of nationality results from a lawful conviction for the commission of a terrorist offence, it is worth questioning the added value that this punishment could actually bring in addition to the imposition of regular criminal sanctions.

[30] See AMBOS, *cit. supra* note 19. The author stresses that the UN SC could have, at the very least, relied on UN SC Res. 1566 (2004), para. 3, which defines terrorist acts as acts (i) committed with the intent to cause death or serious bodily injury, or taking of hostages, (ii) with the purpose to provoke a state of terror in the general public or in a group of persons or particular persons, intimidate a population or compel a government or an international organization to do or to abstain from doing any act, which (iii) constitute offences within the scope of and as defined in the international conventions and protocols relating to terrorism.

currently fighting *against* ISIL, AFN, and other entities associated with Al-Qaida,[31] will end up implementing the obligations enshrined in Resolution 2178 towards everyone who travels, or attempts travel, or facilitates such travel, to join them, presuming the terrorist intent or purpose on the basis of the existing lists.

Furthermore, despite the explicit reference to the need to respect refugee law while countering terrorism, the formulation of the Resolution 2178, by targeting those who cross borders in order to achieve a terrorism-related goal, may lead to the implementation of measures which affect the rights of asylum seekers and refugees.[32] From April 2011 to September 2015, over 500,000 Syrians and thousands of Iraqis have fled to Europe,[33] and this number is expected to climb dramatically. Due the fact that these persons are from Syria and Iraq, where ISIL and other terrorist organizations are based, it is easy to conjure up fears that some jihadi groups have inserted sleeper agents among the refugees who will burrow into host societies and then spring their trap.[34] This may impact not only the overall perception of asylum seekers and refugees, but also the likelihood of States implementing discriminatory practices. Ultimately calling on Member States to prevent the movement of terrorists or terrorist groups by effective border controls and controls on issuing identity papers and travel documents,[35] has contributed to worsening the already complex situation of people trying to escape war-torn countries. As stated in Article 1(F) of the Geneva Convention relating to the Status of Refugees, the provisions of the Convention do not apply to individuals singled out as "not deserving" the refugee status, i.e. those who have committed serious transgressions prior to seeking asylum. Terrorism is not listed explicitly in the exclusion clause, but it is clearly a trigger because, in addition to the fact that terrorist offences may fall under the categories of war crimes and crimes against humanity,[36] UN SC Resolution 1377 (2001) has clarified that acts of international terrorism are contrary to the purposes

---

[31] A significant example is the Turkish PKK, which is still on the list of terrorist groups of the EU and of many countries, including the UK and the US. See KRÄHENMANN, *cit. supra* note 25, p. 240.

[32] On the definition of asylum seekers see UNHCR, "Asylum Trends 2014: Levels and Trends in Industrialized Countries", 26 March 2015, p. 5, available at: <http://reliefweb.int/sites/reliefweb.int/files/resources/551128679.pdf>. On the definition of refugee see Art. 1(A)(2) of the Geneva Convention relating to the Status of Refugees, 28 July 1951, entered into force 22 April 1954.

[33] UNHCR, "Map New Asylum Applications Europe April 2011-September 2015", 26 October 2015, available at: <http://data.unhcr.org/syrianrefugees/asylum.php>.

[34] BYMAN, "Do Syrian Refugees Pose a Terrorism Threat?", Brookings Institute, 27 October 2015, available at: <http://www.brookings.edu/blogs/markaz/posts/2015/10/27-syrian-refugees-terrorism-threat-byman>.

[35] UN SC Res. 2178 (2014), para. 2.

[36] CASSESE, "The Multifaceted Criminal Notion of Terrorism in International Law", JICJ, 2006, p. 933 ff., pp. 943-950. See also KEITH, "Deconstructing Terrorism as a War Crime: The Charles Taylor Case", JICJ, 2013, p. 813 ff., pp. 815-817.

and principles of the UN Charter.[37] Remarkably, measures implemented in recent months pursuant to Resolution 2178 include denying entry to refugees lacking valid passports and identity cards, stricter visa requirements, higher costs for residence renewal, as well as cases of refugees pushed back at official checkpoints or forcibly returned in breach of the principle of non-refoulement.[38]

The third aspect that it is worth addressing concerns the relationship between terrorism and armed conflict, which is blurred by the final sentence of the foreign terrorist fighters' definition enshrined in Resolution 2178. By suggesting that acts outlawed by the resolution may occur "in connection with an armed conflict", the text prompts two possible readings and States are free to implement the one most in line with their own anti-terrorism legislation. The first one entails that Resolution 2178 requests Member States to implement legislative measures in order to prevent and punish the commission, in peace time as well as in war time, of terrorist offences by foreign terrorist fighters. The second one goes as far as presuming that travel or attempted travel for terrorist purposes, including receiving training, and facilitation of such travel, *equates* to engaging in acts of violence during an armed conflict abroad and thus it amounts to a terrorist offence. Both readings may create significant problems. On the one hand, acting in compliance with the first reading would exacerbate a certain confusion between terrorism and IHL, i.e. if conduct is lawful under the law of armed conflict, could it be prosecuted as a terrorist act?[39] In particular, as will be discussed in the following section, anti-terrorism treaties under international law have always excluded acts already governed by IHL, whereas some national legislation adopted in the aftermath of the 9/11 UN SC resolutions have already begun to move in the opposite direction, e.g., by criminalizing acts which are not prohibited by IHL,[40] or proscribing terrorist groups that are currently parties to armed conflicts.[41] Opting for the second

---

[37] UN SC Res. 1377 (2001), para. 5 (emphasis added). See VIETTI and BISI, "Caught in the Crossfire: The Impact of Foreign Fighters on Internally Displaced Persons, Refugees and Asylum Seekers from Syria and Iraq", in DE GUTTRY, CAPONE and PAULUSSEN (eds.), *cit. supra* note 6, p. 489 ff., pp. 509-510.

[38] Art. 33(1) of the Geneva Convention Relating to the Status of Refugees.

[39] See PEJIC, "Armed Conflict and Terrorism: There Is A (Big) Difference", in SALINAS DE FRÍAS, SAMUEL and WHITE (eds.), *Counter-Terrorism. International Law and Practice*, Oxford, 2012, p. 171 ff., p. 173.

[40] For example see the laws of the UK (EWCA Crim 280) and Australia (Commonwealth Criminal Code 1995, s 100.1 and Division 101), cited in SAUL, "Terrorism and International Humanitarian Law", in SAUL (ed.), *Research Handbook on International Law and Terrorism*, Cheltenham, 2014, p. 208 ff., p. 231.

[41] *Ibid.* Saul provides the example of the Liberation Tigers of Tamil Eelam in Sri Lanka. On this point it is worth recalling the important contribution of the Italian jurisprudence: see MANCINI, "Defining Acts of International Terrorism in Time of Armed Conflict: Italian Case Law in the Aftermath of September 11, 2001 Attacks", IYIL, 2009, p. 115 ff.; ALENI, "Distinguishing Terrorism from Wars of National Liberation in the Light of International Law. A View from Italian Courts", JICJ, 2008, p. 525 ff.; and *Corte di Cassazione (Sez. V penale), Criminal proceedings*

reading, on the other hand, would increase the risk of encouraging the adoption of abusive responses to the threat of foreign terrorist fighters, because it means that individuals may face criminal charges under national counter-terrorism laws just for joining or trying to join armed groups that are considered as "terrorist" or even for trying to enter a given territory of a foreign country where terrorist groups are active.[42]

This short analysis has served the purpose of flagging up the problems connected to the implementation of Resolution 2178, which has drawn strong criticism from academics and practitioners.[43] Remarkably, the key issues raised by Resolution 2178, notably affected by an "exceptionally low legal rigor in its drafting",[44] are inherent to the wider counter-terrorism strategy outlined through a number of landmark UN SC resolutions. This article identifies as particularly crucial three aspects, rooted in the existing anti-terrorism framework, that undermine Resolution 2178's capability of effectively countering the phenomenon of foreign terrorist fighters, i.e. the lack of a universally accepted definition of terrorism, the scant attention devoted to counter-terrorism compliance with other regimes of international law, and the current two-tier sanctions system, which have ultimately achieved the – very controversial – goal of singling out terrorists and terrorist groups.

3.   THE INTERPLAY BETWEEN THE "FOREIGN TERRORIST FIGHTERS RESOLUTION" AND THE PRE-EXISTING FRAMEWORK

3.1.   The Lack of a Universally Accepted Definition of Terrorism

Even though the idea of a "general international law of terrorism"[45] is, at the very least, extremely controversial, Resolution 2178 was certainly not adopted in

---

against *Legori Junis Antipuro, Thangavelu Suthaharan and Thevasmajampillai Lowrance*, 21 January 2014, No. 2843, IYIL, 2014, p. 482 ff., with a comment by AMOROSO.

[42] For example, the Australian Counter-Terrorism Legislation Amendment (Foreign Fighters) Act 2014 makes it an offence to enter a "declared" area without a legitimate purpose. According to division 119 the Minister for Foreign Affairs may declare such an area in a foreign country when a listed terrorist organization is engaging in hostile activity on that territory. UN Doc. S/2015/358, para. 54.

[43] See *supra* note 30.

[44] SCHEININ, "The Council of Europe's Draft Protocol on Foreign Terrorist Fighters is Fundamentally Flawed", Just Security, 18 March 2015, available at: <https://www.justsecurity.org/21207/council-europe-draft-protocol-foreign-terrorist-fighters-fundamentally-flawed/>.

[45] The expression "general international law of terrorism" makes reference to a well-known work of Rosalyn Higgins, in which she questioned whether international law has ultimately created a distinct subset of legal principles under the rubric of "counter-terrorism", and ultimately she concluded that it has not. HIGGINS, "The General International Law of Terrorism", in HIGGINS and FLORY (eds.) *Terrorism and International Law*, London, 1997, p. 13 ff., pp. 13-14. More recently, other authors have also expressed their skepticism towards the emergence of a separate,

a legal vacuum. On the contrary, a considerable body of international norms, institutions, and procedures specifically designed to deal with terrorism has emerged over the past 50 years.[46] Since the 1960s, following a series of aircraft hijackings, terrorism became a, if not the, major subject of concern for the UN.[47] In addition to being a burning issue and a controversial topic, it can be easily said that only "few words are plagued by so much indeterminacy, subjectivity and political disagreement as 'terrorism'".[48]

The international community has attempted several times to achieve the goal of agreeing on a generic definition of terrorism for the purposes of prohibition and or criminalization.[49] These attempts[50] so far have led only to the adoption of sectoral treaties that proscribe certain acts or protect specific targets, but do not fill the gap in the transnational repression of terrorist offences.[51] By the end of 2000, the Ad Hoc Committee on Measures to Eliminate International Terrorism established by General Assembly Resolution 51/210 had begun to work on a Draft Comprehensive Convention on International Terrorism.[52] Despite the significant efforts undertaken by the Ad Hoc Committee, the ultimate goal to adopt a single codified international definition of terrorism has not yet been achieved, mainly because it has not been possible to reach an agreement on the exact scope of application of the Draft Comprehensive Convention.[53]

---

or self-contained, regime of "international law of terrorism" or "global anti-terrorism law". See SAUL, "The Emerging International Law of Terrorism", Indian Yearbook of International Law and Policy, 2009, p. 163 ff., pp. 163-166.

[46] See VAN DEN HERIK and SCHRIJVER, "The Fragmented International Legal Response to Terrorism", in VAN DEN HERIK and SCHRIJVER (eds.), Counter-Terrorism Strategies in a Fragmented International Legal Order: Meeting the Challenges, Cambridge, 2013, p. 20 ff., pp. 20-25. See also CONTE, Human Rights in the Prevention and Punishment of Terrorism Commonwealth Approaches: The United Kingdom, Canada, Australia and New Zealand, Berlin/Heidelberg, 2010, p. 7.

[47] CONTE, ibid.

[48] SAUL, "Defining 'Terrorism' to Protect Human Rights", in STAINES (ed.), Interrogating the War on Terror: Interdisciplinary Perspective, Cambridge, 2007, p. 190 ff., p. 190.

[49] In 1926 Romania asked the League of Nations to consider drafting a "convention to render terrorism universally punishable", but the request was not acted on. SAUL, "Attempts to Define 'Terrorism' in International Law", NILR, Vol. 52, 2005-I, p. 57 ff., p. 58.

[50] The most significant early modern attempt to define terrorism as an international crime was undertaken by the League of Nations between 1934 and 1937. See MARSTON, "Early Attempts to Suppress Terrorism: The Terrorism and International Criminal Court Conventions of 1937", BYIL, 2002, p. 293 ff., pp. 293-297; and STARKE, "The Convention for the Prevention and Punishment of Terrorism", BYIL, 1938, p. 214 ff., pp. 214-217.

[51] GROZDANOVA, "'Terrorism' – Too Elusive a Term for an International Legal Definition?", NILR, 2014, p. 305 ff.

[52] See Report of the Ad Hoc Committee established by General Assembly Resolution 51/210 of 17 December 1996, Sixth Session (28 January-1 February 2002), A/57/37, Annex II (at 6).

[53] BIANCHI, "Security Council's Anti-Terror Resolutions and their Implementation by Member States", JICJ, 2006, p. 1044 ff., pp. 1048-1051. UNGA, Ad Hoc Committee, "Finalizing

During the drafting process, while there was a basic consensus on the definition of the offences,[54] disagreement arose with regard to two important aspects, i.e. the relationship between terrorism and self-determination, and the non-applicability of the term terrorism to activities undertaken by the military forces of a State in the exercise of their official duties and to the conduct of States' armed forces in the course of an armed conflict.[55] The latter interplay is also a delicate issue in relation to the scope of Resolution 2178. As mentioned above, in the previous counter-terrorism treaties this problem was resolved by adding an "exclusion clause", i.e. the treaties that cover acts that may occur during an armed conflict typically include provisions excluding acts governed by IHL.[56] In fact, without expressly labelling them as such, IHL does prohibit all acts normally designated as "terrorist" if committed outside an armed conflict, including executions of civilians and persons *hors de combat*, hostage taking, and direct and deliberate attacks against civilians and civilian objects.[57] Interestingly, while international treaty law dealing with terrorism has strived to avoid any interference with IHL and preserve the balance in this complicated relationship, the same sagacity has not guided the efforts of the UN SC, which in both Resolution 1373 (2001) and Resolution 2178 (2014) has blurred the line between armed conflict and terrorism, thus giving rise to adverse consequences that may undermine the effectiveness of IHL and its humanitarian purposes.

Even though there is no formally codified single definition of terrorism, an unofficial "quasi-definition" or at least a common understanding of the key elements of terrorism can be inferred from domestic and international case law,[58] as well as

---

Treaty Requires Agreement on 'Armed Forces', 'Foreign Occupation', Anti-Terrorism Committee Told", PR L/2993, 1 February 2002.

[54] SUBEDI, "The UN Response to International Terrorism in the Aftermath of the Terrorist Attacks in America and the Problem of the Definition of Terrorism in International Law", International Law FORUM du Droit International – The Journal of the International Law Association, 2002, p. 159 ff., pp. 159-165.

[55] See SAUL, *cit. supra* note 49, pp. 70-74.

[56] Art. 12 of the International Convention against the Taking of Hostages, 17 November 1979, entered into force 17 November 1979; Art. 19 of the International Convention for the Suppression of Terrorist Bombings, 15 December 1997, entered into force 23 May 2001; Art. 21 of the International Convention for the Suppression of the Financing of Terrorism, 9 December 1999, entered into force 10 April 2002; and Art. 4 of the International Convention for the Suppression of Acts of Nuclear Terrorism, 13 April 2005, not yet in force. KRÄHENMANN, *cit. supra* note 5, p. 35. See also GIOIA, "The Definition of Terrorism in International Criminal Law", in HEERE (ed.), *From Government to Governance. The Growing Impact of Non-State Actors on the International and European Legal Systems*, Den Haag, 2004, p. 339 ff., p. 344.

[57] GASSER, "Acts of Terror, 'Terrorism' and International Humanitarian Law", IRRC, 2002, p. 547 ff., pp. 559-562.

[58] Significant in this sense is the contribution of the Italian jurisprudence, see *supra* note 41. See also ROACH, *The 9/11 Effect: Comparative Counter Terrorism*, New York, 2011, pp. 161-426. See also Trial Chamber I, *Prosecutor v. Galić*, Case No. IT-98-29-T, Judgment and Opinion of 5 December 2003, paras. 93-138; and *Prosecutor v. Charles Ghankay Taylor* (Case No. SCSL-03-01-A), Appeals Judgment of 26 September 2013.

from legal documents.[59] In relation to the international case law it is worth recalling here the efforts made by the Appeals Chamber of the Special Tribunal for Lebanon (STL), which went as far as arguing for the international customary law nature of the definition adopted.[60] This approach has been strongly criticized on a number of grounds, *in primis* because it rejected the thus far dominant view in the academic literature that there is no universally agreed definition of terrorism;[61] secondly because it imposed an international law definition of terrorism building on the definition and interpretation enshrined in the Lebanese Penal Code;[62] and thirdly because this decision did not reflect the current status of customary international law.[63]

Regardless of whether or not we are witnessing the emergence of an international customary norm that recognizes certain offences as "terrorist" if they have a transnational element and are committed to achieve a given aim, the work of the STL has provided significant guidance in this complex field.

Further assistance to States stems from the non-binding definition contained in UN SC Resolution 1566 (2004).[64] If on the one hand it is important to stress that this definition carries some inherent value and may also be useful to exert pressure on the General Assembly to break the impasse on the Draft Comprehensive Convention, on the other hand it is worth highlighting that the SC has consciously preferred not to offer a definitive version of what terrorism means, thus intentionally and explicitly leaving the task of determining it to the Member States. Despite a well-established accord on the basic components, i.e. typology of acts and intent, embedded in Resolution 1566,[65] which in any case do not shed light on the con-

---

[59] At the national level see for example the US Iran and Libya Sanction Act of 1996, Public Law 104-172, 5 August 1996; the US Antiterrorism and Effective Death Penalty Act of 1996; the UK Terrorism Act 2000, Section 1; Art. 83.01(1) of the Canadian Criminal Code. See CASSESE, *cit. supra* note 36, p. 937.

[60] Case No. STL-11-01/I, Interlocutory Decision on the Applicable Law: Terrorism, Conspiracy, Homicide, Perpetration, Cumulative Charging, 16 February 2011, para. 85. See CASSESE, *International Criminal Law*, 3rd ed., Oxford, 2013, pp. 148-152.

[61] AMBOS, "Judicial Creativity at the Special Tribunal for Lebanon: Is There a Crime of Terrorism under International Law?", Leiden JIL, 2011, p. 655 ff., pp. 665-675.

[62] See CRYER et al., *An Introduction to International Criminal Law and Procedure*, 2nd ed., Cambridge, 2012, p. 338.

[63] POWDERLY, "Distinguishing Creativity from Activism: International Criminal Law and the 'Legitimacy' of a Judicial Development of the Law", in SCHABAS, MCDERMOTT and HAYES (eds.), *The Ashgate Research Companion to International Criminal Law*, Farnham, 2013, p. 223 ff.; and SAUL, "The Special Tribunal for Lebanon and Terrorism as an International Crime: Reflections on the Judicial Function", *ibid.*, p. 79 ff., pp. 79-84.

[64] UN SC Res. 1566 (2004), para. 3, see *supra* note 30. See SETTY, "What's in a Name? How Nations Define Terrorism Ten Years after 9/11", University of Pennsylvania Journal of International Law, 2011, p. 1 ff., pp. 6-15; and BEGORRE-BRET, "The Definition of Terrorism and the Challenge of Relativism", Cardozo Law Review, 2006, p. 1987 ff., pp. 1987-1992. See also SAUL, "Definition of 'Terrorism' in the UN Security Council: 1985-2004", Chinese Journal of International Law, 2005, p. 141 ff., pp. 164-165.

[65] CASSESE, *cit. supra* note 36, pp. 938-941.

troversial aspects that pertain to the definition's scope of application as it emerged during the negotiations of the Draft Comprehensive Convention,[66] a closer look at the historical development of UN actions in this field, and their implementation, reveals that the lack of a binding and universal definition of terrorism has provided too much space for problematic domestic appropriation of this concept, thus encouraging States' unilateral definition and interpretation of the term terrorism.[67] The notion of terrorism has been ultimately overused, and even abused, due to the fact that, since September 2001,[68] it has become too easy to designate someone or some organization or even a State as terrorist on the grounds of political considerations.[69]

In the absence of legal certainty, who ultimately decides whether a group or an individual shall be labelled as "terrorist", and how? The UN SC has embarked on the task,[70] by legislating in the field of counter-terrorism and by establishing two complex sanctions regimes through the adoption of binding resolutions. Even though the UN SC has remarkably tried to fill a dangerous legal blank by setting up a two-tier framework able to dictate[71] or to channel[72] Member States' efforts to identify and thwart terrorist groups, the lack of a universally accepted definition of terrorism constantly undermines, and to some extent discredits, the implementation of the anti-terror resolutions and the sanctions regimes thereof. Without an agreement on such definition, the effectiveness of the measures aimed at fighting terrorism in all its multi-faceted aspects, including foreign terrorist fighters, risks being significantly jeopardized.[73] In particular, since Resolution 2178 refers to terrorism "in all forms and manifestations",[74] and thus is not limited to a specific context or situation, individual States are free to apply vague definitions in order to advance

---

[66] See VAN DEN HERIK and SCHRIJVER, *cit. supra* note 46, p. 22.

[67] On this point see SUBEDI, *cit. supra* note 54, p. 159; and FRIEDRICHS, "Defining the International Public Enemy: The Political Struggle behind the Legal Debate on International Terrorism", Leiden JIL, 2006, p. 69 ff., pp. 71-72.

[68] SCHEININ, "Report of the Special Rapporteur on the Promotion and Protection of Human Rights and Fundamental Freedoms while Countering Terrorism", UN Doc. E/CN.4/2006/98, para. 56(a).

[69] WOOD, "The Role of the UN Security Council in Relation to the Use of Force against Terrorists", in VAN DEN HERIK and SCHRIJVER, *cit. supra* note 46, p. 317 ff., p. 320.

[70] GINSBORG, "The United Nations Security Council's Counter-Terrorism Al-Qaida Sanctions Regime: Resolution 1267 and the 1267 Committee", in SAUL (ed.), *cit. supra* note 40, p. 608 ff., pp. 609-611.

[71] In the case of the sanctions regime established under Res. 1267 (1999) the UN SC has identified the list of individuals and entities to which the sanctions apply.

[72] UN SC Res. 1373 (2001), instead, has given rise to an unprecedented, decentralized sanctioning regime that provides Member States with the task of autonomously identifying terrorist suspects.

[73] BIANCHI, *cit. supra* note 53, p. 1048; and SAUL, *Defining Terrorism in International Law*, New York, 2006, pp. 57-66.

[74] SCHEININ, *cit. supra* note 19.

their own political agenda. This has resulted, for instance, in the selective application of measures aimed at countering the phenomenon of foreign terrorist fighters. Significant in this sense is the example of Lebanon, which has allowed Hezbollah fighters to travel freely to Syria whereas Sunni fighters have been prevented from leaving the country through the adoption of a robust security approach, suggesting that their "terrorist intent" was inherent to their departure in light of the party that they were allegedly going to join.[75]

3.2. Counter-Terrorism Compliance with Other Regimes of International Law in the Security Council's Legislative Efforts

The text of UN SC Resolution 2178 makes explicit reference to States' obligation to act consistently with IHRL, IHL, and international refugee law, also noting that failure to comply with these obligations is one of the factors contributing to increasing the risk of radicalization. Since Resolution 2178 has simply added an extra layer to the existing framework established by the UN SC,[76] it is certainly important to reflect on whether this obligation holds true when implementing a binding decision of the SC and what problems have emerged in relation to the previous SC attempts to legislate in the field of counter-terrorism, in particular with regard to Resolution 1373.[77] By adopting Resolution 1373, the SC has cast itself, for the first time, as the legislature of the entire UN membership. Unlike other resolutions adopted under Chapter VII,[78] Resolution 1373 is not specifically related to any event or situation, even though the 9/11 attacks are mentioned in the preamble.[79] Resolution 1373 also lacks any space or time limitation, and since most of its text establishes binding rules of international law, it seems to be intended that

---

[75] GARTENSTEIN-ROSS and MORENG, "MENA Countries' Responses to the Foreign Fighter Phenomenon", in DE GUTTRY, CAPONE and PAULUSSEN (eds.), *cit. supra* note 6, p. 445 ff., pp. 465-467.

[76] The UN SC has not always been the leading actor in the global anti-terrorism campaign. While the General Assembly has traditionally been the UN body in charge of dealing with terrorism, the UN SC began to expand its role in this sector after the end of the Cold War. See HEUPEL, "Adapting to Transnational Terrorism: The UN Security Council's Evolving Approach to Terrorism", Security Dialogue, 2007, p. 477 ff., p. 478.

[77] UN SC Res. 1373 (2001) was adopted in the aftermath of the 9/11 attacks, acting on a draft proposed by the US and explicitly referring to Chapter VII of the UN Charter.

[78] For instance UN SC Res. 1267 (1999) concerning Al-Qaida and the Taliban and associated individuals and entities; UN SC Res. 1289 (2000) on the situation in Sierra Leone; UN SC Res. 1343 (2001) on the situation in Liberia; UN SC Res. 1479 (2003) on the situation in Côte d'Ivoire; UN SC Res. 1440 (2002) concerning the taking of hostages in Moscow on 23 October 2002; and UN SC Res. 1530 (2004) concerning the bomb attacks in Madrid on 11 March 2004.

[79] BIANCHI, *cit. supra* note 53, p. 1047.

those rules are destined to remain in force indefinitely.[80] The dearth of connection with any particular situation and its general scope are the main reasons why many commentators have characterized Resolution 1373 as a piece of legislation,[81] the same consideration also applies to the other two law-making exercises of the SC, namely Resolution 1540 (2004)[82] and, of course, Resolution 2178. Challenging the legitimacy of the SC's exercise of legislative powers does not fall within the scope of this article, first because the legal effects of *ultra vires* resolutions have been already scrutinized,[83] and secondly because the resolutions of the SC, which is the initial judge of the legality of its own acts,[84] are generally seen as being legal.[85] What is relevant for the purposes of this contribution is to establish whether the SC role of global anti-terrorism legislator is compatible with the requirement, explicitly expressed in Resolution 2178, to comply with IHRL, IHL, and refugee law, and if such compliance can be effectively enforced.

Remarkably, none of the previous resolutions adopted by the SC while acting as the global anti-terrorism legislator have included in their text a reference to States' duty to implement the obligations enshrined in compliance with IHRL, IHL, and refugee law.[86] This approach was consistent with the idea that domestic laws' abidance by human rights law, and other branches of international law potentially hampered by the implementation of binding anti-terrorism resolutions, was not an issue perceived to be as crucial as the maintenance of international peace and security.[87] The inclusion of this express reference in a resolution that poses binding obligations upon States infers that such obligations cannot be implemented in breach

---

[80] Operative paras. 1 and 2 set that all States shall take certain actions against the financing of terrorist activities as well as a miscellany of other actions designed to prevent any support for terrorists and terrorist activities.

[81] See HAPPOLD, "Security Council Resolution 1373 and the Constitution of the United Nations", Leiden JIL, 2003, p. 593 ff., pp. 593-596; GUILLAUME, "Terrorism and International Law", ICLQ, 2004, p. 537 ff., pp. 540-43; and SZASZ, "The Security Council Starts Legislating", AJIL, 2002, p. 901 ff., pp. 902-903.

[82] See LAVALLE, "A Novel, if Awkward Exercise in International Law-Making: Security Council Resolution 1540 (28 April 2004)", Netherlands Journal of International Law, 2004, p. 413 ff., pp. 416-437.

[83] See ROSAND, "The Security Council As 'Global Legislator': Ultra Vires or Ultra Innovative?", Fordham International Law Journal, 2004, p. 542 ff., p. 551.

[84] *Legal Consequences for States of the Continued Presence of South Africa in Namibia (South West Africa) notwithstanding Security Council Resolution 276 (1970)*, Advisory Opinion of 21 June 1971, ICJ Reports, 1971, p. 16 ff., p. 22.

[85] HAPPOLD, *cit. supra* note 81, p. 609.

[86] DOSWALD-BECK, *cit. supra* note 18, p. 147.

[87] BIANCHI, "Assessing the Effectiveness of the UN Security Council's Anti-Terrorism Measures: The Quest for Legitimacy and Cohesion", EJIL, 2006, p. 881 ff., p. 884. Until UN SC Res. 2178 (2014) Member States' obligation to comply with IHRL, refugee law and IHL was embedded only in resolutions not adopted under Chapter VII of the UN Charter. DIVAC ÖBERG, "The Legal Effects of Resolutions of the UN Security Council and General Assembly in the Jurisprudence of the ICJ", EJIL, 2005, p. 879 ff., p. 885.

of IHRL, IHL, and refugee law. In principle the explicit recognition of States' legal duty to respect those regimes of international law while dealing with the threat posed by foreign terrorist fighters carries significant potential as it could contribute to overcoming the conflicts between SC obligations and obligations deriving from other treaties.[88] In fact, since the beginning of the SC's exercise of law making powers the key issues raised have been concerned with whether its resolutions can displace human rights treaties and ultimately which set of norms prevails.[89] As the implementation of the obligations enacted by the SC relies entirely on the Member States, it seems trivial to observe that, in any case, they bear the responsibility to make sure that the incorporation of the relevant SC anti-terror measures is ultimately in line with other obligations undertaken either through customary or treaty law. In the case of Resolution 1373, which imposes upon Member States an obligation of result, leaving them to choose the means by which they give effect to the measures listed therein, it should be presumed, and this has been the dominant approach adopted by the Human Rights Committee as well as the European Court of Human Rights (ECtHR),[90] that the SC does not intend actions taken pursuant to its resolutions to violate human rights, and that SC decisions should be interpreted in light of that presumption.[91] Including in an express manner the obligation to comply with other relevant regimes in the text of a binding resolution, such as Resolution 2178, replaces the presumption with a degree of certainty and this represents a significant step forward. However, what remains unresolved is the issue of the effective supervision of States' implementation, which Resolution 2178 "overcomes" by relying on the existing UN counter-terrorism bodies.[92]

It is worth stressing that the enforcement of the counter-terrorism legal obligations placed on the whole community of States by a political body like the UN SC is monitored by other political organs, *in primis* the Counter-Terrorism Committee[93] and the Counter-Terrorism Executive Directorate,[94] which are the "toothless" su-

---

[88] See ORAKHELASHVILI, "The Acts of the Security Council: Meaning and Standards of Review", Max Planck UNYB, 2007, p. 143 ff., pp. 149-151.

[89] SHEERAN and BEVILACQUA, "The UN Security Council and International Human Rights Obligations: Towards a Theory of Constraints and Derogation", in SHEERAN and RODLEY (eds.), *Routledge Handbook of International Human Rights*, London, 2013, p. 371 ff., p. 393.

[90] See CONTE, "States' Prevention and Responses to the Phenomenon of Foreign Fighters against the Backdrop of International Human Rights Obligations", in DE GUTTRY, CAPONE and PAULUSSEN (eds.), *cit. supra* note 6, p. 283 ff., pp. 293-296.

[91] *Ibid.* See, for example, Human Rights Committee, *Sayadi and Vinck v. Belgium*, Communication No. 1472/2006, UN Doc. CCPR/C/94/D/1472/2006 (2008), para. 4.12; ECtHR, *Al-Jeddah v. United Kingdom*, Application No. 27021/08, Judgment of 7 July 2011, para. 60.

[92] UN SC Res. 2178(2014), paras. 20-24.

[93] UN SC Res. 1373 (2001), para. 6. See ROSTOW, "Before and After: The Changed UN Response to Terrorism since September 11th", Cornell ILJ, 2002, p. 475 ff., pp. 483-84. See also BIANCHI, *cit. supra* note 87, p. 897.

[94] UN SC Res. 1535 (2004). See ROSAND, "Resolution 1373 and the CTC: The Security Council's Capacity-Building", in NESI (ed.) *International Cooperation in Counter-Terrorism.*

pervisory mechanisms established within the framework of Resolution 1373 and whose proactive role is circumscribed to recommending the adoption of implementing measures.[95] Therefore States remain liable for all acts and omissions of their organs arising from the need to enforce SC counter-terrorism resolutions, including Resolution 2178, because, despite explicitly embedding an obligation of compliance with other regimes of international law, the SC decision is not accompanied by effective means of protecting the relevant rights.[96] Thus, there can only be impartial, judicial oversight in the aftermath of an alleged breach of IHRL, refugee law, or IHL. In other words, through Resolution 2178 the UN SC is certainly trying to harmonize what have been perceived so far as "conflicting international obligations",[97] but in practice it is still unable to autonomously provide adequate means of protection and supervision, e.g., by offering judicial guarantees and effective remedies, and for that it must necessarily rely on other legal systems.[98]

3.3. The Current Two-Tier Sanctions Regime and Its Relevance to Foreign Terrorist Fighters

The current two-tier sanctions regime is the third aspect that deserves to be scrutinized while reflecting on the aspects that Resolution 2178 has inherited from the existing UN SC anti-terrorism framework. Resolution 2178 makes explicit reference to both the sanctions regime established by the SC through the adoption of Resolution 1267[99] and the 1373 sanctions regimes, thus indicating their applicability to foreign

---

The United Nations and Regional Organizations in the Fight against Terrorism, Hampshire, 2006, p. 81 ff., pp. 81-86.

[95] It is important to recall that with the adoption of UN SC Res. 1624 (2005), which is dedicated to countering incitement to terrorist acts motivated by extremism and intolerance, the mandate of the CTC has been expanded. In fact, Res. 1624 requests that Member States report their implementing measures, which must conform to their obligations under international law, including human rights, humanitarian law and refugee law, to the CTC (operative para. 4).

[96] TZANAKOPOULOS, "Judicial Dialogue in Multi-Level Governance: The Impact of the Solange Argument", in FAUCHALD and NOLLKAEMPER (eds.), *The Practice of International and National Courts and the (De-)Fragmentation of International Law*, London, 2014, p. 185 ff., pp. 208-211.

[97] See CUYVERS, "The Kadi II Judgment of the General Court: The ECJ's Predicament and the Consequences for Member States", European Constitutional Law Review, 2011, p. 481 ff., pp. 481-490. See also SARVARIAN, "The Kadi II Judgment of the Court of Justice of the European Union: Implications for Judicial Review of UN Security Council Resolutions", in AVBELJ, FONTANELLI and MARTINICO (eds.), *Kadi on Trial. A Multifaceted Analysis of the Kadi Trial*, Oxon, 2014, p. 95 ff.

[98] On the criterion of equivalent protection see ECtHR, *Al-Dulimi and Montana Management Inc. v. Switzerland*, Application No. 5809/08, Judgment of 26 November 2013, para. 113.

[99] The UN SC 1267 (1999) sanctions regime has been modified by subsequent resolutions, all adopted under Chapter VII of the UN Charter, including Res. 1988 (2011), Res. 1989 (2011), and Res. 2161 (2014). Res. 1988 (2011) split the Al-Qaida and Taliban sanctions system into

terrorist fighters as well as to those who finance or otherwise facilitate their travel and subsequent activities.[100] Despite their proclaimed preventive nature, sanctions inflicted through either the centralized regime or the decentralized one have been sharply criticized on human rights grounds, principally for failing to include due process guarantees and independent judicial oversight in the listing and delisting process,[101] as well as for their interference with the fundamental right to freedom of movement, property rights, the right to privacy, and the presumption of innocence.[102]

In contrast to Resolution 1267, which set up a sanctions regime specifically directed at Al-Qaida and the Taliban and associated individuals and entities,[103] thus obliging Member States to implement the regime without the possibility to undertake any autonomous actions,[104] Resolution 1373 has left Member States free to determine those against whom the restrictive measures will be imposed.[105] As a result, despite not having any blacklist attached to it, Resolution 1373 has requested Member States to identify terrorist suspects, not confined to Al-Qaida and the Taliban.[106] The independent listing and delisting responsibility of Member States under the 1373 sanctions regime allows them significant discretion to balance, at least in principle, potential conflicts between human rights and security considerations. But due to the lack of an effective supervisory mechanism, some States have been using their duty to comply with Resolution 1373 as an excuse to

---

two separate regimes, namely a country-specific regime imposing sanctions on those Taliban "constituting a threat to the peace, stability and security of Afghanistan", and the 1267 sanctions measures, as amended by Res. 1390 (2002), which apply to designated individuals and entities associated with Al-Qaida wherever located. Therefore, there has been a significant shift to a sanctioning regime that currently results in a global list of persons associated with Al-Qaida, thus subjecting individuals to sanctions of potentially indefinite duration.

[100] UN SC Res. 2178 (2014), paras. 6-7.

[101] GINSBORG, cit. supra note 70, pp. 612-625; JOHNSTONE, "The UN Security Council, Counterterrorism and Human Rights", in BIANCHI and KELLER (eds.), Counterterrorism: Democracy's Challenge, Oxford, 2008, p. 335 ff., pp. 342-343.

[102] SCHEININ, "Counter-Terrorism and Human Rights", in SHEERAN and RODLEY (eds.), cit. supra note 89, p. 581 ff., p. 591.

[103] BIANCHI, cit. supra note 53, pp. 1056-1058. See also VAN DEN HERIK, "Peripheral Hegemony in the Quest to Ensure Security Council Accountability for Its Individualized UN Sanctions Regimes", Journal of Conflict & Security Law, 2014, p. 427 ff., p. 442.

[104] GINSBORG and SCHEININ, "You Can't Always Get What You Want: The Kadi II Conundrum and the Security Council 1267 Terrorist Sanctions Regime", Essex Human Rights Law Review, 2011, p. 7 ff., pp. 7-10; and KUIJPER et al., The Law of EU External Relations Cases, Materials, and Commentary on the EU as an International Legal Actor, Oxford, 2013, p. 245.

[105] TZANAKOPOULOS, cit. supra note 96, p. 201.

[106] ECKES, EU Counter-Terrorist Policies and Fundamental Rights. The Case of Individual Sanctions, Oxford, 2009, p. 38. See also GINSBORG and SCHEININ, cit. supra note 104, p. 16. An example can help clarifying this difference. In order to implement UN SC Res. 1373 (2001) the EU established a list of persons, groups and entities involved in terrorist acts and subject to restrictive measures. This regime is separate from the EU regime implementing UN SC Res. 1989 (2011) on the freezing of funds of persons and entities associated with Osama Bin Laden, the Al-Qaida network and the Taliban (including ISIL/Da'esh).

justify the introduction of dubious legislation and harsh actions against opposition groups.[107] Moreover, as stressed above, some domestic terrorism laws adopted to fulfil the obligations enshrined in Resolution 1373 proscribe designated terrorist groups, including groups that are involved in an armed conflict,[108] making it a terrorist offence for individuals to be involved in whatever capacity with an outlawed organization and, since the adoption of Resolution 2178, also travel to join it.[109]

An example could help clarifying this point and the relationship between Resolution 2178 and the 1373 sanctions regime. The US, pursuant to Resolution 1373, imposes financial sanctions and penalties on persons who have been indicated in the annex to Executive Order 13224. On September 2015, as part of the effort to counter the threats posed by foreign terrorist fighters, the US Department of State designated ten individuals and five groups. Among the individuals there was also a UK citizen featured in an ISIL video in which he admits to having participated in battles in Syria.[110] This person was included in the US list as a foreign terrorist fighter due to the fact that he left his country of origin to allegedly participate in the hostilities in support of ISIL, even though it has not been ascertained whether he has violated IHL or not, nor whether he has committed any terrorist offence.

Whereas the 1373 sanctions regime is loosely based on Member States' discretion, the one established by Resolution 1267 has envisaged a body specifically tasked with administering the listing and delisting process, i.e. the 1267 Sanctions Committee.[111] The 1267 Sanctions Committee monitors the implementation of the sanctions and maintains a list of individuals and entities to which the sanctions apply. Of course the SC's power to make listing decisions on the basis of nominations by Member States provides a ready means by which individual States can make executive decisions with far-reaching consequences, apparently unconstrained by domestic judicial review, or the IHR treaties by which they are bound.[112] In response to the strong criticism of the 1267 Sanctions Committee,[113] its listing and

---

[107] HEUPEL, "Security Council Legislation in Counter-Terrorism", in POPOVSKI and FRASER (eds.), *The Security Council as Global Legislator*, Oxon, 2014, p. 124 ff., pp. 124-130.

[108] SAUL, *cit. supra* note 49, pp. 230-231. See *supra* section 2.

[109] KRÄHENMANN, *cit. supra* note 25, p. 243.

[110] US Department of State, Office of the Spokesperson, "Designations of Foreign Terrorist Fighters", Media Note, 29 September 2015, available at: < http://www.state.gov/r/pa/prs/ps/2015/09/247433.htm>.

[111] The 1267 Sanctions Committee is comprised of diplomats representing all 15 members of the Security Council and adopts its decisions by consensus. In practice, the Sanctions Committee follows a "no objection" procedure, so that if no State has opposed a listing proposal (or has put it "on hold") within 10 working days, the individual or entity will be added to the list.

[112] EMMERSON, "Promotion and Protection of Human Rights: Human Rights Questions, Including Alternative Approaches for Improving the Effective Enjoyment of Human Rights and Fundamental Freedoms", UN Doc. A/67/396 (2012), para. 14.

[113] International Commission of Jurists, "Assessing Damage, Urging Action: Report of the Eminent Jurists Panel on Terrorism, Counter-Terrorism and Human Rights", Geneva, International Commission of Jurists, 2009.

delisting process has gradually changed with a series of SC resolutions. The most significant reform was the introduction of the Ombudsperson as an external entity with a certain level of scrutiny.[114]

Despite representing an important step towards transparency – but not accountability – the many contradictions that still characterize the 1267 sanctions regime were not resolved through the establishment of the office of the Ombudsperson, whose mandate fails to meet the structural due process requirement of objective independence from the Committee.[115] Under the 1267 sanctions regime the single essential condition for being subjected to it is the association with Al-Qaida, which is, therefore, central to the determination of who is a foreign terrorist fighter. Pursuant to Resolution 2170,[116] the 1267 Sanctions Committee so far has added seven entities and 16 individuals, including two French foreign fighters, to the consolidated list.[117] The association criteria are defined and implemented broadly, i.e. so broadly that ISIL continues to be listed even after Al-Qaida has expressly repudiated it and the two groups are actually competitors in leading the "global jihad".[118] This fundamentally incorrect correlation between the two groups is once again the result of the lack of agreement on the terrorism definition and the consequent inability to determine what exactly it entails. The attempts to overcome this obstacle and reach a common understanding of who is a terrorist beyond the consolidated list have constantly failed,[119] and UN Member States are thus incapable of implementing a uniform approach in relation to groups other than Al-Qaida. The final outcome is that the SC exercises supranational sanctioning powers over individuals and entities,[120] through a permanent global terrorist list based merely on political findings of association, not dependent on any criminal conviction.[121]

---

[114] UN SC Res. 1904 (2009). The mandate of the Ombudsperson extends only to the Al-Qaida sanctions list.

[115] See EMMERSON, *cit. supra* note 112, paras. 32-34.

[116] UN SC Res. 2179 (2014), para. 7. KRÄHENMANN, *cit. supra* note 5, p. 41.

[117] Report of the Security Council Committee pursuant to Res. 1267 (1999) and 1989 (2011) concerning Al-Qaida and associated individuals and entities, S/2014/923, para. 17. The 1267 Sanctions Committee will issue its Annual Report by December 2015, with the updated list of individuals and entities.

[118] According to Al-Qaida's general command ISIL "is not a branch of the al-Qaeda group [...] does not have an organizational relationship with it and [al-Qaeda] is not the group responsible for their actions". Trianni, "Inside ISIS and al-Qaeda's Battle for Brand Supremacy", Time, 5 February 2015, available at: <http://time.com/3695200/islamist-radicals-connections/>. See also STERN and BERGER, *ISIS: The State of Terror*, New York, 2014, p. 43.

[119] See ROSAND, "The UN-Led Multilateral Institutional Response to Jihadist Terrorism: Is a Global Counterterrorism Body Needed?", Journal of Conflict & Security Law, 2007, p. 399 ff., p. 414.

[120] GINSBORG and SCHEININ, *cit. supra* note 104, p. 9.

[121] The breadth of the expression "associated with Al-Qaida" is explained in UN SC Res. 1989 (2011), para. 4. See also VAN DEN HERIK, *cit. supra* note 103, p. 442.

4. CONCLUSION

Resolution 2178 builds extensively on the already complex UN SC framework governing the international community's efforts to counter terrorism, and it fully relies on it, uncritically embracing all its shortcomings and even exacerbating them. The wide array of obligations imposed on Member States by Resolution 2178 has led to an anticipated criminalization that covers both the conduct, i.e. a terrorist offence, and all its preparatory acts, regardless of how remote they are. Thus, several States have been using their national counter-terrorism legislation not only to prosecute and try returning foreign terrorist fighters, but also to arrest and prosecute prospective foreign terrorist fighters, to prevent them from leaving and joining, or attempting to join, armed groups that are considered as "terrorist".[122] Resolution 2178 poses a number of problems in relation to the identification and prosecution of foreign terrorist fighters under national counter-terrorism laws,[123] mainly due to the fact that, in line with the previous legislative attempts of the UN SC, this resolution tackles terrorism without defining it. Central to the resolution are, in fact, the planning, preparation and perpetration of terrorist acts, providing and receiving terrorist training and, ultimately, the detection of a terrorist intent, which are mainly presumed, rather than determined on legal grounds.[124] Thus, the lack of a comprehensive and universally accepted definition of terrorism has been, and still is, an ongoing obstacle to building a unified global stance against terrorism and, on a more practical level, in concretizing and optimising the meaning, implementation, and effect of UN resolutions as well as international treaties involving counter-terrorism issues.[125] In this context a thought expressed in 1974 seems anything but obsolete: "we have caused to neglect that a legal concept of terrorism was ever inflicted upon us. The term is imprecise, it is ambiguous; and, above all, it serves no operative legal purpose".[126] In fact, as Resolution 2178 definitely proves, the concept of terrorism is concretely applied in light of political considerations that guide the designation of who is a terrorist and which groups pursue a terrorist purpose.

Moreover, Resolution 2178, by adding an extra layer to the existing framework, has contributed to perpetuating a strategy that privileges the goal of enhancing security and criminalization over accountability and individuals' rights. Setting aside the question of whether the UN SC has acted *ultra vires* or not, what matters is that in any legal system, even the international legal system, a body exercising power should bear the responsibility that derives from the exercise of this power;

---

[122] KRÄHENMANN, *cit. supra* note 5, p 51-53.

[123] KRÄHENMANN, *cit. supra* note 25, pp. 214-248.

[124] AMBOS, *cit. supra* note 19.

[125] See SETTY, *cit. supra* note 64, p. 7.

[126] BAXTER, "A Skeptical Look at the Concept of Terrorism", Akron Law Review, 1974, p. 380 ff., p. 380.

instead in the case of the current anti-terrorism framework the responsibility is entirely borne by Member States. Consequently, Member States on the one hand are called to implement the new set of obligations embedded in Resolution 2178 abiding by IHRL, refugee law and IHL, but on the other hand are free to determine the means through which the final outcome of thwarting foreign terrorist fighters must be achieved, without a supervisory and enforcement mechanism that can guarantee the application of effective measures and the required compliance with the relevant regime of international law.

THE PROTECTION OF PRIVATE INVESTORS' RIGHTS IN RECENT INTERNATIONAL INVESTMENT AGREEMENTS

STEFANO SILINGARDI[*]

Abstract

A new set of international legal rules has been developed in the recent practice of investment law, intended to balance the promotion of foreign investments with the creation of safeguards for public policies. After a brief introduction, which addresses that trend in the light of the expansion of negotiations on mega-regional agreements as the "new" instrument of investment regulation, the second section of this article discusses the question of the convergence of the protection of private investors and the protection of States' regulatory power in the experience of NAFTA countries and the most recent European investment policy, developed after the entry into force of the Lisbon Treaty. The third section is devoted to an analysis of the substantive provisions of the recently concluded mega-regional agreements concerning three specific elements traditionally linked to investor protection (i.e. the free and equitable treatment standard, "umbrella" clauses, and indirect expropriation) in order to examine how they contribute to setting a new paradigm, or at least a move towards a new paradigm for the protection of investors' rights. Subsequently, investors' obligations – still a major topic under discussion in the practice of investment law – will be examined; and finally the new dispute settlement mechanism which has been proposed by the European Union will be assessed, discussing how it could fit with a reform of the procedural aspects of investor protection to guarantee the State's policy space.

Keywords: international investment agreements; free and equitable treatment; indirect expropriation; "umbrella" clauses; investor-State dispute settlement; mega-regional agreements.

1. INTRODUCTION

International rules on foreign investments were originally developed in the light of the importance of international law as an "insurance" mechanism against the political risk of changes in domestic policy and law of the host State that could adversely affect foreign investors and their rights.[1] However, in the last few years,

---

[*] Adjunct Professor of International Law, University of Modena and Reggio Emilia.
[1] See, in general, SACERDOTI, "Bilateral Treaties and Multilateral Instruments on Investment Protection", RCADI, Vol. 269, 1997-II, p. 251 ff., pp. 298-310; SORNARAJAH, *The International Law on Foreign Investment*, 3rd ed., Cambridge, 2010, p. 187; DOLZER and SCHREUER, *Principles*

that *rationale* seems to have changed and there is now a well aligned front of States moving towards the formulation of a new set of international legal rules intended to balance the promotion of foreign investments with the creation of safeguards for public policies. That policy shift has been further accompanied by a dramatic decline of Bilateral Investment Treaties (BITs) as the typical instrument of investment regulation,[2] with the concurrent expansion of negotiations on mega-regional agreements that have become increasingly prominent especially among OECD countries.[3] There are three predominant reasons for this trend.

First, with the entering into force of the Lisbon Treaty on 1 December 2009, the European Union (EU) acquired a new exclusive competence over foreign direct investments (FDI) in the framework of a broadened Common Commercial Policy.[4] As a consequence, the negotiation and conclusion of International Investment Agreements (IIAs) – with potential implications for almost half of the IIAs actually in force[5] – is now exclusively reserved to the EU Commission, which could stop the conclusion of a turmoil of disparate and fragmented BITs by Member States by the inclusion of investment chapters in negotiations on more comprehensive Free Trade Areas (FTAs).[6]

The second reason is strictly linked to the slow progress of the Doha Round and the more than persistent failure of the World Trade Organization (WTO) as an efficient forum for international trade negotiations over the past decade. In that per-

---

of International Investment Law, 2nd ed., Oxford, 2012, p. 22. For more on the concepts of "insurance" and "political risks" as applied to foreign investments, see HOBER and FELLENBAUM, "Political Risks Insurance and Investment Treaty Protection", in BUGENBERG et al. (eds.), *International Investment Law*, Baden Baden, 2015, p. 1517 ff., pp. 1541-1550.

[2] During the "globalisation decade" of the 1990s the number of BITs increased astonishingly – with just under 2,000 BITs signed in less than a decade. Since 2008 the annual number of BITs has declined down to the 9 signed in 2015. See United Nations Conference on Trade and Development (UNCTAD), *World Investment Report 2015: Reforming International Investment Governance*, New York/Geneva, 2015, p. 107. Actually there are over 3,280 IIAs in force. See UNCTAD, *Investment Policy Monitor No. 15*, March 2016, p. 1.

[3] Of the 34 members of the Organisation for Economic Co-operation and Development (OECD), all but 5 (Iceland, Israel, Norway, Switzerland, and Turkey) would be party to one or more mega-regional agreement. See UNCTAD, *World Investment Report 2014: Investing in the SDGs: An Action Plan*, New York/Geneva, 2014, p. 123.

[4] Consolidated version of the Treaty on the Functioning of the European Union, OJ C 115, 9 May 2008, 2008/C 115/01, Arts. 206 and 207.

[5] The EU is at the very centre of the BITs network, with just under 1,800 BITs signed by its Member States. All but one EU country (the only exception is Ireland) have signed BITs. See at: <http://investmentpolicyhub.unctad.org/IIA>.

[6] The fate of existing BITs by EU Member States as well as of BITs whose negotiation was still open at the date the Treaty of Lisbon entered into force is regulated by Regulation (EU) No. 1219/2012 of 12 December 2012 (OJ L 351/40, 20 December 2012) establishing transitional arrangements for bilateral agreements between Member States and third countries. The Regulation (Art. 7) also allows the Commission to authorise Member States to open formal negotiations with a third country to amend or conclude a BIT under certain conditions.

spective, some countries, with the United States (US) at the forefront, have decided to explore new ways of trade and investment rule making.[7] It is therefore no coincidence that in the Nairobi Declaration, which closed the tenth WTO Ministerial Conference, on 19 December 2015, Ministers released a symptomatic and clearly concerned statement, in which they expressed "the need to ensure that Regional Trade Agreements remain complementary to, not a substitute for, the multilateral trading system".[8]

Finally, because of their increased exposure to Investor-State Dispute Settlement (ISDS) (from 326 cases in 2008 to 662 at the end of 2015, 229 of them still pending),[9] some countries have begun to consider both their "defensive" and "offensive" interests in the investment system. Coupled with the risk of inconsistent and overly expansive interpretations of IIAs by arbitral tribunals, new approaches to key provisions have been adopted (or proposed) with the aim to amend a system that, ultimately, has conveniently served the interests of developed, capital-exporting countries for nearly half a century. The grounds for these changes (i.e. improvements) have been identified, as we shall see in the next section, in the necessity of reaching a balance between the rights of the investors and the rights of host States to regulate in pursuance of public policy objectives.[10]

2. THE CONVERGENCE OF THE PROTECTION OF PRIVATE INVESTORS AND THE PROTECTION OF STATES' REGULATORY POWER IN THE NAFTA-LIKE CLAUSES AND THE EU POSITION

Although BITs were in principle based on reciprocity, in practice, developing countries, in exchange for the promise of increased capital flows from developed countries, agreed to take on internationally binding and enforceable commitments for the protection of foreign investors.[11] Put differently, as investors from devel-

---

[7] PETERSMANN, "Transformative Transatlantic Free Trade Agreements without Rights and Remedies of Citizens?", JIEL, 2015, p. 579 ff., p. 591.

[8] WTO, Nairobi Ministerial Declaration, WT/MIN(15)DEC, 19 December 2015, paras. 3 and 28.

[9] See at: <http://investmentpolicyhub.unctad.org/ISDS>. In the period 2011-2015, an average of 53 cases per annum has been initiated. The total number of cases (265) initiated in this period is only a little bit lower than the sum of all cases brought between 1987 and 2007. See also TITI, "Institutional Developments in Investor-State Dispute Settlement and Arbitration Under the Auspices of the International Centre for Settlement of Investment Disputes", European Yearbook of International Economic Law, 2015, p. 317 ff., p. 319.

[10] LÉVESQUE, "The Challenges of 'Marrying' Investment Liberalisation and Protection in the Canada-EU CETA", in BUNGENBERG, REINISCH and TIETJE (eds.), EU and Investment Agreements: Open Questions and Remaining Challenges, Baden Baden, 2013, p. 121 ff., p. 126.

[11] The preoccupation with investor protection was so strong that some agreements among the older BITs were concluded on an expressly non-reciprocal basis. The 1972 France-Tunisia

oped economies feared the political risks of expropriation and nationalization when investing in developing countries, the protections contained in BITs were perceived by capital-exporting countries to be essential in order to create a climate that would be friendly to foreign investments and would contribute to legal certainty for foreign investors.[12] To this end, ISDS clauses began to be included in BITs at the end of the 1960s,[13] allowing developed countries to avoid the challenges of diplomatic protection by ensuring that their private investors had a private right to arbitration against the host State.

The so-called "Dutch Gold Standard Model BIT"[14] has historically provided the highest standard of investment protection in the BITs arena. *Inter alia* that standard adopts broadly phrased and expansively interpretable definitions of investors and investment,[15] it requires compensation for both direct and indirect expropriation,[16] it places environmental and social objectives in the preamble in a non-binding and non-committal manner,[17] and it also provides for a broad choice of ISDS mechanisms, the fear of reciprocal action being negligible.[18]

Due to the "mounting critique as being excessively investor-friendly, to the detriment of the policy space of developing countries",[19] the Dutch Model BIT

BIT for example (now terminated) was explicitly addressed to "*favoriser le développement des investissements en Tunisie*". See *Décret No. 72.974 du 25 octobre 1972 portant publication de la convention entre le Gouvernement de la République et le Gouvernement de la République tunisienne sur la protection des investissements*, 30 June 1972, Journal officiel, 28 October 1972, p. 11301.

[12] In that perspective, certain investment agreements have even explicitly included a reference to the rights of investors to a "stable business environment". See CALAMITA, "The Making of Europe's International Investment Policy: Uncertain First Steps", Legal Issues of Economic Integration, 2012, p. 301 ff., p. 313.

[13] The first BIT to have incorporated an ISDS provision is the 1968 Netherlands-Indonesia BIT, Art. 11, while the 1969 Chad-Italy BIT is the first agreement to have included in its Art. 7 unqualified State consent to investor-State arbitration. See NEWCOMBE and PARADELL, *Law and Practice of Investment Treaties: Standards of Treatment*, The Hague, 2009, p. 45; and BROWN, "The Evolution of the Regime of International Investment Agreements: History, Economics and Politics", in BUGENBERG et al. (eds.), *cit. supra* note 1, p. 153 ff., p. 180.

[14] LAVRANOS, "In Defence of Member States' BITs Gold Standard: The Regulation 1219/2012 Establishing a Transitional Regime for Existing Extra-EU BITs – A Member State's Perspective", Transnational Dispute Management, 2013, p. 1 ff., p. 2.

[15] Netherlands, BIT Standard Text, March 2004, Art. 1, available at: <https://www.rijksoverheid.nl/binaries/rijksoverheid/documenten/convenanten/2004/08/27/ibo-modelovereenkomst/ibo-modelovereenkomst.pdf.>.

[16] *Ibid.*, Art. 6.

[17] *Ibid.*, preamble: "Considering that these objectives can be achieved without compromising health, safety and environmental measures of general application".

[18] *Ibid.*, Art. 9.

[19] KNOTTNERUS et al., "Socialising Losses, Privatising Gains. How Dutch Investment Treaties Harm the Public Interest", Centre for Research on Multinational Corporations, January 2015, p. 3. That critique has recently led the Dutch Trade Department to announce a review of Dutch BITs with developing countries.

has now been almost completely abandoned. The first developed countries to have shifted towards a different paradigm were the US and Canada, whose experience as respondents in NAFTA investment arbitrations persuaded them to take into account also the "defensive" interests of an FDI-importer country that were, until then, a typical feature of developing countries. That consideration led them to create new model BITs, re-evaluating the balance of rights for investors with other economic and non-economic policy priorities (environment, labour, social welfare, etc.) "in order to restrict the breadth of interpretation by the arbitration and ensure better protection of their public intervention domain".[20] Most importantly, these "new" agreements include a narrower definition of investment and investor, a narrower reading of the free and equitable treatment standard based upon customary international law, the absence of "umbrella" clauses, more detailed provisions on ISDS, and provisions to enhance the transparency of national laws and proceedings.[21] The last review of the US Model BIT, concluded in 2012, further expands obligations on standards related to the environment (Article 12) and labour (Article 13), requiring that Parties not waive or derogate from, or fail to effectively enforce their domestic environmental and labour laws in order to encourage investment.[22] Other significant additions to the 2012 US Model BIT concern dispute resolution, enhancing language regarding the possibility of a future multilateral appellate mechanism for reviewing awards rendered by investment arbitration tribunals (Article 28), as well as the clarification of the concept and scope of application of indirect expropriation (see *infra* Section 3.3).

Europe, which is the only region in the world where the "Dutch Gold Standard" has survived since the beginning of the 1990s, needed more time to rationalise that a change in its role from FDI-exporter to FDI-importer market was on the horizon and that, as a consequence, it was very likely to face a number of claims by foreign investors in the near future. Yet again in 2010, in its "Communication Towards a Comprehensive European Investment Policy", the Commission pledged to "ensure that no EU investor would be worse off than they would be under Member States' BITs",[23] which has the potential to be a very demanding requirement if we consider that the standard of protection spread among EU Member States was the

---

[20] EU Parliament, Resolution on the Future European International Investment Policy, 2010/2203(INI), 6 April 2011, preamble.

[21] See MURPHY, *United States Practice in International Law, Volume 2: 2002-2004*, Cambridge, 2011, p. 163. For an in-depth analysis of the attitude developed by the US since the adoption of the 2004 Model BIT, see ALVAREZ, *The Public International Law Regime Governing International Investment*, Leiden/Boston, 2011, pp. 143-176.

[22] US Model Bilateral Investment Treaty, 2012, Arts. 12-13, available at: <https://ustr.gov/sites/default/files/BIT%20text%20for%20ACIEP%20Meeting.pdf>.

[23] EU Commission, Communication from the Commission to the Council the European Parliament, the European Economic and Social Committee and the Committee of the Regions, Towards a Comprehensive European International Investment Policy, COM(2010)343 final, 7 July 2010, p. 11.

"Dutch Gold Standard". The same stance was shared by the European Council: in its "Conclusions on a Comprehensive European Investment Policy", the Council stressed as a priority "that the new legal framework should not negatively affect investor protection and guarantees enjoyed under the existing agreements".[24]

The main reason behind the highly "conservative" attitude shared by the Council and the Commission was essentially attributable to the near absence of claims brought at that time against pre-2004 enlargement Member States. Indeed, until 2011, only three claims (out of some 450 in total globally) appear to have been brought against them.[25] Put differently, BITs were still continuing to serve the interests of (the private investors of) Western European States.

A sort of "dissociation" among EU institutions therefore began when, on 6 April 2011, just few months after the Council's Conclusions, the EU Parliament released its "Resolution on the Future European International Investment Policy". In that document, the Parliament criticised the Council for its statement as it "could lead to the necessary balance between investor protection and the protection of the right to regulate – in an era of increased inward investment – being put at risk". Instead, the EU Parliament called upon the Commission to "better address the right to protect the public capacity to regulate and meet the EU's obligation to exercise policy coherence for development".[26] Moreover it emphasized that future IIAs concluded by the EU should include the free and equitable treatment standard "defined on the basis of the level of treatment established by international customary law" and a definition of indirect expropriation "that establishes a clear and fair balance between public welfare objectives and private interests".[27]

---

[24] Council of the European Union, Conclusions on a Comprehensive European Investment Policy, 25 October 2010, para. 9.

[25] See CALAMITA, *cit. supra* note 12, p. 315. One of these claims was settled by the parties with no payment to the claimant (*Vattenfall AB v. Germany*, ICSID Case No. ARB/09/6, Award of 11 May 2011); one claim resulted in a rather modest award of $0.3 million to the claimant (*Maffezini v. Spain*, ICSID Case No. ARB/97/7, Award of 13 November 2000), and one claim remained outstanding (*Sanchetti v. United Kingdom*).

[26] EU Parliament, *cit. supra* note 20, paras. 17 and 6. On the protection of the right to regulate, see also paras. 23-26. For more on the EU investment policy and competences post-Lisbon, see BISCHOFF, "Just a Little Bit of 'Mixity'? The EU's Role in the Field of International Investment Protection Law", CML Rev., 2011, p. 1527 ff., pp. 1534-1545; DE LUCA, *La competenza dell'Unione europea sugli investimenti esteri*, Torino, 2012; HOFFMEISTER and ALEXANDRU, "A First Glimpse of Light on the Emerging Invisible EU Model BIT", The Journal of World Investment & Trade, 2014, p. 379 ff., pp. 381-383; REINISCH, "The EU on the Investment Path – Quo Vadis Europe? The Future of EU BITs and Other Investment Agreements", Santa Clara Journal of International Law, 2014, p. 111 ff., pp. 135-148; BUGENBERG and HOBE, "The Relationship of International Investment Law and European Union Law", in BUGENBERG et al. (eds.), *cit. supra* note 1, p. 1602 ff., pp. 1617-1629.

[27] EU Parliament, *cit. supra* note 20, para. 19.

In October 2015, the Commission finally updated its approach on the Parliament's position (which was, in turn, modelled on the most recent US practice). Two main events prompted this change in perspective.

First, in that period, EU Member States became frequent respondents in international investment claims. Since 2012, for example, 22 cases have been filed against Spain.[28] In 2014, Italy faced its first known investor-State claim;[29] in September 2013 France also faced its first known investor-State claim;[30] and the same year, Germany faced an investor-State claim for the third time in its history.[31] Belgium,[32] Cyprus,[33] and Greece[34] too faced their first claims in 2013, all of them having been filed against policies developed by these three countries during the economic and financial crisis in Europe.[35]

Second, given the widespread concerns and oppositions to the Transatlantic Trade and Investment Partnership (TTIP) among EU civil society, the Commission decided to organise a public consultation on investment protection and ISDS. The consultation, which received almost 150,000 replies, took place in the spring of 2014 and its results were published in January 2015 revealing an increasing rejection of investment protection and ISDS among the EU population.[36] In a comment immediately following the public presentation of the Commission's report on that consultation, the Commissioner for Trade, Cecilia Malmström, acknowledged that there was "huge scepticism" among EU civil society on the ISDS mechanism and that for the Commission there is the "need to have an open and frank discussion about investment protection and ISDS in TTIP with EU governments, with the

---

[28] See at: <http://investmentpolicyhub.unctad.org/ISDS/CountryCases/197?partyRole=2>.

[29] The claim, arising under the Energy Charter Treaty, is *Blusun S.A., Jean-Pierre Lecorcier and Michael Stein v. Italy*, ICSID Case No. ARB/14/3, registered on 21 February 2014. Two new cases arising under the Energy Charter Treaty were filed against Italy in 2015: *Silver Ridge Power BV v. Italy*, ICSID Case No. ARB/15/37; and *Greentech Energy Systems and Novenergia v. Italy*, Stockholm Chamber of Commerce Case.

[30] *Erbil Serter v. French Republic*, ICSID Case No. ARB/13/22.

[31] *Vattenfall AB and others v. Federal Republic of Germany*, ICSID Case No. ARB/12/12.

[32] *Ping An Life Insurance Company of China, Limited and Ping An Insurance (Group) Company of China, Limited v. Kingdom of Belgium*, ICSID Case No. ARB/12/29.

[33] *Marfin Investment Group Holdings S.A., Alexandros Bakatselos and others v. Republic of Cyprus*, ICSID Case No. ARB/13/27.

[34] *Poštová banka, a.s. and ISTROKAPITAL SE v. Hellenic Republic*, ICSID Case No. ARB/13/8.

[35] On the recent practice concerning the application of BITs in times of economic crises, see SACERDOTI, "The Application of BITs in Time of Economic Crisis: Limits to Their Coverage, Necessity and the Relevance of WTO Law", in SACERDOTI et al. (eds.), *General Interests of Host States in International Investment Law*, Cambridge, 2014, p. 3 ff.

[36] EU Commission, Online Public Consultation on Investment Protection and Investor-to-State Dispute Settlement (ISDS) in the Transatlantic Trade and Investment Partnership Agreement (TTIP), SWD(2015) 3 final, 13 January 2015.

European Parliament and civil society before launching any policy recommendations in this area".[37]

In its new trade and investment agenda of October 2015, the Commission thus focused its investment policy priority on "putting stronger emphasis on the right of the State to regulate, something which was not sufficiently highlighted in the past", as well as on the commitment "before the end of its mandate [...] [to] review the 2010 communication on international investment".[38]

3.   A "NEW" PARADIGM FOR THE PROTECTION OF INVESTORS' RIGHTS

More than 90 countries are actually involved in negotiations on three mega-regional agreements: the TTIP, the Transpacific Partnership (TPP), and the Regional Comprehensive Economic Partnership (RCEP). While negotiations on the TPP were concluded on 4 October 2015,[39] the two other initiatives are currently under discussion, with considerable doubt as to whether the TTIP negotiations between EU and US will eventually be concluded. The EU has also concluded negotiations on FTAs, with the inclusion of specific chapters on investment protection, with Canada[40] and Singapore[41] in 2014, and more recently, on 2 December 2015, with Vietnam.[42]

The relevant provisions of these agreements concerning three specific elements traditionally linked to investor protection (i.e. the free and equitable treatment standard, "umbrella" clauses, and indirect expropriation) will now be taken into account in order to suggest how they contribute to setting a new paradigm, or at least a move towards a new paradigm for the protection of investors' rights.

---

[37] EU Commission, "Press Release, Report presented today: Consultation on Investment Protection in EU-US Trade Talks", 13 January 2015, available at: <http://trade.ec.europa.eu/doclib/press/index.cfm?id=1234>.

[38] EU Commission, "Trade for All. Towards a More Responsible Trade and Investment Policy", October 2015, pp. 21-22.

[39] See "Trans-Pacific Partnership Ministers' Statement", available at: <https://ustr.gov/about-us/policy-offices/press-office/press-releases/2015/october/trans-pacific-partnership-ministers>.

[40] The Canada-EU summit on 26 September 2014 in Ottawa, marked the end of the negotiations of the EU-Canada trade agreement (CETA). The end of the legal review of the original (English) version of the text was concluded on 29 February 2016. This legally reviewed text was made public the same day, see: <http://trade.ec.europa.eu/doclib/docs/2014/september/tradoc_152806.pdf>. It will now be translated into the other official languages of the EU and Canada before being submitted to the Council and the EU Parliament for approval.

[41] The negotiations for a comprehensive free trade agreement between EU and Singapore were completed on 17 October 2014. On 10 July 2015, the Commission initiated proceedings with the European Court of Justice for an opinion on the EU competence to sign and ratify the FTA.

[42] The official text of the agreement is available at: <http://trade.ec.europa.eu/doclib/press/index.cfm?id=1437>.

3.1. Free and Equitable Treatment Standard

The free and equitable treatment standard is traditionally designed to protect foreign investors from government misconduct not captured by the more specific standards of protection of the most-favoured nation clause and the national treatment obligation.[43] To make this possible, it has traditionally been formulated in general and brief terms. By way of example, it is worded in the "Dutch Gold Standard BIT" as follows:

> "Each Contracting Party shall ensure fair and equitable treatment of the investments of nationals of the other Contracting Party and shall not impair, by unreasonable or discriminatory measures, the operation, management, maintenance, use, enjoyment or disposal thereof by those nationals. Each Contracting Party shall accord to such investments full physical security and protection".[44]

In this perspective it is, therefore, not surprising that that standard has gained particular prominence among the IIA protection elements[45] and that claimants in ISDS proceedings have regularly invoked it with a considerable rate of success.[46]

---

[43] DOLZER and SCHREUER, cit. supra note 1, p. 122. See also MANN, "British Treaties for the Formation and Protection of Investment", BYIL, 1981, p. 241 ff., p. 243, who considered that standard to be a "catch-all clause": "so general a provisions likely to be almost sufficient to cover all conceivable cases, and it may well be that other provisions of the agreements affording substantive protection are no more than examples or specify instances of this overriding duty".

[44] Netherlands, BIT Standard Text, cit. supra note 15, Art. 3(1). That formulation is common to almost all European Western countries' BITs. The Italian 2003 Model BIT (Art. 2(3)), for example, states: "Both Contracting Parties shall at all times ensure just and fair treatment to investments of investors of the other Contracting Party. Both Contracting Parties shall ensure that the management, maintenance, use, transformation, enjoyment or disposal of the investments effected in their territory by investors of the other Contracting Party, as well as by companies and enterprises in which these investments have been effected, shall in no way be the object of unjustified or discriminatory measures". Available at: <http://www.italaw.com/sites/default/files/archive/ITALY%202003%20Model%20BIT%20.pdf>.

[45] See DOLZER, "Fair and Equitable Treatment: Today's Contours", Santa Clara Journal of International Law, p. 7 ff., pp. 10-11. See also PSEG Global Inc. v. Republic of Turkey, ICSID Case No. ARB/02/5, Award of 19 January 2007 (available at: <http://www.italaw.com/documents/ PSEGGlobal-Turkey-Award.pdf>), in which the Court stressed: "The standard of fair and equitable treatment has acquired prominence in investment arbitration as a consequence of the fact that other standards traditionally provided by international law might not in the circumstances of each case be entirely appropriate" (para. 238).

[46] In order to reduce their exposure to investor claims, some States have recently decided to conclude IIAs without referring to that standard or referring to it only in the preamble. See, for example, the 2003 Australia-Singapore FTA, available at: <http://investmentpolicyhub.unctad.org/Download/TreatyFile/2649>; and the 2005 Turkey-United Arab Emirates BIT, available at: <http://investmentpolicyhub.unctad.org/Download/TreatyFile/3332>.

Moreover, the free and equitable treatment standard being closely tied to the notion of legitimate expectations of the investor, there is the risk that it could be applied in order to restrict countries' ability to change investment-related policies or introduce new policies if they have a negative impact on foreign investors (so-called "regulatory chilling effect").

In order to restrict its vagueness[47] and to limit the scope of its application by arbitral tribunals, the recent negotiations on mega-regional agreements have provided a more precise definition of fair and equitable treatment. To this end, two different approaches have been followed.

The TPP Agreement, which is largely built upon the 2012 US Model BIT, anchors the mention of that standard to the customary international law principles. In particular, it qualifies the customary international law minimum standard of treatment of aliens "as the standard of treatment to be afforded to covered instruments", providing that references to that concept "do not require treatment in addition to or beyond that which is required by that standard, and do not create additional substantive rights" (Article 9(6)(2)). The same provision further provides an *illustrative* list of specific situations covered by free and equitable treatment, including: "the obligation not to deny justice in criminal, civil or administrative adjudicatory proceedings in accordance with the principle of due process embodied in the principal legal systems of the world" (Article 9(6)(2)(a)).[48]

Going beyond the 2012 US Model BIT, that neither defined nor delimited that concept, the TPP Agreement further addresses the question of legitimate expectations of investors. Article 9(6)(4) of the TPP clarifies that: "the mere fact that a Party takes or fails to take an action that may be inconsistent with an investor's expectations does not constitute a breach of this Article, even if there is loss or damage to the covered investment as a result".[49]

The approach chosen by the EU and Canada in the Comprehensive Economic and Trade Agreement (CETA) is different as it provides a closed text, which defines the concept of free and equitable treatment through the provision of an exhaustive list of specific obligations which Contracting Parties must commit to. According to CETA Article 8(10), a breach of the free and equitable treatment obligation can only

---

[47] *Saluka Investments B.V. v. Czech Republic*, UNCITRAL Arbitration, Partial Award of 17 March 2006: "The 'ordinary meaning' of the 'fair and equitable treatment' standard can only be defined by terms of almost equal vagueness" (para. 296). See also SALACUSE, *The Law of Investment Treaties*, Oxford, 2010, p. 221, who describes that standard as "maddeningly vague, frustratingly general, and treacherously elastic".

[48] Trans-Pacific Partnership Agreement, Art. 9(6), available at: <https://ustr.gov/tpp>. The text of this Article is exactly the same of Article 5 of the 2012 US Model BIT.

[49] As is explained in the Chapter Summary provided by the Office of the US Trade Representative, this means that an investor cannot win a claim for breach of that standard "merely by showing that a government measure frustrated its expectations (for example, its expectations of earning certain profits)". Available at: <https://medium.com/the-trans-pacific-partnership/investment-c76dbd892f3a#.wzmn8zf12>.

arise when there is: "[d]enial of justice in criminal, civil or administrative proceedings; fundamental breach of due process, including a fundamental breach of transparency, in judicial and administrative proceedings; manifest arbitrariness; targeted discrimination on manifestly wrongful grounds, such as gender, race or religious belief; abusive treatment of investors, such as coercion, duress and harassment".[50]

The idea that the limitation of the meaning of the free and equitable treatment standard would contribute to increased legal certainty is a noteworthy addition to the legal framework of international investment. For a long time, the idea among scholars and States has been that the lack of precision of that standard "may be a virtue rather than a shortcoming. In actual practice, it is impossible to anticipate in the abstract the range of possible types of infringements upon the investor's legal position. [...] Therefore [...] it is susceptible of specification through judicial practice".[51] In that perspective, the need to limit the scope of application of that standard is a clear warning that something has been broken in the decades-long confidence of (developed) States in the interpretative action of arbitral tribunals.[52] If that is true, it will now be up to the negotiations on TTIP to try to resolve the question – at least in an agreement between developed countries with a functioning legal system – whether to adopt a provision on the free and equitable treatment standard which is based on an exhaustive list of obligations or on an illustrative list coupled with reference to the customary international law minimum standard of treatment, whose profile is yet far from clear.[53]

---

[50] Article 8(10) of the CETA, *cit. supra* note 40, also addresses the concept of legitimate expectations, limiting it to those situations where a specific promise or representation was made by the State, upon which the investor relied in deciding to make or maintain the investment which the State subsequently frustrated. The provision also allows for the possibility of extending this list in the future, should the parties agree to do so.

[51] See DOLZER and SCHREUER, *cit. supra* note 1, p. 148. However, the sometimes excessive discretion of arbitral tribunals in interpreting this standard has given rise to criticism even among arbitrators. See, for example, *Suez, Sociedad General de Aguas de Barcelona, S.A. and Vivendi Universal, S.A. v. Argentina*, ICSID Case No. ARB/03/19, and *AWG Group v. Argentina* (joint cases), Decision on Liability of 30 July 2010, Separate Opinion of Arbitrator Pedro Nikken: "I believe that the standard of fair and equitable treatment has been interpreted so broadly that it results in arbitral tribunals imposing upon the Parties obligations that do not arise in any way from the terms that the Parties themselves used to define their commitment [...] Unfortunately, I have not had the intelligence or the ability to convince my colleagues in this Tribunal [...] about the irrationality and the weakness of this jurisprudence, of which I am convinced" (para. 27).

[52] See EU Commission, "Investment Provisions in the EU-Canada Free Trade Agreement (CETA), Factsheet", 26 September 2014, p. 1, stating: "Unlike other agreements, the standard of 'fair and equitable treatment' in CETA is neither a floor or a minimum standard nor an evolving concept. Rather, a clear, closed text defines precisely the standard of treatment *without leaving unwelcome discretion to arbitrators*" (emphasis added).

[53] On 16 September 2015, the text of the EU's proposal to the US for the Investment Chapter to be included in the TTIP was made public. Article 9(3) deals with the free and equitable treatment standard and replies the text of the relevant CETA disposition. See "Text of the Commission's text proposal published on 16 September 2015 on Investment Protection and

3.2. "Umbrella" Clauses

"Umbrella" clauses oblige the host State to respect any undertaking that it has assumed towards its foreign investors regardless of its public-law or private-law nature. These clauses thus bring under the "umbrella" of the BIT also those contractual obligations whose violation by States could not otherwise amount to a violation of the BIT.[54] In that perspective, the more broadly written they are, the greater the ability of "umbrella" clauses to catch every conceivable obligation of the host State under their scope of application. It is, therefore, quite clear why the Dutch Model BIT adopted the broadest possible formulation of that clause, referring it to "any obligation [Each Contracting Party] may have entered into with regard to investments of nationals of the other Contracting Party".[55]

Since 2003, when they appeared for the first time in an ISDS claim, the application of "umbrella" clauses proved to be challenging. Their meaning and scope became the object of interpretative divergences by arbitral tribunals, resulting in contradictory and inconsistent awards concerning what kind of commitment could be elevated to the level of a treaty claim.[56] In order to avoid such uncertainty, in recent years, States are beginning to carve "umbrella" clauses out of their treaties and model BITs. Both the 2004 and 2012 US Model BITs, the Canadian and French Model BITs, the most recent generation of Chinese BITs, Norway's 2015 Draft Model BIT,[57] and the Indian 2016 Model BIT[58] do not include an "umbrella" clause.[59]

Resolution of Investment Disputes and Investment Court System in TTIP", available at: <http://trade.ec.europa.eu/doclib/docs/2014/october/tradoc_152844.pdf>.

[54] From a strict international law point of view, "umbrella" clauses thus contradict the statement according to which "only the State, in the exercise of its sovereign authority, and not as a Contracting party has assumed obligations under the BIT". See *Salini Costruttori SpA and Italstrade SpA v. The Hashemite Kingdom of Jordan*, ICSID Case No ARB/02/13, Decision on Jurisdiction of 29 November 2004, para. 155.

[55] Netherlands, BIT Standard text, *cit. supra* note 15, Art. 3(4).

[56] See DOLZER and SCHREUER, *cit. supra* note 1, pp. 153 ff.; PEREIRA DE SOUZA, "Umbrella Clauses: a Trend towards Its Elimination", Arbitration International, 2015, p. 679 ff., p. 681; TITI, *The Right to Regulate in International Investment Law*, Baden-Baden, 2014, p. 48 ff.; DE LUCA, "Umbrella Clauses and Transfer Provisions in the (Invisible) EU Model BIT", The Journal of World Investment & Trade, 2014, pp. 506-533; and SINCLAIR, "Umbrella Clauses", in BUGENBERG et al. (eds.), *cit. supra* note 1, p. 887 ff., p. 890 ff.

[57] Norway's Draft Model Bilateral Investment Treaty, 13 May 2015, available at: <https://www.regjeringen.no/contentassets/e47326b61f424d4c9c3d470896492623/draft-model-agreement-english.pdf>.

[58] Model text for the Indian Bilateral Investment Treaty, January 2016, available at: <http://finmin.nic.in/the_ministry/dept_eco_affairs/investment_division/ModelBIT_Annex.pdf>.

[59] However, the Japan-Iran BIT, signed on 5 February 2016 (not yet in force) includes in its Art. 6 the classical formulation of an "umbrella" clause. Available at: <http://investmentpolicyhub.unctad.org/Download/TreatyFile/3578>.

With regard to mega-regional agreements, the situation is more varied. Both the CETA and TPP Agreements indeed avoid any reference to an "umbrella" clause in their Investment Chapters. Instead, the 2014 EU-Singapore Free Trade Area (EUSFTA) includes such a clause. According to Article 9(4)(5) of EUFSTA, only "contractual written obligations" that the host State has assumed towards investors of the other Party should be covered by that clause, meaning that "that Party shall not frustrate or undermine the said commitment through the exercise of its governmental authority".[60] The same provision has been included in the EU Commission's "Text Proposal on Investment Protection and Resolution of Investment Disputes and Investment Court System in TTIP".[61] In the CETA, it was, therefore, probably the strong opposition of Canada that caused the exclusion of such a clause from the final text of the agreement, rather than an afterthought of the EU.[62] In this respect, the TTIP negotiations will represent a decisive opportunity to clarify whether "umbrella" clauses should have space in future IIAs, or should be omitted or be applied in a more limited version that could reduce their scope (i.e., by only referring to written obligations and with respect to exercise of sovereign powers by the government).

3.3. Indirect Expropriation

The difficulty of articulating a clear operational definition of indirect expropriation (i.e. of clarifying the acts, or series of acts, whose effects are "tantamount to" or "equivalent to" a direct, formal expropriation) has been traditionally used by investors to challenge a wide range of general non-discriminatory regulations of the host State having a negative effect on their investment.[63] Only recently, some

---

[60] EU-Singapore Free Trade Agreement (EUSFTA) of 29 June 2015, available at: <http://trade.ec.europa.eu/doclib/press/index.cfm?id=961>.

[61] See Commission's TTIP proposal (*cit. supra* note 53), Art. 7. See also Council of the European Union, Declassification of Document ST 11103/13 Restraint UE/EU Restricted dated 17 June 2013 "Directives for the negotiation on the Transatlantic Trade and Investment Partnership between the European Union and the United States of America", 11103/13 DCL 1, 9 October 2014, para. 23, p. 9.

[62] See also Council of the European Union, Partial Declassification of Document 12838/11 of 14 July 2011 "Recommendation from the Commission to the Council on the modification of the negotiating directives for an Economic Integration Agreement with Canada in order to authorise the Commission to negotiate, on behalf of the Union, on investment", 12838/11 EXT 2, 15 December 2015, para. 26(c), p. 5. The text of the negotiating mandate is also consistent with the intentions of the EU Commission outlined in the Communication from the Commission to the Council (*cit. supra* note 23, p. 8) where "umbrella" clauses were outlined as "an important element among others that should inspire the negotiation of investment agreements at the EU level".

[63] Historically, IIAs have not contained any criteria to find a proper limit between unlawful interference in the right to property for which compensation must be paid and what constitutes

States (and the US in particular) have set out a number of criteria that need to be met in order for indirect expropriation to be found. The aim of that clarification is to avoid overly wide interpretations of that clause by arbitral tribunals as well as to allow host States ample policy space to pursue public welfare objectives.

Both in its 2004 and 2012 text versions, the US Model BIT included an annex (Annex B) that curbs the indirect expropriation analysis (e.g. a presumption against the finding of an indirect expropriation)[64] by noting that "except in rare circumstances, non-discriminatory regulatory actions by a Party that are designed and applied to protect legitimate public welfare objectives, such as public health, safety, and the environment, do not constitute indirect expropriations".[65] The annex further tries to limit tribunals' discretion by making reference to a non-exhaustive list of factors that tribunals should take into account when determining whether an action or series of actions by a Party constitutes an indirect expropriation. These factors include: (i) the economic impact of the government action; (ii) the extent to which the government interferes with distinct, reasonable investment-backed expectations; and (iii) the character of the government action.[66]

Annex 9-B of the TPP Agreement adds only a few changes in the wording of the US Model BIT. In particular, two footnotes have been added. The first, in particular, refers to investors' legitimate expectations, clarifying that investor's investment-backed expectations are considered "reasonable" according to some "factors such as whether the government provided the investor with binding written assurances and the nature and extent of governmental regulation or the potential for government regulation in the relevant sector".[67]

Only in recent times has the EU updated its practice on the basis of the US approach, resulting in one of the most significant departures from the classical approach followed by European Western country BITs. Annex 8-A to the CETA

---

legitimate public policymaking for which no compensation is due. See *Impregilo Spa v. Pakistan*, ICSID Case ARB/03/03, Award of 21 June 2011, para. 270.

[64] FONTANELLI and BIANCO, "Converging Towards NAFTA: An Analysis of FTA Investment Chapters in the European Union and the United States", Stanford Journal of International Law, 2014, p. 211 ff., p. 223.

[65] US Model BIT, *cit. supra* note 22, Annex B, Art. 4(b). These criteria were first developed by the US Supreme Court in the case *Penn Central Station Co. v. New York City*, Judgement of 26 June 1978, 438 US 104, p. 124.

[66] US Model BIT, *cit. supra* note 22, Annex B, Art. 4(a). Point (ii) is of particular relevance in attempting to limit tribunals' discretion, as it clarifies that legitimate expectations must be taken into account in order to determine the existence of an indirect expropriation but only if they are "distinct" and "reasonable" in order to exclude expectations merely based on discussions with domestic authorities or presumptions. For more on this, see DE LUCA, "Indirect Expropriations and Regulatory Takings: What Role for the "Legitimate Expectations" of Foreign Investors?", in SACERDOTI et al (eds.), *General Interests of Host States in International Investment Law*, Cambridge, 2014. pp. 58-75.

[67] TPP, *cit. supra* note 48, Annex 9-B, footnote 36.

Agreement[68] appears in fact to be largely identical to the US model, with only three small changes. It adds the requirement to consider the *duration* of the measures by a Party among the factors that shall be taken into account in order to determine whether a measure or a series of measures amount to indirect expropriation. To the same end, it further clarifies that not only the character but also the *object*, *context*, and *intent* of such measure(s) shall be considered. Finally it points out that only measures characterised by a severe impact that appears as *manifestly excessive* could be included in the rare circumstances where a non-discriminatory regulation designed and adopted to protect legitimate public welfare amounts to indirect expropriation.[69]

The same provision was included in the Commission's September 2015 TTIP proposal, with only two differences. The first relates to the character of the measure in determining indirect expropriation, which is now defined only in terms of "object and context", leaving out the "intent" in order to reduce the purposive interpretation suggested in CETA that could foster misunderstanding and overly wide interpretations by arbitral tribunals.[70] The second difference is the longer list of legitimate public welfare objectives, which now includes also measures aiming to protect "public morals, social or consumer protection or promotion and protection of cultural diversity".[71]

3.4. Investors' Obligations

Alongside the clarification of specific terms, three further options have been explored by recent IIA practice in order to better protect States' right to regulate.

First, almost all recent IIAs make clear from the outset (i.e. the preamble) that the Contracting Parties reserve the right to regulate to achieve a number of legitimate policy objectives that may be generally connected to the notion of sustainable development and its three main pillars: society, economy, and the environment.[72] By

---

[68] See also Annex 9-A of the EUSFTA Agreement, *cit. supra* note 60; and EU-Vietnam Free Trade Agreement, *cit. supra* note 42, p. 22.

[69] Consolidated CETA text, *cit. supra* note 40, Annex 8.10.

[70] On the risks connected to the inclusion of the "intent" test in this context, see KRIEBAUM, "FET and Expropriation in the (Invisible) EU Model BIT", The Journal of World Investment & Trade, 2014, p. 455 ff., p. 465. The author points out that "[t]o insist on a manifestation of the intention to expropriate on the part of the host State would impose a virtually impossible burden of proof on the investor who would have to demonstrate the motivations behind government action".

[71] Commission's text proposal, *cit. supra* note 53, Annex 1.

[72] Calls for reform of the international investment legal framework, which could ensure a better protection of the regulatory space of host States, are included in a number of policy proposals that have been submitted in recent years by inter-governmental organizations. See UNCTAD, "Investment Policy Framework for Sustainable Development", 2015, available at: <http://unctad.org/en/PublicationsLibrary/diaepcb2015d5_en.pdf>. See also VAN DUZER, SIMONS

way of an example, the CETA preamble lists "public health, safety, environment, public morals and the promotion and protection of cultural diversity",[73] while the TPP preamble adds "the conservation of living or non-living exhaustible resources [and] the integrity and stability of the financial system"[74] to that list. Considering that the preamble generally serves as one guide for the contextual and teleological interpretation of international treaties,[75] this option may arguably be considered as a useful addition in order to ensure that arbitral tribunals will not state that the purpose of IIAs is the protection of investment only but also take greater account of non-investment policy objectives.[76]

The second option is to complement the Agreement with express public policy exceptions whose formulation is often similar to the language found in the General Agreement on Tariffs and Trade (GATT) Article XX and in the General Agreement on Trade and Services Article XIV. The aim of these GATT Article XX-like provisions is to reduce States' exposure to investor's claims in particularly sensitive sectors,[77] as well as to ensure "that flexibilities are available to the Contracting Parties that guarantee the full right to regulate in the public interest".[78]

Finally, a third issue has emerged in the last decade as a major topic in order to ensure better protection of States' public intervention domain: the possibility to in-

---

and MAYEDA, "Integrating Sustainable Development into International Investment Agreement: A Guide for Developing Countries", Commonwealth Secretariat, August 2012, available at: <https://www.iisd.org/pdf/2012/6th_annual_forum_commonwealth_guide.pdf>.

[73] CETA text, *cit. supra* note 40, preamble.

[74] TPP, *cit. supra* note 48, preamble. It should be noted that the Commission's proposal for TTIP includes reference to States' right to regulate, not in the preamble but in Art. 2(1) of the Investment Chapter, see Commission's text proposal, *cit. supra* note 53, Art. 2(1).

[75] Vienna Convention on the Law of Treaties, 23 May 1969, entered into force 27 January 1980.

[76] See, for example, *Siemens A.G. v. The Argentine Republic*, ICSID Case No. ARB/02/8, Decision on Jurisdiction of 30 August 2004: "The Tribunal shall be guided by the purpose of the Treaty as expressed in its title and preamble. It is a treaty 'to protect' and 'to promote' investments [...] The intention of the parties is clear. It is to create favourable conditions for investments and to stimulate private initiative" (para. 81). For an exhaustive and concise analysis of the "object and purpose" test in investment tribunals case law, see REINISCH, "The Interpretation of International Investment Agreements", in BUGENBERG et al. (eds.), *cit. supra* note 1, p. 372 ff., pp. 396-401.

[77] By a way of example, Chapter 29 of the TPP Agreement, *cit. supra* note 48, includes in Art. 29(5) a separate, explicit recognition of health authorities' right to adopt tobacco control measures in order to protect public health. See also Chapter 28, Art. 28(3) of CETA. CETA also includes carve outs for the audio-visual sector and exceptions for national security, as well as prudential and safeguard measures and balance of payment problems. As has been noted, this incorporation presumably incorporates even the Chapeau of Article XX. See DE MESTRAL, "When Does the Exception Become the Rule? Conserving Regulatory Space under CETA", JIEL, 2015, p. 641 ff., p. 649. See also Norway's Draft Model BIT, *cit. supra* note 57, Art. 24; the Japan-Iran BIT, *cit. supra* note 59, Art. 13; and Model text for the Indian BIT, *cit. supra* note 58, Art. 32, which includes an explicit reference (Art. 33) to GATT Art. XXI ("Security Exceptions").

[78] Chapter summary, *cit. supra* note 49.

corporate investors' obligations into IIAs.[79] To this end, two different categories of provisions can be traced in the recent practice of investment law: the first category refers to direct legal obligations of investors as explicitly stipulated in BITs and other IIAs, whilst the second category concerns non-binding provisions of conduct for foreign investors.

Although the choice of incorporating binding obligations could be seen as the most expected and natural approach, that practice has "until now not gained anything even close to widespread recognition in investment treaty practice".[80] The substantive reasons behind the reluctance of most countries to incorporate such obligations in IIAs are various: from concerns about how detailed such provisions should be, to the need to determine the exact contours of the relationships between these obligations with the corresponding domestic and international legal standards. But the most difficult task, which would significantly modify the rationale behind investment agreements, is generally considered to be the procedural question on how to enforce investors' obligations, as today's IIAs only provide for enforcement by foreign investors of host State obligations.[81]

On the other hand, provisions that mandate the investors to voluntarily incorporate in their practices internationally recognized standards of non-commercial responsibility are gaining ground.[82] Most of the time, these include standards re-

---

[79] On this topic, see HEPBURN and KUUYA, "Corporate Social Responsibility and Investment Treaties", in CORDONIER SEGGER, GEHRING and NEWCOMBE (eds.), *Sustainable Development in World Investment Law*, The Hague, 2011, p. 589 ff.; MUCHLINSKI, "Regulating Multinationals: Foreign Investment, Development, and the Balance of Corporate and Home Country Rights and Responsibilities in a Globalizing World", in ALVAREZ and SAUVANT (eds.), *The Evolving International Investment Regime*, Oxford, 2011, p. 30 ff.; BONFANTI, "Applying Corporate Social Responsibility to Foreign Investments", in TREVES, SEATZU and TREVISANUT (eds.), *Foreign Investment, International Law and Common Concerns*, London/New York, 2014, p. 231 ff.; and NOWROT, "Obligations of Investors", in BUGENBERG et al. (eds.), *cit. supra* note 1, p. 1154 ff., pp. 1173-1185.

[80] NOWROT, "How to Include Environmental Protection, Human Rights and Sustainability in International Investment Law?", The Journal of World Investment & Trade, 2014, p. 612 ff., p. 636. Neither the CETA, nor TPP and the EU Commission's TTIP text proposal, for example, include such obligations.

[81] See WEILER, "Balancing Human Rights and Investor Protection: A New Approach for a Different Legal Order", Boston College International and Comparative Law Review, 2004, p. 429 ff., p. 437.

[82] See, for example, TPP, *cit. supra* note 48, Art. 9(16); Norway's Model BIT, *cit. supra* note 57, Art. 31; Canada-Burkina Faso BIT, 20 April 2015 (not yet in force), Art. 16; and Brazil-Malawi Cooperation and Facilitation Investment Agreement (CFIA), 25 June 2015 (not yet in force), Art. 9. See also the Model text for the Indian BIT, *cit. supra* note 58, Art. 12. However, in terms of investor obligations, the final text of the Indian Model BIT is significantly leaner than the Draft BIT, which was released earlier in 2015. In particular, the draft provisions on "Obligations against Corruption" (stating that the investor would not indulge in any activity amounting to corruption) as well as on "Disclosures" (requiring the investor to maintain all records about its investments) and "Home State Obligations" (requiring home States to prosecute investors for damage or injuries in the host state) have been eliminated. In the CETA Agreement,

sulting from the OECD Guidelines for Multinational Enterprises,[83] the International Labour Organization Tripartite Declaration of Principle Concerning Multinational Enterprises and Social Policy,[84] and the United Nations Guiding Principles on Business and Human Rights.[85] Corporate Social Responsibility (CSR) is also a topic in the EU debate about investment policy. In its "Resolution on the Future European International Investment Policy", the EU Parliament called on the Commission to include in future EU investment agreements a reference to the OECD Guidelines for Multinational Enterprises as well as a provision on CSR.[86]

4. THE PROCEDURAL ASPECTS OF INVESTMENT PROTECTION

A comprehensive set of reforms concerning the substantive investor protection rules is necessary for a better and clearer balancing of investor and State interests, but is insufficient on its own. It is, indeed, the cumulative effect of substantive and procedural rules – namely, those rules whose application can actually lead to a binding legal decision – that drove distinguished scholars to describe investor protection as: "perhaps the most invidious – and most dishonest – part of such agreements. Of course, investors have to be protected against rogue governments seizing their property. But [...] the real intent of these provisions is to impede health, environmental, safety and, yes, financial regulations".[87]

The recent United Nations Independent Expert Report to the Human Rights Council on The Promotion of a Democratic and Equitable International Order re-

---

provisions on CSR shall be found in the preamble and in Chapter 22 ("Trade and Sustainable Development"), Art. 22(3). Instead, no reference to that standard is included in the Commission's text proposal, *cit. supra* note 53.

[83] OECD Guidelines for Multinational Enterprises, 25 May 2011, available at: <http://mneguidelines.oecd.org/text>.

[84] ILO Tripartite Declaration of Principle Concerning Multinational Enterprises and Social Policy, 4th ed., 29 August 2014, available at: <http://www.ilo.org/empent/Publications/WCMS_094386/lang--en/index.htm>.

[85] Guiding Principles on Business and Human Rights, UN Doc. A/HRC/17/31 (2011), available at: <http://www.ohchr.org/Documents/Publications/GuidingPrinciplesBusinessHR_EN.pdf>.

[86] EU Parliament, *cit. supra* note 20, para. 28. More recently, see EU Parliament, Resolution of 9 October 2013 on the EU-China Negotiations for a Bilateral Investment Agreement (2013/2674(RSP)), para. 33. See also the Communication from the Commission to the Council (*cit. supra* note 23, p. 9) where the OECD Guidelines for Multinational Enterprises are described as "an important instrument to help balance the rights and responsibilities of investors".

[87] Stiglitz, "The Secret Corporate Takeover of Trade Agreements", The Guardian, 13 May 2015, available at: <http://www.theguardian.com/business/2015/may/13/the-secret-corporate-takeover-of-trade-agreements>. See also an open letter signed by 100 professors, judges, and lawyers from Trans-Pacific Partnership countries, available at: <https://tpplegal.wordpress.com/open-letter>.

flects a particular example of such criticism. In that Report, ISDS has been described as:

> "[A] challenge to democracy and the rule of law [...]. Among the major threats to a democratic and equitable international order is the operation of arbitral tribunals that act as if they were above the international human rights regime [...] corporate arbitrators are not natural guardians of the public interest, but of business interests and of a new 'industry' that, as experience shows, has privileged investors over the public".[88]

If this criticism is excessive in some ways, it would certainly be naïve to deny that there is a risk that multinational companies may use the specific instrument of investor protection rules to achieve corporate aims, with developing countries facing major risks since they often lack the resources to defend themselves against such major transnational enterprises.

A shared view has, therefore, emerged in the recent years on the need for a reform on the procedural aspects of investor protection to guarantee the State's policy space. In that perspective, one should note that developed countries, once the strongest supporters of ISDS, are now the most active in proposing improvements that could reflect their "new" role of capital-importing countries and frequent respondents in investment claims.

Differences, however, exist among those advocating for a new start[89] – with proposals swinging from exclusive reliance on domestic dispute resolution, to replacing ISDS with a WTO-like State-State dispute settlement system, or with a standing international investment court which would hear private investors' claim against host States – and those considering that improvements are necessary but the essence of the existing ISDS mechanism should be retained.[90]

While the TPP embraces the latter position, relying on reforms of the current system,[91] the final version of the CETA Agreement, made public on 29 February

---

[88] DE ZAYAS, Report of the Independent Expert on the Promotion of a Democratic and Equitable International Order, UN Doc. A/HRC/30/44 (2015), para. 15.

[89] KRAJEWSKI, "Modalities for Investment Protection and Investor-State Dispute Settlement (ISDS) in TTIP from a Trade Union Perspective", Friedrich-Ebert-Stiftung, EU Office, 2014, p. 24, available at: <http://library.fes.de/pdf-files/bueros/bruessel/11044.pdf>.

[90] WEILER, "European Hypocrisy: TTIP and ISDS", EJIL: Talk!, 21 January 2015, available at: <http://www.ejiltalk.org/european-hypocrisy-ttip-and-isds>.

[91] Among them, there are provisions about transparency, ensuring that arbitration hearings and documents will be open and available to the public as well as ensuring *amicus curiae* submissions by NGOs and other interested stakeholders; provisions to address conflicts of interest by arbitrators as well as the establishment of a binding code of conduct; the exclusion of parallel proceedings before ISDS and other fora, such as domestic courts (the so-called "fork in the road" clause); statutory limits (three and a half years) for bringing claims from the date of knowledge

2016, replaces the current ISDS system with a new dispute settlement mechanism and move towards establishing a permanent multilateral investment court.[92]

Before moving to a brief analysis of some of these "new" rules, it is noteworthy that, waiting for the entry into force of both the CETA Agreement and the recently signed EU-Vietnam Agreement,[93] only one country – Brazil – has until now departed from the traditional ISDS paradigm, starting to conclude a number of treaties that provide for State-State arbitration procedure only.[94]

4.1. The New Dispute Settlement Mechanism in CETA

The new dispute settlement system would be composed of a tribunal and an appeal tribunal.[95] A central pillar of the new system would be the accompanying CETA joint committee, established under Article 26(1), a political mechanism comprising representatives of the EU and Canada, which shall be co-chaired by the Minister

---

of an alleged breach; the right for the Parties to adopt at any time interpretations of the agreement that are binding on tribunals; and, finally, a fast track system for rejecting unfounded or trivial claims. As for the creation of an appellate mechanism, which was included in the CETA text before the conclusion of the legal review, the US approach on that issue is based on the proposal of an appeal body only in the event of such a mechanism being introduced at global level. The text of the TPP (*cit. supra* note 48) is therefore missing reference to an appellate mechanism. However, it provides for States to make certain counterclaims against investors challenging investment authorisations or investment agreements (Art. 9(18)).

[92] On the EU and Canada's commitment to join efforts with other trading partners to set up a permanent multilateral investment court with a standing appellate mechanism, see in particular the CETA text, *cit. supra* note 40, Art. 8(29). As has been noted, however, "the prospects for such an ambitious project are not good under present circumstances" and the "vision of a global forum for the settlement of investment disputes between host States and foreign investors remain distant and elusive". SCHREUER, "The Future of International Investment Law", in BUGENBERG et al. (eds.), *cit. supra* note 1, p. 1904 ff., p. 1908.

[93] Even the EU-Vietnam Free Trade Agreement (*cit. supra* note 42) has accepted the standing international investment court as its method for dispute resolution of investment disputes. See Chapter II ("Investment"), Sub-Section 3 ("Resolution of Investment Disputes"), Arts. 12 and 13.

[94] See Brazil-Mozambique CFIA, 30 March 2015, Art. 15(6); Brazil-Angola CFIA, 1 April 2015, Art. 15(6); Brazil-Mexico CFIA, 26 May 2015, Art. 19(4); Brazil-Malawi CFIA (*cit. supra* note 82), Art. 13(6). The texts of these agreements are available at: <http://investmentpolicyhub.unctad.org/IIA/CountryBits/27#iiaInnerMenu>.

[95] The Commission's TTIP proposal (*cit. supra* note 53) includes a new dispute settlement mechanism almost identical to the CETA model. However, the US does not seem to agree with such proposal. See the declaration of the US Trade Representative, Michael Froman, "US Wary of EU Proposal for Investment Court in Trade Pact", Reuters, 29 October 2015, available at: <http://www.reuters.com/article/us-trade-ttip-idUSKCN0SN2LH20151029>. For a detailed overview of the EU internal debate about the proposal of a standing investment tribunal, see BRONCKERS, "Is Investor-State Dispute Settlement (ISDS) Superior to Litigation Before Domestic Courts? An EU View on Bilateral Trade Agreements", JIEL, 2015, p. 655 ff., p. 656.

for International Trade of Canada and the Member of the EU Commission responsible for Trade, or their respective designees. The CETA joint committee, which shall meet once a year or at the request of a Party, is not only entitled with the general responsibility "for all questions concerning trade and investment between the Parties and the implementation and application of this Agreement", but may also adopt, in a manner which likely resembles the WTO Ministerial Conference and General Council model, interpretations of the provisions of the CETA Agreement that shall be binding on both the tribunal and the appeal tribunal.[96] The CETA joint committee shall also appoint the fifteen members of the tribunal, for a five year term, renewable once, according to the "one third rule": five shall be nationals of a EU Member State, five shall be nationals of Canada, and five shall be nationals of third countries.[97]

The tribunal shall hear cases in divisions consisting of three members, of whom one shall be a national of a EU Member State, one a national of Canada, and one a national of a third country (who shall be appointed as chairman of the division). Notably, investors do not take part in this process as the decision about the composition of divisions is made by the president of the tribunal "on a rotation basis, ensuring that the composition of the divisions is random and unpredictable, while giving equal opportunity to all members of the tribunal to serve".[98] If the investor is a small or medium-sized enterprise, or the compensation or damages claimed are relatively low, the investor may propose, when submitting its claim, that a sole member of the tribunal, at random from among the members who are nationals of third countries, should hear the claim, and the respondent shall give sympathetic consideration to that request.[99]

The tribunal shall issue its final award within 24 months of the date the claim is submitted.[100] Rules about submission of claims are included in Article 8(23), whilst Article 8(22) stipulates that a claim is inadmissible before the tribunal if it concerns the same treatment that has been brought before a tribunal or court under domestic or international law. Finally, the tribunal may only award, separately or in combination, monetary damages and any applicable interests, or restitution of property; it shall also order that the costs of the proceedings be borne by the unsuccessful disputing party.[101]

As for the appeal tribunal – whose mandate is to consider whether the tribunal has erred in the interpretation or application of the applicable law or whether it

---

[96] CETA text, *cit. supra* note 40, Art. 26(1)(5)(e).

[97] *Ibid.*, Art. 8(27)(2).

[98] *Ibid.*, Art. 8(27)(7). The President "will be appointed for a two-year term and shall be drawn by lot from among the members of the tribunal who are nationals of third countries" (Art. 8(27)(8)).

[99] *Ibid.*, Art. 8(23)(5).

[100] *Ibid.*, Art. 8(39)(7).

[101] *Ibid.*, Art. 8(39)(1-5).

has manifestly erred in the appreciation of the facts, including the appreciation of relevant domestic law[102] – the administrative and organisational matters regarding its functioning shall be established in a future decision of the CETA joint committee.[103] Moreover, the CETA joint committee shall also determine a monthly retainer fee for members of the tribunal and the appeal tribunal in order to ensure their availability.[104]

A sensitive point where CETA achieves significant improvements compared to traditional arbitral tribunals concerns the need to guarantee complete transparency of proceedings. On that issue, CETA goes even further than the UNCITRAL "Rules on Transparency in Treaty-Based Investor-State-Arbitration", which came into effect in April 2014.[105] According to Article 8(36) CETA, a number of documents shall be included in the list of those to be made available under Article 3(1) of the UNCITRAL Transparency Rules, such as the request for consultations, the notice requesting a determination of the respondent, the notice of determination of the respondent, the agreement to mediate, the notice of intent to challenge a member of the tribunal, and the decision on a challenge to a member of the tribunal. Recalling Article 6 of the UNCITRAL Rules, the CETA text states that "hearings shall be open to the public" unless "there is a need to protect confidential or protected information".[106] This is a notable change to the EU's negotiating direction, as the Commission's draft TTIP text submitted to the US does not mention this.

Other significant improvements concern independence and impartiality. In this regard, Article 8(30), which is fully dedicated to "Ethics", provides stringent rules aimed at avoidance of conflicts of interest *inter alia* stipulating that judges "upon appointment [...] shall refrain from acting as counsel or as party-appointed expert

---

[102] *Ibid.*, Art. 8(28)(2).

[103] In the Commission's TTIP proposal (*cit. supra* note 53) it is provided that the appellate tribunal shall be composed of six members, of whom two shall be nationals of a EU Member State, two shall be nationals of the US and two shall be nationals of third countries. The appellate tribunal shall have a president and a vice-president who shall be selected for a two-year term from among the members who are nationals of third countries. Finally, it shall hear appeals in divisions consisting of three members, chaired by the member who is a national of a third country. Resemblances to the WTO Appellate Body are clear. On this, see VENZKE, "Investor-State Dispute Settlement in TTIP from the Perspective of a Public Law Theory of International Adjudication", Amsterdam Center for International Law Research Paper 2016-06, p. 19.

[104] In the Commission's TTIP proposal (*cit. supra* note 53) retainer fees are currently proposed as €2,000 per month for judges at the tribunal of first instance and €7,000 per month for judges at the appellate level.

[105] UNCITRAL Rules on Transparency in Treaty-Based Investor-State-Arbitration, January 2014, available at: <http://www.uncitral.org/pdf/english/texts/arbitration/rules-on-transparency/Rules-on-Transparency-E.pdf>.

[106] CETA text, *cit. supra* note 40, Art. 8(36)(2).

or witness in any pending or new investment dispute under this or any other inter-national agreement".[107]

Finally, there are two specific points that would be emphasized as they make clear that the CETA dispute settlement system mainly operates within the realm of international public law.[108] First, judges of the tribunal and the appeal tribu-nal shall not only "possess the qualifications required in their respective countries for appointment to judicial office, or be jurists of recognised competence", but they are specifically required to "have demonstrated expertise in public interna-tional law".[109] Second, according to Article 8(31) the tribunal shall apply the CETA Agreement in accordance with the principles of international law enshrined in the Vienna Convention on the Law of Treaties,[110] and can only look at EU or Member State law as a matter of fact not interpreting domestic law in a manner binding on EU courts or EU governments.[111]

5. CONCLUSIONS

However controversial and reprehensible the limitation posed by investor pro-tection rules on States' right to regulate may be, for half a century capital-exporting countries have had no problem in imposing on developing countries the payment of such an unpredictable price in return for investment flows. After all, both BITs and other IIAs are still, at their core, treaties about the liberalization of investment flows and it is mainly on that ground that their merits are to be evaluated.

The increase in the number of ISDS in recent years – with some "spectacular" and highly contested cases that, sometimes, have hit the headlines[112] – together with the starting negotiations of mega-regional agreements (such as the TTIP and TPP) that could affect the lives of millions of people, have indeed provoked a mounting public concern that governments may have allowed foreign investors too much scope to challenge their decision. In that perspective, the recent approach of IIAs

---

[107] On that issue, see also the Commission's TTIP proposal (*cit. supra* note 53), Art. 11 and Annex II, "Code of Conduct for Members of the Tribunal, the Appeal Tribunal and Mediators". CETA only has a Code of Conduct for Arbitrators and Mediators (Annex 29-B).

[108] See also VENZKE, *cit. supra* note 103, p. 22.

[109] CETA text, *cit. supra* note 40, Art. 8(27)(4).

[110] *Cit. supra* note 75.

[111] See EU Commission, "CETA – Summary of the Final Negotiating Results", 29 February 2016, p. 12, available at: <http://trade.ec.europa.eu/doclib/docs/2014/december/tradoc_152982.pdf>.

[112] See, for example, *Philip Morris Brands Sàrl, Philip Morris Products S.A. and Abal Hermanos S.A. v. Oriental Republic of Uruguay*, ICSID Case No. ARB/10/7 (pending); and *Philip Morris Asia Limited v. The Commonwealth of Australia*, UNCITRAL, PCA Case No. 2012-12. On 17 December 2015, the tribunal in *Philip Morris v. Australia* issued its award (not yet published) declining jurisdiction.

towards substantive investment protection rules contains a number of improve-ments, if compared to traditional BITs, in order to reduce the sometime excessive interpretative ambiguity by arbitral tribunals.[113]

In that perspective, there are, however, some cases where clarifications could have been more satisfactory. The notion of legitimate expectations of the investors, for example, has been linked in the CETA to all those situations where a specific promise or representation was made by the State (see *supra* Section 3.1). On the contrary, it would have been better if the text specified that only representations by competent authorities could create legitimate expectations so as to avoid overly expansive interpretations of that provision by arbitral tribunals.[114] Again, whilst the carving out of the "intent" test from the indirect expropriation provision in the Commission's TTIP proposal text shall be evaluated as a positive step, the same cannot be said for the "manifestly excessive" test, whose preservation could bestow on arbitral tribunals an overly broad authority to review both legislative and admin-istrative measures by host States through the lens of the proportionality principle.

Alongside the need to balance the right of investors with the right of host States (i.e. to allow host States ample policy space to pursue public welfare objectives) there is a further point that may perhaps be raised but has not yet been sufficiently explored by the recent IIA practice: that is the question of investors' obligations. In that perspective, more stringent reference in IIAs to provisions which mandate the investors to voluntarily incorporate internationally recognized standards of non-commercial responsibility in their practices and internal policies would perhaps contribute to give positive evidence to the requirement that private investors should be evaluated not only as rights-holders but also as duty-bearers.

---

[113] DE MESTRAL, *cit. supra* note 77, p. 645.
[114] KRAJEWSKI, *cit. supra* note 89, p. 13.

THE ACHIEVEMENTS AND LIMITS OF ITALIAN ANTI-CORRUPTION LEGISLATION IN LIGHT OF THE INTERNATIONAL LEGAL FRAMEWORK

LEONARDO BORLINI*

Abstract

The past twenty years have seen unprecedented international initiatives aimed at combatting corrupt practices. Over the same period, Italy has ratified and implemented within its legal system five international anti-corruption treaties and amended its domestic legislation on different occasions. However, despite considerable efforts, corruption remains a serious challenge in the country. With particular reference to the aforementioned conventions, this article explores the main international rules on criminalisation and prevention of corruption in order to assess achievements and limits of the Italian legislation in light of such provisions. The article is thus divided into two main sections. The first considers the development of the regional and other anti-corruption initiatives which culminated in the United Nations Convention against Corruption; the second examines the main achievements and shortcomings of the Italian anti-corruption legislation in light of the outcomes of the monitoring procedures set by the international instruments ratified by Italy.

Keywords: international anti-corruption treaties; monitoring systems; bribery; trading in influence; liability of legal persons; valued-based confiscation; statute of limitations.

* Assistant Professor of European Union Law, Bocconi University, Milan, Ph.D, LL.M (Cantab.). The author was part of the Italian delegation at the Fifth Conference of State Parties to the United Nations Convention against Corruption (UNCAC) in November 2013, and to the UNCAC Implementation Review Group (IRG) on Prevention and Asset Recovery in September 2014. The author also participated as an expert invited to the Working Group of the Organisation for Economic Co-operation and Development (OECD) on Bribery's on-site evaluation (phase three) of the national implementing law of the 1997 OECD Convention on Combating Bribery of Foreign Public Officials in International Business Transactions, and to the on-site Third Mutual Evaluation of Italy by the Group of States Against Corruptions (GRECO). The views expressed are the author's alone.

1. THE DEVELOPMENT AND SCOPE OF ANTI-CORRUPTION TREATIES RATIFIED BY ITALY

Approximately a quarter of century after the adoption of the US Foreign Practices Act (FCPA)[1] – the first domestic legislation criminalising corruption of foreign public officials – a substantial and evolving array of international instruments to combat corruption is now in force. The most intensive phase of international legislation is known to have lasted from the mid-1990s to the early 2000s, when several global and regional treaties to combat corruption were adopted in rapid succession. Regarding the emergence of international legal standards on anti-corruption, the Chief of Crime Conventions Section of the United Nations Office on Drugs and Crime (UNODC) maintains that:

> "[T]he gradual understanding of both the scope and seriousness of the problem of corruption can be seen in the evolution of international action against it, which has progressed from general consideration and declarative statements, to the formulation of practical advice, to the development of binding legal obligations and the emergence of numerous cases in which countries have sought assistance from other countries in investigating and prosecuting corruption and in tracing, freezing, confiscating and recovering proceeds of corruption offences".[2]

The international anti-corruption framework is rather fragmented and not comprised only of treaties.[3] The international financial institutions have played a cata-

---

[1] Foreign Corrupt Practices Act, 15 USC, § 78dd-1 (1977), as amended by the International Anti-Bribery and Fair Competition Act, Pub. L. No. 105-366 (1998). The FCPA represents the foundation upon which the subsequent international anti-corruption framework has been built, providing an original way of dealing with bribery across national boundaries.

[2] VLASSIS, "The United Nations Convention against Corruption: A Way of Life", in PASSAS and VLASSIS (eds.), *The United Nations Convention against Corruption as a Way of Life. Selected Papers and Contributions from the International Conference on "The United Nations Convention against Corruption as a Way of Life" Courmayeur Mont Blanc, Italy 15-17 December 2006*, Milano, 2007, p. 15 ff., p. 17.

[3] See, *ex multis*, POSADAS, "Combating Corruption under International Law", Duke Journal of Comparative and International Law, 2000, pp. 345-414; STESSENS, "The International Fight against Corruption", International Review of Penal Law, 2002, pp. 891-938; SACERDOTI (ed.), *Responsabilità d'impresa e strumenti internazionali anti-corruzione. Dalla Convenzione OCSE 1997 al Decreto n. 231/2001*, Milano, 2003; SAYED, *Corruption in International Trade and Commercial Arbitration*, The Hague, 2004, p. 5 ff.; WOUTERS, RYNGAERT and CLOOTS, "The International Legal Framework against Corruption: Achievements and Challenges", Melbourne Journal of International Law, 2013, pp. 205-280; DEL VECCHIO and SEVERINO (eds.), *Il contrasto alla corruzione nel diritto interno e nel diritto internazionale*, Padova, 2014; LLAMZON, *Corruption in International Investment Arbitration*, Oxford, 2014; ARNONE and BORLINI,

lytic role in promoting multilateral initiatives to fight corruption and related crimes like money laundering (ML), making public the negative impact of such offences, and stimulating governments to take a more pro-active role in this fight.[4] Moreover, non-binding instruments (mainly sectoral in nature) have also, on occasion, influenced domestic legal systems.[5] However, the present study does not address the latter initiatives, but focuses on the international anti-corruption treaties ratified by Italy with a view to assessing the adherence of its legislation to such instruments.

1.1. The Council of Europe Conventions on Corruption

In 1999, the Council of Europe (CoE) adopted two regional treaties against corruption, the Criminal Law Convention on Corruption (CoECLCC),[6] and the Civil Law Convention on Corruption (CoECivLCC).[7] The drafters of the CoECLCC chose not to articulate a definition of corruption[8] but instead require State Parties to criminalise bribery, trading in influence, ML when the predicate offence consists of any of the convention offences, and "account offences".[9] As regards bribery, active and passive bribery are considered as separate offences with State Parties being required to criminalise, on the basis of a set of common elements, the active bribery of domestic, foreign and international public servants, members of legislatures, and judges, including prosecutors and holders of judicial office,[10] and the passive bribery of domestic public officials and judges, including prosecutors

---

Corruption. Economic Analysis and International Law, Cheltenham, 2014; and FERGUSON, *Global Corruption. Law, Theory and Practice*, Victoria, 2015.

[4] See further ARNONE and BORLINI, *cit. supra* note 3, pp. 270-310. See also World Bank, *Strengthening World Bank Group Engagement on Governance and Anticorruption. Main Report*, Washington DC, 2007. For the IMF's tools to improve the legal and institutional frameworks of its members and assisted countries and for improving governance and reducing corruption, see SIEL, "Governance/Anti-corruption. Legal Issues in the Work of the IMF", in PASSAS and VLASSIS (eds.), *cit. supra* note 1, p. 47 ff.

[5] See ROSE, *International Anti-Corruption Norms. Their Creation and Influence on Domestic Legal Systems*, Oxford, 2015, pp. 15-27, 133-175, 177-215.

[6] 27 January 1999, ETS No. 173, entered into force 1 July 2002. Ratified by Italy on 13 June 2013.

[7] 4 November 1999, ETS No. 174, entered into force 1 November 2003. Ratified by Italy on 13 June 2013.

[8] See further Council of Europe, Criminal Law Convention on Corruption: Explanatory Report, para. 2. It is worth nothing that most international instruments use the term "corruption" in their titles, though the focus lies (sometimes exclusively) on bribery. On the distinction between corruption and bribery see JOHNSON and SHARMA, "About Corruption", in JOHNSON (ed.), *The Struggle against Corruption: A Comparative Study*, New York, 2004, p. 1 ff., p. 2.

[9] In other words, acts or omissions designed to commit, conceal or disguise the commission of any convention offence. See CoECLCC, Art. 14.

[10] *Ibid.*, Arts. 2, 4-6, 9-11.

and holders of judicial office.[11] Articles 7 and 8 also capture the conduct of private actors, requiring State Parties to criminalise both active and passive bribery of "any persons who direct or work for, in any capacity, private sector entities".[12] The CoECLCC is supplemented by an Additional Protocol,[13] which extends the scope of the Convention to arbitrators in commercial, civil and other matters, as well as to jurors, thus complementing the Convention's provisions aimed at protecting judicial authorities from corruption.[14]

Chapter IV of the CoECLCC addresses international cooperation issues. In particular, Article 25 provides that for the purposes of the investigation and prosecution of Convention offences, State Parties agree to cooperate with one another to the widest extent possible on the basis of relevant international instruments on international cooperation in criminal matters or other arrangements. In practice, there are a range of CoE instruments[15] as well as other treaties already covering this area and "in essence the Chapter is a safety net designed to provide a basis for international cooperation in the absence of any other international treaty or agreement".[16]

It is noteworthy that Contracting Parties are allowed to make reservations as regards specific Convention provisions. This mirrors the intention of its drafters that Parties assume obligations under the CoECLCC only to the extent consistent with their constitution and the fundamental principles of their legal system.

Well-known corruption cases such as the *Fininvest v. CIR* saga in Italy, or the outcomes of the *Abacha* case in Switzerland are evidence that civil remedies complement the criminal prosecution of corruption and can even be, on occasion, more effective than penal sanctions.[17] The manifest advantage of the civil law approach is that it makes corruption controls partly self-enforcing by empowering victims to take action on their own initiative. This is mirrored by the CoE's approach that is not limited to criminalisation. Instead, it follows different patterns of regulation,

---

[11] *Ibid.*, Arts. 3, 4, 11.

[12] The drafter of the CoECLCC deliberately assumed a pioneering role when opting for the criminalisation of such offences. This was deemed to be necessary in order to avoid gaps in the comprehensive strategy to fight corruption. See Council of Europe, *cit. supra* note 8, para. 52.

[13] 15 May 2003, ETS No. 191, entered into force 1 February 2005.

[14] *Ibid.*, Arts. 2-6.

[15] In particular, the Council of Europe Convention on Mutual Assistance in Criminal Matters, 20 April 1959, ETS No. 30, entered into force 12 June 1962, and the Council of Europe Convention on Extradition, 13 December 1957, ETS. No 24, entered into force 18 April 1960.

[16] HATCHARD, "Criminalizing Corruption: The Global Initiatives", in BOISTER and CURRIE (eds.), *Routledge Handbook of Transnational Criminal Law*, 2015, p. 347 ff., p. 349.

[17] In *Cir v. Fininvest* (*Tribunale di Milano (Sez. X civile)*, 7 July 2015, No. 8537/2015), the industrial group CIR, through a civil action, managed to recover almost €0.5 billion in damages resulting from the corruption of a judge by the competitor Fininvest despite the eventual failure of the criminal proceedings. Regarding the *Abacha* case (Swiss Federal Court, No. 1A.215/2004/col, 7 February 2005), by making use of the so-called *parte civile* within the Swiss criminal proceedings, Nigeria recovered a sum in excess of US$ 0.5 billion.

the CoECLCC being complemented by the CoECivLCC, the first attempt to define common international rules in the field of civil law and compensation for damages due to corruption crimes.

The CoECivLCC thus requires State Parties to provide in their internal law effective remedies for persons who have suffered damage as a result of corruption, in order to enable them to defend their rights and interests, including the possibility of obtaining compensation for damage. To this end, the Convention deals with different elements of the discipline of damages recovery actions in corruption cases, including: liability; contributory negligence; reduction or disallowance of compensation; validity of contracts; acquisition of evidence; court orders to preserve the assets necessary for the execution of the final judgement and for the maintenance of the *status quo* pending resolution of the points at issue; and international cooperation. The extent of the compensation is to be fixed by the court, which can provide for the compensation of material damages, loss of profits, and non-pecuniary loss.[18]

The CoE's anti-corruption efforts have received substantial attention mainly because of the anti-corruption implementation mechanism. Monitoring the implementation of both conventions is the responsibility of the Group of States against Corruption (GRECO).[19] To date GRECO has launched four evaluation rounds. GRECO evaluation procedures involve the collection of information through questionnaire(s), on-site country visits enabling evaluation teams to solicit further information during high-level discussions with domestic key players, and drafting of evaluation reports.[20]

1.2. The European Union Initiatives

The European Union (EU) started off with modest anti-corruption instruments tackling mainly the misdirection of EU funds: the protection of financial interests

---

[18] CoECivLCC, Art. 3.2.

[19] Like the OECD and UNCAC monitoring systems, GRECO is a paradigmatic case of international supervision, i.e. *non-contentieux* monitoring systems of inducing compliance with international rules. On international supervision see *ex multis* CASSESE, *Il controllo internazionale. Contributo alla teoria delle funzioni di organizzazione dell'ordinamento internazionale*, Milano, 1972; and, more recently ID., "Supervision and Fact-Finding as Alternatives to Judicial Review", in ID. (ED.), *Realising Utopia. The Future of International Law*, Oxford, 2012, p. 295 ff.; and GRACE and BRUDERLEIN, "On Monitoring, Reporting and Fact-finding Mechanism", ESIL Reflections, Vol. 1, Issue 2, 15 July 2012.

[20] For a detailed analysis of the monitoring systems established by the anti-corruption conventions see WEBB, "The United Nations Convention against Corruption: Global Achievements or Missed Opportunities?", JIEL, 2005, p. 191 ff., pp. 222-27; ARNONE and BORLINI, *cit. supra* note 3, pp. 443-78; and NICCHIA, "I Meccanismi di controllo delle convenzioni internazinali in tema di lotta alla corruzione", in DEL VECCHIO and SEVERINO (eds.), *cit. supra* note 3, pp. 451-462.

through criminal law has represented a high priority for the European Community since the mid-seventies. In support of this objective, the 1995 Convention on the Protection of the European Union's Financial Interests[21] requires Member States to criminalise fraud affecting the EU's financial interests, covering the misappropriation of EU funds through fraudulent statements or false documents, whilst the First Protocol to the 1995 Convention specifically contains definitions of, and harmonised penalties for, offences of corruption by or against national and Community officials "which damages or is likely to damage the European Communities' financial interests".[22]

In addition, on 26 May 1997 the Council of the European Union took specific measures to tackle corruption amongst European Community officials. Although it does not explicitly deal with transnational bribery, the Convention on the Fight against Corruption involving Officials of the European Communities or Officials of Member States of the European Union,[23] requires Member States to criminalise corrupt conduct involving officials of both the Community and Member States even if the conduct took place in its own territory or was instigated by one of their own nationals. There is currently no evaluation and monitoring system in place.[24] Over the years, however, the EU has broadened its focus, with the latest step being a comprehensive two-year review process of Member States' general anti-corruption achievements, the so-called "EU Anti-Corruption Report" by the Commission.[25]

As corruption seriously hinders competition and the functioning of the internal market, the EU legislature could have acted on this legal basis. However, it opted for the (more straightforward) legal basis of providing an area of freedom, security and justice.[26] EU action against corruption is thus articulated through further different instruments, ranging from former "third pillar" acts aimed at strengthening and easing judicial cooperation in criminal matters, to the anti-corruption safeguards included in the EU Public Procurement directives[27] or the recently adopted Fourth Anti-Money Laundering Directive.[28] In terms of governance mechanisms

---

[21] OJ 1995, C316/49.

[22] OJ 1996, C313, Arts. 1-2.

[23] Council Act 97/C OJ 1997 C 195/01.

[24] See, more extensively, ARNONE and BORLINI, *cit. supra* note 3, pp. 460-461.

[25] Commission Decision of 6 June 2011, COM (2011) 3673 final.

[26] See, e.g., Council Framework Decision 2003/568/JHA of 22 July 2003 on combatting corruption in the private sector, OJ L 192, 31 July 2003, pp. 54-56.

[27] Directive 2004/18/EC of 31 March 2004 on the coordination of procedures for the award of public works contracts, public supply contracts and public service contracts, OJ L 134, 30 April 2004, pp. 114-240; and Directive 2004/17/EC of 31 March 2004 coordinating the procurement procedures of entities operating in the water, energy, transport and postal services sectors, OJ L 134, 30 Avril 2004, pp. 1-113.

[28] Directive 2015/849/EU of 20 May 2015 on the prevention of the use of the financial system for the purposes of money laundering or terrorist financing, amending Regulation (EU) 648/2012, and repealing Directive 2005/60/EC and Directive 2006/70, OJ L 141, 5 June 2015, pp. 73-117.

the EU has also responded by establishing a series of EU criminal justice agencies whose remit includes the fight against transnational crime including corruption.[29] Furthermore, the EU is negotiating membership of GRECO.[30] Other measures include a legislative instrument for the harmonisation of asset recovery rules across the EU.[31]

Space precludes here an assessment of these different initiatives.[32] It suffices to note that, notwithstanding the fact that "[t]he EU's legal order provides a benchmark for regional integration in regard to legal responses to transnational organised crime, in terms of both the volume and diversity of the measures adopted and the high standards of compliance and enforcement underpinning EU law",[33] the various anti-corruption instruments have been rather fragmented and success on this issue would be enhanced by streamlining a coherent anti-corruption policy in all its activities. In this respect, the Commission's anti-corruption report is a first promising step.

Finally, with the entry into force of the Treaty of Lisbon, the EU Institutions, through secondary law, can intervene in "the areas of particularly serious crime with a cross-border dimension resulting from the nature or impact of such offences or from a special need to combat them on a common basis" and, hence, influence national criminal law systems by establishing "minimum rules concerning the definition of criminal offences and sanctions".[34] Corruption is explicitly listed in the text of the Treaty as belonging to the area of such "Euro crimes". The harmonisation here seeks to create those definitions that act as a starting point for Member States to take criminal offences further. However, such development of EU criminal law – based on the premise that it will facilitate the mutual recognition of judicial decisions and other forms of mutual legal assistance – is not an easy process: "extensive harmonization in this sensitive area [...] ends up with in the fire of constitutional objections and political obstacles to further development of this policy

---

[29] See MITSILEGAS, *EU Criminal Law*, Oxford, 2009, pp. 161-234.

[30] European Commission, Communication from the Commission to the European Parliament, the Council and the European Economic and Social Committee Participation of the European Union in the Council of Europe Group of States against Corruption (GRECO), Communication COM (2012) 604 final, 19 October 2012.

[31] Directive 2014/42/EU of 3 April 2014 on the freezing and confiscation of instrumentalities and proceeds of crime in the European Union, OJ L 127, 29 Avril 2014, pp. 39-50.

[32] For more in-depth illustrations see MITSILEGAS, "The Aims and Limits of EU Anti-Corruption Law", in HORDER and ALLDRIDGE (eds.), *Modern Bribery Law. Comparative Perspectives*, Cambridge, 2013, p. 160 ff.; and ARNONE and BORLINI *cit. supra* note 3, pp. 229-244.

[33] MITSILEGAS, "Regional Organisations and the Suppression of Transnational Crime", in BOISTER and CURRIE (eds.), *cit. supra* note 16, p. 73 ff., pp. 73-74.

[34] Treaty on the Functioning of the European Union, OJ C 326, 26 October 2012, Art. 83(1).

in practice".[35] It thus comes as no surprise that the then Commissioner for Home Affairs Malmström stated in late 2013 that: "for the time being, the Commission does not [...] intend to propose new legislation on the definition of corruption or approximation of statutes of limitations of corruption offences or protections of whistle-blowers".[36]

1.3. The OECD Anti-Bribery Convention

In 1997, the Organisation for Economic Co-operation and Development (OECD) adopted the Convention on Combating Bribery of Foreign Public Officials in International Business Transactions (OECD Convention).[37] As of 7 March 2015, it had been ratified by 41 States.[38]

The OECD Convention is plainly influenced by the fair trade approach adopted by the United States (US). It adopted an economic lens and focused on the market distorting effects of corruption in order to assure a "level playing field", that is to say, common rules for companies of different origins in international markets, as stated in its preamble. As its name reveals, this Convention addresses exclusively the issue of transnational bribery and related accounting offences (*recte:* active bribery of foreign or international public officials in transnational business transactions).[39] Despite the limited scope *ratione materiae*, the OECD Convention was a catalyst for further action. As Sacerdoti observes, its importance lies in the fact that the State Parties to the Convention are home to just about all the major multinational/international companies.[40] Thus, their undertakings to counter the bribery of foreign public officials by companies based in their jurisdictions can have a direct effect on international trade generally and on good governance in specific trading partners in particular.[41]

The OECD Convention follows the classical model of penal law conventions, in that it defines the offences (Articles 1 and 7), the jurisdictional bases (Article 4), the secondary rules, and the means of mutual cooperation between the Contracting States in matters of assistance and extradition (respectively, Articles 9 and 10).

---

[35] PEERS, "EU Justice and Home Affairs Law (Non-Civil)", in CRAIG and DE BÙRCA (eds.), *The Evolution of EU Law*, Oxford, 2011, p. 269 ff., p. 297.

[36] See at: <http://ec.europa.eu/avservices/video/shotlist.cfm?ref=94671>.

[37] 17 December 1997, entered in force 15 February 1999. Ratified by Italy on 15 December 2000.

[38] See further at: <http://www.oecd.org/daf/anti-bribery/WGBRatificationStatus.pdf>.

[39] See OECD Convention, Art. 1.

[40] See SACERDOTI, "The 1997 OECD Convention on Combating Bribery in International Business Transactions. An Example of Piece-Meal Regulation of Globalization", IYIL, 1999, p. 26 ff., p. 27; and BORLINI and MAGRINI, "La lotta alla corruzione internazionale dall'ambito OCSE alla dimensione ONU", DCI, 2007, p. 15 ff., pp. 17-18.

[41] WOUTERS, RYNGAERT and CLOOTS, *cit. supra* note 3, p. 227.

Nonetheless, it distances itself from this model in other respects. Most importantly, the Convention includes non-criminal provisions, by requiring each State Party to adopt adequate accounting and auditing standards with a view to facilitating the identification and prosecution of individuals and entities involved in the bribery of foreign public officials.[42] This provision assumes fundamental importance, because a system aimed at eliciting reliable financial data is imperative in combatting "supply-side bribery". Moreover, a key feature of the Convention is its effective and systematic monitoring system undertaken by the OECD Working Group on Bribery (WGB), which replaces the dispute settlement procedures frequently envisaged by multilateral penal treaties.[43]

1.4. The United Nations Convention against Corruption

On the heels of the United Nations Convention against Transnational Organized Crime,[44] the desire for a global, comprehensive international legal instrument through which to combat corruption in both the public and private sectors led in 2003 to the development of the United Nations Convention against Corruption (UNCAC).[45] As of 1 December 2015, it had been ratified by 178 State Parties. The agreement presents several important innovations with respect to existing international anti-corruption conventions. There are nevertheless a number of constant features, starting with the consideration that corruption is a socio-political and economic phenomenon, which acquires an extraordinarily aggressive impact, by extending its reach beyond the frontiers of individual States.

In structure, it thus comprises four operative chapters that reflect the four "pillars" in the fight against corruption: (i) prevention (Chapter II); (ii) criminalisation and law enforcement (Chapter III); (iii) international cooperation (Chapter IV); and (iv) asset recovery (Chapter V).[46] The scope *ratione materiae* of the UNCAC is the widest among anti-corruption treaties. Not only does it deal with the full gamut of topics – from prevention to civil and criminal enforcement – but it also encompasses a wide range of criminal offences, which only *lato sensu* may be classified as corruption.

---

[42] OECD Convention, Art. 8(1).

[43] On the three-phase process for monitoring implementation of the Convention see BONUCCI, "Article 12: Monitoring and Follow Up", in PIETH, LOW and CULLEN (eds.), *The OECD Convention on Bribery. A Commentary*, Cambridge, 2007, p. 445 ff.

[44] 15 November 2000, entered into force 29 September 2003. Ratified by Italy on 2 August 2006.

[45] 31 October 2003, entered into force 14 December 2005. Ratified by Italy on 5 October 2009.

[46] Chapter I contains "General Provisions", whilst Chapter VI addresses technical assistance and information exchange.

Despite its sweeping reach, binding status and review mechanism, the formulation of its provisions reduces its potential to contribute to international anti-corruption initiatives by penetrating domestic legal systems. Many of the UNCAC's provisions, indeed, do not impose firm obligations on the State Parties. Instead the different provisions of the Convention fall into several graduations, ranging from mandatory to non-mandatory, precise to vague (and, hence, open to varying interpretations),[47] and absolute to qualified.[48]

Regarding criminalisation, it contains provisions (only a few of which mandatory) that concern a range of additional corruption-related offences, including: embezzlement, misappropriation or other diversion of property by a public official;[49] trading in influence;[50] embezzlement in the private sector;[51] abuse of functions;[52] illicit enrichment;[53] concealment of property resulting from corruption;[54] and obstruction of justice.[55]

Also, the UNCAC enumerates a wide range of preventive measures directed at both the public and private sector. Keeping in mind that most of the related provisions are phrased in non-mandatory terms, their typology varies considerably. State Parties are called to set up anti-corruption bodies; establish appropriate procurement systems; prevention of ML; strengthen the integrity of the judiciary; take measures to prevent private sector corruption; promote the active participation of civil society; enhance transparency in the financing of election campaigns and political parties; institute a comprehensive regulatory regime for banks and other financial institutions to prevent ML; and disallow the tax deductibility of expenses

---

[47] This is manifest in the UNCAC's provisions (Arts. 34-35) on how States should address the consequences of corruption and ensured that injured actors may seek compensation.

[48] This is the case of the provisions (like Art. 23 on the criminalisation of ML) that include qualifying language, with the effect that State Parties are only required to adopt certain measures where necessary or where doing so does not conflict with the basic tenets of their legal systems. On the implications of the liberal use of non-mandatory, vague and qualified language in the Convention see further SCHROTH, "The United Nations Convention against Doing Anything Serious about Corruption", Journal of Legal Studies in Business, pp. 1-21; and ROSE, *cit. supra* note 5, pp. 97-99, 106-132.

[49] UNCAC, Art. 17, mandatory. Reading late judicial reporting, it emerges that cases of misappropriation and diversion of public funds/assets are frequent also among the apical positions of governments: on 31 March 2016, at the time of revising the present article, the eleven judges of the Constitutional Court of South Africa unanimously ruled that President Jacob Zuma violated the constitution when he failed to repay government money spent on his private home. See Constitutional Court of South Africa, Cases CCT 143/15 and CCT 171/15, 31 March 2016.

[50] UNCAC, Art. 18, optional.

[51] *Ibid.*, Art. 22, optional.

[52] *Ibid.*, Art. 19, optional.

[53] *Ibid.*, Art. 20, optional.

[54] *Ibid.*, Art. 24, optional.

[55] *Ibid.*, Art. 25, mandatory.

that constitute bribes, an issue to which the OECD has devoted a specific but non-binding recommendation.[56]

Another remarkable feature of the UNCAC is its extensive and detailed array of provisions relating to jurisdictional bases, international cooperation in criminal matters and mutual legal assistance, which are particularly important in that law enforcement is strictly territorial in nature and corruption crimes are often transnational.[57] One of the most original features of the Convention is represented by its provisions on asset recovery.[58] Accordingly, Chapter V is entirely dedicated to the restitution of assets originating from one of the Convention offences. Chapter VII sets out "Mechanisms for Implementation" with Article 63 establishing a review process through the Conference of the State Parties to the Convention (COSP) to be convened regularly and assisted by the Implementation Review Group (IRG) set up in 2009. The monitoring mechanism is conceived as a review cycle, focusing on specific parts of the UNCAC.[59]

2. THE ITALIAN ANTI-CORRUPTION LEGISLATION IN LIGHT OF THE INTERNATIONAL COMMITMENTS

2.1. An Outlook of Corruption and Recent Legislative Reforms in Italy

In Italy, for some time corruption has assumed the character, both in its proportions and qualitative features, of a "systemic" phenomenon that infects vast sectors of administration and public life, not to mention a non-negligible part of business and finance.[60] As emerges from the data provided by the Court of Auditors (Corte dei Conti) at the inauguration of the judicial year, the number of judgments

---

[56] *Ibid.*, Arts. 6-14. While the basic thrust of these provisions is that States Parties "shall" adopt such measures, this requirement is often weakened by adding qualifiers such as "in accordance with the fundamental principles of its domestic law". See, e.g., UNCAC, Art. 13(1).

[57] See further ARNONE and BORLINI, *cit. supra* note 3, pp. 406-414.

[58] UNCAC, Arts. 51-59.

[59] On the structure, functioning and limits of the UNCAC monitoring mechanism see ARNONE and BORLINI, *cit. supra* note 3, pp. 467-478.

[60] Italian scholars are in agreement regarding the structural character of corruption. See, *ex multis*, FIANDACA, "Esigenze e prospettive di riforma dei reati di corruzione e concussione", Rivista Italiana di diritto e procedura penale, 2000, p. 883 ff., p. 883; COLOMBO, "Le indagini della magistratura italiana nei reati contro la pubblica amministrazione. Il danno conseguente alla corruzione", Questione Giustizia, 1994, p. 467 ff., p. 467; VIVARELLI, "Il fenomeno della corruzione", Foro amministrativo, 2008, p. 2928 ff., p. 2928; FORTI (ed.), *Il prezzo della tangente. La corruzione come sistema a dieci anni da "mani pulite"*, Milano, 2003; DAVIGO, *La giubba del re. Intervista sulla corruzione*, Bari, 2004; DAVIGO and MANNOZZI, *La corruzione in Italia, percezione sociale e controllo penale*, Bari, 2007; and ALESSANDRI, "I reati di riciclaggio e corruzione nell'ordinamento italiano: linee generali di riforma", Diritto penale contemporaneo, 2013, p. 133 ff., p. 134.

pronounced against public employees for corruption-related offences has risen dramatically.[61]

Recently, moreover, the Italian press has given great prominence to the last report drafted by the non-governmental organisation Transparency International (a global network with headquarters in Berlin of which more than ninety associations are members on a national basis), that every year compiles a ranking of the most corrupt countries based on the so-called corruption perception index. In this ranking, Italy is not only placed in the "lower part" of the list, it is also one of the Western countries to have lost most ground in the last decade.[62] Leaving aside the debated limits of such assessment methodology,[63] it remains the case that the situation in Italy is alarming, above all when one considers that corruption is a phenomenon "with a high degree of concealment" and therefore difficult to quantify.[64] Also, beyond the mere figures and statistical data, it is easy to see how the recent level of attention to the phenomenon of corruption has grown considerably in Italy, both at the governmental-institutional level and in public opinion.[65]

Against this background and the evidence of defects and inadequacies in the 1990 reforms,[66] the Italian legislator, although not always appropriately and rarely in an organic fashion, has intervened on several occasions to amend the domestic anti-corruption legislation as regards both repression and, more recently, prevention, with a view to confronting the phenomenon in a more effective manner. This intense legislative activity has also been conducted to facilitate the implementation of the international anti-bribery treaties ratified by Italy[67] as well as to address the critiques and recommendations made by the CoE, OECD, and the UN's competent bodies subsequent to monitoring procedures conducted to date and those in the EU Anti-Corruption Report.[68]

These reforms have been grafted onto legislation traditionally leaning towards criminal repression and law enforcement only. As noted by the EU Commission:

---

[61] See the data analysed in the report written by the Attorney General Martino Colella at the *Cerimonia inaugurale dell'anno giudiziorio 2016*, 18 February 2016. In his last five annual reports, also the President of the Court of Auditors has constantly reiterated concerns as to the impact of corruption on the national economy.

[62] Today Italy is positioned in 61 place, having dropped six positions since 2008, and as many as 21 positions since 2005.

[63] See, e.g., OMAN and ARNDT, "Measuring Governance", Policy Brief No. 39, Paris, 2010.

[64] DAVIGO and MANNOZZI, *cit. supra* note 60, p. 99. On the diffusion of the phenomenon see also Autorità Nazionale Anticorruzione, Relazione Annuale 2014, Rome, 2 July 2015.

[65] For an effective representation of the phenomenon of corruption in Italy see also VANNUCCI, *Atlante della corruzione*, Torino, 2012.

[66] Law No. 86 of 26 April 1990.

[67] The national legal framework against corruption includes the relevant provisions of the Criminal Code and Criminal Procedure Code, the Civil Code, as well as specific legislation on the public sector, money-laundering, and liability of legal persons.

[68] See European Commission, Annex Italy to the EU Anti-Corruption Report, 3 February 2014, COM (2014) 38 final, Annex 12.

"Italy's drivers for anti-corruption measures have for long time been limited to law enforcement, prosecution, the judiciary and, to some extent, the Court of Auditors".[69]

However, the absence of an all-encompassing strategy underscored how a reform limited to penal norms could not represent an effective obstacle to the spread of illegality and corruption. Particularly, with the outbreak of the so-called phenomenon of "*Tangentopoli*" and the resulting wide-ranging judicial inquiry "*Mani pulite*",[70] it appeared clear to most observers that the Criminal Code system resulting from the reforms of 1990 was inadequate to address the emerging "morphology" of corruption activities. The features of corruption have actually changed significantly over the course of time to the point that today we can hardly speak of side-payments in the traditional sense, since corruption resorts to other instruments of reward, and has metamorphosed, more generally, into a network of exchanges of favours and utility or profit.[71] In the majority of cases, moreover, corruption does not have as its object a single action bought or sold, but an entire functioning relationship.[72]

Notwithstanding the above and the ratification of the first anti-bribery treaties, before the current legislative apparatus settled, on a number of occasions, the Italian Parliament passed or attempted to pass laws hampering a legal framework that would ensure effective processing and finalisation of court proceedings in complex cases. One example is the draft law on a "short limitation period" ("*prescrizione breve*"), which would have increased the risk of dismissing cases involving defendants with no prior convictions. Another one was the law allowing for the suspension of criminal proceedings until the end of the term of office for offences committed prior to or while in office by a certain categories of high-level officials,[73] which was later found to be unconstitutional.[74] Decriminalisation of certain offences, such as certain forms of false accounting as established by Legislative Decree 61/2002, could also be mentioned in this context.

---

[69] *Ibid.*, p. 3.

[70] "Mani pulite" (Italian for "clean hands") was a nationwide judicial investigation into political corruption in Italy undertaken in the 1990s. *Mani pulite* led to the demise of the so-called "First Republic", resulting in the disappearance of many "historical" Italian political parties. In some accounts, as many as 5,000 public figures fell under suspicion. At one point, more than half of the members of the Italian Parliament were under indictment. More than 400 city and town councils were dissolved because of corruption charges. The corrupt system uncovered by these investigations was usually referred to as "Tangentopoli" (the expression derives from *tangente*, which means kickback and in this context refers to kickbacks given for public works contracts, and from "polis", the ancient Greek word for city).

[71] See VIVARELLI, *cit. supra* note 60, p. 2936.

[72] Textually GUERRINI and GUIDI, "Bribery in Italy: An Outlook on Present Law and Perspective of Reforms", in HORDER and ALLDRIDGE (eds.), *cit. supra* note 32, p. 97 ff., p. 114.

[73] Law No. 124 of 23 July 2008.

[74] *Corte Costituzionale*, 21 October 2009, No. 262.

The subsequent reforms in Italy, partly prompted by the international community, follow three main directions: on the repressive front, (i) the modernisation of sanctions; and (ii) the reorganisation and rationalisation of the offences in the penal code, (especially with regards to the problematic coexistence of the two contiguous criminal offences of corruption and *concussione* and the introduction of the new offence of trading in influence); and, on prevention, (iii) the strengthening of the preventative controls of an administrative nature by aligning the Italian legislation to the UNCAC and the CoECLCC requirements.

With a view to identifying its achievements and shortcomings, the main traits of the Italian legislation resulting from the aggregate of such reforms will be weighed against the central principles of the international treaties and the indications emerging from the monitoring procedures conducted by the competent international bodies.

2.2. The State of the Italian Legislation vis-à-vis the International Anti-Corruption Conventions

2.2.1. Criminalisation of Corruption Offences

Criminalisation is one of the areas which has been most incisively influenced by the international anti-corruption conventions. The majority of the offences contained in the anti-corruption treaties are today covered by the Italian penal law.[75]

First, although through a rather fragmented configuration, Articles 317 to 322 of the Italian Criminal Code criminalise the domestic active and passive bribery of public officials envisaged by the international anti-bribery treaties.[76] Participatory conduct and attempts are also duly criminalised.[77] However, the international dimension of the offence essentially covers active bribery of foreign public officials in international businesses transactions as well as bribery acts committed by EU officials and foreign officials of EU Member States in so far as those acts are committed against the financial interests of the EU.[78] Also, the relevant notions of public official and persons in charge of a public office as established by Articles 357 and

---

[75] See UNODC, Implementation Review Group, Country Review Report of Italy, Vienna, 2014, available at: <http://www.unodc.org/unodc/en/treaties/CAC/country-profile/index.html>.

[76] In the Italian penal system, the concept of bribery, far from being identified in a single criminal typology, turns out to be fragmented in several subtypes distinguished on the basis of action bought or sold and the moment in which the corruption pact is stipulated, forming a sort of "unitary mini-system". The expression is from ROMANO, *Commentario sistematico del codice penale. I delitti contro la pubblica amministrazione*, Milano, 2006, p. 128.

[77] These are covered, respectively, by the general provisions contained in Arts. 110 and 56 of the Criminal Code.

[78] See Art. 322 bis of the Criminal Code introduces by Law 300/2000. Note that para. 5 bis of Art. 322 bis, introduced in 2012, criminalising bribery of the judges, public prosecutors, deputy

358 of the Criminal Code cover the different categories referred to in the relevant treaty provisions. The Italian jurisprudence, moreover, interprets "public function" to the widest possible extent and may also include employees of public enterprises and companies which have been officially granted licenses to perform public services.[79]

Second, the Italian criminal legislation also covers the other corruption offences prohibited by the UNCAC.[80] Moreover, Article 346 bis introduced in the Criminal Code by Law 190/2012, contemplates the new criminal typology of "traffic of illicit influences" directed at punishing the conduct of subjects that propose themselves as intermediaries in the settlement of matters of corruption, alongside those who seek out collaboration. Without entering into the domestic debate regarding the final formulation and the implications of such provision, we note that the novelty is appropriate in order to adapt the outline of the doctrine to the recent changes in the corruption phenomenon.[81] The offence indeed targets not the public official/decision-maker, but those persons who are in the neighbourhood of power and who try to obtain advantages from their situation by influencing the public official decision-maker and, hence, addresses the so-called "background corruption".[82]

Third, Italy considered but decided not to criminalise the offence of illicit enrichment due to incompatibility with the fundamental principles of its legal system. In this respect, however, as the COSP also observes, Italy provides for mandatory confiscation of assets where a person who has been convicted for a number of serious offences (including corruption offences) cannot justify their origin. There are also specific rules imposing patrimonial disclosure obligations on elected officials and top public officials, and stipulating sanctions for non-disclosure.[83]

Finally, the COSP appreciated the "all-crime" approach[84] taken with regard to predicate offences for ML.[85] Repression of ML is indeed of great importance in the fight against corruption. The two crimes are often interlinked. Corruption offences

---

public prosecutors, and officials of the International Criminal Court, addresses GRECO's criticism on the limited scope of Art. 322 bis.

[79] This is acknowledged, for instance, by OECD, Working Group of Bribery, Review of the Implementation of the Convention and 1997 Recommendation. Phase 1 Report, Paris, 2001, p. 8.

[80] See UNODC, *cit. supra* note 75, pp. 34-36, 40-42, 52-54.

[81] The same position is voiced, for instance, by GUERRINI and GUIDI, *cit. supra* note 72, p. 124.

[82] Council of Europe, *cit. supra note* 8, paras. 64-66.

[83] See UNODC, *cit. supra* note 75, p. 37.

[84] There are three main models for identifying predicate crimes of ML. A first system may encompass all crimes as predicate crimes of ML (so-called "all crimes approach"). Another way is defining ML as a crime related to a specific list of offences (so-called "list approach"). Finally, ML can be defined in relation to "serious crime", that is all offences punishable by a sanction beyond a certain threshold (so called "threshold-approach").

[85] UNODC, *cit. supra* note 75, pp. 47-52. Also the controversial introduction of self-laundering in the new Art. 348 ter of the Criminal Code goes in the direction indicated by the inter-

are normally committed for the purpose of obtaining private gains; by laundering the proceeds of corruption offences, such illicit gains can be enjoyed without fear of being confiscated. On the other hand, the illicit proceeds generated by corruption breed illicit financial flows, the proceeds of corruption being among the largest sources of laundered funds.[86] Further, the perpetration of a ML offence frequently includes a transnational element, which can favour the prosecution of launderers and their "allies" in foreign States in cases where a criminal prosecution for corruption in their home State is improbable. The case of James Ibory, mentioned by Hatchard, Daniel, and Maton,[87] is most telling in this respect: seemingly because of considerable ongoing domestic political support, the former Governor of Delta State in Nigeria was not prosecuted successfully in Nigeria although there was substantial evidence of corrupt practices on his part. However, in 2012 he was convicted in a London court of conspiracy to defraud and money laundering involving sums totalling almost £50 million. Hence, an effective anti-corruption legislation must also prohibit such activities, which is a consolidated principle in the anti-bribery conventions,[88] as well as in the Italian legislation.

By contrast, few but significant challenges for the implementation of the provisions on criminalisation of the international treaties endure and have been duly underscored by the international monitoring systems. Apart from the complex and fragmented configuration of bribery offences, the major shortcomings of the Italian legislation concern the problematic coexistence of the contiguous criminal typologies of corruption and *concussione*,[89] and certain persisting limits on the prosecution of the offence of bribery between private persons.

As to the former issue, to date the distinction between the two criminal typologies seems to have produced more failures than advantages in relation to both trial and evidence. Furthermore, above all due to its uncertain contours, the crime of *concussione* could represent an improper shield for bribe-givers.[90] In this re-

---

national anti-bribery monitoring systems. See, e.g., OECD, Report on Implementing the OECD Anti-Bribery Convention in Italy, Paris, 2011, p. 33.

[86] See, *ex multis*, KYRIAKOS-SAAD, ESPOSITO and SCHWARZ, "The Incestuous Relationship between Corruption and Money Laundering", Revue Internationale de Droit Pénal, 2012, pp. 161-172.

[87] HATCHARD, *cit. supra* note 18, p. 358; and DANIEL and MATON, "Is the UNCAC an Effective Deterrent to Grand Corruption", in HORDER and ALLDRIDGE (eds.), *cit. supra* note 32, p. 293 ff., pp. 306-309.

[88] See OECD Convention, Art. 7; CoECLCC, Arts. 6(1)-(2) and 13; UNCAC, Arts. 2(h) and 23.

[89] The crime of *concussione* is peculiar to the Italian Criminal Code. It represents an extortion committed by civil servants in two ways: by constriction and by induction.

[90] *Concussione* can be indeed used as defence for an individual if a public official abuses his/her functions or power to oblige or induce the individual to unduly give or promise money or other assets to the official or a third party.

spect, the WGB has reiterated concerns as to the nebulous scope of *concussione*.[91] Noting that the defence was inconsistent with the OECD Convention as interpreted in light of its Commentary 7, the WGB recommended that Italy amend "its legislation to exclude the defence of *concussione* from the offence of foreign bribery".[92] However, after the amendment to the Criminal Code introduced by Law 190/2012, the WGB recognised the efforts taken in narrowing the scope of the offence of *concussione* and establishing a new offence of undue inducement.[93] The WGB, thus, decided to follow-up on the implementation of the redefined offence of *concussione* and the scope and impact of the new offence of undue inducement as the case law develops.[94]

The domestic provisions on bribery between private persons as resulting from the reform of 2012[95] also seem not to be fully consistent with the offences defined by Article 21 of the UNCAC and Articles 7 and 8 of the CoECLCC. The fact that the offence is not prosecuted *ex officio* but only upon complaint, except for the cases where it leads to distortions of competition in the procurement of goods and services, is criticized by both GRECO and COSP.[96] For similar reasons, the EU Commission has recently remarked that Italy has not yet fully transposed the Framework Decision 2003/568/JHA on combatting corruption in the private sector in that the new provisions introduced with the 2012 anti-corruption law still do not address all the deficiencies related to the scope of corruption offences in the private sector and to the sanctioning regime.[97]

---

[91] OECD, "Italy: Phase 2 Report on the Application of the Convention on Combating Bribery of Foreign Public Officials in International Business Transactions and the 1997 Recommendation On Combating Bribery", Paris, 2004, pp. 33-35, noted also that the definition of *concussione* is further blurred by the concept of *concussione ambientale*, and that magistrates may be tempted to characterise a case as *concussione* rather than bribery, so that the private individual faces no proceedings and may thus be encouraged to offer testimony against the public official.

[92] *Ibid.*, Recommendation 7(a).

[93] According to the WGB, "the offence of *concussione* now restricts the defence to situations where the will of the person who pays the bribe has been 'radically limited'", whilst the separate offence of undue inducement "cannot be used as a defence but provides for lower sanctions for the briber and hence a shorter period of limitation". See OECD, Italy: Follow-up to the Phase 3 Report & Recommendations, Paris, 2014, p. 4.

[94] To the same extent see GRECO, Third Evaluation Round. Compliance Report on Italy, "Incrimination (ETS 173 and 191, GPC 2)". Transparency of Public Funding, GRECO RC III (2014) 9E, Strasbourg, 2014, Recommendation viii, p. 9.

[95] This is a species placed outside the Criminal Code, but included within the range of the so-called "corporate crimes" in Title XI, Book V of the Civil Code ("Penal dispositions in the matter of companies and consortia"). See Art. 2635 of the Civil Code. On the new configuration of the offence see BELLACOSA, "La corruzione privata societaria", in DEL VECCHIO and SEVERINO (eds.), *cit. supra* note 3, pp. 11 ff., and the vast literature referred to therein.

[96] See UNODC, *cit. supra* note 75, p. 9. See also European Commission, *cit. supra* note 68, p. 14, and GRECO, Council of Europe, Joint First and Second Evaluation Rounds. Evaluation Report on Italy, GRECO Eval I/II (2008) 2E, p. 5.

[97] See European Commission, *cit. supra* note 68, p. 14.

2.2.2. Accounting Offences

Regarding accounting offences, GRECO noted that the accounting system in Italy does not comply with the CoECLCC. This was evident in particular as regards the thresholds for liability, the limited scope of accounting requirements (i.e. applicable only to listed companies, State-owned companies and insurance companies), the setting of penalties and the scope of false accounting offences.[98] Such remarks were reiterated before the adoption of Italian Law 69/2015 reforming crimes against the public administration, mafia-type associations, and false accounting.[99] Although it did not meet the expectations of those who called for a comprehensive redefinition of such crimes, this law, taking up part of GRECO's recommendation, at least raises the sanctioning response.

2.2.3. Sanctions and Liability of Legal Persons

Corruption offences are generally regarded as serious offences with correspondingly proportionate punishment, aggravating circumstances, and possible additional sanctions like disqualification. In principle, therefore, the Italian sanctioning regime has been considered in line with the basic tenets of the anti-corruption treaties.[100] This comes as no surprise when considering that the treaty-approach regarding criminalisation has unquestionably contributed to calibrating the national responses and to the design of innovative sanctions such as value-based confiscation[101] and the promotion, for the first time in the Italian legal system, of forms of *ex crimine* liability for legal entities, formulating them *ex novo*.[102]

The sanctioning regime for corruption offences has been recently strengthened by Law 69/2015, which, *inter alia*, provides for a general increase of the duration of imprisonment (with positive effects also on the statute of limitations), and an increase in the duration of the prohibition on participating in public tenders (up to

---

[98] See, e.g., GRECO, Council of Europe, Joint First and Second Evaluation Rounds. Addendum to the Compliance Report on Italy, GRECO RC-I/II (2011) 1E Addendum, Strasbourg, 2013, p. 13. See also European Commission, *cit. supra* note 68, p. 13.

[99] Such offences are now governed by Arts. 2621, 2621 bis, 2621 ter, and 2622 of the Civil Code. An examination of such legislative amendments evidently goes beyond the limits of the present contribution. For a comprehensive discussion, see SEMINARA, "La riforma dei reati di false comunicazioni sociali", Diritto penale e processo, 2015, p. 813 ff.

[100] See, for example, UNODC, *cit. supra* note 75, pp. 5, 9.

[101] This sanction, introduced with Law 300/2000, which ratified the EU and OECD anti-bribery conventions, is governed by Art. 322 ter of the Criminal Code and complements the provisions on confiscation contained in Arts. 240, 322, 325, and 355, as well as in D.Lgs. 395/1992, and Law No. 97/2001.

[102] As is widely known, it was only through Law 300/2000 and D.Lgs. 231/2001 (as amended by D.Lgs. 146/2006 and, subsequently, Laws 190/2012 and 69/2015) that Italy introduced an organic system of sanctions for legal entities.

five years) for any entrepreneur found guilty of such crimes. Remarkably, with a view to stimulating the individual propensity towards denunciation,[103] it also introduced a strategy of rewards, that is, a reduction of sanctions for the individual offenders who *post delictum* effectively strive to avoid corruption activities, or to prevent the production of further illicit effects or to those who effectively cooperate in gathering evidence and identifying other offenders.[104]

Still, certain remarkable flaws remain. Criticism is made regarding the deterrence of pecuniary sanctions on legal persons, which appear relatively low, especially for large companies to which they may be "fairly insignificant" (whereas the arsenal of disqualifying sanctions are recognised as far more dissuasive);[105] and the absence of financial sanctions alongside imprisonment for individuals, which may constitute a useful additional deterrent.[106]

2.2.4. Statute of Limitations

The most serious concern, however, is unanimously thought (and pointedly documented) to be the effectiveness of the sanctions and, especially, their enforcement in practice: the effective, proportionate, and dissuasive character of sanctions based on conviction becomes highly theoretical when a large proportion of cases never reach a conviction, due to the expiry of the limitation periods.[107] The WGB Phase 3 Report, for instance, remarked that, although sixty defendants had been prosecuted and nine cases were under investigation at that time, final sanctions were imposed only against three legal persons and nine individuals in all cases through "*patteggiamento*" (a sort of plea bargain). Cases against numerous other legal persons and individuals had been dismissed, mostly, as time-barred under Italy's statute of limitations, which includes all stages of a trial through to appeals.[108]

---

[103] Such strategy is advocated by, among others, DAVIGO and MANNOZZI, *cit. supra* note 60, pp. 286-287; and MATTARELLA and PELLISSERO, *La legge anticorruzione. Prevenzione e repressione*, Torino, 2013, pp. 351-353.

[104] See Section 1 of Law 69/2014, and Art. 323 bis of the Italian Criminal Code.

[105] See OECD, *cit. supra* note 91, p. 20, and pp. 22-23, adding that "in the very rare instances where a fine was imposed on legal persons in a foreign bribery case, the level of the fine was far from the maximum available under the law (EUR 900,000 or EUR 300,000)", this being of particular concern as "comparable statutory maximum fines were deemed too low by the Working Group in other G8 countries".

[106] *Ibid.*, p. 19.

[107] See GRECO, *cit. supra* note 96, pp. 30-35; OECD, *cit. supra* note 91, pp. 20-32; UNODC, *cit. supra* note 75, pp. 6-7, 9; European Commission, *cit. supra* note 68, pp. 8-9.

[108] See Arts. 157-161 of the Italian Criminal Code. The inadequacy of Italy's statute of limitation regime for bribery offences is also authoritatively voiced, *ex multis*, by PULITANÒ, "La novella in materia di corruzione", Cassazione Penale, 2012, Suppl. al No. 11, p. 15 ff.; and ALESSANDRI, *cit. supra* note 60, p. 13. The OECD has recently underlined the necessity of modi-

GRECO advanced virtually identical concerns, claiming that the combination of the calculation method for the statute of limitations and other factors (such as delays, an overload in criminal justice, the length of criminal proceedings and complexity of investigation for corruption cases) increase the risk that corruption cases becomes time-barred.

Despite such remarks, and even with an increase in the maximum penalty for certain offences, the new anti-corruption laws do not modify the statute of limitations systemically. In short, lengthy proceedings and the current statute of limitations remain highly controversial issues in Italy. More so, in light of the anti-corruption treaties (which also stipulate provisions in this respect)[109] and other international obligations in contiguous fields. The domestic statute of limitations, indeed, has been violently shaken by the EU Court of Justice (ECJ) in the *Taricco* case,[110] referred by the Court of Cuneo. In this case the ECJ issued a landmark (and controversial)[111] judgment on the parallel issue of whether the domestic provisions on limitation periods can be considered as an impediment to the effective fight against VAT fraud[112] and other illegal activities affecting the financial interests of the EU, as provided by Article 325(1) and (2) of the Treaty on the Functioning of the European Union (TFEU), and, in the affirmative, whether they should be disregarded by national courts in order to give EU law its full effect.

Given the complexity of cases such as this which has now been referred back to the Court of Cuneo, the ECJ agreed that the rules constraining the maximum period of limitation, even in the presence of procedural acts which interrupt the course of the term, can be considered contrary to the obligations deriv-

---

fying such regime with a view of impeding delaying tactics. See OECD, Economic Survey: Italy 2013, Paris, 2013, pp. 36-38.

[109] See, e.g., OECD Convention, Art. 6; and UNCAC, Art. 29.

[110] Case No. C-105/14, *Criminal proceedings against Taricco and others*, 8 September 2015, paras. 34-58. For an assessement of the ruling see VIGANÒ, "Disapplicare le norme vigenti sulla prescrizione nelle frodi in materia di IVA? Primato del diritto UE e *nullum crimen sine lege* in una importante sentenza della Corte di giustizia (sent. 8 settembre 2015 (Grande Sezione), Taricco, causa C-105/14)", Diritto penale contemporaneo, 2015, pp. 1-16.

[111] Even if the Italian Supreme Court upheld the jurisprudence of the ECJ (*Corte di Cassazione (Sez. III penale), Crimiminal proceedings against Pennacchini*, 17 September 2015, No. 12999/2015), the Court of Appeal of Milano, the day after, on 18 September 2015, raised a question of constitutional validity of Law No. 130/2008 which ratified and implemented the Lisbon Treaty, with a view to stimulating the application, for the first time in Italian constitutional history, of the "counter-limits" doctrine as applied to EU law. The question submitted to the Constitutional Court assumes the substantive nature of statutes of limitations and refers to a possible breach by the ECJ jurisprudence of the principle *nullum crimen sine lege* and, specifically, its corollary of the prohibition of retroactive application of penal law. See *Corte di Appello di Milano (Sez. II penale), Criminal proceedings against De Bortoli and others*, 18 September 2015, No. 6421/2014.

[112] It must be recalled that a small percentage of VAT revenues collected by Member States accrues to the EU budget.

ing from Article 325 TFEU. Accordingly, even if the national court considers that the limitation period has expired under national law, it should be obliged to give EU law its full effect by setting aside the provisions of national law which conflict with Article 325 TFEU (*in casu*, the last paragraph of Article 160(3), read in conjunction with Article 161(2), of the Italian Criminal Code) and thus deny the possibility for the defendant to be acquitted as a result of the domestic rules on limitation periods. It is of note that, given the very wording of Article 325(1) TFEU ("[...] other illegal activities affecting [...]"), the far-reaching consequences of the ruling cover also corruption offences affecting the financial interests of the EU.

2.2.5. *Consequences of Acts of Corruption. Compensation for Damage*

The system of sanctions is complemented by the provisions on civil and other non-criminal consequences. Article 1418 of the Italian Civil Code establishes a general provision on the nullity of contracts. Article 135 of Legislative Decree No. 163/2006 containing the Code of Public Contracts and amendments introduced by the 2012 law foresees the termination of a contract or withdrawal of qualification where the contractor has been convicted of corruption offences. The National Anti-Corruption Authority for Evaluation and Transparency of Public Administrations (ANAC) is tasked with transmitting the relevant case files to competent judicial authorities and can impose administrative sanctions. The Criminal Code contains general provisions on compensation for damage under Articles 185 and 186, and entitlement to civil claims are foreseen in Articles 74 and 75 of the Criminal Procedure Code. This legal framework seems fully consistent with the relevant provisions of the UNCAC and the CoECivLCC: no specific criticism is advanced by the respective monitoring mechanisms in this regard.

2.2.6. *The Recent Focus on Prevention*

It is only with Law 190/2012 on the prevention and repression of corruption and illegal activities in the public administration that Italy has implemented the anti-corruption treaties' provisions on prevention. This Law constitutes the reference point for Italian policies in this area and puts into effect a complex institutional and organisational design that refers to models based on prevention which have been advocated by international organisations for years. Essentially, it comprises a twofold strategy.

First, addressing the concerns expressed by several international organisations, it includes provisions on ethics (i.e. the adoption of a code of conduct for all public officials, the infringement of which may entail disciplinary action), conflicts of interest and the receipt of gifts for all public officials within public administration (including managers and consultants),[113] whistleblowing protection for public servants and *pantouflage*, and transparency of public administration processes (e.g. information on public administration activities and budgets, and details on public tenders and contractors).[114]

With a view to implementing Article 6 of the UNCAC and Articles 20 and 21 of the CoECLCC, the second part of the strategy articulates an institutional framework for monitoring, coordinating and assessing the effectiveness of the anti-corruption measures developed by each administration at central and local levels, which is today centred around ANAC. Accordingly, ANAC's main functions are the following: to approve the National Anti-Corruption Plan;[115] to analyse the causes and factors of corruption and identify measures to prevent it; to monitor the implementation and effectiveness of public administration's anti-corruption plans and compliance with transparency rules.

Such reforms bring Italy closer to the models designed by the anti-corruption treaties. However, as also remarked by the OECD and the EU, there is still work to be done, for example, regarding protection of whistle-blowers in the private sector, financing of political parties, and the regulation of conflict of interests.[116]

3.   CONCLUDING REMARKS

The fight against corruption and the crimes closely correlated to it has been among the priorities at European and international levels for the past twenty years now. The net effect of the international anti-corruption agreements and the other international initiatives undertaken over such period is that today there exists a sort of "hyper-norm", or a global standard repudiating corruption that transcends national boundaries.

As a result, relevant steps have undeniably been made. To cite the most significant examples, the array of provisions dealing with the criminalisation of corruption of foreign public officials and officials of international public organisations, liability of legal persons, value-based confiscation, disallowance of tax deductibility of bribes to foreign officials, and a comprehensive apparatus of preventive measures, represent a common facet of most of the anti-bribery treaties and further provides an example for the States Parties to such treaties.

---

[113] See also D.Lgs No. 33 and No. 39 of 2013.

[114] See, more extensively, MATTARELLA and PELLISSERO, *cit. supra* note 102.

[115] According to Law 190/2012, each entity operating in the public sector is expected to identify areas vulnerable to corruption risk and formulate annually a (rolling) three-year corruption prevention plan. It applies to both central and local governments.

[116] See OECD, *cit. supra* note 91, pp. 46-47; and EU Commission, *cit. supra* note 68, pp. 7, 11-12.

The case of Italy is most telling. Except for certain phases of manifest asynchrony between the international and domestic normative initiatives, the anti-corruption treaties Italy has ratified have stimulated several remarkable innovations in its legal system, first in the field of criminal repression and, eventually, on prevention. Moreover, the international monitoring mechanisms they set up have thoroughly scrutinised Italy's implementation of these treaties. On the one hand, such mechanisms have acknowledged the steps made by Italy in its anti-corruption actions and also underscored a range of already-existing good practices such as in the area of international cooperation.[117] On the other hand, more importantly, they have repeatedly shown where the Italian legal framework (still) fails to meet the international standards and evidenced the main obstacles for an effective fight against corruption.

---

[117] For instance, UNODC, *cit. supra* note 75, pp. 11-12, commends Italy for its membership to a range of bilateral treaties on extradition and mutual legal assistance; its continuing efforts to conclude treaties with other States to that effect; its participation to law enforcement cooperation networks (like Europol and INTERPOL) and a large number of bilateral agreements on police cooperation.

THE PARIS AGREEMENT ON CLIMATE CHANGE:
BALANCING "LEGAL FORCE" AND "GEOGRAPHICAL SCOPE"

CHRISTINE BAKKER*

Abstract

The Paris Agreement on Climate Change has been acclaimed as a "historic turning point", but it has also been dismissed as "an epic failure". This note presents some critical considerations on this Agreement, focusing on two questions: first, to what extent will the Paris Agreement be legally binding for its Parties; and second, which of two essential concerns has a higher weight when balancing "legal force" and "geographical scope"? The author concludes that, while the Paris Agreement in itself will be legally binding on its States Parties, its individual provisions provide little scope for their judicial enforcement. In order to restore the balance, which has tipped towards the geographical scope, considerable weight must now be put on the scales in the next phase of the process, so as to render the modalities of the Agreement's transparency and facilitation mechanisms as effective as possible.

Keywords: climate change; climate negotiations; Paris Agreement; Nationally Determined Contributions (NDCs); legally binding nature; geographical scope; transparency and facilitation mechanisms.

1. INTRODUCTION

The Paris Agreement on Climate Change adopted on 12 December 2015[1] has been acclaimed as a "historic turning point"[2] and a "renaissance for humankind",[3] but it has also been dismissed as "a farce"[4] and "an epic failure".[5] The media have highlighted these different viewpoints in the immediate aftermath of the Paris

---

* Research Associate, LUISS University, Rome, formerly Research Fellow, European University Institute, Florence.

[1] Annex to Decision FCCC/CP/2015/L.9/Rev.1, available at: <https://unfccc.int/resource/docs/2015/cop21/eng/l09.pdf> (hereinafter "Agreement" or "Paris Agreement").

[2] Laurent Fabius, French Minister for Foreign Affairs and President of COP 21, see at: <http://www.reuters.com/article/us-climatechange-summit-idUSKBN0TV04L20151212>.

[3] Mogens Lykketoft, President of the 70th session of the UN General Assembly, see at: <http://www.un.org/pga/70/2015/12/12/statement-on-adoption-of-paris-climate-agreement/>.

[4] David Goldtooth, Indigenous Environmental Network, see at: <http://newint.org/features/web-exclusive/2015/12/12/cop21-paris-deal-ep-fail-on-planetary-scale/>.

[5] New Internationalist, *ibid.*

Conference (COP 21),[6] and the discussion is being pursued among scholars from different perspectives.[7]

As a small contribution to this discussion, this note will present some critical considerations on the outcome of COP 21, focusing on two questions. First, to what extent will the Paris Agreement, after its ratification, be legally binding for its Parties (section 2). Second, how important is its legal nature for achieving its objectives in light of the virtually universal acceptance of the agreement, i.e. which has a higher weight when balancing "legal force" and "geographical scope"? (section 3). The author concludes with some remarks on the critical next steps in the process towards the achievement of the goals agreed in Paris.

Two essential points on which the Paris Agreement differs from its predecessor, the Kyoto Protocol, provide the context for the questions to be considered in this note. On the one hand, in the new agreement, all 196 Parties (195 States and the European Union as a regional organization) have committed themselves to reducing their greenhouse gas (GHG) emissions, whereas in the Kyoto Protocol, only 37 industrialized States had agreed to determine quantified emission reductions. In the Paris Agreement, also the United States (US) and the main economies in transition (China, Brazil, South-Africa, and India, which account for a large share of global GHG emissions) have agreed to play their part, thereby broadening the geographical scope of these efforts to a near universal level.

On the other hand, the new agreement is based on *voluntary* commitments on GHG emission reductions by the participating States, referred to as "Nationally Determined Contributions" (NDCs), instead of legally binding emission reduction commitments as included in Annex B of the Kyoto Protocol. Indeed, the NDCs themselves are not included in the agreement itself, but in a separate, non-legally binding document. Even though it was agreed to establish a transparency framework and a committee that will monitor State's compliance with their voluntary commitments, the exact modalities thereof still need to be defined.

2.   To What Extent Will the Paris Agreement Be Legally Binding for Its Parties?

As is well known, the legally binding nature of the outcome of COP 21 has been a controversial subject of discussions until the last moments of the negotiations. The three options agreed upon at COP 17 in Durban (2011), "a protocol, another le-

---

[6] The 21st Conference of the Parties to the United Nations Framework Convention on Climate Change, held in Paris from 30 November till 12 December 2015.

[7] See, for example, MONTINI, "The Paris Agreement on Climate Change: Miracle or Disaster?", Environmental Liability, Vol. 23, Issue 5, 2015, p. 161 ff.; and SAVARESI, "The Paris Agreement: A New Beginning?", Journal of Energy & Natural Resources Law, 2016, Vol. 34, No. 1, pp. 16-26.

gal instrument or agreed outcome with legal force under the Convention applicable to all Parties" were still on the table in Paris. Also the diverging positions among those favouring an agreement that would be legally binding in all its aspects, including the emission reduction commitments (especially the European Union and the Least Developed States), and those in favour of a more flexible solution – and outright opposing an overall binding document (US, China, India, and others), persisted throughout the Paris conference.[8] In this section, the following aspects will be considered: (i) the legally binding nature of the Agreement as a whole; and (ii) the legally binding nature of the Agreement's individual provisions.[9]

2.1. The Legally Binding Nature of the Agreement as a Whole

There is no doubt that the Paris Agreement as such is a treaty under international law, which will be binding on its Parties when the necessary procedural conditions have been fulfilled. After the adoption of the Agreement, 175 States have signed it at an official ceremony held in New York on 22 April 2016,[10] after which it needs to be ratified in accordance with the applicable domestic procedures. Before addressing the question to what extent the Agreement is legally enforceable by courts (section 2.1.2), a brief look will be taken at the conditions for the Agreement's entry into force, and the role of the US in the ratification process, which differs from that in most other Parties to the Agreement.

2.1.1. Entry Into Force of the Agreement and the Role of the US in the Ratification Process

The Paris Agreement will enter into force "on the thirtieth day after the date on which at least 55 Parties to the United Nations Framework Convention on Climate Change (UNFCCC) accounting in total for at least an estimated 55 per cent of the total global greenhouse gas emissions have deposited their instruments of ratification, acceptance, approval or accession".[11]

---

[8] For more details on the positions of the EU and the US in the climate negotiations, see also BAKKER, "Climate Governance Towards 'Paris-2015' and Beyond: EU and US Perspectives", IYIL, 2015, pp. 143-158.

[9] For a more exhaustive analysis of the different dimensions of the legal force of the Paris Agreement, including its enforceability by courts, and the acceptance procedures and legal status of the Agreement at the national level, see BODANSKY, "The Legal Character of the Paris Agreement", RECIEL, forthcoming, available at: <http://ssrn.com/abstract=2735252> or <http://dx.doi.org/10.2139/ssrn.2735252>.

[10] Paris Agreement, Art. 20. States can still sign the Agreement until 21 April 2017.

[11] Paris Agreement, Art. 21(1). Art. 21(2) states that: "[s]olely for the limited purpose of paragraph 1 of this Article, 'total global greenhouse gas emissions' means the most up-to-date

Interestingly, a similar threshold was also set in the Kyoto Protocol.[12] Due to the changing political context in the US at the time, which led to a decision *not* to ratify it, the threshold of 55 per cent of global GHG emissions could not be easily reached and ultimately depended on ratification by Russia, so that the entry into force of the Kyoto Protocol was severely delayed until 2005, eight years after its adoption. Today, the active role played by the Obama Administration in the run-up to, and during the Paris Conference has been vital for reaching agreement among the 195 States Parties and the EU. Nevertheless, persisting domestic resistance within the US Congress and Senate, the recent decision of the US Supreme Court to stay the implementation of the ambitious Clean Power Plan (2015) pending judicial review,[13] and the uncertainties related to the upcoming presidential elections, are factors that may endanger a continuation of this positive role during the implementation of the Paris Agreement.

The attention paid by the US negotiators to ensure that the Agreement itself only reflected international obligations already ratified by the US (through its ratification of the UNFCCC), or provisions that concern the implementation of existing legal obligations, seem to indicate a strategy to avoid submitting the Paris Agreement for approval by the US Senate. As explained by an authoritative US expert, a similar path, namely acceptance by the President based on existing statutory, treaty, or constitutional authority, has been followed with respect to other environmental treaties before.[14]

It will be interesting to see how these internal problems will be solved, and to what extent they will influence the above mentioned requirement for the Agreement's entry into force. In any case, the threshold of 55 States accounting for 55 per cent of global GHG emissions will certainly be met more easily after Paris than it was met after Kyoto, considering the high percentages accounted for by China and the other BRICS, compared to the situation at the end of the 1990s.

---

amount communicated on or before the date of adoption of this Agreement by the Parties to the Convention".

[12] However, in the Kyoto Protocol, these 55 per cent related to "the carbon dioxide emissions for 1990 of the Parties included in Annex I" (i.e. the industrialized countries and the economies in transition according to the definition of the time, which did not include China, Brazil, and South-Africa, for example).

[13] Barnes and Mufson, "Supreme Court Freezes Obama Plan to Limit Carbon Emissions", The Washington Post, 9 February 2016, available at: <https://www.washingtonpost.com/politics/courts_law/supreme-court-freezes-obama-plan-to-limit-carbon-emissions/2016/02/09/ac9d-fad8-cf85-11e5-abc9-ea152f0b9561_story.html?tid=a_inl>.

[14] See BODANSKI, "Legal Options for U.S. Acceptance of a New Climate Change Agreement", Center for Climate and Energy Solutions, May 2015, p. 14 ff., available at: <http://www.c2es.org/publications/legal-options-us-acceptance-new-climate-change-agreement>. Bodanski mentions the 1991 Air Quality Agreement with Canada, several protocols under the 1979 Long-Range Transboundary Air Pollution Convention (including the 1999 Gothenburg Protocol to Abate Acidification, Eutrophication and Ground-level Ozone), and the Minamata Convention on Mercury (signed and accepted by the US in 2013).

2.1.2. Can the Paris Agreement Be Legally Enforced?

Despite the fact that after its entry into force the Agreement will have legally binding force under international law, the question arises what is the scope of the Parties' obligations, which depends essentially on the wording of its individual provisions. The Agreement has a "hybrid" character, containing both binding and non-binding provisions. This clearly affects the enforceability of the Agreement by judicial mechanisms, either at the national or at the international level.

The problem of limited enforceability also exists with respect to the UNFCCC, which still constitutes the overarching legal context for international efforts to address climate change. In legal terms the Paris Agreement is in fact an implementing agreement of this framework convention. Despite its significance in terms of a broad international consensus on the recognition of climate change as a threat to humankind, on the need to take measures, and on the objectives to pursue, the obligations of States are formulated in such general terms that render their enforcement by a court virtually impossible. This limitation exists both with regard to national courts and to the International Court of Justice, the only international court before which, in theory, a case of non-compliance by a State with the UNFCCC could be brought, subject to fulfilment of the applicable conditions of jurisdiction. However, this does not exclude that the Agreement could play a role also in other fora where it could be considered relevant to solve preliminary or incidental questions, e.g., in investment arbitration, WTO dispute settlement, or human rights courts.

So far, few cases have been brought before national courts to hold a State accountable for non-compliance with this convention. In the sporadic instances where national courts have found a State responsible for its failure to comply with its obligations under international law to reduce its GHG emissions, the UNFCCC was only one out of several legal sources on which these judgments were based.[15] The same limitations exist with respect to the Paris Agreement, as will be discussed below.

2.2. The Legally Binding Nature of the Agreement's Individual Provisions

The above mentioned hybrid nature of the Paris Agreement can be seen in its individual provisions, which are formulated in different ways.

Some provisions contain *collective goals*, which are formulated in terms of aims, and can therefore not be considered as legally binding per se, but which express an international consensus on far-reaching and ambitious objectives. These

---

[15] See, in particular, Hague District Court, *Urgenda Foundation v. The Netherlands*, Judgment of 24 June 2015, ECLI:NL:RBDHA:2015:7196. A similar procedure was launched on 11 June 2016 by the Belgian NGO Klimaatzaak against Belgium, and another case is being prepared in Norway.

include, in particular: (i) a long term goal to keep the "increase in the global average temperature to well below 2°C above pre-industrial levels and to pursue efforts to limit the temperature increase to 1.5°C above pre-industrial levels";[16] (ii) the aim to reach global peaking of greenhouse gas emissions as soon as possible, and to undertake rapid reductions thereafter in accordance with best available science, so as to achieve a balance between anthropogenic emissions by sources and removals by sinks of greenhouse gases in the second half of this century;[17] (iii) the "global goal on adaptation of enhancing adaptive capacity, strengthening resilience and reducing vulnerability to climate change, with a view to contributing to sustainable development and ensuring an adequate adaptation response in the context of the temperature goal referred to in Article 2".[18]

The Agreement also contains *collective obligations*, which pertain to all its States Parties, for example: (i) to have a "global stocktake" every five years to evaluate progress and to set progressively ambitious targets through Nationally Determined Contributions (NDCs);[19] (ii) and to establish, and adopt common modalities, procedures and guidelines for a transparency framework for reporting to each other and the public on the progress achieved in implementing the national targets.[20]

Moreover, certain collective obligations pertain only to *a group of States*, namely the developed countries, such as the duty to provide continued and enhanced international support to developing countries' mitigation and adaptation efforts, through financial support, transfer of technologies, and capacity-building.[21]

Other provisions include clear *obligations for individual Parties*, such as the obligation to "prepare, communicate and maintain successive NDCs that it intends to achieve",[22] the obligation to communicate a successive NDC every five years, which will represent a progression beyond the Party's current NDC,[23] the obligation to provide the information necessary for clarity, transparency, and understanding, when communicating their NDCs,[24] and the obligation to regularly provide a national greenhouse gas inventory and the information necessary to track progress in implementing and achieving its NDC.[25] Yet another type of provisions in the Agreement have a *facilitating character*, such as Article 6, which refers to mechanisms and modalities for voluntary co-operation among Parties on the implementation of their NDCs.

It is interesting to note that most, if not all provisions that are formulated in stringent terms, using the term "shall", and which can be considered to contain

---

[16] Paris Agreement, Art. 2(1)(a).
[17] Paris Agreement, Art. 4(1).
[18] Paris Agreement, Art. 7(1).
[19] Paris Agreement, Art. 14.
[20] Paris Agreement, Art. 13, in particular paras. (1) and (13)
[21] Paris Agreement, Art. 9(1), Art. 10(6), and Art. 11(3).
[22] Paris Agreement, Art. 4(2).
[23] Paris Agreement, Art. 4(3).
[24] Paris Agreement, Art. 4(8).
[25] Paris Agreement, Art. 13(7)(b).

legally binding procedural obligations, are of a procedural nature, whereas the provisions dealing with substantive matters are formulated rather as aims, or as non-binding commitments, using the verbs "should" or "encourage".

In this context, it should finally be noted that in the Preamble of the Paris Agreement, the recognition of the linkage between climate change and States' obligations to respect and promote human rights has been formulated more explicitly than in previous agreements:

> "Acknowledging that climate change is a common concern of humankind, Parties should, when taking action to address climate change, respect, promote and consider their respective obligations on human rights, the right to health, the rights of indigenous peoples, local communities, migrants, children, persons with disabilities and people in vulnerable situations and the right to development, as well as gender equality, empowerment of women and intergenerational equity".

The placement of this paragraph in the Preamble already excludes any legally binding force of this provision, which also uses the non-stringent verb "should". Considering the hybrid nature of the Agreement as a whole, it would arguably have been desirable to include it in the core of the text, thereby giving it more weight, if not in legal terms, than at least from a political or moral perspective. However, it should also be noted that in accordance with Article 31(2) of the Vienna Convention on the Law of Treaties, the preamble of a treaty provides, together with, *inter alia*, the treaty's text and annexes, the *context* for the interpretation of the treaty's purpose. Therefore, also a statement included in the preamble, such as the above-mentioned paragraph, can be an important element in the interpretation of the treaty itself.[26]

In any case, the explicit recognition of the relationship between climate change and human rights in the Paris Agreement is significant, since it highlights the need for States to ensure that when adopting and implementing policies and measures to address climate change, they must ensure that these actions are in line with the State's obligations under human rights law. By specifically mentioning certain human rights, such as the right to health and the right to development, as well as vulnerable groups, including indigenous peoples and migrants, this acknowledgment goes further than a mere general statement. Also the explicit reference to the relationship

---

[26] See also Art. 31(1) of the Vienna Convention on the Law of Treaties (23 May 1969, entered into force 27 January 1980): "A treaty shall be interpreted in good faith in accordance with the ordinary meaning to be given to the terms of the treaty in their context and in the light of its object and purpose". Art. 31(2) provides: "The context for the purpose of the interpretation of a treaty shall comprise, in addition to the text, including its *preamble* and annexes: (a) any agreement relating to the treaty which was made between all the parties in connexion with the conclusion of the treaty; (b) any instrument which was made by one or more parties in connexion with the conclusion of the treaty and accepted by the other parties as an instrument related to the treaty" (emphasis added).

between climate change and the rights of children and intergenerational equity is, in this author's view, a positive step towards a more integrated approach when addressing these interrelated concerns.[27] In practical terms, it provides an authoritative point of reference for policy makers and civil society groups to urge governments to take these linkages into account from the planning stage of climate mitigation and adjustment policies. As also noted by others, the abovementioned paragraph in the Preamble covers two distinct dimensions: on the one hand, it (implicitly) recalls that States must comply with their due diligence obligations under human rights law to prevent that the impacts of climate change adversely affect human rights (such as the right to health, and, arguably, the right to life).[28] On the other hand, it urges them to ensure that their *policies and actions aiming to address climate change* do not affect either substantive or procedural human rights. This entails many aspects, and there are many obstacles to overcome before this can be fully realized in practice. Nevertheless, the recognition of these linkages is certainly an important step.[29]

3.   BALANCING "LEGAL NATURE" WITH "GEOGRAPHICAL SCOPE"

The outcome of the Paris conference is not surprising, considering the positions of the main Parties in the climate negotiations. In particular, the strong resistance of those States that are responsible for the largest percentages of global GHG emissions (China and the US) to sign up to an agreement that would be legally binding in all its aspects, including their national commitments, virtually blocked any other result. In this section, a closer look will be taken at the voluntary nature of the nationally determined contributions and what this means in practice (section 3.1.), before addressing the question whether it was a "mistake" to give more importance to getting more States on board than to the legal status of the Agreement (section 3.2.).

3.1.   The Voluntary Nature of NDCs

One of the main points of criticism of the Paris Agreement is the fact that the commitments of States on the reduction of their GHG emissions are entirely voluntary, and that States are free to choose the means by which they will achieve their

---

[27] For an analysis of the relationship between climate change and children's rights, including on State's obligations under human rights law, see BAKKER, "Children's Rights Challenged by Climate Change: Is a Reconceptualization Required?", in LENZERINI and VRDOLJAK (eds.), *International Law for Common Goods: Normative Perspectives on Human Rights, Culture and Nature*, Oxford, 2014, p. 361 ff.

[28] On this point, see also BAKKER, "Climate Change and the Right to Life: Potentialities and Limits of the International Human Rights System", in QUIRICO and BOUMGHAR (eds.), *Climate Change and Human Rights: An International Law Perspective*, London/New York, 2015, p. 71 ff.

[29] See also SAVARESI, *cit. supra* note 7, at pp. 24-25.

self-imposed goals. By departing from the Kyoto system of binding, quantified commitments, also the possibility to determine, within the UNFCCC institutional context, an overall percentage of emission reductions to be achieved by a fixed deadline has been abandoned. As noted by several commentators, this entails the risk that it "could lead to a situation where a 'race to the bottom' approach prevails; most parties have no interest in setting ambitious targets that they might not be able to meet later on".[30] A first confirmation of this risk can be found in recent reports, demonstrating that the total GHG emission reductions, based on the indicated nationally determined commitments communicated to the UNFCCC Secretariat prior to the Paris conference, the goal of keeping global warming under 2 degrees centigrade above pre-industrial levels will not be achieved. Indeed, according to a report published by the UNFCCC Secretariat, based on the Indicative Nationally Determined Contributions (INDCs) from 147 Parties communicated by 1 October 2015, projections indicate that if no additional action is taken to reduce GHG emissions, a temperature rise of 2.7 degrees will already be reached by 2030.[31]

Moreover, the Paris Agreement's provisions that address Parties' efforts to put their NDCs into practice, again allow for some flexibility. The relevant provision, referring to these NDCs, provides that "Parties shall *pursue* domestic mitigation measures, with the aim of achieving the objectives of such contributions", which is less stringent than an obligation to *implement* such measures.[32] On the other hand, as mentioned above, States do have an obligation to regularly provide, in the context of the Enhanced Transparency Framework, "[i]nformation necessary to track progress made in implementing and achieving its nationally determined contribution under Article 4".[33] This indicates that while the implementation of the NDCs itself is indeed voluntary, by accepting an obligation to regularly provide information on the progress achieved, at least an effort towards transparency – with the potential political embarrassment of exposing a State's failure to comply with its own commitments – has been accepted. However, all the efforts made during the Paris conference to protect States' flexibility on their national policies and measures, seem to contradict – or at least weaken – the ambitious overall goals included in the Agreement, and the recognition that climate change poses an "urgent threat".[34] As noted by another author, also the fact that the first "global stocktake" to assess

---

[30] MONTINI, *cit. supra* note 7, p. 162.

[31] UNFCCC, "Synthesis Report on the Aggregate Effect of the Intended Nationally Determined Contributions", FCCC/CP/2015, 30 October 2015, available at: <http://unfccc.int/resource/docs/2015/cop21/eng/07.pdf>. The term "Indicative Nationally Determined Contributions" was used in the run-up to the Paris Conference, whereas in the Agreement itself the term "Nationally Determined Contributions" was included.

[32] Paris Agreement, Art. 4(2) (emphasis added). For a more detailed analysis on this point, see BODANSKI, *cit. supra* note 9, p. 8.

[33] Paris Agreement, Art. 13(7)(b).

[34] Paris Agreement, Preamble, para. 4.

progress in the implementation of the Agreement is set for 2023,[35] seems to be at odds with the stated recognition of urgency.[36]

3.2. A Balancing Act with an Unbalanced Outcome?

The hybrid nature of the Agreement, and the "bottom-up" approach of voluntary NDCs, was the only realistic way to reach the goal of broadening the geographical scope of international efforts to mitigate climate change. On balance, the necessity of a wider geographical scope has outweighed the concerns about the Agreement's legal nature. Does this mean that the balance has tipped too far towards the aim to have a near-universal agreement, thereby abandoning any certainty about its actual implementation? This question can only be answered by considering any indications of how this implementation will be ensured in practice. Indeed, the need to create an effective monitoring and verification mechanism, allowing to track progress in the implementation of States' voluntary commitments, was among the main negotiating points, both in the run-up to the Paris conference, and at COP 21 itself. When looking at the relevant provisions in the Agreement, once again, a mixed picture emerges.

On the one hand, the Agreement foresees the establishment of several mechanisms to promote its effective implementation: an enhanced transparency framework,[37] a facilitation mechanism,[38] and a five-yearly "global stocktake".[39] As mentioned above (section 2), the Agreement also formulates the collective obligations and individual obligations to create these mechanisms, to decide on their modalities, and to regularly provide the required information in a constringent manner. In this regard, also the provision stating that the outcome of the five-yearly global stocktake "shall inform Parties in updating and enhancing, in a nationally determined manner, their actions and support [...], as well as in enhancing international cooperation for climate action"[40] should be mentioned. Undoubtedly these are, by themselves, positive achievements, with great political significance.

On the other hand, the numerous references included in these provisions to the need to ensure "flexibility",[41] and to the fact that both the transparency framework, and the facilitation mechanism shall be "*facilitative* in nature and function in a manner that is [...] *non-adversarial* and *non-punitive*",[42] considerably weaken their ca-

---

[35] Paris Agreement, Art. 14(2).

[36] See MONTINI, *supra* note 7, p. 164.

[37] Paris Agreement, Art. 13.

[38] Paris Agreement, Art. 15.

[39] Paris Agreement, Art. 14.

[40] Paris Agreement, Art. 14(3).

[41] Paris Agreement, Art. 13(1) and (2).

[42] Paris Agreement, Art. 15(2) (emphasis added). See also Art. 13(3): "The transparency framework shall [...] be implemented in a facilitative, non-intrusive, non-punitive manner, respectful of national sovereignty, and avoid placing undue burden on Parties".

pacity to function effectively, and to strongly "condemn" any non-compliance with stated commitments. Much will depend on the exact modalities and procedures of these mechanisms, which still need to be adopted by the Conference of the Parties, serving as the meeting of the Parties to the Paris Agreement, at its first meeting.[43] The fact that several elements to be considered in the context of these mechanisms are already included in the Agreement provides useful guidance in this regard.

4. CONCLUDING REMARKS

The considerations outlined in this note confirm that, despite the fact that the Paris Agreement in itself will be legally binding on its Parties after its entry into force, its individual provisions provide little scope for their judicial enforcement. The fact that virtually all the provisions that are formulated in constringent terms (using the verb "shall") contain *procedural* obligations, severely limits the possibilities to hold States accountable, in terms of their legal responsibility, for non-compliance with the substantive commitments in the Agreement, which are the ones that matter most for achieving its objectives.

An agreement with legally binding force in all its aspects, including the national commitments for mitigation measures and GHG emission reductions, would have provided more certainty and predictability for all Parties involved, including States, the private sector, investors, NGOs, and – most importantly – for people around the globe who suffer the consequences of climate change. It will depend on the willingness of the participating States, first, to adopt progressively ambitious targets through their INDCs, and second, to comply with their own voluntary commitments.

Returning to the question of weighing the vital concerns of "legal force" versus "geographical scope", it can be expected that such balancing acts will continue to characterize international efforts to address climate change also in the future. Nevertheless, now that the broader geographical scope has been achieved, as much weight as possible should be put on the scales in the next phase of the process, in order to render the modalities of the Agreement's transparency and facilitation mechanisms as effective as possible. This would be a vital element in restoring the balance.

---

[43] Paris Agreement, Arts. 13(13) and 15(3).

IN PRAISE OF SUSTAINABILITY: THE ENCYCLICAL LETTER
LAUDATO SÌ AND ITS LEGAL-ECONOMIC IMPLICATIONS

MASSIMILIANO MONTINI[*] and FRANCESCA VOLPE[**]

Abstract

The Encyclical Letter "Laudato Sì. On Care For Our Common Home", issued by Pope Francis in May 2015, contains some legal and economic aspects that go beyond a purely religious relevance, touching upon the political, social, and ethical spheres. The present contribution aims to identify these aspects of the Encyclical Letter, providing a brief reasoned analysis of its most interesting and relevant features, namely the emergence and the human origin of the ecological crisis, the critique of the dominant technocratic paradigm, the weakness of the institutional and legal international response, and the major paths of dialogue proposed by the Encyclical Letter to overcome "the spiral of self-destruction" which humanity is currently confronting. This contribution then focuses on integral ecology as the proposed solution to tackle the present ecological crisis and the call for an ecological conversion. On the basis of the analysis, a final section highlights some tipping points which are worthy of further comment, and contextualises Pope Francis' views in the light of the most relevant scientific literature on these topics.

Keywords: Encyclical Letter *Laudato Sì*; ecological crisis; integral ecology; ecological conversion.

1. THE ECOLOGICAL CRISIS AND THE WEAKNESS OF THE INTERNATIONAL RESPONSE

The Encyclical Letter "Laudato Sì. On Care For Our Common Home", issued by Pope Francis in May 2015, contains some legal and economic aspects that go beyond a purely religious relevance, touching upon the political, social, and ethical spheres.[1] The present article aims at identifying these aspects of the Encyclical Letter and providing a legal appraisal of its most interesting and relevant features.

The Encyclical Letter is a particularly timely document which encourages humanity to reconsider its role on the planet and its relationship with the other living

---

[*] Professor of European Union Law, Co-Director of Regulation for Sustainability (R4S) Research Group, University of Siena.

[**] Research Fellow in European Union Law, Researcher of Regulation for Sustainability (R4S) Research Group, University of Siena.

[1] POPE FRANCIS, *Encyclical Letter Laudato Sì. On Care For Our Common Home*, 2015.

species. It begins with the recognition of the compelling necessity of addressing the severe ecological crisis that is affecting our common home and which has been largely caused by the "irresponsible use and abuse" of the resources of planet Earth by human beings.

Pope Francis argues that "[n]othing in this world is indifferent to us", and calls for "a new dialogue about how we are shaping the future of our planet" (para. 14). He starts by reviewing the most relevant aspects of the current ecological crisis (para. 15). To this effect, he provides a brief overview of "what is happening to our common home" (para. 17). The attention is mostly devoted to the main forms of pollution affecting our planet, such as the exposure to air pollution (para. 20), pollution caused by waste (para. 21), and, more generally, pollution linked to the "throwaway culture" which characterises our society (para. 22).

The Encyclical Letter deals with the climate change issue. It interestingly identifies climate as a "common good, belonging to all and meant for all" (para. 23). Climate change is then recognised as "a global problem with grave implications: environmental, social, economic, political and for the distribution of goods. It represents one of the principal challenges facing humanity in our day" (para. 25). While acknowledging various natural factors influencing global warming, Pope Francis takes a clear stance on the anthropogenic nature of climate change, by clearly stating that "a number of scientific studies indicate that most global warming in recent decades is due to the great concentration of greenhouse gases [...] released mainly as a result of human activity" (para. 23). Furthermore, Pope Francis warns that the negative effects of climate change "will continue to worsen if we continue with current models of production and consumption" and expresses "an urgent need to develop policies so that, in the next few years, the emission of carbon dioxide and other highly polluting gases can be drastically reduced" (para. 26).

Subsequently, the attention shifts to the issue of water (para. 27 ff.), with references to both the qualitative as well as quantitative aspects. The Encyclical Letter takes a very strong position by affirming that "*access to safe drinkable water is a basic and universal human right, since it is essential to human survival and, as such, is a condition for the exercise of other human rights*" (para. 30; italics in the original text). It continues by saying that "our world has a grave social debt towards the poor who lack access to drinking water, because *they are denied the right to a life consistent with their inalienable dignity*" (para. 30; italics in the original text). In this context, Pope Francis also denounces water waste, highlighting that "the problem of water is partly an educational and cultural issue" (para. 30).

The Encyclical Letter then focuses on the loss of biodiversity, underlining that "the earth's resources are also being plundered because of short-sighted approaches to the economy, commerce and production" (para. 32).

Pope Francis then underlines the close connection between environmental degradation and the decline in the quality of human life (para. 43 ff.). In particular, he addresses both the individual dimension, warning that "we cannot fail to consider the effects on people's lives of environmental deterioration, current models of development and the throwaway culture" (para. 43), and the societal one, stressing that "we cannot adequately combat environmental degradation unless we attend to causes related to human and social degradation" (para. 48).

In addition, Pope Francis highlights that, despite the gravity of the current ecological crisis, "the problem is that we still lack the culture needed to confront this crisis. We lack leadership capable of striking out on new paths and meeting the needs of the present with concern for all and without prejudice towards coming generations" (para. 53). This wording resembles the quest for intra- and inter-generational equity initiated several decades ago by the Brundtland Report.[2] The Encyclical Letter goes further by underlining the necessity of establishing an appropriate legal framework to promote and support the shift needed in the ecological culture. In this respect, Pope Francis calls for the "establishment of a legal framework which can set clear boundaries and ensure the protection of ecosystems", "otherwise, the new power structures based on the techno-economic paradigm may overwhelm not only our politics but also freedom and justice" (para. 53).

It is within such a context that the Pope stigmatises the grave weakness of the international responses to the ecological crisis thus far demonstrated by the "failure of global summits on the environment" (para. 54). In the Pope's view, this is directly related to the fact that "our politics are subject to technology and finance" (para. 54). This entails two negative consequences. On the one side, "there are too many special interests, and economic interests easily end up trumping the common good and manipulating information" (para. 54). On the other side, "the alliance between the economy and technology ends up side-lining anything unrelated to its immediate interests" (para. 54). As a result, we are witnessing both a "superficial rhetoric" aimed at environmental protection and the failure of any attempt to introduce change. In the Pope's wording this is expressed as follows: "the most one can expect is superficial rhetoric, sporadic acts of philanthropy and perfunctory expressions of concern for the environment, whereas any genuine attempt by groups within society to introduce change is viewed as a nuisance based on romantic illusions or an obstacle to be circumvented" (para. 54).

On the same line of reasoning, Pope Francis highlights that "economic powers continue to justify the current global system where priority tends to be given to speculation and the pursuit of financial gain, which fail to take the context into account, let alone the effects on human dignity and the natural environment" (para. 56). Within such a framework, Pope Francis calls for a greater effort to address the challenges posed by the ecological crisis and warns about the risks of "a false or superficial ecology which bolsters complacency and a cheerful recklessness" (para. 59). In other words, humanity seems neither ready nor willing to take courageous decisions to tackle the profound ecological crisis, thus showing a certain degree

---

[2] United Nations Commission on Environment and Development, *Our Common Future*, Oxford, 1987.

of "evasiveness", which "serves as a licence to carrying on with our present life-styles and models of production and consumption. This is the way human beings contrive to feed their self-destructive vices: trying not to see them, trying not to acknowledge them, delaying the important decisions, and pretending that nothing will happen" (para. 59).

2. THE HUMAN ORIGIN OF THE ECOLOGICAL CRISIS

Following the analysis of the ecological crisis, Pope Francis argues that "it would hardly be helpful to describe symptoms without acknowledging the human origins of the ecological crisis"; to this effect, his analysis focuses in particular on the "dominant technocratic paradigm" (para. 101). Notwithstanding the positive outcomes brought about by the scientific and technological progress in the last two centuries, Pope Francis raises a fundamental issue related to the globalisation of the technocratic paradigm, by arguing that the problem is not represented by technological progress as such, but the issue to be addressed is rather "the way that humanity has taken up technology and its development according to an undifferentiated and one-dimensional paradigm" (para. 106). In other words, as the Encyclical Letter points out, "many problems of today's world stem from the tendency [...] to make the method and aims of science and technology an epistemological paradigm which shapes the lives of individuals and the workings of society" (para. 107). In fact, relying on such a paradigm, humanity has developed a destructive approach, which legitimises an excessive exploitation of natural resources. This is in line with the "idea of infinite or unlimited growth, which proves so attractive to economists, financiers and experts in technology", and which is "based on the lie that there is an infinite supply of the Earth's goods, and this leads to the planet being squeezed dry beyond every limit" (para. 106). Moreover, "the technocratic paradigm also tends to dominate economic and political life" (par. 109).

Pope Francis takes a clear stance against the widespread belief that "current economics and technology will solve all environmental problems" (para. 109). Therefore, the question implicitly raised by Pope Francis is essentially the following: what can be done to react against the dominant technocratic paradigm and prevent its negative consequences? He calls for a "resistance to the assault of the technocratic paradigm", which should be based on a new and "distinctive way of looking at things", which also implies a new "way of thinking, policies, an educational programme, a lifestyle and a spirituality" (para. 111). Otherwise, as Pope Francis correctly points out, "even the best ecological initiatives can find themselves caught up in the same globalized logic" (para. 111). In fact, "to seek only a technical remedy to each environmental problem which comes up is to separate what is in reality interconnected and to mask the true and deepest problems of the global system" (para. 111). In sum, it may be said that in order to overcome the presently dominant technological paradigm, the Encyclical Letter proposes a fundamental shift in the ecological culture, which is currently limited "to a series of urgent and partial responses to the immediate problems of pollution, environmental decay and the depletion of natural resources" (para. 111), suggesting "to slow down and look at reality in a different way, to appropriate the positive and sustainable progress which has been made, but also to recover the values and the great goals swept away by our unrestrained delusions of grandeur" (para. 114).

3. MAJOR PATHS OF DIALOGUE

In order to address the human origin of the ecological crisis, the Encyclical Letter proposes a series of "major paths of dialogue", which may be relied upon to overcome "the spiral of self-destruction" which humanity is currently confronting (para. 163).

Firstly, the importance of a "dialogue on the environment in the international community" is stressed. Pope Francis notes that "beginning in the middle of the last century and overcoming many difficulties, there has been a growing conviction that our planet is a homeland and that humanity is one people living in a common home" (para. 164). At the same time, he acknowledges that "interdependence obliges us to think of *one world with a common plan*" (para. 164; italics in the original text) and that:

> "[A] global consensus is essential for confronting the deeper problems, which cannot be resolved by unilateral actions on the part of individual countries. Such a consensus could lead, for example, to planning a sustainable and diversified agriculture, developing renewable and less polluting forms of energy, encouraging a more efficient use of energy, promoting a better management of marine and forest resources, and ensuring universal access to drinking water" (para. 164).

However, as highlighted by Pope Francis, despite the increased concern for the widespread environmental degradation at international level, "recent World Summits on the environment have not lived up to expectations because, due to lack of political will, they were unable to reach truly meaningful and effective global agreements on the environment" (para. 166). In particular, the Encyclical Letter, while acknowledging the partial success of the 1992 Rio Summit (para. 167), points out the "wide-ranging but ineffectual outcome document" that emerged from the 2012 Rio+20 Summit (para. 169). It underlines that with regard to climate change "the advances have been regrettably few", remarking that "reducing greenhouse gases requires honesty, courage and responsibility, above all on the part of those countries which are more powerful and pollute the most" (para. 169). Pope Francis concludes the dialogue on the environment arguing that:

"[A] more responsible overall approach is needed to deal with both problems: the reduction of pollution and the development of poorer countries and regions. The twenty-first century, while maintaining systems of governance inherited from the past, is witnessing a weakening of the power of nation states, chiefly because the economic and financial sectors, being transnational, tends to prevail over the political. Given this situation, it is essential to devise stronger and more efficiently organized international institutions, with functionaries who are appointed fairly by agreement among national governments, and empowered to impose sanctions" (para. 175).

Secondly, the attention is shifted to the "dialogue for new national and local policies", needed to address both the environmental and economic development challenges (para. 176). Pope Francis focuses on two fundamental elements, namely the centrality of the State and the centrality of the law (para. 177). As for the centrality of the State, he observes that "given the real potential for a misuse of human abilities, individual States can no longer ignore their responsibility for planning, coordination, oversight and enforcement within their respective borders" (para. 177). As for the centrality of the law, he underlines that:

"[O]ne authoritative source of oversight and coordination is the law, which lays down rules for admissible conduct in the light of the common good. The limits which a healthy, mature and sovereign society must impose are those related to foresight and security, regulatory norms, timely enforcement, the elimination of corruption, effective responses to undesired side-effects of production processes, and appropriate intervention where potential or uncertain risks are involved" (para. 177).

Pope Francis concludes this part by highlighting the creative role of law, affirming that "political and institutional frameworks do not exist simply to avoid bad practice, but also to promote best practice, to stimulate creativity in seeking new solutions and to encourage individual or group initiatives" (para. 177). A particularly relevant role is assigned to the local dimension:

"[L]ocal individuals and groups can make a real difference. They are able to instil a greater sense of responsibility, a strong sense of community, a readiness to protect others, a spirit of creativity and a deep love for the land. They are also concerned about what they will eventually leave to their children and grandchildren" (para. 179).

Thirdly, the Encyclical Letter presents the necessity of a "dialogue and transparency in decision-making". In fact, "an assessment of the environmental impact of business ventures and projects demands transparent political processes involving a free exchange of views" (para. 182). In particular, it stresses the importance of the involvement of the local population in decision-making:

> "[T]he local population should have a special place at the table; they are concerned about their own future and that of their children, and can consider goals transcending immediate economic interest. We need to stop thinking in terms of 'interventions' to save the environment in favour of policies developed and debated by all interested parties" (para. 183).

Finally, the Encyclical Letter addresses the issue of a "dialogue between politics and economy for human fulfilment". "Politics must not be subject to the economy, nor should the economy be subject to the dictates of an efficiency-driven paradigm of technocracy" (para. 189). With reference to the ecological crisis, Pope Francis clearly affirms: "environmental protection cannot be assured solely on the basis of financial calculations of costs and benefits. The environment is one of those goods that cannot be adequately safeguarded or promoted by market forces" (para. 190).[3] It is underlined that it is not realistic "to hope that those who are obsessed with maximizing profits will stop to reflect on the environmental damage which they will leave behind for future generations" (para. 190). In fact, "where profits alone count, there can be no thinking about the rhythms of nature, its phases of decay and regeneration, or the complexity of ecosystems which may be gravely upset by human intervention" (para. 190). It is therefore necessary to embrace a new development path, which may pave the way "to different possibilities which do not involve stifling human creativity and its ideals of progress, but rather directing that energy along new channels" (para. 191). In this sense, "[f]or new models of progress to arise, there is a need to change 'models of global development'; this will entail a responsible reflection on 'the meaning of the economy and its goals with an eye to correcting its malfunctions and misapplications'" (para. 194).[4] Pope Francis states the necessity of clear-cut choices, focusing on a correct definition of progress:

> "It is not enough to balance, in the medium term, the protection of nature with financial gain, or the preservation of the environment with progress. Halfway measures simply delay the inevitable disaster. Put simply, it is a matter of redefining our notion of progress. A technological and economic development which does not leave in its wake a better world and an integrally higher quality of life cannot be considered progress" (para. 194).

---

[3] Originally in Pontifical Council for Justice and Peace, *Compendium of the Social Doctrine of the Church*, 2004, p. 470.

[4] Originally in BENEDICT XVI, *Message for the 2010 World Day of Peace*, 2010, p. 43.

From the Encyclical Letter it is clear that the gravity of the problem requires a certain degree of courage in the definition and implementation of correct solutions. In this sense, Pope Francis warns against inadequate solutions by taking, for instance, a very critical position towards sustainable growth, as an example of a misleading concept. In this respect, Pope Francis states that talking of "sustainable growth usually becomes a way of distracting attention and offering excuses. It absorbs the language and values of ecology into the categories of finance and technocracy, and the social and environmental responsibility of businesses often gets reduced to a series of marketing and image-enhancing measures" (para. 194).

4. The "Integral Ecology" and the Call for an Ecological Conversion

Starting from the assumption that "everything is closely interrelated, and today's problems call for a vision capable of taking into account every aspect of the global crisis" (para. 137), Pope Francis proposes to embrace an "integral ecology" as a possible solution. Such an integral ecology is composed by an environmental, economic, social, cultural ecology, and an ecology of daily life.

The environmental ecology, which "studies the relationship between living organisms and the environment in which they develop", "entails reflection and debate about the conditions required for the life and survival of society, and the honesty needed to question certain models of development, production and consumption" (para. 139). In this context, Pope Francis highlights the importance of trying to devise effective and "comprehensive solutions which consider the interactions within natural systems themselves and with social systems" (para. 139). This is closely related to the recognition that there are not "two separate crises, one environmental and the other social", rather "one complex crisis which is both social and environmental" (para. 139). In order to properly address such a complex crisis, adequate solutions must be based on an integrated approach "to combating poverty, restoring dignity to the excluded, and at the same time protecting nature" (para. 139). The comprehensive and integrated approach proposed by the Encyclical Letter should be relied upon also to determine the environmental impact of business activities on ecosystems. In such a sense, "we take these systems into account not only to determine how best to use them, but also because they have an intrinsic value independent of their usefulness" (para. 140). Furthermore, there is "the need for an 'economic ecology' capable of appealing to a broader vision of reality. The protection of the environment is in fact 'an integral part of the development process and cannot be considered in isolation from it'" (para. 141).[5] Moreover, the Encyclical Letter stresses the need for a

---

[5] Originally in *Rio Declaration on Environment and Development*, 1992, Principle 4.

social ecology as "the health of a society's institutions has consequences for the environment and the quality of human life. [...] In this sense, social ecology is necessarily institutional, and gradually extends to the whole of society, from the primary social group, the family, to the wider local, national and international communities" (para. 142).

The integral ecology comprises also a cultural ecology, which expresses itself in "protecting the cultural treasures of humanity in the broadest sense. More specifically, it calls for greater attention to local cultures when studying environmental problems, favouring a dialogue between scientific-technical language and the language of the people" (para. 143). Eventually, the Encyclical Letter proposes an ecology of daily life as a prerequisite for an "authentic development", whose attainment "includes efforts to bring about an integral improvement in the quality of human life, and this entails considering the setting in which people live their lives" (para. 147). This applies both to urban and rural settings, as "interventions which affect the urban or rural landscape should take into account how various elements combine to form a whole which is perceived by its inhabitants as a coherent and meaningful framework for their lives" (para. 151).

Furthermore, "an integral ecology is inseparable from the notion of the common good, a central and unifying principle of social ethics" (para. 156), which "also extends to future generations" recognising the existence of "our common destiny, which cannot exclude those who come after us" (para. 159). This remark recalls the already mentioned necessity of solidarity among generations (commonly referred to as the inter-generational equity principle) as a precondition of sustainable development (para. 159).

The quest for an integral ecology is accompanied by the recognition that "many things have to change course, but it is we human beings above all who need to change"; in fact, we "lack an awareness of our common origin, of our mutual belonging and of a future to be shared with everyone" (para. 202). In the view of Pope Francis, "a great cultural, spiritual and educational challenge stands before us, and it will demand that we set out on the long path of renewal" by developing "new convictions, attitudes and forms of life" (para. 202).

Pope Francis notes that "since the market tends to promote extreme consumerism in an effort to sell its products, people can easily get caught up in a whirlwind of needless buying and spending. Compulsive consumerism is one example of how the techno-economic paradigm affects individuals" (para. 203). This entails two main consequences: on the one hand, "when people become self-centred and self-enclosed, their greed increases [and] a genuine sense of the common good also disappears"; on the other hand, "obsession with a consumerist lifestyle [...] can only lead to violence and mutual destruction" (para. 204). There is only one solution to overcome this negative situation: a decisive "change in lifestyle". In fact, this "could bring healthy pressure to bear on those who wield political, economic and social power", also increasing the value of consumer social responsibility (para. 206). It is worth noting that the Encyclical Letter recalls the challenge posed by the 2000 Earth Charter,[6] according to which "common destiny beckons us to seek a new beginning" (para. 207).

Finally, the Encyclical Letter states that "an awareness of the gravity of to-day's cultural and ecological crisis must be translated into new habits" and this compels us to address the "educational challenge" we are facing (para. 209). In this sense, Pope Francis notes that "[e]nvironmental education has broadened its goals. Whereas in the beginning it was mainly centred on scientific information, consciousness-raising and the prevention of environmental risks, it tends now to include a critique of the 'myths' of a modernity grounded in a utilitarian mind-set (individualism, unlimited progress, competition, consumerism, the unregulated market)" (para. 210). The new environmental education "needs educators capable of developing an ethics of ecology, and helping people, through effective pedagogy, to grow in solidarity, responsibility, and compassionate care" (para. 210). It should promote the creation of an "ecological citizenship" and "encourage ways of acting which directly and significantly affect the world around us" (para. 211). Therefore, "the ecological crisis is also a summons to profound interior conversion", identified by Pope Francis as an "ecological conversion" (para. 217).

5.   THE MAIN TIPPING POINTS OF THE ENCYCLICAL LETTER

After a brief reasoned analysis of the most relevant legal and institutional is-sues raised by the Encyclical Letter, some tipping points which deserve further comment will now be discussed, and the views of Pope Francis will be contextual-ised in the light of the most relevant scientific literature on these topics.

The first of the main tipping points emerging from the reading of the Encyclical Letter is the very harsh critique of the dominant technocratic paradigm made by Pope Francis. In the Encyclical Letter, it is clearly stated that the problem is not technology as such. The main problem lies in the way in which humanity is devel-oping and making use of technology, according to the above-mentioned paradigm, that is legitimising a destructive approach towards nature and an over-exploitation of natural resources, which is putting pressure on the planet above any reasonable limits. As already mentioned, Pope Francis takes a clear stance against the belief that "current economics and technology will solve all environmental problems". In this sense, his position can be read also as a critique of the widespread idea of an infinite or unlimited growth that unfortunately still finds broad support in contem-porary politics and economics. It should be underlined that this position echoes the warnings raised in the scientific literature by many scholars, such as Schumacher, Daly, Tiezzi, Costanza, Georgescu-Roegen, Capra, and Luisi.[7] According to such

---

[6] Earth Charter, The Hague, 2000.

[7] On this issue see, for instance, SCHUMACHER, *Small is Beautiful. A Study of Economics as if People Mattered*, London, 1973; DALY, *Steady-State Economics. The Economics of*

authors, it is well demonstrated that limitless economic growth can hardly be sustainable on a planet characterised by limited natural resources and sinks for waste.[8] This is also in line with the Planetary Boundaries theory, which defines the Earth's biosphere as the "safe-operating space" for humanity.[9]

Pope Francis' critique also includes a call for a resistance to the assault of the technocratic paradigm, which should be based on a new way of thinking, on the promotion of different policies, on the revision of our education programmes and most interestingly on a change in ecological culture and lifestyle. The Encyclical Letter argues that should such changes not occur, even the best ecological initiatives will end up being captured in the same globalised logic and therefore will not produce any satisfactory results.

The second main tipping point which may be detected in the Encyclical Letter is the recognition by Pope Francis that the institutional and legal response, undertaken at international level to deal with the global ecological crisis, has been generally quite weak and certainly not sufficient to cope in an adequate way with the gravity of the problems humanity faces. It is worth noting the clear acknowledgement about the failure of the global summits on the environment that have characterised the last few decades. This, in Pope Francis' view, is directly related to the fact that politics is substantially subject to technology and finance. In this context, Pope Francis notes that special interests, and most notably economic interests, easily end up trumping the common good and manipulating information. As a consequence, not only has humanity not been able to put up an adequate legal framework to deal with the widespread ecological crisis, but we are also witnessing the triumph of a superficial rhetoric aimed at environmental protection, which is coupled with the failure to introduce any substantial change to the present situation.

Biophysical Equilibrium and Moral Growth, San Francisco, 1977; TIEZZI, *Tempi storici. Tempi biologici*, Milano, 1984; GEORGESCU-ROEGEN, "The Entropy Law and the Economic Process in Retrospect", Eastern Economic Journal, 1986, p. 3 ff.; COSTANZA and DALY, "Natural Capital and Sustainable Development", Conservation Biology, 1992, vol. 6, pp. 37-46; and CAPRA and LUISI, *The Systems View of Life. A Unifying Vision*, Cambridge, 2014, p. 362 ff.

[8] On the impossibility of limitless growth on a limited planet see, for instance, DALY, *Beyond Growth. The Economics of Sustainable Development*, Boston, 1996.

[9] ROCKSTRÖM, STEFFEN, NOONE, PERSSON, STUART III CHAPIN, LAMBIN, LENTON, SCHEFFER, FOLKE, SCHELLNHUBER, NYKVIST, DE WIT, HUGHES, VAN DER LEEUW, RODHE, SÖRLIN, SNYDER, COSTANZA, SVEDIN, FALKENMARK, KARLBERG, CORELL, FABRY, HANSEN, WALKER, LIVERMAN, RICHARDSON, CRUTZEN and FOLEY, "Planetary Boundaries: Exploring the Safe Operating Space for Humanity", Ecology and Society, 2009, available at: <www.ecologyandsociety.org/vol14/iss2/art32>; ROCKSTROM, STEFFEN, NOONE, PERSSON, STUART III CHAPIN, LAMBIN, LENTON, SCHEFFER, FOLKE, SCHELLNHUBER, NYKVIST, DE WIT, HUGHES, VAN DER LEEUW, RODHE, SÖRLIN, SNYDER, COSTANZA, SVEDIN, FALKENMARK, KARLBERG, CORELL, FABRY, HANSEN, WALKER, LIVERMAN, RICHARDSON, CRUTZEN and FOLEY, "A Safe Operating Space for Humanity", Nature, 2009, Vol. 461, No. 7263, pp. 472-475. See also WIJKMAN and ROCKSTRÖM, *Bankrupting Nature: Denying Our Planetary Boundaries*, New York, 2011.

It is within this framework of analysis that Pope Francis warns about the risks of a false or superficial ecology which promotes a certain degree of complacency with the present situation and of evasiveness that serves as a license to continue present lifestyles and models of production and consumption. According to Pope Francis, this is how humanity feeds its self-destructive vices: "trying not to see them, trying not to acknowledge them, delaying the important decisions and pretending that nothing will happen". The solution suggested by Pope Francis to overcome the weakness of the international response consists in the establishment of an appropriate legal framework that will promote and support the shifts needed in the ecological culture mentioned above. Such a legal framework should allow us to set clear boundaries and to ensure the protection of the ecosystems upon which life and human prosperity are based.

A good example of the urgent need to improve the institutional and legal response is represented by the climate change issue. As mentioned above, the Encyclical Letter recognises a need to develop adequate policies coupled with a decisive change in lifestyle and the abandonment of the "current models of production and consumption". Pope Francis more recently commented in a cautious way on the Agreement on climate change adopted in December 2015 in Paris. The Pope, rather than adding his voice to those simplistically celebrating the outcome of the Paris summit as "historic",[10] in the immediate aftermath of the conclusion of the Conference affirmed that "[t]he climate conference has just ended in Paris with the adoption of an agreement, which many are defining as historic".[11] The careful choice of words would seem to indicate that Pope Francis intends to postpone his opinion on the Paris Agreement, while urging "the entire international community to continue with solicitude the path taken, in a sign of solidarity that will become more and more active".[12]

The third main tipping point which, in our opinion, may be detected and should be highlighted, is directly related to the critique of the technocratic paradigm and the proposal of a paradigm shift. It consists in the necessity of reassessing and re-defining the respective rights and duties of the most relevant actors involved: the State, the business community, and the population.

As regards the State, Pope Francis notes that, within the present globalised world, individual States have somehow failed to fully exercise their regulatory powers with respect to environmental protection. In fact, in the contemporary world "it is the case that some economic sectors exercise more power than States

---

[10] See UNFCCC, "Historic Paris Agreement on Climate Change: 195 Nations Set Path to Keep Temperature Rise Well Below 2 Degrees Celsius", available at: <http://newsroom.unfccc.int/unfccc-newsroom/finale-cop21>.

[11] POPE FRANCIS, *Angelus*, Saint Peter's Square, 13 December 2015, available at: <https://w2.vatican.va/content/francesco/en/angelus/2015/documents/papa-francesco_angelus_20151213.html>.

[12] Ibid.

themselves". Pope Francis highlights the pivotal role that States should play, calling for a renewed responsibility of individual States for "planning, coordination, oversight and enforcement within their respective borders" (para. 177). In particular, he stresses that each individual State, within its borders, has a responsibility to promote and implement national policies contributing to combating the global ecological crisis. The Encyclical Letter makes clear that States should also contribute to putting in place adequate political and institutional frameworks, not only aimed at preventing and avoiding bad practices, but also striving to develop and implement best practices to proactively address the ecological challenges.

With reference to the business community, Pope Francis warns that the immediate interest of the economy often overwhelms the general public interest. As a consequence, environmental protection is often limited to a "superficial rhetoric" and characterised by "sporadic acts", rather than by a comprehensive approach aimed at introducing an effective change. Although Pope Francis recognises the positive outcomes that business may bring for society as a whole, he notes that the dominant principle of the maximization of profits, if considered and applied in isolation from other competing interests, may lead to "a misunderstanding of the very concept of the economy" (para. 195). Within such a context, the economy is today dominated by multinationals, which often perform in an unsustainable way, mostly in developing countries. In particular, Pope Francis highlights that in some cases the environmental and social responsibility of economic actors may be reduced to mere marketing initiatives without any substantial contribution to environmental protection. Instead, the Encyclical Letter contains a strong call for the need to change the development model, going beyond the simple balancing of the protection of nature with financial gains, towards an ecological conversion.

As regards the population, they may be involved in the ecological conversion first of all as by enhancing the role of ecological citizens, that should promote environmentally sound behaviours and new patterns of consumption. In fact, the gravity of the present situation with regard to environmental degradation and the widespread ecological crisis challenges people to re-examine and reconsider their lifestyles. To this end, people should be promoters and actors of a decisive "change in lifestyle", which could exercise a certain pressure on the political, economic and social forces by enhancing the relevance of consumers social responsibility. Equally, the population should play a more relevant role within decision-making processes. The Encyclical Letter calls for a full involvement of the population in the assessment of the environmental impact of business activities and projects. Pope Francis highlights, in particular, the importance of the involvement of the local population, insofar they are directly concerned with their own land and can be in a position to better balance the competing interests at stake, not being overwhelmed by immediate economic interests.

In sum, Pope Francis, by calling to action the State, the business community, and the population, seems to promote in parallel both a top-down approach and a bottom-up perspective. The advocated paradigm shift, in fact, needs a set of comprehensive initiatives to be undertaken at different levels.

6. CONCLUSION

On the basis of what has been discussed, it emerges clearly from the Encyclical Letter that there is an urgent need for a change in the ecological culture, which should be based on a profound paradigm shift, inspired by Pope Francis' call for an integral ecology. Obviously, the required shift should not be performed abruptly or all at once. Should this occur, in fact, there would be a high risk of impairment of existing investments and of an overall negative interference with the development strategies of many countries. This could in turn endanger the stability of the economic and financial systems. Therefore, the required changes should be gradual. However, they should be conceived as inescapable progressive steps and should be framed within a clear long-term ecological sustainability approach.[13]

The patterns proposed in the Encyclical Letter should be coupled with the actions to be taken in order to implement the Sustainable Development Goals (SDGs) adopted by the United Nations General Assembly in September 2015.[14] The SDGs, in fact, despite their shortcomings,[15] are the main driver for the global development agenda up to 2030 and are meant to represent an unprecedented attempt to contribute to "transforming our world" towards a more sustainable future. However, such a transformative change will be possible only if underpinned by the deep ecological conversion advocated by Pope Francis, both at individual and societal level, with a view to promote and create a new alliance between humanity and the environment which should replace the present dominant "alliance between the economy and technology".

---

[13] On the concept of ecological sustainability see BOSSELMANN, *The Principle of Sustainability*, Aldershot, 2008, p. 53; MONTINI, "Revising International Environmental Law through the Paradigm of Ecological Sustainability", in LENZERINI and VRDOLJAK (eds.), *International Law for Common Goods. Normative Perspectives in Human Rights, Culture and Nature*, Oxford, 2014, p. 271 ff.

[14] Transforming Our World: The 2030 Agenda For Sustainable Development, UN Doc. A/RES/70/1 (2015).

[15] MONTINI and VOLPE, "Sustainable Development Goals: 'Much Ado About Nothing'?", Environmental Liability, 2015, p. 141 ff.

PRACTICE OF INTERNATIONAL COURTS
AND TRIBUNALS

THE JUDICIAL ACTIVITY OF THE INTERNATIONAL COURT OF JUSTICE IN 2015

DANIELE AMOROSO[*]

1. OVERVIEW

2015 was quite a busy year for the International Court of Justice (ICJ). In addition to holding public hearings in three cases,[1] the Court was able to deliver as many judgments (two on the merits and one on preliminary objections), which are – for different reasons – worthy of note. In particular, at the beginning of the year, the ICJ rendered the much awaited judgment in the case concerning the *Application of the Convention on the Prevention and Punishment of the Crime of Genocide (Croatia v. Serbia)*, where it dealt with several controversial issues including the *mens rea* requirement for genocide. In the judgment on preliminary objection in the case concerning the *Obligation to Negotiate Access to the Pacific Ocean (Bolivia v. Chile)*, on the other hand, the Court addressed (although not completely satisfactorily) the question relating to the characterization of an objection as non-exclusively preliminary. Finally, the judgment on the joined cases *Certain Activities carried out by Nicaragua in the Border Area (Costa Rica v. Nicaragua)* and *Construction of a Road in Costa Rica along the San Juan River (Nicaragua v. Costa Rica)* provided some interesting insights as to the customary regime on environmental impact assessment.

Moreover, the ICJ issued an order on the modification of provisional measures in the case on *Questions relating to the Seizure and Detention of Certain Documents and Data (Timor-Leste v. Australia)*, which ultimately led to the settlement of the dispute before it, and resumed the proceedings with regard to issue of reparation in the case concerning *Armed Activities on the Territory of the Congo (Democratic Republic of the Congo v. Uganda)*.

---

[*] Lecturer in International Law, University of Napoli "Federico II".

[1] Namely, the case concerning the *Obligation to Negotiate Access to the Pacific Ocean (Bolivia v. Chile)*; the joined cases *Certain Activities carried out by Nicaragua in the Border Area (Costa Rica v. Nicaragua)* and *Construction of a Road in Costa Rica along the San Juan River (Nicaragua v. Costa Rica)*; and the case on *Alleged Violations of Sovereign Rights and Maritime Spaces in the Caribbean Sea (Nicaragua v. Colombia)*.

2. GENOCIDE CASE "REVISITED": THE JUDGMENT IN THE CASE CONCERNING THE
   *APPLICATION OF THE CONVENTION ON THE PREVENTION AND PUNISHMENT OF
   THE CRIME OF GENOCIDE (CROATIA V. SERBIA)*

Some eight years after its judgment in the *Bosnian Genocide* case,[2] the ICJ returned to the issue of the application of the 1948 Convention for the Prevention and Punishment of the Crime of Genocide ("Genocide Convention") in the context of the break-up of the Socialist Federal Republic of Yugoslavia (SFRY). At the end of one of the longest proceedings in its history,[3] on 3 February 2015 the ICJ delivered the judgment on the merits in the (so-called)[4] *Croatian Genocide* case. As we will see, although the outcome of the case (dismissal of both claim and counter-claim) has been described as "entirely predictable",[5] the majority's approach to procedural and substantive issues did not fail to elicit a lively debate within and outside the Court.

2.1. *Jurisdiction and Admissibility Ratione Temporis*

As it is known, the Court was asked to rule on the mutual allegations of genocide by Croatia and Serbia (formerly Federal Republic of Yugoslavia – FRY), the former claiming that Serbia directly perpetrated, was accomplice in, or in any case failed to prevent and punish the acts of genocide which occurred, between 1991 and 1995, in a number of Croatian regions; the latter accusing in turn Croatia of having committed genocide in the context of the counter-offensive aimed at reconquering the Krajina region ("Operation Storm"). Preliminarily, however, it had to pronounce on Serbia's second objection on jurisdiction and admissibility, whose treatment had been postponed to the merits phase because, in the Court's opinion, it did not possess an exclusively preliminary character.[6]

Serbia's second objection basically revolved around the fact that most of the events relied on by the applicant State had occurred before the FRY (and, in some

---

[2] *Application of the Convention on the Prevention and Punishment of the Crime of Genocide (Bosnia and Herzegovina v. Serbia and Montenegro)*, Judgment of 26 February 2007, ICJ Reports, 2007, p. 43 ff. ("*Bosnian Genocide*").

[3] See, critically, the Dissenting Opinion of Judge Cançado Trindade, paras. 6-18.

[4] This caution is in order because the Court in fact found that the tragic events occurring during the Croatian Independence War did not amount to genocide.

[5] MILANOVIC, "On the Entirely Predictable Outcome of Croatia v. Serbia", *EJIL: Talk!*, 6 February 2015, available at: <http://www.ejiltalk.org/on-the-entirely-predictable-outcome-of-croatia-v-serbia/>.

[6] *Application of the Convention on the Prevention and Punishment of the Crime of Genocide (Croatia v. Serbia)*, Judgment of 18 November 2008, ICJ Reports, 2008, p. 412 ff., paras. 129-130.

cases, even Croatia) came into existence. Notably, it unfolded in three arguments, one concerning jurisdiction, two the admissibility of Croatia's claim.

As to jurisdiction, the respondent State observed that, since the provisions of the Genocide Convention (including the compromissory clause contained in Article IX) were not retroactive, they could not apply to events taking place before the FRY became a party to the Convention.[7] Croatia's reply to this objection was three-fold. First, it invoked "a presumption in favour of the retroactive effect of compromissory clauses" as well as the absence of any temporal limitation in Article IX of the Genocide Convention.[8] Second, it argued that, although most of the genocidal acts were carried out by SFRY armed forces and paramilitary groups before the FRY came into existence, they were nonetheless attributable to the latter by virtue of the customary principle codified by Article 10(2) of the Articles on the Responsibility of States for Internationally Wrongful Acts of the International Law Commission (ILC), for these forces could be characterized as "a movement [...] which succeed[ed] in establishing a new State", namely the FRY.[9] Third and finally, it maintained that, in any case, the FRY succeeded to the responsibility of the SFRY under the Genocide Convention.[10]

The Court analysed Croatia's counter-arguments in turn. In the first place, it dwelt upon the temporal scope of Article IX. At the outset, it ruled out that the latter could yield – *as a compromissory clause* – retroactive effects, and maintained that its scope was necessarily linked to that of the other provisions of the Genocide Convention.[11] Then, basing itself on textual and logical elements,[12] as well as on the drafting history of the Convention,[13] the Court reached the conclusion that, contrary to Croatia's contention, the provisions of the Genocide Convention (and thus also Article IX) were not retroactive.[14]

---

[7] Judgment of 3 February 2015, para. 79.

[8] *Ibid.*, para. 92.

[9] *Ibid.*, para. 82.

[10] *Ibid.* Serbia contested the admissibility of this argument, by arguing that Croatia introduced it for the first time at the oral phase (*ibid.*, para. 107). The Court, however, dismissed this objection in the light of the observation that Croatia's argument did not substantively changed the subject-matter of the dispute (*ibid.*, para. 109). For a critical appraisal of the majority's approach to this issue, see Declaration of Judge Xue, para. 7.

[11] Judgment of 3 February 2015, para. 93.

[12] The logical argument was employed, in particular, in order to exclude the retroactivity of the obligation to *prevent* genocide (*ibid.*, para. 95: "[t]he Court considers that a treaty obligation that requires a State to prevent something from happening cannot logically apply to events that occurred prior to the date on which that State became bound by that obligation; what has already happened cannot be prevented").

[13] *Ibid.*, para. 97.

[14] *Ibid.*, para. 100. The Court's reasoning on this point has been considered "not entirely persuasive" by AKHAVAN, "Balkanizing Jurisdiction: Reflections on Article IX of the Genocide Convention in *Croatia* v. *Serbia*", Leiden JIL, 2015, p. 893 ff., p. 895.

The argument based on Article 10(2) of the ILC Articles on State Responsibility was dismissed in the light of similar considerations. The Court observed that the rule of attribution set forth by Article 10(2), regardless of whether it actually corresponds to customary international law,[15] is not meant to introduce an exception to the *tempus regit actum* principle under Article 13 of the ILC Articles on State Responsibility.[16] Therefore, even assuming that the acts committed by SFRY armed forces and Serb paramilitary groups were attributable to Serbia, the fact remained that they took place at a time when the Genocide Convention was not binding upon the FRY (and thus Serbia).[17]

Yet, the Court found that it had jurisdiction under Article IX to the extent that the dispute at hand concerned Serbia's succession to the responsibility of the SFRY for acts of genocide. In this connection, it pointed out that the controversy before it, if framed in the terms of succession to responsibility, entailed the resolution of three, intertwined questions, namely: (1) whether the acts relied on by Croatia took place; and, if they did, whether they were contrary to the Convention; (2) if so, whether those acts were attributable to the SFRY at the time that they occurred and engaged its responsibility; and (3) if the responsibility of the SFRY had been engaged, whether the FRY succeeded to that responsibility.[18]

Each of these questions, in the Court's view, involved a dispute "relating to the interpretation, application, or fulfilment of the [...] Convention" and, in particular, "to the responsibility of a State for genocide", in line with the requirements of Article IX,[19] without implying, on the other hand, a retroactive application of the Genocide Convention (the SFRY was a party to the Convention when the relevant facts allegedly occurred).[20] This finding on jurisdiction, however, left untouched the issue of whether Serbia *actually* succeeded to the responsibility of the SFRY (as well as the more general question concerning the existence of a customary rule on State succession to responsibility). As the Court was eager to stress, these ques-

---

[15] The Court carefully avoided taking stance on this issue. For a negative view, see Separate Opinion of Judge *ad hoc* Kreća, para. 67.

[16] Judgment of 3 February 2015, para. 104.

[17] *Ibid.*, para. 105.

[18] *Ibid.*, para. 112.

[19] *Ibid.*, paras. 113-115.

[20] *Ibid.*, para. 113. According to the Court, the exercise of jurisdiction on alleged misconducts by the SFRY did not raise a problem of admissibility in the light of the "third-party" rule (also known as "Monetary Gold" principle), whereby the ICJ will not adjudicate on a case where it would be required, as a necessary prerequisite, to pass a judgment on the rights or responsibilities of a non-consenting third State (*Monetary Gold Removed from Rome in 1943 (Italy v. France, United Kingdom of Great Britain and Northern Ireland and United States of America)*, Judgment of 15 June 1954, ICJ Reports, 1954, p. 19 ff., p. 32). This is because "[t]hat rationale has no application to a State which no longer exists, as is the case with the SFRY" (Judgment of 3 February 2015, para. 116). This finding was criticized by Judge *ad hoc* Kreća (Separate Opinion of Judge *ad hoc*, paras. 81-83) as well as, although to a minor extent, by Judge Tomka (Separate Opinion of President Tomka, paras. 28-33).

tions belonged to the realm of the merits and were to be dealt with only once it was established that acts contrary to the Genocide Convention took place in Croatia and that they were attributable to the SFRY.[21]

As to admissibility, Serbia contended (i) that Croatia's claim was inadmissible as it was related to facts which happened before the FRY came into existence; and (ii) that, in any case, Croatia could not maintain a claim with regard to facts predating its accession to the Genocide Convention on 8 October 1991. The Court quickly disposed of both arguments. On the one hand, it observed that the first argument raised an issue of attribution which pertained to the merits. On the other hand, it noted that Croatia did not make discrete claims with regard to acts occurring before 8 October 1991, but made reference to a general pattern of violence occurring throughout the course of 1991, which constituted, as such, an element to be taken into account in order to establish whether acts of genocide had been carried out in Croatia between 1991 and 1995.[22]

The Court's ruling on jurisdiction and admissibility *ratione temporis* turned out to be divisive, as shown by the fact that only a majority of eleven out of seventeen judges voted in its favour. A first point of disagreement concerned the construction of Article IX, which some judges stigmatized as overly expansive. It was evidenced, in particular, that that provision does not cover "*any dispute* that concerns interpretation, application, and fulfilment of the Convention", but only those "between the Contracting Parties".[23] Furthermore, it was anything but foregone that the term "responsibility" employed by Article IX encompassed the concept of "succession to responsibility".[24] The compromissory clause under Article IX, therefore, would not have provided the ICJ with the power to adjudicate the (allegedly) genocidal acts committed by the SFRY, which at the time of the commencement of the proceedings "[was] no longer in existence and [was] no longer a Contracting Party".[25]

Even more controversial was the issue of succession to responsibility. Here we may discern three lines of criticism. First, the Court would have shown an excessive openness as to the possibility to ascertain the existence of a rule of general international law on State succession to responsibility, notwithstanding the complete lack of State practice in this matter.[26] Second, the majority would have obliterated the distinction between "successor State" and "continuator State", which would have offered a far more clear standard against which to assess the issue of succes-

---

[21] Judgment of 3 February 2015, para. 117.

[22] *Ibid.*, paras. 118-119.

[23] Separate Opinion of President Tomka, paras. 9-23; Declaration of Judge Xue, para. 20; and Separate Opinion of Judge Sebutinde, para. 15.

[24] Separate Opinion of President Tomka, para. 24; and Declaration of Judge Xue, para. 19.

[25] Separate Opinion of Judge Sebutinde, para. 15.

[26] Separate Opinion of Judge *ad hoc* Kreća, paras. 60-65; and Separate Opinion of Judge Owada, paras. 17-21.

sion to responsibility.[27] Third, the Court would have artificially subverted the logical order of the questions with a view to finding that it had jurisdiction to entertain the merits of Croatia's claim, while avoiding taking a clear stance on the delicate issue of State succession to responsibility. The latter point was put forth with particular strength by Judge *ad hoc* Kreća:

> "The applied methodology cannot be denied a certain judicial elegance which served, in fact, to sweep under the carpet the complex issue of the admissibility of the claim in relation to the facts that occurred prior to the date on which the FRY came into existence as a separate State, involving, in addition, questions of attribution, and to link it with the issue as to whether the principal claim and counter claim are founded in law and fact. Qualifying tacitly the issue of admissibility of the claim not as incidental to, but rather as coincident with, the principal claim, the majority reduced the fundamental issue of the jurisdiction of the Court to the level of a technical question, and the jurisdictional decision to some kind of accessory consequence of the decision as regards the principal claim and counter claim. In this way, the procedure as established by the law of the Court has been turned on its head".[28]

At a formal level, all these criticisms certainly hit the mark. The Court's finding on jurisdiction is basically grounded on the assumption – to be verified at a later moment (which never came) – that Serbia could succeed to the responsibility of the SFRY. But such an assumption could easily have been disproved, without going to the merits. As suggested by the minority, it would have sufficed to note that there is no such a thing as a customary regime on State succession to responsibility; that the only case where succession to responsibility can be established is with regard to the continuator State; and that Serbia (and, before it, the FRY) was never considered by the international community (including by Croatia)[29] as the continuator of the SFRY. Against this background, the Court's decision to examine the merits of Croatia's claims concerning the period prior to 27 April 1992 not only comes

---

[27] Notably, it has been maintained that only if Serbia had been considered the continuator of the SFRY (which it was not), would it have been possible to hold the former responsible for the breaches committed by the latter. See Separate Opinion of Judge Sebutinde, para. 13; Declaration of Judge Xue, para. 8; and Separate Opinion of Judge Skotnikov, para. 5.

[28] Separate Opinion of Judge *ad hoc* Kreća, para. 56. See also Separate Opinion of Judge Skotnikov, para. 3.

[29] According to some judges, this circumstance alone would have prevented Croatia from invoking Serbia's succession to the responsibility of the SFRY. See Declaration of Judge Xue, para. 15; and Separate Opinion of President Tomka, para. 25.

across as legally flawed, but is also difficult to reconcile with the principle of judicial economy.[30]

On the other hand, however, one should not underestimate that the ICJ was not merely invested with the task of settling a legal dispute between two States. Rather, it was asked to give an answer to the demand for truth and justice coming from the thousands of people who lost their loved ones or were victims of violence during the Croatian Independence War, as well as to help Croatia and Serbia to put those tragic events to rest and finally turn the page. The Court's unwillingness to dispose of (most of) Croatia's claims on purely jurisdictional grounds is therefore fully understandable.[31] Perhaps, the Court could have striven to make its reasoning more legally sound. In this respect, a convenient alternative was suggested by Judge Tomka in his Separate Opinion. According to the latter, although the Court did not have jurisdiction *ratione temporis* with regard to events occurred *before* 27 April 1992, it was not prevented from considering them with a view to ascertaining the genocidal character of the acts carried out *after* 27 April 1992.[32] Such an alternative appears all the more reasonable if we consider that, as seen above, a similar approach was followed by the majority with regard to the events taking place before Croatia's accession to the Genocide Convention.[33]

2.2. The Merits: Questions of General Character

Before considering the merits of the parties' respective claims and counterclaims, the Court lingered on some questions of a general character, concerning the applicable law, the definition of genocide, and the evidentiary standards to be adopted.

As to the applicable law, it is worth recalling the Court's analysis of the relationship between the Genocide Convention and international criminal law. In this

---

[30] In this respect, some judges also underscored the futility of the Court's decision to join Serbia's second objection to the merits. In fact, it is in no way clear how the "new elements" which the Court received during the lengthy merits phase helped it in settling the issues of jurisdiction and admissibility *ratione temporis*. After all, the Court crafted its reasoning so as to avoid addressing all the substantive aspects (both in fact and in law) of the doctrine of State succession to responsibility, namely the only reason which would have justified a joinder to the merits. See Separate Opinion of Judge Owada, para. 11; Separate Opinion of President Tomka, para. 4; and Separate Opinion of Judge Skotnikov, para. 1. On this issue, see *infra* the analysis of the Judgment on Preliminary Objection in the case concerning *The Obligation to Negotiate Access to the Pacific Ocean (Bolivia v. Chile)*.

[31] FOURNET, "The *Actus Reus* of Genocide in the *Croatia v. Serbia* Judgment: Between Legality and Acceptability", Leiden JIL, 2015, p. 915 ff., p. 916.

[32] Separate Opinion of President Tomka, para. 26.

[33] See *supra* note 22 and accompanying text.

respect, the ICJ drew a conceptual distinction which appeared, at first glance, very neat:

> "State responsibility and individual criminal responsibility are governed by different legal régimes and pursue different aims. The former concerns the consequences of the breach by a State of the obligations imposed upon it by international law, whereas the latter is concerned with the responsibility of an individual as established under the rules of international and domestic criminal law, and the resultant sanctions to be imposed upon that person".[34]

In the very next sentence, however, the Court somehow diluted the sharpness of this distinction, by underscoring the need to "take account, where appropriate, of the decisions of international criminal courts or tribunals, in particular those of the ICTY, as it did in 2007, in examining the constituent elements of genocide in the present case".[35]

As regards the definition of genocide, the Court largely relied on the views it expressed in the *Bosnian Genocide* case.[36] Nevertheless, since there was a disagreement between the parties as to certain aspects of the *mens rea*, it deemed it necessary to return on three definitional and methodological issues, namely (i) the meaning and scope of "destruction" of a group under Article II of the Genocide Convention; (ii) the meaning of destruction of a group "in part" under the same provision; and (iii) the way to demonstrate the existence of the genocidal intent. In relation to each question, Croatia urged the Court to slightly revise the stance it took in 2007 in favour of a more liberal approach. First, it recommended that the "intent to destroy a group" should not be construed literally, as a physical destruction, being sufficient the intent to prevent the group from functioning as a unit. Second, it invited the Court to downplay, in the assessment of the "substantiality" of the part of the targeted group, the numerical criterion, by giving more weight to other factors such as the geographical location of the group and the opportunities presented to the perpetrators to destroy it. Third, it asked the ICJ to abandon the test it adopted in 2007 to infer the *mens rea* of genocide from a pattern of conduct

---

[34] Judgment of 3 February 2015, para. 129. The Court expressed a similar view with regard to the relationship between the Convention and international humanitarian law (*ibid.*, paras. 151-153). In particular, it observed that, although it had not jurisdiction "on breaches of obligations under international humanitarian law [...] the rules of international humanitarian law might be relevant in order to decide whether the acts alleged by the Parties constitute genocide within the meaning of Article II of the Convention" (*ibid.*, para. 153).

[35] *Ibid.*, para. 129.

[36] In this respect, the Court explained that the 2007 Judgment would have been taken into account "to the extent necessary for its legal reasoning", but that this would not have prevented it "from elaborating upon this jurisprudence, in light of the arguments of the Parties in the present case" (*ibid.*, para. 125).

(viz., that the pattern at hand is "such that it could only point to the existence of such intent")[37] and to endorse the test worked out by the International Criminal Tribunal for the former Yugoslavia (ICTY) in the *Tolimir* case, whereby the existence of the intent to destroy should be "the only reasonable [inference] available on the evidence".[38]

The Court declined to follow up Croatia's suggestions. In the first place, it reaffirmed – also in the light of the *travaux préparatoires* of the Genocide Convention – that the "intent to destroy" must concern the physical, not the cultural, existence of the group.[39] It also reiterated its view whereby the numerical criterion remains "critical" in evaluating the "substantiality" of the part of the group, while acknowledging that qualitative factors (namely "the geographic location and the prominence of the allegedly targeted group") may also be taken into account.[40] Finally, it observed that, despite some differences in terminology, the "only reasonable inference" test applied by the ICTY "is in substance identical" with (and certainly not less stringent than) that laid down in the 2007 Judgment.[41]

The last part of this introductive analysis was devoted to evidentiary issues. In this regard, the most interesting observations were made in relation to (i) the applicable standard of proof, and (ii) the probative value of some of the evidence produced by the parties.[42] The discussion of the standard of proof was rather concise. Indeed, the Court limited itself to reiterating the view – already expressed in 2007[43] – whereby, given "the exceptional gravity" of the charges made by the parties, it would consider a fact to be proven only if it was supported "by evidence that is fully conclusive".[44]

---

[37] *Bosnian Genocide, cit. supra* note 2, para. 373.

[38] Trial Chamber II, *Prosecutor v. Zdravko Tolimir*, Case No. IT-05-88/2-T, Judgment of 12 December 2012, para. 745.

[39] Judgment of 3 February 2015, para. 136. For a critical appraisal of this finding, see BERSTER, "The Alleged Non-Existence of Cultural Genocide: A Response to the *Croatia v. Serbia* Judgment", JICJ, 2015, p. 677 ff.

[40] Judgment of 3 February 2015, para. 142. As noted by Judge Bhandari, this represents a slight – but welcome – move from the 2007 precedent "in favour of a more equal balancing effort" between quantitative and qualitative elements. See Separate Opinion of Judge Bhandari, para. 11.

[41] Judgment of 3 February 2015, para. 148. This conclusion was strongly criticized by Judge Bhandari in his Separate Opinion (paras. 15-23).

[42] For a more comprehensive analysis of the evidentiary issues dealt with in the present Judgment, see GATTINI and CORTESI, "Some New Evidence on the ICJ's Treatment of Evidence: The Second Genocide Case", Leiden JIL, 2015, p. 899 ff.

[43] *Bosnian Genocide, cit. supra* note 2, para. 209.

[44] Judgment of 3 February 2015, para. 178 (quoting *Corfu Channel (United Kingdom of Great Britain and Northern Ireland v. Albania)*, Judgment of 9 April 1949, ICJ Reports, 1949, p. 4 ff., p. 17). For a sharp criticism of the majority's reliance on the *Corfu Channel* precedent, see Separate Opinion of Judge Gaja, para. 4. See also TZENG, "Proving Genocide: The High Standards of the International Court of Justice", Yale JIL, 2015, p. 419 ff., p. 421.

As to the second aspect, the ICJ focused on two methodological issues, which were controversial between the parties. First, it dwelled on the inferences to be drawn from the ICTY Prosecutor's decisions not to include a charge of genocide in an indictment. Although the Court had already pronounced on this question in 2007, when it deemed these decisions as "significant",[45] in the present case Croatia urged a reconsideration of the issue in the light of the circumstance that the Prosecutor's decision not to indict a defendant for genocide could be dictated by factors unrelated to the actual occurrence of that crime, such as for instance the will to avoid a lengthy and expensive proceedings.[46] The Court rejected Croatia's arguments on the basis of the following observation:

> "The persons charged by the Prosecutor included very senior members of the political and military leadership of the principal participants in the hostilities which took place in Croatia between 1991 and 1995. The charges brought against them included, in many cases, allegations about the overall strategy adopted by the leadership in question and about the existence of a joint criminal enterprise. In that context, the fact that charges of genocide were not included in any of the indictments is of greater significance than would have been the case had the defendants occupied much lower positions in the chain of command".[47]

The second issue concerned the admissibility of out-of-court statements made by people who were not subsequently called to give oral testimony. Also in this respect, the Court upheld its previous case law, by clarifying that, in order to be taken into account, these statements must be signed or, if unsigned, must be at least confirmed by supplementary signed statements.[48] In the light of this assumption, the ICJ found that many of the statements produced by Croatia were "deficient" and thus bereft of any evidentiary weight.[49]

Later in the judgment,[50] the Court dealt with a further question of evidence, which is appropriate to analyze here for consistency of exposition, namely whether the findings of a unanimous Trial Chamber of the ICTY should be accorded some probative value when they are reversed in appeal only by a majority vote.[51]

---

[45] *Bosnian Genocide, cit. supra* note 2, para. 217.

[46] Judgment of 3 February 2015, para. 185.

[47] *Ibid.*, para. 187. This conclusion was strongly contested by Judge Sebutinde in her Separate Opinion (paras. 16-21). In a similar vein, see also Separate Opinion of Judge Bhandari, paras. 51-53; and Dissenting Opinion of Judge Cançado Trindade, paras. 505-506.

[48] Judgment of 3 February 2015, para. 198.

[49] *Ibid.* For a more in-depth discussion of this issue, see Declaration of Judge Donoghue.

[50] Judgment of 3 February 2015, paras. 464-475.

[51] Notably, this question arose in relation to the conflicting judgments handed down, respectively, by the Trial Chamber I and the Appeals Chamber in the *Gotovina* case (Trial Chamber II,

According to Serbia, there was no reason to give more weight to the findings of the Appeals Chamber, since the main difference between the two benches would not lie in the "greater experience or authority" of the appellate judges, but only in their number (five instead of three).[52] The Court was not persuaded by this reasoning. In its view, whatever "the manner in which the members of the Appeals Chamber are chosen" the fact remains that its judgments "represent the last word of the ICTY on the cases before it".[53] Accordingly, in case of disagreement between Trial Chamber and Appeal Chamber, the ICJ "is bound to accord greater weight" to the latter's findings, "while ultimately retaining the power to decide the issues before it on the facts and the law".[54]

Underlying the Court's reasoning on most (if not all) of the aforementioned points is the issue concerning the relationship between State responsibility and individual criminal responsibility for genocide.[55] This question was pivotal in the case at hand because, unlike in 2007, no conviction for genocide had been handed down by the ICTY in relation to the facts alleged by the parties.[56] As we have just seen, the Court repeatedly vindicated, in the clearest terms, the autonomy of the regime governing State responsibility,[57] as well as its own liberty to depart from the findings made by the ICTY. In fact, it remained well anchored to the international criminal law's understanding of genocide (and, relatedly, to the jurisprudence of the ICTY).[58] In this respect, the adoption of extremely high, criminal-like standard of proof is quite revealing. Indeed, if the proclaimed autonomy between the two regimes is to mean something, that is precisely with regard to evidentiary standards which, in cases concerning State responsibility for genocide, should be less

---

Prosecutor v. Ante Gotovina, Ivan Čermac and Mladen Markač, Case No. IT-06-90-A, Judgment of 15 April 2011; and Appeals Chamber, *Prosecutor v. Ante Gotovina and Mladen Markač*, Case No. IT-06-90-A, Judgment of 16 November 2012).

[52] Judgment of 3 February 2015, para. 470.

[53] *Ibid.*, para. 471.

[54] *Ibid.*

[55] On this issue, see BUFALINI, "La responsabilità internazionale dello Stato per atti di genocidio: un regime in cerca di autonomia", DUDI, 2015, p. 571 ff. For a general appraisal on the interplay between State and individual responsibility in relation to international crimes, see BONAFÉ, *The Relationship between State and Individual Responsibility for International Crimes*, Leiden/Boston, 2009.

[56] BONAFÉ, "Responsabilità dello Stato e dell'individuo per crimine di genocidio: persistenti incertezze nella giurisprudenza della Corte internazionale di giustizia", *SIDIBlog*, 20 February 2015, available at: <http://www.sidi-isil.org/sidiblog/?p=1344>.

[57] For a criticism on this distinction, see GATTINI, "Evidentiary Issues in the ICJ's *Genocide* Judgment", JICJ, 2007, p. 889 ff., p. 894.

[58] In relation to the *Gotovina* judgment (*cit. supra* note 51), for instance, the Court stated that it "would only be in exceptional circumstances that it would depart from the findings reached by the ICTY". See Judgment of 3 February 2015, para. 472. On the Court's excessive deference to the ICTY, see GATTINI and CORTESI, *cit. supra* note 42, p. 911. For a contrary view, however, see Separate Opinion of Judge Skotnikov, para. 14.

stringent than those applied in the context of a criminal proceedings.[59] After all, the need to shield the reputation of a State from a "charge of exceptional gravity" is far less pressing than that to avoid a deprivation of personal liberty on the basis of a groundless conviction.[60]

2.3. The Merits: Claim and Counter-Claim

The examination of the merits of both claim and counter-claim was two-pronged. In the first place, the Court verified whether, in the light of the evidence produced by the parties, the material conducts ascribed, respectively, to Serbia and Croatia fell within one (or more) of the categories listed by Article II of the Genocide Convention (*actus reus*).[61] In the case it was so established, it then assessed whether those conducts were carried out with the intent to destroy, in whole or in part, a protected group (*mens rea*).[62]

As mentioned above, Croatia's claim concerned a large series of violent incidents which had allegedly taken place, between 1991 and 1995, in six localities (Eastern Slavonia, Western Slavonia, Banovina/Banija, Kordun, Lika, and Dalmatia). Faced with a very high number of allegations, the Court refrained from examining them in detail, but chose to focus only on those episodes from which, in the Applicant's view, it was possible to infer Serbia's genocidal intent.[63] It thus found the *actus reus* proven in relation to the conducts proscribed by Article II(a) ("Killing members of the group")[64] and (b) ("Causing serious bodily or mental harm to members of the group"),[65] but not with regard to those envisaged by Article II(c) ("Deliberately inflicting on the group conditions of life calculated to bring about its physical destruction in whole or in part")[66] and (d) ("Imposing measures intended to prevent births within the group").[67]

This part of the Judgment is eminently devoted to questions of fact and will not be examined in particular depth. Only two points deserve to be briefly addressed

---

[59] Separate Opinion of Judge Gaja, para. 4. See also Dissenting Opinion of Judge Cançado Trindade, paras. 122-124, 467-471.

[60] In this sense, BUFALINI, *cit. supra* note 55, p. 583; TZENG, *cit. supra* note 44, pp. 420-421; BONAFÉ, *cit. supra* note 56; and LANDI, "Mens rea e responsabilità dello Stato per illecito di genocidio (ancora sulla sentenza della Corte internazionale di giustizia)", *SIDIBlog*, 12 May 2015, available at: <http://www.sidi-isil.org/sidiblog/?p= 1445>.

[61] Judgment of 3 February 2015, para. 201.

[62] *Ibid.*, para. 202.

[63] *Ibid.*, para. 203.

[64] *Ibid.*, para. 295.

[65] *Ibid.*, para. 360.

[66] *Ibid.*, para. 394.

[67] *Ibid.*, para. 400.

here, namely the issue of missing persons and the legal characterization of the acts of rape and sexual violence.

Regarding the first point, it should be noted that, although the Court ruled out that the psychological pain suffered by the relatives of missing persons amounted to a "serious [...] mental harm" under Article II(b),[68] it proved sensitive to their situation. Indeed, having noted that both Croatia and Serbia voiced their willingness to co-operate in order to shed light on the fate of the people who had disappeared during the civil war, it encouraged the parties "to pursue that co-operation in good faith and to utilize all means available to them in order that the issue of the fate of missing persons can be settled as quickly as possible".[69] As to the second point, the ICJ held that the acts of rape and sexual violence committed against Croat women, while causing a serious bodily or mental harm under the terms of Article II(b),[70] could not be qualified as deliberate infliction of conditions of life calculated to bring about the physical destruction of the targeted group (Article II(c)) nor as measures intended to prevent births within the group (Article II(d)) because they did not occur on a sufficient "scale" to achieve (or, at least, to threaten) the destruction of the group.[71] The Court's reliance on a "scale factor" was met with some criticism. It has been noted, in particular, that the introduction of an additional, objective requirement – which was not expressly envisaged by the Convention – would end up making it exceedingly difficult to demonstrate the commission of the *actus reus* of genocide, at least as far as acts of sexual violence are concerned.[72]

With regard to the *mens rea*, the main question before the Court was whether, in the absence of an express genocidal plan, the acts proved to have occurred between 1991 and 1995 "represented a pattern of conduct from which the only reasonable conclusion to be drawn is an intent on the part of the Serbian authorities to destroy 'in part' the protected group".[73] To support this conclusion, Croatia marshalled seventeen factors, which included both quantitative (e.g., the scale and systematic nature of the attacks, or the sheer number of Croat casualties not justified by military

---

[68] *Ibid.*, para. 356.

[69] *Ibid.*, para. 359. See also Separate Opinion of Judge Keith, paras. 35-36.

[70] Judgment of 3 February 2015, para. 360: "the Court considers it established that during the conflict in a number of localities in Eastern Slavonia, Western Slavonia, and Dalmatia, the JNA and Serb forces [...] perpetrated acts of [...] sexual violence and rape. These acts caused such bodily or mental harm as to contribute to the physical or biological destruction of the protected group".

[71] *Ibid.*, paras. 364 and 397.

[72] PECORELLA, "Rape and Sexual Violence in the ICJ's Judgment in *Croatia* v. *Serbia*", Leiden JIL, 2015, p. 945 ff., pp. 950-950. See also Dissenting Opinion of Judge Cançado Trindade, paras. 259-276 (making the case for the adoption by the ICJ of "a Gender Analysis"). The Court's attitude to construe genocide as a large-scale phenomenon will appear even clearer from its analysis of the *mens rea* element. See *infra* notes 87-90 and accompanying text.

[73] Judgment of 3 February 2015, para. 407.

necessity) and qualitative elements (e.g., the use of ethnically derogatory language by Serb soldiers, or the demonization of Croats by Serbian propaganda).[74] Of all these factors, however, the Court considered only those having quantitative character[75] and, on this basis, established the existence of a pattern of violent conduct against the Croat population.

It then passed to verify whether the only reasonable inference which could be drawn from such pattern of conduct was the intent to destroy the Croat group. The Court focused on the context in which those violent acts were committed[76] and the opportunity that Serb military and paramilitary forces had of destroying the Croat group.[77] In the light of this analysis, the ICJ contended that the existence of a genocidal intent was not the only reasonable inference to be drawn, since the violent conduct of Serb forces seemed more geared towards the ethnic cleansing of the regions under control[78] and the punishment of the vanquished enemy[79] than the destruction of (a part of) the Croat group. Before concluding on this point, the Court quickly added that no inference whatsoever could be drawn from the fact that, during the siege of Vukovar, the Serb paramilitary group known as "Arkan's Tigers" was instructed by one of its leader to take care not to kill Serbs (thus implying that only Croats were to be targeted). For, even supposing that the actions of Arkan's Tigers were attributable to Serbia, "[i]t is difficult to infer anything from one isolated instance".[80]

Having ruled out the existence of the *mens rea* (and thus the violation of the Genocide Convention), the ICJ found it unnecessary to consider whether acts occurring before 27 April 1992 were attributable to the SFRY, and whether Serbia succeeded to the responsibility of the latter.[81]

Turning to the counter-claim, the Court found the *actus reus* under Article II(a) and (b) to be established in relation to some of the facts alleged by Serbia, namely the attacks on columns of Serbs fleeing from Knin[82] and the summary executions, as well as the ill-treatment, of Serbs who had remained in the Krajina United Nations Protected Area.[83] As to the *mens rea* element, the discussion was mainly

---

[74] *Ibid.*, para. 408.

[75] *Ibid.*, para. 413. As Judge Bhandari pointed out, the majority "provide[d] no *ratio*" to explain why certain factors were less important than others (Separate Opinion of Judge Bhandari, paras. 47-48). For a more detailed analysis of Croatia's claim on this point, see Separate Opinion of Judge Keith, paras. 2-23. The Court's exclusive reliance on quantitative factors is indicative of its tendency to conceive of genocide as a "macro-phenomenon" (see *infra* notes 87-90 and accompanying text).

[76] Judgment of 3 February 2015, paras. 419-430.

[77] *Ibid.*, paras. 431-437.

[78] *Ibid.*, paras. 424-428 and 435.

[79] *Ibid.*, 429-430 and 436.

[80] *Ibid.*, para. 438.

[81] *Ibid.*, para. 442.

[82] *Ibid.*, para. 485.

[83] *Ibid.*, paras. 493 and 496.

centred on the transcript of the high-level meeting held on 31 July 1995 in Brioni in order to plan Operation Storm ("Brioni Transcript").[84] According to Serbia, indeed, on that occasion Croat leaders clearly expressed their willingness to destroy a substantial part of the Serb national group, i.e. the Serbs living in Krajina, as evidenced – among other things – by President Tudjman's declared intention "to inflict such blows that the Serbs will to all practical purposes *disappear*".[85] This argument was dismissed by the Court, which observed that the Brioni Transcript, taken as a whole, only indicated the military objective pursued by Croat leaders, namely to cause "the flight of the great majority of the Serb population of the Krajina", but did not provide "a sufficient basis [...] to make a finding of the existence of the specific intent which characterizes genocide".[86]

The majority's analysis of the *mens rea* requirement proved controversial. First, it has been critically observed that the ICJ tended to characterize genocide as a macro-phenomenon, namely as "a large scale event whose establishment can be divorced from the circumstances of individual perpetrators".[87] This would emerge, among other things, from the invocation of the existence of a wide-scale "pattern of conduct" as the only way to demonstrate the genocidal intent and from the downplaying, as isolated incidents, of the arguably genocidal acts carried out by the Arkan's Tigers during the siege of Vukovar.[88] In this way, the Court ended up turning "objective magnitude" from a circumstantial evidence of the *mens rea* to a veritable element of the concept of genocide – a hermeneutical operation which was anything but warranted by the text and purpose of the Genocide Convention.[89] Had the ICJ adopted an "individualized approach" (thus paying more attention to the individual perpetrator's personal reach), the argument goes, the ICJ would have perhaps ascertained that the violent conducts of the Arkan Tigers – regardless of their isolated nature – had been put in place with the required mental element.[90]

Secondly, as noted by Judge Bhandari, the majority would have conflated "the distinct legal concepts of *motive* and *intent*".[91] To be criticized, in particular,

---

[84] *Ibid.*, paras. 501-507.

[85] *Ibid.*, para. 502 (emphasis added).

[86] *Ibid.*, para. 505.

[87] BEHRENS, "Between Abstract Event and Individualized Crime: Genocidal Intent in the Case of Croatia", Leiden JIL, 2015, p. 923 ff., p. 925. A similar point was made by BONAFÉ, *cit. supra* note 56.

[88] On the genocidal character of the deliberate targeting of the members of a particular group "while excluding the members of other groups", see Trial Chamber I, *Prosecutor v. Jean-Paul Akayesu*, Case No. ICTR-96-4-T, Judgment of 2 September 1998, para. 523; and Trial Chamber III, *Prosecutor v. Laurent Semanza*, Case No. ICTR-97-20-T, Judgment of 15 May 2003, para. 429.

[89] BEHRENS, *cit. supra* note 87, pp. 926-929.

[90] Judgment of 3 February 2015, pp. 391-392. This would have left open, however, the distinct question concerning the attribution of those conduct to Serbia.

[91] Separate Opinion of Judge Bhandari, para. 50.

was the idea whereby the existence of the genocidal intent was not "the only reasonable inference" which could be drawn from the available evidence because both parties demonstrably pursued non-genocidal objectives, notably ethnic cleansing and enemies' punishment (Serbia) and the military defeat of the opponent (Croatia). It has been pointed out, indeed, that all these non-genocidal *motives* do not rule out, as such, the presence of specific genocidal *intent*, but may on the contrary coexist with it.[92] The Court, therefore, should not have contented itself with establishing the existence of these motives, but should have verified, in the light of the circumstances of the case, whether they "occupy such prominent place in the mind of the perpetrator[s]" to replace the *dolus specialis* of genocide.[93]

In the light of all these shortcomings, one may legitimately question – as Judge Skotnikov did in his Separate Opinion – whether the ICJ is "ill-equipped" to deal with the elements of the crime of genocide and, accordingly, whether it should substantively defer to international criminal tribunals (*in casu*, the ICTY).[94] In our view, these queries should be given a negative answer. In the first place, as seen above,[95] if State responsibility and individual criminal responsibility for genocide are conceived of as interrelated but *autonomous* regimes, such a judicial deference would be unwarranted. In any case, moreover, the alleged lack of institutional competence of the ICJ is more asserted than demonstrated. Indeed, both the Statute and the Rules "provide the Court with the tools to deal with questions of high factual complexity and to acquire all the information necessary to decide upon the allegations of the parties",[96] as shown by the length of the discovery phase in the case at hand.[97] Thirdly and finally, such deference would be hardly reconcilable with the ICJ's role as the "principal judicial organ of the United Nations".[98]

---

[92] BEHRENS, *cit. supra* note 87, pp. 932-933. See also Dissenting Opinion of Judge Cançado Trindade, para. 241; and STEINFELD, "When Ethnic Cleansing Is Not Genocide: A Critical Appraisal of the ICJ's Ruling in *Croatia* v. *Serbia* in relation to Deportation and Population Transfer", Leiden JIL, 2015, p. 937 ff., p. 941 (observing that the Court made ethnic cleansing become "a rather cruel 'trump card' that could be used as a comprehensive defence against any allegation [...] of genocide").

[93] BEHRENS, *cit. supra* note 87, p. 933.

[94] Separate Opinion of Judge Skotnikov, paras. 12-14.

[95] See *supra* notes 55-60 and accompanying text.

[96] HALINK, "All Things Considered: How the International Court of Justice Delegated Its Fact-Assessment to the United Nations in the *Armed Activities* Case", New York University Journal of International Law and Politics, 2008, p. 13 ff., p. 50.

[97] For an overview, see Judgment of 3 February 2015, paras. 17-48.

[98] Art. 92 of the Charter of the United Nations; and Art. 1 of the Statute of the International Court of Justice.

3. WHAT MAKES AN OBJECTION "NON-EXCLUSIVELY PRELIMINARY"? THE JUDGMENT ON PRELIMINARY OBJECTIONS IN THE CASE CONCERNING THE *OBLIGATION TO NEGOTIATE ACCESS TO THE PACIFIC OCEAN (BOLIVIA V. CHILE)*

When, in 1970, legal experts[99] and States were asked to suggest ways to improve the 1946 Rules of Court, one of the most recurring answers was that the provisions governing preliminary objections should have been amended with a view to ensuring that preliminary issues were settled "as soon as feasible" and to avoiding that the same questions be discussed "at both the preliminary stage and the stage of the merits".[100] Underlying this call for reform there was widespread criticism on the way the Court (mis-)used the discretion enjoyed under the 1946 Rules[101] in the *Barcelona Traction* case.[102] On that occasion the ICJ, after joining the preliminary objections to the merits and requiring the parties to plead their case fully, ended up disposing of the dispute on a purely preliminary ground – which was perceived of as an unnecessary waste of time.[103]

The Committee for the Revision of the Rules took account of these suggestions and crafted the relevant provision, Article 67(7) (now Article 79(9)), so as to circumscribe the Court's discretion in this respect. Notably, it removed the (unqualified) power to join the preliminary objections to the merits and replaced it with the possibility for the Court to declare that an objection does not possess "an exclusively preliminary character". While this new wording is plainly meant to limit the discretion of the Court (which is bound to dispose of an objection having

---

[99] This survey involved, in particular, former ICJ judges (including *ad hoc* judges) and lawyers who had pleaded before the ICJ in at least three cases.

[100] JIMÉNEZ DE ARÉCHAGA, "Amendments to the Rules of Procedure of the International Court of Justice", AJIL, 1973, p. 1 ff., pp. 1, 11-21.

[101] As it is well known, under Art. 62(5) of the 1946 Rules, the Court could uphold the objection, reject it or join it to the merits. In the absence of a clear indication as to the reasons for which a joinder should be decided, the ICJ felt at liberty to adopt such a measure whenever it considered that the interests of the good administration of justice so required. See THIRLWAY, *The Law and Procedure of the International Court of Justice: Fifty Years of Jurisprudence*, Oxford, 2013, Vol. I, p. 983; TOMUSCHAT, "Article 36", in ZIMMERMANN et al. (eds.), *The Statute of the International Court of Justice: A Commentary*, 2nd ed., Oxford, 2012, p. 633 ff., p. 706; and TALMON, "Article 43", in ZIMMERMANN et al. (eds.), *ibid.*, p. 1088 ff., p. 1167.

[102] *Barcelona Traction, Light and Power Company, Limited (Belgium v. Spain)*, Judgment of 24 July 1964, ICJ Reports, 1964, p. 6 ff.; and *Barcelona Traction, Light and Power Company, Limited (Belgium v. Spain)*, Judgment of 5 February 1970, ICJ Reports, 1970, p. 3 ff.

[103] THIRLWAY, *cit. supra* note 101, p. 982; and TALMON, *cit. supra* note 101, p. 1167. For a convincing defence of the ICJ's choice, however, see *Barcelona Traction, Light and Power Company, Limited (Belgium v. Spain)*, Judgment of 5 February 1970, *cit. supra* note 102, Separate Opinion of Judge Sir Gerald Fitzmaurice, p. 64 ff., pp. 110-112.

an "exclusively preliminary character" at the preliminary stage),[104] the question has remained open as to what makes an objection non-exclusively preliminary.[105]

The judgment on preliminary objection of 24 September 2015 in the case concerning the *Obligation to Negotiate Access to the Pacific Ocean (Bolivia v. Chile)* shows that the problem is still there. In this case, indeed, the main point of divergence between majority and minority was precisely whether Chile's jurisdictional objection could be characterized as "exclusively preliminary" for the purposes of Article 79(9) of the Rules. Furthermore, the minority itself proved divided on the reason why such an objection was non-exclusively preliminary.

The terms of the dispute may be summarized as follows. As it is known, Bolivia lost its coast as a consequence of the War of the Pacific (1879-1884), which opposed Bolivia and Peru, on the one side, to Chile, on the other side. The transfer of Bolivian coastal territory under Chilean sovereignty was formalized in 1904 with the Treaty of Peace and Friendship between the two countries ("1904 Peace Treaty"), which also governed some aspects of Bolivia's access to the sea (i.e. the right of commercial transit and that to establish customs agencies in Chilean ports). Since then, however, both States have made a number of declarations and undertaken diplomatic exchanges on the issue of Bolivian access to the Pacific Ocean. In Bolivia's view, these acts would have given rise to an obligation on Chile to negotiate an agreement aimed to grant Bolivia "a fully sovereign access" to the Pacific Ocean – an obligation which Chile would have breached by discontinuing ongoing negotiations on this matter. Accordingly, it instituted proceedings against Chile before the ICJ and grounded the jurisdiction of the Court on Article XXXI of the American Treaty on Pacific Settlement of 30 April 1948 ("Pact of Bogotá").

Chile filed a preliminary objection contesting the jurisdiction of the Court on the basis of Article VI of the Pact of Bogotá. This provision rules out the application of the dispute settlement procedures set forth in the Pact in relation to "matters already settled by arrangement between the parties [...] or which are governed by agreements or treaties in force on the date of the conclusion of the present Treaty". According to Chile, the case brought before the Court fell squarely within the scope of Article VI as the question concerning Bolivia's access to the Pacific Ocean had already been settled by the 1904 Peace Treaty, which was still in force at the time of the adoption of the Pact of Bogotá. It further argued that the applicant State's reliance on an (alleged) obligation to negotiate was only an artificial attempt to introduce a disguised request for a substantial revision of the 1904 Peace Treaty, since the outcome of the negotiations was already established: to obtain a sovereign access to the Pacific Ocean. Bolivia replied to this objection by asserting that the dispute at hand did not concern, as Chile erroneously maintained, its sovereignty

---

[104] THIRLWAY, *cit. supra* note 101, p. 984.

[105] For an accurate overview of ICJ's case law on this issue, see THIRLWAY, *cit. supra* note 101, pp. 980-994; and THIRLWAY, *The Law and Procedure of the International Court of Justice: Fifty Years of Jurisprudence*, Oxford, 2013, Vol. II, pp. 1816-1824.

on a certain portion of Pacific coast. The subject matter of the dispute, instead, was whether Chile had an obligation to negotiate in good faith Bolivia's sovereign access to the Ocean, an obligation which existed independently of the 1904 Peace Treaty.

Confronted with a different characterization of the dispute by the parties, the ICJ proceeded to determine, autonomously and in an objective manner, the subject matter of the controversy before it.[106] The Court observed, in particular, that nowhere in the Application did Bolivia ask for a judicial finding as to the legal status of the 1904 Peace Treaty, as it limited itself to invoking Chile's obligation to negotiate in good faith.[107] On the other hand, the circumstance that Bolivia's ultimate goal was to obtain a sovereign access to the Pacific Ocean would be immaterial because "a distinction must be drawn between that goal and the related but distinct dispute presented by the Application".[108] It then concluded that the case submitted to it only related to whether Chile was obliged to negotiate in good faith and, if so, whether it had breached this obligation.[109] Having so defined the subject matter of the dispute, it was all too easy for the Court to dismiss Chile's objection. Indeed, since the 1904 Peace Treaty does not make any reference to an obligation to negotiate Bolivia's sovereign access to the Pacific Ocean, the dispute at hand could not be said to have been settled or governed by it. Accordingly, Article VI of the Pact of Bogotá did not apply.[110]

Before concluding, the ICJ briefly dwelled on Bolivia's alternative argument whereby, had the Court accepted Chile's characterization of the dispute, the objection should have been dealt with at the merits phase because it was not exclusively preliminary. Although the rejection of Chile's thesis made this argument inevitably moot,[111] the Court was at pains to stress that the objection at issue had an exclusively preliminary character, in light of the fact "that it ha[d] all the facts necessary to rule on Chile's objection and that the question whether the matters in dispute [were] matters 'settled' or 'governed' by the 1904 Peace Treaty [could] be answered without determining the dispute, or elements thereof, on the merits".[112]

The approach followed by the majority has been stigmatized as "a triumph of form over substance" by Judge *ad hoc* Arbour, who emphasized that there is no point in distinguishing between Bolivia's ultimate goal (i.e. to put in question the 1904 Peace Treaty and obtain sovereign access to the Ocean) and the subject matter of the dispute before the Court (i.e. whether Chile is obliged to negotiate

---

[106] Judgment of 24 September 2015, para. 26.

[107] *Ibid.*, para. 31.

[108] *Ibid.*, para. 32.

[109] *Ibid.*, para. 34.

[110] *Ibid.*, para. 50.

[111] *Ibid.*, para. 52. Precisely for this reason, Judge Bennouna deemed that the analysis carried out by the Court on this point was "redundant and misconceived" (Declaration of Judge Bennouna, p. 2).

[112] Judgment of 24 September 2015, para. 53.

Bolivia's sovereign access to the Ocean).[113] As Judge Gaja explained in his dissenting opinion, "although the request put the stress on negotiations, these are only a means for enabling Bolivia to acquire a sovereign access to the sea"[114] – something not provided for by the 1904 Peace Treaty, which would be inevitably revised as a consequence of a judgment favourable to the applicant State.

Both dissenting judges, however, agreed that this would not necessarily have implied the application of Article VI of the Pact of Bogotá and, thus, the upholding of Chile's objection. On the contrary, they held that the Court should have declared that the objection did not possess an exclusively preliminary character and joined it to the merits[115] – a point which was also shared by Judge Cançado Trindade in his separate opinion.[116]

Judges Arbour and Cançado Trindade, in particular, argued that the application of Article VI to the case at hand depended ultimately on whether the alleged obligation to negotiate incumbent upon Chile was qualified as an obligation of result or of means – an issue which should have been resolved at the merits stage.[117] According to Judge Gaja, on the other hand, while it was true that the issue of Bolivia's sovereign access to the sea was settled by the 1904 Peace Treaty, it could not be ruled out that it "may [have] subsequently become unsettled" as a result of the conduct of the parties.[118] In fact, this is precisely the gist of Bolivia's case before the ICJ: after 1904 Chile would have behaved in a way suggesting the intention to reopen the question of Bolivia's access to the Pacific Ocean (which, in turn, would have given rise to an obligation to negotiate stemming from the principle of good faith). In assessing Chile's objection, therefore, the Court should have verified whether Chile's behaviour had "unsettled" the issue of Bolivia's access to the sea before the critical date of 30 April 1948 (entry into force of the Pact of Bogotá).[119] But this inquiry, Judge Gaja concluded, would have entailed a deep incursion into the merits of Bolivia's claim, hence the need for a joinder.[120]

There is much truth in the criticism coming from the minority. The distinction drawn by the Court between the goal pursued by Bolivia (viz. a sovereign access to the Pacific Ocean) and the subject matter of the dispute (viz. the existence of an obligation to negotiate) appears, at a closer inspection, fairly weak. Indeed, it does not take into account that, if the obligation incumbent upon Chile is qualified as one of result (as the formula "obligation to negotiate a sovereign access" seems to

---

[113] Dissenting Opinion of Judge *ad hoc* Arbour, para. 24.

[114] Dissenting Opinion of Judge Gaja, para. 1.

[115] Dissenting Opinion of Judge *ad hoc* Arbour, paras. 18-30; and Dissenting Opinion of Judge Gaja, para. 4.

[116] Separate Opinion of Judge Cançado Trindade, paras. 59-67.

[117] Dissenting Opinion of Judge *ad hoc* Arbour, para. 19; and Separate Opinion of Judge Cançado Trindade, para. 64.

[118] Dissenting Opinion of Judge Gaja, para. 3.

[119] *Ibid.*

[120] *Ibid.*, para. 4.

suggest), this ultimately means that "Chile has an obligation to cede sovereignty over part of its territory to Bolivia, on terms to be negotiated",[121] an outcome which would be facially incompatible with what established by the 1904 Peace Treaty.

But what led the minority to deem Chile's objection as "non-exclusively preliminary"? Here the argumentative paths of the minority judges split again. Notably, Judge *ad hoc* Arbour focused on the *impossibility* to adopt an adequately informed decision without fully hearing the case on the merits.[122] Judge Gaja, instead, underlined that Chile's objection raised issues which were "also part of the merits of the case", with the consequence that it would have been *improper* to deal with them at the preliminary stage.[123] Judge Cançado Trindade, finally, swayed between the two lines of considerations.[124]

According to a learned author, this "dichotomy" between "possibility" and "property" has been running through the whole ICJ's jurisprudence on the handling of preliminary objections.[125] In his view, underlying the Court's decision not to rule on an objection at the preliminary stage there are two distinct (but often intertwined) rationales: on the one hand, the awareness of not being able to rule correctly upon the objection "in the existing state of the case-file"; on the other hand, the unwillingness to "embark on the 'merits' in the context of a preliminary proceeding".[126] It is certainly not the place to analyze this issue in detail. One may note, however, that the two rationales (although equally rooted in ICJ's case law)[127] are not convincing in the same way. Notably, the idea whereby there is a category of questions which can be labelled as "merits" and which, *for this sole reason*, cannot be treated at the preliminary phase is fairly problematic. Once the Court has the *possibility* to decide on a given preliminary objection because it has before it all the relevant elements (in fact and in law), it is difficult to see why it should be *proper* to postpone its examination to the merits stage. Indeed, such a delay would be plainly in contrast with the principle of sound (and expeditious) administration

---

[121] Dissenting Opinion of Judge *ad hoc* Arbour, para. 25.

[122] *Ibid.*, paras. 18, 29-30.

[123] Dissenting Opinion of Judge Gaja, para. 4.

[124] Separate Opinion of Judge Cançado Trindade, para. 67: "May I conclude that the objection raised by Chile appears as a defence to Bolivia's claim as to the merits, inextricably interwoven with this latter. And the Court, anyway, does not count on all the necessary information to render a decision on it as a 'preliminary' issue".

[125] THIRLWAY, *cit. supra* note 101, p. 991.

[126] *Ibid.*, p. 992.

[127] See, among others, *Territorial and Maritime Dispute (Nicaragua v. Colombia)*, Judgment of 13 December 2007, ICJ Reports, 2007, p. 832 ff., para. 51: "In principle, a party raising preliminary objections is entitled to have these objections answered at the preliminary stage of the proceedings unless the Court does not have before it all facts necessary to decide the questions raised or if answering the preliminary objection would determine the dispute, or some elements thereof, on the merits". As we have seen above (notes 107-112 and accompanying text), the majority relied on both rationales to affirm that Chile's objection had an exclusively preliminary character.

of justice, which should inform every procedural decision of the ICJ, including those concerning the disposal of preliminary objections.[128]

It would therefore be advisable that, in the future, the ICJ returns to the topic and makes clear that the characterization of an objection as non-exclusively preliminary should not depend on some abstract notion of what is purely preliminary and what relates (also) to the merits, but on the practical consideration as to whether the Court has before it all the relevant elements to make a decision.[129] In this respect, both the judgment under comment and the individual opinions attached thereto undoubtedly represent a lost opportunity.

4. The Judgment in the Joined Cases *Certain Activities Carried Out by Nicaragua in the Border Area (Costa Rica v. Nicaragua)* and *Construction of a Road in Costa Rica along the San Juan River (Nicaragua v. Costa Rica)*

On 16 December 2015, the ICJ rendered its judgment on the merits in the joined cases *Certain Activities Carried out by Nicaragua in the Border Area* and *Construction of a Road in Costa Rica along the San Juan River*. Although both cases concerned the lawfulness of works "being carried out in, along, or in close proximity to the San Juan River" (a circumstance which ultimately justified the joinder),[130] the legal issues raised therein are basically different. For this reason, they will be dealt separately.

4.1. *The Case Concerning Certain Activities Carried Out by Nicaragua in the Border Area (Costa Rica v. Nicaragua): An Exhibition of Judicial Timidity*

Writing in 1961 about the contribution made by Hersch Lauterpacht as a judge of the ICJ, Sir Gerald Fitzmaurice sketched "the two main possible approaches to the task of a judge". On the one hand, there is the idea whereby "the primary, if not the sole duty of the judge [is] to decide the case in hand, with the minimum of verbiage necessary for this purpose"; on the other hand, we have the approach conceiving of the "proper function of the judge" not to be limited to settle the case at hand, but "to utilize those aspects of it which have a wider interest or connotation,

---

[128] On this point, see Separate Opinion of Judge Cançado Trindade, paras. 23-40.

[129] THIRLWAY, *cit. supra* note 101, pp. 993-994.

[130] *Certain Activities Carried Out by Nicaragua in the Border Area (Costa Rica v. Nicaragua)*, Order of 17 April 2013, ICJ Reports, 2013, p. 166 ff.; and *Construction of a Road in Costa Rica along the San Juan River (Nicaragua v. Costa Rica)*, Order of 17 April 2013, ICJ Reports, 2013, p. 184 ff. See AMOROSO, "The Judicial Activity of the International Court of Justice in 2013: Procedural Law Issues Before the ICJ", IYIL, 2013, p. 325 ff., pp. 341-343.

in order to make general pronouncements of law and principle that may enrich and develop the law".[131] The approach followed by the Court in the case concerning *Certain Activities Carried out by Nicaragua in the Border Area* best epitomizes the first strand of thought. Having been asked to rule on a number of important questions of procedure and substance, indeed, the Court disposed of the case on the narrowest grounds, by carefully avoiding ruling on the most controversial issues.

As the case title suggests, Costa Rica pleaded, on various grounds, the illegality of a series of activities carried out by Nicaragua since 2010 with the declared intent of improving the navigability of the San Juan River (and its effluents). In its first – and perhaps main – claim, Costa Rica argued that Nicaragua infringed its sovereignty by digging an artificial channel ("*caño*") within its national borders, as defined by the Treaty of Territorial Limits between Costa Rica and Nicaragua of 15 April 1858 ("the 1858 Treaty"), the arbitral award rendered by the (then) President of the United States of America, Grover Cleveland, on 22 March 1888 ("the Cleveland Award"), and the arbitral awards issued by Umpire Edward Porter Alexander between 1897 and 1900 on the basis of the 1896 Pacheco-Matus Convention on border demarcation ("the Alexander Awards").[132] The respondent State, on its part, contended that it was not creating *ex novo* an artificial channel, but was simply dredging an (already existing and naturally formed) effluent of the San Juan River in order to improve its navigability.[133]

The question concerning the artificial or natural character of the *caño*, as well as its navigability, was crucial to the territorial issue. The boundary line between the two countries in the disputed area, in fact, was defined in the first Alexander award by making reference to "the first channel met" by the waters of the Harbor Head Lagoon, namely – at least at that time – the northerly branch of the San Juan River ("lower San Juan River"), whose right bank was placed under Costa Rica's sovereignty.[134] In its second award, however, Umpire Alexander conceded that the banks of that river, as well as its channels, could have undergone "wholesale changes" and that these changes would inevitably have affected the boundary line, in a way to be determined "on a case-by-case basis in accordance with such principles of international law as may be applicable".[135] The third award made it clear that the "first channel met" formed the boundary on the assumption that it was

---

[131] FITZMAURICE, "Hersch Lauterpacht – The Scholar as Judge", BYIL, 1961, p. 1 ff., p. 1.

[132] Reference was made, in particular, to the first three awards, rendered by Umpire Alexander on 30 September 1897, 20 December 1897, and 22 March 1898.

[133] Judgment of 16 December 2015, para. 63.

[134] *First Award under the Convention between Costa Rica and Nicaragua of 8 April 1896 for the Demarcation of the Boundary between the Two Republics*, 30 September 1897, Reports of International Arbitral Awards, 2006, p. 215 ff., p. 220.

[135] *Second Award under the Convention between Costa Rica and Nicaragua of 8 April 1896 for the Demarcation of the Boundary between the Two Republics*, 20 December 1897, Reports of International Arbitral Awards, 2006, p. 223 ff., p. 224.

"navigable by ships and general-purpose boats".[136] This is because "throughout the [1858 Treaty] the river is treated and regarded as an outlet of commerce".[137]

By arguing that the *caño* at hand was natural (and navigable), therefore, Nicaragua was in fact contending that, following non-human induced changes, the boundary line in the disputed area would have moved from the lower San Juan River to the newly formed channel. As a consequence, its dredging activities would have occurred entirely within its territory.[138] Contrariwise, Costa Rica submitted that, since the *caño* was artificial, it did not alter the boundary line between the two countries, which was still the lower San Juan River.[139]

While admitting that "only an inspection on the ground could provide certainty regarding the *caño*",[140] Nicaragua tried to demonstrate the existence (and the navigability) of the channel before 2010 by relying on the following sources of evidence: (i) a satellite picture dating from 1961; (ii) a series of affidavits of Nicaraguan officers showing both the navigability of the *caño* and the effective exercise of sovereign powers in the dispute territory; and (iii) two maps of the National Geographic Institute of Costa Rica. The Court did not find this evidence persuasive. By way of premise, it stated that "an inspection would hardly be useful for reconstructing the situation prevailing before 2010".[141] It then observed that the aerial images provided by Nicaragua were not particularly helpful because of their "general lack of clarity".[142] As to the affidavits, it recalled that, as a general rule, the statements made by State officials for purposes of litigation are to be treated "with caution".[143] With specific regard to the argument based on the effective exercise of sovereign power, moreover, the Court maintained that, regardless of the probative value of the affidavits produced by Nicaragua, *effectivité* was "of limited significance" and could not impair "the title of sovereignty resulting from the 1858 Treaty and the Cleveland and Alexander Awards".[144] Also, the maps invoked by the respondent State did not straightforwardly support its claim and were "contradicted by several official maps of Nicaragua".[145] As an additional remark, the Court noted that the long-standing existence of a *navigable* channel in the location claimed by Nicaragua was disproved by the number of trees "of considerable size and age" lying at its bed before the start of the (allegedly) dredging activities in 2010, as well

---

[136] *Third Award under the Convention between Costa Rica and Nicaragua of 8 April 1896 for the Demarcation of the Boundary between the Two Republics*, 22 March 1898, p. 227 ff., p. 230

[137] *First Award, cit. supra* note 134, pp. 218-219.

[138] Judgment of 16 December 2015, para. 78.

[139] *Ibid.*, para. 77.

[140] *Ibid.*, para. 80.

[141] *Ibid.*, para. 81.

[142] *Ibid.*

[143] *Ibid.*, para. 83.

[144] *Ibid.*, para. 89.

[145] *Ibid.*, paras. 84-85.

as by the fact that, by mid-summer 2011, the channel was no longer connected to the lagoon.[146]

In light of the above, the Court concluded that there was not sufficient proof that the *caño* did form naturally and that, in any case, it could not be regarded as the navigable "outlet of commerce" envisaged by the 1858 Treaty.[147] Accordingly, it ruled that the *caño* was not part of the boundary between Nicaragua and Costa Rica; that the disputed area fell under the sovereignty of Costa Rica; and that Nicaragua's dredging activities violated the territorial sovereignty of Costa Rica, with the consequence that the latter was entitled to reparation for the damages suffered.[148]

The operative paragraph ascertaining Costa Rica's sovereignty over the disputed territory was approved with the contrary vote of Judge Gevorgian and Judge *ad hoc* Guillaume. While agreeing with the bulk of the majority's reasoning, both judges stressed that the Court was not originally asked to determine which State was sovereign on the disputed territory, but only whether Nicaragua's dredging activities amounted to a breach of Costa Rica's territorial sovereignty.[149] The request to establish Costa Rica's sovereignty on that area was formulated by the Applicant State only in its final pleadings, thus ending up transforming *"un contentieux de la responsabilité en un contentieux territorial"*.[150] Yet, the Court was unable to address this issue appropriately because the parties did not provide it with adequate information, as evidenced by the fact that the majority "deliberately refrained from establishing the geographical limits of the 'disputed territory'".[151] Costa Rica's request to ascertain its sovereignty over the area, hence, should have been declared inadmissible because it contained an entirely new claim.[152]

The second claim was strictly related to the first one. Indeed, since the dredging of the *caño* had been carried out by Nicaragua with the support of military personnel, Costa Rica denounced also the breach of the prohibition of the use of force under Article 2(4) of the UN Charter and Article 21 of the Charter of the Organization of American States ("OAS Charter"). The Court, however, declined to render a judgment on this claim on the ground that, since the unlawful character of Nicaragua's activities had already been established, the injury suffered by Costa Rica was "suf-

---

[146] *Ibid.*, para. 90.

[147] *Ibid.*

[148] *Ibid.*, paras. 92-93, as well as points 1 and 2 of the operative clause. The Court left the determination of the amount of compensation to the negotiations between the parties. However, it reserved its power to assess the question at the request of either parties, in case they will not reach an agreement within 12 months (*ibid.*, para. 142 and point 5(b) of the operative clause).

[149] Declaration of Judge Gevorgian, para. 3; and Declaration of Judge *ad hoc* Guillaume, para. 16.

[150] Declaration of Judge *ad hoc* Guillaume, para. 16.

[151] Declaration of Judge Gevorgian, para. 5.

[152] Declaration of Judge *ad hoc* Guillaume, para. 17, arguing that Nicaragua's acquiescence on this point was wholly immaterial as "[i]l incombait à la Cour de s'interroger proprio motu sur la recevabilité des nouvelles conclusions du Costa Rica".

ficiently addressed".[153] Such an elusive approach – which, as anticipated above, runs throughout the whole judgment – was severely criticized by Judges Yusuf and Robinson who described it as "rather inadequate and too economical",[154] as well as "somewhat summary, dismissive and indiscriminate".[155] Echoing the distinction set out at the outset of this sub-section, Vice-President Yusuf underscored that

> "As the principal judicial organ of the United Nations, the function of the Court is not only to 'decide in accordance with international law such disputes as are submitted to it', but also, in the exercise of such judicial functions, to contribute to the elucidation, interpretation and development of the rules and principles of international law".[156]

This should be all the more true "in relation to a claim that 'a cornerstone of the United Nations Charter' [viz., the prohibition on the use of force] has been removed".[157] Moreover, it should not be taken for granted that the finding that Nicaragua violated Costa Rica's territorial sovereignty "sufficiently addresses" also the claim concerning the use of force, as "the norms prohibiting the use of force and requiring respect for sovereignty and territorial integrity serve distinct functions".[158] Indeed, in the light of "the prolonged Nicaraguan presence on Costa Rican territory", the Court could have considered it appropriate, as suggested by Judge Robinson, to order Nicaragua to offer formal apologies as a form of satisfaction.[159]

In its third claim, Costa Rica contended that Nicaragua performed the dredging of the lower San Juan River in violation of the procedural and substantial obligations incumbent on it under international environmental law, namely (i) the customary law obligation to conduct an environmental impact assessment concerning activities that risk causing significant transboundary harm; (ii) the obligation to notify and consult, in case of risk of transboundary harm, with potentially affected States, (allegedly) set forth by Articles 3(2) and 5 of the 1971 Convention

---

[153] Judgment of 16 December 2015, para. 97, quoting *Land and Maritime Boundary between Cameroon and Nigeria (Cameroon v. Nigeria: Equatorial Guinea intervening)*, Judgment of 10 October 2002, ICJ Reports, 2002, p. 303 ff., para. 319. For a distinction between the two cases, however, see Separate Opinion of Judge Owada, para. 12.

[154] Declaration of Vice-President Yusuf, para. 2.

[155] Separate Opinion of Judge Robinson, para. 38. See also, although with a milder tone, Separate Opinion of Judge Owada, paras. 11-12; and Separate Opinion of Judge *ad hoc* Dugard, para. 3.

[156] Declaration of Vice-President Yusuf, para. 3.

[157] Separate Opinion of Judge Robinson, para. 38, quoting *Armed Activities on the Territory of the Congo (Democratic Republic of the Congo v. Uganda)*, Judgment of 19 December 2005, ICJ Reports, 2005, p. 168, para. 148.

[158] Separate Opinion of Judge Robinson, para. 39.

[159] *Ibid.*, para. 68.

on Wetlands of International Importance ("the Ramsar Convention") and Articles 13(g) and 33 of the Convention for the Conservation of Biodiversity and Protection of Priority Wildlife Areas in Central America; and (iii) the obligation to exercise due diligence to avoid causing significant transboundary harm provided by both the 1858 Treaty and customary international law. In relation to the latter claim, in particular, it was argued that Nicaragua's activities resulted in a significant diversion of water from the Colorado River (an effluent of the San Juan River flowing in the territory of Costa Rica).

The Court rejected all these claims. In the first place, it found that Nicaragua was not required to carry out an environmental impact assessment because the dredging programme planned in 2006 did not raise a risk of significant transboundary harm – a point that was confirmed by both parties' experts.[160] The absence of such a risk prompted the ICJ to rule out that Nicaragua was under an obligation to notify, and consult with, Costa Rica in relation to its dredging programme.[161] Finally, the Court considered – again on the basis of the reports of the parties' experts – that a causal link between Nicaragua's dredging programme and the reduction in flow complained of by Costa Rica was not established.[162]

The majority's discussion of environmental issues was supplemented by a number of separate opinions and declarations. Since they also relate to the main claim in the case concerning the *Construction of a Road in Costa Rica along the San Juan River*, their analysis will be postponed to the following sub-section.

In its final submissions to the ICJ, Costa Rica added two further claims. On the one hand, it complained of the infringement, in at least five instances, of its "perpetual rights of free navigation" of the San Juan River provided by the 1858 Treaty. The Court addressed this claim very briefly. Having noted that the occurrence of two of the five incidents invoked by Costa Rica was undisputed, it concluded that Nicaragua had violated the 1858 Treaty, deeming it unnecessary to examine the other episodes.[163]

On the other hand, Costa Rica asked the Court to declare that Nicaragua violated the Order on provisional measures of 8 March 2011. In this regard, it should be recalled that the 2011 Order required both parties to "refrain from sending to, or maintaining in the disputed territory [...] any personnel, whether civilian, police or security".[164] Nicaragua, however, not only kept up its excavation activities after the 2011 Order, by creating two additional *caños*, but also installed a military encampment in the disputed area. Since these facts had already been ascertained in the

---

[160] Judgment of 16 December 2015, para. 105.

[161] *Ibid.*, para. 108.

[162] *Ibid.*, para. 119. For a contrary view, see Separate Opinion of Judge *ad hoc* Dugard, paras. 21-45.

[163] Judgment of 16 December 2015, para. 136.

[164] *Certain Activities Carried Out by Nicaragua in the Border Area (Costa Rica v. Nicaragua)*, Order of 8 March, 2011, ICJ Reports, 2011, p. 6 ff., point 1 of the operative clause.

Order of 22 November 2013,[165] the respondent State did not contest them. Rather, it suggested that a finding on this point would have been superfluous, as the Court would have in any case pronounced on it by adjudging the violation of Costa Rica's territorial sovereignty.[166] The ICJ did not accept this view. In ruling that "Nicaragua acted in breach of its obligations under the 2011 Order by excavating the second and third *caños* and by establishing a military presence in the disputed territory", it clarified that this finding was independent of the conclusion "that the same conduct also constitutes a violation of the territorial sovereignty of Costa Rica".[167]

Since the breach of the 2011 Order had made it necessary to request the adoption of new provisional measures, Costa Rica asked the Court to condemn Nicaragua to bear the costs of the proceedings thereof. This request was dismissed. By displaying a blend of extreme laconicism and (again) judicial restraint, the ICJ limited itself to observing that "taking into account the overall circumstances of the case, an award of costs to Costa Rica [...] would not be appropriate".[168] Judges Tomka, Greenwood and Sebutinde, as well as Judge *ad hoc* Dugard voted against this decision by explaining their dissent in a joint declaration. The dissenting judges did not question that, under Article 64 of the Statute, the general rule whereby "each party shall bear its own costs" should be derogated only in exceptional circumstances.[169] However, they contended that these circumstances were certainly present in the case at hand whose features were unprecedented in the Court's history.[170] Here, indeed, the conduct in bad faith of one party forced the other one to sustain the costs of a further incidental proceedings. The consequences of the Court's decision not to uphold Costa Rica's request, therefore, were wholly illogical and inconsistent with the principle of the sound administration of justice. As the dissenting judges point-

---

[165] *Certain Activities Carried Out by Nicaragua in the Border Area (Costa Rica v. Nicaragua); Construction of a Road in Costa Rica along the San Juan River (Nicaragua v. Costa Rica)*, Order of 22 November 2013, ICJ Reports, 2013, p. 354 ff., paras. 45-46. See AMOROSO, *cit. supra* note 130, pp. 347-350.

[166] Judgment of 16 December 2015, para. 126.

[167] *Ibid.*, para. 129.

[168] *Ibid.*, para. 144. It should be acknowledged, however, that such a laconicism is perfectly in line with ICJ's previous case law on the issue. See *Application for Review of Judgement No. 158 of the United Nations Administrative Tribunal*, Advisory Opinion of 12 July 1973, ICJ Reports, 1973, p. 166 ff., para. 98, where it was stated: "Account must also be taken of the basic principle regarding the question of costs in contentious proceedings before international tribunals, to the effect that each party shall bear its own in the absence of a specific decision of the tribunal awarding costs [...]. An award of costs in derogation of this general principle, and imposing on one of the parties the obligation to reimburse expenses incurred by its adversary, requires not only an express decision, but also a statement of reasons in support. On the other hand, the decision merely to allow the general principle to apply does not necessarily require detailed reasoning, and may even be adopted by implication".

[169] Joint Declaration of Judges Tomka, Greenwood, Sebutinde and Judge *ad hoc* Dugard, para. 2, quoting approvingly ROSENNE, *The Law and Practice of the International Court 1920-2005*, 4th ed., Leiden/Boston, 2006, Vol. III, p. 1281.

[170] *Ibid.*, para. 8.

ed out, in this way the "party which has been the victim of a breach of provisional measures indicated by the Court is treated less favourably if it incurs expense in coming back to the Court to seek redress than if it takes unilateral action to remedy the damage caused by that breach".[171]

4.2. The Case Concerning the Construction of a Road in Costa Rica along the San Juan River (Nicaragua v. Costa Rica): Towards a Customary Regime on Environmental Impact Assessment

The case brought by Nicaragua was specular, in its structure, to the environmental claims put forth by Costa Rica. In its Application of 22 December 2011, indeed, it complained of the violation of both procedural and substantive obligations under international environmental law in connection to the construction of a road along the San Juan River. Similarly to its counterpart, in particular, it invoked (i) the obligation, envisaged by general international law, to conduct an environmental impact assessment (EIA) concerning activities that risk causing significant transboundary harm; (ii) the obligation to notify, and consult with, potentially affected States, in case of risk of transboundary harm; and (iii) the obligation not to cause significant transboundary harm, provided by both customary international law and the 1858 Treaty.

As regards the first issue, Costa Rica's objected that it was not obliged to prepare an EIA because the works at hand did not pose any serious risk of transboundary harm; alternatively, that it was exempted from this obligation because of the state of emergency created by the military activities carried out by Nicaragua; in any case, that it fulfilled its obligations under international law by conducting a number of environmental studies, including the "Environmental Diagnostic Assessment" in 2013.[172]

The Court was not persuaded by any of these arguments. In the first place, it maintained that, contrary to what was argued by Costa Rica, the scale of the project, the planned location of the road and the geographic condition of the river basin all indicated that the construction works along the San Juan River posed a risk of significant transboundary harm, so triggering the obligation to evaluate its environmental impact.[173]

---

[171] Ibid., para. 7. In this respect, the (pretty eccentric) stance taken by Judge Cançado Trindade should be briefly recalled. In his view, the Court should have determined ex officio the breach of the Order of 8 March 2011, without waiting "until the completion of the proceedings as to the merits" (Separate Opinion of Judge Cançado Trindade, para. 44). As a consequence, its decision not to award costs was not objectionable because "[a]fter all, the prolongation of the proceedings (as to provisional measures) was due to the hesitation of the Court itself", not to Nicaragua behaviour (ibid., para. 50).

[172] Judgment of 16 December 2015, paras. 147-149.

[173] Ibid., paras. 155-156.

In relation to the alleged existence of a state of emergency, the Court's reasoning was twofold. On the one hand, it rebutted Costa Rica's argument whereby, since international law contains a *renvoi* to domestic law as to the "specific content of the environmental impact assessment required in each case",[174] it would have been dispensed from carrying out such an assessment by virtue of the emergency exemption provided under its own law. It was indeed clarified that "this reference to domestic law does not relate to the question of whether an environmental impact assessment should be undertaken [at all]".[175] On the other hand, the ICJ observed that there was no emergency dispensing Costa Rica from evaluating the impact of the construction of the road. This was evidenced by the fact that the completion of the work would have required a long time; that, when the works started, the situation in the disputed territory was already before the Court; and that, because of its route, the road could constitute a response to the possible emergency "only to a limited extent".[176] Having ruled out the existence of a state of emergency, the Court did not find it necessary to decide whether customary international law provides for "an emergency exemption from the obligation to carry out an environmental impact assessment in cases where there is a risk of significant transboundary harm".[177]

Finally, the Court contended that the studies prepared by Costa Rica – which analysed, *ex post facto*, the adverse effects caused by the construction of the road – did not meet the standards required by international law. While reaffirming that "the obligation to carry out an environmental impact assessment is a continuous one, and that monitoring of the project's effects on the environment shall be undertaken, where necessary, throughout the life of the project", the Court underscored that an *ex ante* evaluation of the risk of significant transboundary harm must be conducted in any event, otherwise it would be impossible to evaluate the risk of *future* harm.[178]

In light of the foregoing, the Court concluded that Costa Rica had not complied with its obligation under general international law to perform an EIA.[179] Having established this, it decided not to examine Nicaragua's submission concerning the obligation to notify and consult.[180] While this passage does not stand out for its clarity, the Court seemed to argue that the obligation to notify, and consult with, the potentially affected State arises as a consequence of the performance of an EIA, when the latter confirms the existence of a risk of significant transboundary harm.

---

[174] In this sense, see *Pulp Mills on the River Uruguay (Argentina v. Uruguay)*, Judgment of 20 April 2010, ICJ Reports, 2010, p. 14 ff., para. 205.

[175] Judgment of 16 December 2015, para. 157.

[176] *Ibid.*, para. 158.

[177] *Ibid.*, para. 159.

[178] *Ibid.*, para. 161 (quoting *Pulp Mills*, *cit. supra* note 174, para. 205).

[179] *Ibid.*, para. 162.

[180] *Ibid.*, para. 168.

Since, the argument goes, such an assessment was not made in the case at hand, it was not possible to ascertain whether the obligation to notify and consult had been complied with.

Nicaragua's third claim, namely that the construction of the road caused significant transboundary harm (by increasing sediment concentration in the river and by affecting its morphology, water quality, and ecosystem), was not upheld by the Court.[181] Since the parties largely relied on the views of their appointed experts, the ICJ was called on – again, after the *Whaling* case – to appreciate their evidential value.[182] In performing this task, the ICJ adopted the following methodology. First, it gave particular weight to the fact that the opinion of one party's expert was not contested by the counterpart.[183] Second, in case of divergence, the Court tried to avoid taking sides, by verifying whether such a scientific discord could have any bearing on the legal appraisal of the claim. This happened with regard to the measurement of the total amount of sediment contributed by the road, on which there was "considerable disagreement" between the parties. Instead of adjudging which expert was right or wrong, the Court limited itself to noting that "the amount of sediment in the river due to the construction of the road represents *at most* 2 per cent of the river's total load" and that "significant harm cannot be inferred therefrom".[184] Third, the probative value of experts' statements was tested against the scientific evidence adduced in support of them. The assertion by Nicaragua's expert that sediment eroded from the road created "huge" deltas, for instance, was given no weight because it was completely unsubstantiated.[185]

The most intriguing feature of the judgment under comment is no doubt the discussion of the customary obligation to conduct on EIA. As it is known, the gradual emergence of this norm in international environmental law is eminently the product of a judicial lawmaking process.[186] In the case at hand, the Court

---

[181] *Ibid.*, para. 217. The issue was analysed in paras. 181-216.

[182] *Whaling in the Antarctic (Australia v. Japan: New Zealand intervening)*, Judgment of 31 March 2014, ICJ Reports, 2014, p. 226 ff. On this issue, see LIMA, "Weighing the Evidential Value of Expert Opinion: The *Whaling* Case", QIL, Zoom-in 14, 2015, p. 31 ff.

[183] This criterion was applied in relation to both cases. See Judgment of 16 December 2015, paras. 105, 119, 186, and 198. A similar approach was adopted in the *Whaling* case. See LIMA, *ibid.*, p. 37.

[184] Judgment of 16 December 2015, para. 186. Also on this point, see LIMA, *cit. supra* note 182, p. 38.

[185] Judgment of 16 December 2015, para. 206.

[186] The key steps of this process may be found in the individual opinions rendered by Judge Weeramantry in the *Nuclear Test II* and *Gabcikovo-Nagymaros* cases (*Request for an Examination of the Situation in Accordance with Paragraph 63 of the Court's Judgment of 20 December 1974 in the Nuclear Tests (New Zealand v. France) Case*, Order of 22 September 1995, Dissenting Opinion of Judge Weeramantry, ICJ Reports, 1995, p. 317 ff., pp. 344-345; and *Gabčíkovo-Nagymaros Project (Hungary v. Slovakia)*, Judgment of 25 September 1997, Separate Opinion of Vice-President Weeramantry, ICJ Reports 1997, p. 88 ff., pp. 111-113), the *Pulp Mills* Judgment

pushed this process another step forward, by expounding on the content of this obligation. While reiterating that international law would operate a *renvoi* to domestic law, the Court pinpointed, in the words of Judge Bhandari, "three cumulative stages that must be fulfilled when it comes to assessing the impact of a proposed project in a case of possible transboundary harm".[187] In the first place, a preliminary assessment has to be performed with a view to establishing whether the projected activity is potentially dangerous to the environment of other States. If this preliminary analysis shows that such a risk is actually present, *and only in that case*, States are required to conduct an EIA. The third stage is represented by the post-project assessment, namely the continuous monitoring of the environmental impact of the activities undertaken. This latter activity, as the Court was keen to clarify, should be kept distinct from (and could not in any case replace) the performance of an *ex ante* EIA.

In this connection, three remarks are in order. On the one hand, it is regrettable that the ICJ refrained from ruling on the existence of an emergency exemption to the obligation to conduct an EIA – a topical (and controversial) issue on which it would have been important to have clearer guidance. As we have seen above, such self-restraint is consistent with the overly-cautious attitude shown in other parts of the judgment. On the other hand, the Court's analysis of the obligation to notify and consult is not wholly persuasive. In this respect, the majority seemed to assume that such an obligation would arise only if an EIA is performed and shows the actual existence of a risk of transboundary harm. Yet, as one judge aptly noted, in some cases "input from a potentially affected State may be necessary in order for the State of origin to make a reliable assessment of the risk of transboundary environmental harm".[188] In this hypothesis, notification and consultation should be performed before the EIA is complete.[189]

At a more theoretical level, it is still unclear whether, in the Court's opinion, the obligation to perform an EIA should be regarded as a freestanding obligation under customary international law or as a specification of the due diligence principle. This point was dealt with in particular depth by Judge Donoghue. In her view, the current status of State practice and *opinio juris* does not warrant the conclusion whereby general international law would impose the detailed procedural and substantial prescriptions of the kind laid down by the judgment.[190] Rather, positive international law would only envisage a general principle oblig-

---

(*cit. supra* note 174, paras. 204-205), and the Advisory Opinion delivered by the International Tribunal for the Law of the Sea on 1 February 2011 (*Responsibilities and Obligations of States with respect to Activities in the Area*, Advisory Opinion of 1 February 2011, ITLOS Reports, 2011, p. 10 ff., paras. 141-150).

[187] Separate Opinion of Judge Bhandari, para. 31.

[188] Separate Opinion of Judge Donoghue, para. 21.

[189] *Ibid.*, para. 22.

[190] *Ibid.*, para. 13.

ing States to exercise due diligence, from which more specific prescriptions could be inferred, in the light of the circumstances, on a case-by-case basis.[191] A (radically) different point of view was put forth by Judge *ad hoc* Dugard. According to him, the conceptualization of "the due diligence obligation as the source of the obligation to perform an environmental impact assessment" paves the way for a dangerous "backward looking approach".[192] In fact, States would be allowed "to argue, retrospectively, that because no harm has been proved at the time of the legal proceedings, no duty of due diligence arose at the time the project was planned".[193]

This is certainly not the place to take a definitive stance on such a complex issue. One may note, however, that the position of Judge Donoghue, to the extent that it focuses on general principles of law, more accurately grasps the way judicial law making is actually performed in contemporary international law.[194] Moreover, reliance on the due diligence principle does not necessarily imply the "backward looking approach" stigmatized by Judge *ad hoc* Dugard. As underlined by Judge Donoghue,

> "In the planning phase, a failure to exercise due diligence to prevent significant transboundary environmental harm can engage the responsibility of the State of origin even in the absence of material damage to potentially affected States. [...] If, at a subsequent phase, the failure of the State of origin to exercise due diligence in the implementation of a project causes significant transboundary harm, the primary norm that is breached remains one of due diligence, but the reparations due to the affected State must also address the material damage caused to the affected State".[195]

In other words, the absence of a material damage would not preclude the ascertainment of a breach of the due diligence obligation, but would only affect the kind of the reparation to be accorded – an idea which is more consistent with the view, also endorsed by the International Law Commission, whereby "damage" does not represent an element of State responsibility.[196]

---

[191] *Ibid.*, paras. 10 and 24.

[192] Separate Opinion of Judge *ad hoc* Dugard, para. 10.

[193] *Ibid.*

[194] IOVANE, "La participation de la société civile à l'élaboration et à l'application du droit international de l'environnement", RGDIP, 2008, p. 465 ff., pp. 492-495.

[195] Separate Opinion of Judge Donoghue, para. 9.

[196] ILC, Articles on Responsibility of States for Internationally Wrongful Acts, 2001, Commentary on Art. 2, para. 9.

5. OTHER DECISIONS

5.1. The Orders of 22 April 2015 and 11 June 2015 in the case on Questions relating to the Seizure and Detention of Certain Documents and Data (Timor-Leste v. Australia)

The year under review saw the (amicable) end of the "hot" dispute between Timor-Leste and Australia, which concerned – as it is well-known – the forcible seizure, by Australian intelligence agents, of certain documents and data relating to a proceedings brought by Timor-Leste against Australia before the Permanent Court of Arbitration.[197]

Just over a year after the ICJ directed Australia, with the Order on provisional measures of 3 March 2014, to ensure that the content of these documents was not used "to the disadvantage of Timor-Leste" (first operative paragraph), as well as to "keep under seal the seized documents and electronic data [...] until further decision of the Court" (second operative paragraph),[198] the defendant State manifested its intention to return those materials. Accordingly, it asked for a modification of the 2014 Order under Article 76 of the Rules of Court, in order for the restitution of the documents and data to be authorized.[199]

Although this request was not objected to by Timor-Leste, the ICJ did nevertheless verify whether the conditions for a modification of the provisional measures under Article 76 were met. To this end, it applied the two-step approach ushered in the *Costa Rica v. Nicaragua* case.[200] Notably, it assessed (i) whether a change in the situation occurred and, in the affirmative case, (ii) whether this change was such as to justify a modification of the provisional measures. The Court considered both conditions to be present. On the one hand, it observed that Australia's shift in position on the return of the seized materials could be deemed as a change in the situation that prompted the adoption of the Order.[201] On the other hand, it noted

---

[197] For a summary of the facts of the case, see BETTAUER, "Case Report: Questions Relating to the Seizure and Detention of Certain Documents and Data (Timor-Leste v. Australia), Provisional Measures Order", AJIL, 2014, p. 763 ff., pp. 763-764.

[198] *Questions Relating to the Seizure and Detention of Certain Documents and Data (Timor-Leste v. Australia)*, Order of 3 March 2014, ICJ Reports, 2014, p. 147 ff. The Court also ordered Australia not to interfere "in any way in communication between Timor-Leste and its legal advisers" in connection with the dispute before the Permanent Court of Arbitration (third operative paragraph). See AMOROSO, "The Judicial Activity of the International Court of Justice in 2014", IYIL, 2014, p. 317 ff., pp. 321-328.

[199] Order of 22 April 2015, para. 7.

[200] *Certain Activities Carried Out by Nicaragua in the Border Area (Costa Rica v. Nicaragua)* and *Construction of a Road in Costa Rica along the San Juan River (Nicaragua v. Costa Rica)*, Order of 16 July 2013, ICJ Reports, 2013, p. 230 ff., paras. 23-29. That was the first time the Court was invested of a request for modification under Article 76. See AMOROSO, *cit. supra* note 130, pp. 343-346.

[201] Order of 22 April 2015, para. 14.

that, under the second operative paragraph of the 2014 Order, any operation on the sealed documents and data could have been effected only on the basis of a "further decision": hence the need for a modification of the previously adopted measure.[202]

In the light of the foregoing, the Court unanimously[203] (i) authorized the return "still sealed" of the documents at issue "under the supervision of a representative of Timor-Leste"; (ii) requested the parties to keep it informed as to whether and when the restitution took place; and (iii) decided that, upon the completion of the restitution procedures, the provisional measure under the second operative paragraph would have ceased to have effect.

The return was actually performed on 12 May 2015 and, on 2 June 2015, Timor-Leste notified its intention to discontinue the proceedings. In the absence of an objection by Australia, the Court, by an Order of 11 June 2015, removed the case from its docket. At first sight, this outcome could come across as a complete removal of any source of disagreement between the parties. It should be noted, however, that both Timor-Leste and Australia expressed pretty different positions as to the legal significance of the latter's decision to return the seized documents. In fact, while Timor-Leste characterized it as an "implicit recognition by Australia that its actions were in violation of Timor-Leste's sovereign rights",[204] Australia was keen to emphasize that it constituted just "an affirmation of [its] commitment to the peaceful settlement of the dispute in a constructive and positive manner to put it behind the Parties", by adding that "[n]o other implication should be drawn from [it]".[205]

5.2. The Order of 1 July 2015 in the Case Concerning Armed Activities on the Territory of the Congo (Democratic Republic of the Congo v. Uganda)

On 1 July 2015, some ten years after the merits judgment in the case concerning *Armed Activities in Congo* was handed down,[206] the Court resumed the proceedings with regard to the question of reparations, since the parties proved unable to reach a negotiated solution on this issue.[207] While the Order, being merely procedural, does not deserve to be commented upon, it is worth briefly recalling the Declaration appended by Judge Cançado Trindade. Although voting in favour of the order, the

---

[202] *Ibid.*, paras. 18-19.
[203] While voting in favour of the Order, Judge Cançado Trindade and Judge *ad hoc* Callinan appended, respectively, a Separate Opinion and a Declaration.
[204] Order of 11 June 2015, p. 3.
[205] *Ibid.*
[206] *Armed Activities on the Territory of the Congo (Democratic Republic of the Congo v. Uganda)*, Judgment of 19 December 2005, ICJ Reports, 2005, p. 168 ff.
[207] Order of 1 July 2015, para. 7.

Brazilian judge criticized the ICJ's decision not to fix, in 2005, a time limit to the negotiation between the parties.[208] In his opinion, indeed,

> "Reparations, in cases involving grave breaches of the International Law of Human Rights and of International Humanitarian Law, cannot simply be left over for 'negotiations' without time-limits between the States concerned, as contending parties. Reparations in such cases are to be resolved by the Court itself, within a reasonable time, bearing in mind not State susceptibilities, but rather the suffering of human beings, – the surviving victims, and their close relatives, – prolonged in time, and the need to alleviate it. The aforementioned breaches and prompt compliance with the duty of reparation for damages, are not be separated in time: they form an indissoluble whole".[209]

---

[208] Declaration of Judge Cançado Trindade, paras. 3-4.
[209] *Ibid.*, para. 7.

THE INTERNATIONAL TRIBUNAL FOR THE LAW OF THE SEA AND OTHER LAW OF THE SEA JURISDICTIONS (2015)

TULLIO TREVES[*]

1. INTRODUCTORY NOTES

1. 2015 has been an extraordinarily active year for disputes concerning the law of the sea.[1] The International Tribunal for the Law of the Sea (ITLOS or "the Tribunal") has handed out one advisory opinion and two provisional measures orders in the marine delimitation case between Ghana and Côte d'Ivoire,[2] and the *Enrica Lexie Incident* case between Italy and India.[3] Annex VII arbitration tribunals have handed out three awards on the *Chagos Marine Protected Area* case between Mauritius and the United Kingdom,[4] on the *Arctic Sunrise* case between the Netherlands and Russia,[5] and on the *South China Sea* case between the Philippines and China.[6]

---

[1] Previous instalments of the present work are: TREVES, "The International Tribunal for the Law of the Sea (1996-2000)", IYIL, 2000, p. 233 ff.; ID., "The International Tribunal for the Law of the Sea (2001)", IYIL, 2001, p. 165 ff.; ID., "The International Tribunal for the Law of the Sea (2002)", IYIL, 2002, p. 207 ff.; ID., "The International Tribunal for the Law of the Sea (2003)", IYIL, 2003, p. 157 ff.; ID., "The International Tribunal for the Law of the Sea (2004)", IYIL, 2004, p. 289 ff.; ID., "The International Tribunal for the Law of the Sea (2005)", IYIL, 2005, p. 255 ff.; ID., "The International Tribunal for the Law of the Sea and Other Law of the Sea Jurisdictions (2006)", IYIL, 2006, p. 227 ff.; ID., "The International Tribunal for the Law of the Sea and Other Law of the Sea Jurisdictions (2007)", IYIL, 2007, p. 175 ff.; ID., "The International Tribunal for the Law of the Sea and Other Law of the Sea Jurisdictions (2008-2009)", IYIL, 2009, p. 315 ff.; ID., "The International Tribunal for the Law of the Sea and Other Law of the Sea Jurisdictions (2010)", IYIL, 2010, p. 315 ff.; ID., "The International Tribunal for the Law of the Sea and Other Law of the Sea Jurisdictions (2011)", IYIL, 2011, p. 275 ff.; ID., "The International Tribunal for the Law of the Sea and Other Law of the Sea Jurisdictions (2012)", IYIL, 2012, p. 245 ff.; ID., "The International Tribunal for the Law of the Sea and Other Law of the Sea Jurisdictions (2013)", IYIL, 2013, p. 354 ff. ("TREVES, ITLOS 2013"); and ID., "The International Tribunal for the Law of the Sea and Other Law of the Sea Jurisdictions (2014)", IYIL, 2014, p. 341 ff. ("TREVES, ITLOS 2014").

[2] *Dispute Concerning Delimitation of the Maritime Boundary between Ghana and Côte d'Ivoire in the Atlantic Ocean (Ghana/Côte d'Ivoire)*, ITLOS Case No. 23, Order of 25 April 2015.

[3] *The "Enrica Lexie" Incident (Italy v. India)*, ITLOS Case No. 24, Order of 24 August 2015.

[4] PCA Arbitral Tribunal, *Chagos Marine Protected Area Arbitration (Mauritius v. United Kingdom)*, Award of 18 March 2015.

[5] PCA Arbitral Tribunal, *The Arctic Sunrise Arbitration (Netherlands v. Russia)*, Award of 14 August 2015.

[6] PCA Arbitral Tribunal, *The Republic of Philippines v. The People's Republic of China*, Award on Jurisdiction and Admissibility of 29 October 2015.

It is worth noting, although outside the scope of the present article, that, while the International Court of Justice (ICJ) did not issue any decisions concerning the law of the sea in 2015 – unless we classify as a law of the sea case *Obligation to Negotiate Access to the Pacific Ocean (Bolivia v. Chile)*[7] – various law of the sea cases are nonetheless presently pending before the Court: two cases brought by Nicaragua against Colombia, on which the decision on preliminary objections should be handed out in 2016, and the delimitation cases between Costa Rica and Nicaragua and between Somalia and Kenya. Before the ITLOS, the merits phase of the dispute between Ghana and Côte d'Ivoire is also pending before a Chamber, and the *Norstar* case, between Panama and Italy, was submitted on 17 December 2015 to the full Tribunal. Within the framework of the Permanent Court of Arbitration (PCA) three cases are presently pending: the merits phase of the arbitration between Philippine and China, for which hearings were held in November 2015, the *Duzgit Integrity Arbitration (Malta v. São Tomé and Príncipe)*, for which hearings are scheduled for February 2016, and the *Enrica Lexie Incident* case between Italy and India.

So, 2015 has seen two judgments on the merits, one judgment on jurisdiction, one advisory opinion and two provisional measures orders in this field. Nine cases are pending.

2. In all the cases brought to the ITLOS and to Annex VII arbitration, the plaintiff invoked the compulsory jurisdiction provisions of UNCLOS. The cases before the ICJ were brought invoking compulsory jurisdiction of the ICJ under the Pact of Bogotá (the two *Nicaragua v. Colombia* cases), or declarations under Article 36(2) of the ICJ Statute: *Costa Rica v. Nicaragua*, also invoking the Pact of Bogota, and *Somalia v. Kenya*, stating that jurisdiction is "underscored" by Article 282 of UNCLOS.

The fact that all the pending or decided cases before ITLOS and Annex VII Arbitration Tribunals have been brought to adjudication at the request of one party, shows that States are increasingly realizing the potential of the UNCLOS jurisdictional clauses. Even though compulsory adjudication under these jurisdictional clauses is not unrestrained, it remains true that compulsory jurisdiction clauses are binding for all 167 parties. There probably exists no other treaty binding so many parties which permits the unilateral triggering of adjudication.

Consequently, it is often the case that the only agreement providing for compulsory adjudication in force between two States in a dispute is UNCLOS. This causes the party submitting the case to shape its arguments in order to fit the jurisdictional requirements of the Convention even though there may be a dispute separating the parties broader than, or different from, the dispute which it is legally

---

[7] Judgment on Preliminary Objections of 24 September 2015. See the review by Amoroso, *supra* in this *Volume*, pp. 343-348.

possible to submit to a judge or arbitrator under UNCLOS. This was notably the case in *Philippines v. China*, in *Mauritius v. United Kingdom*, and in *Italy v. India*.

The Philippines and China have different views concerning sovereignty on islands and on the delimitation of maritime areas.[8] Questions of sovereignty are, nevertheless, not questions concerning the interpretation and application of UNCLOS and questions of delimitation have been excluded from the compulsory jurisdiction of courts and tribunals by a declaration made by China under Article 298(1). In order for an adjudicating body (an Annex VII arbitral tribunal) to examine this dispute and in light of the fact that UNCLOS was the only treaty binding the parties providing for compulsory adjudication, the Philippines shaped its request around these two difficulties and requested the Annex VII arbitral tribunal to declare that China's rights and obligations in the South China Sea are those set out in UNCLOS and not those deriving from a "nine-dash line" put forward by China, and to determine the legal nature of certain features (islands, low tide elevations or submerged banks) claimed by both China and the Philippines. These requests were further elaborated and modified during the proceedings, but the cautionary remarks set out in the Philippines' notification of claim of 22 January 2012 have not been withdrawn. In these remarks the Philippines stresses that it "does not seek in this arbitration a determination of which Party enjoys sovereignty over the islands claimed by both of them. Nor does it request a delimitation of any maritime boundaries".[9]

The Award on Jurisdiction of 29 October 2015 basically follows the Philippines and affirms jurisdiction on many of the latter's submissions, notwithstanding China's position that the "real" dispute between the parties was a sovereignty and a delimitation dispute.

In *Mauritius v. the United Kingdom*, Mauritius shaped one of the submissions in its application as concerning a question of interpretation of the term "coastal State" in UNCLOS, in order to support the conclusion that the United Kingdom, not being a "coastal State" of the Chagos Archipelago, was not entitled to proclaim a "marine protected area" in the archipelago. The United Kingdom objected that this was an indirect way to have the Tribunal make a statement as to sovereignty on the archipelago, which would be beyond its jurisdiction, as it would not concern the interpretation or application of UNCLOS. The Tribunal accepted the United Kingdom's position on this point. In light of the record of the discussions between the parties, it stated that the "real" dispute concerned sovereignty of the Chagos archipelago.[10]

In *Italy v. India*, while the parties agreed that there was a dispute, they did not agree as to whether the dispute concerned the interpretation or application of

---

[8] Award of 29 October 2015: "There is no question that there exists a dispute between the parties concerning land sovereignty over certain maritime features in the South China Sea" (para. 152).

[9] *Ibid.*, para. 26.

[10] Award of 18 March 2015, paras. 211-212.

UNCLOS. This will be the main subject of contention, as regards jurisdiction, of the proceedings on the merits once the case is examined by the Annex VII arbitral tribunal. All the ITLOS considered it fit to say, at the provisional measures phase, was that the Italian view that the dispute concerns a violation by India of certain provisions of UNCLOS was "plausible".[11]

3. With one exception (*Panama v. Italy*), all contentious cases unilaterally submitted to adjudication under UNCLOS have been submitted to an arbitration tribunal. This is the effect of Article 287 of UNCLOS which, through the well-known "Montreux formula", makes Annex VII Arbitration the default mechanism for the exercise of compulsory jurisdiction under the Convention. Annex VII arbitration is the competent adjudication mechanism whenever one or both parties have not made a declaration indicating either the ITLOS or the ICJ as the preferred adjudicating body. As a matter of fact, more than two thirds of the parties to UNCLOS have made no declaration and are consequently deemed, under Article 287(3) to have accepted arbitration under Annex VII. Since the entry into force of UNCLOS, disputes for which the applicant – because of the above mentioned constraint of Article 287 – has requested the constitution of an arbitral tribunal under Annex VII, have sometimes been transferred to the Tribunal or a chamber thereof by an agreement of the parties. This happened in the *M/V "Saiga"* case, in the *Swordfish* case, and, in different legal forms, in the *Delimitation of the Maritime Boundary between Bangladesh and Myanmar* case, in the *M/V "Virginia G"* case, and, in 2015, in the marine delimitation case between Ghana and Côte d'Ivoire.

2015 is notable because it seems to bring about a change, or perhaps to announce a change, in the pattern observed thus far. Three facts have to be observed in this connection. First, for the first time a case has been submitted to ITLOS on the basis of concomitant declarations of preference made by the parties under Article 287 (*Panama v. Italy*) without direct connection to a specific case, as was the situation in the *MV Louisa (St. Vincent and the Grenadines v. Spain)* case, and in the *Delimitation of the Maritime Boundary between Bangladesh and Myanmar* case. Second, for the first time a judge of the ICJ has been called to sit as an ad hoc judge in the ITLOS. Third, the previous practice of transferring to ITLOS or a chamber thereof, by agreement of the parties, cases in which Annex VII arbitration had been started by one party has been confirmed in the dispute between Ghana and Côte d'Ivoire.

The fact that ICJ Judge (and President) Abraham is serving as ad hoc judge in the ITLOS Special Chamber proceedings in *Ghana/Côte d'Ivoire* balances the fact that often ITLOS judges have served as ad hoc judges in the ICJ and shows that the

---

[11] Order of 24 August 2015, para. 85.

initial tension and competition between the ICJ and the Tribunal has subsided and has been replaced by cooperation.

While the transfer agreement concerning *Ghana/Côte d'Ivoire* confirms a previous practice, it seems, nevertheless, remarkable that in 2015 there were three occasions on which transfer agreements could have been made, but in fact to the cases remained with the Annex VII arbitral tribunal. These were the *Arctic Sunrise*, the *South China Sea*, and the *Enrica Lexie Incident* cases. The high political visibility of these cases probably made negotiations for transfer difficult or impossible.

4. The compulsory dispute-settlement provisions of UNCLOS have, however, met resistance, especially from the big powers. Such resistance is not limited to the fact that the USA has still not acceded to UNCLOS, and that among the reasons given by opponents to accession are indeed the dispute-settlement provisions. This is also due to the use of the optional exceptions declarations under Article 298 made by important countries such as Russia, China, and the Republic of Korea.

Big powers' resistance emerged more spectacularly in the decision of the Russian Federation not to accept arbitration and not to participate in the *Arctic Sunrise* case both in its provisional measures phase before ITLOS and its jurisdiction and merits phases before the Annex VII Arbitration Tribunal,[12] and in the previous decision of China not to accept the arbitration and not to participate in the Annex VII arbitration proceedings initiated by the Philippines against it.[13]

The decisions addressing this aspect take as a given the right of Russia and of China not to appear in the proceedings. Both ITLOS and the arbitral tribunals refer to the relevant provisions according to which non-appearance shall not constitute a bar to the proceedings and that the adjudicating body, before making its decision, "must satisfy itself not only that it has jurisdiction over the dispute but also that the claim is well founded in fact and law" (Article 28 ITLOS Statute, Article 9 annex VII).

The adjudicating bodies adopted procedures aimed at ensuring the equality of the parties, in particular by affording the absent party every possibility to enter the proceedings. Both the ITLOS and the Philippines-China arbitral tribunal underscored, however, that the absence of the defendant should not result in a disadvantage for the applicant party. It is interesting to note that neither in the *Arctic Sunrise* ITLOS provisional measures order nor in the Philippine-China judgment on jurisdiction, notwithstanding the presence both in ITLOS and in the arbitral tribunal of Judge Wolfrum, one finds any visible echo of the separate opinion signed by him (together with Judge Kelly) in the former case in which it was argued that:

---

[12] TREVES, ITLOS 2013, pp. 359-361.
[13] TREVES, ITLOS 2013, pp. 364-365; and TREVES, ITLOS 2014, pp. 362-363.

"In the case of States having consented to a dispute settlement system in general such as the Netherlands and the Russian Federation by ratifying the Convention on the Law of the Sea non-appearing is contrary to the object and purpose of the dispute-settlement system under Part XV of the Convention. Surely as stated in Article 28 of the Statute of the Tribunal, the non-appearing State remains a party to the proceedings and is bound by the decisions taken. However essential as this may be, this does not cover the core of the issue. Judicial proceedings are based on a legal discourse among the parties and the co-operation of both parties with the international court or tribunal in question. Non-appearance cripples this process".[14]

While both China and Russia remained firm in their non-participation in the cases they were involved in, both States made their position known through memoranda made available to the arbitrators.

2. The Decisions Handed Down by ITLOS in 2015

5. In the provisional measures order in the maritime delimitation case between Ghana and Côte d'Ivoire, a Special Chamber of ITLOS found that its *prima facie* jurisdiction was uncontroverted between the parties. Addressing a kind of *fumus boni juris* requirement that it had not addressed in its early provisional measures orders, it also found that the claims put forward by Côte d'Ivoire, the requesting party, were "plausible".[15]

Examining the requirement of urgency, the Chamber found that Côte d'Ivoire had not adduced sufficient evidence that the continuation of oil activities by Ghana was such as to create an imminent risk of serious harm to the environment. It found, however, that "drilling may create irreversible damage, as it could result in significant and permanent modification of the physical character of the area in dispute".[16] It consequently prescribed, as a provisional measure, the prohibition of drilling by Ghana in the disputed area.[17]

The general suspension of all Ghana's ongoing activities in the disputed area requested by Côte d'Ivoire was not considered an acceptable provisional measure. Ghana argued that it would have suffered "considerable financial loss" as a result.[18] This argument was not specifically addressed by the Chamber, which preferred to

---

[14] ITLOS Reports, 2013, p. 256, separate opinion annexed to the Order of 22 November 2013, *ibid.*, p. 230.

[15] Order of 25 April 2015, para. 62.

[16] *Ibid.*, para. 89.

[17] *Ibid.*, operative para. 108(1)(a).

[18] *Ibid.*, para. 84.

base its decision on other arguments. The Chamber further prescribed that Ghana should take the necessary steps to prevent information resulting from past, ongoing or future exploration activities from being used in any way whatsoever to the detriment of Côte d'Ivoire.[19] In its reasons, the Chamber stated that "the exclusive right to access to information about the resources of the continental shelf is plausibly" among "the rights of the coastal State necessary for and connected with the exploration and exploitation of the natural resources of the continental shelf".[20]

6. In the *Enrica Lexie Incident* case, the positions of the parties were described as follows by the PCA in a press release:

> "According to Italy, the Parties' dispute arises from an incident approximately 20.5 nautical miles off the coast of India involving the MV Enrica Lexie, an oil tanker flying the Italian flag, and India's subsequent exercise of criminal jurisdiction over two Italian Marines from the Italian Navy [...] in respect of that incident. According to India, the 'incident' in question concerns the killing of two Indian fishermen, on board an Indian vessel named the St. Antony, allegedly by two Italian marines stationed on the Enrica Lexie, and the subsequent exercise of jurisdiction by India".[21]

The marines were detained by India in an Indian port, under the accusation of having killed two Indian fishermen outside Indian territorial waters. The marines were in service on an Italian tanker, and shot at the Indian fishermen approaching the tanker in a small vessel, as they appeared to them to be pirates.

The case was submitted by Italy to an Annex VII arbitral tribunal, the adjudicating body which in its view could exercise jurisdiction under Article 287 of UNCLOS. Pending the establishment of the arbitral tribunal, ITLOS was seized by Italy of a request for provisional measures under UNCLOS Article 290(5). In its Order of 24 August 2015,[22] ITLOS confirmed that the rights claimed on the merits must be, and were, plausible.[23]

The Tribunal rejected the argument submitted by India that the fact that Italy had chosen to seize the Indian Courts precluded it from resorting to ITLOS under

---

[19] *Ibid.*, operative para. 108(1)(b).

[20] *Ibid.*, para. 94.

[21] PCA Press Release of 30 January 2016.

[22] For a comment, with references to the abundant literature raised by the dispute, which has attracted considerable media attention in Italy and India, see CANNONE, "L'ordinanza del Tribunale internazionale del diritto del mare sulla vicenda della *Enrica Lexie*", RDI, 2015, p. 1144 ff.

[23] Order of 24 August 2015, paras. 84 and 85.

Article 290. In rejecting this argument, based on the principle (well developed in international investment arbitration) of *electa una via*, ITLOS stated:

> "Considering that the Tribunal is of the view that Article 290 of the Convention applies independently of any other procedures that may have been instituted at the domestic level and Italy is therefore entitled to have recourse to the procedures established in that article and, if proceedings are instituted at the domestic level, this does not deprive a State of recourse to international proceedings".[24]

The Tribunal considered that the measures requested by Italy that India refrain from taking or enforcing judicial or administrative measures against the two detained marines and from exercising any form of jurisdiction over the *Enrica Lexie Incident*, and that it lift all restrictions to liberty, security and movement of the detained marines, would not "equally preserve the respective rights of both parties until the constitution of the Annex VII arbitral tribunal" and consequently the measures were not "appropriate".[25] The Italian request was rejected even though "during the hearing Italy undertook to abide by any decision the Annex VII Arbitral Tribunal will render and to return Sargeant Latorre and Sargeant Girone to India following the final determination of rights by the Annex VII tribunal, if that is requested by the award of the tribunal".[26]

The provisional measure prescribed by the Tribunal required both parties to suspend or refrain from initiating proceedings which might aggravate the dispute submitted to the Annex VII arbitral tribunal.[27] The Tribunal declined to prescribe measures relating to the situation of the detained marines as this would concern the merits.[28] On 11 December 2015, Italy submitted a new request for provisional measures to the Annex VII arbitral tribunal, the content of which has not been publicized.[29] According to the press, it concerns the freedom of the two marines.

7. The ITLOS Advisory Opinion of 2 April 2015 is the first opinion requested from the Tribunal as a whole.[30] The request came from a seven-member West

---

[24] *Ibid.*, para. 73.

[25] *Ibid.*, paras. 126-127.

[26] *Ibid.*, para. 118. In para. 124 ITLOS recalls that India had observed during the hearing that it had "legitimate apprehensions on Italy's ability to fulfil its promises". See the pleading of Pellet on 11 August 2015 (ITLOS/PV.15/C24/4), pp. 15-16, with reference to the jurisprudence of the Italian Constitutional Court and the Court of Cassation.

[27] Order of 24 August 2015, operative para. 141(1).

[28] *Ibid.*, para. 132.

[29] See the Arbitral Tribunal's Procedural Order No. 1 of 19 January 2016.

[30] For a comment see MAROTTI, "Sulla funzione consultiva del Tribunale internazionale del diritto del mare", RDI, 2015, p. 1171 ff.; and TANAKA, "Reflections on the Advisory Jurisdiction

African fisheries organization, the Sub-Regional Fisheries Commission (SRFC) whose statute, adopted on 8 June 2012, provides – in connection with Article 33 of the Convention on Minimum Access Conditions for the Exploitation of Resources within the Maritime Zones Under the Jurisdiction of the SFRC Member States of 14 July 1983 (MAC Convention) – that "the Conference of Ministers shall author- ize the Permanent Secretary of the SFRC to seize the International Tribunal on a specific legal matter for an advisory opinion". The request was made according to this provision.

As is well known, UNCLOS, including the Statute of the Tribunal in its Annex VI, does not provide for advisory opinions by the Tribunal in its full formation. Article 138 of the Rules, however, provides that an advisory opinion may be giv- en by the Tribunal "if an international agreement related to the purposes of the Convention specifically provides for the submission to the Tribunal of a request for such an opinion" (paragraph 1). Paragraph 2 adds that the request shall be transmit- ted to the Tribunal "by whatever body is authorized by or in accordance with the agreement to make the request to the Tribunal".

A majority of the States presenting oral and written pleadings argued that the Tribunal lacked jurisdiction because no provision in the Convention granted the Tribunal the power to give advisory opinions and consequently, Article 138 had been adopted *ultra vires*. These States further argued that Article 21 of the Statute, by including in the Tribunal's jurisdiction "all matters specifically provided for in any other agreement which confers jurisdiction on the Tribunal", refers to conten- tious cases as may be seen from the use of the same words in Article 36(1) of the ICJ Statute.[31] This argument was rejected by the Tribunal, which stated that Article 21, in referring to "disputes" and "matters", "must include something more than only 'disputes'" and that "[t]hat something more must include advisory opinions".[32] Thus, according to ITLOS, the jurisdiction of the Tribunal was based on Article 21 of the Statute in conjunction with the "other agreement", namely the MAC Convention.[33] As regards Article 138 of the Rules, this provision "does not estab- lish the advisory jurisdiction of the Tribunal. It only furnishes the prerequisites that need to be satisfied before the Tribunal can exercise its advisory jurisdiction".[34] The Tribunal found that these prerequisites were satisfied.[35]

The Tribunal specified that its jurisdiction in the present case was "limited to the exclusive economic zone of the SFRC Member States".[36] However, the ques-

---

of ITLOS as a Full Court: The ITLOS Advisory Opinion of 2015", The Law and Practice of International Courts and Tribunals, 2015, p. 318 ff.

[31] Advisory Opinion of 2 April 2015, para. 46.
[32] *Ibid.*, para. 56.
[33] *Ibid.*, para. 58.
[34] *Ibid.*, para. 59.
[35] *Ibid.*, para. 61.
[36] *Ibid.*, para. 69.

tions submitted to the Tribunal are of a general nature. In consideration of this, and in view of the advisory, non-binding, character of the Opinion, the presence of this limitation is not likely to have a significant impact.

The SFRC submitted four questions to the Tribunal concerning: (1) the obligations of the flag State when illegal, unreported and unregulated (IUU) fishing is conducted in the EEZ of third States; (2) the liability of the flag State for IUU fishing activities conducted by vessels flying its flag; (3) the liability of the contracting State or of the international organization for violation of the fishing legislation of the coastal State if fishing is conducted under a licence within the framework of an international agreement or within an international organization; (4) the rights and obligations of the coastal State in ensuring the sustainable management of shared stocks and stock of common interest.

In answering question (1), the Tribunal, while underscoring that primary responsibility for combatting IUU fishing in the EEZ lies with the coastal State, observed that there are various provisions in UNCLOS setting out obligations of the flag State. Of particular interest are Articles 58(3), 62(4), and 192, from which it follows "that flag States are obliged to take the necessary measures to ensure that their nationals and vessels flying their flag are not engaged in IUU fishing activities".[37] The Opinion then recalls the arguments set out in the Seabed Chamber Advisory Opinion of 2011 as to the meaning of the expression "responsibility to ensure" and "ensure".[38] The obligation "to ensure" applies also to States not parties to the MCA Convention exercising IUU fishing in the EEZ of the SRFC States.[39]

Answering question (2), the Opinion stated that violation of the laws and regulations of the coastal State in the EEZ "is not per se attributable to the flag State. The liability of the flag State arises from its failure to comply with its 'due diligence' obligations concerning IUU fishing activities conducted by vessels flying its flag in the exclusive economic zones of the SRFC Member States".[40]

The answer to question (3) is interesting as regards fishing licenses given to the European Union (EU), the only international organization party to UNCLOS to which Member States have transferred competences on fisheries. The Opinion stated that "an international organization which in a matter of its competence undertakes an obligation, in respect of which compliance depends on the conduct of its Member States, may be held liable if a member State fails to comply with such obligation and the organization did not meet its obligation of 'due diligence'".[41] If an international organization such as the EU concludes a fisheries access agreement

---

[37] *Ibid.*, para. 124.

[38] Responsibilities and Obligations of States Sponsoring Persons and Entities with respect to Activities in the Area, Advisory Opinion of 1 February 2011, ITLOS, Reports 2011, p. 10, paras. 107-120.

[39] Advisory Opinion of 2 April 2015, para. 129.

[40] *Ibid.*, para. 146.

[41] *Ibid.*, para. 169.

providing for access of vessels flying the flag of Member States, "the obligations of the flag State become the obligations of the international organization [...]. The international organization [...] must therefore ensure that vessels flying the flag of a member State comply with the fisheries laws and regulations of the SRFC Member State and do not conduct IUU fishing activities within the exclusive economic zone of that State".[42] The Tribunal then affirmed:

> "173. Accordingly, only the international organization may be held liable for any breach of its obligations arising from the fisheries access agreement, and not its Member States. Therefore, if the international organization does not meet its 'due diligence' obligations, the SRFC Member States may hold the international organization liable for the violation of their fisheries laws and regulations by a vessel flying the flag of a member State of that organization [...]".

The answer to question (4) indicated the various articles in UNCLOS providing for the obligation of cooperation between Member States for fishing shared stocks and stocks of common interest.

The position of the EU as regards these advisory proceedings is worth noting.[43] The EU Commission participated in the proceedings, submitting written observations and intervening orally at the hearing. It proposed answers to the questions submitted to the Tribunal, and addressed only in very general terms the issue of the jurisdiction of ITLOS. Seven Member States participated in the proceedings.[44] All of them but one, addressed the question of jurisdiction only. France – perhaps because it exercises sovereignty over certain territories not included in the EU – also addressed briefly two of the questions submitted to ITLOS. Six out of seven of these Member States considered, although with nuances, that ITLOS had no jurisdiction. Of these the most elaborate was that of the United Kingdom. Only Germany argued in favour of the jurisdiction of ITLOS.

A judgment of the EU Court of Justice of 6 October 2015 throws some light on the attitude of the EU and its Member States. This judgment is the outcome of a case submitted by the Council against the Commission[45] arguing that the Commission had infringed Article 16 of the Treaty on the European Union in submitting on be-

---

[42] *Ibid.*, para. 172.

[43] For some observations made before the Advisory Opinion was handed out see TREVES, "Union Européenne et règlement des différends dans le cadre de la Convention des Nations Unies sur le droit de la mer. Aspects récents", in Institut du droit économique de la mer (ed.), *Droit international de la mer et droit de l'Union Européenne. Cohabitation, Confrontation, Coopération*, Paris, 2014, p. 339 ff., pp. 344-346.

[44] France, Germany, Ireland, the Netherlands, Portugal, Spain, and the United Kingdom.

[45] Case C-73/14, *Council v. Commission*, Judgment of the Grand Chamber of 6 October 2015.

half of the EU a written statement to ITLOS without the approval of the Council. The Court rejected the request observing, *inter alia*, that

> "[…] it can be seen from the written statement submitted on behalf of the European Union to ITLOS in Case Nr. 21 that the statement consisted in suggesting answers to the questions raised in that case, by setting out the manner in which the European Union envisaged the interpretation and application of the relevant provisions of UNCLOS, of the FAO Compliance Agreement, and of the United Nations Fish Stocks Agreements in relation to IUU fishing, and by describing the measures contained, in that connection , in the partnership agreements and the EU legislation […]. The purpose of the statement was therefore not to formulate a policy in relation to IUU fishing, for the purpose of the second sentence of Article 16 (1) TEU, but to present ITLOS, on the basis of an analysis of the provisions of international and EU law relevant to that subject, a set of legal observations aimed at enabling that court to give, if appropriate, an informed advisory opinion on the questions put to it". [46]

From the narrative in the judgment and from what the participating States did (including the intervention of nine Member States in support of the Council in the EU Court proceedings) it appears that there was agreement that the Commission was exclusively competent to submit positions on the substance of the four questions, and that the Member States (perhaps with the exception of France for the reason noted above) would abstain from doing so. The Commission in turn would not take a stand on the jurisdiction of ITLOS, and on this the Member States would be free to take positions, including divergent positions. The question separating the Council and some Member States from the Commission concerned the need for approval by the Council of the pleading to be submitted by the Commission, but the Court held that there was no need for such approval.

3. DECISIONS OF ANNEX VII ARBITRAL TRIBUNALS

8. The *Arctic Sunrise* case concerned the conduct of the Russian Federation in reacting to the protest of Greenpeace activists based on the Netherlands-flagged vessel Arctic Sunrise and attempting to board a Russian platform in Russia's continental shelf.[47] The Netherlands claimed, *inter alia*, that Russia in boarding, inves-

---

[46] *Ibid.*, paras. 70-71.
[47] The Netherlands had requested and obtained provisional measures from ITLOS under Art. 290(5). ITLOS Order of 22 November 2013, ITLOS Reports 2013, p. 230. See also TREVES, ITLOS 2013, pp. 358-363.

tigating and seizing the Arctic Sunrise had violated various UNCLOS provisions and deprived the Netherlands of its right to exercise diplomatic protection. Among the many interesting points made in the *Arctic Sunrise* award the following are of particular interest.

As regards the Netherlands' standing, the Award did not consider it necessary to deal with the contention that the violations of UNCLOS imputed to Russia were violations of *erga omnes* obligations according to Article 42 of the ILC Articles on State Responsibility, because the Netherlands had standing under the Convention.[48] It is to be noted that, in similar circumstances, the ICJ, in its judgment on the *Questions relating to the Obligation to Prosecute or Extradite (Belgium v. Senegal)* case, followed a different logic. The Court did not consider it necessary to explore Belgium's argument that it had standing to claim violation by Senegal of the Convention Against Torture as a specially interested party, because it found that the obligations violated by Senegal were of an *erga omnes* character.[49]

Staying with the issue of standing, the Award confirmed the jurisprudence of ITLOS that a vessel "is a unit such that its crew, all persons and objects on board as well as its owner and every person involved or interested in its operations" and was linked in the specific case to the Netherlands as the flag State. Consequently, the Netherlands had standing to invoke Russia's responsibility for injury caused to all persons on board the ship flying its flag regardless of their nationality.[50]

As regards the applicable law, the Award stated that provisions of the International Covenant on Civil and Political Rights in force between the parties could not be applied directly as "that treaty has its own enforcement regime and it is not for this Tribunal to act as a substitute for that regime".[51] However, the reference to "other rules of international law" in Article 293 of UNCLOS permits the consideration of general international law in order to determine whether law enforcement action "was reasonable and proportionate". Article 293 permits the Tribunal to

> "have regard to the extent necessary to rules of customary international law, including international human rights standards, not incompatible with the Convention, in order to assist in the interpretation of the Convention's provisions that authorize the arrest or detention of a vessel and persons, even though the Tribunal has no jurisdiction to determine breaches of specific provisions of the International Covenant on Civil and Political rights".[52]

---

[48] Award of 14 August 2015, para. 186.
[49] *Ibid.*, para. 197.
[50] *Ibid.*, para. 170-172.
[51] *Ibid.*
[52] *Ibid.*, para. 198.

As regards the right of the coastal State under Article 60(4) UNCLOS to take measures in the safety zones around installations in the EEZ "to ensure the safety both of navigation and of the artificial islands and structures", in the view of the arbitral tribunal, it goes "beyond its rights in the EEZ at large".[53]

On one of the key issues before it, the Award stated that "[p]rotest at sea is an internationally lawful use of the sea related to the freedom of navigation". This right, exercised in conjunction with the freedom of navigation, derives from the freedom of expression and the freedom of assembly, both recognized in several international law instruments to which both the Netherlands and Russia are parties.[54] There are limitations to such rights which derive from the law of the sea. In particular, the rule of Article 88 reserving the high seas for peaceful purposes, and the rule in Article 58 according to which, in exercising its freedoms in the EEZ, States must "have due regard for the rights and duties of the coastal State".[55] In the EEZ a State enjoys, under Articles 82(1) and 58(2) of UNCLOS, exclusive jurisdiction over ships flying its flag "which include ships used for the exercise of the right to protest".[56] No permission had been given to Russia to derogate this exclusive jurisdiction. The alleged characterization of the Arctic Sunrise behaviour as pirate activity could not apply because piracy under the Convention requires the presence of two ships, while in the case under consideration one ship and a fixed platform were involved.[57] On the merits the Tribunal found that

> "by boarding, investigating, inspecting, arresting, detaining, and seizing the Arctic Sunrise without the prior consent of the Netherlands, and by arresting, detaining, and initiating judicial proceedings against the Arctic 30, the Russian Federation breached obligations owed by it to the Netherlands as the flag State under Articles 56(2), 58(1), 58(2), 87(1)(a), and 92(1) of the Convention".[58]

The arbitral tribunal reached the conclusion that the coastal States' enforcement powers explicitly set out in Article 73, as regards fishing activities, and, implicitly in Article 77 as regards enforcement of the coastal States' laws concerning the exploration and exploitation of the living resources of the continental shelf, did not apply to the case as it did not concern resource-oriented activities.[59] Similarly, Article 220 concerning enforcement powers in cases of pollution from vessels in the EEZ did not apply to the case for lack of clear grounds for Russia to believe that

---

[53] *Ibid.*, para. 211.
[54] *Ibid.*, para. 227.
[55] *Ibid.*, para. 228.
[56] *Ibid.*, para. 231.
[57] *Ibid.*, para. 238.
[58] *Ibid.*, para. 404 C.
[59] *Ibid.*, paras. 281-285.

the Arctic Sunrise had committed a violation of applicable international rules and standards for the prevention, reduction and control of vessel-source pollution.[60]

Among the other points of the operative part, it seems worth noting point D, finding that Russia had violated obligations under Article 290 (6) and (1) of UNCLOS by failing to comply with its obligations to the Netherlands under paragraphs 1 and 2 of the *dispositif* of the provisional measures Order adopted by ITLOS in the case under Article 290(5) of UNCLOS.

9. The *Chagos* award contains elaborate discussions on a number of provisions of UNCLOS concerning jurisdiction. The discussion and decision concerning whether the United Kingdom could be considered the "coastal State" for the purpose of adopting a marine protected area around the Chagos Archipelago has already been mentioned above.[61] The Tribunal underlined that the "real issue in the case" did not relate to the interpretation or application of the Convention and specified that "an incidental connection between the dispute and some matter regulated by the Convention [was] insufficient to bring the dispute, as a whole, within the ambit of article 288(1)".[62] The Award does not, however, "categorically exclude that in some instances a minor issue of territorial sovereignty could indeed be ancillary to a dispute concerning the interpretation or application of the Convention", but this was not the case in the dispute under discussion.[63]

The only submission by Mauritius over which the Tribunal found that it had jurisdiction was the fourth one, concerning the compatibility of the establishment of a Marine Protected Area (MPA) with the United Kingdom's substantive and procedural obligations under the Convention. The Tribunal found that the MPA had an object broader than fisheries because it included preservation of biodiversity in order to address the risk of irreversible damage to the oceans.[64] The question of jurisdiction had thus to be addressed not only from the point of view of Article 297(3), as the United Kingdom argued, but also from the point of view of Article 297(1)(c), as argued by Mauritius. The Tribunal adopted a reading of Article 297(1) according to which this provision restricts compulsory jurisdiction only "in enumerated cases" and "does not restrict a tribunal from considering disputes concerning the exercise of sovereign rights and jurisdiction in other cases".[65] As regards Article 297(1)(c), the Tribunal holds the view that the reference to international rules and standards does not concern only substantive rules and standards. According to the Tribunal, it may also concern obligations such as that of consultation or giving re-

---

[60] *Ibid.*, para. 290-291.
[61] *Supra* section 2.2.
[62] Award of 18 March 2015, para. 220
[63] *Ibid.*, para. 221.
[64] *Ibid.*, paras 286-292.
[65] *Ibid.*, para. 317.

gard to the rights of other States. These procedural rules, according to the Tribunal, may be "of equal or even greater importance than the substantive standards existing in international law". In the Tribunal's view, the "obligation to consult with and have due regard for the rights of other States, set out in multiple provisions of the Convention, is precisely such a procedural rule and its alleged contravention is squarely within the terms of Article 297 (1)(c)".[66]

Turning to the merits of Mauritius' fourth submission, the Tribunal – in light of preparatory work and of a comparison of the linguistic versions – came to the conclusion that Article 2(3) UNCLOS, according to which the "sovereignty over the territorial sea is exercised subject to this Convention and to other rules of international law", is not a descriptive provision but gives rise to obligations.[67] In the view of the Tribunal, the United Kingdom had not acted in good faith in its relationship with Mauritius as regards the territorial sea and failed to pay due regard, under Article 56, to Mauritius' rights as a prospective coastal State especially comparing the scant consultations with Mauritius about the MPA with those held with the United States.[68] The obligation in Article 194(4) to refrain from unjustifiable interference is, according to the Tribunal, "functionally equivalent to the obligation to give 'due regard', set out in Article 56(2), or the obligation of good faith that follows from Article 2(3)".[69] The Tribunal thus concluded, *inter alia*, that, in establishing the MPA, the United Kingdom "breached its obligations under article 2(3), 56(2) and 194 (4) of the Convention".[70]

10. In the *Philippines v. China* award the arbitral tribunal addressed numerous questions, of which the most important will be examined. One of these is the question whether the Philippines were abusing compulsory dispute settlement procedures. The Tribunal noted that the "mere act of unilaterally initiating an arbitration under part XV in itself cannot constitute an abuse of rights".[71] Further, having stated that it was entitled to determine *proprio motu* whether the Philippines's claim constituted an abuse of legal process under Article 294 of UNCLOS, the Tribunal declined to do so: "[i]n light of the serious consequences of a finding of abuse of process or of *prima facie* unfoundedness, the Tribunal considers that the procedure is appropriate in only the most blatant cases of harassment".[72]

---

[66] *Ibid.*, para. 322.

[67] *Ibid.*, paras. 499-516. The Tribunal bases its argument on the comparison between the different linguistic versions of the provision (paras. 500-502), on its placement (paras. 503-504), and on the negotiation history (paras. 505-516).

[68] *Ibid.*, para. 534-536.

[69] *Ibid.*, para. 540.

[70] *Ibid.*, para. 541.

[71] Award of 29 October 2015, para. 126. The Award quotes in support the Arbitral Award of 11 April 2006, *Barbados v. Trinidad and Tobago*, RIAA, Vol. XXVII, p. 147, para. 208.

[72] Award of 29 October 2015, para. 128.

The disagreement between the parties as regards the definition of the dispute, or disputes, separating them has already been mentioned, as has the decision of the Tribunal that there were disputes concerning the interpretation or application of UNCLOS it could decide upon notwithstanding that the parties had a broader dispute concerning sovereignty and delimitation.[73] The main reasons given were the following:

> "150. Where a dispute exists between parties to the proceedings, it is further necessary that it be identified and characterised. The nature of the dispute may have significant jurisdictional implications, including whether the dispute can fairly be said to concern the interpretation or application of the Convention or whether subject-matter based exclusions from jurisdiction are applicable. Here again, an objective approach is called for, and the Tribunal is required to 'isolate the real issue in the case and to identify the object of the claim'. In so doing it is not only entitled to interpret the submissions of the parties, but bound to do so. [...] In the process, a distinction should be made 'between the dispute itself and arguments used by the parties to sustain their respective submissions on the dispute'.
>
> 151. In the present case, the Philippines argues that it has submitted to the Tribunal a series of concrete disputes concerning the interpretation or application of specific articles of the Convention to Chinese activities in the South China Sea and to certain maritime features occupied by China. The Philippines also considers that it has submitted a dispute concerning the interaction of 'historic rights' claimed by China with the provisions of the Convention. China's Position Paper sets out two overarching characterisations of the Parties' dispute that, in China's view, exclude it from the Tribunal's jurisdiction. In its Position Paper, China argues, first, that the Parties' dispute concerns 'territorial sovereignty over several maritime features in the South China Sea' and, second (in what the Tribunal understands to be an alternative argument), that the Parties' dispute concerns matters that are 'an integral part of maritime delimitation'. The former characterisation would, in China's view, mean that the dispute is not one concerning the interpretation or application of the Convention; the latter would bring it within the ambit of the jurisdictional exceptions created by China's declaration under Article 298 of the Convention [...].
>
> 152. There is no question that there exists a dispute between the Parties concerning land sovereignty over certain maritime features

---

[73] *Supra* section 2.1.

in the South China Sea. [...] The Tribunal does not accept, however, that it follows from the existence of a dispute over sovereignty that sovereignty is also the appropriate characterisation of the claims the Philippines has submitted in these proceedings. In the Tribunal's view, it is entirely ordinary and expected that two States with a relationship as extensive and multifaceted as that existing between the Philippines and China would have disputes in respect of several distinct matters. Indeed, even within a geographic area such as the South China Sea, the Parties can readily be in dispute regarding multiple aspects of the prevailing factual circumstances or the legal consequences that follow from them. [...]

153. The Tribunal might consider that the Philippines' Submissions could be understood to relate to sovereignty if it were convinced that either (a) the resolution of the Philippines' claims would require the Tribunal to first render a decision on sovereignty, either expressly or implicitly; or (b) the actual objective of the Philippines' claims was to advance its position in the Parties' dispute over sovereignty. Neither of these situations, however, is the case. The Philippines has not asked the Tribunal to rule on sovereignty and, indeed, has expressly and repeatedly requested that the Tribunal refrain from so doing. The Tribunal likewise does not see that any of the Philippines' Submissions require an implicit determination of sovereignty. The Tribunal is of the view that it is entirely possible to approach the Philippines' Submissions from the premise – as the Philippines suggests – that China is correct in its assertion of sovereignty over Scarborough Shoal and the Spratlys. The Tribunal is fully conscious of the limits on the claims submitted to it and, to the extent that it reaches the merits of any of the Philippines' Submissions, intends to ensure that its decision neither advances nor detracts from either Party's claims to land sovereignty in the South China Sea. Nor does the Tribunal understand the Philippines to seek anything further. The Tribunal does not see that success on these Submissions would have an effect on the Philippines' sovereignty claims and accepts that the Philippines has initiated these proceedings with the entirely proper objective of narrowing the issues in dispute between the two States. In this respect, the present case is distinct from the recent decision in Chagos Marine Protected Area. The Tribunal understands the majority's decision in that case to have been based on the view both that a decision on Mauritius' first and second submissions would have required an implicit decision on sovereignty and that sovereignty was the true object of Mauritius' claims. For the reasons set out in this paragraph, the Tribunal does not accept the objection set out in China's

Position Paper that the disputes presented by the Philippines concern sovereignty over maritime features. [...]

155. Turning now to the question of maritime boundaries, the Tribunal is likewise not convinced by the objection in China's Position Paper that the Parties' dispute is properly characterised as relating to maritime boundary delimitation. The Tribunal agrees with China that maritime boundary delimitation is an integral and systemic process. In particular, the Tribunal notes that the concepts of an 'equitable solution', of 'special circumstances' in respect of the territorial sea, and of 'relevant circumstances' in respect of the exclusive economic zone and continental shelf may entail consideration of a wide variety of potential issues arising between the parties to a delimitation. It does not follow, however, that a dispute over an issue that may be considered in the course of a maritime boundary delimitation constitutes a dispute over maritime boundary delimitation itself.

156. In particular, the Tribunal considers that a dispute concerning the existence of an entitlement to maritime zones is distinct from a dispute concerning the delimitation of those zones in an area where the entitlements of parties overlap. While fixing the extent of parties' entitlements and the area in which they overlap will commonly be one of the first matters to be addressed in the delimitation of a maritime boundary, it is nevertheless a distinct issue. A maritime boundary may be delimited only between States with opposite or adjacent coasts and overlapping entitlements. In contrast, a dispute over claimed entitlements may exist even without overlap, where – for instance – a State claims maritime zones in an area understood by other States to form part of the high seas or the Area for the purposes of the Convention.

157. In these proceedings, the Philippines has challenged the existence and extent of the maritime entitlements claimed by China in the South China Sea. This is not a dispute over maritime boundaries. The Philippines has not requested the Tribunal to delimit any overlapping entitlements between the two States, and the Tribunal will not effect the delimitation of any boundary. Certain consequences, however, do follow from the limits on the Tribunal's competence in this respect and the limited nature of the dispute presented by the Philippines. China correctly notes in its Position Paper that certain of the Philippines' Submissions (Submissions No. 5, 8 and 9) request the Tribunal to declare that specific maritime features 'are part of the exclusive economic zone and continental shelf of the Philippines' or that certain Chinese activities interfered with the Philippines' sovereign rights in its exclusive economic zone. Because the Tribunal has not been requested to – and will not delimit a maritime boundary between the Parties, the Tribunal will be able address those of the Philippines' Submissions

based on the premise that certain areas of the South China Sea form part of the Philippines' exclusive economic zone or continental shelf only if the Tribunal determines that China could not possess any potentially overlapping entitlement in that area [...]."

The Tribunal, after stating that "the existence of a dispute must be evaluated objectively",[74] came to the conclusion that each of the submissions of the Philippines reflected a dispute. Such dispute concerned in some cases "the source of marine entitlements in the South China seas and interaction of China's claimed 'historic rights' with the provisions of the Convention".[75] Other submissions reflected "a dispute concerning the status of the marine features and the source of marine entitlements in the South China Sea".[76] Another group of disputes concerned "Chinese activities on the South China Sea", in particular as regards petroleum survey, fishing, building of installations, action of Chinese law enforcement vessels, and Philippine military presence on a specific feature.[77]

The Tribunal award came to the conclusion that they had jurisdiction as regards seven of the fifteen submissions of the Philippines, while on seven others the determination of jurisdiction "would involve consideration of issues that do not possess an exclusively preliminary character", so that their consideration was reserved for the merits phase. The Tribunal requested that the Philippines clarify the content of one of the submissions and narrow its scope in the merits phase.

The submission on which the Tribunal found that it had jurisdiction are the following (the original number is kept): (3) Scarborough Shoal generates no entitlement to an exclusive economic zone or continental shelf; (4) Mischief Reef, Second Thomas Shoal and Subi Reef are low-tide elevations that do not generate entitlement to a territorial sea, exclusive economic zone or continental shelf, and are not features that are capable of appropriation by occupation or otherwise; (6) Mischief Reef, Second Thomas Shoal and Subi Reef are low-tide elevations that do not generate entitlement to a territorial sea, exclusive economic zone or continental shelf, and are not features that are capable of appropriation by occupation or otherwise; (7) Johnson Reef, Cuarteron Reef and Fiery Cross Reef generate no entitlement to an exclusive economic zone or continental shelf; (10) China has unlawfully prevented Philippine fishermen from pursuing their livelihoods by interfering with traditional fishing activities at Scarborough Shoal; (11) China has violated its obligations under the Convention to protect and preserve the marine environment at Scarborough Shoal and Second Thomas Shoal; (13) China has breached its obligations under the Convention by operating its law enforcement

---

[74] Award of 29 October 2015, para. 163.
[75] *Ibid.*, paras. 164 and 172.
[76] *Ibid.*, para. 169
[77] *Ibid.*, para. 173.

vessels in a dangerous manner causing serious risk of collision to Philippine vessels navigating in the vicinity of Scarborough Shoal.

Submissions (3), (4), (6), and (7) concern the status of the mentioned feature respectively as "island" or "rock" under UNCLOS Article 121 (submissions 3 and 7), or as "low tide elevation" under Article 13 (submissions 4 and 6). With language similar for the three submissions the Tribunal stated:

> "This is not a dispute concerning sovereignty over the features, notwithstanding any possible question concerning whether low-tide elevations may be subjected to a claim of territorial sovereignty. Nor is this a dispute concerning sea boundary delimitation: the status of a feature as a 'low-tide elevation', 'island', or a 'rock' relates to the entitlement to maritime zones generated by that feature, not to the delimitation of such entitlements in the event that they overlap".[78]

As regards submissions 10, 11, and 13, the Tribunal observed that they do not concern boundaries or sovereignty so that its jurisdiction is not precluded. The reasons given on submission 11 are particularly interesting:

> "The Philippines' Submission No. 11 reflects a dispute concerning the protection and preservation of the marine environment at Scarborough Shoal and Second Thomas Shoal and the application of Articles 192 and 194 of the Convention. This is not a dispute concerning sovereignty or maritime boundary delimitation, nor is it barred from the Tribunal's consideration by any requirement of Section 1 of Part XV. Depending on the Tribunal's ultimate decision on the status of these features, the basis for its jurisdiction may differ: (a) To the extent that the alleged harmful activities took place in the territorial sea surrounding Scarborough Shoal, or in any territorial sea generated by Second Thomas Shoal, the Tribunal notes that the environmental provisions of the Convention impose obligations on States Parties including in the territorial sea. The Tribunal's jurisdiction is thus not dependent on a prior determination of the status of Second Thomas Shoal or of sovereignty over either feature, and Articles 297 and 298 of the Convention have no application in the territorial sea. (b) To the extent that the alleged harmful activities took place in the exclusive economic zone of the Philippines, of China, or in an area of overlapping entitlements, the Tribunal notes that Article 297(1)(c) expressly affirms the Tribunal's jurisdiction over disputes concerning the alleged violation of ' specified interna-

---

[78] *Ibid.*, para. 403. See also paras. 400, 401 and 404.

tional rules and standards for the protection and preservation of the marine environment' in the exclusive economic zone.

Under neither circumstance, however, is jurisdiction precluded. The Tribunal's jurisdiction is thus not dependent on a prior determination of the status of any maritime feature, on the existence of an entitlement by China to an exclusive economic zone in the area, or on the prior delimitation of any overlapping entitlements. Accordingly, the Tribunal concludes that it has jurisdiction to address the matters raised in the Philippines' Submission No. 11".[79]

The submissions for which the Tribunal reserved the decision on jurisdiction to the merits phase are the following (the original numbering has been kept): (1) China's maritime entitlements in the South China Sea, like those of the Philippines, may not extend beyond those permitted by UNCLOS; (2) China's claims to sovereign rights and jurisdiction, and to "historic rights", with respect to the maritime areas of the South China Sea encompassed by the so-called "nine-dash line" are contrary to the Convention and without lawful effect to the extent that they exceed the geographic and substantive limits of China's maritime entitlements under UNCLOS; (5) Mischief Reef and Second Thomas Shoal are part of the exclusive economic zone and continental shelf of the Philippines; (8) China has unlawfully interfered with the enjoyment and exercise of the sovereign rights of the Philippines with respect to the living and non-living resources of its exclusive economic zone and continental shelf; (9) China has unlawfully failed to prevent its nationals and vessels from exploiting the living resources in the exclusive economic zone of the Philippines; (12) China's occupation and construction activities on Mischief Reef (a) violate the provisions of the Convention concerning artificial islands, installations and structures; (b) violate China's duties to protect and preserve the marine environment under the Convention; and (c) constitute unlawful acts of attempted appropriation in violation of the Convention; (14) Since the commencement of this arbitration in January 2013, China has unlawfully aggravated and extended the dispute by, among other things: (a) interfering with the Philippines' rights of navigation in the waters at, and adjacent to, Second Thomas Shoal; (b) preventing the rotation and resupply of Philippine personnel stationed at Second Thomas Shoal; and (c) endangering the health and well-being of Philippine personnel stationed at Second Thomas Shoal; and (15) China shall desist from further unlawful claims and activities.

The Tribunal's reasons for joining consideration of jurisdiction to that of the merits on submissions 1 and 2 (possibly the most far-reaching of the Philippines's submissions) are stated in very similar terms as follows:

---

[79] *Ibid.*, para. 408.

"The Philippines' Submission No. 1 reflects a dispute concerning the
source of maritime entitlements in the South China Sea and the role
of the Convention. This is not a dispute concerning sovereignty or
maritime boundary delimitation, nor is it barred from the Tribunal's
consideration by any requirement of Section 1 of Part XV. The
Philippines' Submission No. 1 does, however, require the Tribunal
to consider the effect of any historic rights claimed by China to
maritime entitlements in the South China Sea and the interaction of
such rights with the provisions of the Convention. This is a dispute
concerning the interpretation and application of the Convention. The
Tribunal's jurisdiction to consider this question, however, would be
dependent on the nature of any such historic rights and whether
they are covered by the exclusion from jurisdiction over 'historic
bays or titles' in Article 298".[80]

Among the reasons given on other submissions in which the question of jurisdiction was joined to the merits, those given as regards submission 12 are of
particular interest:

"The Philippines' Submission No. 12 reflects a dispute concerning
China's activities on Mischief Reef and their effects on the marine environment. This is not a dispute concerning sovereignty or maritime
boundary delimitation, nor is it barred from the Tribunal's consideration by any requirement of Section 1 of Part XV. However, the
Tribunal's jurisdiction to address these questions is dependent on
the status of Mischief Reef as an 'island', 'rock', or 'low-tide
elevation'. If the Tribunal were to find – contrary to the premise
of the Philippines' Submission – that Mischief Reef is an 'island'
or 'rock' and thus constitutes land territory, the Tribunal would lack
jurisdiction to consider the lawfulness of China's construction activities or the appropriation of the feature. The status of Mischief
Reef is a matter for the merits. Additionally, Article 298 excludes
disputes concerning military activities from the Tribunal's jurisdiction. The Tribunal considers that the specifics of China's activities
on Mischief Reef and whether such activities are military in nature
to be a matter best assessed in conjunction with the merits. The
possible jurisdictional objections with respect to the dispute underlying Submission No. 12 therefore do not possess an exclusively

---

[80] *Ibid.*, para. 398, as regards submission 1. As regards submission 2, para. 399, after stating
that this submission "directly requires the Tribunal to determine the legal validity of any claim
by China to historic rights is the South China Sea", repeats the last two sentences of para. 398
reproduced in the text.

> preliminary character. Accordingly, the Tribunal reserves a decision
> on its jurisdiction with respect to the Philippines' Submission No. 12
> for consideration in conjunction with the merits of the Philippines'
> claims".[81]

Before reaching its conclusions on jurisdiction, the Award examined various
preliminary questions. While there is no space to discuss them all, one in particular
seems worthy of note. This concerned whether the China/ASEAN declaration on
the Conduct of Parties in the South China Sea of 4 November 2002 (the DOC) may
be considered as an agreement which excludes "any further procedure" according
to Article 281(1) of UNCLOS. The relevant provision (Article 4) is as follows:

> "The Parties concerned undertake to resolve their territorial and
> jurisdictional disputes by peaceful means, without resorting to the
> threat of force, through friendly consultations and negotiations by
> sovereign states directly concerned, in accordance with universally
> recognized principles of international law, including the 1982 UN
> Convention on the Law of the Sea".

The Tribunal came to a negative conclusion, arguing as follows:

> "As stated above, the Parties disagree on whether an express exclu-
> sion is required. The Philippines argues that the intent to exclude
> further procedures under the Convention must be evident from the
> terms of the agreement itself. China considers an express exclusion
> unnecessary and subscribes to the view of the majority of the Annex
> VII tribunal in *Southern Bluefin Tuna*. The Tribunal considers that
> the better view is that Article 281 requires some clear statement of
> exclusion of further procedures. This is supported by the text and
> context of Article 281 and by the structure and overall purpose
> of the Convention. The Tribunal thus shares the views of ITLOS
> in its provisional measures orders in the *Southern Bluefin Tuna* and
> *MOX Plant* cases, as well as the separate opinion of Judge Keith in
> *Southern Bluefin Tuna* that the majority's statement in that matter
> that 'the absence of an express exclusion of any procedure [...] is
> not decisive' is not in line with the intended meaning of Article 281.
> The text of Article 281 provides that when parties agree to resolve
> their dispute by other peaceful means, Part XV dispute procedures
> 'will apply' where the parties' agreement 'does not exclude any
> further procedure'. This requires an 'opting out' of Part XV proce-

---

[81]*Ibid.*, para. 409. Similar reasons are given in para. 411 as regards submission 14.

dures. It does not contain an 'opting in' requirement whereby the Parties must positively agree to Part XV procedures. Such an 'opting in' is only required where the parties have chosen an alternative compulsory and binding procedure, as set out in Article 282. Pursuant to Article 282, the chosen binding procedure will apply 'in lieu of' the Part XV procedures 'unless the parties to the dispute otherwise agree'. In other words, the Part XV procedures are excluded by the alternative compulsory binding procedure, and the only way to make them available is for the parties to opt back in to them by 'agreeing otherwise'. That distinction between Article 281 and 282 is consistent with the overall design of the Convention as a system whereby compulsory dispute resolution is the default rule and any limitations and exceptions are carefully and precisely defined in Section 3 of Part XV".[82]

---

[82] *Ibid.*, paras. 223-224.

INTERNATIONAL CRIMINAL JUSTICE (2015)

CARLO FOCARELLI[*]

1. INTRODUCTION

On 27 January 2015, the International Criminal Tribunal for the former Yugoslavia (ICTY) began the handover of judicial records to the Mechanism for International Criminal Tribunals (MICT).[1] Addressing before the UN General Assembly on 13 October 2015, President Meron reported on the Tribunal's progress in completing the last of its proceedings. He anticipated that two trials are expected to be completed by the first quarter of the 2016, one further trial and one appeal during the remainder of 2016, and the final two cases of the ICTY completed before the end of 2017.[2] On 3 June 2015, Prosecutor Brammertz presented to the UN Security Council its 23rd completion report strategy. He briefed the Council on the current status of trials and appeals at the ICTY, on the cooperation of Bosnia and Herzegovina, Croatia, and Serbia with the Prosecutor, and on the situation regarding national war crimes prosecutions. As to the latter, in particular, the Prosecutor recognized the significant results in regional cooperation on high-profile cases, also noting that only a limited number of the outstanding cases at the national level have been prosecuted to date and that more should be done on the most complex and highest-priority cases.[3] Then, on 9 December 2015 the Prosecutor presented to the UN Security Council its 24rd completion strategy report discussing the status of the final four trials and three appeals before the ICTY.[4]

As for the International Criminal Tribunal for Rwanda (ICTR), on 14 December 2015 it delivered its last judgment in the *Nyiramasuhuko et al.* case. On 31 December 2015, it formally concluded its judicial function and only liquidation activities will remain to be completed during the first half of 2016.[5] In so doing, the

[*] Professor of International Law, University of Perugia and LUISS Guido Carli University, Rome. The author would like to thank Amina Maneggia and Raffaella Nigro for their invaluable research assistance.

[1] See at: <http://www.icty.org/en/press/tribunal-begins-transfer-judicial-records-mict>.

[2] See at: <http://www.icty.org/en/press/president-meron%E2%80%99s-address-united-nations-general-assembly-2>.

[3] See at: <http://www.icty.org/en/press/completion-strategy-report-prosecutor-brammertz-addresses-united-nations-security-council>.

[4] See at: <http://www.icty.org/en/press/completion-strategy-report-prosecutor-brammertz-addresses-united-nations-security-council-0>.

[5] See the Final Report on the Completion Strategy of the International Criminal Tribunal for Rwanda by its President, Judge Vagn Joensen, of 9 December 2015, available at: <http://unictr.unmict.org/en/news/address-united-nations-security-council-final-report-completion-strategy-international-criminal>. On the ICTY and the ICTR see BURKE and WEISS, "The Security Council and Ad

ICTR is the first *ad hoc* international criminal tribunal to complete its mandate and hand its remaining functions over to its residual mechanism, the MICT.

With regard to the activity of the International Criminal Court (ICC) in 2015, proceedings and investigations continued in the nine pre-existing situations. No new situations have been referred to the Court.

As regards to the activity of the hybrid criminal tribunals in 2015, noteworthy are the Extraordinary Chambers in the Courts of Cambodia (ECCC) decision to charge Meas Muth in absentia; the Residual Special Court for Sierra Leone (RSCSL) Decision on Charles Ghankay Taylor's Motion for Termination of Enforcement of Sentence in the United Kingdom and for Transfer to Rwanda; and finally the decisions of the Special Tribunal for Lebanon (STL) on its jurisdiction to hear cases against legal persons.

2. THE ICTY'S CASE LAW[6]

In 2015, the ICTY handed down three Appeals Chamber judgments in *Popović et al.*, *Tolimir*, and *Stanišić and Simatović*.

2.1. *Popović et al.*

On 30 January 2015, the Appeals Chamber issued a judgment concerning five military officials serving in the Army of Republika Srpska (VRS) for crimes perpetrated by Bosnian Serbian forces in July 1995, following the takeover of the protected areas of Srebrenica and Žepa.[7] In particular, the Appeals Chamber affirmed the sentences of life imprisonment of Popović and Beara after founding them guilty of genocide, conspiracy to commit genocide, violations of the laws or customs of war, and crimes against humanity, through their participation in a Joint Criminal Enterprise (JCE). Also the Chamber affirmed the Nicolić's sentence of 35 years of

---

Hoc Tribunals: Law and Politics, Peace and Justice", in POPOVSKI and FRASER (eds.), *The Security Council as Global Legislator*, London, 2014, p. 241 ff.; KELDER, HOLÁ and WIJK, "Rehabilitation and Early Release of Perpetrators of International Crimes: A Case Study of the ICTY and ICTR", International Criminal Law Review, 2014, p. 1177 ff.; and MUTABAZI, *The United Nations "Ad Hoc" Tribunals' Effectiveness in Prosecuting International Crimes*, Pretoria, 2014.

[6] Judgments and decisions of the ICTY are available at: <http://www.icty.org>. On the ICTY, see CLARK, "Elucidating the *Dolus Specialis*: An Analysis of ICTY Jurisprudence on Genocidal Intent", Criminal Law Forum, 2015, p. 497 ff.; ARIAV, "Hardly the *Tadić* of Targeting: Missed Opportunities in the ICTY's *Gotovina* Judgments", Israel Law Review, 2015, p. 329 ff.; and PONTI, "The Crime of Indiscriminate Attack and Unlawful Conventional Weapons: The Legacy of the ICTY Jurisprudence", Journal of International Humanitarian Legal Studies, 2015, p. 118 ff.

[7] *Prosecutor v. Vujadin Popović, Ljubiša Beara, Drago Nikolić, Radivoje Miletić, Vinko Pandurević*, Case No. IT-05-88-A, Judgment of 30 January 2015.

imprisonment for aiding and abetting genocide, and crimes against humanity and violations of the laws of war through his participation in a JCE. As to Miletić, he was found guilty of crimes against humanity and violations of the laws and customs of war, through his participation in a JCE and his sentence of imprisonment was reduced from 19 to 18 years. Finally, the Appeals Chamber affirmed the Pandurević's sentence of 13 years of imprisonment for aiding and abetting violations of the laws and customs of war and crimes against humanity and for failing to prevent and punish the crimes of his subordinates as well.

2.2. Tolimir

On 8 April 2015, the Appeals Chamber issued its judgment in the case of Tolimir, a former Assistant Commander and Chief of the Sector for Intelligence and Security Affairs of the Army of the Republica Srpska, accused of crimes committed in the Srebrenica and Žepa enclaves in 1995.[8] The Appeals Chamber confirmed the Trial Chamber's finding that Tolimir participated in two JCEs: one to murder the able-bodied men of Srebrenica and the other to forcibly remove the Bosnian Muslim population from Srebrenica and Žepa. The Appeals Chamber's judgment also confirmed Tolimir's convictions for genocide, conspiracy to commit genocide, extermination, murder, persecutions, and inhumane acts, and forcible transfer. The Chamber affirmed that Tolimir actively participated in and significantly contributed to these JCEs, which resulted in the mass executions of thousands of Bosnian Muslims in Srebrenica and the forcible displacement of thousands of civilians from the two enclaves. Although the Chamber partly reversed Tolimir's conviction for genocide, it upheld his sentence to life imprisonment.

2.3. Stanišić and Simatović

In its judgment of 9 December 2015, the Appeals Chamber quashed the Trial Chamber's decision to acquit Stanišić – formerly Deputy Chief of the State Security Service (SDB) of the Ministry of Interior of the Republic of Serbia – and Simatović – formerly Deputy Chief of the Serbian SDB and special advisor in the SDB.[9] According to the indictment, Stanišić and Simatović were accused of participating in a JCE the purpose of which was the forcible and permanent removal of the majority of non-Serbs from large areas of Croatia and Bosnia and Herzegovina. The indictment also alleged that the JCE involved the commission of murder as a violation of the laws or custom of war and as a crime against humanity as well

---

[8] *Prosecutor v. Zdravko Tolimir*, Case No. IT-05-88/2-A, Judgment of 8 April 2015.

[9] *Prosecutor v. Jovica Staniši, Franko Simatoviš*, Case No. IT-03-69-A, Judgment of 9 December 2015.

as deportation, other inhumane acts, and persecutions a crimes against humanity. On 30 May 2013, the Trial Chamber found that neither Stainišić nor Simatović were responsible for committing the alleged crimes because it was not established beyond reasonable doubt that they possessed the requisite intent to further the common criminal purpose.

The Appeals Chamber observed that the Trial Chamber did not first adjudicated whether the elements of the *actus reus* of JCE liability were fulfilled and that in the absence of a thorough analysis on the existence and scope of a common criminal purpose shared by a plurality of persons as well as on Stainišić and Simatović's contribution to it, the Trial Chamber could not have properly adjudicated their intent. The Appeals Chamber also concluded that the Trial Chamber erred in law in requiring that the aider and abettor be specifically directed to assist the commission of a crime. In this regard it recalled its previous findings in the *Šainović et al.* and *Popović et al.* cases wherein the Appeals Chamber had affirmed that "specific direction" is not an element of aiding and abetting liability under customary international law.

On the basis of the identified errors, the Appeals Chamber, by majority (Judge Agius partially dissenting and Judge Afande dissenting), found that the case gave rise to appropriate circumstances for retrial pursuant to Rule 117(C) of the Tribunal's Rules of Procedure and Evidence and it ordered a retrial of Stanišić and Simatović under all counts of the indictment.

3.   THE ICTR'S CASE LAW[10]

In 2015, the ICTR delivered one judgment by the Appeals Chamber of the International Residual Mechanism for Criminal Tribunals in *Nyiramasuhuko et al.*

3.1.   Nyiramasuhuko et al.

On 14 December 2015 the Appeals Chamber delivered the last judgment in *Nyiramasuhuko et al.*, which brings an end to the Tribunal's judicial activity.[11]

The Appeals Chamber found that the six appellants' right to be tried without undue delay had been violated, and it reduced the life sentences imposed by the Trial Chamber on Nyiramasuhuko, Ntahobali, and Ndayambaje, to 47 years of imprison-

---

[10] Judgments and decisions of the ICTR are available at: <http://www.unictr.org/en/cases>. On the ICTR, see COMBS, "A New Look at Fact-Finding at the ICTR: Advances in Judicial Acknowledgement", Criminal Law Forum, 2015, p. 387 ff.; and WINDRIDGE, "Assessing Circumstantial Evidence and Inference at the ICTR", Criminal Law Forum, 2015, p. 403 ff.

[11] *Prosecutor v. Pauline Nyiramasuhuko, Arsène Shalom Ntahobali, Sylvain Nsabimana, Alphonse Nteziryayo, Joseph Kanyabashi, Élie Ndayambaje*, Case No. ICTR-98-42-A, Judgment of 14 December 2015.

ment for each of them. With respect to Nsabimana, Nteziryayo, and Kanyabashi, the Appeals Chamber further found errors in the Trial Chamber's determination of their respective sentences, and reduced Nsabimana's sentence to 18 years of imprisonment, Nteziryayo's sentence to 25 years of imprisonment, and Kanyabashi's sentence to 20 years of imprisonment. Considering the time already served, the Appeals Chamber ordered Nsabimana's and Kanyabashi's immediate release.

The Appeals Chamber affirmed Nsabimana's convictions for aiding and abetting the killing of Tutsis by failing to discharge his duty to provide assistance to people in danger and to protect civilians against acts of violence. It also affirmed Nteziryayo's convictions for direct and public incitement to commit genocide for their speeches that constituted direct appeals to the population to kill Tutsis. By majority, the Appeals Chamber affirmed Kanyabashi's convictions for committing direct and public incitement to commit genocide and reversed his convictions based on his superior responsibility for the killings of Tutsis. The Chamber affirmed Ndayambaje's conviction for committing direct and public incitement to commit genocide, and also his convictions for aiding and abetting the killings of Tutsis at Mugombwa Church on 20 and 21 April 1994. It also upheld Ndayambaje's convictions on the basis of instigating the killings of Tutsi women and girls, but the Chamber reversed his conviction based on direct and public incitement to commit genocide.

4. THE ICC'S JUDICIAL ACTIVITY[12]

In 2015, proceedings before the Court and investigations continued in the nine pre-existing situations: two situations regarding the Central African Republic (CAR) relating to events of 2002-2003 and to alleged crimes committed since 2012 respectively, Côte d'Ivoire, the Democratic Republic of the Congo (DRC), Kenya, Libya, Mali, Darfur (Sudan), and Uganda.

---

[12] Judgments and decisions of the ICC are available at: <http://www.icc-cpi.int/EN_Menus/icc/Pages/default.aspx>. On the ICC, see BECKMANN-HAMZEI, *Child in ICC Proceedings*, Cambridge, 2015; BIRNBAUM, "Predictive Due Process and the International Criminal Court", Vanderbilt Journal of Transnational Law, 2015, p. 307 ff.; BUFALINI, "The Principle of Legality and the Role of Customary International Law in the Interpretation of the ICC Statute", The Law & Practice of International Courts and Tribunals, 2015, p. 233 ff.; CHAZAL, *The International Criminal Court and Global Social Control: International Criminal Justice in Late Modernity*, New York, 2015; CIAMPI, "Il meccanismo di cooperazione della Corte penale internazionale alla prova dei fatti: che cosa, e perché, non ha funzionato", DUDI, 2015, p. 151 ff.; COLLINS, *Admissibility in the Rome Statute of the International Criminal Court*, Oxford, 2015; COURTNEY and KAOUTZANIS, "Proactive Gatekeepers: The Jurisprudence of the ICC's Pre-Trial Chambers", Chicago Journal of International Law, 2015, p. 518 ff.; DANGNOSSI, *La Cour pénale internationale à l'épreuve de la répression en Afrique: des préjugés aux réalités*, Paris, 2015; DASTUGUE, "The Faults in 'Fair' Trials: An Evaluation of Regulation 55 at the International Criminal Court",

The Office of the Prosecutor continued preliminary examinations of the situations in Afghanistan, Colombia, Guinea, Iraq/UK, and Nigeria; opened one new preliminary examination relating to the situation in Palestine; and completed preliminary examinations in relation to Honduras and Georgia. As regards Honduras, the Office concluded that it lacked a reasonable basis to believe that crimes within the jurisdiction of the Court have been or are being committed. Conversely, the preliminary examination on the situation in Georgia, conducted since August 2008 and relating to alleged crimes committed in and around South Ossetia during the armed conflict between South Ossetian forces, the Georgian army and the Russian armed forces, was closed on 13 October 2015 when the Prosecutor submitted a request to Pre-Trial Chamber I for authorisation to initiate an investigation pursuant to Article

---

Vanderbilt Journal of Transnational Law, 2015, p. 273 ff.; DE VOS, KENDALL and STAHN (eds.), *Contested Justice: The Politics and Practice of the International Criminal Court Interventions*, Cambridge, 2015; DEPREZ, "The Authority of Strasbourg Jurisprudence from the Perspective of the International Criminal Court", Journal européen des droits de l'homme, 2015, p. 278 ff.; FOFÉ DJOFIA MALEWA, *L'administration de la preuve devant la Cour pénale internationale. Règles procédurales et méthodologiques*, Paris, 2015; FREELAND, *Addressing the Intentional Destruction of the Environment During Warfare under the Rome Statute of the International Criminal Court*, Cambridge, 2015; GIL GIL and MACULAN, "Current Trends in the Definition of 'Perpetrator' by the International Criminal Court: From the Decision on The Confirmation of Charges in the *Lubanga* Case to the *Katanga* Judgment", Leiden JIL, 2015, p. 349 ff.; HAMILTON, "Case Admissibility at the International Criminal Court", The Law & Practice of International Courts and Tribunals, 2015, p. 305 ff.; JOYCE, "Duress: From Nuremberg to the International Criminal Court, Finding the Balance between Justification and Excuse", Leiden JIL, 2015, p. 623 ff.; KAMAGATÉ, *La Cour pénale internationale et la lutte contre l'impunité en Afrique*, Paris, 2015; KENDALL, "Commodifying Global Justice: Economies of Accountability at the International Criminal Court", JICJ, 2015, p. 113 ff.; KJELDGAARD-PEDERSEN, "What Defines an International Criminal Court? A Critical Assessment of the Involvement of International Community as a Deciding Factor", Leiden JIL, 2015, p. 113 ff.; MARINIELLO (ed.), *The International Criminal Court in Search of Its Purpose and Identity*, London, 2015; MENNECKE, *International Criminal Court: The Politics and Practice of Prosecuting Atrocity Crimes*, London, 2015; MOFFETT, "Elaborating Justice for Victims at the International Criminal Court: Beyond Rhetoric and the Hague", JICJ, 2015, p. 281 ff.; NTUBE NGANE, *The Position of Witnesses before the International Criminal Court*, Leiden, 2015; RIGNEY, "The Fractured Relationship between Fairness, the Rights of the Accused, and Disclosure at the International Criminal Court", in PETROVIC (ed.), *Accountability for Violations of International Humanitarian Law: Essays in Honour of Tim Mccormack*, London, 2015, p. 198 ff.; ROBINSON, "Inescapable Dyads: Why the International Criminal Court Cannot Win", Leiden JIL, 2015, p. 323 ff.; STAHN (ed.), *The Law and Practice of the International Criminal Court*, Oxford, 2015; STEINBERG (ed.), *Contemporary Issues Facing the International Criminal Court*, Leiden, 2016; TRIFFTERER and AMBOS (eds.), *The Rome Statute of the International Criminal Court: A Commentary*, 3rd ed., München, 2016; VAGIAS and FERENCZ, "Burden and Standard of Proof in Defence Challenges to the Jurisdiction of the International Criminal Court", Leiden JIL, 2015, p. 133 ff.; and WEGNER, *The International Criminal Court in Ongoing Intrastate Conflicts: Navigating the Peace-Justice Divide*, Cambridge, 2015.

15(3) of the Statute covering the period from 1 July 2008 to 10 October 2008.[13] As a result of its examination the Office concluded that war crimes and crimes against humanity falling within the Court's jurisdiction had reasonably been committed by the three parties to the conflict, in particular: killings, forcible displacements and persecution of ethnic Georgian civilians, and destruction and pillaging of their property, by South Ossetian forces (with possible participation by Russian forces); and the crimes of intentionally directing attacks against Georgian peacekeepers by South Ossetian forces; and against Russian peacekeepers by Georgian forces.[14] The authorisation to proceed with an investigation for the crimes committed in and around South Ossetia, Georgia, was granted by Pre-Trial Chamber I on 27 January 2016.[15]

On 16 January 2015, the Office opened a preliminary examination on the basis of an Article 12(3) declaration lodged by the Government of Palestine on 1 January 2015, accepting the jurisdiction of the Court over alleged crimes committed in the occupied Palestinian territory, including East Jerusalem, since 13 June 2014.[16]

As regards the preliminary examination on the situation of the Registered Vessels of Comoros, Greece and Cambodia (arisen in relation to the 31 May 2010 Israeli raid against the "Gaza Freedom Flotilla"), closed in November 2014 for lack of sufficient gravity,[17] on 29 January 2015 the representatives of the Government of the Comoros filed an application for review of the Prosecutor's decision not to proceed, pursuant to Article 53(3)(a) of the ICC Statute, based on two main grounds: (i) the failure to take into account facts which did not occur on the three vessels over which the Court has territorial jurisdiction; and (ii) the errors in addressing the factors relevant to the determination of gravity under Article 17(1)(d) of the Statute.[18]

---

[13] See ICC, "The Prosecutor of the International Criminal Court, Fatou Bensouda, requests judges for authorisation to open an investigation into the Situation in Georgia", Press Release No. ICC-OTP-20151013-PR1159, 13 October 2015. See TSERETELI, "Pre-Trial Chamber of the International Criminal Court Authorizes Initiation of Investigation in Georgia", EJIL: Talk!, 1 February 2016, available at: <http://www.ejiltalk.org/pre-trial-chamber-of-the-international-criminal-court-authorizes-initiation-of-investigation-in-georgia/>.

[14] ICC-OTP, Report on Preliminary Examination Activities 2015, 12 November 2014, paras. 19, 232-251, available at: <https://www.icc-cpi.int/iccdocs/otp/OTP-PE-rep-2015-Eng.pdf>.

[15] See ICC, "ICC Pre-Trial Chamber I authorises the Prosecutor to open an investigation into the situation in Georgia", Press Release No. ICC-CPI-20160127-PR1183, 27 January 2016.

[16] See Report of the International Criminal Court on its Activities in 2014/15 (A/70/350), 28 August 2015, para. 21. The Palestine declaration accepting the jurisdiction of the ICC of 31 December 2014 is available at: <www.icc-cpi.int/iccdocs/PIDS/press/Palestine_A_12-3.pdf>.

[17] ICC-OTP, Statement of the Prosecutor of the International Criminal Court, Fatou Bensouda, on concluding the preliminary examination of the situation referred by the Union of Comoros: "Rome Statute Legal Requirements Have Not Been Met", 6 November 2014.

[18] *Situation on Registered Vessels of the Union of the Comoros, the Hellenic Republic and the Kingdom of Cambodia*, Case No. ICC-01/13-3-Red, Public Redacted Version of Application for Review pursuant to Article 53(3)(a) of the Prosecutor's Decision of 6 November 2014 not to initiate an investigation in the Situation, 29 January 2015.

The application was granted on 16 July 2015 by Pre-Trial Chamber I, which re-quested the Prosecutor to reconsider the decision, Judge Péter Kovács partly dis-senting. The Chamber argued, firstly, that the commencement of an investigation should not be made contingent on the information available at the pre-investigative stage being already clear, univocal or not contradictory since the purpose of an investigation is precisely to provide clarity, and stated accordingly that in the pres-ence of several plausible explanations of the available information, the presumption of Article 53(1) of the Statute is that the Prosecutor investigates in order to be able to properly assess the relevant facts.[19] Moreover, the Chamber stressed that Article 53(1), paras. (a) and (b), set exacting legal requirements limiting the Prosecutor's discretion in deciding whether or not to initiate an investigation.[20]

As to the first ground of appeal, the Chamber held that the rules of jurisdiction in the Statute do not preclude the Court from considering facts that in themselves occur outside of its jurisdiction for the purpose of establishing crimes and their gravity, and observed accordingly that the Prosecutor erred in holding that, for the assessment of gravity, no information in relation to facts occurring elsewhere than on the three vessels over which the Court may exercise territorial jurisdiction can be considered. However, the Chamber found that the Prosecutor did not in fact apply the erroneous principle she announced, but took into account certain facts outside of the Court's jurisdiction, and therefore the validity of her assessment of gravity was not affected.[21] As to the second ground – the alleged failure to properly address the factors relevant to the determination of gravity under Article 17(1)(d) of the Statute – the Chamber stated that the determination of gravity in the deci-sion not to investigate was affected, first of all, by the Prosecutor's failure to take into account whether the persons likely to be the object of the investigation would include those who bear the greatest responsibility for the identified crimes;[22] the Chamber also contested as erroneous and flawed the Prosecutor's assessment as to the *scale* of the crimes in respect to the total number of victims;[23] as to the *nature* of the crimes, finding that she erred in excluding the possibility of torture or inhu-man treatment having been committed;[24] as to the manner of commission of the

---

[19] *Situation on Registered Vessels of the Union of the Comoros, the Hellenic Republic and the Kingdom of Cambodia*, Case No. ICC-01/13-34, Decision on the request of the Union of the Comoros to review the Prosecutor's decision not to initiate an investigation, 16 July 2015, para. 13. See SKANDER GALAND, "The Situation Concerning the *Mavi Marmara* at the ICC: What Might the Next Move of the Prosecutor Be?", EJIL: Talk!, 22 March 2016, available at: <http://www.ejiltalk.org/the-situation-concerning-the-mavi-marmara-at-the-icc-what-might-be-the-next-move-of-the-prosecutor/>.

[20] Para. 14.

[21] Paras. 16-19.

[22] Paras. 22-24.

[23] Paras. 25-26.

[24] Paras. 27-30.

identified crimes;[25] and as to the *impact* of the crimes on the lives of the people in Gaza.[26] The Prosecutor appealed the Pre-Trial Chamber's decision on 27 July 2015. On 6 November 2015, the Appeals Chamber by majority, Judge Silvia Fernández de Gurmendi and Judge Christine Van den Wyngaert dissenting, dismissed the Prosecutor's appeal as inadmissible *in limine*, finding that the impugned decision was not by its nature a decision determining admissibility which could be appealed under Article 82(1)(a) of the Statute.[27]

The most important developments in the ICC's activities during 2015 concerned: (a) with regard to the situation in the Central African Republic, the Appeals Chamber reversal of the decisions ordering the interim release of Jean-Pierre Bemba Gombo, Aimé Kilolo Musamba, Jean-Jacques Mangenda Kabongo, Fidèle Babala Wandu, and Narcisse Arido; and the opening of the trial of Aimé Kilolo Musamba, Jean-Jacques Mangenda Kabongo, Fidèle Babala Wandu, and Narcisse Arido for offences against the administration of justice in connection with witnesses' testimonies in the case *Prosecutor v. Jean-Pierre Bemba Gombo*; (b) with regard to the situation in Darfur (Sudan), the judgment of the Appeals Chamber confirming Abdallah Banda Abakaer Nourain's warrant of arrest; a non-compliance decision against Sudan for its failure to surrender Omar Al Bashir to the Court, and several measures adopted by the Court attempting to obtain the enforcement of the arrest warrants of the Sudanese President; (c) with regard to the situation in the DRC, the Appeals' Chamber judgment on reparations in the *Lubanga* case, establishing the elements of reparations order and the principles governing the reparations for victims; the transferral of Thomas Lubanga Dyilo and Germain Katanga to a prison facility in the DRC, as the first State designated by the ICC for the enforcement of imprisonment's sentences; the confirmation of the acquittal of Mathieu Ngudjolo Chui and the opening of the trial against Bosco Ntaganda; (d) with regard to the situation in Kenya, the confirmation of the arrest warrant against Walter Osapiri Barasa for offences against the administration of justice; the arrest warrants issued against Paul Gicheru and Philip Kipkoech Bett for offences against the administration of justice, and their arrest by the Kenyan police in Nairobi; the termination of the proceedings in the case against Mr. Kenyatta, and the reversal of the decision on Kenya's non-

---

[25] Paras. 31-45.

[26] Paras. 46-48.

[27] *Situation on Registered Vessels of the Union of the Comoros, the Hellenic Republic and the Kingdom of Cambodia*, Case No. ICC-01/13-51, Decision on the admissibility of the Prosecutor's appeal against the "Decision on the request of the Union of the Comoros to review the Prosecutor's decision not to initiate an investigation", 6 November 2015, paras. 50-51 and 66. Conversely, Judge Silvia Fernández de Gurmendi and Judge Christine Van den Wyngaert were of the view that the Impugned Decision was necessarily a "decision with respect to [...] admissibility" within the meaning of Article 82(1)(a) of the Statute, holding that neither the previous jurisprudence of the Appeals Chamber, nor the scheme of the Statute contradict this conclusion. Case No. ICC-01/13-51-Anx, Joint dissenting opinion of Judge Silvia Fernández De Gurmendi and Judge Christine Van Den Wyngaert, 6 November 2015.

compliance with its obligations of cooperation under the Rome Statute, with remand to the Trial Chamber for a new determination; (e) with regard to the situation in Côte d'Ivoire, the joining of the cases against Laurent Gbagbo and Charles Blé Goudé, followed by the start of the joint trial on 28 January 2016; and the rejection of Côte d'Ivoire's appeal against the admissibility of the case against Simone Gbagbo; (f) with regard to the situation in Mali, the warrant of arrest against Ahmad Al Faqi Al Mahdi for war crimes of intentionally directing attacks against buildings dedicated to religion and historic monuments in Timbuktu, and his surrender to the Court by the authorities of Niger; (g) with regard to the situation in Uganda, the surrender of Dominic Ongwen to the ICC's custody by the Central African authorities.

4.1. Central African Republic

The situation in the CAR was referred to the ICC by the country's government in December 2004, and presents two related cases: *Prosecutor v. Jean-Pierre Bemba Gombo* (the trial started on 22 November 2010), and *Jean-Pierre Bemba Gombo, Aimé Kilolo Musamba, Jean-Jacques Mangenda Kabongo, Fidèle Babala Wandu, and Narcisse Arido* (the trial started before Trial Chamber VII on 29 September 2015).[28]

Aimé Kilolo Musamba, Jean-Jacques Mangenda Kabongo, Fidèle Babala Wandu, and Narcisse Arido were granted interim release by Pre-Trial Chamber II on 21 October 2014.[29] Mr. Bemba was granted interim release by Pre-Trial Chamber II on 23 January 2015, but remains in custody in connection with ongoing proceedings in the case of *Prosecutor v. Jean-Pierre Bemba Gombo.*[30] All the suspects were released on the basis that the time they had spent in detention pending trial had become unreasonable. The ICC Prosecutor appealed the Trial Chamber decisions.

On 29 May 2015, the Appeals Chamber reversed and remanded to Trial Chamber VII the 2014 decision of Pre-trial Chamber II ordering the interim release of Mr. Kilolo Musamba, Mr. Mangenda Kabongo, Mr. Babala Wandu, and Mr. Arido.[31] The Appeals Chamber held that, in order to determine whether a person has been in pre-trial detention for an unreasonable amount of time pursuant to

---

[28] See ICC, "Bemba, Kilolo et al. trial opens at International Criminal Court", Press Release No. ICC-CPI-20150929-PR1155, 29 September 2015.

[29] See ICC, "Bemba, Kilolo et al. case: ICC Pre-Trial Chamber II grants interim release to four suspects", Press Release No. ICC-CPI-20141021-PR1053, 21 October 2014.

[30] *Prosecutor v. Jean-Pierre Bemba Gombo, Aimé Kilolo Musamba, Jean-Jacques Mangenda Kabongo, Fidèle Babala Wandu and Narcisse Arido*, Case No. ICC-01/05-01/13-798, Decision on "Mr Bemba's Request for provisional release", 23 January 2015.

[31] *Prosecutor v. Jean-Pierre Bemba Gombo, Aimé Kilolo Musamba, Jean-Jacques Mangenda Kabongo, Fidèle Babala Wandu and Narcisse Arido*, Case No. ICC-01/05-01/13-969, Judgment on the appeals against Pre-Trial Chamber II's decisions regarding interim release in relation to Aimé Kilolo Musamba, Jean-Jacques Mangenda, Fidèle Babala Wandu, and Narcisse Arido and order for reclassification.

Article 60(3) of the Statute, which provides for regular reviews of detention, a Chamber must balance the duration of detention against the risks listed in Article 58(1)(b) of the Statute justifying detention. According to the Appeals Chamber, the Pre-Trial Chamber erred by not conducting a proper assessment of the risks justifying detention and did not carried out appropriately the necessary balancing exercise. However, the Appeals Chamber concluded that, taking into account the length of time that has passed since the release of the four suspects, it would not be in the interests of justice for them to be re-arrested, and maintained their release until the Trial Chamber now seized of the case decides on the matter.[32]

In a separate judgment also rendered on 29 May 2015, the Appeals Chamber on the same grounds reversed and remanded to Trial Chamber VII the decision of Pre-Trial Chamber II, issued on 23 January 2015, ordering Mr. Bemba's interim release.[33]

4.1.1.   Bemba Gombo, Kilolo Musamba, Mangenda Kabongo, Babala Wandu, and Arido

The trial of Jean-Pierre Bemba Gombo, Aimé Kilolo Musamba, Jean-Jacques Mangenda Kabongo, Fidèle Babala Wandu, and Narcisse Arido started on 29 September 2015 for offences against the administration of justice committed between the end of 2011 and 14 November 2013 in connection with witnesses' testimonies in the case of *Prosecutor v. Jean-Pierre Bemba Gombo*, including corruptly influencing witnesses by giving them money and instructions to provide false testimony, presenting false evidence, and giving false testimony in the courtroom.[34] The charges had been confirmed by Pre-Trial Chamber II on 11 November 2014.[35] The four accused are appearing before the Court freely, since on 21 October 2014 they were granted interim release subject to the condition that they appear for trial or whenever summoned.[36]

---

[32] See ICC, "ICC Appeals Chamber delivers its judgments on the appeals regarding the interim release of Mr Jean-Pierre Bemba Gombo, Mr Aimé Kilolo Musamba, Mr Fidèle Babala Wandu, Mr Jean Jacques Mangenda Kabongo and Mr Narcisse Arido", Press Release No. ICC-CPI-20150529- PR1113, 29 May 2015.

[33] *Prosecutor v. Jean-Pierre Bemba Gombo, Aimé Kilolo Musamba, Jean-Jacques Mangenda Kabongo, Fidèle Babala Wandu and Narcisse Arido*, Case No. ICC-01/05-01/13-970, Judgment on the appeal of the Prosecutor against the decision of Pre-Trial Chamber II of 23 January 2015 entitled "Decision on 'Mr Bemba's Request for provisional release'".

[34] See ICC, "Bemba, Kilolo et al. trial opens at International Criminal Court", Press Release No. ICC-CPI-20150929-PR1155, 29 September 2015.

[35] See ICC, "Bemba, Kilolo et al. case: Pre-Trial Chamber II commits five suspects to trial", Press Release No. ICC-CPI-20141111-PR1062, 11 November 2014.

[36] See ICC, "Bemba, Kilolo et al. case: ICC Pre-Trial Chamber II grants interim release to four suspects", Press Release No. ICC-CPI-20141021-PR1053, 21 October 2014.

4.2. Darfur (Sudan)

The situation in Darfur was referred to the ICC by the UN Security Council, acting under Chapter VII of the UN Charter, by Resolution 1593 (2005) of 31 March 2005. Pre-Trial Chamber I issued arrest warrants (all not executed yet) for Ahmad Muhammad Harun (2007), Ali Muhammad Ali Abd-Al-Rahman (2007), Omar Hassan Ahmad Al Bashir (2009 and 2010), Abdel Raheem Muhammad Hussein (2012), and Abdallah Banda Abakaer Nourain (2014).

On 15 April 2015, Pre-Trial Chamber II ordered the Registrar, each and every time that information of travel as regards persons at large who are the subject of a warrant of arrest issued by the Court is relayed to the Court or one of its organs, to remind with a *Note verbale* States affected by such travel of their obligation to cooperate with the Court in the arrest and surrender of that person, stemming from Articles 86 and 89 of the Statute (for States Parties), or from a resolution of the Security Council (in cases arising from a situation referred to the Court pursuant to Article 13(b) of the Statute), or, if no request for arrest and surrender of the relevant suspect had already been transmitted pursuant to a Chamber's order, to transmit such request to the State affected by that suspect's travel, and to proceed in the same way in all cases arising from future situations which could be assigned to the Chamber. The Chamber also ordered the Registrar to prepare a report on the information received as regards travels, whether planned or ongoing, by persons at large for whom a warrant of arrest has been issued by the Court and the action taken in respect of it, as well as on any follow-up which might be received from States, to be filed in the relevant case record, as appropriate.[37]

4.2.1. Abdallah Banda Abakaer Nourain[38]

On 3 March 2015, the Appeals Chamber delivered its judgment rejecting Abdallah Banda's appeal against Trial Chamber IV's decision replacing the summons to appear by a warrant of arrest, issued on 11 September 2014.[39] The Appeals

---

[37] Case No. ICC-02/05-01/09-235-Corr, Corrigendum of "Orders to the Registrar concerning action to be taken in case of information relating to travel of suspects", 15 April 2015.

[38] Abdallah Banda Abakaer Nourain, Commander-in-Chief of *Justice and Equality Movement* Collective-Leadership, faces three charges of war crimes (violence to life in the form of murder; intentionally directing attacks against personnel, installations, material, units or vehicles involved in a peacekeeping mission; and pillaging) allegedly committed in an attack carried out on 29 September 2007 against African Union Peacekeeping Mission in Sudan, in the Umm Kadada locality of North Darfur. The case initially involved also Saleh Mohammed Jerbo Jamus, proceedings against whom were terminated on 4 October 2013 upon evidence of his death.

[39] *Prosecutor v. Abdallah Banda Abakaer Nourain*, Case No. ICC-02/05-03/09-632-Red, Public redacted version of Judgment on the appeal of Mr Abdallah Banda Abakaer Nourain against Trial Chamber IV's issuance of a warrant of arrest, 3 March 2015, para. 31. See also ICC,

Chamber noted that Mr. Banda did not put forth any legal argument in support of the contention that the procedural step of inviting further submissions before issuing an arrest warrant was required as a matter of law; and stated that, in such circumstances as those of the case, no internationally recognised human right to file further submissions appeared to exist.[40] The Appeals Chamber also noted that the Trial Chamber's decision left open the possibility to "revisit […] the conditions of [Mr. Banda's] stay in The Netherlands during trial" in the case of his voluntary appearance after the issuance of the warrant of arrest.[41]

4.2.2. Al Bashir

On 9 March 2015, Pre-Trial Chamber II issued a decision on the Prosecution's request of 19 December 2014 for a finding of non-compliance against the Republic of the Sudan in the case of *Prosecutor v. Omar Hassan Ahmad Al Bashir*, pursuant to Article 87(7) of the Rome Statute. Having registered the clear and persistent refusal of the Sudanese authorities to cooperate with the Court in the arrest and surrender of Omar Al Bashir, the Chamber stressed that, as a member of the UN, Sudan is bound by the terms of the Charter including Article 25 according to which members of the UN agree to accept and carry out the decisions of the Security Council; reminded that in Security Council Resolution 1593 (2005) it was decided that the Government of Sudan shall cooperate fully with and provide any necessary assistance to the Court and the Prosecutor, and averted that this resolution has the legal effect to make the Statute and the relevant Rules governing State Party cooperation applicable vis-à-vis Sudan.[42] The Chamber concluded that Sudan not only disregarded the 2009 and 2010 requests related to its obligation to cooperate in the arrest and surrender of Omar Al Bashir, but also Resolution 1593 (2005), stressing that this course of action calls upon the Security Council to take the nec-

---

"ICC Appeals Chamber confirms decision issuing an arrest warrant for Abdallah Banda", Press Release No. ICC-CPI-20150303-PR1091, 3 March 2015. A leave to appeal the issue arising from the arrest warrant – namely whether the Trial Chamber should have provided Mr. Banda with a further opportunity to present submissions on the appropriateness of replacing the summons to appear with a warrant of arrest after being satisfied that Mr. Banda would not appear voluntarily for his trial – had been granted by the Court on 19 December 2014 (*Prosecutor v. Abdallah Banda Abakaer Nourain*, Case No. ICC-02/05-03/09-619-Red, Public Redacted Version of Corrigendum to Decision on defence application for leave to appeal the decision on "Warrant of arrest for Abdallah Banda Abakaer Nourain" and, in the alternative, request for reconsideration, 19 December 2014, para. 48; and Case No. ICC-02/05-03/09-619-Red-Corr, Corrigendum, 13 January 2015).

[40] Case No. ICC-02/05-03/09-632-Red, para. 31.

[41] Para. 33.

[42] *Prosecutor v. Omar Hassan Ahmad Al Bashir*, Case No. ICC-02/05-01/09-227, Decision on the Prosecutor's Request for a Finding of Non-Compliance against the Republic of the Sudan, 9 March 2015, paras. 14-15.

essary measures they deem appropriate. In this respect, it claimed that since the Security Council, acting under Chapter VII of the Charter, referred "the situation in Darfur, Sudan to the Court as constituting a threat to international peace and security, it must be expected that the Council would follow-up by way of taking such measures which are considered appropriate, if there is an apparent failure on the part of Sudan to cooperate in fulfilling the Court's mandate as entrusted to it by the Council", stressing that absent any follow up action on the part of the Security Council, "any referral by the Council to the ICC under Chapter VII of the UN Charter would never achieve its ultimate goal, namely, to put an end to impunity. Accordingly, any such referral would become futile".[43] The Chamber, in accordance with Article 109(4) of the Regulations, referred the non-compliance decision to the President of the Court for transmission to the Security Council pursuant to Article 17(3) of the Relationship Agreement.[44]

Moreover, during 2015 Pre-Trial Chamber II adopted decisions concerning the travel of President Al Bashir to several African States. In decisions of 23 January 2015, 24 February 2015, and 24 March 2015, the Chamber invited the competent authorities of the addressee States not parties to the Statute (Ethiopia, the United Arab Emirates, Saudi Arabia, Kuwait, Bahrain, and Egypt) to arrest Omar Al Bashir, in the event he entered their respective territory and to surrender him to the Court, recalling that the situation in Resolution 1593 (2005) referring the situation in Darfur to the Court, the Security Council, although recognizing that non-party States (apart from Sudan) have no obligation under the Statute, still urged *all States* and concerned regional and other international organizations to cooperate fully with the Court.[45]

On 26 October 2015, acting in compliance with the aforementioned Chambers' Orders of 15 April 2015,[46] the Registrar transmitted the Republic of India – also a State not Party to the Statute and which had not previously been transmitted a request for arrest and surrender – a request to this end during Omar Al Bashir's travel to India; and issued several reports on Al Bashir's travels to other countries.[47]

---

[43] Paras. 16-17.

[44] Operative para. b.

[45] *Prosecutor v. Omar Hassan Ahmad Al Bashir*, Case No. ICC-02/05-01/09-222, Decision on the Prosecution's Notification of Travel in the Case of The Prosecutor v. Omar Al Bashir, para. 8; and Case No. ICC-02/05-01/09, Decision Regarding Omar Al Bashir's Travel to the United Arab Emirates and His Potential Travel to the Kingdom of Saudi Arabia, the State of Kuwait and the Kingdom of Bahrain, 24 February 2015, para. 9; and Case No. ICC-02/05-01/09-232, Decision Regarding Omar Hassan Ahmad Al Bashir's Travel to the Kingdom of Saudi Arabia and the Arab Republic of Egypt, 24 March 2015, para. 9.

[46] See *supra* section 4.2.

[47] *Prosecutor v. Omar Hassan Ahmad Al Bashir*, Case No. ICC-02/05-01/09-246, Report of the Registry on Omar Al Bashir's Travels to the Kingdom of Saudi Arabia, the State of Qatar and the Arab Republic of Egypt, 12 August 2015; *Prosecutor v. Omar Hassan Ahmad Al Bashir*, Case No. ICC-02/05-01/09-251, Report of the Registry on Omar Al-Bashir's Travels to the Islamic Republic of Mauritania, the Federal Democratic Republic of Ethiopia, the People's Republic

On 28 May 2015, also pursuant to the Orders of 15 April 2015, the Registrar notified a *Note verbale* to the Embassy of South Africa in the Netherlands reminding it of the obligation of South Africa, as a State Party to the Statute, to arrest Omar Al Bashir during its travel to Johannesburg to attend the African Union Summit scheduled from 7 to 15 June 2015 and surrender him to the Court, and, in case of any difficulties in implementing the request for cooperation, to consult with the Court without any delay in accordance with Article 97 of the Statute.[48] On 12 June 2015, upon request of the Republic of South Africa, the Presiding Judge of the Court met with the Ambassador of South Africa to the Netherlands for consultations under Article 97 of the Statute, during which the Ambassador of South Africa made the argument that there was lack of clarity in the law and that the Republic of South Africa was subject to competing obligations. In response, the Presiding Judge explained that there is no ambiguity in the law and that the Republic of South Africa is under the obligation to arrest and surrender to the Court Omar Al Bashir. In particular, he reiterated that the immunities granted to Al Bashir under international law and attached to his position as a Head of State have been implicitly waived by the UN Security Council by Resolution 1593 (2005) referring the situation in Darfur to the Court, and that the Republic of South Africa cannot invoke any other decision, including that of the African Union, providing for any obligation to the contrary.

On 14 June 2015, pending the deliberation of an application filed before the High Court of Justice in Pretoria requesting the South African authorities to arrest Omar Al Bashir, the Court issued a provisional order compelling the same authorities to prevent Al Bashir from leaving the country. On 15 June 2015, the Sudanese President flew out of South Africa from a military base while hearings relating to the adjudication of the application were taking place before the South African bench. On 23 June 2015, in Pretoria, the High Court of South Africa issued a judgment finding, *inter alia*, that the departure of Omar Al Bashir from the country was in non-compliance with the ICC Order of 14 June.[49] On 4 September 2015, the Chamber requested the competent authorities of South Africa to submit, no later than 5 October 2015, their views on the events surrounding Omar Al

---

of China and the Republic of South Sudan, 23 October 2015; and *Prosecutor v. Omar Hassan Ahmad Al Bashir*, Case No. ICC-02/05-01/09-255, Report of the Registry on Omar Al Bashir's Travels to the People's Democratic Republic of Algeria, the Republic of India and the Kingdom of Saudi Arabia, 27 November 2015.

[48] *Prosecutor v. Omar Hassan Ahmad Al Bashir*, Case No. ICC-02/05-01/09-247, Order requesting submissions from the Republic of South Africa for the purposes of proceedings under Article 87(7) of the Rome Statute, 4 September 2015, para. 5.

[49] *Prosecutor v. Omar Hassan Ahmad Al Bashir*, Order, *ibid.* A report summarising the events and circumstances surrounding the consultations held on 12 June 2015 and subsequent developments was filed by the Registrar on 17 June 2015: *Prosecutor v. Omar Hassan Ahmad Al Bashir*, Case No. ICC-02/05-01/09-243, Registry Report on the consultations undertaken under Article 97 of the Rome Statute by the Republic of South Africa and the departure of Omar Al Bashir from South Africa on 15 June 2015, 17 June 2015.

Bashir's attendance of the African Union Summit in Johannesburg in June 2015, with particular reference to their failure to arrest and surrender Omar Al Bashir, for the purposes of the Chamber's determination pursuant to Article 87(7) of the Statute.[50] On 5 October 2015, the Republic of South Africa requested an extension of the time limit for the submission of its views until the finalisation of the judicial process in South Africa. Such an extension was granted on 15 October 2015 by Pre-trial Chamber II, which also ordered the competent South African authorities, should no such developments occur prior to 15 December 2015, to submit a report detailing the status of the relevant domestic judicial proceedings no later than 31 December 2015.[51] Such reports where submitted by the Embassy of South Africa on 21 December and on 24 December 2015.[52]

On 19 October 2015, the Legal Representative of eight victims participating in the case against Omar al-Bashir notified their withdrawal from the case in light of the inability to advance the prosecution of the case since 2009 and in light of the Prosecutor's decision to suspend active investigations into the Darfur situation in late 2014.[53]

4.3. Democratic Republic of the Congo[54]

In April 2004, the DRC Government referred the situation of grave crimes allegedly committed on its territory since 1 July 2002 to the ICC. In relation to this situation, six cases have been brought before the relevant Chambers against Thomas Lubanga Dyilo, Germain Katanga, Bosco Ntaganda, Mathieu Ngudjolo Chui, Callixte Mbarushimana, and Sylvestre Mudacumura. One accused, Bosco Ntaganda, remains in ICC custody after his voluntary surrender to the Court on 22 March 2013. His trial started on 2 September 2015 and the hearings are scheduled to resume in January 2016. Sylvestre Mudacumura remains at large, while Mathieu Ngudjolo Chui has been acquitted by Trial Chamber II, and the charges were not confirmed against Callixte Mbarushimana.

---

[50] *Prosecutor v. Omar Hassan Ahmad Al Bashir*, Order, *cit. supra* note 48, paras. 10-13.

[51] *Prosecutor v. Omar Hassan Ahmad Al Bashir*, Case No. ICC-02/05-01/09-249, Decision on the request of the Republic of South Africa for an extension of the time limit for submitting their views for the purposes of proceedings under Article 87(7) of the Rome Statute, 15 October 2015.

[52] *Prosecutor v. Omar Hassan Ahmad Al Bashir*, Case No. ICC-02/05-01/09-256, Decision of 21 December 2015, and Case No. ICC-02/05-01/09-257, 24 December 2015.

[53] *Prosecutor v. Omar Hassan Ahmad Al Bashir*, Case No. ICC-02/05-01/09-250, Victims' notification of withdrawal from the case against Omar Hassan Ahmed Al-Bashir, 19 October 2015.

[54] On the situation in the DRC before the ICC see MUZUNGU, *La Cour pénale internationale face à la crise en République démocratique du Congo: étude critique et prospective*, Paris, 2015.

On 24 November 2015, the ICC and the DRC finalised an *ad hoc* Agreement in respect of each sentenced person, expressing the willingness of the DRC to accept Mr. Lubanga and Mr. Katanga for the enforcement of their sentences of imprisonment and providing a framework to govern such enforcement. On 8 December 2015, the Presidency of the ICC designated the DRC as the State of enforcement for the sentences pursuant to Article 103 of the Rome Statute, after Mr. Lubanga and Mr. Katanga expressed the preference to serve their sentences of imprisonment in their home country. This constitutes the first time that the ICC has designated a State for the enforcement of imprisonment's sentences. On 19 December 2015, with the close cooperation of the DRC authorities and the support of the Dutch and French authorities, Thomas Lubanga Dyilo and Germain Katanga were transferred to a prison facility in the DRC.[55]

4.3.1. *Lubanga*[56]

On 14 March 2012, Mr. Lubanga was found guilty of the war crimes of enlisting and conscripting children under the age of fifteen years into the *Force patriotique pour la libération du Congo* (FPLC) and using them to participate actively in hostilities. He was sentenced on 10 July 2012 to 14 years of imprisonment, and, on 1 December 2014, the Appeals Chamber confirmed, by majority, the verdict declaring Mr. Lubanga guilty as well as the sentencing decision.

On 22 September 2015, a Panel of three Judges of the Appeals Chamber decided not to reduce Mr. Lubanga Dyilo's sentence pursuant to the review conducted under Article 110(3) of the Statute – which provides that when the person has served two thirds of the sentence the Court shall review the sentence to determine whether it should be reduced.[57] The Panel found, *inter alia*, that Mr. Lubanga's cooperation with the Court did not qualify as "an early and continuing willingness to cooperate" within the meaning of Article 110(4)(a) of the Statute;[58] that he has not provided any voluntary assistance to the Court within the meaning of Article 110(4)

---

[55] See ICC, "Thomas Lubanga Dyilo and Germain Katanga transferred to the DRC to serve their sentences of imprisonment", Press Release No. ICC-CPI-20151219-PR1181, 19 December 2015.

[56] Thomas Lubanga Dyilo was one of the founding members and President of the *Union des Patriotes Congolais* (UPC), created on 15 September 2000. The UPC and its military wing, the *Force Patriotique pour la Libération du Congo* (FPLC), took power in Ituri in September 2002. The UPC/FPLC, as an organised armed group, was involved in an internal armed conflict against the *Armée Populaire Congolaise* (APC) and other Lendu militias, including the *Force de Résistance Patriotique en Ituri* (FRPI), between September 2002 and 13 August 2003.

[57] *Prosecutor v. Thomas Lubanga Dyilo*, Case No. Decision on the review concerning reduction of sentence of Mr. Thomas Lubanga Dyilo, 22 September 2015.

[58] Paras. 36-37.

(b) of the Statute;[59] that he has not genuinely dissociated from his crimes;[60] and that he took no significant action for the benefit of the victims within the meaning of Rule 223(d) of the Rules of Procedure and Evidence (RPE).[61] Although the Panel determined in accordance with Rule 223(c) RPE, that there is a prospect for the re-socialisation and successful resettlement of Mr. Lubanga in the DRC, it considered that in the absence of any other factors in favour of reduction, a reduction of Mr. Lubanga's sentence could not be justified.[62]

As regards the proceedings on reparations, it is recalled that on 7 August 2012, Trial Chamber I decided, for the first time in proceedings at the ICC, on the principles to be applied to reparations for victims in the context of the case against Thomas Lubanga Dyilo and ordered collective reparations to victims to be made through the Trust Fund for Victims. Both Mr. Lubanga and the Prosecutor appealed against the reparations Order.

On 3 March 2015, the Appeals Chamber by majority, Judge Anita Ušacka dissenting, delivered its judgment on the appeals against the Trial Chamber's "decision establishing the principles and procedures to be applied to reparations" in the case against Thomas Lubanga Dyilo.[63] The Appeals Chamber amended the Trial Chamber's order for reparations and instructed the Trust Fund for Victims (TFV) to present a draft implementation plan for collective reparations to the newly constituted Trial Chamber I within six months. The TVF presented the plan on 3 November 2015, and on 9 February 2016 Trial Chamber II ordered the TFV to add information to the plan by 31 December 2016.

In the judgment and the amended order, the Appeals Chamber established the necessary minimum elements required of a reparations order, and the principles governing the reparations for victims. The Appeals Chamber clarified that an order for reparations under Article 75 of the Statute must contain, at a minimum, five essential elements: (1) it must be directed against the convicted person; (2) it must establish and inform the convicted person of his or her liability with respect to the reparations awarded in the order; (3) it must specify, and provide reasons for, the type of reparations ordered, either collective, individual or both; (4) it must define

---

[59] Para. 40.

[60] Paras. 46-47.

[61] Para. 76

[62] Para. 77.

[63] *Prosecutor v. Thomas Lubanga Dyilo*, Case No. ICC-01/04-01/06-3129, Judgment on the appeals against the "Decision establishing the principles and procedures to be applied to reparations" of 7 August 2012 with amended order for reparations (Annex A) and public annexes 1 and 2, 3 March 2015. See also ICC, "Lubanga case: ICC Appeals Chamber amends the Trial Chamber's order for reparations to victims", Press Release No. ICC-CPI-20150303-PR1092, 3 March 2015. See STAHN, "Reparative Justice after the Lubanga Appeals Judgment on Principles and Procedures of Reparation", EJIL: Talk!, 7 April 2015, available at: <http://www.ejiltalk.org/reparative-justice-after-the-lubanga-appeals-judgment-on-principles-and-procedures-of-reparation/>.

the harm caused to direct and indirect victims as a result of the crimes for which the person was convicted, as well as identify the modalities of reparations that the Trial Chamber considers appropriate based on the circumstances of the specific case before it; and (5) it must identify the victims eligible to benefit from the awards for reparations or set out the criteria of eligibility based on the link between the harm suffered by the victims and the crimes for which the person was convicted.[64]

With regard to the first element, the Appeals Chamber determined that reparations orders are intrinsically linked to the individual whose criminal liability is established in a conviction, since they must ensure that offenders account for their acts, and therefore should always be made *against* the convicted person, although they can be made *through* the Trust Fund. Consequently, the Appeals Chamber found that the Trial Chamber erred in not making Mr. Lubanga personally liable for the collective reparations due to his current state of indigence.[65]

The Appeals Chamber confirmed the principle established by the Trial Chamber that reparations are to be awarded based on the harm suffered as a result of the commission of any crime within the jurisdiction of the Court. In this respect, it considered that, for the purpose of reparations, and considering the nature of proceedings on reparations which are different from proceedings at trial, the applicant must provide only sufficient proof of the causal link between the crime and the harm suffered.[66]

As to the nature of the reparations awarded, the Appeals Chamber found that the Trial Chamber did not err in deciding to award reparations only on a collective basis, and not on an individual basis, and highlighted that the number of victims is an important factor in determining that reparations on a collective basis are more appropriate.[67] The Appeals Chamber upheld the Trial Chamber's finding that the victims of the crimes, whether or not they participated in the trial or filed requests for reparations, should be able to participate in the collective reparation awards.[68] The Appeals Chamber amended the Trial Chamber's order to include an instruction to the TFV that it consult with victims who participated at trial and submitted individual requests, in order to acquire their views regarding the appropriate modalities and programmes for reparations awarded on a collective basis.[69]

One question considered by the Appeals Chamber was whether sexual violence could be defined as a "harm" resulting from the crimes for which Mr. Lubanga was convicted. The Appeals Chamber considered that it could not, as Mr. Lubanga was not convicted for crimes of sexual violence and because sexual and gender-based violence was not included as an aggravating factor of the crimes for which he was

---

[64] Para. 1.
[65] Paras. 64-76.
[66] Paras. 79-81.
[67] Paras. 151-157.
[68] Para. 155.
[69] Para. 204.

convicted. However, it held that this did not preclude victims of sexual violence from being able to benefit from assistance activities of the TFV, according to the discretionary assistance mandate of the Fund.[70]

As regards the methods and types of reparations, the Appeals Chamber confirmed the Trial Chamber's finding that reparations programmes should include measures to reintegrate former child soldiers in order to eradicate the victimisation, discrimination and stigmatisation of these young people.[71] With respect to the "community-based approach" adopted by the Trial Chamber in awarding collective reparations, the Appeals Chamber considered that it is appropriate to award collective reparations to a community, understood as a group of victims, if there is a sufficient causal link between the harm suffered by members of that community and the crimes of which Mr. Lubanga was found guilty. Indeed, the Appeals Chamber recalled that only victims who suffered harm as a result of the commission of the crimes of which Mr. Lubanga was found guilty, may claim reparations against him. In this respect, the Appeals Chamber found that in granting an award for reparations to communities the Trial Chamber did not set out any criteria for distinction between those members who suffered harm as a result of the commission of the crimes of which Mr. Lubanga was found guilty, and other members of the communities.[72]

Finally, the Appeals Chamber determined that the draft implementation plan that the TFV is instructed to submit should include the anticipated monetary amount that it considers would be necessary to remedy the harm caused by the crimes for which Mr. Lubanga was convicted;[73] and also a referral process to competent NGOs in the affected areas that offer services to victims of sexual and gender-based violence.[74]

4.3.2. Katanga[75]

On 7 March 2014, Trial Chamber II, ruling in the majority (Judge Christine Van den Wyngaert dissenting), found Germain Katanga guilty of murder as a crime against humanity and murder, attacking a civilian population, destruction of property and pillaging as war crimes, committed on 24 February 2003 during the attack

---

[70] Paras. 196-199.

[71] Para. 202.

[72] Paras. 210-214.

[73] Para. 242.

[74] Para. 199.

[75] Germain Katanga and Mathieu Ngudjolo Chui were respectively the highest-ranking FRPI commander and the former leader of the *Front des nationalistes et intégrationnistes* in the DRC. Upon his acquittal on 18 December 2012 by Trial Chamber II and release from ICC's custody on 21 December 2012, Mr. Ngudjolo Chui applied for asylum in the Netherlands, where he currently remains.

on the village of Bogoro, in the Ituri district of the DRC. On 23 May 2014, Trial Chamber II sentenced Mr. Katanga to a total of twelve years imprisonment.[76] The judgment became final on 25 June 2014, when the Defence and the Office of the Prosecutor discontinued their appeals against it.[77]

The time spent by Mr. Katanga in detention prior to being convicted was deducted from the sentence imposed. Accordingly, on 18 September 2015, Mr. Katanga had served the statutory two-thirds of his sentence. On 13 November 2015, a Panel of three Judges of the Appeals Chamber, specifically appointed by the Appeals Chamber, reviewed Mr. Katanga's sentence pursuant to Article 110 of the Rome Statute, which provides that "[w]hen the person has served two thirds of the sentence; […] the Court shall review the sentence to determine whether it should be reduced", and decided to reduce it by 3 years and 8 months, setting to 18 January 2016 the date for the completion of his sentence, on the basis of the following factors: (i) an early and continuing willingness by Mr. Katanga to cooperate with the Court in its investigations and prosecutions;[78] (ii) a genuine dissociation from his crimes demonstrated by his conduct while in detention, in particular as he repeatedly and publically took responsibility for the crimes for which he was convicted, as well as expressed regret for the harm caused to the victims by his actions;[79] (iii) the prospect of re-socialisation and successful resettlement of Mr. Katanga;[80] and (iv) a clear and significant change in Mr. Katanga's individual circumstances, namely his change in familial responsibilities after the death of his father and brother.[81] The Panel also considered that Mr. Katanga's early release would give rise to some social instability in the DRC, but found no evidence to suggest that it would be of a significant level.[82]

On 19 December 2015, Germain Katanga was transferred to a prison facility in the DRC to serve his sentence of imprisonment.

The reparations proceedings in this case are currently before Trial Chamber II and a decision on reparations for victims will be rendered in due course.

---

[76] *Prosecutor v. Germain Katanga*, No. ICC-01/04-01/07-3484, Décision relative à la peine (Article 76 du Statut), 23 May 2014; and Case No. ICC-01/04-01/07-3484-Anx1, Dissenting opinion of Judge Christine Van den Wyngaert. See also ICC, "Germain Katanga sentenced to 12 years' imprisonment", Press Release No. ICC-CPI-20140523-PR1008, 23 May 2014.

[77] ICC, "Defence and Prosecution discontinue respective appeals against judgment in Katanga case", Press Release No. ICC-CPI-20140625-PR1021, 25 June 2014.

[78] *Prosecutor v. Germain Katanga*, Decision on the review concerning reduction of sentence of Mr Germain Katanga, No. ICC-01/04-01/07-3615, paras. 26-35. See also ICC, "Germain Katanga's sentence reduced and to be completed on 18 January 2016", Press Release No. ICC-CPI-20151113-PR1174, 13 November 2015.

[79] Paras. 47-51.

[80] Paras. 57-61.

[81] Paras. 108-110.

[82] Paras. 74-79.

4.3.3. Ngudjolo Chui[83]

On 27 February 2015, the Appeals Chamber issued its judgment confirming, by majority, Trial Chamber II's decision of 18 December 2012 acquitting Mathieu Ngudjolo Chui of charges of crimes against humanity and war crimes.[84] The Appeals Chamber rejected the three grounds of appeal raised by the Prosecutor against the acquittal decision: firstly, it concluded that the Trial Chamber correctly applied the "beyond reasonable doubt" standard of proof – and not a more exacting standard requiring proof beyond any doubt – in relation to Mr. Ngudjolo Chui's role in the attack on Bogoro; secondly, the Appeals Chamber found that, contrary to the Prosecutor's allegations, the Trial Chamber adopted a correct approach in its decision-making process, taking into account the entirety of the evidence presented. Under the third ground of appeal, which dealt with allegations of witness tampering by Mr. Ngudjolo Chui whilst he was in detention, the Appeals Chamber held, *inter alia*, that even though the Trial Chamber erred in refusing to allow the Prosecutor to use information gleaned from Mr. Ngudjolo Chui's recorded telephone conversations, to cross-examine the accused and two other key witnesses, this error did not materially affect the outcome of the acquittal decision.[85]

Judges Ekaterina Trendafilova and Cuno Tarfusser adopted a joint dissenting opinion and found that the Appeals Chamber should have amended or reversed the Trial Chamber's decision and ordered a new trial before a different Chamber.[86]

4.3.4. Ntaganda[87]

The trial against Bosco Ntaganda opened on 2 September 2015 before Trial Chamber VI, and is expected to take several months. Mr. Ntaganda is accused of thirteen counts of war crimes and five crimes against humanity allegedly committed in Ituri, DRC, in 2002-2003, as part of a widespread and systematic at-

---

[83] The proceedings against Mr. Chui were severed from the proceedings against Mr. Katanga in 2012 (Case No. ICC-01/04-01/07-3319-tENG/FRA, Decision on the implementation of regulation 55 of the Regulations of the Court and severing the charges against the accused persons, 21 October 2012).

[84] *Prosecutor v. Mathieu Ngudjolo Chui*, Case No. ICC-01/04-02/12-271, Judgment on the Prosecutor's appeal against the decision of Trial Chamber II entitled "Judgment pursuant to article 74 of the Statute" of 27 February 2015.

[85] See ICC, "Ngudjolo Chui case: ICC Appeals Chamber confirms the acquittal decision", Press Release No. ICC-CPI-20150227-PR1089, 27 February 2015.

[86] *Prosecutor v. Mathieu Ngudjolo Chui*, Case No. ICC-01/04-02/12-271-AnxA, Joint Dissenting Opinion of Judge Ekaterina Trendafilova and Judge Cuno Tarfusser. See also ICC, "Ngudjolo Chui case: ICC Appeals Chamber confirms the acquittal decision", Press Release No. ICC-CPI-20150227-PR1089, 27 February 2015.

[87] Allegedly, Bosco Ntaganda, born in Rwanda, is the former Deputy Chief of the Staff and FPLC commander.

tack against the civilian population by the *Union des Patriotes Congolais/Forces Patriotiques pour la Libération du Congo* (UPC/FPLC). The accused pleaded not guilty to the charges.[88]

4.4. Kenya[89]

On 31 March 2010, the Prosecution opened an investigation *proprio motu* into crimes against humanity allegedly committed in the Republic of Kenya in the context of the post-electoral violence of 2007 and 2008. On 23 January 2012, Pre-Trial Chamber II confirmed the charges against William Samoei Ruto (Deputy President of Kenya since 2013), Joshua Arap Sang (Head of operations at Kass FM in Nairobi), Francis Kirimi Muthaura (former Head of the Public Service), and Uhuru Muigai Kenyatta (current President of Kenya since 2013) for crimes against humanity, including murder, forcible transfer of population, and persecution (plus rape and other inhumane acts as regards Mr. Muthaura and Mr. Kenyatta), allegedly committed in Kenya between December 2007 and January 2008. The charges against Mr. Muthaura and Mr. Kenyatta were withdrawn on 18 March 2013 and 5 December 2014 respectively, for lack of sufficient evidence. On 2 October 2013, Pre-Trial Chamber II unsealed an arrest warrant against Walter Osapiri Barasa, for several offences against the administration of justice consisting in corruptly or attempting to corruptly influencing ICC witnesses. A challenge submitted by Mr. Barasa, whose arrest and surrender have not yet taken place, to the warrant of arrest against him was rejected by Pre-Trial Chamber II on 10 September 2015, and leave to appeal the rejection was denied on 29 October 2015.[90] On 10 March 2015, Single Judge Ekaterina Trendafilova, acting on behalf of Pre-Trial Chamber II, issued warrants of arrest against Paul Gicheru and Philip Kipkoech Bett for offences against the administration of justice, in particular for corruptly influencing a witness under Article 70(1)(c) of the Statute in conjunction with Article 25(3). According to the Single Judge, there are reasonable grounds to believe that an organised and well-coordinated scheme existed, involving with different roles both Paul Gicheru and Philip Kipkoech Bett, aiming at the corruption of six witnesses of

---

[88] See ICC, "Ntaganda trial opens at International Criminal Court", Press Release No. ICC-CPI-20150902-PR1143, 2 September 2015; and ICC, "Opening statements in Ntaganda trial conclude at International Criminal Court; trial hearings to resume on 15 September 2015", Press Release No. ICC-CPI-20150903-PR1144, 3 September 2015.

[89] On the situation in Kenya before the ICC see MATERU, *The Post-Election Violence in Kenya: Domestic and International Legal Responses*, The Hague, 2015; and NICHOLS, *The International Criminal Court and the End of Impunity in Kenya*, Heidelberg, 2015.

[90] *Prosecutor v. Walter Osapiri Barasa*, Case No. ICC-01/09-01/13-35, Decision on the "Defence challenge to the warrant for the arrest of Walter Osapiri Barasa", 10 September 2015; and *Prosecutor v. Walter Osapiri Barasa*, Case No. ICC-01/09-01/13-41, Decision on the "Defence request for leave to appeal decision ICC-01/09- 01/13-35", 29 October 2015.

the Prosecutor.[91] The Single Judge also found that the requirements of Article 58(1) of the Statute were met for the issuance of warrants of arrest against Mr. Gicheru and Mr. Kipkoech Bett, their arrest appearing necessary for all three reasons articulated in Article 58(1)(b), namely: to ensure their appearance at trial; to ensure that they do not obstruct or endanger the investigation or court proceedings; and to prevent the further exercise of corrupt influence on the witnesses of the Court.[92] Paul Gicheru and Philip Kipkoech Bett were arrested on 30 July 2015 by the Kenyan police in Nairobi, in execution of the Court's request for arrest and surrender. After their arrest, Pre-Trial Chamber II unsealed the warrants of arrest against them.[93]

4.4.1. Samoei Ruto and Arap Sang

On 19 August 2015, in the context of the trial against Mr. Ruto and Mr. Sang, started on 10 September 2013, Trial Chamber V(A) granted the Prosecutor's request for admission of prior recorded testimony into evidence for the truth of its contents, pursuant to amended rule 68 of the Rules of Procedure and Evidence (RPE).[94] The decision was reversed on 12 February 2016 by the Appeals Chamber, which considered that the amended rule could not apply to this case pursuant to Article 51(4) of the Rome Statute, providing that amendments to the RPE shall not be applied retroactively to the detriment of the accused. Indeed, amended Rule 68 of the RPE was adopted by the Assembly of States Parties on 27 November 2013 after the start of the trial, and its retroactive application negatively affected the overall position of Mr. Sang and Mr. Ruto in the proceedings.[95]

4.4.2. Kenyatta

On 29 November 2013, the Prosecution filed an application for a finding of non-cooperation against the Kenyan Government and referral of the matter to the Assembly of States Parties (ASP), alleging that the Government had failed to com-

---

[91] *Prosecutor v. Paul Gicheru and Philip Kipkoech Rett*, Case No. ICC-01/09-01/15-1-Red, Public redacted version of Decision on the "Prosecution's Application under Article 58(1) of the Rome Statute", 10 September 2015.

[92] Paras. 24-29.

[93] *Prosecutor v. Paul Gicheru and Philip Kipkoech Rett*, Case No. ICC-01/09-01/15-11, Order unsealing the warrant of arrest and other documents, 10 September 2015.

[94] *Prosecutor v. William Samoei Ruto and Joshua Arap Sang*, Case No. ICC-01/09-01/11-1938-Corr-Red2, Public Redacted Version of Corrigendum: Decision on Prosecution Request for Admission of Prior Recorded Testimony, 19 August 2015.

[95] ICC, "Ruto and Sang case: ICC Appeals Chamber reverses Trial Chamber V(A)'s decision on admission of prior recorded testimony", Press Release No. ICC-CPI-20160212-PR1189, 12 February 2016.

ply with a request to produce records relating to Mr. Kenyatta. On 3 December 2014, Trial Chamber V(B) rejected the Prosecutor's application for referral of the matter to the ASP. The Prosecutor appealed this decision on 20 March 2015.

On 5 December 2014, the Prosecutor withdrew the charges against Mr. Kenyatta, declaring it had no alternative given the state of the evidence in this case, but without prejudice to the possibility of bringing a new case should additional evidence become available.[96] On 13 March 2015, Trial Chamber V(B), noting the Prosecution's withdrawal of charges against Mr. Kenyatta, decided to terminate the proceedings in the case and to vacate the summons to appear against him.[97] In the Decision on the withdrawal of the charges, the Chamber stressed, *inter alia*, that, although the proceedings shall be terminated, the Court retains jurisdiction over any interference with a witness or with the collection of evidence and that the protective measures ordered for witnesses and/or victims shall continue, subject to the review by the Court. The Chamber recalled that, in its previous decision of 3 December 2014, it had indicated that, in the event of a withdrawal of charges by the Prosecution, the principle of *ne bis in idem* would not attach, and it would be open to the Prosecution to bring new charges against the accused at a later date, based on the same or similar factual circumstances, should it obtain sufficient evidence to support such a course of action.[98] The Chamber also considered that, although the proceedings were being terminated, it might be necessary to resume a residual jurisdiction on the case depending on the manner in which the Prosecution's appeal of the decision of 3 December 2014 declining to refer to the ASP the matter in relation to non-compliance of the Kenyan Government with its obligations under the Rome Statute, is resolved.[99]

---

[96] *Prosecutor v. Uhuru Muigai Kenyatta*, Case No. ICC-01/09-02/11-983, Notice of withdrawal of the charges against Uhuru Muigai Kenyatta, 5 December 2014. See also ICC, "Statement of the Prosecutor of the International Criminal Court, Fatou Bensouda, on the withdrawal of charges against Mr. Uhuru Muigai Kenyatta", Press Release, 5 December 2014.

[97] *Prosecutor v. Uhuru Muigai Kenyatta*, Case No. ICC-01/09-02/11-1005, Decision on the withdrawal of charges against Mr Kenyatta, 13 March 2015. See also ICC, "Kenyatta case: Trial Chamber V(B) terminates the proceedings", Press Release No. ICC-CPI-20150313-PR1099, 13 March 2015.

[98] Para. 9.

[99] Para. 11. On 9 March 2015, the Chamber granted the Prosecutor's request to appeal the decision of 3 December 2014 (*Prosecutor v. Uhuru Muigai Kenyatta*, Case No. ICC-01/09-02/11-1004, Decision on the Prosecution's request for leave to appeal, 9 March 2015). In granting leave, the Trial Chamber, taking into account the Prosecutor's mandate under Article 54(1) of the Statute, found that the Prosecutor's capacity "to secure future or ongoing cooperation would be significantly affected by whether or not [it] had appropriately exercised its discretion" in not referring the matter to the Assembly of States Parties (para. 8). On March 2015, 839 victims in the case filed a request to participate in the Prosecutor's appeal against the Decision on Prosecution's application for a finding of non-compliance under Article 87(7) of the Statute. On 24 April 2015, the Appeals Chamber granted the victims the right to participate for the purpose of presenting their views and concerns with respect to their personal interests in the issues raised on appeal, finding that the four cumulative criteria set in Article 68(3) of the Statute for victims' participa-

Indeed, on 9 August 2015 the Appeals Chamber, though rejecting the Prosecutor's grounds of appeal, reversed Trial Chamber V(B)'s decision of 3 December 2014 regarding the Kenyan Government's alleged non-compliance with its obligations under the Rome Statute, due to errors in the Trial Chamber's assessment, and remanded it for the Trial Chamber for a new determination as to whether Kenya has failed to comply with a cooperation request that has prevented the Court from exercising its functions and powers and, if so, to make an assessment of whether it is appropriate to refer Kenya's non-compliance to the ASP.[100] Under the first ground of appeal, the Prosecutor had argued that, once the Trial Chamber made a finding on Kenya's non-compliance with the request for cooperation that prevented the Court from exercising its functions and powers, the Trial Chamber, having no discretion not to do so, should have automatically referred the matter to the ASP.[101] Contrary to the Prosecutor's stance, and also in the light of the Court's jurisprudence,[102] the Appeals Chamber found that the Trial Chamber did not err in law by not automatically referring Kenya to the ASP once it had made a factual determination of a failure to cooperate that affected the Trial Chamber's ability to exercise its functions and powers under the Statute. The Appeals Chamber considered that, since the object and purpose of Article 87(7) is to foster cooperation, a referral is not an automatic consequence of a finding of a failure to comply with a request for cooperation, but rather this determination falls within the discretion of the Chamber, which will often need to take into account considerations that are distinct from the factual assessment of whether the State has failed to comply with a request to cooperate.[103] The Appeals Chamber also rejected the Prosecutor's second ground of appeal, under which it was argued that, if the Trial Chamber did have discretion regarding whether to refer the matter, it erred in the exercise of its discretion by considering irrelevant factors and by failing to consider other relevant factors.[104] The Appeals Chamber found that the Trial Chamber erred in the exer-

---

tion in appeals brought under Article 82(1)(d) had been fulfilled, namely: (i) the individuals seeking participation must be victims in the case; (ii) their personal interests must be affected by the issues on appeal; (iii) their participation must be at an appropriate stage of the proceedings; and (iv) the manner of participation should neither cause prejudice to nor be inconsistent with the rights of the accused and a fair and impartial trial. (*Prosecutor v. Uhuru Muigai Kenyatta*, Case No. ICC-01/09-02/11-1015, Decision on the victims' request to participate in the appeal proceedings, 24 April 2015, para. 8).

[100] *Prosecutor v. Uhuru Muigai Kenyatta*, Case No. ICC-01/09-02/11-1032, Judgment on the Prosecutor's appeal against Trial Chamber V(B)'s "Decision on Prosecution's application for a finding of non-compliance under article 87(7) of the Statute", 19 August 2015, paras. 94 and 98. See also ICC, "ICC Appeals Chamber reverses decision on Kenya's cooperation and remands issue to Trial Chamber for new determination", Press Release No. ICC-CPI-20150819-PR1139, 19 August 2015.

[101] Para. 29.

[102] Analysed in paras. 45-49.

[103] Paras. 51-54.

[104] Para. 54.

cise of its discretion by conflating the non-compliance proceedings against Kenya with the criminal proceedings against Mr. Kenyatta, by failing to address whether judicial measures had been exhausted and by assessing the sufficiency of evidence and the conduct of the Prosecutor in an inconsistent manner, and concluded that these errors materially affected the Trial Chamber's decision not to refer the matter of Kenya's non-compliance, and also prevented the Trial Chamber from making a conclusive determination on the existence of a failure to comply with a request to cooperate by the Court which prevents the Court from exercising its functions and powers under the Statute, as required by the first clause of Article 87(7) of the Statute.[105] Taking the view that the Chamber of first instance is generally better placed to identify and assess the relevant facts and circumstances in order to decide whether engaging external actors under Article 87(7) of the Statute would foster cooperation, the Appeals Chamber considered it appropriate to remand the decision to Trial Chamber.[106]

4.4.3. Barasa

On 21 August 2015, the defence for Walter Osapiri Barasa challenged the warrant of arrest against the suspect, requesting Pre-Trial Chamber II to revoke it and issue in its place a summons to appear pursuant to Article 58(7) of the Statute. The request was framed by relying on Rule 117(3) of the Rules of Procedure and Evidence (RPE), which provides for a challenge as to whether the warrant of arrest was properly issued in accordance with Article 58(1), paras. (a) and (b), of the Statute.[107] On 10 September 2015, Pre-Trial Chamber II dismissed the request. The Chamber considered it dispositive that, irrespective of whether challenges under Rule 117(3) of the RPE are inadmissible as such in proceedings with respect to offences under Article 70 of the Statute, in any case Rule 117 does not become applicable until the person for whom a warrant of arrest has been issued is detained in the custodial State, which is not the case with Walter Osapiri Barasa.[108]

On 15 September 2015, the counsel for Mr. Barasa requested leave to appeal the Decision dismissing the challenge to the arrest warrant, pursuant to Article 82(1)(d) of the Rome Statute.[109] The Prosecutor responded on 18 September 2015 submitting that the Request should be rejected *in limine* because the Defence has

---

[105] Paras. 90-91.

[106] Paras. 93-94.

[107] *Prosecutor v. Walter Osapiri Barasa*, Case No. ICC-01/09-01/13-31, Defence challenge to the warrant for the arrest of Walter Osapiri Barasa, 21 August 2015.

[108] *Prosecutor v. Walter Osapiri Barasa*, Case No. ICC-01/09-01/13-35, Decision on the "Defence challenge to the warrant for the arrest of Walter Osapiri Barasa", 10 September 2015, paras. 1-2.

[109] *Prosecutor v. Walter Osapiri Barasa*, Case No. ICC-01/09-01/13-37, Defence request for leave to appeal decision ICC-01/09-01/13-35, 15 September 2015.

no standing until Walter Barasa is detained in the custodial State.[110] On 29 October 2015, Pre-Trial Chamber II rejected Mr. Barasa's leave to appeal.[111] The Chamber noted the Prosecutor's argument, but considered it appropriate to examine the merits of the Request, as this aimed to obtain leave to appeal precisely the Chamber's ruling on the applicability of Rule 117 to the proceedings.[112] The Chamber noted that proceedings under Rule 117 are not intermediate in the sense of ultimately leading to a decision or judgment which would be appealable pursuant to Articles 81 or 82 of the Statute. Indeed, a decision of the Chamber on a challenge to the warrant of arrest under Rule 117 constitutes the outcome of a separate, distinct proceeding under that Rule. In this sense, it determined that issues raised with respect to these proceedings cannot be said to have a significant impact on the fairness and expeditiousness of the proceedings, or on the outcome of trial. Accordingly, the leave to bring an interlocutory appeal against the Decision was rejected.[113]

4.5. Côte d'Ivoire

On 15 February 2013, Côte d'Ivoire ratified the Rome Statute. Before becoming party to the Statute, on 18 April 2003 the country accepted ICC's jurisdiction. It had reconfirmed such acceptance on 14 December 2010 and 3 May 2011.

On 3 October 2011, Pre-Trial Chamber III authorized the Prosecutor to open investigations *proprio motu* into the situation in Côte d'Ivoire, with respect to alleged crimes against humanity and war crimes committed since 28 November 2010, as well as with regard to "continuing crimes" committed in the context of the ongoing situation in the country. On 22 February 2012, the Chamber expanded its authorization to also include crimes allegedly committed between 19 September 2002 and 28 November 2010.[114]

On 11 December 2014, Pre-Trial Chamber I rejected Côte d'Ivoire's challenge to the admissibility of the case against Simone Gbagbo, on the grounds that Côte d'Ivoire had not demonstrated that the case is currently subject to domestic proceedings within the meaning of Article 17(1)(a) of the Statute.[115] The Chamber

---

[110] *Prosecutor v. Walter Osapiri Barasa*, Case No. ICC-01/09-01/13-38, Prosecution's Response to "Defence challenge to the warrant for the arrest of Walter Osapiri Barasa" (ICC-01/09-01/13-31, 21 August 2015), 18 September 2015.

[111] *Prosecutor v. Walter Osapiri Barasa*, Case No. ICC-01/09-01/13-41, Decision on the "Defence request for leave to appeal decision ICC-01/09- 01/13-35", 29 October 2015.

[112] Para. 6.

[113] Para. 8.

[114] Decision on the "Prosecution's provision of further information regarding potentially relevant crimes committed between 2002 and 2010", 22 February 2012.

[115] *Prosecutor v. Simone Gbagbo*, Case No. ICC-02/11-01/12-47-Red, Public redacted Decision on Côte d'Ivoire's challenge to the admissibility of the case against Simone Gbagbo, 11 December 2014.

found the investigative activities undertaken by the domestic authorities to be sparse and disparate, rather than tangible, concrete and progressive; and the information available on the scope of the national proceedings against Simone Gbagbo unclear with respect to the alleged crimes. The decision also resulted in the termination of the effects of Article 95 of the Statute which, as of the filing of the Admissibility Challenge on 30 September 2013, had allowed Côte d'Ivoire to postpone the execution of the request for the surrender of Simone Gbagbo to the Court. The Court therefore ordered Côte d'Ivoire to proceed to surrender Simone Gbagbo to the Court without delay. On 17 December 2014 Côte d'Ivoire appealed the decision and requested for suspensive effect of the appeal pursuant to Article 82(3) of the Statute.[116] On 20 January 2015, the Appeals Chamber rejected the request for suspensive effect in respect to the State's obligation to surrender Simone Gbagbo to the Court without delay. The arrest warrant remains pending and Ms. Gbagbo is not yet in the ICC's custody.[117]

On 27 May 2015 the Appeals Chamber rejected Côte d'Ivoire's appeal and confirmed the ICC Pre-Trial Chamber I's decision of 11 December 2014 declaring the case against Simone Gbagbo admissible before the Court.[118] As regards Côte d'Ivoire's main arguments submitted under the first ground of appeal, the Appeals Chamber held that Pre-Trial Chamber: had not violated the principle of complementarity by setting overly rigorous criteria in determining that no relevant investigations or prosecutions were ongoing at the national level;[119] and had not erred in applying the "same person/same conduct" test by undertaking a purely formal examination of the proceedings in Côte d'Ivoire.[120] The Appeals Chamber also rejected the main arguments put forward under the second ground of appeal, finding that Côte d'Ivoire failed to demonstrate that it was unreasonable for the Pre-Trial Chamber to conclude that, on the basis of the available documentation, the factual parameters of the case or cases being investigated domestically were unclear.[121] Moreover, regarding the Pre-Trial Chamber's assessment of the nature of the conduct underlying crimes being investigated domestically, namely economic crimes and crimes against the State, the Appeals Chamber found that it was not unreason-

---

[116] *Prosecutor v. Simone Gbagbo*, Case No. ICC-02/11-01/12-48-tENG, Appeal of the Republic of Côte d'Ivoire against Pre-Trial Chamber I's Decision on Côte d'Ivoire challenge to the admissibility of the case against Simone Gbagbo, dated 17 December 2014 and registered on 27 January 2015.

[117] See ICC, "Appeals Chamber confirms admissibility of the ICC's Simone Gbagbo case", Press Release No. ICC-CPI-20150527- PR1112, 27 May 2015.

[118] *Prosecutor v. Simone Gbagbo*, Case No. ICC-02/11-01/12-75-Red, Judgment on the appeal of Côte d'Ivoire against the decision of Pre-Trial Chamber I of 11 December 2014 entitled "Decision on Côte d'Ivoire's challenge to the admissibility of the case against Simone Gbagbo", 27 May 2015.

[119] Paras. 58-61.

[120] Para. 71.

[121] Para. 92

able for the Pre-Trial Chamber to find this conduct to be "clearly of a different nature" from the conduct alleged in the proceedings before the Court, and related to the crimes against humanity of murder, rape and other forms of sexual violence, persecution and other inhumane acts, on the basis of which the warrant of arrest against Ms. Gbagbo was issued.[122] The Appeals Chamber also found that, contrary to Côte d'Ivoire's argument, it was not unreasonable for the Pre-Trial Chamber to conclude that the investigative steps, in view of their number and frequency, were "sparse and disparate".[123]

4.5.1. Laurent Gbagbo[124] and Charles Blé Goudé[125]

On 11 March 2015, Trial Chamber I decided to join the cases concerning Laurent Gbagbo and Charles Blé Goudé, deeming a joint trial appropriate to ensure the efficacy and expeditiousness of the proceedings. The Chamber noted that the conduct of Mr. Gbagbo and Mr. Blé Goudé is closely linked, that largely the same

---

[122] Paras. 98-100.

[123] Para. 131.

[124] On 23 November 2011, Pre-Trial Chamber III had unsealed an arrest warrant against Laurent Gbagbo, former Ivorian President, for crimes against humanity allegedly committed in the context of post-electoral violence in Côte d'Ivoire between 16 December 2010 and 12 April 2011. He was surrendered to the Court by the Ivorian authorities on 30 November 2011, and made his initial appearance on 5 December 2011. On 12 June 2014, Pre-Trial Chamber I by majority (Judge Christine Van den Wyngaert dissenting) confirmed the charges against Laurent Gbagbo. He is accused of having engaged his individual criminal responsibility for committing the crimes against humanity of murder, rape, other inhumane acts, or – in the alternative – attempted murder, and persecution, against pro-Ouattara supporters, jointly with members of his inner circle and through members of the pro-Gbagbo forces (Article 25(3)(a) of the Rome Statute), or, in the alternative, for ordering soliciting and inducing the commission of these crimes (Article 25(3)(b) of the Rome Statute), or, in the alternative, for contributing in any other way to the commission of these crimes (Article 25(3)(d) of the Rome Statute). On 11 September 2014, the Appeals Chamber denied the Defence application for leave to appeal the Decision Confirming Charges, thereby concluding the pre-trial proceedings in the case.

[125] Charles Blé Goudé, an Ivorian political leader, was surrendered to the ICC on 22 March 2014 by the national authorities of Côte d'Ivoire following a warrant of arrest issued by the ICC on 21 December 2011 and unsealed on 30 September 2013. On 11 December 2014, Pre-Trial Chamber I confirmed four charges of crimes against humanity against Charles Blé Goudé (murder, rape, other inhumane acts or, in the alternative, attempted murder and persecution) allegedly committed in Abidjan, Côte d'Ivoire, between 16 December 2010 and or around 12 April 2011, in the context of a widespread and systematic attack carried out by the pro-Gbagbo forces against civilians perceived to be Alassane Ouattara's supporters, pursuant to an organisational policy aimed at keeping Laurent Gbagbo in power. Mr. Blé Goudé is accused of having engaged his individual criminal responsibility for committing these crimes, alternatively, as indirect co-perpetrator (under Article 25(3)(a) of the Rome Statute), ordering, soliciting or inducing (Article 25(3)(b)), aiding, abetting or otherwise assisting (Article 25(3)(c)), or contributing in any other way to the commission of these crimes (Article 25(3)(d)).

evidence has been and will be presented in both cases, and that they both have had charges confirmed against them which arise from the same allegations, namely crimes allegedly committed during the same incidents by the same direct perpetrators who targeted the same victims because they were perceived to be supporters of Alassane Ouattara. The Chamber also vacated the commencement date for the trial in the Gbagbo case, originally set for 7 July 2015.[126]

On 28 October 2015 Trial Chamber I rescheduled the opening of the trial, previously scheduled for 10 November 2015, to 28 January 2016, finding it appropriate to order the attendance of the experts appointed by the Chamber to report on Mr. Gbagbo's health condition, as requested by the Defence.[127] The trial of Laurent Gbagbo and Charles Blé Goudé opened at ICC on 28 January 2016.[128]

4.6. Libya

The situation in Libya since 15 February 2011 was referred to the ICC on 26 February 2011 by Resolution 1970 (2011) by the UN Security Council, acting under Chapter VII of the UN Charter and Article 13(b) of the Rome Statute.[129] Warrants of arrest were issued in 2011 for Saif Al-Islam Gaddafi (former *de facto* Head of Libyan Government), Abdullah Al-Senussi (former Head of Libyan Military Intelligence, whose case was declared inadmissible on 24 July 2014 and formally terminated on 7 August 2014),[130] and Muammar Mohammed Abu Minyar Gaddafi (the former Libyan President, whose case was formally terminated on 22 November 2011 after his death).[131]

Saif Al-Islam Gaddafi was arrested by the Libyan authorities on 19 November 2011 and remains in detention in Zintan. On 10 December 2014, Pre-Trial Chamber II made a finding of non-compliance by Libya with the Court's requests to surrender Saif Al-Islam Gaddafi and to return to the Defence the originals of the privileged documents seized from his former counsel in Zintan by the Libyan au-

---

[126] See ICC, "ICC Trial Chamber I joins the cases concerning Laurent Gbagbo and Charles Blé Goudé", Press Release No. ICC-CPI-20150311-PR1097, 11 March 2015.

[127] See ICC, "The trial of Laurent Gbagbo and Charles Blé Goudé to open on 28 January 2016", Press Release No. ICC-CPI-20151028-PR1163, 28 October 2015.

[128] See ICC, "Trial of Laurent Gbagbo and Charles Blé Goudé opens at International Criminal Court", Press Release No. ICC-CPI-20160128-PR1184, 28 January 2016.

[129] UN Security Council Resolution 1970 of 26 February 2011 on Peace and Security in Africa.

[130] *Prosecutor v. Saif Al-Islam Gaddafi and Abdullah Al-Senussi*, Case No. ICC-01/11-01/11-567, Decision following the declaration of inadmissibility of the case against Abdullah Al-Senussi before the Court, 7 August 2014.

[131] ICC, Warrant of Arrest for Abdullah Al-Senussi, No. ICC-01/11-01/11-4, 27 June 2011; ICC, Warrant of Arrest for Saif Al-Islam Gaddafi, No. ICC-01/11-01/11-3, 27 June 2011; and ICC, Warrant of Arrest for Muammar Mohammed Abu Minyar Gaddafi, No. ICC-01/11-01/11-2, 27 June 2011.

thorities and destroy any copies thereof, and referred the matter to the UN Security Council.[132] The English and Arabic versions of the Decision on non-compliance were notified by the Registry to the Focal point of Libya for the Court on 2 March 2015.[133]

4.6.1. *Gaddafi*

Saif Al-Islam Gaddafi is allegedly responsible as indirect co-perpetrator for two counts of crimes against humanity (murder and persecution) committed across Libya from 15 February 2011 until at least 28 February 2011, through the State apparatus and security forces. On 21 May 2014, the Appeals Chamber issued by majority – Judge Anita Ušacka dissenting and with a separate concurring opinion by Judge Sang-Hyun Song – its judgment confirming the decision of Pre-Trial Chamber I rejecting Libya's challenge to the admissibility of the case against Saif Al-Islam Gaddafi and declaring it admissible.[134]

Mr. Gaddafi was sentenced to death by the Tripoli Court of Appeal on 28 July 2015 along with several other co-accused for their roles during Libya's 2011 uprising.

On 30 July 2015 the Prosecution requested that the Pre-Trial Chamber I order Libya to refrain from carrying out Mr. Gaddafi's sentence, surrender him to the Court, and inform the Security Council of the death sentence handed down to Mr. Gaddafi by the Tripoli Court of Appeal.[135] In its Response of 20 August 2015 to the Prosecution's request the Libyan Government advanced several reasons making

---

[132] *Prosecutor v. Saif Al-Islam Gaddafi and Abdullah Al-Senussi*, Case No. ICC-01/11-01/11-577, Decision on the non-compliance by Libya with requests for cooperation by the Court and referring the matter to the United Nations Security Council, 10 December 2014. As from 7 August 2014, the case is referred to as "*The Prosecutor v. Saif Al-Islam Gaddafi*", to reflect that the proceedings against Abdullah Al-Senussi before the Court have come to an end. See Decision following the declaration of inadmissibility of the case against Abdullah Al-Senussi before the Court, No. ICC-01/11-01/11-567, 7 August 2014, *cit. supra* note 130.

[133] *Prosecutor v. Saif Al-Islam Gaddafi*, Case No. ICC-01/11-01/11-587, Registrar's Report on the referral to the United Nations Security Council and the notification of the Decision on the non-compliance by Libya with requests for cooperation, 18 March 2015.

[134] *Prosecutor v. Saif Al-Islam Gaddafi*, Case No. ICC-01/11-01/11-547-Red, Judgment on the appeal of Libya against the decision of Pre-Trial Chamber I of 31 May 2013 entitled "Decision on the admissibility of the case against Saif Al-Islam Gaddafi", 21 May 2014; Case No. ICC-01/11-01/11-547-Anx1, Separate Opinion of Judge Sang-Hyun Song; and Case No. ICC-01/11-01/11-547-Anx2, Dissenting Opinion of Judge Anita Ušacka. See also ICC, "ICC Appeals Chamber confirms the admissibility before the ICC of the case against Saif-Al-Islam Gaddafi", Press Release No. ICC-CPI-20140521-PR1005, 21 May 2014.

[135] *Prosecutor v. Saif Al-Islam Gaddafi*, Case No. ICC-01/11-01/11-611, Prosecution Request for an Order to Libya to Refrain from Executing Saif Al-Islam Gaddafi, Immediately Surrender Him to the Court, and Report His Death Sentence to the United Nations Security Council, 30 July 2015.

it currently impossible for Libya to comply with the obligation to surrender Mr. Gaddafi or to otherwise cooperate with the Court, and requested accordingly that the Prosecutor's request be rejected.[136] The Libyan Government stressed that the Prosecutor's request for an order that Libya refrain from executing Mr. Gaddafi is not necessary because the death sentence is not final: first, because it arises from a trial *in absentia*, but once Mr. Gaddafi is transferred from Zintan into the custody of the State, he will have an absolute right to a new trial in person; secondly, because any judgment against Mr. Gaddafi will in any case be subject to appeal before the Supreme Court of Libya.[137]

With regard to the request for Libya to immediately surrender Mr. Gaddafi to the Court, the State representatives stressed that Mr. Gaddafi's continued custody in Zintan precludes any possibility for him to be surrendered to the Court.[138] Moreover, the Government put forward the deterioration of the security situation in recent months, alleging that bombing campaigns and other acts of terrorism have disrupted effective communication and negotiations between Zintan and Tripoli concerning transfer of the custody of Mr. Gaddafi to the Libyan Government, and stated that until a unified Libyan Government can be established, there is no authority in Libya that can properly make and implement a decision in respect of the situation of Mr. Gaddafi.[139]

4.7. Mali

The situation in Mali was referred to the ICC by the government of Mali on 13 July 2012 in relation to crimes against humanity and war crimes (murder, mutilation, cruel treatment and torture, intentionally directing attacks against protected objects, the passing of sentences and the carrying out of executions without previous judgment pronounced by a regularly constituted court, pillaging, and rape) allegedly committed since January 2012 in the north of the country. On 16 January 2013, following the results of preliminary examination, the Prosecutor formally opened an investigation into alleged crimes committed on the territory of Mali since 2012.[140] Only the case against Ahmad Al Faqi Al Mahdi has been brought and is actually before the Court in relation to the situation in Mali.

---

[136] Paras. 15-16.
[137] Para. 2.
[138] Paras. 3-4.
[139] Paras. 11-15.
[140] ICC, "ICC Prosecutor opens investigation into war crimes in Mali: 'The legal requirements have been met. We will investigate'", Press Release No. ICC-OTP-20130116-PR869, 13 January 2013.

4.7.1. Al Faqi Al Mahdi

On 18 September 2015, Pre-Trial Chamber I issued an arrest warrant against Ahmad Al Faqi Al Mahdi (Abu Tourab) for war crimes allegedly committed in Timbuktu, Mali, between about 30 June 2012 and 10 July 2012, through intentionally directing attacks against buildings dedicated to religion and/or historic monuments.[141] The case against Mr. Al Faqi is the first to be brought before the ICC concerning the destruction of buildings dedicated to religion and historic monuments.

According to the arrest warrant there are reasonable grounds to believe that an armed conflict of non-international character began in January 2012 and was still ongoing in Mali throughout the period of the alleged facts, which all took place in Timbuktu. Throughout this period, the city would have been under the control of armed groups, Al Qaeda in the Islamic Maghreb (AQIM), and Ansar Eddine, a mainly Tuareg movement associated with AQIM. Mr. Al Faqi, from the Ansar Tuareg tribe, was an active personality in the context of the occupation of Timbuktu. He was a member of Ansar Eddine, working closely with the leaders of the two armed groups and in the context of the structures and institutions established by them. It is alleged that, until September 2012, he was at the head of the "Hesbah" ("Manners' Brigade"), operational from May 2012. The Chamber found that the evidence presented by the Prosecutor establish reasonable grounds to believe that Mr. Al Faqi is criminally responsible for having committed, individually and jointly with others, facilitated or otherwise contributed to the commission of war crimes regarding intentionally directing attacks against ten religious buildings and historic monuments protected by UNESCO in Timbuktu.[142]

On 26 September 2015 Mr. Al Faqi was surrendered to the ICC by the authorities of Niger and arrived at the Court's Detention Centre in the Netherlands. The confirmation of charges hearing is scheduled to open on 1 March 2016.[143]

4.8. Uganda

On 16 December 2003, the Government of Uganda referred the situation concerning the Lord's Resistance Army to the Office of the Prosecutor. On 29 July 2004, the Prosecutor determined a reasonable basis to open an investigation into the situation concerning northern Uganda.

---

[141] *Prosecutor v. Ahmad Al Faqi Al Mahdi*, Case No. ICC-01/12-01/15-1-Red, Mandat d'arrêt à l'encontre d'Ahmad Al Faqi Al Mahdi, Version publique epurgée, 28 September 2015.

[142] See ICC, "Situation in Mali: Ahmad Al Faqi Al Mahdi surrendered to the ICC on charges of war crimes regarding the destruction of historical and religious monuments in Timbuktu", Press Release No. ICC-CPI-20150926-PR1154, 29 September 2015.

[143] See ICC, "Al Mahdi case: Confirmation of charges hearing to open on 1 March 2016", Press Release No. ICC-CPI-20160113-PR1182, 13 January 2016.

On 8 July 2005, Pre-Trial Chamber II issued warrants of arrest under seal against Joseph Kony, Vincent Otti, Raska Lukwiya, Okot Odhiambo, and Dominic Ongwen for the commission of crimes against humanity and war crimes. The warrants of arrest were unsealed by Pre-Trial Chamber II on 13 October 2005. On 11 July 2007, the proceedings against Raska Lukwiya were terminated following his death. On 10 September 2015, Pre-trial Chamber II also terminated proceedings against Okot Odhiambo, alleged Deputy Army Commander of the Lord's Resistance Army (LRA), following the forensic confirmation of his passing.[144] According to these decisions, the warrants of arrest are rendered without effect and the names of the two suspects were removed from the case.

There are currently two cases before the Court related to the situation in Uganda: the case against Joseph Kony and Vincent Otti – respectively alleged Commander-in-Chief, and Vice-Chairman and Second-in-Command of the LRA, who are still at large – and the case against Dominic Ongwen – alleged Commander of the Sinia Brigade of the LRA.

4.8.1. Ongwen

As the alleged Brigade Commander of the Sinia Brigade of the LRA, Dominic Ongwen is suspected of three counts of crimes against humanity (murder, enslavement, inhumane acts of inflicting serious bodily injury and suffering) and four counts of war crimes (murder, cruel treatment of civilians, intentionally directing an attack against a civilian population, pillaging) allegedly committed on or about 20 May 2004 at the Lukodi IDP Camp in the Gulu District, northern Uganda.

On 16 January 2015, nearly ten years after the issuance of the warrant of arrest, Dominic Ongwen was surrendered to the ICC's custody by the Central African Authorities in Bangui,[145] he was transferred to the ICC on 21 January and made his initial appearance before the Single Judge of Pre-Trial Chamber II on 26 January 2015. On 6 February 2015, Single Judge Ekaterina Trendafilova, on behalf of Pre-Trial Chamber II, deemed it necessary to separate the proceedings against Dominic Ongwen from the case of *Prosecutor v. Joseph Kony, Vincent Otti, Okot Odhiambo and Dominic Ongwen* so as not to delay the pre-trial proceedings against Mr. Ongwen, having the other suspects in the case not been apprehended yet.[146]

---

[144] See ICC, "ICC terminates proceedings against Okot Odhiambo following forensic confirmation of his passing", Press Release No. ICC-CPI-20150910-PR1147, 10 September 2015.

[145] Case No. ICC-02/04-01/05-419, Report of the Registry on the voluntary surrender of Dominic Ongwen and his transfer to the Court, 22 January 2015, reclassified as public pursuant to Pre-Trial Chamber II's Decision ICC-02/04-01/15-260, 7 July 2015.

[146] ICC, "ICC Pre-Trial Chamber II separates Dominic Ongwen case from Kony et al. case", Press Release No. ICC-CPI-20150206-PR1088, 6 February 2015.

On 6 March 2015, Pre-Trial Chamber II postponed to 21 January 2016 the commencement of the confirmation of charges hearing, which had been provisionally scheduled for 24 August 2015, in order to allow the Prosecutor to prepare adequately for the hearing and to comply with the Chamber's instructions.[147] On 28 October 2015, the Presidency of the ICC decided that the confirmation of charges hearing would be held at the seat of the Court at The Hague, and not in Uganda as recommended by Pre-Trial Chamber II on 10 September 2015. Although it recognized that holding the hearing in Uganda would in principle contribute to a better perception of the Court and bring the proceedings closer to the communities affected by the alleged crimes, the Presidency noted the possibility, expressed by Uganda itself, that political tensions may increase during an upcoming electoral period, especially during January 2016, which may have an adverse impact on the Court.[148]

The confirmation of charges hearing opened at the ICC in The Hague before Pre-Trial Chamber II on 21 January 2016.

5. THE ECCC'S JUDICIAL ACTIVITY[149]

On 3 March 2015, the Co-Investigating Judges of the ECCC decided to charge *in absentia* Mea Muth, one of the individuals allegedly responsible for the crimes committed during the period from April 1975 to January 1979.[150] The Judges affirmed the compatibility of *in absentia* proceedings with human rights law referring to the principles established by the European Court of Human Rights and the interpretation of Article 14 of the 1966 International Covenant on Civil and Political Rights by the Human Rights Committee. The Judges also took into account the

---

[147] *Prosecutor v. Dominic Ongwen*, Case No. ICC-02/04-01/15-206, Decision Postponing the Date of the Confirmation of Charges Hearing, 6 March 2015. See also ICC, "Ongwen case: Confirmation of charges hearing postponed to 21 January 2016", Press Release No. ICC-CPI-20150306-MA179, 6 March 2015.

[148] *Prosecutor v. Dominic Ongwen*, Case No. ICC-02/04-01/15-330, Decision on the recommendation to the Presidency to hold the confirmation of charges hearing in the Republic of Uganda, 28 October 2015. See also ICC, "Ongwen case: the confirmation of charges hearing to be held at the seat of the ICC in The Hague", Press Release No. ICC-CPI-20151028-PR1162, 28 October 2015.

[149] Judgments and decisions of the ECCC are available at: <http://www.eccc.gov.kh/en/caseload>. On the ECCC, see WILLIAMS, "The Severance of Case 002 at the ECCC: A Radical Trial Management Technique or a Step Too Far?", JICJ, 2015, p. 815 ff.; and LAMB, "Access to Justice before International Criminal Tribunals: An Evaluation of the Scheme of Victim Participation Adopted by the Extraordinary Chambers in the Courts of Cambodia (ECCC)", in KEYZER, POPOVSKY and SAMPFORD (eds.), *Access to International Justice*, London, 2015, p. 128 ff.

[150] Case No. 003/07-09-2009-ECCC/OCIJ, Decision to charge Meas Muth in absentia, 3 March 2015.

procedural rules established at the international level, in particular by the STL, ICTY, ICTR, and ICC. Eventually, they concluded that *in absentia* proceedings are admissible under human rights law in the presence of certain circumstances. These include (i) the refusal of the person subject to criminal proceedings to appear before the competent court, and (ii) the fact that procedural rules at the international level allow for *in absentia* proceedings when a person has waived expressly and in writing his or her right to be present or when all reasonable steps have been taken to secure his or her appearance before the competent court and to inform him or her of the charges, but these efforts have been unsuccessful. The Judges also recalled that when holding *in absentia* proceedings, a court needs to ensure that the absent accused or charged person is adequately and effectively represented. Following this decision, the arrest warrant against Mea Muth was issued on 4 June 2015.[151]

6. THE RESIDUAL SPECIAL COURT FOR SIERRA LEONE (RSCSL)'S JUDICIAL ACTIVITY[152]

On 30 January 2015, the Trial Chamber of the RSCSL issued a decision on the Taylor's request that the RSCSL terminate the enforcement of his sentence in the United Kingdom and transfer him to Rwanda to serve the remainder of his 50-years prison sentence.[153] After reasoning that Taylor's case is an exceptional one in that he was the first setting Head of State to be indicted and convicted of international crimes since the Nuremberg Trial, the Chamber found that Taylor's inability to receive visits from his wife and two daughters is not due to any interference with his right to family life (under Article 8 of the ECHR) by the United Kingdom authorities or by the RSCSL. According to the Chamber, such inability is due purely to his wife's failure to comply with UK visa requirements and to her ignoring the assistance offered to her to re-apply. The Chamber also affirmed that Taylor had failed to establish any violation of his Article 3 of the ECHR rights and that the conditions of his imprisonment accord to international standards.

---

[151] Case No. 003/07-09-2009-ECCC/OCIJ, Arrest Warrant, 4 June 2015.

[152] Decisions of the RSCSL are available at: <http://www.rscsl.org/RSCSL-Decisions.html>. On the SCSL, see KLIP, FREELAND and LOW (eds.), *Annotated Leading Cases of International Criminal Tribunals: Special Court for Sierra Leone*, Vol. XLV, Cambridge, 2015; MUJUZI, "The Conditional Early Release of Offenders from the Special Court for Sierra Leone to Serve their Sentences in Designated States: Some Observations and Recommendations", African Yearbook on International Humanitarian Law, 2015, p. 154 ff.; and RODMAN, "Intervention and the 'Justice Cascade': Lessons from the Special Court of Sierra Leone on Prosecution and Civil War", Human Rights Review, 2015, p. 39 ff.

[153] *In the Matter of Charles Ghankay Taylor* (Case No. SCSL-03-01-ES), Decision on Public with Public and Confidential Annexes Charles Ghankay Taylor's Motion for Termination of Enforcement of Sentence in the United Kingdom and for Transfer to Rwanda, 30 January 2015.

On 21 May 2015 the President of the RSCSL denied the Taylor's application to appeal against the decision of the Trial Chamber on his request to be transferred to Rwanda.[154]

7. THE SPECIAL TRIBUNAL FOR LEBANON[155]

According to Article 8(2) of the STL Statute and Rule 31 of the Rules of Procedure and Evidence, on 19 February 2015 Judge Ivana Hrdličková of the Czech Republic has been elected President of the Special Tribunal for Lebanon for a period of 18 months, starting from 1 March 2015.[156]

On 23 January 2015, the Appeals Panel issued its decision on the case against Ibrahim Mohamed Ali Al Amin and Al Akhbar Beirut S.A.L., where it unanimously decided that the Tribunal does have jurisdiction to hear cases of obstruction of justice against legal persons.[157] The Panel emphasized that the same reasoning of the New TV S.A.L. Jurisdiction Appeal Decision of 2 October 2014 applies since the legal issue is the same in both cases.

On 18 September 2015, the Contempt Judge at the STL issued a judgment in the contempt case against Al Jadeed (CO.) and Ms Karma Mohamed Tahsin Al Khayat.[158] Judge Lettieri found Ms Al Khayat guilty of knowingly and wilfully interfering with the administration of justice by failing to remove from Al Jadeed TV's website information on purported confidential witnesses in the *Ayyash et al.* case, thereby violating the Order issued by the Pre-Trial Judge on 10 August 2012.[159] To the contrary, the Judge found Al Jadeed TV not guilty with respect to the same charge. As to the corporate liability of the latter, the Judge affirmed that the Appeals Panel provided no clear guidance as to the applicable material elements

---

[154] *In the Matter of Charles Ghankay Taylor* (Case No. SCSL-03-01-ES), Decision on Charles Ghankay Taylor's Motion for Termination of Enforcement of Sentence in the United Kingdom and for the Transfer to Rwanda and on Defence Application for Leave to Appeal Decision for Termination of Enforcement of Sentence in the United Kingdom and for Transfer to Rwanda, 21 May 2015.

[155] Decisions of the STL are available at: <http://www.stl-tsl.org>. See BERNAZ, "Corporate Criminal Liability under International Law: The New TV S.A.L. and Akhbar Beirut S.A.L. Cases at the Special Tribunal for Lebanon", JICJ, 2015, p. 313 ff.

[156] See at: <http://www.stl-tsl.org/en/news-and-press/press-releases/3814-election-of-judge-ivana-hrdlickova-as-new-stl-president>.

[157] *In the case against Akhbar Beirut S.A.L. Ibrahim Mohamed Ali Al Amin*, Case No. STL-14-06/PT/AP/AR126.1, Decision on Interlocutory Appeal Concerning Personal Jurisdiction in Contempt Proceedings of 23 January 2015.

[158] *In the case against Al Jadeed [CO.] S.A.L./ New TV S.A.L. (N.T.V.) Karma Mohamed Tahsin Al Khayat*, Case No. STL-14-05/T/CJ, Judgment of 18 September 2015.

[159] On 28 September 2015, the Contempt Judge sentenced Ms Khayat to a fine of 10,000 Euros: *In the case against Karma Mohamed Tahsin Al Khayat*, Case No. STL-14-05/S/CJ, Reasons for Sentencing Judgment of 6 October 2015.

in attributing liability to legal persons charged with contempt before the Tribunal, including with respect to the relationship between the modes of responsibility in the Statute and accusations against corporations. Confirming that no international model of corporate criminal liability has emerged, the Judge concluded that it was appropriate in the circumstances of the case to look to Lebanese law on corporate liability. He found to be significant that the corporate accused was domiciled in and substantially operated in Lebanon, considering that looking to the material elements of the pertinent Lebanese law would not violate the rights of the accused.

8. CONCLUSION

While President Meron confirmed that the ICTY is expected to complete its mandate by 2017, the ICTR delivered its last judgment on 14 December 2015 in the *Nyiramasuhuko et al.* case and on 31 December 2015 it formally concluded its judicial function.

The judicial activity of the ICC continued on the proceedings and investigations in the nine pre-existing situations, and a Prosecutor's request for authorization to initiate investigation in the situation in Georgia, submitted in 2015, was granted in January 2016. The most relevant events in the 2015 ICC activity are: the judgment in the *Lubanga* case setting the principles governing the reparations for victims; the opening of two trials in cases related to the situations in the CAR and in the DRC; and the arrest and transferal to the Court of two accused persons in relation to the situations in Mali and Uganda. However, the Court's weakness, lacking States' cooperation in enforcing arrest warrants, emerged clearly in the *Al Bashir* case.

Among the hybrid criminal tribunals, noteworthy are the ECCC decision to charge Meas Muth in absentia; the RSCSL Decision on Charles Ghankay Taylor's Motion for Termination of Enforcement of Sentence in the United Kingdom and for Transfer to Rwanda; and finally the decisions of the STL on its jurisdiction to hear cases against legal persons.

THE WTO DISPUTE SETTLEMENT SYSTEM IN 2015

edited by Giorgio Sacerdoti[*]

1. Introduction

1.1. A Short Overview of 2015

On 10 November 2015, just when the WTO was reaching its 20th anniversary, the WTO website featured within its news items the statement of Director General (DG) Roberto Azevêdo celebrating the WTO Dispute Settlement System (DSS) having reached the 500 mark (of which 282 had been brought to litigation). The receipt of the 500th trade dispute for settlement, said the DG, "shows that the WTO's dispute settlement system enjoys tremendous confidence among the membership, who value it as fair, effective and efficient mechanism to solve trade problems". As of the end of 2014, 201 panel reports had been issued, of which 136 had been appealed (68% of the total, on average).[1]

As a victim of its own success, the major problem affecting the DSS in 2015 was the delays in proceedings due precisely to the increasing number and complexity of disputes brought to the system by an increasing number of members.

This overload has affected also this Review, since it has been necessary to select the Appellate Body reports to be reviewed while in past years the Yearbook was able to host a review of all Appellate Body reports.

1.1.1. Consultations and Panel Composition

In 2015 WTO members filed a total of thirteen requests for consultations, slightly down from the fourteen requests filed the year before. The Dispute Settlement Body (DSB) established eight panels, some of which were still not composed at

---

[*] Of the Board of Editors. This contribution was carried out within the framework of the Ph.D. program in International Law and Economics of the Ph.D. School of Bocconi University in Milan. Professor Giorgio Sacerdoti coordinated the individual reviews of WTO cases. These were authored by Ph.D. candidates Carlo de Stefano, Loly Aylu Gaitan Guerrero, Elisa Longoni, Francesco Montanaro, Niall Moran, Giacomo Tagiuri, and Laura Zoboli.

[1] These data are drawn from those provided by the DG in his statement to the DSB of 22 October 2015, those annexed to the AB Report for 2014, and those included in the news item of 12 November 2015 on the 500 mark. Some data are not easy to compare, especially since there is a difference with regard to the relevant year between panel and AB reports *issued* and *adopted* by the DSB. See also the statement on the Dispute Settlement Workload by the DSB chairman at the DSB meeting of 25 November 2015, WT/DSB/M/370.

the end of the year. Additionally, it established and composed ten panels, and composed one that had been established the year before.[2]

1.1.2.   Panel and Appellate Body Reports

Eight panel reports were circulated in 2015, covering nine disputes. Of these, five were adopted, two after appeal[3] and three without appeal;[4] the DSB also adopted in 2015 five panel reports circulated in 2014 and appealed, together with the corresponding appeal report. Seven Appellate Body reports were circulated in 2015, covering eleven disputes, of which six are reviewed hereafter; all were adopted in 2015,[5] in addition to one Appellate Body report circulated in 2014, not reviewed hereafter.[6] This is an increase in output compared to 2014, during which five reports covering eight disputes were circulated.

1.1.3.   Compliance Disputes (Article 21.5 DSU)

Of the eight panel reports circulated in 2015, three concerned compliance disputes.[7] Two of these reports were adopted, one after appeal (*US – Tuna II*) and the other without appeal (*China – GOES*), whereas two (*EC – Fasteners* and *Argentina – Financial Services*) were under appeal at the end of 2015. The Appellate Body also circulated one report on two compliances disputes (*US – COOL*) by Canada and Mexico, adopted together with the Panel report on the same disputes circulated in 2014. At the end of the year, other than the *EC – Fasteners* appeal, the only other compliance disputes pending concerned the two *Large Civil Aircraft* cases, for which compliance panels, established in 2012, have not yet produced a report.[8]

---

[2] *Brazil – Certain Measures Concerning Taxation and Charges (EU)*, DS472.

[3] Panel Report, *US – Tuna II (Mexico)*, DS381; and Panel Report, *China – HP-SSST*, DS454.

[4] Panel Report, *China – GOES*, DS414; Panel Report, *US – Animals*, DS447; and Panel Report, *Ukraine – Passenger Cars*, DS468.

[5] Appellate Body Report, *Argentina – Import Measures*, DS438 (reviewed hereafter); Appellate Body Report, *US – Shrimp II (Vietnam)*, DS429; Appellate Body Report, *US – COOL*, Article 21.5, DS384 (reviewed hereafter); Appellate Body Report, *India – Agricultural Products*, DS430 (reviewed hereafter); Appellate Body Report, *Peru – Agricultural Products*, DS457 (reviewed hereafter); Appellate Body Report, *China – HP-SSST*, DS454; and Appellate Body Report, *US – Tuna II (Mexico)*, Article 21.5, DS381 (reviewed hereafter).

[6] Appellate Body, *United States – Countervailing Duty Measures on Certain Products from China*, adopted on 16 January 2015, WT/DS437/AB (reviewed hereafter).

[7] Panel Report, *EC – Fasteners*, Article 21.5, DS397; Panel Report, *China – GOES*, Article 21.5, DS414; and Panel Report, *US – Tuna II (Mexico)*, Article 21.5, DS381.

[8] DS353, *US – Large Civil Aircraft (Second Complaint)*; and DS316, *EC and Certain Member States – Large Civil Aircraft*. This extraordinary delay, accepted by both parties, is due to their

1.1.4. Arbitration under Articles 21.3 and 22.6 DSU

In 2015, three arbitral awards (an unprecedented number for a single year) were issued concerning the determination of reasonable periods of time (RPT) for implementation of DSB recommendations under Article 21.3(c) DSU.[9] Additionally, one arbitration award on the level of nullification or impairment pursuant to Article 22.6 DSU (also reviewed hereafter) was issued in 2015 (in the *COOL* dispute), which is reviewed hereafter – the first of its kind since 2009.[10] This dispute gave rise to a somehow quixotic dispute at the DSB as to whether under Article 22.2 DSU it is the DSB that has to refer a dispute to arbitration upon request of the party which has prevailed in the compliance dispute or whether the request can be referred to arbitration even without a formal decision of the DSB, the meeting of the DSB having been cancelled.[11] This having been the solution recorded in the DSB documents, the EU forcefully opposed it while the arbitrator, entering in the matter without a real need (according to Canada and Mexico, but not the EU), confirmed that it had jurisdiction and that the text did not require in its view a DSB meeting to refer the matter to arbitration.[12] The discussion on the issue raised the question of third party rights in Article 22.6 arbitration, which are generally considered not to exist, but that the EU asserts are not prevented by the silence of the text.

1.1.5. Concluded Disputes

The only dispute formally terminated in 2015 was the withdrawal of the requests for consultations brought by the EU against Indonesia for its request, in *US – Clove Cigarettes*, to be authorized to suspend concessions under Article 22.2

---

factual and legal complexity. On 11 December the panel in DS316, which had been composed on 17 April 2012, informed that it would complete its work by the end of June 2016.

[9] Award of the Arbitrator, *US – Countervailing Measures on Certain Products from China*, Article 21.3(c), 9 October 2015, WT/DS436/16 (RPT: 14 months and 16 days; Arbitrator: Mr. Georges Abi-Saab, appointed by the DG); Award of the Arbitrator, *US – Shrimp II (Vietnam)*, Article 21.3(c), 15 December 2015, WT/DS429/12 (RPT: 15 months; Arbitrator: Mr Simon Farbenbloom, appointed by the parties); Award of the Arbitrator, *Peru – Agricultural Products*, Article 21.3(c), 16 December 2015, WT/457/15 (RPT: 7 months and 29 days; Arbitrator: Mr Ricardo Ramírez-Hernández, appointed by the parties).

[10] Decisions by the Arbitrator, *US – Certain Country of Origin Labelling (COOL) Requirements*, 7 December 2015, WT/DS384/ARB, WT/DS386/ARB and Add.1.

[11] See the EU Communication of 9 July 2015, WT/DS386/38.

[12] See Decisions by the Arbitrator, *United States – Certain Country of Origin Labelling (COOL) Requirements*, Recourse to Art. 22.6 of the DSU by the United States, WT/DS384/ARB, WT/DS386/ARB and Add.1, paras. 2.1 to 2.18. The discussion on the issue took place at the DSB meeting of 21 December 2015 where the DSB agreed on request of Canada and Mexico to authorize the suspension of tariff concessions to the US consistent with Arbitrator's decision, WT/DSB/M/372.

DSU, when the existence of an assertion of implementation by the United States would have, the EU alleged, obliged it to have recourse first to Article 21.5 (compliance panel).[13]

In 2015 the EU implemented in stages the reports in the *EC – Seal Products* which included complex recommendations concerning the non-conformity of the EU Seal regime with various GATT provisions.[14] The EU first amended the "Basic Regulation" 1007/2009 by Regulation 2015/1775 of 6 October 2015, abolishing the exception for maritime resource management. The new Commission Implementing Regulation 2015/1850 of 13 October (just before the expiration of the reasonable period of time of 16 months that had been agreed by the parties) lays down detailed rules for the implementation of the Inuit exception, in particular setting up an attestation body system to allow the entering of seal products in the EU market under this exception. It is notable that this system is based on the recognition by the EU of the Government of Nuvanut (Canada) as an attestation body pursuant to negotiations between the EU and Canada.[15]

1.2. Systemic Issues[16]

1.2.1. Addressing the Delays Due to the Increasing Case Load of the DSS

The issue of the delays in panel proceeding, which had been addressed for the first time in 2014 in an unprecedented intervention of the DG at the DSB of 26 September 2014,[17] has become a major concern for the WTO membership and the Secretariat in 2015 due to their increase to a level that appears to be incompatible with the basic features of an efficient dispute settlement system.

The direct cause of this situation affecting especially the panel stage and which has been raised more than once by countries concerned at the DSB, is the lack of le-

---

[13] *Indonesia – Recourse to Article 22.2 of the DSU in the US – Clove Cigarettes Dispute*, DS481.

[14] See SACERDOTI (ed.), "The WTO Dispute Settlement System in 2014", IYIL, 2014, p. 395 ff., p. 408 ff.

[15] See WT/DS400/16 and DS/401/17 Add.7 of 16 October 2015.

[16] Besides the issues covered in the text, it is interesting to note the following active example of management of a pending dispute by the parties with a view to find an amicable solution. In *India – Certain Measures Relating to Solar Cells and Modules* (WT/DS/456) the parties (US and India) asked the panel not to circulate its report, which had been issued to the parties on 28 August 2015, to allow discussions between them in view of finding an agreement. The panel granted a number of delays, the last one until 24 February 2016. The parties were ultimately unable to agree so that the Panel report was circulated on 24 February 2016 and was appealed by India in due course on 20 April 2016 (WT/DS456/9).

[17] See SACERDOTI (ed.), *cit. supra* note 14, p. 400 ff.

gal resources in the Secretariat to staff the many panels that are being established.[18] As a result, panel proceedings may well take now between two or three years from the formal establishment of the panel by the DSB to the circulation of their report. This is without considering the additional time needed to conclude a dispute until full implementation.[19] The Appellate Body has faced similar increasing difficulties in respecting the short 90-day period prescribed for issuing its own reports and has announced in advance that it would not be able to complete its task within the due period in certain disputes both because of the shortage in legal staff and of several appeals pending at the same time.[20]

It is curious, however, that members which complained did not ask for more effective remedies than those initiated by the DG, beyond increased transparency and information from the Secretariat as to the reasons for the "queue", and as to the situation in the line and the outlook for "their" case being decided. The same attitude prevailed in the discussion that followed the DG's lengthy and detailed statement at the DSB of 28 October 2015 where he made the point that the problems would not be resolved just through administrative measures[21] such as shifting of resources within the Secretariat and hiring junior lawyer for servicing the panels and the Appellate Body.[22] Several members acknowledged this issue and decried the negative consequences of the current set on the effectiveness of

---

[18] At the DSB of 31 August 2015, Korea complained that in DS488 (where Korea challenged US anti-dumping measures) the Secretariat had notified Korea that the panel established on 25 March 2015 would not begin its work before the end of 2016, "not because the panelist were unavailable, but due to the constraints affecting the Secretariat".

[19] As an example, at a DSB meeting in June 2015 Canada complained that four and a half years after the establishment of the panel, the *COOL* dispute with the US was still settled (this would occur in the following December after the issuance of the Art. 22.6 arbitration reviewed here under).

[20] See the communication of the Appellate Body (WT/DS453/9) of 22 December 2015 explaining the reasons for the Appellate Body expecting to be able to issue its report in *Argentina – Measures Relating to Trade in Goods and Services (Panama)* beyond the 90-days deadline, expiring on 26 January 2016 (the report was issued on 14 April 2016). The Appellate Body has also issued directions to the parties in order to limit the page number of the submissions.

[21] An important initiative of the Legal Affairs Division has been the launch of the WTO Digital Dispute Settlement Registry, which will allow electronic filing of submissions and secure access to briefs and documents by the parties.

[22] In his address to the DSB on 28 October 2015, the DG explained in detail the steps he had taken and was taking to mitigate delays, consisting mostly of reallocating of personnel; hiring new legal staff; adjusting the grades and salaries to the competence of the lawyers, taking into account the competition by law firms; increasing internal mobility; and pooling junior lawyers of both divisions assisting panels. This should result in more efficiency and has already nearly doubled the relevant positions – from 30 to 57 – since 2013.

the DSS, but abstained from launching any ideas for tackling the problems more seriously.[23]

1.2.2. The Renewal of the Mandate of Appellate Body Members

The first term of two Appellate Body members, Ujal Singh Bhatia (India) and Thomas Graham (United States) was due to expire at the end of 2015. Although reappointment is not automatic, the practice is generally that absent any opposition – an occurrence that has never explicitly happened – after some consultation by the chairman, the DSB would formally agree to the reappointment, as provided by Article 13 DSU, but without an in depth examination of the matter, least this appear as putting pressure on the independence and impartiality of the Appellate Body members.

For the first time in this instance some WTO members, principally the United States, asked a previous meeting with the two Appellate Body members.[24] This request prompted formal and informal discussions, within the DSB, the Appellate Body and between the chairs of the two bodies on a format and type of questioning that would safeguard the independence of the Appellate Body members while responding positively to the interest of the WTO members to meet the two judges. At the end a compromise was found in that it was agreed that the encounter, where only questions on general issues concerning the functioning of the Appellate Body could be put to them, would take place at an informal meeting of the DSB. This meeting took place on 12 November 2015 and was attended by 28 delegations; the strict rules concerning the questioning which had been announced in advance by the Chairman of the DSB were respected.[25] The resulting dialogue appears to have been positive in general terms. As was stated by Canada, the meeting "provided a rare and valuable opportunity for delegations to hear from the Appellate Body members some of their preoccupation with the workload and other process issues", to the point that "the DSB may wish to reflect further, as Brazil and the EU had suggested, on whether or not there was merit in organizing a similar set of exchanges on a regular basis [...] not related to the reappointment process".[26] Thereupon the reappointment was approved at the meeting of 25 November 2015.

GIORGIO SACERDOTI

---

[23] See the minutes of the meeting at WT/DSB/M/369, p. 20. The present author has addressed the issue of how to fix the current problems in a broader perspective *de iure condendo*, see SACERDOTI, "The Future of the WTO Dispute Settlement System: Consolidating a Success Story", in BRAGA and HOEKMAN (eds.) *The Future of the Global Trade Order*, 2016, p. 45 ff.

[24] DSB, 28 October 2015, WT/DSB/M/369.

[25] The list is found in the minutes of 25 November 2015, para. 7.2.

[26] *Ibid.*, para. 7.7.

2. APPELLATE BODY REPORT, *UNITED STATES – COUNTERVAILING DUTY MEASURES ON CERTAIN PRODUCTS FROM CHINA (US – COUNTERVAILING MEASURES (CHINA))*[27]

2.1. Introduction and Main Facts of the Dispute

Between 2007 and 2012, the United States Department of Commerce (USDOC) conducted seventeen countervailing duties investigations concerning products imported from China, which according to China, violated several dispositions of the Agreement on Subsidies and Countervailing Measures (SCM Agreement). China requested the establishment of a panel whose report was circulated on 14 July 2014 and was subsequently appealed by the United States and China. The Appellate Body Report was finally adopted by the DSB on 16 January 2015. Subsequently, to determine the implementation period in absence of agreement between the parties, China requested for arbitration under Article 21.3(c) DSU. On 9 October 2015, the arbitrator determined the reasonable period of time to expire on 1 April 2016 (14 months and 16 days).

2.2. The Panel Report

Given the limited space available, the present comment focuses on the Panel's findings on the merits that were subsequently challenged before the Appellate Body.

First of all, the Panel held that the USDOC correctly ascertained whether the firms subject to investigation had received a benefit under Articles 14(d) and 1.1(b) of the SCM Agreement. In particular, it found that, since China's State owned enterprises (SOEs) were the principal suppliers of inputs for such companies, in-country prices were inevitably distorted and, therefore, the USDOC had rightly resorted to an out-of-country benchmark.[28] Then, the Panel went on to assess whether the USDOC's acted consistently with Article 2.1 of the SCM Agreement. Notably, the Panel held that, when assessing the specificity of a given subsidy, one should not scrutinize it under each and every paragraph of the said article. Consequently, the *de facto* specificity assessment under Article 2.1(c) may

---

[27] Appellate Body Report, *United States – Countervailing Duty Measures on Certain Products from China*, adopted on 16 January 2015, WT/DS/437/AB/R.

[28] Appellate Body Report, *United States – Final Countervailing Duty Determination with respect to certain Softwood Lumber from Canada (US – Softwood Lumber IV)*, adopted on 19 January 2004, WT/DS257/AB/R, paras. 425-458 and 611; Appellate Body Report, *United States – Definitive Anti-Dumping and Countervailing Duties on Certain Products from China (US – Anti-Dumping and Countervailing Duties (China))*, adopted on 25 March 2011, WT/DS379/AB/R, para. 286.

be carried without a previous evaluation under Articles 2.1(a) and 2.1(b). In addition, the Panel addressed the claim that the USDOC's determinations failed to identify a "subsidy programme" and a "jurisdiction granting authority" under the same provision. In terms of the former, the Panel observed that the phrase "subsidy programme" should be broadly construed. Thus, it concluded that China had established a "subsidy programme" by providing inputs on a regular basis for less than adequate remuneration to the companies under investigation. By the same token, it found that such determinations implicitly but unequivocally referred to China's jurisdiction.

Finally, the Panel turned to consider whether the USDOC erred in applying Article 12.7 of the SCM Agreement, whereby an investigating authority is entitled to make a determination on the basis of the facts available when an interested party refuses to provide the information requested. In China's view, the USDOC's based its determinations on assumptions rather than on the facts available in forty-eight instances. The Panel rejected this claim by affirming that China did not provide sufficient evidence in support of its assertions.

2.3. The Appellate Body Report

China challenged the findings concerning USDOC's determinations of benefit, *de facto* specificity, and the use of "adverse" facts in case of non-cooperation of the interested Member with the investigating authority.

As to the first issue, the Appellant maintained that the Panel erroneously upheld USDOC recourse to out-of-country benchmark. In particular, it argued that USDOC's determinations rested upon a wrong interpretation according to which China's SOEs were equated with its government or a public body under Article 1.1(a)(1). The Appellate Body dismissed this argument by adopting a different market distortion test. In fact, when conducting such an assessment, the investigating authorities need to consider a number of factors and, notably, the structure of the market and the behaviour of the firms operating therein. On the basis of these principles, the Appellate Body resolved to complete the legal analysis and concluded that four USDOC's determinations were inconsistent with Articles 1.1(b) and 14(d).

The Appellate Body addressed thereafter the claims based on Article 2.1 of the SCM Agreement. To begin with, the Appellate Body, following the Panel's approach, found that the assessment of the *de facto* specificity under Article 2.1(c) should not be preceded by the evaluation of the of the *de jure* specificity pursuant to Articles 2.1(a) and 2.1(b). Then, it addressed the claim that USDOC did not provide evidence as to the existence of a subsidy programme. Although it concurred with the Panel's view that a systematic series of activities may amount to a subsidy programme, it nonetheless concluded that the Panel did not correctly apply Article 2.1(c) by not engaging in a case-specific analysis. However, the Appellate Body in this case refused to complete the analysis owing to the insufficient factual basis. With respect to the last claim, it made clear that, contrary to what China asserted, the granting authority should be determined through a holistic approach by taking into account both the granting authority and its jurisdiction. With this in mind, it found nonetheless that the Panel erred in finding that the USDOC had sufficiently identified the granting authority. Notwithstanding that, it refrained from completing the legal analysis because of the limited importance of this issue with respect to the decision of the case.

Finally, the Appellate Body examined the complaint under Article 12.7 of the SCM Agreement and Article 11 DSU. In this respect, it held that the Panel, instead of ascertaining whether the USDOC's determinations rested upon facts, had only engaged in an analysis of the language contained therein. Consequently, the Appellate Body concluded that the Panel failed in establishing that the USDOC acted inconsistently with these provisions, but it once again refused to complete the legal analysis owing to the limited factual basis.

2.4. Comment

The present case is likely to have an impact on subsequent case law in two respects. First, the Appellate Body seems to reaffirm that, when reviewing anti-subsidies measures, Panels should not lower the intensity of scrutiny, even though the latter is limited to the issues examined before the national investigating authorities.[29] Second, the Appellate Body elucidated the concepts of "benefit" by clarifying under which circumstances an investigating authority may adopt an external benchmark to carry out the test under Article 14.1(d) of the SCM Agreement. What is more, it made clear that SOEs are also subject to this rule, as they are capable of distorting market prices regardless of their market share dimension. In this respect, it has been noted that this approach leaves unresolved two important issues: whether investigating authorities must prove a minimum degree of distortion and to what extent such authorities are free to choose out-of-country benchmarks.[30] Be that as it may, such an approach seems nonetheless suitable to prevent the circumvention of the SCM Agreement through SOEs, which, despite the commitments undertaken

---

[29] RUIZ FABRI, "Le Juge de l'OMC: Ombres et Lumières d'une Figure Judiciaire Singulière", RGDIP, 2006, p. 39 ff., pp. 76-77.

[30] DU, "State-Owned Enterprises in the WTO Law: An Analysis of United States-Definitive Anti-Dumping and Countervailing Duties on Certain Products from China", in LIU and SHAN (eds.), *China and International Commercial Dispute Resolution*, Leiden, 2015, p. 306 ff., p. 328.

by China at the time of its accession to the WTO,[31] still represents an obstacle to the application of WTO law.[32]

FRANCESCO MONTANARO[*]

3. APPELLATE BODY REPORT, *ARGENTINA – MEASURES AFFECTING THE IMPORTATION OF GOODS*[33]

3.1. Introduction and Main Facts of the Dispute

The dispute stems from the complaint of the European Union (EU), the United States (US) and Japan concerning certain measures adopted by Argentina on importation of goods. The complainants challenged two measures. First, the procedure for the Advance Sworn Import Declaration (*Declaración Jurada Anticipada de Importación* – DJAI) established by Resolution 3252/12 of the Federal Administration of Public Revenues of Argentina, which obliged importers to inform governmental authorities of their intent to introduce foreign goods to Argentina by any means. If the cargo arrived without the DJAI having been presented by the importer in advance, goods could be refused by customs and returned to sender. The second measure consisted of certain actions or trade-related requirements (TRRs) introduced to induce economic operators in Argentina to achieve either a trade balance or an export surplus as a result of their transactions. The EU contested that 23 different requirements by the Argentinian government acted as a single TRR.

After consultations and following the US, the EU and Japan's request, a single Panel was composed on May 2013. The complainants raised a number of claims concerning the measures and their alleged inconsistence with various provisions of the GATT 1994. The panel reports were circulated in August 2014 and appealed by Argentina, Japan, and the EU. The Appellate Body issued as a single report for the three separately appeals which was circulated in January 2015. In the report substantially all panel findings with practical implications where upheld with the exception of the Panel's finding that the 23 "specific instances" of application of the

---

[31] *Report of the Working Party on the Accession of China*, WT/ACC/CHN/49, para. 46.

[32] YA QIN, "WTO Regulation of Subsidies to State-Owned Enterprises (SOEs) – A Critical Appraisal of the China Accession Protocol", JIEL, 2004, p. 863 ff., pp. 871-874; and HUFBAUER, "China as An Economic Actor on the World Stage: An Overview", in ABBOTT (ed.), *China in the World Trading System: Defining the Principle of Engagement*, The Hague/London/New York, 1998, p. 47 ff., p. 50.

[*] Dual Ph.D. candidate at Bocconi University (Milan) and Panthéon-Assas University (Paris).

[33] Appellate Body Reports, *Argentina – Measures Affecting the Importation of Goods*, adopted on 15 January 2015, WT/DS438/AB/R, WT/DS444/AB/R, WT/DS445/AB/R.

TRRs had not been clearly identified in the EU Panel Request and did not, therefore, constitute measures at issue in the dispute.[34]

Argentina expressed its intention to comply with the DSB recommendations and requested a "reasonable period of time" for the implementation. It was agreed by the parties that the reasonable period of time would expire on 31 December 2015. On 16 January 2016 Argentina and the EU "informed the DSB of agreed procedures under Articles 21 and 22 of the DSU".[35]

3.2. Findings of the Panel and the Appellate Body

3.2.1. The Panel's Terms of Reference – A Single or "Overarching" Measure and the Identification of 23 Specific Measures: An Analysis from Article 6.2 DSU

According to Argentina's contentions in the appeal, the Panel erred in finding that the single or "overarching" TRRs measure was within the Panel's terms of reference and so that the Panel had acted inconsistently with Article 6.2 DSU. Argentina's argument was based on the fact that the complainants' requests for consultations did not identify a single "overarching" TRRs measure while in their panel requests they had added a "single" TRR measure as a measure at issue. Argentina considered such inconsistency an expansion of the scope of the dispute or change in its essence,[36] since the "overarching" measure could be considered a new measure. The complainants argued in turn that they were not requested to identify the TRRs measure with "precise and exact identity" in the two requests.[37]

Under Article 6.2 DSU a panel request should identify the "specific measure at issue" while the "measure at issue" must be identified in a consultation request. Accordingly, in identifying the measure at issue, complainants should include greater specificity in the panel request than in a consultations request.[38] Moreover, the panel request is the one governing the panel's terms of reference, and therefore its legal basis may be "expected to be shaped by, and thereby constitute a natural evolution of, the consultations process".[39]

As a result of the analysis above, the Appellate Body saw no error in the Panel's finding that the single or "overarching" TRRs measure did not expand or change

---

[34] These Panel Reports were in the form of a single document constituting three separate Panel Reports: WT/DS438/R, WT/DS444/R, and WT/DS445/R.

[35] DSB Communication of 20 January 2016, WT/DS438/24.

[36] See *Argentina – Measures Affecting the Importation of Goods, cit. supra* note 33, para. 5.1.

[37] *Ibid.*, para. 5.18.

[38] *Ibid.*, para. 5.9.

[39] *Ibid.*, para. 5.10.

the scope and essence of the dispute and was within the Panel's terms of reference. The Appellate Body considered also that the identification in the panel requests of the single or "overarching" TRRs measure could be considered as an evolution of the language, and as a more precise enunciation of the consultations requests.

Regarding the specific issues raised in the EU panel report, the EU appealed the findings of the Panel that the 23 specific instances of application of the TRRs were not precisely identified in the EU Panel Request and did not, therefore, constitute a measure at issue in the dispute. The Panel reasoned that "on its face", the list provided by the EU in the Annex III of its panel request did not identify any "specific measures at issue".[40] On the contrary, EU argued in the appeal that it was possible to identify the specific measure at issue from the information contained in the title of each of the 23 press releases and their contents listed in Annex III of the panel request.[41]

In reversing the Panel's conclusion, the Appellate Body began by recalling its jurisprudence on the definition of a "measure at issue" according to Article 6.2 DSU.[42] The Appellate Body examined each of the 23 individual measures and found that they were identified in a manner consistent with Article 6.2 DSU and that the narrative of the EU Panel Request was conclusive to consider them as "the measure at issue".[43]

3.2.2. Identification of the Single Unwritten TRRs Measure: Consistency with Articles XI(1) and III(4) GATT 1994

In its appeal Argentina argued that the Panel should have applied the criteria listed by the Appellate Body in *US – Zeroing (EC)*[44] in order to prove the existence of a single unwritten measure challenged "as such", as well as its detailed content, and its general and prospective application.[45] The Appellate Body clarified that even if it was to consider that the Panel did not apply the criteria formulated in

---

[40] *Ibid.*, para. 5.46.

[41] *Ibid.*, para. 5.35.

[42] The following are the relevant cases recalled by the Appellate Body: Appellate Body Report, *United States – Definitive Anti-Dumping and Countervailing Duties on Certain Products from China*, adopted on 25 March 2011, WT/DS379/AB/R; Appellate Body Report, *European Communities – Selected Customs Matters*, adopted on 11 December 2011, WT/DS315/AB/R; and Appellate Body Report, *European Communities and Certain Member States – Measures Affecting Trade in Large Civil Aircraft*, adopted on 1 June 2011, WT/DS316/AB/R.

[43] See *Argentina – Measures Affecting the Importation of Goods, cit. supra* note 33, paras. 5.81, 5.83, 5.84.

[44] Appellate Body Report, *United States – Laws, Regulations and Methodology for Calculating Dumping Margins ("Zeroing")*, adopted on 18 April 2006, WT/DS294/AB/R.

[45] See *Argentina – Measures Affecting the Importation of Goods, cit. supra* note 33, para. 5.94.

US – Zeroing (EC), these criteria cannot be understood as a general legal standard to consider the existence of an unwritten measure challenged in WTO dispute settlement as proven.[46]

When analyzing the alleged TRRs the Panel found that the individual impositions on several economic operators by Argentina were interacting in a manner that constituted a single measure, which was acting as a condition to import.[47] As a consequence, the Appellate Body upheld the Panel's finding that the Argentina Government's impositions on economic operators operated as a single TRRs measure attributable to Argentina, and therefore upheld the Panel's finding that the measure was inconsistent with Article XI(1) and Article III(4) of the GATT 1994.

3.2.3. *Japan: Article 11 DSU and Article X(1) GATT 1994*

With respect of a particular "as such" and "as applied" claim by Japan, the Panel found that the TRRs measure "as such" was inconsistent with Articles III(4) and XI(1) of the GATT 1994. Argentina contended that the Panel had found that Japan had established the existence of the TRRs measure without an examination regarding the sufficient evidentiary basis provided by Japan on the measure's "precise content" and "general and prospective application" so that the Panel had acted inconsistently with Article 11 DSU.

The Appellate Body dismissed Argentina's argument and it held, on the contrary, that the Panel findings were based on a record of evidence with a sufficient reasoning to determine the content and the general and prospective application of the alleged TRRs measure.

3.2.4. *The DJAI Procedure: Inconsistency with Articles VIII and XI(1) GATT 1994*

The Panel considered that regardless of the nature of the DJAI, application of Article XI(1) of the GATT 1994 to the measure was not excluded and concluded the DJAI was an import restriction having restrictive effects on imports, in breach of Article XI(1) of the GATT 1994.

---

[46] *Ibid.*, paras. 5.130-5.133.

[47] The Panel found five different trade measures acting as one inconsistent with Article III:4 of the GATT 1994 for aiming to modify Argentina's market competition with a detrimental impact on imports: (1) ensuring that imports present themselves only after a trade balance if reached; (2) limiting imports in general under volume or value considerations; (3) requiring levels of domestic content in production; (4) requiring investments in Argentina; and (5) requiring not to repatriate profits from Argentina.

The Appellate Body in assessing the interpretation by the Panel of Article XI(1) GATT 1994 concluded that not all conditions or burdens related to imports are inconsistent with Article XI(1) of the GATT 1994, but only those that directly limit the importation or export of products, as results from the design of the measure. The Appellate Body found that Argentina had failed in proving that the Panel was wrong. While the "effects of the formality or requirement itself" were limiting trade, the Appellate Body considered that the application of the DJAI measure would generate a detrimental impact on imports.

The Appellate Body also rejected Argentina's claim that a trade restriction is required to include a quantitative threshold to be in breach of WTO rules.[48]

3.3. Comment

Overall, the analysis and proceedings conducted by the Panel were upheld by the Appellate Body in *Argentina – Measures Affecting the Importation of Goods*, except for the EU others appeal regarding the identification of 23 Specific Measures in accordance with Article 6.2 DSU. This case presents an interesting reasoning on the application of TRRs measures in an "apparently" isolated fashion, while they concur in having a single detrimental impact on international trade in breach of the WTO rules.

Furthermore, while the EU reached an agreement on the application of the Appellate Body recommendations, some trade actors both in Argentina and abroad consider that the DJAI and TRRs inconsistent measures were replaced with bureaucratic internal measures that possibly restricted even more the import process into Argentina.[49] This raises the question on how the WTO should handle bureaucratic requirements that even though apparently not in clear breach of a specific WTO provision evidently, when analyzed under an international trade liberation perspective result in a trade restriction even if disguised.

LOLY AYLU GAITAN GUERRERO*

---

[48] *Ibid.*, paras. 5.276-5.286.

[49] Riggi, "El Gobierno reemplazó las DJAI por nuevas barreras burocráticas para frenar importaciones", Cronista.com, 23 December 2015, available at: <http://www.cronista.com/economiapolitica/El-Gobierno-reemplazo-las-DJAI-por-nuevas-barreras-burocraticas-para-frenar-importaciones-20151223-0079.html>.

* Ph.D. candidate in International Law and Economics, Bocconi University, Milan.

4. APPELLATE BODY REPORT, *UNITED STATES – CERTAIN COUNTRY OF ORIGIN LABELLING (COOL) REQUIREMENTS, ARTICLE 21.5 APPELLATE BODY REPORT AND RECOURSE TO ARTICLE 22.6 ARBITRATION REPORT*[50]

4.1. Introduction to the Dispute

The *US-COOL* cases dealt with a technical regulation adopted by the US requiring retailers to provide country of origin information for certain meat products including beef and pork. On 23 July 2012, the DSB adopted the Panel and Appellate Body Reports for this case.[51] On 13 September 2012, Canada requested binding arbitration pursuant to Article 21.3(c) to determine a "reasonable period of time" for the US to implement measures in response to the DSB's recommendations. After arbitration on the reasonable periods of time (RPT) Canada and Mexico challenged the changes made by the US Department of Agriculture (USDA), which they claimed were more restrictive and caused further harm. On 10 June 2013, a compliance Panel was established under Article 21.5 DSU.

4.2. Main Findings of the Compliance Panel

On 20 October 2014, the compliance Panel report was circulated to Members. The complainants challenged the treatment accorded to imported meat and livestock under the amended COOL rules. The amended measure consisted of the addition of the "2013 Final Rule" (78 Fed. Reg. 31367) to the original COOL statute (7 U.S.C. §1638).

The compliance Panel found that imported meat was accorded less favourable treatment under the amended measure and thus the US remained in violation of Article 2.1 of the Agreement on Technical Barriers to Trade (TBT Agreement).[52] Furthermore, the amended COOL measure was deemed to increase the detrimental impact on the competitive opportunities for imported livestock as it necessitated increased segregation according to origin. The Panel also found that the detrimental impact did not stem exclusively from legitimate regulatory distinctions.[53] It followed the approach of the Appellate Body in the original dispute[54] by having regard

---

[50] *United States – Certain Country of Origin Labelling (COOL) Requirements*, Art. 21.5 Appellate Body Report, 29 May 2015, WT/DS384/AB/RW, WT/DS386/AB/RW, and Recourse to Art. 22.6 Arbitration Report, circulated 7 December 2015 WT/DS384/ARB, WT/DS386/ARB.

[51] For a summary of the Panel and Appellate Body Reports of the *US-COOL* case, see SACERDOTI (ed.), "WTO Case Law in 2012", IYIL, 2012, p. 299 ff., p. 332 ff.

[52] Article 21.5 Panel Report, *United States – Certain Country of Origin Labelling (COOL) Requirements*, 29 May 2015, WT/DS384/RW, WTDS386/RW, para. 7.284.

[53] *Ibid.*, para. 7.284.

[54] Appellate Body Report, *United States – Certain Country of Origin Labelling (COOL) Requirements*, 29 June 2012, WT/DS384/AB/R, WTDS386/AB/R, para. 342.

to factors such as the recordkeeping burden associated with the measure. In light of these considerations, the Panel deemed that the detrimental impact was not offset by the legitimate aim of informing consumers.

The compliance Panel determined on the other hand that the complainants had not made a *prima facie* case that the amended COOL measure was more trade restrictive than necessary under Article 2.2 of the TBT Agreement (subsequently overturned by the Appellate Body).[55] It further found however that the amended COOL measure had increased the "considerable degree of trade-restrictiveness" of the measure that the Appellate Body had found in the original dispute.[56] The Panel concluded that it was unable to ascertain the gravity of the consequences of non-fulfilment of the objective.[57] Consumer demand for labelling was considered an indicator and there was not enough evidence on the record to make a determination.[58] The Panel reviewed four alternative measures proposed by the complainants and found that none of them made a *prima facie* case that the amended COOL measure was more trade restrictive than necessary under the TBT Agreement. The Panel found moreover that the amended COOL measure continued to violate GATT Article III:4 as it increased the original COOL measure's detrimental impact on the competitive opportunities for imported livestock in comparison with like US products.

4.3.   Key Legal Issues Before the Appellate Body

The US appealed the Panels' findings that the amended COOL measure was inconsistent with Article 2.1 of the TBT Agreement and Article III:4 of the GATT 1994. Canada and Mexico appealed the Panels' findings that they had not presented a *prima facie* case that the amended COOL measure was more trade restrictive than necessary under Article 2.2 of the TBT Agreement.

4.3.1.   Article 2.1 of the TBT Agreement

In its report, the Appellate Body upheld the Panel's conclusions and found that the amended COOL measure increased the record-keeping burden for imported livestock entailed by the original COOL measure. The Appellate Body rejected the arguments of the US that the Panel's conclusions were based on "incorrect hypothetical" scenarios that were not based on actual, or the most common, trade situations. The Appellate Body reminded that Article 2.1 is concerned with competitive

---

[55] Article 21.5 Panel report *US-COOL*, *cit. supra* note 50, para. 7.356.
[56] *Ibid.*, para. 7.611.
[57] *Ibid.*, para. 7.424.
[58] *Ibid.*, para. 7.418.

opportunities wherein analysis should not be limited to actual patterns of trade.[59] The Appellate Body similarly dismissed the argument that the Panel's finding regarding the potential for inaccuracy in labels was based on hypothetical scenarios. It found that the Panel did not rely on these scenarios but rather considered a wide range of scenarios and disregarded those unlikely to occur.[60]

The Appellate Body upheld the Panel's finding that the recordkeeping and verification requirements of the amended COOL measure impose a disproportionate burden on producers and processors of livestock that cannot be explained by the need to provide information to consumers. The US argued that the exemptions provided were applied equally to imported and domestic livestock. However the pertinent issue was deemed to be that the exemptions demonstrated that the relevant regulatory distinctions were not designed and applied in an even-handed manner as part of the overall architecture of the amended COOL measure since most of the time that did not convey relevant information to the consumers as to the origin of the meat.[61]

4.3.2. Article 2.2 of the TBT Agreement

The Appellate Body reversed the Panel's conclusion that Canada and Mexico failed to make a *prima facie* case that the amended COOL measure was more trade restrictive than necessary and thus violated Article 2.2 of the TBT Agreement. However, the Appellate Body made no finding as to whether the amended COOL measure is inconsistent with Article 2.2.

The Appellate Body found that the Panel had erred by failing to take into consideration the proposed alternative measures in assessing the respective overall degrees of contribution. The Panel had incorrectly excluded two types of COOL labels when reaching its conclusion that the amended COOL measure makes a "considerable but necessarily partial" contribution to its objective of providing consumer information on origin. The Appellate Body was however unable to complete its legal analysis as there were insufficient undisputed facts on the record. It found that the Panel had also erred in concluding that it was unable to ascertain the gravity of the consequences of non-fulfilment of the amended COOL measure's objective. Although such a determination was acknowledged to be difficult, this does not "relieve a Panel from its duty to assess this factor".[62]

---

[59] Article 21.5 Appellate Body Report, *United States – Certain Country of Origin Labelling (COOL) Requirements*, 29 May 2015, WT/DS384/AB/RW, WTDS386/AB/RW, para. 5.58.

[60] *Ibid.*, para. 5.55.

[61] *Ibid.*, para. 5.121.

[62] *Ibid.*, para. 5.310.

4.4. Decisions by the Arbitrator

In view of the fact that the US had taken no compliance measure after the adoption of the Appellate Body compliance report on 29 May 2015, Canada and Mexico requested authorization from the DSB to suspend concessions under Article 22.2 DSU to an annual value of CAD 3.068 billion and USD 713 million respectively. The US objected to the suspension of concessions and so the matter was referred to arbitration as required under Article 22.6 DSU.

The arbitration was carried out by the original Panel and the proceedings for DS384 and DS386 were joined. The Panel assessed the complainants' proposed levels of suspension of and although flaws were found, they were not deemed fatal to the claims. Lost export revenues were calculated as the difference between export revenue with and without the COOL measure. The Panel followed the complainants' price estimation but rejected their quantity estimation. On 7 December 2015, the arbitrator's decision was circulated where it was determined that the level of nullification or impairment for Canada amounted to CAD 1.054.729 million annually. The level of nullification or impairment for Mexico was calculated to be USD 227.758 million annually. On the same date, Canada and Mexico requested authorization from the DSB to suspend the application of certain tariff concessions and related obligations in conformity with the Arbitrator's Decisions pursuant to Article 22.7 DSU. At its meeting on 21 December 2015, the DSB authorized Canada and Mexico to suspend concessions or other obligations to the US. However at the same meeting, the US announced that on 18 December the COOL legislation had been repealed by the US Congress. As there were no longer any WTO-inconsistent measures in place, the request for retaliation was "obsolete".[63] In response, Mexico said that it was analyzing the repeal of the COOL legislation. Canada said it did not accept that the dispute had been completely resolved as more steps need to be completed. Hoping in any case that "no retaliatory action will be needed in future".[64]

4.5. Comment

Under Article 2.2 of the TBT Agreement, the Appellate Body found that the Panel was not relieved of its duty to ascertain the gravity of the consequences of non-fulfilment of the amended COOL measures because of the difficulty of the task. The Panel considered consumer demand for labelling to be an indicator and

---

[63] See minutes of the DSB for 21 December 2015, available at: <https://www.wto.org/english/news_e/news15_e/dsb_18dec15_e.htm> (as of 12 April 2016).

[64] "Statement from Ministers Freeland and MacAulay on U.S. Country of Origin Labelling", 21 December 2015, Ottawa/Ontario, Global Affairs Canada, available at: <http://news.gc.ca/web/article-en.do?nid=1025819> (as of 12 April 2016).

that there was not enough evidence of this on the record to make a determination. The Appellate Body found that the Panel should proceed with a "holistic weighing and balancing" of all relevant factors and reach a conclusion.[65] The Appellate Body recalled the language "taking account of the risks non-fulfilment would create" and that this calls for an active and meaningful consideration of the risks of non-fulfilment.[66] The requirement was deemed flexible enough to adapt to the particularities of a given case and future Panels should bear this in mind.

NIALL MORAN[*]

5.   APPELLATE BODY REPORT, *INDIA – MEASURES CONCERNING THE IMPORTATION OF CERTAIN AGRICULTURAL PRODUCTS*[67]

5.1.   *Factual Background*

Avian Influenza (hereinafter also AI), commonly called as Bird Flu, is an infectious viral disease of birds. Most AI viruses do not cause disease in humans; risks for human health are limited to two subtypes of AI, the high pathogenicity A(H5N1) virus and the low pathogenicity A(H7N9) virus.[68] The H5N1 virus has, since 1997, spread through most of Asia and Europe and it is considered to constitute a serious pandemic threat.

The organization in charge for establishing health standards for international trade in animals and animal products, including regulation of Avian Influenza, is the Organization for Animal Health, previously known as Office International des Epizooties (OIE). Under Chapter 10(4) of the OIE Terrestrial Code,[69] State Parties have a duty to notify the OIE of all cases of High Pathogenicity Avian Influenza (HPAI) occurring in all birds, as well as of certain types of Low Pathogenicity Avian Influenza (LPAI) when occurring in poultry. As mentioned in the Appellate Body Report, between 2004 and January 2014, the US did not notify the OIE of any

---

[65] Article 21.5 Appellate Body Report *US-COOL*, *cit. supra* note 50, para. 5.306.

[66] *Ibid.*, para. 5.28.

[*] Ph.D. candidate in International Law and Economics, Bocconi University, Milan.

[67] Appellate Body Report, *India – Measures Concerning the Importation of Certain Agricultural Products*, adopted on 19 June 2015, WT/DS430/AB/R.

[68] World Health Organization Website, "Avian Influenza in Humans", available at: <www.who.int/influenza/human_animal_interface/avian_influenza/en/>. As specified by the WHO, the primary risk factor for human infection appears to be direct or indirect contact with infected (live or dead) poultry or eggs. While eating properly cooked meat or eggs does not seem to constitute a risk factor, preparation of contaminated food does.

[69] OIE, "Terrestrial Animal Health Code", available at: <http://www.oie.int/international-standard-setting/terrestrial-code/access-online/>.

outbreaks of HPAI, but did notify occurrences of LPAI in poultry.[70] Over a similar ten years period, from the end of 2003 to March 2013, India notified to the OIE 95 outbreaks of HPAI in poultry, but no outbreak of LPAI.[71]

Given the high number of outbreaks on its territory, India adopted measures aimed at protecting its animal and human population from risks of AI. Section 3 of its Livestock Act 1898, as amended in 2001, allows the Indian Government to regulate or prevent "the import into India of live-stock which is liable to be affected by contagious disorders". In exercise of this power, on 19 July 2011, the Indian Department of Animal Husbandry adopted Statutory Order 1663, establishing a total ban on the import of wild birds (except those bred in captivity) from all foreign countries, as well as a ban on the import of a list of live stock products from countries reporting occurrences of both high and low pathogenicity avian influenza.[72] As the US is one of the world's largest exporters of chicken meat, the interests of the American poultry industry were seriously harmed by the Indian ban.[73]

5.2. Procedural History

After consultations with India on 11 May 2012, the US requested the establishment of a Panel whose report, circulated on 14 October 2014, accepted almost all of the US claims – including claims that the ban was not based on a risk assessment or scientific evidence, did not conform to international standards, and failed to take into account regional characteristics in the US – and ruled the Indian measures incompatible with the SPS provisions. On 18 November 2014, the DSB agreed to allow an extension to the period for appeal, as requested by India and the US. On 26 January 2015, India filed an appeal challenging several key findings of the Panel. On 4 June 2015, the Appellate Body circulated its report that upheld most of the Panel's findings. On 19 June 2015, the DSB adopted the report.

5.3. Key Legal Issues

The case concerns the adoption, by India, of certain SPS measures. It is worth recalling, by way of introduction, that SPS measures typically take the form of tech-

---

[70] Appellate Body Report, *India – Measures Concerning the Importation of Certain Agricultural Products (India – Agricultural Products)*, adopted on 4 June 2015, WT/DS430/AB/R, para. 4.13.

[71] *Ibid.*

[72] The text of the Statutory Order is reproduced in the Appellate Body Report, *India – Agricultural Products, cit. supra* note 67, para. 4.6.

[73] See Roy, "Cheap US Chicken Leaves Indian Poultry Farmers in a Flap", The Wall Street Journal, 13 July 2015, estimating that the value of US chicken exports into India could exceed $300 millions a year once India removes its restrictions.

nical barriers to trade but are regulated by a different set of WTO rules, contained in the SPS Agreement often linked to agricultural trade, a sector where Members have traditionally resisted liberalization.[74]

The legal questions emerging in the case at issue concern India's exercise of its right to introduce SPS measures. Among the many issues considered by the Appellate Body,[75] three appear particularly interesting for their link to current debates or for their relative novelty in the WTO case law: the relationship of SPS measures with *scientific evidence* (Articles 2(2), 5(1) and 5(2) SPS Agreement); their compliance with *international standards* (Articles 3(1) and 3(2) SPS Agreement); and their adaptation to *regional conditions* (Article 6 SPS Agreement).

5.3.1. Scientific Evidence

Article 2(2) SPS Agreement requires that measures adopted by Members "be based on scientific principles and not be maintained without sufficient scientific evidence". The scientific evidence requirement is elaborated by Article 5(1), specifying that the SPS measures must be based on a risk assessment, while Article 5(2) further qualifies the kind of scientific evidence that can be used in the assessment of risk. Since India did not conduct any risk assessment, the Panel found the measures to be inconsistent with Articles 5(1) and 5(2) and consequently also to violate Article 2(2) SPS Agreement.

In its appeal, India contends that the Panel erred in interpreting the relationship between Article 2(2) and Article 5(1): these are independent legal provisions and "the close link between the two does not mean they are identical".[76] In the interpretation favoured by India, the presence of a risk assessment is not always required, as a member may still prove that its measures are based on scientific evidence under Article 2(2): failure to respect Articles 5(1) and 5(2) simply creates a presumption of inconsistency with Article 2(2), but this presumption is rebuttable.[77]

The Appellate Body partly accepts India's contentions. While restating that the Panel's interpretation of the relationship between Articles 2(2) and 5(1) is formally correct, the Appellate Body finds that the Panel erred in its application of Article 2(2) to the Indian measures as it automatically derived a violation of Article

---

[74] See VAN DEN BOSSCHE and ZDOUC, *The Law and Policy of the World Trade Organization*, Cambridge, 2013, p. 895. See more broadly GRUSZCZYNSKI, *Regulating Health and Environmental Risk under WTO Law: A Critical Analysis of the SPS Agreement*, Oxford, 2010.

[75] Both the Panel and Appellate Body also found the measure to be more trade restrictive than necessary (thus to violate Arts. 5(6) and 2(2) SPS Agreement) and to violate national treatment (Art. 2.3 SPS Agreement).

[76] Appellate Body Report, para. 2.2.

[77] As stated by the Panel and confirmed by the Appellate Body, this interpretation of Art. 2.2 is confirmed by previous cases: *Australia – Salmon*, *EC – Hormones* and *Australia – Apples*. See Appellate Body Report, *India – Agricultural Products*, *cit. supra* note 67, para. 5.34.

2(2) from the absence of a risk assessment. The Panel should have considered the evidence and arguments produced by India to assess if the presumption had been rebutted. The Appellate Body consequently reverses the Panel's findings with regard to India's prohibitions on fresh poultry meat and eggs from countries reporting LPAI, since the Panel had failed to analyze the scientific evidence brought by India in relation to these measures. However, as the Report clarifies, "SPS measures adopted by members must comply with all of the requirements of Articles 2(2), 5(1) and 5(2)":[78] a Member cannot, as India suggests, elect either to base its measure on Article 2(2) or to conduct a risk assessment basing its measure on Articles 5(1) and 5(2).

5.3.2. International Standards

Pursuant to Article 3(1), Members of the SPS Agreement always have to "base their measures" on "international standards, guidelines or recommendations". Article 3(2) establishes a rebuttable presumption of compliance with the SPS and GATT Agreement rules for measures which "conform to" international standards. The Panel found the Indian measures to violate both provisions: they did not "conform to" nor they were "based on" international standards.

India's claims with regard to these findings are particularly interesting as they allow discussing the relationship between the WTO judicial bodies and other global standard setting bodies. In particular, India claims that the Panel exceeded the permissible scope of consultation with the OIE as prescribed by Article 11(2) SPS Agreement and 13(2) DSU, because it consulted with the OIE not only on scientific or technical matters but also on the legal interpretation of the OIE code.[79]

In its decision, the Appellate Body re-states the centrality of Article 3 in the architecture of the SPS Agreement. By quoting from *EC – Hormones*, the Appellate Body clarifies that the purpose of Article 3 is to "promote the harmonization of SPS measures [...] on as wide a basis as possible, while recognizing and safeguarding the right and duty of Members to protect the life and health of their people".[80] The Appellate Body further clarifies that Article 3 establishes "an obligation concerning harmonization with relevant standards"[81] and that it is up to the Panel to interpret the international standards that serve as benchmarks. In doing so the Panel can rely

---

[78] Appellate Body Report, *India – Agricultural Products, cit. supra* note 67, para. 5.32.

[79] *Ibid.*, para. 2.14.

[80] *Ibid.*, para. 5.77. The AB recalls the finding of *EC – Hormones*, that a measure is to be considered "based on international standards" when it adopts "some, but not necessarily all the elements of that standard" and drew on *EC – Sardines* to find that when a measure contradicts an international standard (even while reproducing some of its elements) cannot be deemed as being "based upon" it.

[81] Appellate Body Report, para. 5.79.

on "any relevant interpretative principle" but also may find additional sources to be useful, including "the views of the relevant standard setting body".[82] The Appellate Body discusses more generally the limits of the authority of the panel to seek advice, which is defined by Article 13 DSU, entitled "Right to Seek Information". By quoting its decision in *US – Shrimp*, the Appellate Body underlines the wide discretion enjoyed by the Panel, which can decide whether to seek advice, to what extent and from which body.[83] Furthermore, Article 11(2) SPS Agreement provides that the panel "should seek advice" from experts in disputes involving scientific or technical issues. The Appellate Body rejects the contention that Article 11(2) SPS Agreement could work to restrain the discretion of the Panel and consequently establishes that the Panel legitimately consulted the OIE with regard to the legal interpretation of the OIE Code. Furthermore, the Appellate Body concludes that the Panel did not accept a-critically the opinion of the OIE and thus upholds the Panel findings that the Indian measures cannot enjoy the presumption of compliance of Article 3(2) and that they additionally violate Article 3(1) SPS Agreement.

5.3.3. *Regional Conditions*

The assessment of the compliance of the Indian measure with Article 6 SPS is particularly interesting because it represents the first WTO interpretation of this provision. The article requires Members to adapt their rules to the geographic sanitary conditions of the exporting country in particular by recognizing the concept of disease free areas (Article 6(2) SPS Agreement) and it establishes that exporting countries must provide the necessary evidence to prove the existence of such areas (Article 6(3) SPS Agreement). In other words, Members cannot ban products irrespective of the geographic conditions of the exporting countries. As India had banned poultry products from the US as a whole without distinction, even if cases of LPAI were detected only in the State of Virginia in 2007,[84] the Panel ruled that India had failed to recognize "disease free areas and areas of low disease prevalence" under the definition of Article 6(2) SPS Agreement so that it breached Article 6(1).

The Appellate Body here reaches the same conclusions of the Panel but with a different reasoning. In its first interpretation of Article 6 SPS, the Appellate Body clarifies that this provision establishes an "obligation that is not static, but rather ongoing, requiring that SPS measures be adjusted over time so as to establish and maintain their continued suitable in respect of the relevant SPS characteristics of

---

[82] *Ibid.*

[83] Appellate Body Report, *United States – Import Prohibition of Certain Shrimp and Shrimp Products* (*US – Shrimp*), adopted on 12 October 1998, WT/DS58/AB/R, para. 104.

[84] "US Wins on Almost All Claims in WTO Case Against India Poultry Ban", Inside US Trade, 17 October 2014.

the relevant areas".[85] The Appellate Body however suggests that Members enjoy a wide degree of latitude in meeting this obligation: there is not one correct manner to adapt to regional conditions and a case-specific analysis is required. In particular, the Appellate Body seems to disagree with the Panel insofar as it considers that the requirement of Article 6(2) can be met also without need of previous formal recognition of the concept of disease free area, but it still rejects India's claim that the Panel erred in its application of Article 6(2) by not relying solely on the Livestock Act.[86] With regard to the relationship between 6(1) and 6(3), the Appellate Body rejects India's claim but recognizes that it would normally be very difficult to prove a violation of Article 6(1) without a previous action by the exporting Member.[87]

5.4. Comment

The case at issue is a telling example of some key tensions in the application of SPS measures. It shows that as the world grows more interconnected and risk of pandemic outbreaks increases, hygiene or health standards growingly become avenues to introduce protectionist measures. More specifically the judgment appears relevant because of the wide discretion recognized by the Appellate Body to Panels in consulting with global standard setters and because it constitutes the first judicial application of Article 6 SPS Agreement, which imposes a duty to adapt measures to regional conditions prevailing in the exporting country. Article 6 might appear marginal but it actually becomes very important in the architecture of the SPS Agreement, clarifying that if the Agreement recognizes the right of importing countries to protect the health of their animals and humans, it also forces them to accept the claims of exporters with regard to areas that are free from animal diseases.

GIACOMO TAGIURI[*]

6. APPELLATE BODY REPORT, *PERU – ADDITIONAL DUTIES ON IMPORTS OF CERTAIN AGRICULTURAL PRODUCTS*[88]

6.1. Introduction and Factual Background

The dispute *Peru – Agricultural Products* arose out of complaints brought by Guatemala against the Peruvian Price Range System (PRS), a mechanism con-

---

[85] *Ibid.*, para. 5.132.
[86] *Ibid.*, para. 5.144.
[87] *Ibid.*, para. 5.156.
[*] Ph.D. candidate in International Law and Economics, Bocconi University, Milan.
[88] Appellate Body Report, *Peru – Additional Duty on Imports of Certain Agricultural Products*, adopted on 31 July 2015, WT/DS457/AB/R.

ceived to minimize fluctuations in the international price for certain agricultural products.[89] It operated on the basis of a reference price, which reflected the average international price over the preceding two weeks, along with a range composed by a floor price and a ceiling price.

In practical terms, the PRS imposes additional duties to the tariff when the reference price is below the floor-price level, it applies tariff reductions in case the reference price exceeds the ceiling price and leaves tariffs unaltered if the reference price is below the ceiling price and above the floor price.

The relevant legal instrument for the case is a Free Trade Agreement (FTA), the parties being Guatemala and Peru, which was signed in December 2011 and which, in Annex 2.3 paragraph 9, states that "Peru may maintain its PRS".[90] It should be noted that the FTA was approved by Guatemalan Congress in July 2013 and subsequently, was formally ratified by the Guatemalan President in February 2014. Peru, however, had not ratified the agreement yet, so that it was not in force at the time of the dispute.

6.2. Procedural History

Following an unsuccessful attempt to find a mutually agreed solution in consultations and consistent with Article 4(7) DSU, a Panel was established in July 2013. The Panel report was circulated on 27 November 2014 and appealed against by both Parties to the dispute. On 31 July 2015, the DSB adopted the Appellate Body Report and on 1 October 2015 Guatemala requested and obtained a determination of the reasonable period of time through a binding arbitration pursuant to Article 21(3)(c) DSU. The award was circulated on 16 December 2015 and the expiration for the implementation of the DSB's recommendations was determined to be 29 March 2016.

6.3. The Panel Report

The Panel addressed first as a preliminary matter the admissibility of Guatemala's proceedings as Peru had asserted that they were brought in a manner contrary to good faith and therefore inconsistent with Article 3(7) and Article 3(10) DSU. In this respect, the Panel confirmed that a Member that resorts to the DSB enjoys the presumption of good faith, excluding that the Panel "can[not] question

---

[89] The agricultural products concerned with the application of the PRS were milk, yellow maize, rice, and sugar. See Panel Report, *Peru – Additional Duties on Imports of Certain Agricultural Products*, adopted 27 November 2014, WT/DS457/R, para. 2.2.

[90] Tratado de Libre Comercio Guatemala-Perù (Guatemala-Peru Free Trade Agreement), 6 December 2011, Art. 9 of Annex 2.3.

a Member's exercise of judgement as to whether initiation of a dispute settlement procedure would be fruitful".[91] Additionally, the Panel clarified that a violation of Article 18 of the Vienna Convention on the Law of Treaties (VCLT) that prohibits States from acting against the object and the purpose of treaties subject to acceptance, does not constitute *per se* evidence of lack of good faith. Furthermore, the Panel ruled that Peru had not adduced sufficient evidence to show breach of Article 18 VCLT and of good faith obligations.

As to the merit, the Panel assessed two substantive aspects, the first being the nature of the measure at issue and the second its compatibility with the multilateral agreements. With regard to the former, the PRS was found to be a "variable import levy", meaning a border duty characterized by "an inherent variability" and specific features such as the lack of transparency and predictability.[92] Such features differentiated this kind of measures from ordinary customs duties.

Turning to the consistency with WTO obligations, Guatemala claimed a breach of both Article 4(2) of the Agreement on Agriculture and Article II(1)(b) of the GATT. With respect to the first claim, the Panel considered that maintaining variable import levies, which were explicitly required to be converted into ordinary customs duties under Article 4(2) of the Agreement on Agriculture, was a violation of WTO obligations. Since the PRS was held to be a variable import levy, it was applied in a manner inconsistent with WTO commitments. By the same token, the additional duties applied through the PRS corresponded to "other duty or charge" that were not recorded in Peru's Schedule of Concession and, thus, were also implemented in violation of Article II(1)(b) of the GATT.

6.4. *Arguments on Appeal*

The Parties in the dispute appealed multiple findings of the panel report. Indeed, Peru's claims concerned various issues of law and legal interpretations. First, it requested that the Appellate Body reverse the Panel's conclusions regarding Guatemala's presumption of good faith in light of Guatemala's relinquishment of its DSU right to a Panel contained in the Peru-Guatemala FTA. Second, Peru claimed that additional duties resulting from the PRS constituted ordinary customs duties so that the measure was consistent with WTO obligations. Furthermore, it challenged the Panel's interpretation of Article 4(2) of the Agreement on Agriculture which, in Peru's view, did not take into consideration Article 31 of the VCLT and Articles 20 and 45 of the International Law Commission's Articles on State Responsibility (ASR). On the other hand, Guatemala requested the Appellate Body to find that the

---

[91] Panel Report, *Peru – Additional Duties on Imports of Certain Agricultural Products*, para. 7.74.

[92] *Ibid.*, para. 7.291.

Panel erred in its analysis since the measure at issue constituted a minimum import price rather than a variable import levy.

6.5. Key Appellate Body Findings

6.5.1. Good Faith Obligations and the Relinquishment of the Right to Initiate WTO Dispute Settlement Proceedings

Peru asserted that Guatemala had acted inconsistently with the good faith principle as it had initiated legal proceedings despite having waived its right to have recourse to the DSU in the FTA. In addressing this issue, the Appellate Body first established that Peru's arguments did not constitute "new claims". On the contrary, the Appellate Body held that the arguments pertained to the issue of law covered previously by the Panel and accordingly, fell within the scope of appeal.

On the merit, the Appellate Body observed that although Article 3(7) DSU confers a considerable discretion to a Member in exercising its right to initiate WTO dispute settlement, this discretion is not unbounded. However, recalling the *EC – Banana* case,[93] the Appellate Body restated that a relinquishment or a waiver of Members' right to have recourse to the DSU to be effectively stipulated must be clearly stated in a mutually agreed solution that is consistent with the covered agreements. The Appellate Body concluded that the FTA at issue, independently from its legal status, did not constitute a clear stipulation of the relinquishment of Guatemala's right to initiate WTO proceedings. For these reasons, it was held that the claimant did not act contrary to its good faith obligations.[94]

6.5.2. The Determination of the Measure at Issue and Its Consistency with Article 4(2) of the Agreement of Agriculture and Article II(1)(b) GATT 1994

Peru claimed that the Panel erred in its assessment of the variability of the measure. Indeed, according to Peru, the Panel analysis should have considered only the additional duties resulting from the Peruvian system rather than the PRS meth-

---

[93] Appellate Body Reports, *European Communities – Regime for the Importation, Sale and Distribution of Bananas (Article 21.5 – Ecuador II / Article 21.5 – US)*, adopted on 26 November 2008, WT/DS27/AB/RW2/ECU and WT/DS27/AB/RW/USA, paras. 217, 228.

[94] The Appellate Body observed that the FTA presented various ambiguities concerning the maintenance of the PRS, which prevent the agreement from being a mutually accepted solution. The unclear aspects concerned the wording in Annex 2.3 para. 9, which states "Peru may maintain" instead of "Peru shall maintain" the presence of a fork-in-the-road clause in Art. 15.3, and the existence of a provision affirming the FTA primacy over WTO obligations in Art. 1.3(2). See Appellate Body Report, *Peru – Additional Duties on Imports of Certain Agricultural Products*, adopted on 31 July 2015, WT/DS457/AB/R (*Peru – Agricultural Products*), paras. 5.26-5.28.

odology and formula used to calculate them. On the other hand, Guatemala challenged the Panel findings and claimed that the PRS was a minimum import price within the meaning of footnote 1 of Article 4(2) of the Agreement of Agriculture.

The Appellate Body upheld the Panel's assessment of the measure where it had established the PRS to be a variable import levy due to the inherent variability of the Peruvian System which "[...] incorporated a scheme that caused automatic and continuous change in the applicable duties".[95] It also observed that the additional features were not absolute characteristics and should not be given more relevance than the inherent variability in the determination that the levy was variable.[96] The Appellate Body found that in the Panel's examination of whether the measure was a minimum import price "the structure, design and operation of the PRS"[97] was not sufficiently assessed, though the Appellate Body could not satisfy Guatemala's request for the completion of the analysis.

6.5.3. Relationship between WTO and FTA Provisions

In its claims in appeal Peru asserted that, in accordance with Article 31(3) VCLT, the Panel should have interpreted the term "shall not maintain" in Article 4(2) of the Agreement of Agriculture as meaning "may maintain" in light of the Peru-Guatemala FTA. Indeed, according to Peru, the FTA constituted a subsequent agreement, which modified WTO obligations exclusively in the relations between the treaty parties, in accordance with Article 41 VCLT, and consequently allowed Peru to maintain the PRS. Furthermore, Peru argued that Guatemala's ratification represented a formal expression of consent, which precluded the Peruvian system from being considered wrongful, consistently with Articles 20 and 45 of the ASR.

The Appellate Body observed that Article 31 VCLT "[...] aims at establishing the ordinary meaning of the treaty terms reflecting the common intention of the parties to the treaty and not just the intentions of some of the parties" and it accordingly rejected Peru's position according to which "[...] WTO provisions can be interpreted differently, depending on the Members to which they apply and on their rights and obligations under an FTA to which they are parties".[98]

Moreover, the Appellate Body noted that the key issue in the dispute was determining whether the additional duties applied through the PRS were variable import levies, minimum import prices or ordinary customs duties. Therefore, it did not consider the FTA and Articles 20 and 45 ASR as "relevant" rules of international

---

[95] Ibid., para. 5.33.

[96] Additional features are referred to the transparency and predictability of a duty, as well as the distortion of international prices into the domestic market. Appellate Body Report, Peru – Agricultural Products, adopted on 31 July 2015, WT/DS457/AB/R, para. 5.41.

[97] Ibid., para. 5.142.

[98] Ibid., para. 5.106.

law within the meaning of Article 31(3)(c) of the VCLT since these provisions did not concern the same subject matter as Article 4(2) of the Agreement of Agriculture and Article II(1)(b) of the GATT.

Finally, the Appellate Body held that the FTA did not constitute a subsequent agreement "regarding the interpretation" of Article 4(2) of the Agreement of Agriculture and that, in any case, the FTA had not produced legally binding effects upon the Parties since it had not yet entered into force. In this regard, it further clarified that even assuming, *arguendo*, that the FTA had established modifications to the multilateral treaties, those modifications would not be subject to Article 41 of the VCLT but rather to Article XXIV of the GATT. For these reasons, it concluded by upholding the Panel's findings.

6.6. *Comment*

Although the present case undoubtedly offers important guidance on the definition of "variable import levy", it however sheds more prominently light on the systemic relation between WTO and non-WTO agreements as results from report's innovative analyses. Despite the fact that the FTA was not in force, the Appellate Body offered significant clarifications on two main issues: whether Members can waive their WTO rights through understandings concluded outside the covered agreements and whether an FTA, as a treaty, can modify the interpretation or the application of the WTO agreements.

With regard to the first issue, the Appellate Body reaffirmed that the right to initiate legal proceedings is a fundamental principle from which the Panel cannot derogate.[99] The Appellate Body admitted the possibility for Members to waive their right to have recourse to the DSB but on condition that the relinquishment is clearly stated "by means of a solution mutually acceptable to the parties that is consistent with the covered agreements".[100] Thus, the reports included FTAs as being among the valid legal instrument which may stipulate a relinquishment of WTO rights. However, within the current dispute, the FTA was ambiguous and Guatemala's consent, rather than being considered as absolute, was deemed to be contingent upon Peru's ratification.[101] Although the theoretical distinction between

---

[99] Appellate Body Report, *Mexico – Tax Measure on Soft Drinks and Other Beverages*, adopted 24 March 2006, WT/DS308/AB/R, paras. 5.26-5.28. For a detailed explanation of the primacy of the WTO settlement system see KWAK and MARCEAU, "Overlaps and Conflicts of Jurisdiction between the World Trade Organization and Regional Trade Agreements", in BARTELS and ORTINO (eds.), *Regional Trade Agreement and WTO Legal System*, Oxford, 2006, p. 465 ff.

[100] Appellate Body Report, *Peru – Agricultural Products, cit. supra* note 88, para. 5.25.

[101] The articulation of members' relinquishment of their WTO rights in FTAs should meet three requirements: should be clearly stipulated, should refer explicitly to the DSU, and the waiver should be limited to "specific disputes" (Appellate Body Report, *Peru – Agricultural Products, cit. supra* note 88, para. 5.25). NATENS and DESCHEEMAEKER, "Say It Loud, Say It Clear: Article

procedural and substantial good faith was irrelevant to address Peru's claims under Article 3(10) DSU, Guatemala's acceptance of substantive FTA provisions could have been weighed differently in the assessment of the wrongfulness of Peru's actions, based on Articles 20 and 45 of the ASR.[102]

With regard to the question of whether an FTA can modify WTO obligations, the Appellate Body answered negatively. First, it clarified that, in an interpretative exercise, Article 31 of the VCLT "[...] could not be used to develop interpretation based on asserted agreements or asserted relevant rules of international law applicable in the relations between the parties to subvert the common intention of the treaty parties", implicitly alluding to the need of a larger consent to modify WTO commitments.[103] Second, the Appellate Body expressly excluded *inter se* modifications of the WTO multilateral agreements from being subject to Article 41 of VCLT since "[...] specific provisions addressing amendments, waivers or exceptions for regional trade agreements, prevail over general provisions of VCLT".[104] In other words, the WTO adjudicative body appeared to "lock down" WTO agreements, precluding subsequent agreements from influencing the interpretation or the application of the former. Indeed, as the Appellate Body clearly stated "[...] the proper route for assessing whether a provision of the FTA may depart from certain WTO rules were the legal provisions specifically addressing regional trade agreements, namely Article XXIV of the GATT".[105] Undoubtedly, the limited application of Articles 31 and 41 of the VCLT in respect of subsequent FTAs made by the Appellate Body can be considered controversial, especially in comparison with *US – Clove Cigarette* and *US – Tuna II* where the Appellate Body applied Article 31(3)(a) of the VCLT to subsequent practice of the WTO.[106]

3.10 DSU's Clear Statement Test as a Legal Impediment to Validly Established Jurisdiction", JWT, 2015, p. 873 ff.

[102] According to the author, Guatemala's intention to admit Peruvian PRS was openly expressed in the FTA substantial provisions and also proved by Guatemala's ratification. For a critical analysis consult PAUWELYN, "Interplay between the WTO Treaty and Other International Legal Instruments and Tribunals: Evolution after 20 Years of WTO Jurisprudence", 10 February 2016, available at: <http://ssrn.com/abstract=2731144>.

[103] Appellate Body Report, *Peru – Agricultural Products*, para. 5.94.

[104] *Ibid.*, para. 5.112.

[105] The validity of FTA obligations is conditional upon two requirements: first, that the measure is introduced upon to the formation of free trade area; and second, that the measure is unavoidable to the realization of the free trade area itself. Appellate Body Report, *Turkey – Restrictions on Imports of Textile and Clothing Products*, adopted on 22 October 1999, WT/DS34/AB/R, paras. 58-61.

[106] In the cases *US – Clove Cigarette* and *US – Tuna II* the approach adopted by the Appellate Body was different. Respectively the Doha Ministerial Declaration and the TBT Committee Decision were considered subsequent agreements even if both lack explicit reference to Art. IX(2) of the WTO and legally binding effects. Appellate Body Report, *United States – Measures Affecting the Production and Sale of Clove Cigarettes*, adopted 24 April 2012, WT/DS406/AB/R, paras. 262-267; and Appellate Body Reports, *United States – Measures Concerning the*

To conclude, although the contours of the FTA-WTO relation cannot be deemed as definitive yet, the present case has shed considerable light on the central question of the compatibility between WTO regime and other international legal instruments.

ELISA LONGONI*

7. PANEL REPORTS AS MODIFIED BY APPELLATE BODY REPORTS, *CHINA – MEASURES IMPOSING ANTI-DUMPING DUTIES ON HIGH-PERFORMANCE STAINLESS STEEL SEAMLESS TUBES FROM JAPAN*[107]

7.1. Factual Background

On 8 November 2012 the Ministry of Commerce of the People's Republic of China (MOFCOM) came to the conclusion that dumping concerning imports of certain high-performance stainless steel seamless tubes from the EU and Japan was in place.[108] Thus, an anti-dumping duty on the imports of HP-SSST from the EU and Japan was issued at a rate of from 9.2% to 14.4% for 5 years.

7.2. Procedural History

In December 2012 Japan requested consultations with China, soon joined by EU. Thereafter – upon Japan and EU requests – two panels with the same panelists were established. In February 2015, a single Panel report was circulated among members. On May 2015, Japan, China, and the EU notified the DSB of their decision to appeal and – in October 2015 – the Appellate Body report was circulated.

7.3. Key Legal Issues

7.3.1. The Panel Report

The Panel report recognized that China's imposition of anti-dumping duties was inconsistent with Articles 3.1, 3.2, 3.4, and 3.5 of the Anti-Dumping Agreement, because of defects in the determination of injury to China's domestic industry and

---

Importation, Marketing and Sale of Tuna and Tuna Products, adopted 16 May 2012, WT/DS381/AB/R, paras. 371-372.

* Ph.D. candidate in International Law and Economics, Bocconi University, Milan.

[107] Appellate Body Reports, *China – HP-SSST*, adopted on 28 October 2015, WT/DS454/AB/R, WT/DS460/AB/R and Add. 1.

[108] Notice No. 21 [2012] and Notice No. 72 [2012].

of the weakness of the causal relationship between such an injury and the dumped exports. China's decision has also been considered as inconsistent with Articles 6.5, 6.5.1, 7.4, 12.2, and 12.2.2 of the Anti-Dumping Agreement because of certain concerns in the investigation procedure, such as in the disclosure of essential facts. With respect to the fulfilment of requirements in Article 6.8 of the Anti-Dumping Agreement, the Panel found that there was no factual basis to conclude that MOFCOM had failed to inform unknowing exporters of the information required of them, since MOFCOM had posted the exporter questionnaire on its website. The Panel also rejected claims concerning MOFCOM's use of narrative description to disclose the essential facts with which it had reached its dumping determination, because it noted that MOFCOM had provided narrative descriptions of essential facts that referred to factual information already in the exporters' possession.

In the end, the Panel upheld the consequential claims based on the circumstance that by failing to comply with the provisions of the Anti-Dumping Agreement, China had consequently acted in a manner inconsistent with Article 1 of the Anti-Dumping Agreement and Article VI of the GATT 1994.

7.3.2.   The Appellate Body Report

A. Showing of Good Cause

In agreement with the Panel, the Appellate Body stated that it could not ascertain the objectivity of MOFCOM's *good cause* assessment, as the evidences provided in support of its request for confidential treatment were deemed insufficient. Therefore, the Appellate Body upheld the Panel's finding that China acted inconsistently with Article 6.5 of the Anti-Dumping Agreement, since MOFCOM had kept the four reports at issue mostly confidential without objectively assessing the petitioners' showing of *good cause*. In addition, the Appellate Body noted that an investigating authority should "objectively assess the *good cause* alleged for confidential treatment, and scrutinize the party's showing in order to determine whether the submitting party has sufficiently substantiated its request".[109]

B. MOFCOM's Price Effects Analysis

Contrary to the Panel, the Appellate Body found that Article 3.2 of the Anti-Dumping Agreement requires an assessment of price trends in the relationship between prices of the dumped imports and those of their domestic counterparts,

---

[109] *China – HP-SSST, cit. supra* note 107, para. 5.3.

and that the investigating authority may not disregard evidence suggesting that the prices of dumped imports have little or no effect on domestic prices.

C. MOFCOM's Impact Analysis

The Appellate Body disagreed with the Panel's interpretation of Articles 3.1 and 3.4 of the Anti-Dumping Agreement, which regarded the results of the inquiries under Article 3.2 to be unnecessary for the impact analysis under Article 3.4. It recalled that, according to Article 3.4, an examination of the state of the domestic industry cannot suffice and that an investigating authority, instead, should use such an examination as the basis for an analysis of the impact of subject imports. In particular, the Appellate Body observed that said authority is required, when it has discovered a price undercutting, to take into consideration the relative market shares of the affected product types as well as the duration and extent of price undercutting, price depression, or price suppression. The Appellate Body therefore reversed the Panel's findings on Japan's claim and it stated that China acted inconsistently with Articles 3.1 and 3.4, because MOFCOM had not undertook such an analysis.

D. MOFCOM's Causation Analysis

The Appellate Body, in agreement with the Panel's findings, stated that China acted inconsistently with Articles 3.1 and 3.5 of the Anti-Dumping Agreement, since MOFCOM erroneously relied on the market share of dumped imports, and its flawed price effects and impact analyses, in determining a causal link between dumped imports and material injury to the domestic industry, and made no finding of cross-grade price effects whereby price undercutting by Grade B and C imports might be shown to affect the price of domestic Grade A HP-SSST.[110] According to the Appellate Body – which upheld the Panel's findings – MOFCOM failed to exclude that the injury caused by other factors was attributed to the dumped imports and thus China acted inconsistently with Articles 3.1 and 3.5 of the Anti-Dumping Agreement. In addition, the Appellate Body confirmed the Panel's finding that claimants had not advanced any independent Article 3.5 claims – apart from those regarding MOFCOM's reliance on market shares and MOFCOM's non-attribution analysis – concerning MOFCOM's price effects and impact analyses.[111]

---

[110] The MOFCOM carried out an investigation on 3 categories of these steel tubes (Grade A, B and C).

[111] *China – HP-SSST, cit. supra* note 107, para. 5.5.3.

7.4. Comment

If we look at the bigger picture, we can see that the dispute at hand exemplifies a more general trend occurring in trade relations recently. China's shift in its traditional stance has been twofold. First, contrary to its usual role as target of anti-dumping measures, China itself has started to react to such trade defences.[112] Secondly, China's presence in WTO disputes has become more and more assertive in order to safeguard its growing trade interests, thus effectively signalling an end to its traditional "light" approach.[113] Nowadays, anti-dumping policies have a major role in trade protection enforcement.[114] There is strong evidence that an anti-dumping measure implemented in one country will provoke a similar response by the restricted country.[115] The case we have analyzed could be seen as a – not isolated – prime example: the EU had imposed anti-dumping duties on imports of certain seamless tubes and stainless steel pipes from China on 29 June 2011, nearly two months before the start of China anti-dumping investigation on HP-SSST.[116]

LAURA ZOBOLI*

---

[112] GHORI, "The Dumping Dragon: Analyzing China's Evolving Anti-Dumping Behavior", The Business and Management Review, International Trade & Academic Research Conference, 2013, pp. 114-125.

[113] HSIEH, "China's Development of International Economic Law and WTO Legal Capacity Building", JIEL, 2010, p. 997 ff.

[114] Antidumping Publishing, Summary Statistics of Global Trade Protection Activity between 1995 and 2014.

[115] CHEN and KAO, "Anti-Dumping Policy and Anti-Dumping Retaliation", Institute of Economics, Academia Sinica, 2016 (forthcoming); and FEINBERG and REYNOLDS, "The Spread of Anti-Dumping Regimes and the Role of Retaliation in Filings", Southern Economic Journal, 2006, pp. 877-890.

[116] In this sense, the EU Trade Spokesman John Clancy said: "The EU continues its fight against unjustified Chinese trade defence measures, which do not comply with WTO rules and often seem to be motivated by retaliation. The Chinese case was brought shortly after a European case against Chinese steel imports. Given its obvious technical weaknesses, we are confident that the WTO will support our claims against these anti-dumping duties". See European Commission, Press Release (IP/13/772), "EU Requests WTO Panel on Chinese Anti-Dumping Duties on Steel Tubes", 16 August 2013, available at: <http://europa.eu/rapid/press-release_IP-13-772_en.htm>.

* Ph.D. candidate in International Law and Economics, Bocconi University, Milan.

8. REPORT OF THE APPELLATE BODY, *UNITED STATES – MEASURES CONCERNING THE IMPORTATION, MARKETING AND SALE OF TUNA AND TUNA PRODUCTS (US – TUNA II (MEXICO)) – RECOURSE TO ARTICLE 21.5 OF THE DSU BY MEXICO*[117]

8.1. US – Tuna II: Main Facts and Procedural History

This compliance dispute[118] under Article 21.5 DSU concerns the US "dolphin-safe" labelling regime affecting the importation, marketing, and sale of tuna and tuna products ("tuna measure"). In the original dispute, Mexico challenged the tuna measure under the GATT 1994 and the TBT Agreement. In particular, the "measure at issue" was represented by: (i) the Dolphin Protection Consumer Information Act (DPCIA) of 1990 (enabling statute);[119] (ii) its implementing regulation, and;[120] (iii) the ruling by the US Court of Appeals of the Ninth Circuit in *Earth Island Institute v. Hogarth* ("*Hogarth* ruling").[121] On 16 May 2012, the Appellate Body circulated its report.[122] It found that the tuna measure was a "technical regulation" within the meaning of Annex 1.1 to the TBT Agreement, as such inconsistent with Article 2.1 TBT Agreement, but not with Article 2.2 TBT Agreement. On 13 June 2012, the DSB adopted the original panel and Appellate Body reports. At the DSB meeting of 25 June 2012, the US declared that it intended to implement the DSB recommendations and rulings in a manner that respects its obligations and that it would need a reasonable period of time (RPT) to do so.[123] On 17 September 2012, the US and Mexico informed the DSB that they had agreed pursuant to Article 21(3)(b) DSU that the RPT for the US to implement the DSB recommendations and rulings should be 13 months (expiring on 13 July 2013).[124] On 9 July 2013, the US passed the Enhanced Document Requirements to Support Use of the Dolphin Safe Label on Tuna Products ("2013 Final Rule"), which partially amended the implementing regulation. The 2013 Final Rule embodies the new measure, which, together with the remaining parts of the tuna measure, specifically forms the basis of this compli-

---

[117] Appellate Body Report, *United States – Measures Concerning the Importation, Marketing and Sale of Tuna and Tuna Products – Recourse to Article 21.5 of the DSU by Mexico (US – Tuna II (Mexico) (Article 21.5))*, adopted on 3 December 2015, WT/DS381/AB/RW.

[118] GUZMAN and PAUWELYN, *International Trade Law*, 2nd ed., New York, 2012, pp. 136-137; VAN DEN BOSSCHE and ZDOUC, *The Law and Policy of the World Trade Organization*, 3rd ed., Cambridge, pp. 293-295; and MATSUSHITA, SCHOENBAUM, MAVROIDIS and HAHN, *The World Trade Organization. Law, Practice, and Policy*, 3rd ed., Oxford, 2015, pp. 127-131.

[119] 16 USC § 13855.

[120] 50 US CFR §§ 216.91-216.92.

[121] *Earth Island Institute et al. v. William T. Hogarth*, 494 F.3d 757 (9th Cir. 2007).

[122] Appellate Body Report, *United States – Measures Concerning the Importation, Marketing and Sale of Tuna and Tuna Products*, adopted on 16 May 2012, WT/DS381/AB/R (*US – Tuna II (Mexico)*). See SACERDOTI (ed.), *cit. supra* note 51, p. 317 ff.

[123] On the determination of the RPT pursuant to DSU Art. 21(3), see SACERDOTI (ed.), "WTO Case Law in 2013", IYIL, 2013, p. 391 ff., pp. 418-425.

[124] WT/DS381/17.

ance dispute ("amended tuna measure").[125] The amended tuna measure results in comprising three main sets of labelling conditions, namely (i) the "eligibility criteria", (ii) the "certification requirements", and (iii) the "tracking and verification requirements".

On 14 November 2013, Mexico requested the establishment of a compliance panel considering that the above measures had not brought the US in compliance with the findings of the Appellate Body.[126] On 14 April 2015, the original panel circulated its report.[127] The panel found that the amended tuna measure remained inconsistent with Article 2.1 TBT Agreement, in relation to the "certification requirements" and the "tracking and verification requirements". In addition, the panel ruled that it was inconsistent with Articles I:1 and III:4 GATT 1994, nevertheless provisionally justified under Article XX(g) GATT, but ultimately inconsistent with the chapeau of the same provision. On 20 November 2015, following appeal by the US, the Appellate Body circulated its report, which forms the object of this comment. The Appellate Body reversed the panel's findings under Article 2.1 TBT Agreement by establishing that the amended tuna measure remained in breach also with regard to its "eligibility criteria". As a result, the Appellate Body found the whole amended tuna measure as being inconsistent with Article 2.1 TBT Agreement. In addition, the Appellate Body established that the tuna amended measure, to the inclusion of its "eligibility criteria", was inconsistent with Article I:1 and III:4 GATT 1994, nevertheless provisionally justified under Article XX(g) GATT (a finding that was not appealed by any Party), but ultimately inconsistent with the chapeau of Article XX GATT.[128]

---

[125] "These amendments required that all tuna sought to be entered into the United States as 'dolphin-safe', regardless of where it was caught or the nationality of the fishing vessel, must be accompanied by a certification that (a) no nets were intentionally set on dolphins in the set in which the tuna was caught; and (b) no dolphins were killed or seriously injured in the sets in which the tuna was caught. However, other documentation and tracking and verification requirements continued to differ depending on where the tuna was caught. Additionally, the measure continued to bar tuna caught by setting on dolphins from being labelled as 'dolphin-safe'". See at: <https://www.wto.org/english/tratop_e/dispu_e/cases_e/ds381_e.htm>.

[126] WT/DS381/20.

[127] WT/DS381/RW.

[128] In the aftermath of this compliance dispute, Mexico filed a request on 10 March 2016 seeking authorization from the DSB pursuant to DSU Art. 22.2 to suspend tariff concessions and other obligations in the goods sector for an amount of USD 472.3 million annually (WT/DS381/29). After the US objected on 22 March 2016 to the level of suspension of concessions proposed by Mexico, Mexico's request was referred to arbitration under DSU Art. 22.6. On 11 April 2016, the US submitted a request for a new compliance panel under DSU Art. 21.5 to examine measures adopted by the US in March 2016 with a view to bringing itself into conformity with the recommendations and rulings of the Appellate Body Report adopted on 3 December 2015 (WT/DS381/32).

8.2. *Key Legal Issues*

In the *US – Tuna II* compliance dispute, the Appellate Body has followed the canonical two-step analysis required by Article 2.1 TBT Agreement for a finding of "less favourable treatment" as comprising both (i) modification of the conditions of competition to the detriment of imported products vis-à-vis like products of domestic origin and/or like products originated in any other country (detrimental impact on imports) and, (ii) detrimental impact on imports not stemming exclusively from a legitimate regulatory distinction but rather reflecting discrimination against the group of imported products.[129] With regard to the claims of violation of Articles I:1 and III:4 GATT 1994, plus the chapeau of Article XX, the Appellate Body decided in line with its established case law, notably *EC – Seal Products*.[130] Indeed, the Appellate Body provided insightful comparisons between claims of discrimination under the TBT Agreement and the GATT 1994. While acknowledging a significant overlap of *rationes* (i.e., protection of the expectation of equal competitive opportunities for like imported products), it nevertheless recognised that the legal standards applicable under Article 2.1 TBT Agreement and the chapeau of Article XX GATT 1994 differ.[131] This comment specifically focuses on three issues that recurrently crosscut this report of the Appellate Body.

8.2.1. *Scope of Article 21.5 DSU Proceedings*

The Appellate Body preliminarily clarified the scope of the proceedings under Article 21.5 DSU. First, a compliance dispute should not be treated as being in isolation from the original dispute ("both proceedings form part of a continuum of events").[132] Second, the Appellate Body defined in greater detail the meaning of "measure taken to comply" pursuant to Article 21.5 DSU. While such proceedings canonically involve "a new and different measure which was not before the original panel",[133] nonetheless the modification or amendment by a member of specific

---

[129] Appellate Body Report, *United States – Measures Affecting the Production and Sale of Clove Cigarettes*, adopted on 24 April 2012, WT/DS406/AB/R, para. 182; *US – Tuna II (Mexico)*, para. 202; and Appellate Body Reports, *United States – Certain Country of Origin Labelling (COOL) Requirements*, adopted on 23 July 2012, WT/DS384/AB/R, WT/DS386/AB/R, para. 268.

[130] Appellate Body Reports, *European Communities – Measures Prohibiting the Importation and Marketing of Seal Products*, adopted on 18 June 2014, WT/DS400/AB/R, WT/DS401/AB/R, para. 5.86.

[131] *US – Tuna II (Mexico) (Article 21.5)*, paras. 7.278 and 7.345.

[132] *US – Tuna II (Mexico) (Article 21.5)*, para. 5.9.

[133] Appellate Body Report, *Canada – Measures Affecting the Export of Civilian Aircraft – Recourse by Brazil to Article 21.5 of the DSU*, adopted on 4 August 2000, WT/DS70/AB/RW, para. 41.

aspects of the original measure is susceptible to turn it in its totality into a new and different measure.[134] As a general rule, compliance proceedings should not be used to re-open issues decided in substance in the original dispute, in consistency with the principles of prompt settlement of disputes ex Article 3.3 DSU and prompt compliance ex Article 21.1 DSU.[135] There is indeed a rule of preclusion establishing that a member is prevented in a compliance dispute to raise claims that it could have pursued in the original proceedings, but did not.[136] In addition, the "measure taken to comply" may incorporate components of the original measure that remain unchanged and are not separable from the other (new or amended) elements of the same. Hence, it is possible that an (original) element of the measure at issue is challenged for the first time in the compliance phase, depending on the "critical question" whether such an element forms an integral part of the "measure taken to comply".[137] This scenario inevitably triggers considerations of double-jeopardy (*ne bis in idem*; *res judicata*),[138] which should nevertheless be calibrated to the prospective nature of the remedy provided by the WTO dispute settlement system, since a compliance dispute exactly pertains to the hypothesis of a persisting violation of the covered agreement by the violating Member.[139]

8.2.2. *Segmented Analysis*

The Appellate Body criticized the panel for having embarked on a segmented analysis ("distinction-by-distinction"), by separately addressing the three elements of the amended tuna measures.[140] In particular, the panel had found that the "eligibility criteria", as being considered in isolation, did not result in a finding of inconsistency under Article 2.1 TBT Agreement and did meet the requirements of the chapeau of Article XX, differently from the "certification requirements" and

---

[134] *US – Tuna II (Mexico) (Article 21.5)*, para. 5.7, quoting Appellate Body Report, *United States – Laws, Regulations and Methodology for Calculating Dumping Margins ("Zeroing") – Recourse to Article 21.5 of the DSU by the European Communities*, adopted on 11 June 2009, WT/DS294/AB/RW and Corr.1, para. 432; Appellate Body Report, *United States – Import Prohibition of Certain Shrimp and Shrimp Products – Recourse to Article 21.5 of the DSU by Malaysia*, adopted on 21 November 2001, WT/DS58/AB/RW, para. 87.

[135] Appellate Body Report, *European Communities – Anti-Dumping Duties on Imports of Cotton-Type Bed Linen from India – Recourse to Article 21.5 of the DSU by India*, adopted on 24 April 2003, WT/DS141/AB/RW, paras. 96-98.

[136] Appellate Body Report, *United States – Subsidies on Upland Cotton – Recourse to Article 21.5 of the DSU by Brazil*, adopted on 20 June 2008, WT/DS267/AB/RW, para. 434.

[137] *US – Tuna II (Mexico) (Article 21.5)*, para. 5.8.

[138] PALMETER and MAVROIDIS, *Dispute Settlement in the World Trade Organization: Practice and Procedure*, 2nd ed., Cambridge, 2004, p. 41.

[139] VIDIGAL, "Re-Assessing WTO Remedies: The Prospective and the Retrospective", JIEL, 2013, p. 505 ff.

[140] *US – Tuna II (Mexico) (Article 21.5)*, para. 7.11.

the "tracking and verification requirements". The Appellate Body observed that "analysing a measure in a segmented manner may raise concerns when the constituent parts of the measure are interrelated and operate in an integrated way".[141] Accordingly, the Appellate Body considered that the panel failed to examine it as a whole and in an integrated manner.[142] Therefore, the Appellate Body held that the amended tuna measure, by virtue of its structure, required a holistic assessment of the entirety of its labelling conditions, which the panel failed to exercise.[143]

8.2.3. Burden of Proof

The Appellate Body elucidated the functioning of the allocation of the burden of proof before it.[144] As a general principle, each Party to international proceedings should prove the facts, on which its allegations are grounded (*onus probandi incumbit ei dicit, non ei qui negat*).[145] In the context of the WTO dispute settlement system, the Appellate Body, while asserting that "[o]f course, there is no set formula as to how a complainant must make out its case", generally established that "[w]hile the complaining party bears the burden of making its prima facie case, the responding party must prove the case it seeks to make in response, and each party bears the burden of substantiating the assertions that it makes".[146] Nevertheless, when the scrutiny of State conducts is at issue, a responding Member is clearly better situated to adduce evidence pertaining to the same.[147] In addition, the Appellate Body noted with criticism that the panel had ultimately upheld the parties' agree-

---

[141] *Ibid.*, para. 7.13.

[142] *Ibid.*, para. 7.21.

[143] Cf. Appellate Body Report, *European Communities – Measures Affecting Asbestos and Asbestos-Containing Products*, adopted on 5 April 2001, WT/DS135/AB/R, para. 64; and Appellate Body Report, *Brazil – Measures Affecting Imports of Retreaded Tyres*, adopted on 17 December 2007, WT/DS332/AB/R, paras. 122-127; *EC – Seal Products, cit. supra* note 130, para. 5.20.

[144] See MARTINES, *L'onere della prova nell'Organizzazione Mondiale del Commercio e valori del sistema*, Santarcangelo di Romagna, 2012, p. 75.

[145] CHENG, *General Principles of Law as Applied by International Courts and Tribunals*, London, 1953, p. 326 ff. See *Military and Paramilitary Activities in and against Nicaragua (Nicaragua v. United States of America)*, Jurisdiction and Admissibility, Judgment of 26 November 1984, ICJ Reports, 1984, p. 392 ff., p. 437, para. 101; and *Avena and Other Mexican Nationals (Mexico v. United States of America)*, Judgment of 31 March 2004, ICJ Reports, 2004, p. 12 ff., p. 41, para. 55.

[146] *US – Tuna II (Mexico) (Article 21.5)*, para. 7.33, quoting *US – Tuna II (Mexico)*, para. 283; Appellate Body Report, *Japan – Measures Affecting the Importation of Apples*, adopted 10 December 2003, WT/DS245/AB/R, paras. 154, 157; and Appellate Body Report, *EC – Measures Concerning Meat and Meat Products (Hormones)*, adopted 13 February 1998, WT/DS26/AB/R and WT/DS48/AB/R, para. 98.

[147] *US – Tuna II (Mexico) (Article 21.5)*, para. 7.34.

ment on the assignment of the burden of proof.[148] Instead, the Appellate Body resorted to the general principles, as above described, without recognising itself as being compelled by the parties' joint endorsement with regard to the issue of the burden of proof.

8.3. Comment

The *US – Tuna II* compliance dispute displays various elements of analysis and understanding of the proceedings under Article 21.5 DSU. The Appellate Body's determinations on the two interconnected issues of the scope of the jurisdiction of a compliance panel, on one side, and of the "segmented analysis", on the other side, reveal its tendency to consider the extent of the "measure taken to comply" as comprising also aspects of the measure at issue in the original dispute, provided that such elements are not promptly separable. Indeed, this may trigger issues of "double-jeopardy", which should nevertheless be assessed in light of the quasi-judicial nature of WTO panel and Appellate Body reports, and of the prospective nature of the remedies provided by the WTO dispute settlement system. Finally, the Appellate Body's treatment of the issue of the allocation of the burden of proof corroborates the view of the non-isolation of the WTO regime from customary international law and general principles of international law.[149] Indeed, the Appellate Body seems to apply the issue of the allocation of the burden of proof in consistency with the case law of international courts and Tribunals. Accordingly, it upholds a general rule that the violating Member is usually more proximate to the measures it enacted and accordingly may be subject to a more flexible allocation of the evidentiary burden, which it may be required to partially discharge.

CARLO DE STEFANO[*]

---

[148] *Ibid.*, para. 7.35.

[149] BACCHUS, "Not in Clinical Isolation", in MARCEAU (ed.), *A History of Law and Lawyers in the GATT/WTO. The Development of the Rule of Law in the Multilateral Trading System*, Cambridge, 2015, p. 507 ff., clearly referring to Appellate Body Report, *United States – Standards for Reformulated and Conventional Gasoline*, adopted on 29 April 1996, WT/DS2/AB/R, p. 17.

[*] Ph.D. candidate in International Law and Economics, Bocconi University, Milan.

THE ARBITRAL PRACTICE OF THE INTERNATIONAL CENTRE FOR SETTLEMENT OF INVESTMENT DISPUTES (ICSID) IN 2015

EDUARDO SAVARESE[*]

1. INTRODUCTION

Treaty-based investment arbitration, with specific regard to ICSID arbitration, has acquired an unprecedented weight in delineating the current features of international economic law and the juridical foundation of the relationship between public international and international commercial law.[1] This is demonstrated, on the one hand, by the increasing number of arbitral decisions which concern questions of jurisdiction *ratione personae* arising out of highly controversial nationality issues. On the other hand, ICSID tribunals, by means of an increasingly in-depth analysis, seek to define and settle technically complicated issues on the merits. In particular, there are three relevant factors that deserve due attention.

First, as far as jurisdiction *ratione personae* is concerned, a thorough examination of the factual background is currently regularly carried out by ICSID tribunals in order to find the effective and ultimate layers behind the formal chain of companies incorporated under foreign laws. Indeed, ICSID arbitral tribunals have been empowered to settle international investment disputes and not to substitute domestic courts or arbitrations in deciding purely domestic controversies. Moreover, certain important principles have been authoritatively delineated as a result of annulment proceedings in the field of beneficial ownership.

Second, respondent States have begun to have recourse to revision of arbitral awards according to Article 51 of the Washington Convention. Thus, ICSID tribunals have clarified the legal requirements for revision under the ICSID arbitration system, which considers of utmost importance the principle of finality of arbitral awards under Article 53 of the Convention.

Third, the relevance of ICSID arbitration in shaping principles and rules of public international law is emphasised by the case law involving expropriation with regard to questions of compensation and attribution.

We have selected some decisions which appear to be significant in the light of what has been outlined above. In this regard, we will pay due attention to the most controversial questions of jurisdiction, which concern the requirement of foreign

---

[*] Ph.D. in International Law; Civil and Criminal Judge at the Tribunal of Nola, Napoli.
[1] In 2015, 52 new cases were registered under the ICSID Convention and Additional Facility Rules, whereas 38 new cases had been registered in 2014: it is the highest number in the history of ICSID Arbitration. As to the outcomes of ICSID proceedings, 64 of pending disputes were decided by ICSID Tribunals, whereas 36 were settled or otherwise discontinued. See *The ICSID Caseload – Statistics*, Issue 2016-1.

nationality for claimant investors (section 2) and beneficial ownership for the purposes of asserting or denying ICSID jurisdiction (section 3). As far as revision is concerned, the case *Tidewater* will be analysed extensively since it correctly points out the notion of "new fact" as the main basis for the admissibility of a claim for revision (section 4). Finally, as to issues on the merits, four decisions will be examined: the cases *Tidewater* and *Quiborax*, with the important dissenting opinion of Professor Brigitte Stern, which concern the difference between lawful and unlawful expropriation in the assessment and quantification of damages (section 5); the case *Al Hamadi*, where the ICSID Tribunal has established the relationship between the ILC Articles on State responsibility and the applicable Bilateral Investment Treaty (section 6); and the case *Dan Cake*, regarding an interesting dispute that involves domestic insolvency law (section 7).

2. *RATIONE PERSONAE* JURISDICTION

Both the decisions in the cases *Venoklim v. Venezuela*[2] and *Guardian v. Macedonia*[3] concern issues surrounding the requirement of foreign nationality for claimant companies.[4]

2.1. *The* Venoklim *Award*

In the case *Venoklim v. Venezuela*, the ICSID Tribunal examined the controversial issue of its jurisdiction *ratione personae*. The dispute concerned the alleged expropriation of five companies under the direct control of the claimant, Venoklim Holding B.V., which was a company duly registered under the laws of the Netherlands. The latter had acquired its shares in the expropriated companies before the expropriation had been perpetrated by the host State in 2010.

The claimant investor's request for arbitration relied on Article 22 of the Venezuelan Investment Law.[5] However, such a provision does not confer jurisdic-

---

[2] *Venoklim Holding B.V. v. Republica Bolivariana de Venezuela*, ICSID Case No. ARB/12/22, "Laudo" of 14 April 2015. The members of the Tribunal were Dr. Enrique Gomez Pinzòn (President), Dr. Rodrigo Oreamuno Blanco (Arbitrator), and Prof. Yves Derains (Arbitrator).

[3] *Guardian Fiduciary Trust, Ltd, f/k/a Capital Conservator Savings & Loan, Ltd v. Macedonia, former Yugoslav Republic of*, ICSID Case No. ARB/12/31, Award of 22 September 2015. The members of the Tribunal were Dr. Veijo Heiskanen (President), Prof. Andreas Bucher (Arbitrator), and Prof. Brigitte Stern (Arbitrator).

[4] On this issue, DUGAN, WALLACE JR., RUBINS and SABAHI, *Investor-State Arbitration*, Oxford, 2011, p. 291 ff.

[5] In its original version, Article 22 reads as follows: "*Las controversias que surjan entre un inversionista internacional, cuyo país de origen tenga vigente con Venezuela un tratado o acuerdo sobre promoción y protección de inversiones, o las controversias respecto de las cuales*

tion upon ICSID tribunals, insofar as it does not contain the written consent by the State as required by Article 25 of the Washington Convention. The Tribunal followed the consistent interpretation of ICSID tribunals, according to which Article 22 merely served to confirm Venezuela's offers to arbitrate made under other legal instruments, such as BITs – but could not have been considered an independent, clear and general offer to arbitrate.[6]

In the case under consideration, the obligation to submit investment disputes to ICSID is set forth in the BIT between Venezuela and the Netherlands at Article 9. The tribunal based its jurisdiction on the twofold basis of Article 9 of the applicable BIT and of Article 22 of the Venezuelan Investment Law. However, this approach divided the tribunal.

On the one hand, the majority maintained that the BIT should have been interpreted in a way that assured the fulfillment of the requirements stemming from domestic law.[7] Venezuelan domestic law, in the majority's view, makes it clear that an investor can be considered as a foreign investor if property or control of the investment are in the hands of foreigners. Since the parties had not discussed the aspect which concerned property, the majority focused on whether the claimant investor was under a real and effective foreign control.

The tribunal ascertained that the ultimate layers behind the corporate veil of the claimant were Venezuelan companies and citizens. Therefore, it concluded that Venezuela did not give its consent to submit such a dispute to ICSID under Article 22 of the Investment Law, coupled with Article 9 of the BIT. Moreover, as far as the Washington Convention's goal lies in the settlement of international disputes between foreign investors and host States, the Tribunal stressed that the ICSID Convention itself requires to be interpreted in the light of a substantive

---

sean aplicables las disposiciones del Convenio Constitutivo del Organismo Multilateral de Garantía de Inversiones (OMGI -MIGA) o del Convenio sobre Arreglo de Diferencias Relativas a Inversiones entre Estados y Nacionales de Otros Estados (CIADI), serán sometidas al arbitraje internacional en los términos del respectivo tratado o acuerdo, si así éste lo establece, sin perjuicio de la posibilidad de hacer uso, cuando proceda, de las vías contenciosas contempladas en la legislación venezolana vigente". It can be translated as follows: "Disputes arising between an international investor whose country of origin has in effect with Venezuela a treaty or agreement on the promotion and protection of investments, or disputes to which are applicable the provisions of the Convention Establishing the Multilateral Investment Guarantee Agency (OMIGI-MIGA) or the Convention on the Settlement of Investment Disputes between States and Nationals of Other States (ICSID), shall be submitted to international arbitration according to the terms of the respective treaty or agreement, if it so provides, without prejudice to the possibility of making use, when appropriate, of the dispute resolution means provided for under the Venezuelan legislation in effect".

[6] *Ibid.,* paras. 102-111. See SCHREUER, "Investment Arbitration based on National Legislation", in HAFNER, MATSCHER and SCHMALENBACH (eds.), *Volkerrecht und die Dynamik der Menschenrechte, Liber Amicourm Wolfram Karl,* Berlin, 2012, p. 527 ff.

[7] *Venoklim, cit. supra* note 2, paras. 129, 137.

methodology: purely domestic disputes are outside the scope of the Convention. Conclusively, the majority maintained that to look solely at Venoklim's incorporation in the Netherlands to consider it a foreign investor, even though the investment was ultimately owned by Venezuelans, "would be to allow formalism to prevail over reality and to betray the object and purpose of the ICSID Convention".[8]

On the other hand, the dissenting arbitrator Enrique Gómez Pinzón contested these conclusions on three main grounds. First, in his view Article 22 had simply no weight in assessing ICSID jurisdiction, the sole basis being the nationality requirements of the BIT. Second, the ICSID Convention does not give a definition of nationality precisely because it left the contracting parties free to choose nationality criteria in more specific instruments. Accordingly, the Venezuela-Netherlands BIT chose "incorporation" as the applicable criterion, so that the majority erred in disregarding that choice. Finally, piercing Venoklim's corporate veil only could have been based on a detailed analysis of whether its incorporation in the Netherlands had been fraudulent or done to evade legal requirements. Yet, the majority did not carry out any analysis of this nature.

It is noteworthy that, after eight years since the division between the majority and the dissenting arbitrator in the case *TSA Spectrum v. Argentina*[9] emerged, another ICSID Tribunal did not reach a unanimous conclusion on the identical issue.

2.2. Guardian Trust v. Macedonia

Also in the case *Guardian v. Macedonia*, the scope and weight of the notion of effective control for nationality purposes was at the heart of the reasoning of the ICSID tribunal. Having determined that the issue of control was ultimately a matter of evidence, and not something to be determined solely on the basis of an analysis of New Zealand law, the Tribunal concluded that the claimant had failed to provide that necessary evidence.

In effect, the tribunal noted that there was no dispute between the parties, that the claimant, Guardian Fiduciary Trust Limited, was organized under the law of New Zealand and therefore did not qualify as a national of the Netherlands under Article 1(b)(II) of the applicable BIT. However, the claimant argued that it was indirectly controlled by Stichting Intetrust, a foundation organized under the law of the Netherlands and, thus, it qualified as a national of the Netherlands under Article 1(b)(III) of the BIT. More specifically, Guardian was wholly owned by Capital Conservator Trustee Limited (CCT), a trustee company incorporated in New

---

[8] *Ibid.*, para. 156 (our translation from Spanish).
[9] *TSA Spectrum de Argentina S.A. v. Argentine Republic*, ICSID Case No. ARB/05/5, Award of 19 December 2008 (with the Dissenting Opinion of Arbitrator Grant D. Aldonas).

Zealand. CCT was, in turn, a wholly owned subsidiary of IN Asset Management Limited (IN Asset Management), a company incorporated in New Zealand and wholly owned by Stichting Intetrust, a Dutch foundation having its registered office in the Netherlands.

The tribunal pointed out that, while ownership generally implies the legal right or the capacity to exercise control, the issue was complicated in the case by the fact that different aspects of the ownership of CCT, i.e. the claimant's immediate holding company, were divided between IN Asset Management and Capital Conservator Group (CCG), a Marshall Islands company that fell outside the corporate chain of which Stichting Intetrust formed part.

Pursuant to the deed of 1 October 2008 between IN Asset Management and CCG, the former became the legal owner of CCT, the immediate holding company of the claimant, whereas the latter retained beneficial ownership over CCT. The question therefore arose whether CCT could have been said to be controlled by IN Asset Management, given that the beneficial ownership of CCT had been retained by CCG. From the respondent's point of view, a legal owner merely possesses formal ownership. It could not be said to control its subsidiary. Conversely, the beneficial owner retains the power or the capacity of control. The claimant argued, in turn, that legal ownership was sufficient in order to find a form of control.

It is noteworthy that, far from being based on the weight of the notion of legal ownership rather than of beneficial ownership, the Tribunal's decision concluded that the claimant simply failed to prove that it was controlled by Stichting Intetrust. It did not qualify as a national of the Netherlands within the meaning of Article 1(b) (III) of the BIT and, as a consequence, ICSID jurisdiction was denied.

The tribunal recalls that, in order to assert jurisdiction *ratione personae*, the claimant would have to qualify as a national of the Netherlands under both the BIT and the ICSID Convention. As the claimant failed to establish that it met the nationality requirements of the BIT, the tribunal need not consider whether the claimant would meet the nationality requirements of the ICSID Convention.[10] Albeit the reasoning of the decision lies in the failure of evidence, the decision shows the possible legal relevance arising out from the difference between legal and beneficial ownership.

---

[10] *Guardian Fiduciary Trust, cit. supra* note 3, para. 140.

3. *OCCIDENTAL V. ECUADOR*: THE PARTIAL ANNULMENT OF THE AWARD[11]

3.1. *The Factual Background and the Award*

The dispute concerned the termination of a Participation Contract between Occidental Exploration and Production Company (OEPC) and PetroEcuador, a State agency, for the exploration and exploitation of hydrocarbons in Block 15 in the Ecuadorian Amazon. Under the Participation Contract, OEPC received a share of the oil produced from Block 15, in return for undertaking the obligation to explore, develop and exploit Block 15. The Participation Contract also provided that the transfer of rights or obligations without authorization of the Minister could result in termination of that Contract. In 2000, OEPC and City Investing Company Limited (AEC), a Bermuda company, explored the possibility of a transaction over Block 15 and, as a result, executed the Farmout Agreement. Thereafter, in compliance with the obligations assumed in the Farmout Agreements, AEC regularly paid to OEPC 40% of the expenditure incurred in the exploitation and development of Block 15 and received 40% of the oil produced.

OEPC sent a letter to the Minister requesting consent with respect to the transfer of economic interests in favor of AEC. Ecuador's Minister of Mines and Energy answered OEPC's letter noting the company's intention to transfer in the future 40% of the rights and obligations of Block 15, and indicating that such a future transfer would have required prior government approval. However, the approval sought by OEPC was not granted. Rather, the Attorney General of Ecuador ordered the Ministry of Mines and Energy to terminate the Participation Contract through a declaration of *caducidad.* The proceedings against OEPC culminated on 15 May 2006 with the issuance of a *Caducidad* Decree. In the meanwhile, Ecuador enacted Law 42, which required all companies operating under participation contracts to contribute 50% of their windfall revenues to the State.

On 5 October 2012, the ICSID Tribunal issued its Award, by stating that Ecuador failed to accord a fair and equitable treatment, and that the investment was indirectly expropriated in breach of the applicable BIT. It also declared the *Caducidad* Decree to be in breach of Ecuadorian Law and customary international law as well. Yet, Arbitrator Brigitte Stern dissented from the conclusions of the majority.[12]

---

[11] *Occidental Petroleum Corporation Occidental Exploration and Production Company v. The Republic of Ecuador*, ICSID Case No. ARB/06/11, Decision on Annulment of the Award of 2 November 2015. The members of the *ad hoc* Committee were Prof. Juan Fernandez-Armesto (President), Judge Florentino P. Feliciano (Member of the Committee), and Mr. Rodrigo Oreamuno B. (Member of the Committee).

[12] *Occidental Petroleum Corporation Occidental Exploration and Production Company v. The Republic of Ecuador*, ICSID Case No. ARB/06/11. Members of the Tribunal were Mr. L. Yves Fortier, C.C., Q.C. (President), Mr. David A.R. Williams, Q.C. (Arbitrator), and Prof. Brigitte Stern (Arbitrator).

Respondent invoked as first ground for annulment that the tribunal had manifestly exceeded its powers. The Annulment Committee partially annulled the Award on that ground. It is to this specific aspect that we will focus our attention.

3.2. Excess of Powers and the Violation of the Ecuadorian Constitution

In the first place, it is to be noted that the *ad hoc* Committee dismissed the "arbitrability objection" submitted by Ecuador. Such an argument was based on the following legal aspects: (a) the Ecuadorian Constitution is the most important legal source in Ecuador and prevails over international treaties, including bilateral investment treaties; and, (b) Article 196 of the Constitution attributes exclusive jurisdiction to the administrative tribunals of Ecuador to adjudicate any dispute concerning *actos administrativos*, including disputes over *Caducidad* decrees.

The Committee concurred with the tribunal that the arguments of Ecuador had no value, because they simply disregarded the basic principle of international law that a State cannot invoke its domestic law, including its constitutional provisions, for the purpose of avoiding treaty obligations.

3.3. The Legal Effects of the Farmout Agreements: The Partial Annulment of the Award

In the Award, the majority of the Tribunal accepted the approach of awarding 100% of the value of the investment: it found that, since the assignment of rights from the Participation Contract had not been authorized by the Ecuadorian Minister, such assignment was null and void. The assignment was therefore disregarded by the Tribunal for purposes of determining the compensation to which claimants were entitled. As a result, in the Tribunal's opinion, OEPC continued to own, as of the date of the *Caducidad* Decree, 100% of the rights under the Participation Agreement and had to be compensated for 100% of the value of Block 15.

To the contrary, in the opinion of Arbitrator Professor Brigitte Stern, at the time of the *Caducidad* Decree the rights under the Participation Contract were owned 60% by OEPC and 40% by AEC. Professor Stern then found that both under New York and under Ecuadorian law the Farmout Agreement, not having been invalidated either by a New York Court or an Ecuadorian court, should have been considered as still in force and binding, and that the ICSID Tribunal exceeded its powers in annulling AEC's rights thereunder. Arbitrator Stern added that title to AEC's 40% interest in Block 15 was split, the nominal legal title belonging to OEPC and the beneficial interest to AEC. In accordance with international law, only the beneficial owner, AEC, could have claimed compensation for expropriation.

The Committee noted that, although the Farmout Agreements foresaw a transfer of ownership, the transfer was timed to occur in two phases, and it was agreed that

AEC was only to acquire formal title over its 40% share in the Farmout Property in a second phase. During the first phase (when the *Caducidad* Decree was issued) the parties agreed that title to the 40% interest in the Farmout Property was to be split: AEC would have been the beneficial owner, while OEPC would be acting as a "nominee" for AEC, appearing as formal owner *vis-à-vis* third parties (including *vis-à-vis* the Ecuadorian public administration).

The Committee agreed with Professor Stern's analysis. The Farmout Agreements had indeed provided that, at the time when the *Caducidad* Decree was issued, the claimants only retained full title over 60% of their investment in Block 15. For the remaining 40%, OEPC was simply a "nominee", who held apparent ownership, but in substance was acting on behalf and for the benefit of the true beneficiary, AEC. The Annulment Committee found that, in view of the clear language of the Farmout Agreements, the Tribunal's conclusion that AEC did not acquire any interest – beneficial or otherwise – in the Participation Contract was simply untenable.

As far as 40% of that investment did not belong to OEPC, the US corporation was protected by the BIT and was also party to the Participation Contract. In other terms, the tribunal compensated a protected investor for an investment which was beneficially owned by a non-protected investor. In doing so, the tribunal – the Committee concluded – illicitly expanded the scope of its jurisdiction and acted with an excess of powers.

As far as the *Caducidad* Decree was concerned, the Committee noted that each and every declaration of *caducidad* was subject to Article 79 of the Ecuadorian Hydrocarbons Law, a rule establishing that transfers of contract or assignment of rights, executed without prior administrative authorization, shall be null and void and without validity.

The majority of the tribunal accepted that, although not expressly stated in the Ecuadorian Civil Code, the Ecuadorian Supreme Court had confirmed on a number of occasions that Ecuadorian law recognizes automatic nullity or inexistence, without a judicial decision or declaration being necessary.

Arbitrator Stern dissented. In her opinion under New York law (which was the contractually relevant law), the Farmout Agreements, not having been invalidated by a New York court, should be considered as still in force and binding. Under this aspect also, the Committee agreed with the dissenting opinion.

Two final considerations have to been made. First, the *ad hoc* Committee excluded that beneficial ownerships are left without an international law protection. A final *caveat*: neither the international law principles nor the Committee's decision imply that investors holding beneficial ownership are left unprotected from interferences by host States. Such investors will enjoy the protection granted under the treaties which benefit their nationality. In the present case, AEC/Andes are entitled to the protection which investors from Bermuda/China enjoy, when investing in Ecuador, under applicable bilateral investment treaties or under general principles of international law. What they are not entitled to – because they are not US nationals or companies – is to the protection offered to US investors investing in Ecuador under the US-Ecuador BIT.[13] Second, the *ad hoc* Committee carried out an in-depth examination of the relevant case law. It is to be noted that, insofar as an annulment proceedings is concerned, the principle delineated in the decision under review is particularly important to guide future ICSID awards. It can be formulated with the words of the *ad hoc* Committee as follows: "[…] under international law legal standing pertains to beneficial owners and not necessarily to nominees, and […] unprotected parties cannot receive compensation, even if claimed on their behalf by protected investors".[14]

4. *VENEZUELA HOLDINGS V. VENEZUELA*: ICSID REVISION UNDER ARTICLE 51 OF THE WASHINGTON CONVENTION

Bolivia submitted to ICSID a request for revision of the Award delivered by the ICSID Tribunal on 9 October 2014.[15] The respondent State claimed that the investors' actions after the Award had showed that they had no intention of honoring representations made before the Award was rendered. Indeed, the investors had assured that, in order to avoid double recovery in the event of an award in their favor, they were willing to reimburse the host State agency *Petroleos de Venezuela* for the compensation already received in the ICC arbitration.

However, after the ICSID decision on the merits, on request of the investors a US federal court issued an order in the full amount of the arbitral award without referring to the double recovery question. Accordingly, the Applicant requests the following revisions of the Award: "Paragraph 404(e) of the Award should be revised to add the following sentence as the second sentence of the subparagraph: 'The required reimbursements to PDVSA will be made simultaneously with the satisfaction of this Award'".

It is noteworthy that the ICSID Secretary-General, once registered the application for revision, provisionally granted the stay of enforcement of the ICSID award. The investors maintained that the application of Bolivia was an abuse of revision and requested that the stay of enforcement be entirely or partially lifted. Article 51 of the ICSID Convention reads as follows:

> "(1) Each Party may request revision of the award by an application in writing addressed to the Secretary-General on the ground of discovery of some fact of such a nature as decisively to affect the award,

---

[13] *Occidental Petroleum Corporation, cit. supra* note 11, para. 272.

[14] *Ibid.*, para. 273.

[15] *Venezuela Holdings B.V., Mobil Cerro Negro Holding, Ltd., Mobil Venezolana de Petroleos, Inc. v. The Bolivarian Republic of Venezuela*, ICSID Case No. ARB/07/27, Award of 9 October 2014. The members of the Tribunal were H.E. Judge Gilbert Guillaume (President), Prof. Gabrielle Kaufmann-Kohler (Arbitrator), and Dr. Ahmed Sadek El-Kosheri (Arbitrator).

provided that when the award was rendered that fact was unknown to the tribunal and to the applicant and that the applicant's ignorance of the fact was not due to negligence".

The tribunal dismissed the request.[16] First, the Tribunal noted that, under Article 51 an application for revision ought to cumulatively satisfy the following conditions: (a) the application should be based upon the discovery of a fact; (b) the fact, the discovery of which is relied on, must be of such a nature as decisively to affect the award; (c) the fact should have been unknown to the tribunal and to the applicant when the award was rendered; (d) the applicant's ignorance of the fact must not be due to negligence; and (e) the application for revision must be made within 90 days after the discovery of the fact and in any event within three years after the date on which the award was rendered. Second, the Tribunal yielded to the conclusion that an additional requirement exists that the discovered facts must predate the ICSID award, as confirmed by the literal interpretation of Article 51 in the light of its object and purpose. According to the Tribunal,

> "Article 51 presupposes that the relevant fact *could have been known when the award was rendered* and that, had it not been known, said ignorance *could have been due to negligence when the award was rendered*. Only a fact that existed when the award was rendered could have been known when the award was rendered. Only ignorance of a fact that existed when the award was rendered could be due to negligence. It follows that only a fact that existed when the award was rendered may form the basis for a request for revision under Article 51(1) of the ICSID Convention".[17]

On the other hand, revision of arbitral awards, far from being allowed in all arbitral rules, seeks to impair the stability of legal relations. Hence, it is an exceptional remedy. Case law of international tribunals brings to the surface that revision exclusively rests on facts antedating the delivery of final judgments. This rule was stated by the European Court of Justice in the case *Riseria Modenese S.r.l.*,[18] and by the International Court of Justice when interpreting Article 61 of its Statute after the request for revision of the judgment in the case *Bosnia Herzegovina v.*

---

[16] *Venezuela Holdings B.V., Mobil Cerro Negro Holding, Ltd., Mobil Venezolana de Petroleos, Inc. v. The Bolivarian Republic of Venezuela*, ICSID Case No. ARB/07/27, Decision on Revision of 12 June 2015. The members of the Tribunal were H.E. Judge Gilbert Guillaume (President), Prof. Gabrielle Kaufmann-Kohler (Arbitrator), and Dr. Ahmed Sadek El-Kosheri (Arbitrator).

[17] *Ibid.*, para. 3.1.11.

[18] Case 267/80, *Riseria Modenese Srl v. Council and Commission of the European Communities and Birra Peroni SpA*, ECR, 1985, p. 3499 ff.

Yugoslavia.[19] At the same vein, the principle of irrelevance of new facts postdating the final judgment was held by the Franco-Bulgarian Mixed Arbitral Tribunal in 1929.[20] Therefore, the Tribunal concluded that an application that relies on post-award facts is not admissible.

In the case under examination, Bolivia maintained that, even if the main fact having legal effects on the double recovery issue was the relief obtained by the investors in US courts after the ICSID award, this was part of a more comprehensive strategy already existing during the arbitral proceedings. According to Bolivia, when the investors represented to the ICSID Tribunal that they would have eliminated the risk of double recovery by means of an obligation to duly reimburse, they already intended to seek the enforcement of the full amount granted by the ICSID Tribunal without recognition of the compensation already paid in 2012 in accordance to the ICC award. However, in the tribunal's view:

> "Intentions and strategy characterise a state of mind and do not constitute events that may be considered facts in the sense of Article 51(1) of the ICSID Convention. Accordingly, even if the Tribunal were minded to find that an application for revision under Article 51(1) of the ICSID Convention may be based on the discovery of post-award facts relied on as evidence of pre-award facts, the Application would still be dismissed for want of pre-award facts".[21]

As a consequence, the Tribunal dismissed the application for revision in its entirety and the stay of enforcement was automatically terminated.

5. UNLAWFUL EXPROPRIATION AND PROVISIONALLY LAWFUL EXPROPRIATION

The analysis of ICSID case law highlights the difference between an unlawful expropriation and a provisionally lawful expropriation. The former is perpetrated by the violation of the requirements usually set forth in BITs, i.e. the existence of public interests, the respect for the principles of non-discrimination and due process, and an adequate compensation. The latter occurs when, while all the requirements of a lawful expropriation have been met, compensation has not been paid

---

[19] *Application for Revision of the Judgment of 11 July 1996 in the Case Concerning Application of the Convention on the Prevention and Punishment of the Crime of Genocide (Bosnia and Herzegovina v. Yugoslavia), Preliminary Objections (Yugoslavia v. Bosnia and Herzegovina)*, Judgment of 3 February 2003, ICJ Reports, 2003, p. 7 ff.

[20] *Battus* case, Franco-Bulgarian Mixed Arbitral Tribunal, 6 June 1929, RDTAM, Vol. IX, 1929, pp. 284-286. Cf. also *Creange* case, Franco-German mixed Arbitral Tribunal, RDTAM, Vol. V, 1924, pp. 114-116; and *Guillaume Krichel* case, RDTAM, Vol. VIII, 1928, p. 764; *Otzenberger* case, RDTAM, Vol. IX, 1929, p. 272.

[21] *Venezuela Holdings, cit. supra* note 16, para. 3.1.21.

(for lack of agreement between the host State and foreign investors, or for other reasons either). The difference entails important legal effects as to the quantum of compensation. In the first case, the criterion of full reparation is to be applied. In the second case, a fair and equitable indemnification should be assured. The cases *Quiborax v. Bolivia* and *Tidewater v. Venezuela* illustrate such a difference.[22]

5.1. Quiborax v. Bolivia

5.1.1. Factual Background and Questions

In the case *Quiborax v. Bolivia*,[23] a preliminary assessment of the factual background is opportune. As a result of a process of privatization, Bolivia adopted the *Ley Valda*, following which 43 new mining concessions were requested between 1998 and 2004 in an area that had previously been a fiscal reserve. Seven of these concessions were granted to the Bolivian company *Compañía Minera Río Grande Sur S.A.* (RIGSSA), owned by Bolivian businessmen David Moscoso and Álvaro Ugalde.

As a consequence of negotiations between Quiborax and RIGSSA, on 12 January 2001 both companies entered into an Exclusive Supply Contract for fifteen years. Quiborax decided to create a new Bolivian company (Non-Metallic Minerals S.A., NMM) that would act as its investment vehicle. The corporate structure of Quiborax's investment vehicle in Bolivia did not change until the events giving rise to the dispute submitted to ICSID: the shareholders of NMM are Quiborax (50.995%), Mr. David Moscoso (49%), and Mr. Allan Fosk (0.005%).

Following the political instability in the country in 2003-2004, on 23 June 2004 the President of Bolivia issued a decree revoking the claimants' mining concessions. On 23 July 2004, in compliance with the decree, NMM handed over its eleven mining concessions to the Prefect of the Department of Potosí. On 28 October 2004, Bolivia annulled the revoked concessions on the grounds that there had been errors in the requests for concessions.

However, the revocation decree was successively abrogated because of legal defects, since the Mining Code does not provide for the revocation of mining

---

[22] As to the issues of expropriation and compensation in international investment law, see BROWN, "The End of the Affair? Hulley Enterprises Ltd (Cyprus) v Russian Federation; Yukos Universal Ltd (Isle of Man) v Russian Federation; Veteran Petroleum Ltd (Cyprus) v Russian Federation, UNCITRAL, PCA Nos AA 226, 227, 228, Final Awards, 18 July 2014 (Yves Fortier, Charles Poncet, Stephen Schwebel)", Journal of World Investment & Trade, 2016, p. 126 ff. On the *Tidewater* case, see TOMUSCHAT, "Case Comment, Tidewater v Venezuela", ICSID Review, 2016, p. 1 ff.

[23] *Quiborax S.A. and Non Metallic Minerals S.A. v. Plurinational State of Bolivia*, ICSID Case No. ARB/06/2, Award of 16 September 2015. The members of the Tribunal were Prof. Gabrielle Kaufmann-Kohler (President), Hon.Marc Lalonde, P.C., O.C., Q.C., (Arbitrator), and Prof. Brigitte Stern (Arbitrator).

concessions, but rather for the "*caducidad*" or annulment of mining concessions after an administrative proceeding under the competence and jurisdiction of the Superintendence of Mines.

In December 2008, Bolivia initiated criminal proceedings against Allan Fosk, David Moscoso and others on the ground that these individuals allegedly fabricated evidence for the purpose of allowing the claimants to establish jurisdiction in ICSID arbitration. Bolivia maintained that the claimants' investments were affected by both an illegality in connection with the establishment of the investment (i.e. an original illegality) and an illegality in its subsequent administration and operation. (i.e. an ongoing illegality).

According to the respondent State, the acquisition of the claimants' mining concessions was illegal and therefore the concessions were null and void *ab initio*. As a result, such concessions could have not been subject to expropriation. In any case, according to Bolivia, the revocation and subsequent annulment of the claimants' concessions were punitive measures against the investors', which were justified by breaches of Bolivian law in the establishment and operation of these concessions.

5.1.2. The Majority Decision

The Tribunal carried out a thorough examination of the alleged grounds of illegality. In particular, the Tribunal stressed that annulment was stated four months after the concessions were revoked. Since revocation had been questioned in lack of a legal provision which allowed it, the concessions were annulled. In this regard, far from being the proportionate sanction against relevant breaches of domestic law, annulment (which concerned exclusively formal grounds) was deemed by the Tribunal an *ex post* attempt to improve Bolivia's defense in ICSID arbitration rather than a legitimate exercise of Bolivia's police powers.

At this point, the Tribunal analyzed whether an expropriation occurred in the light of Article VI.1 of the applicable BIT, which provides:

> "1. Neither of the Contracting Parties shall take measures depriving, directly or indirectly, an investor of the other Contracting Party of its investment unless the following conditions are met: a) the measures are taken for reasons of public purpose or national interest and in accordance with the law; b) the measures are not discriminatory; c) the measures are accompanied by provisions for payment of immediate, adequate and effective compensation".

In the Tribunal's view, the standard for an indirect expropriation to be assessed requires that the State measure deprives the investor of its investment by means of a permanent deprivation which does not find any justification under the police powers doctrine. The Tribunal stated that:

"This is particularly true in the case of rights of exploitation (such as licenses or concessions) that depend on the fulfillment of certain requirements by the foreign investor. If a State cancels a license or a concession because the investor has not fulfilled the necessary legal requirements to maintain that license or concession, or has breached the relevant laws and regulations that are sanctioned by the loss of those rights, such cancellation cannot be considered to be a taking by the State".[24]

In the Tribunal's understanding, four main aspects emerged from the arbitration: (a) Bolivian Law only allowed the Executive to annul concessions for breaches that were sanctioned by nullity pursuant to the laws and regulations in force: the Tribunal found that the legal flaws affecting the concessions were either non-existent or were not subject to the sanction of annulment; (b) the Revocation Decree simply was not justified under Bolivian law; (c) the revocation of the claimants' concessions did not comply with minimum standards of due process, whether under international law or Bolivian law; and (d) the date on which NMM was definitively deprived of the economic benefits of its concessions was 23 July 2004.

Since Quiborax qualified as an investor holding an investment under the BIT, the question for the Tribunal was thus whether the revocation of the concessions had the effect of substantially depriving Quiborax of the value of its investment in Bolivia, i.e. of its shares in NMM. The Tribunal considered that in the absence of the concessions the claimants' investment in NMM was virtually worthless. To the extent that such a deprivation was permanent and not justified by the police powers doctrine, it indirectly expropriated Quiborax of the value of its investments.

Moreover, the Tribunal yielded to the conclusion that the revocation decree discriminated against NMM, since other mining companies, such as Copla and Tecno Química, while being fined for alleged errors in their export declarations, kept their concessions. Evidence on record showed the discriminatory intent underlying the revocation decree because of the Chilean nationality of the main shareholder of NMM, i.e. Quiborax.

Finally, insofar as Bolivia neither paid nor offered compensation to NMM for the revocation of its mining concessions, the Tribunal reached the conclusion that NMM and Quiborax were unlawfully expropriated of their investments by the Respondent.

Having underlined that Article VI(2) of the BIT only sets out the standard of compensation for lawful expropriations, the Tribunal applied the full reparation principle provided for unlawful expropriations by the Permanent Court of International Justice (PCIJ) in the *Chorzów* case and Article 31 of the ILC Draft Articles on Responsibility of States for Internationally Wrongful Acts. According

---

[24] *Ibid.*, para. 206.

to these principles and rules, the reparation must eliminate all consequences of the internationally wrongful act and restore the injured party to the situation that would have existed if the act had not been committed, as set forth in ILC Draft Article 36.

As to the methodology to calculate Fair Market Value (FMV), the tribunal noted that the Discounted Cash Flow (DCF) method is widely accepted as the appropriate method to assess the FMV of going concerns with a proven record of profitability. Moreover, the majority of the tribunal considered that the final assessment of *quantum* damage required valuing the damage on the date of the award and taking into consideration information available then.

Having analyzed the PCIJ's reasoning in *Chorzów*, the ICSID Tribunal pointed out that

> "Although the Court was using an asset-based valuation rather than a DCF method, the purpose of the exercise is clear: either valuation would have allowed the Court to award the dispossessed companies the value of their losses on the date of the judgment. The Tribunal thus concludes by majority that, dealing with an expropriation that is unlawful not merely because compensation is lacking, its task is to quantify the losses suffered by the claimant on the date of the award (or on a proxy for that date). This is easily explained by a reference to restitution: damages stand in lieu of restitution which would take place just following the award or judgment. It is also easy to understand if one keeps in mind that what must be repaired is the actual harm done, as opposed to the value of the asset when taken".[25]

Such an approach entailed a legal effect of utmost importance: the tribunal took into consideration *ex post* data, i.e. information available after the date of the expropriation, which would have allowed to better reflect reality (including market fluctuations) when attempting to re-establish the situation which would, in all probability, have existed if that act had not been committed. At the same time, the majority asked itself the question whether *ex post* valuation or data should not have been used because they were unforeseeable on the date of the breach. In this regard, the tribunal underlined that, if the factual link between the act and the damage is composed of an atypical chain of events that could objectively not have been foreseen to ensue from the act, the damage may not be recoverable:

> "Subject possibly to special circumstances, the expropriation of a going concern appears objectively capable of causing the loss of future profits which may fluctuate according to the evolution of the econo-

---

[25] *Ibid.*, para. 377.

my and the market. If one focuses on foreseeability in this context, then it is equally clear that losses of future profits determined by the fluctuations of the market are objectively foreseeable. As a result, the majority is satisfied that the test of foreseeability (to the extent that it is deemed part of causation) is met in the circumstances before it".[26]

And it was precisely for the latter statement that a dissenting opinion was attached by Professor Stern.

5.1.3. The Dissenting Opinion

While Professor Stern agreed with the majority as to the difference between compensation for a lawful expropriation and reparation for an unlawful expropriation, she maintained that this full reparation is the one foreseen in all probability at the time of the expropriation and not at the time of the award, as decided by the majority. More specifically, Professor Stern deemed that any lost profits after the date of the judgment could not be taken into account. In the same vein, the possibility to use *ex post* information ought to have been ruled out: "[t]he purpose of the reparation is to compensate the consequences of the illegal act of the State, as appreciated at the time of such expropriation, not the consequences of some posterior evolution of prices or evolution of demand or other circumstances".[27]

In Professor Stern's view, it is enough to look at the international tribunals' case law to reach the conclusion that the approach adopted by the majority was an "ultraminority position" which unfairly favors foreign investors. Indeed, the dissenting opinion contested the legal interpretation according to which, while investors can enjoy the benefits of unanticipated events that increase the value of an expropriated asset up to the date of the judicial decision, they do not bear the risk of unanticipated events decreasing the value of an expropriated asset over that time period:

> "[…] A legal solution cannot just be based on what is more favorable to one of the parties. […] This comforts my view that the fair solution is to be based on what was foreseeable at the date of the expropriation, which is indeed in line with the respect of the investor's legitimate expectations. This does not mean that the investor should not receive full compensation, which for the PCIJ in the *Chorzów* case was not restricted to *damnum emergens*, but had also to include the

---

[26] *Ibid.*, para. 445.
[27] Dissenting Opinion, para. 43.

probable *lucrum cessans*, until the time of the judgment. The vocabu-
lary has changed, but the basic ideas remain".[28]

5.2. Tidewater v. Venezuela

The dispute between Tidewater and Venezuela concerned the adoption of the
Reserve Law and subsequent State actions against foreign investors in the field
of exploitation and service provision of hydrocarbons.[29] Indeed, on 7 May 2009,
the Government of Venezuela enacted the organic law that reserved to the State
the assets and services related to primary activities of hydrocarbons (the Reserve
Law). The following day, the Ministry of Popular Power for Energy and Petroleum
issued a resolution that identified the claimants, along with 38 other service providers, as subject to the Reserve Law. In the same day, the investors' assets on Lake
Maracaibo, and specifically the assets of SEMARCA, a company wholly controlled by the claimants, were seized, including its headquarters at *La Cañada* and 11
vessels. The claimant investors continued to provide services in the Gulf of Paria
following that seizure, but on 12 July 2009 four vessels were also seized. At this
juncture, the investment substantially terminated. The claimant investors sought
relief for unlawful expropriation.

Article 5 of the applicable BIT is in a form commonly found in many investment treaties. It does not prohibit the expropriation of investments. Rather, each
Contracting Party undertakes only to expropriate if certain specified conditions are
met. The expropriation must be: (a) for a public purpose related to the internal
needs of that Party; (b) on a non-discriminatory basis; and (c) against prompt, adequate and effective compensation. The Contracting States extend these protections to measures having effect equivalent to nationalization or expropriation. They
also undertake to provide prompt judicial or independent review of an investor's
case or the valuation of its investment in accordance with the principles set out in
Article 5.

Four measures were relied upon by the claimant investors as constituting acts
by which Respondent expropriated its investments in Venezuela: (i) Reserve Law
of 7 May 2009; (ii) Ministerial Resolution No. 51 of 8 May 2009; (iii) physical seizure of business operations at *La Cañada* on 9 May 2009; and (iv) physical seizure
of business operations at *Corocoro* on 12 July 2009.

As to the first measure, the Tribunal noted that the Reserve Law had two functions: on the one hand, the reservation to the State in the public interest of the oil

---

[28] *Ibid.*, paras. 56-60.
[29] *Tidewater Investment SRL and Tidewater Caribe, C.A. v. The Bolivarian Republic of
Venezuela*, ICSID Case No. ARB/10/5, Award of 13 March 2015. The members of the Tribunal
were Prof. Campbell McLachlan Q.C. (President), Dr. Andrés Rigo Sureda (Arbitrator), and
Prof. Brigitte Stern (Arbitrator).

industry support functions; and, on the other hand, the nationalization of the assets and operations of private companies then carrying out such activities and services. Without such a nationalization, the purpose of the Reserve Law could not then have been achieved. As far as the Ministerial Resolution is concerned, the Tribunal pointed out that it instructed competent State agencies to take control of the operations and immediate possession of the facilities, documentation, assets and equipment related to the activities to which it referred. Accordingly, physical seizures occurred. The tribunal yielded to the conclusion that the investors' assets were expropriated after those measures were delivered and implemented. It excluded that the expropriation was discriminatory and stated that it pursued public policy purposes. Yet, the tribunal ascertained that no compensation was paid by the State.

By citing scholarship and international case law,[30] as well as the World Bank guidelines,[31] the tribunal reached the conclusion that an expropriation wanting only a determination of compensation by an international tribunal could have not been treated as an illegal expropriation. Thus, once an arbitral tribunal has had the opportunity to make its determination as to compensation, the expropriation will not be illegal. In these terms, an expropriation only wanting fair compensation should be considered as a provisionally lawful expropriation. As the tribunal pointed out, "[t]he essential difference between the two is that compensation for a lawful expropriation is fair compensation represented by the value of the undertaking at the moment of dispossession and reparation in case of unlawful expropriation is restitution in kind or its monetary equivalent".[32]

Yet, claimants submitted that the taking was illegal, since the Reserve Law mandated a level of compensation that was limited to the book value of the assets and it prohibited the taking into account of lost profits or indirect damages, so violating Article 5 of the BIT. In the Tribunal's view, this provision merely refers to "fair market value" and, insofar as it entrusts to arbitral tribunals to evaluate and determine the amount of compensation, it cannot be ruled out that, in some cases, the appropriate valuation is the book value of the assets.

Having so stated, the tribunal found in the World Bank Guidelines reasonable guidance as to the content of the standard chosen by the State Parties to the BIT to compensate cases of lawful compensation, where the investment constituted a going concern at the time of the taking. The Guidelines prescribe the fair market value of the taken asset as such value is determined immediately before the time at which the taking occurred. The Guidelines provide for a distinction to be drawn between a going concern with a proven record of profitability and other enterprises not having this characteristic. Where the enterprise meets this criterion, the Guidelines indicate

---

[30] *Ibid.*, paras. 136-137; SALACUSE, *The Law of Investment Treaties*, 2009, p. 328.

[31] World Bank Guidelines on the Treatment of Foreign Investment Law, available at: <http://www.italaw.com/documents/WorldBank.pdf>.

[32] *Tidewater* case, *cit. supra* note 29, para. 142.

that compensation will be reasonable if determined on the basis of the discounted cash flow value. On this basis, the Tribunal conclusively pointed out:

> "[...] [I]t is appropriate to determine the fair market value of Claimants' investment in SEMARCA by reference to a discounted cash flow analysis for the following reasons: (a) SEMARCA was, immediately prior to the date of the taking, a going concern with a proven track record of profitability; (b) it had been operating successfully in Venezuela for some fifty years, and (c) in the five years prior to the taking, it had recorded substantial operating income as recorded in its income statements. Thus, in the Tribunal's view, it is not appropriate to determine the fair market value by reference to either the liquidation value of the assets of the SEMARCA Enterprise, or the book value of those assets, as Respondent contends. Such methods would likely only be appropriate, as the World Bank Guidelines point out, where the enterprise was not a proven going concern".[33]

6. *HAMADI V. OMAN*: EXPROPRIATION AND ISSUES OF ATTRIBUTION TO THE HOST STATE

This arbitration arises out of the claimant's investment in the development and operation of a limestone quarry in the Jebel Wasa mountain range, located in the municipality of Mahda, Oman.[34] The claimant was Mr. Al Tamimi and his investment was created through two lease agreements signed between, respectively, his companies Emrock Aggregate & Mining LLC (Emrock) and SFOH Limited (SFOH), and the Omani State-owned enterprise Oman Mining Company LLC (OMCO). Both these contracts provided that OMCO would have sought to obtain the requisite environmental and operating permits for the quarry. Emrock and SFOH agreed to comply with all obligations imposed by relevant permits, and with all environmental, mining and crushing requirements as well.

Very quickly, however, the relationship between the claimant, OMCO and State agencies protecting environment deteriorated. This situation culminated in the decision of OMCO to terminate the OMCO-Emrock Lease Agreement by letter of 20 July 2008. In addition, OMCO informed the claimant on 2 June 2008 that it regarded the OMCO-SFHO Lease Agreement as "null and void", as a result of the claimant's failure to register SFOH in accordance with the laws of Oman. A second termination letter from OMCO to Emrock followed on 17 February 2009.

---

[33] *Ibid.*, para. 165.

[34] *Adel A Hamadi Al Tamimi v. Sultanate of Oman*, ICSID Case No. ARB/11/33, Award of 3 November 2015. Members of the Tribunal were Prof. David A R Williams, Q.C. (President), Judge Charles N Brower (Arbitrator), and Mr. J Christopher Thomas, Q.C. (Arbitrator).

Ultimately, on 23 May 2009, the Royal Oman Police arrested Mr. Al Tamimi for allegedly conducting operations outside of his permitted boundaries and operating without the necessary permits. A criminal trial was subsequently commenced against Mr. Al Tamimi in the Mahda Court of First Instance. By virtue of his position as chairman of Emrock, Mr. Al Tamimi was tried and convicted by the Court on 8 November 2009.

We will focus here exclusively on the issue of attribution. Indeed, the claimant submitted that the actions of OMCO could have been attributed to Oman for the purposes of State responsibility under the US-Oman FTA. It is to be noted that investment protection under Chapter 10 of the US-Oman FTA applies only to "measures adopted or maintained by a Party". In the claimant's view, on the one hand, OMCO could have been considered as an organ of the Omani State by virtue of its being a governmental company exercising "governmental authority" under Article 10.1.2 of the US-Oman FTA. On the other hand, OMCO terminated the lease agreement with Emrock under the direction of State regulatory authorities, relying on alleged non-payment of fines in order to conceal a politically-motivated decision.

The tribunal maintained that the US-OMAN FTA derogates from ILC Articles on State Responsibility, by requiring a higher criterion for the purpose of attribution than that underlying ILC Articles 4, 5 and 8. Under Article 10.1.2 of the cited FTA, the fact that OMCO is a State enterprise is insufficient, since its conduct must occur in the exercise of "regulatory, administrative, or other governmental authority delegated to it" by Oman.

The Tribunal noted that, according to the ILC Articles, responsibility may be imputed to a State where the conduct of a person or entity is closely directed or controlled by the State. However, it found that there was no evidence that in making the decision to terminate the OMCO-Emrock Lease Agreement, OMCO was exercising any regulatory, administrative or governmental authority, and it was acting under direction from state regulatory authorities either. As far as the legal relationship between the FTA and customary international law as codified by the ILC Articles is concerned, the Tribunal

> "accepts the Respondent's submission that contracting parties to a treaty may, by specific provision (*lex specialis*), limit the circumstances under which the acts of an entity will be attributed to the State. To the extent that the parties have elected to do so, any broader principles of State responsibility under customary international law or as represented in the ILC Articles cannot be directly relevant. Most significantly, the Claimant has been unable to identify any relevant law that specifically delegates any regulatory, administrative or governmental authority or powers to OMCO. [...] The Tribunal finds that OMCO's conduct in terminating the OMCO-Emrock Lease Agreement was nothing more than what it was expressed to be: a com-

mercial response to Emrock's alleged various and repeated breaches of contract".[35]

It followed that the claimant's claim under international law for expropriation of his primary investment in Oman, i.e. the right to operate a limestone quarry at the Jebel Wasa quarry site, failed. In other terms, the Tribunal concluded that Mr. Al Tamimi's investment was lost not as the result of a sovereign expropriation, but as the result of a contractual dispute with a private commercial actor.

However, the claimant submitted also a creeping expropriation claim for facts occurred after the termination of the OMCO-Emrock Lease Agreement. The investor complained of his arrest, the alleged coerced undertaking to cease operations at the quarry site, the subsequent prosecution of Mr. Al Tamimi himself and the alleged police harassment of Emrock employees at the quarry site. The Tribunal dismissed this claim as well. To the extent that, after the termination of the contract, the investor had no covered investment under the applicable FTA, these facts could not in practice have had any expropriatory effect.

7. *DAN CAKE V. HUNGARY*: EXPROPRIATION AND INSOLVENCY PROCEEDINGS[36]

In 1996, the Portuguese company Dan Cake acquired a majority of the shares in a Hungarian company, later renamed Danesita, whose business consisted in supplying biscuits and cookies to Eastern European, Southern European, and Scandinavian countries. In 2006, Danesita's creditors pursued the company for unpaid debts, and the liquidation of the company was ordered. With the help of Dan Cake, Danesita reached agreements with various creditors to settle its debts, and was in the process of concluding agreements with other creditors, including MKB Bank, whose loan was secured by a lien.

The Metropolitan Court of Budapest, sitting as a bankruptcy court, issued a decision by which it served Danesita a copy of Florena's request for liquidation and ordered it to declare, within 8 days, whether it admitted the contents of the request. It warned Danesita that if it failed to make the declaration by the above deadline, its insolvency would be presumed, based on Section 24(3) of the Hungarian Bankruptcy Act. Danesita did not respond to the Court's order. Consequently, on 18 January 2007, the Court issued an order declaring Danesita insolvent and appointing a liquidator.

According to Hungarian insolvency law, liquidation proceedings are opposed to bankruptcy proceeding and the only way for the debtor company to avoid the

---

[35] *Ibid.*, paras. 321-322.

[36] *Dan Cake (Portugal) S.A. v. Hungary*, ICSID Case No. ARB/12/9, Award of 24 August 2015. Members of the Tribunal were Prof. Pierre Mayer (President), Prof. Jan Paulsson (Arbitrator), and Mr. Toby Landau, Q.C. (Arbitrator).

sale of its assets is to enter into an agreement with its creditors. The liquidator is under the obligation to proceed with the public sale of the debtor company's assets within 120 days from the date of the liquidation order, unless a creditors' committee is formed and decides to postpone the commencement of the sale process. In the course of liquidation proceedings, Danesita and Dan Cake tried to enter into an agreement with Danesita's creditors. The Bankruptcy Act provides the possibility for the debtor company to request from the Bankruptcy Court, under certain conditions, the convening of a composition hearing during which the creditors may vote on and approve, by a qualified majority, an agreement with the debtor. If the agreement is approved by the Court, the sale of the assets will be avoided.

Danesita requested that the Metropolitan Court of Budapest convened a "composition hearing", during which it hoped that its creditors would have voted in its favor. However, on 22 April 2008, the Metropolitan Court of Budapest declined to convene a composition hearing. It considered that Danesita's request in its current form was not suitable to be served on the creditors and to convene a composition hearing, and ordered Danesita to make several supplementary filings. At the same time it insisted that the liquidator was obliged to proceed to the sale of the assets within 120 days from the publication of the liquidation proceedings. Danesita did not satisfy these conditions. Shortly thereafter, the liquidator announced the sale of Danesita's factory. Dan Cake thus lost its investment.

Dan Cake claimed before ICSID that Hungary violated the BIT's provisions on fair and equitable treatment, full protection and security, arbitrary and discriminatory measures impairing investment, and expropriation without compensation.

The ICSID Tribunal highlighted that the prompt convening of a composition hearing was the only way for Danesita and Dan Cake to avoid the sale of Danesita's assets and the disappearance of Danesita, which was the Dan Cake's investment in Hungary. Since under Hungarian bankruptcy law, there is no hierarchy between a composition hearing and the sale of assets – the tribunal observed – the debtor has a right that the composition hearing be at least convened by the court, provided the request is accompanied by the documents required by law, or deemed necessary. According to Hungarian law, only three documents must be submitted with the request: a program for restoring solvency, a composition proposal, and a list of creditors. Thus, the Tribunal additionally observed that, if a composition satisfies both the interests of the debtor and those of the creditors – who would only be bound if a qualified majority of them voted in favor of its adoption – there is no reason to refuse to convene a composition hearing. In this regard, the Tribunal clarified that:

> "It is not the task of this Tribunal to determine whether it agrees, or disagrees, with the Metropolitan Court of Budapest as to whether the items required were indeed necessary. The Tribunal is not a court of appeal. A mere disagreement with what the Metropolitan Court of Budapest decided on one or another point would not establish that the decision was unfair or inequitable if it found that some of the

requirements were *obviously unnecessary* or *impossible to satisfy*, or in *breach of a fundamental right*, having in mind that since many employees had been laid off by the liquidator, the factory was not running at full capacity, as underlined in the request, so that unnecessarily postponing the convening could but ruin the possibility of a successful hearing, thereby dooming the investment to disappear".[37]

While the Tribunal deemed that it was impossible to determine whether a composition agreement would have been reached if a composition hearing had been convened, it had no doubt that each and every chance of a successful composition hearing was destroyed by the Bankruptcy Court's decision to refuse to convene a hearing, as required by the law.

Specifically, the ICSID Tribunal brought at the surface that the judicial domestic order was rendered in flagrant violation of the Bankruptcy Act, since it conditioned the mandatory convening of the hearing upon several requirements, all of which were unnecessary. Moreover, in the tribunal's view, the accumulation of unjustified obstacles, coupled with the reminder of the liquidator's obligation to proceed with the sale of Danesita's assets, demonstrated the uncontestable will of the Court not to do what was mandatory. The tribunal concluded that such a violation of the obligation to treat the investor in a fair and equitable manner took the form of a denial of justice.[38]

---

[37] *Ibid.*, para. 117.
[38] See PAULSSON, *Denial of Justice in International Law*, Cambridge, 2005. Prof. Paulsson was one of the arbitrators in the case under examination.

ITALIAN PRACTICE
RELATING TO INTERNATIONAL LAW

Classification Scheme

JUDICIAL DECISIONS

(edited by *Daniele Amoroso* and *Andrea Caligiuri*)

V. IMMUNITIES

Immunity of foreign States from Jurisdiction – Judgment No. 238/2014 of the Italian Constitutional Court – International Crimes – Reparation – Universal Civil Jurisdiction – UN Convention on Jurisdictional Immunities of States and Their Property of 2 December 2004

Corte Costituzionale, 3 March 2015, No. 30 (order)
Donati v. Scheungraber, Stommel and Germany

Corte di Cassazione (Sezioni Unite Civili), 6 May 2015, No. 9097
Germany v. Sterea Ellada Region

Corte di Cassazione (Sezioni Unite Civili), 6 May 2015, No. 9098
Germany v. Sterea Ellada Region

Tribunale di Firenze (Sez. II), 6 July 2015, No. 2468
Bergamini v. Germany and Italy

Tribunale di Firenze (Sez. II), 6 July 2015, No. 2469
Simoncioni v. Germany and Italy

Corte di Cassazione (Sezioni Unite Civili), 28 October 2015, No. 21946
Flatow and others v. Iran and Ministry of Intelligence and Security of Iran

Corte di Cassazione (Sezioni Unite Civili), 28 October 2015, No. 21947
Eisenfeld and others v. Iran and Ministry of Intelligence and Security of Iran

Corte di Cassazione (Sez. I penale), 29 October 2015, No. 43696
Criminal proceedings against Dobrivoje Opačić

In 2015, a number of Italian courts addressed the issue of the jurisdictional immunities of the State in light of Judgment No. 238/2014 of the *Corte Costituzionale* (CHECHI, ILDC 2237 (IT 2014); FRANCIONI, "From Deference to Disobedience: The Uncertain Fate of Constitutional Court Decision No. 238/2014", IYIL, 2014, p. 1 ff.; PISILLO MAZZESCHI, "Access to Justice in Constitutional and International Law: The Recent Judgment of the Italian Constitutional Court", *ibid.*, p. 9 ff.;

BOTHE, "The Decision of the Italian Constitutional Court Concerning the Jurisdictional Immunities of Germany", *ibid.*, p. 25 ff.; CATALDI, "A Historic Decision of the Italian Constitutional Court on the Balance Between the Italian Legal Order's Fundamental Values and Customary International Law", *ibid.*, p. 37 ff.; PALCHETTI, "Can State Action on Behalf of Victims Be an Alternative to Individual Access to Justice in Case of Grave Breaches of Human Rights?", *ibid.*, p. 53 ff.).

As is well known, the *Corte Costituzionale* relied on a strictly dualist approach to the relationship between international and domestic law in concluding that the customary norm on State immunity from jurisdiction, as interpreted by the International Court of Justice (ICJ), could not display any legal effects in the Italian legal order, insofar as it relates to claims stemming from war crimes and crimes against humanity that affect inviolable fundamental human rights, as this would impair the right of the victims, or their heirs, to effective judicial protection (CANNIZZARO, "Jurisdictional Immunities and Judicial Protection: The Decision of the Italian Constitutional Court No. 238 of 2014", RDI, 2015, p. 126 ff., p. 127; KOLB, "The Relationship between the International and the Municipal Legal Order: Reflections on the Decision No. 238/2014 of the Italian Constitutional Court", QIL, Zoom out II, 2014, p. 5 ff., p. 5). Moreover, Article 3, Law No. 5/2013 (the Italian legislation implementing the ICJ Judgment in *Jurisdictional Immunities of the State (Germany v. Italy)*, 3 February 2012, ICJ Reports, 2012, p. 99 ff.) was deemed unconstitutional; and even the law implementing the UN Charter was held to be incompatible with the fundamental principles of the Constitution insofar as it bound Italy to comply with the ICJ Judgment.

As noted by Tomuschat in his critical appraisal of the consequences of Judgment No. 238/2014 on the dispute between Germany and Italy, "the ball is in the court of Italy but cannot be resolved by its courts" (TOMUSCHAT, "The National Constitution Trumps International Law", Italian Journal of Public Law, 2014, p. 189 ff., p. 195). However, absent any significant step by the Italian Government to address these matters, the ball has indeed come back to Italian courts to deal with.

In the first decision under review, the *Corte Costituzionale* reconsidered the problem when deciding a further referral by the *Tribunale di Firenze*. The *Corte Costituzionale* dismissed the referral as being manifestly inadmissible since the request had lost its object as a consequence of its previous findings in Judgment No. 238/2014. This outcome was to be expected and Order No. 30 does not bring much new in this context; however, it is worth noting that, according to paragraph 1 of its operative part, the request for a ruling on the customary norm on immunity is inadmissible insofar as the latter denies jurisdiction over crimes committed by the Third Reich *at least in part in the forum State*. The Order, expressly refers this qualification to customary norms which would in principle fall under the scope of Article 10 of the Constitution. Although its wording reflects *verbatim* the order whereby the *Tribunale di Firenze* referred the issue to the *Corte Costituzionale*, also the relevant parts of the orders that led to Judgment No. 238 were formulated in almost identical terms, whereas no similar qualification was included in the operative part of Judgment No. 238 (see, e.g., *Tribunale di Firenze*, 21 January 2014, *Alessi*, para. 1 of the operative part; CHECHI, ILDC 2725 (IT 2014)). Only the latter's reasoning posited, albeit marginally, that the incompatibility with fundamental principles enshrined in the Constitution relates to the obligation for Italian courts to "deny their jurisdiction over actions for damages for crimes against humanity, committed jure imperii by a foreign State on Italian territory, without any other form of judicial redress for the fundamental rights violated" (Judgment No. 238, para. 5.1 of the conclusions on points of law). This holding was, however, included in the part of the judgment concerning Law No. 5/2013; no specification was made in this regard with reference to the implementation of customary international law. Order No. 30 would seem to imply that the issue of whether international customary norms on State immunity could be implemented in Italy in cases concerning international crimes could, at the very least, be reassessed by the *Corte Costituzionale* as regards crimes which were not perpetrated on Italian territory.

Moreover, the need for a restrictive reading of the consequences of Judgment No. 238 finds some support also in the latter's reference to the "last resort" argument, whereby the individual right of access to a court would prevail over the right of foreign States to enjoy immunity from contentious jurisdiction only if no alternative, effective means of redress were provided before other national jurisdictions, notably those of the State to which the crime is attributed. This argument was raised by Italy in the proceedings before the ICJ (Judgment of 3 February 2012, *cit. supra*, paras. 98 ff.; see PISILLO MAZZESCHI, *cit. supra*, p. 13). Also the *Corte Costituzionale* relied on it (e.g., in para. 5.1 quoted *supra*) but this point was not made with sufficient clarity (see the criticism of CONFORTI, "La Cour constitutionnelle italienne et les droits de l'homme méconnus sur le plan international", RGDIP, 2015, p. 353 ff., p. 356), nor was it included in the operative part of the judgment. Still, arguably the Italian Constitution, as interpreted by the *Corte Costituzionale*, requires ordinary courts to pursue a careful balance of all relevant circumstances before upholding jurisdiction against foreign States, even in cases concerning war crimes and crimes against humanity (see also DE SENA, "The Judgment of the Italian Constitutional Court on State Immunity in Cases of Serious Violations of Human Rights and Humanitarian Law: A Tentative Analysis Under International Law", QIL, Zoom out II, 2014, p. 17 ff.; *contra* see PINELLI, "Decision No. 238/2014 of the Constitutional Court: Between Undue Fiction and Respect for Constitutional Principles", *ibid.*, p. 33 ff.). Not all the judicial pronouncements discussed below have taken these problems into account. In fact, Judgment No. 238 entails a high cost in terms of respect for Italy's international obligations and the task of reconciling the *Corte Costituzionale*'s findings with the need to ensure, as far as possible, compliance with those obligations was left mainly in the hands of ordinary courts (see CANNIZZARO, *cit. supra*, p. 133; PALCHETTI, *cit. supra*, p. 54; TANZI, "Il difficile dialogo tra Corte internazionale di giustizia e Corte costituzionale", CI, 2015, p. 13 ff.). The issue arose in a series of cases directly related to war crimes committed by Germany in the Second World War, on which the *Corte Costituzionale*'s judgment had an immediate bearing, whereas other decisions had no connection whatsoever to those events.

As to the first group of decisions (*Germany v. Sterea Ellada Region*, 6 May 2015, Nos. 9097 and 9098), the *Corte di Cassazione* (*Sezioni Unite*) ruled on two parallel claims whereby Germany sought revocation of judgments upholding a declaration of enforceability in Italy of a Greek judgment on compensation for the Distomo massacre as regards respectively the parts concerning the award of costs (*Corte di Cassazione (Sezioni Unite)*, 6 May 2008, No. 14199 (order), Giustizia civile, 2009, 6, I, p. 1385 ff.) and the main claim (*Germany v. Prefecture of Vojotia (Greece)*, 20 May 2011, No. 11163, IYIL, 2011, p. 357 ff., with a comment by AMOROSO; AMOROSO, ILDC 1815 (IT 2011)). In the revocation proceedings, Germany relied on the ICJ judgment and on Law No. 5/2013. The *Corte di Cassazione* deemed the claim inadmissible in light of the finding of the *Corte Costituzionale* that Article 3 of that law, specifically providing for a ground of revocation of domestic judgments incompatible with ICJ judgments, was unconstitutional. Thus, the third shift of the *Corte di Cassazione*'s stance on State immunity in a decade apparently took place in a very straightforward way (SCISO, "Brevi considerazioni sui primi seguiti della sentenza della Corte Costituzionale 238/2014", RDI, 2015, p. 887 ff., p. 889).

A much more complex reasoning lies at the basis of two twin judgments rendered by the *Tribunale di Firenze* in *Bergamini* and *Simoncioni*, that is, two of the cases that were at the origin of the 2014 *Corte Costituzionale*'s Judgment. The *Tribunale di Firenze* ruled in favour of the applicants and awarded compensation to be paid by Germany in the amount of 50.000 and 30.000 Euros (plus interests), respectively – whereas the request by Germany to be released of liability by Italy was rejected. In discussing the implications of such findings in international law the *Tribunale di Firenze* expressly acknowledged that, while the ruling of the *Corte Costituzionale* did not formally imply an exercise of jurisdiction over Germany, its own judgments may in themselves constitute an internationally wrongful act attributable to Italy:

> "It is for this judge to decide not only, as a court of first instance, on the preliminary exception of lack of jurisdiction, but also to strike a balance, *in concreto*, between customary international law [on immunity of States from jurisdiction] – which is incompatible with the Constitution – and the domestic legal regime of State immunity, as aligned with the Constitution by Judgment No. 238/2014, which is however unlawful under international law in light of the ICJ Judgment of 3 February 2012".

Therefore, the *Tribunale* did not consider that Judgment No. 238 would automatically lead to a denial of Germany's immunity, and took great care in justifying its assessment from several points of view, while critically analysing the *Corte*

Costituzionale's Judgment No. 238 and Order No. 30/2015 of the same Court (paras. 1-2 of the judgments), and their consequences for the cases at hand. According to *Bergamini* and *Simoncioni*, a first implication of the *Corte Costituzionale*'s findings is that also the implementing order of the 1957 European Convention for the Peaceful Settlement of Disputes (Law No. 411/1958) cannot transpose in Italy Article 39 of that Convention, insofar as it binds Italy to respect the 2012 ICJ Judgment. In the *Tribunale*'s view, there is no need to seek a new ruling by the *Corte Costituzionale*, as Judgment No. 238 "binds Italy, not only its courts, not to decline civil jurisdiction over war crimes or crimes against humanity, albeit committed *iure imperii*, by other States on Italian territory" (para. 2).

As regards specifically the discussion on jurisdiction, the *Tribunale* relied on a number of arguments to justify its decisions. First, it stressed that both Germany and Italy belong to the European Union (EU): while EU law does not apply as such to the cases at hand, it sets a particularly high standard of protection of fundamental rights which, it is suggested, should influence the attitude of EU Member States also as a matter of international law. This, in turn, could be conducive to a reading of customary rules on immunity in line with the interpretation of the *Corte Costituzionale*, at least within the territorial scope of the EU Charter of Fundamental Rights (para. 3; for the suggestion that a regional custom may be emerging in this regard see DE SENA, *cit. supra*, p. 31).

Furthermore, the judgments emphasised that "strains which may amount also to internationally wrongful acts" could actually contribute to enhancing the protection of values that lie at the basis of the EU legal order, "in line with the best European tradition" (*Bergamini* and *Simoncioni*, para. 3). This clearly echoes the *Corte Costituzionale*'s hint to the fact that apparent infringements of existing international legal rules may cause custom to develop accordingly (Judgment No. 238/2014, para. 3.3; GRADONI, "Corte Costituzionale italiana e Corte internazionale di giustizia in rotta di collisione sull'immunità dello Stato straniero dalla giurisdizione civile", SIDIblog, 27 October 2014; see also *Flatow* and *Eiselfeld*, para. 4.1; *Opačić*, para. 5.2). The *Tribunale di Firenze* also considered that

> "[T]he radical choice the *Corte Costituzionale* had to face was caused, in the first place, by the behaviour of the Federal Republic of Germany which, albeit acknowledging its responsibility for the crimes of the Third Reich, relied on jurisdictional immunity and, moreover, did not pursue any negotiations with either the victims and their close relatives, or with the Italian State" (para. 3).

According to the *Tribunale*, the ICJ had justified its findings on the unlimited scope of immunities for acts *iure imperii* also on the basis of an *obligation* for Germany to negotiate a settlement (*ibid.*) – although the *Tribunale* did acknowledge later (para. 4.6) that the 2012 Judgment had not actually assessed the existence of such an obligation. Indeed, the ICJ, which had already declined jurisdiction *ratione temporis* on the issue of reparations in its Order concerning Italy's counter-claims of 6 July 2010 (ICJ Reports, 2010, p. 310 ff.), merely considered that the outstanding claims "could be the subject of further negotiation involving the two States concerned" (ICJ Reports, 2012, para. 104) while expressing its surprise and regret notably as regards the position of the Italian military internees, who where deemed not to be eligible under the reparations schemes established by Germany as they were prisoners of war, although their status had not been recognized by the Third Reich (*ibid.*, para. 99).

Be that as it may, the *Tribunale di Firenze* further recalled that, in the parallel case of *Alessi*, it had invited the parties to negotiate and suggested a settlement whereby Germany would grant the plaintiffs (who were not direct victims) or to a member of their family a scholarship of 15.000 Euros for a study period or cultural visit to Germany (Order of 23 March 2015; see also the parallel decision in *Donati v. Scheungraber, Stommel and Federal Republic of Germany*, which is reproduced in part in the merits judgment, No. 691 of 22 February 2016, para. 3). The terms of the order clearly called into question also the position of Italy, as they implicitly pointed to the only option for that State to avoid incurring international responsibility vis-à-vis Germany: paying compensation to the victims or their heirs (see SCISO, *cit. supra*, p. 891; FORLATI, "International Judgments and the Italian Legal Order: Some Comments on the Italian Constitutional Court's Ruling on the Issue of the *Jurisdictional Immunities of the State*", Romanian Journal of Comparative Law, 2014, p. 248 ff., p. 265). However, "neither Germany nor Italy gave any sign of being ready to reach an agreement, or even to pursue a minimal negotiation, be it in the framework of these proceedings or out of court" (*Bergamini* and *Simoncioni*, para. 3).

A further element, which had some relevance in striking the balance between Germany's right to enjoy immunity and the victims' rights to judicial protection, was the remedy sought. In this respect, the *Tribunale di Firenze* discarded the argument whereby the right to judicial redress should enjoy higher standards of protection when the plaintiff seeks restitution, rather than compensation (CONSOLO and MORGANTE, "Immunità e crimini di guerra: la Consulta decreta un plot-twist, abbraccia il dualismo e riapre alle azioni di danno", Corriere giuridico, 2015, p. 100 ff., pp. 105 and 108). On the contrary, it stressed that the seriousness of the crimes under discussion, allowing for no reparation in kind, rather militate in favour of the exercise of jurisdiction. At the same time, it considered that a domestic judgment awarding monetary compensation would, as a matter of principle, be less intrusive on foreign States' sovereignty than one awarding *restitutio in integrum*. Furthermore, the *Tribunale* highlighted that its findings are merely in the form of "a declaratory judgment and an award of reparation", i.e. an exercise of contentious jurisdiction, whereas "States may still promote negotiations on the implementation of the judgment" (*ibid.*). This would seem to imply that immunity could be upheld in the enforcement phase. The judgments concluded that

> "[T]he fundamental right of access to a judge, a supreme principle of the domestic legal order enshrined in Article 24 of the Constitution, may not, in the case at hand, suffer the complete nullification that would ensue from upholding the jurisdictional immunities of the Federal Republic of Germany also in proceedings concerning the assessment and award of damages" (*ibid.*).

As to the merits of the claims, the judgments considered the allegations of fact made by the plaintiffs and Germany's responsibility for those facts to be proven, as they were never challenged by the Respondent. The *Tribunale di Firenze* further held that the claims were not time-barred, relying on a customary rule of international law whereby statutory limitations do not apply to international crimes (para. 4.4), and, moreover, that they did not fall under the scope of the waiver included in Article 77 of the Peace Treaty concluded by Italy in 1947 and of Article 2 of the Bonn Agreement of 1961 (this is in line with several previous stances by Italian courts: see para. 3). Therefore, Germany's claim that Italy be held liable to pay compensation on the basis of the latter clause was dismissed (para. 4.6).

Finally, the judgments also dismissed the argument that Italy should release the Respondent from liability, since an award of damages would constitute an internationally wrongful act attributable to Italy. While acknowledging that an exercise of jurisdiction would be incompatible with international law, the *Tribunale di Firenze* considered that wrongfulness was precluded under the specific circumstances of the case. The judgments did not amount to a countermeasure, as Germany was not infringing a fully-fledged obligation to negotiate under international law. Rather, a legal basis for rejecting Germany's claim was identified with the need to ensure respect for the key constitutional principles of the Italian legal order, notably fundamental human rights. These are enshrined as "supreme principles" also in the German and EU legal orders, as part of a "complex, inter-constitutional legal framework" (para. 4.6).

The outcome of these judgments is not surprising, as it could hardly be expected that an ordinary court would disregard or limit, even indirectly, the impact of a judgment of the *Corte Costituzionale* in a case upon which it has a direct bearing (BOTHE, *cit. supra*, p. 26). While the reasoning of the *Tribunale di Firenze* is not always entirely consistent, the efforts to reconcile the findings of the *Corte Costituzionale* with the need to prevent an infringement by Italy of its international obligations as assessed by the ICJ are in keeping with Italy's constitutional tradition of compliance with international obligations and the values enshrined in Articles 10 and 11 of the Italian Constitution. However, coming to the second group of cases under review, other Italian courts have adopted a more sweeping interpretation of the *Corte Costituzionale*'s Judgment No. 238/2014 and upheld jurisdiction without attempting to strike a balance between the requirement to respect fundamental rights and the (constitutionally protected) interest in complying with international law even in cases involving war crimes and crimes against humanity. As recalled above, this probably had little practical impact on the outcome of proceedings directly involving events of the Second World War. However, the approach of the *Corte di Cassazione* in cases unrelated to Germany's war crimes is less obvious, and more worrisome, in this respect.

Jurisdiction was upheld in *Opačić*, a criminal case, which involved the civil liability of Serbia. The defendant, a former colonel of the National Yugoslav Army, had been sentenced to 28 years of detention by the *Corte d'assise d'appello di Roma* for ordering to shoot down, in 1992, an Italian military helicopter participating in the European Community Monitoring Mission, which was flying over Podrute, in the territory now belonging to Croatia. The *Corte d'assise d'appello* had provisionally awarded damages for over one million Euros in total, plus costs, to be paid jointly and severally by Mr. Opačić, other members of the former Yugoslav Army, and the Republic of Serbia. Only Mr. Opačić referred the case to the *Corte di Cassazione* on grounds related to the treatment of evidence that were, however, rejected. Serbia had not taken part to the proceedings before the *Corte d'appello*, which did not raise the issue *ex officio*, contrary to the provision of Article 11 of Law No. 218/1995 (see also *Jurisdictional Immunities, cit. supra*, para. 130). Furthermore, Serbia had become time-barred from challenging the findings concerning its liability for damages caused by the defendants other than Mr. Opačić; it did, however, appear before the *Corte di Cassazione*, seeking a review of the appeals judgment insofar as its liability for the crime attributed to Mr. Opačić was concerned. Serbia unsuccessfully relied on several arguments drawn from domestic and international law.

Specifically as regards immunity, Serbia maintained that the alleged facts did not amount to an international crime but the *Corte di Cassazione* took the opposite view, qualifying them as a war crime (para. 5.2.1 of the conclusions on points of law). Serbia further relied on the "last resort" argument (see again para. 5.2.1). In dealing with the latter challenge, the *Corte di Cassazione* acknowledged that Judgment No. 238 concerned "war crimes committed, at least in part, in the forum State" (para. 5.2), but the problem of the *locus commissi delicti* was not considered at all when discussing the existence of Italian jurisdiction. The *Corte di Cassazione* endorsed the overall approach of the *Corte Costituzionale*, insofar as it raised no explicit criticism as regards the assessment of customary international rules on immunity made by the ICJ (para. 5.2). At the same time, according to the judgment, it is for domestic courts to ensure full respect for fundamental rights enshrined in national constitutions and the fundamental principles of national legal orders, even by disregarding customary international law if necessary.

Moreover, the *Corte di Cassazione* stressed that Judgment No. 238 requires to ensure *effective* judicial protection in respect of particularly serious crimes; this implies that victims should be able to enforce their right to reparation as against entities that are actually within their reach, and that are financially sound – this is easier when damages are awarded as against "public entities", whereas individuals' economic means could easily be insufficient to cover reparations (*ibid.*).

Of course, the requirement that any judicial remedies be effective is a key feature of the individual right to reparation for international crimes. This is emphasised, *inter alia*, by Article 2 of the Resolution of the Institut de Droit International on *Universal Civil Jurisdiction with regard to Reparation for International Crimes* (Tallinn Session, 30 August 2015). In *Opačić*, however, the argument relating to effectiveness was apparently used only as a justification of the decision to uphold jurisdiction as against a foreign State, rather than as a criterion under which to assess the availability of any alternative remedies to the victims' relatives. The judgment did recall that enquires were pursued also by Yugoslav authorities and that, after the end of the conflict, Mr. Opačić had been sentenced to 20 years of detention by Croatian courts (para. 3). However, it did not explain in any way why no alternative, effective remedies would be available in the context of those proceedings or, indeed, before Serbian courts. While this may well have been the case, the issue is apparently of no relevance: according to the *Corte di Cassazione*, precluding access to judicial redress to victims of international crimes, as defined by the Statute of the International Criminal Court, would imply a disproportionate restriction on the enjoyment of fundamental rights regardless of the circumstances of each specific case. Jurisdiction as against foreign States should therefore be upheld regardless of whether any alternative remedy exists:

> "[T]here is no mention of such condition in the operative part of the judgment of the *Corte Costituzionale*, neither is there any legal argument in the [latter's] reasoning supporting such a reading [...]; the parts of the reasoning that dwell on the complete lack of alternative forms of judicial protection [...] seem to merely reinforce the soundness of the decision by highlighting the extremely unfair consequences to which a denial of justice would lead in the specific cases for which the constitutional referral was raised" (para. 5.2.1).

The *Sezioni Unite* adopted the same approach in *Flatow* and *Eisenfeld*, two parallel proceedings concerning requests that decisions of the United States District Court for the District of Columbia (respectively No. 97-396 (RCL) of 11 March 1998, and No. 98-1945 (RCL) of 11 July 2000) be declared enforceable in Italy. These decisions awarded damages, including punitive damages, for the death of United States citizens in consequence of terrorist attacks by Hamas in Israel, which, according to the US District Court, had been perpetrated under the direction and control of Iran. The *Corte d'Appello di Roma* had rejected the claim and upheld Iran's immunity, relying on the 2012 ICJ judgment. The *Corte di Cassazione (Sezioni Unite)* reversed this part of the finding, in light of Judgment No. 238/2014 of the *Corte Costituzionale*, since immunity for acts *jure imperii* would not apply to "claims stemming from war crimes and crimes against humanity, impinging on human rights, as this is a qualifying principle of the Italian constitutional system, which is firmly grounded on the protection of human dignity and inalienable rights, and on principles of peace and justice in international relations" (para. 4 of both judgments' conclusions on points of law). The terrorist attacks at stake were deemed to be crimes against humanity, as they were perpetrated "in the framework of a systematic and conscious attack to unarmed civil population, inspired by reasons of racial, ethnic, political and religious hate and extremely dangerous for international order and security" (*ibid.*). This notwithstanding, the US decisions were not declared enforceable in Italy as the grounds of jurisdiction which the District Court for the District of Columbia had relied upon were not in line with those set forth by the Italian legal system for similar cases – whereas this is an obstacle to enforceability in Italy under Article 64(1)(a) of Law No. 218/2015 (para. 6; on this issue see further below).

The approach adopted in *Opačić*, *Flatow* and *Eisenfeld* is in line with the 2004 *Corte di Cassazione*'s stance in *Ferrini* (IYIL, 2004, p. 341 ff., with a comment by IOVANE, "The *Ferrini* Judgment of the Italian Supreme Court: Opening Up Domestic Courts to Claims of Reparation for Victims of Serious Violations of Fundamental Human Rights", *ibid.*, p. 165 ff.; and STIRLING-ZANDA, ILDC 19 (IT 2004)) and, moreover, with the Italian constitutional tradition, whereby striking a balance between competing interests is not a task (openly) entrusted to the courts but is rather for the legislature, under the supervision of the *Corte Costituzionale* (BIN, "L'adattamento dell'ordinamento italiano al diritto internazionale non scritto dopo la sent. 238/2014", speech delivered at the XX Conference of the Italian Society of International Law, Macerata, 5-6 June 2015). It is also coherent with the idea that the monopoly of any decision concerning the compatibility of customary law with the Italian legal order should lie with the *Corte Costituzionale*, which was far from obvious before Judgment No. 238 (SALERNO, "Giustizia costituzionale versus giustizia internazionale nell'applicazione del diritto internazionale generalmente riconosciuto", Quaderni costituzionali, 2015, p. 33 ff., pp. 36-38). Nonetheless, as a direct consequence of Judgment No. 238, Italy is infringing the customary rule on State immunity from contentious jurisdiction, whereas the prospects for a modification of customary law on this point are dim at the moment (see only KOLB, *cit. supra*, p. 6). The problem will sooner or later arise also as regards immunity from enforcement, which is not formally covered by Judgment No. 238/2014 (PALCHETTI, *cit. supra*, p. 57). By endorsing the reading of Judgment No. 238 discussed above, the *Corte di Cassazione* may pave the way for a proliferation of civil claims against foreign States also in cases not connected to crimes of the German Third Reich, with respect to which Judgment No. 238 did leave some room for reappraisal. .The approach whereby jurisdiction against foreign States is automatically upheld in cases involving international crimes, without even trying to verify whether these crimes were committed in Italy, or (more importantly, in this writer's view) whether any alternative, effective means of redress would have been available to the victims is not a satisfactory development. This approach arguably goes beyond the stance of the *Corte Costituzionale*, thus unduly enhancing the difficulties that Italy will face in its international relations. Moreover, the fact that no relevance is given to conditions for denying immunity such as those related to the tort exception or to the last resort argument, which were mentioned in Judgment No. 238 and that could more easily lead to a development of customary international law on immunity from jurisdiction in the future, hinders the *Corte di Cassazione*'s chances to meaningfully contribute to setting higher standards of human rights protection in international law..

In light of the *Corte di Cassazione*'s pronouncements the only, albeit significant, limitation to the exercise of Italian civil jurisdiction on claims against foreign States relating to international crimes is the requirement that a suitable ground of jurisdiction exists under Italian law. The existence of a ground of jurisdiction under this Law was not discussed in any of the instances mentioned above, but no difficulties seem to arise in this regard.

Personal grounds of jurisdiction such as residence or domicile (set forth by Article 3(1) Law No. 218/1995) could not apply; moreover, the *Corte di Cassazione* considered that foreign States could not be sued on the basis of the *forum actoris*, as provided by Article 18 of the Italian Code of Civil Procedure when the defendant is neither resident, nor domiciled, nor has an abode in Italy, as this is only a residual criterion (see *Flatow* and *Eisenfeld*, para. 6.4; compare SALERNO, *cit. supra*, p. 54). On the other hand, *Flatow* and *Eisenfeld* posit that the ground of jurisdiction based on the presence of "a representative in this country who is enabled to appear in court" would be satisfied whenever diplomatic relations exist with the respondent State (whereas those between the US and Iran were interrupted in 1979: see para. 6.5). This is consistent with previous case law of the *Corte di Cassazione*, such as *Islamic Republic of Iran v. Racing Pictures and Titanus*, 5 December 1992, No. 12951; although in that instance Iran was the plaintiff, the stance expressed therein as to the capacity of heads of diplomatic missions to act on behalf the State in domestic judicial proceedings is set out in general terms (Foro It., 1994, I, p. 562 ff., with a comment by SALERNO).

In the cases under discussion, other criteria establishing Italian jurisdiction existed: as regards *Simoncioni* and *Bergamini*, Article 3(2) Law No. 218/1995 stipulates that, in matters not covered by the Brussels Convention on Jurisdiction and the Enforcement of Judgments in Civil and Commercial Matters, Italian jurisdiction "shall be also determined according to the criteria laid down for territorial jurisdiction". This provision should be read together with Article 20 of the Italian Code of Civil Procedure, which sets forth that jurisdiction on claims relating to (contractual and non-contractual) obligations lies with the courts of the place where those obligations were originated or where they had to be executed; as recalled above, the *Tribunale di Firenze* assumed that the obligation to provide reparation was originated, at least in part, in Italy (although in the case of Mr. Bergamini, who was a military internee, deportation to Germany was actually not per se unlawful). In *Opačić*, jurisdiction could be established under Article 3(2) Law 218/1995 read together with Article 74 of the Italian Code of Criminal Procedure, stipulating that claims for damages against defendants in a criminal trial or against the liable third party may be raised in the criminal proceedings. In *Germany v. Sterea Ellada Region*, *Flatow*, and *Eiselfeld* jurisdiction on requests to declare respectively the Greek and the US judgments enforceable in Italy was based on Article 67 Law 218/1995: "Whenever foreign judgements [...] are not complied with or challenged as to their recognition, as well as where forceable execution is required, any person concerned may request the Court of appeals of the district where enforcement is sought to determine the prerequisites for recognition". While in *Flatow* and *Eisenfeld* the *Corte di Cassazione* refused to declare the US decisions enforceable because US jurisdiction was established on a ground that would not apply under Italian Law, the absence of the "mirror clause" was an obstacle to upholding the claim on the merits, not an issue of jurisdiction. Before reaching this conclusion, the *Corte di Cassazione* examined several possible heads of jurisdiction set forth by Italian law (para. 6.5), and specifically the *forum delicti* under Article 20 of the Code of Civil Procedure. In this respect, the place where a non-contractual obligation arises is where a wrongful act "produced its effects as against the direct victim", not where indirect victims suffered prejudice (*ibid.*).

It is also noteworthy that these judgments include an express reference to Article 12 of the 2004 UN Convention on Jurisdictional Immunities of States and their Property, albeit not as a justification for the exercise of jurisdiction. In *Ferrini* (*cit. supra*, para. 10) the *Corte di Cassazione* had also relied on the tort exception, as a means to reinforce the main line of reasoning on the issue of immunity, based on the peremptory nature of norms prohibiting international crimes (see GAJA, "The Protection of General Interests in the International Community", RCADI, Vol. 364, 2014, p. 19 ff., p. 148). Moreover, although other heads of jurisdiction existed also in that case, *Ferrini* purported that the principle of universal civil jurisdiction should rather be applied (*cit. supra*, para. 12; see IOVANE, *cit. supra*, p. 185 ff.; on the issue see also BUCHER, "La compétence universelle civile", RCADI, Vol. 372, 2015, p. 21 ff., p. 115). *Flatow* and *Eisenfeld* took a different stance, holding that "the need to identify a ground of jurisdiction in keeping with those enshrined in the Italian legal order is not removed by [...] the *Corte Costituzionale*'s Judgment No. 238", and that it would not be possible to "draw from that pronouncement [...] a principle of universal civil jurisdiction on claims for reparations arising from *delicta imperii*" (para. 6.6). In this respect, therefore, in *Flatow* and *Eisenfeld* the approach was more restrictive than in *Ferrini*. While the issue was discussed as a matter of domestic rather than international law, the former judgments implicitly ruled out the existence of an international obligation to exercise universal civil jurisdiction on international crimes, from which Italian courts could draw a head of jurisdiction not expressly set forth by domestic law.

At the same time if, as the *Corte di Cassazione* confirms, the existence of diplomatic relations is sufficient to establish a head of jurisdiction in Italy against foreign States in cases concerning international crimes, suits could successfully be brought before Italian courts also as regards international crimes having little or no connection with Italy; States wishing to avoid any risk in this regard may eventually choose to interrupt diplomatic relations with Italy (for the Italian text of the decisions under comment see RDI, 2015, p. 1020 ff. (*Corte Costituzionale*, 3 March 2015, No. 30); RDI, 2015, p. 1039 ff. (*Corte di Cassazione*, 6 May 2015, No. 9097); the other decisions by the *Corte di Cassazione* are available at: <http://www.italgiure.giustizia.it>; the text of the judgments by the *Tribunale di Firenze* is available at: <www.questionegiustizia.it>).

SERENA FORLATI

Immunity of foreign States from jurisdiction – UN Convention on Jurisdictional Immunities of States and Their Property of 2 December 2004 – Restrictive immunity – Distinction between acta jure imperii and acta jure gestionis

Corte di Cassazione (Sezioni Unite Civili), 1 April 2015, No. 6603 (order)
Brazil v. Italplan Engineering Environment & Transports s.p.a.

In the order under scrutiny, the *Corte di Cassazione* dealt with the issue of setting the borders between *acta jure imperii* and *acta jure gestionis* in order to determine the extent of a foreign State's immunity from jurisdiction. In particular, the Court held that a foreign State's obligation, set forth by its own Constitution, as guarantor of all debts of insolvent public companies fell into the realm of *acta jure privatorum*. This decision was one of the stages of a dispute involving the breach of a contract between Italplan Engeneering Environment & Transports s.p.a., an Italian company, and Valec, a Brazilian public company responsible for the expansion of Brazil's railways. Italplan had drafted the construction plans of a high-speed railway project between the cities of Rio de Janeiro and São Paulo. After Valec failed to pay the amount due under the contract, Italplan asked the *Tribunale di Arezzo* to issue an injunction ordering the payment of the debt, to which Valec did not object. A second enforcement proceedings was initiated against the Federative Republic of Brazil by virtue of its position of guarantor under Article 37(XXI)(6) of the Brazilian Constitution. Following the summons, a new payment injunction was issued against Brazil. The latter filed an opposition to the payment injunction and then asked the *Corte di Cassazione* to deliver a preliminary ruling on jurisdiction, claiming to enjoy immunity under international law.

The Court rejected Brazil's plea of sovereign immunity and affirmed the jurisdiction of the Italian courts. The grounds for the Court's decision, however, do not appear to be entirely persuasive and deserve a more detailed analysis.

The Court summarily dismissed any arguments based on the UN Convention on Jurisdictional Immunities of States and Their Property (UN Convention). Indeed, the *Cassazione* pointed out that the UN Convention had not entered into force and that, in any case, Brazil had not ratified it. It is striking, however, that in three recent decisions that have been analysed in the previous Volume of this Yearbook the *Corte di Cassazione* dealt with the UN Convention in a totally different fashion (see

Corte di Cassazione (Sezioni Unite Civili), Embassy of Spain to the Holy See v. De la Grana Gonzales, 18 April 2014, No. 9034; *Corte di Cassazione (Sezioni Unite Civili), Académie de France à Rome v. Galamini di Recanati*, 18 September 2014, No. 19674; *Corte di Cassazione (Sezioni Unite Civili), Lasaracina v. Embassy of the United Arab Emirates*, 27 October 2014, No. 22744, IYIL, 2014, p. 468 ff., with a comment by ROSSI). In disputes concerning State immunity relating to contracts of employment, the *Cassazione* applied Article 11 of the UN Convention by assuming that it reflected customary international law in its entirety, and that it could therefore be applied pursuant to Article 10(1) of the Italian Constitution, which incorporates customary international law into Italian law. Such an approach to Article 11 was faulty on many scores, because – among other reasons – it was based on no survey of State practice whatsoever. Yet, one could have expected the Court to adopt the same attitude towards the UN Convention in the case at hand, thus verifying (and, if appropriate, rejecting) the consistency with customary international law of the treaty provision possibly relevant to the case.

However, as stated above, the Court took a radically different approach and did not look into Article 10 of the UN Convention. The reasoning of the *Cassazione* ultimately revolved around the notorious distinction between *acta jure imperii* and *acta jure gestionis*. On this ground, the Court denied State immunity because it found that Brazil's obligation as guarantor had to be considered as undertaken *jure privatorum*. In the Court's words:

> "In the present case, both the obligation assumed by the Brazilian company and the guarantee obligation of the foreign State undeniably pertain to the field of private law and of the legal relationships between individuals. In particular, the guarantee relationship, arising from the law at its highest level (the Brazilian Constitution), relates to a relationship between the Brazilian State and the foreign contractor that entered into a construction design contract with the company of that State. Given the unquestionably collateral nature of the guarantee, the legal relationship falls inevitably and irredeemably in the field of private law and there is no question of *acta jure imperii* because the guarantee was set out by the law. Indeed, the Brazilian State did not adopt any sovereign acts excluding the effects of the guarantee [...]" (pp. 6-7).

The Court clarified its stance by drawing a distinction between the current dispute and its case law related to the Argentine bonds. On that occasion, the *Cassazione* held that, although the issuance of bonds fell into the field of the acts done by the State in a private capacity, the extension of the payment terms of the bonds through legislation had to be regarded as an exercise of sovereign authority, thus exempting Argentina from the jurisdiction of the Italian courts (*Corte di Cassazione (Sezioni Unite Civili), Borri v. Argentina*, 27 May 2005, No. 11255, IYIL, 2005, p. 315 ff., with a comment by PALOMBINO). In the present case, the

Court applied a similar scheme and affirmed that the guarantee set forth by Article 37(XXI)(6) of the Brazilian Constitution, just like the issuance of bonds, constituted a private act. On the contrary, a State's legislative act excluding the effects of the guarantee would have constituted an exercise of sovereign powers, like the Argentine legislation concerning the payment terms of its bonds. Since no such act was adopted, Brazil did not enjoy immunity from jurisdiction.

As previously mentioned, the Court's arguments do not seem to be entirely conclusive. There are very few similarities between the issuance of a bond and the guarantee set forth by Article 37(XXI)(6). While the former creates a legal relationship (easily ascribable to the field of commercial transactions) between the State and the buyer of the bond lending money to the State, the latter provides for a guarantee of all damages caused by agents of public legal entities or private entities rendering public services; a guarantee obligation that, in the lower court's interpretation, apparently extends to the State as a whole and covers all damages caused by public companies, including insolvencies. Such an all-encompassing guarantee obligation can hardly boil down to a purely commercial transaction, not least because it has not contractual nature, being prescribed in general and abstract terms by the Constitution, and because it clearly reflects a pursuit of public goals and an (at least partial) exercise of sovereign authority.

As is well known, the concepts of *acta jure imperii* and *acta jure gestionis* are not always easily distinguishable and provide no reliable guidance in "borderline cases" (FOX and WEBB, *The Law of State Immunity*, 3rd ed., Oxford, 2013, p. 411), so much so that it has been pointed out that the choices made by the courts are not infrequently arbitrary (HIGGINS, "Certain Unresolved Aspects of the Law of State Immunity", NILR, 1982, p. 265 ff., pp. 268-272). Nevertheless, regardless of whether one wants to attach greater importance to the nature or to the purpose of the State act, the case under review was far from being as clear-cut as the wording of Order No. 6603 suggests and arguably rested in one of the "grey areas" between the two above-mentioned concepts. Indeed, it should be kept in mind that, in cases of doubt, the foreign State's immunity should be upheld (CONFORTI, *Diritto internazionale*, 10th ed., Napoli, 2014, p. 271) (the Italian text of the decision is available at: <http://www.italgiure.giustizia.it>).

PIERFRANCESCO ROSSI

Immunity of foreign States from jurisdiction – Restrictive immunity – Distinction between acta jure imperii and acta jure gestionis – 1970 Convention on the Means of Prohibiting and Preventing the Illicit Import, Export and Transfer of Ownership of Cultural Property of 14 November 1970 – UNIDROIT Convention on Stolen or Illegally Exported Cultural Objects of 24 June 1995 – Implied waiver of immunity

Corte di Cassazione (Sezioni Unite Civili), 5 October 2015, No. 19784 (order)
Consulate General of Peru in Milan v. Moshe Tabibnia

In the order under comment, the *Corte di Cassazione* provided an application of the doctrine of restrictive immunity by holding that a Consulate's refusal to return seized property that it had voluntarily accepted for safekeeping, as a result of an interim measure, fell outside the field of *acta jure imperii*, and therefore that the Italian courts retained jurisdiction on the matter. Moreover, the Court stated that the acceptance for safekeeping amounted to an implied waiver of immunity from jurisdiction.

The facts of the case may be summarized as follows. As a result of a report made by the Consulate of Peru, the *Pubblico Ministero* at the *Tribunale di Milano* had impounded a number of pre-Columbian artifacts purchased by Moshe Tabibnia, owner of an art gallery in Milan, and had charged him with handling stolen goods. The *Pubblico Ministero* had also adopted an interim measure handing over the seized property to the consulates of Chile and Peru. Some time later, all criminal charges against Tabibnia were dropped and the *Tribunale di Milano* ordered the artifacts to be returned to their owner, but the two consulates did not comply. Tabibnia then requested and obtained an interim measure ordering the restitution of the property and started a proceeding to obtain a declaratory judgment that he was the legitimate owner of the goods. While the Consulate of Chile did not appear before the Court, the Peruvian Consulate brought the issue of jurisdiction before the *Corte di Cassazione* for a preliminary ruling, claiming that it had acted in a public capacity and hence that it was entitled to immunity from jurisdiction.

The claim for immunity was dismissed by the *Cassazione* on two grounds: the private law character of the Consulate's actions and the implied waiver of immunity on the part of Peru. As for the first argument, the Court applied the *acta jure imperii/ acta jure gestionis* distinction and held that the taking possession of seized property by virtue of an interim measure fell into the latter category. As the Court put it:

> "After the goods were released from seizure […], the dispute that arose on the subject of property had to be regarded as falling – quite legitimately – under Italy's civil jurisdiction, not revealing any connection with the typical exercise of governmental powers by the foreign State through its consular representation. The dispute over which the immunity from the Italian courts is invoked does not interfere with either the sovereign function of the foreign State, or the typical exercise of its governmental power, or the interest of maintaining good international relations" (p. 2).

The customary international law doctrine of restrictive immunity has been consistently applied by the *Cassazione* under Article 10 of the Italian Constitution, which incorporates generally recognized norms of international law into Italian law (see, for instance, *Corte di Cassazione (Sezioni Unite Civili)*, *Borri v. Argentina*, 27 May 2005, No. 11255, IYIL, 2005, p. 315 ff., with a comment by PALOMBINO). Although the outcomes of the *Cassazione*'s previous decisions have not always been entirely persuasive, the qualification of the actions taken by the Peruvian Consulate as *acta jure privatorum* in the case at hand appears to be solidly grounded. In this respect, the Court underlined that a procedure (which instead would have amounted to an exercise of public authority) for the recovery of stolen cultural property is set forth by the 1970 Convention on the Means of Prohibiting and Preventing the Illicit Import, Export and Transfer of Ownership of Cultural Property (1970 Convention; ratified by Italy in 1978 and by Peru in 1979), whose Article 7(b)(ii) provides that a State

> "at the request of the State Party of origin, [shall] take appropriate steps to recover and return any [stolen cultural property] […], provided, however, that the requesting State shall pay just compensation to an innocent purchaser or to a person who has valid title to that property. Requests for recovery and return shall be made through diplomatic offices. The requesting Party shall furnish, at its expense, the documentation and other evidence necessary to establish its claim for recovery and return".

The above requires a caveat. The *Cassazione* neglected to mention the most important treaty in the field of recovery of cultural property, namely the 1995 UNIDROIT Convention on Stolen or Illegally Exported Cultural Objects (1995 Convention), to which Italy and Peru are both also parties. Making a reference to the 1995 Convention would have appeared more appropriate because it provides for "an unconditional duty of restitution of stolen cultural property" (see PAVONI, "Sovereign Immunity and the Enforcement of International Cultural Property Law", in FRANCIONI and GORDLEY (eds.), *Enforcing International Cultural Heritage Law*, Oxford, 2013, p. 79 ff., p. 81), while the procedure set forth by the 1970 Convention only refers to "cultural property stolen from a museum or a religious or secular public monument or similar institution" (Article 7(b)(i)). From the text of the decision under scrutiny it is not evincible whether the 1970 Convention was actually applicable to Tabibnia's impounded property. This notwithstanding, the Court seems to have reached a right result in the application of the distinction between *acta iure imperii* and *acta iure gestionis*.

As for the Court's second argument, that is to say the implied waiver of immunity, it appears to be well-grounded under customary international law as well. The *Cassazione* argued that, by accepting to profit from the interim measure and take custody of the goods, the Consulate had implicitly but unequivocally accepted the jurisdiction of the Italian courts on the matter. It is undisputed, indeed, that the bar of immunity can be removed by consent of the foreign State and that the consent can be implied; this is true, incidentally, even under the doctrine of absolute immunity (FOX and WEBB, *The Law of State Immunity*, 3rd ed., Oxford, 2013, pp. 35-36) (the Italian text of the decision is available at: <http://www.italgiure.giustizia.it>).

PIERFRANCESCO ROSSI

VII. LAW OF THE SEA

Criminal jurisdiction over crimes committed at sea by foreigners on foreign ships – Article 1 of the Convention for the Unification of Certain Rules Relating to Penal Jurisdiction in matters of Collision or Other Incidents of Navigation of 10 May 1952 – Articles 27, 97 and 311 of the UN Convention on the Law of the Sea of 10 December 1982 – Scope of the expression "collision or any other incidents of navigation" – Death caused by the collision of two ships in the UK territorial sea

Corte di Cassazione (Sez. VI penale), 5 January 2015, No. 48
Criminal proceedings against Pasquale Miccio

The key – and internationally relevant – legal question of the case under review is whether a coastal State is permitted to exercise criminal jurisdiction over crimes committed at sea by foreigners on foreign ships.

The factual and procedural background of the decision at hand may be summarized as follows. On 7 July 2014 the Sheriff Court of Lothian and Borders at Edinburgh issued a European arrest warrant seeking Mr. Miccio's extradition from Italy to the UK to face a trial on the charges of culpable homicide and "conduct endangering ships, structures or individuals" (Art. 58(2)(b)(iii) of the 1995 Merchant Shipping Act). The charges pertained to the death of Mr. Stewart McNeil caused by the collision, occurring on 5 August 2010 in the UK territorial sea, between the *Scottish Viking*, an Italian-flag vessel steered by Mr. Miccio, and the *Homeland*, a fishing boat whose crew included Mr. Stewart McNeil.

By a judgment of 30 October 2014 the *Corte d'Appello di Roma* decided to surrender the accused person to the Scottish authorities holding that there were no grounds for refusing to execute the European arrest warrant. Notably, among the causes of refusal cited by the requested person before the *Corte d'Appello* there was the one set forth in Article 18(b) of the Law 69/2005 (adopted in implementation of the 2002/584/JHA Council Framework Decision of 13 June 2002 on the European arrest warrant and the surrender procedures between Member States), which provides that the surrender may be refused where the European arrest warrant relates to offences which (i) are regarded by the Italian law as having been committed in whole or in part in the Italian territory or in a place treated as such; or (ii) have been committed outside the territory of the issuing Member State and the Italian law does not allow prosecution for the same offences when committed outside its territory.

The defendant's case in support of Italian exclusive jurisdiction was two-fold. On the one hand, he argued that the coastal State could not claim jurisdiction under the exceptions envisaged by Article 27 UNCLOS ("Criminal jurisdiction on board a foreign ship") because that provision applies only when the foreign ship is "passing through the territorial sea" and not when, as in the present case, the ship has already left it. On the other hand, he maintained that the offences with which he was charged clearly fell under the jurisdiction of the flag State (Italy) pursuant to

Article 1 of the 1952 Convention for the Unification of Certain Rules Relating to Penal Jurisdiction in matters of Collision or Other Incidents of Navigation (1952 Convention). This Article reads as follows:

> "In the event of a collision or any other incident of navigation concerning a sea-going ship and involving the penal or disciplinary responsibility of the master or of any other person in the service of the ship, criminal or disciplinary proceedings may be instituted only before the judicial or administrative authorities of the State of which the ship was flying the flag at the time of the collision or other incident of navigation".

The *Corte d'Appello* dismissed the defendant's claim, maintaining that the UK had jurisdiction given the reservation it made in accordance with Article 4 of the 1952 Convention, under which the Parties "[…] shall be at liberty […] to reserve to themselves the right to take proceedings in respect of *offences committed within their own territorial waters*" (emphasis added). Moreover, the *Corte* observed that the flag State jurisdiction generally provided in Article 1 of the 1952 Convention concerns only facts and offences relating to navigation and not offences against the person – such as culpable homicide – resulting in a hazardous situation that require the coastal State's intervention. Finally, with regard to Article 27 UNCLOS, the *Corte d'Appello*, while agreeing with the defendant's position on its non-applicability in this case, rejected the interpretation put forth by the accused and extended the actual scope of the Article in question. In particular, the *Corte* firstly pointed out that only events occurring on board the ship – and not events that have an external impact over the coastal State (such as the case of a collision of two ships resulting in the death of the victim) – fall within the exclusive jurisdiction of the flag State under Article 27. Secondly, it acknowledged that criminal jurisdiction referred to in Article 27 UNCLOS concerns the power of the coastal State to arrest persons and conduct investigations on board the ship passing through the territorial sea ("enforcement jurisdiction"), and not the power to take proceedings or hold a trial ("adjudicative jurisdiction"), which does not necessarily require the presence of the ship within the coastal state's territorial sea.

In the proceeding before the *Corte di Cassazione*, the accused person essentially raised the same arguments as to the question of jurisdiction. By upholding the decision taken by the *Corte d'Appello*, the Court predictably quashed these arguments. Interestingly, even though the Supreme Court took for granted the coastal State jurisdiction in the case at hand – having taken note of the UK reservation to the 1952 Convention –, it nonetheless adopted a restrictive interpretation of Article 1 of the Convention. Such an interpretation deserves a close look. The *Corte di Cassazione* first noted that the *Corte d'Appello*'s reading – which, as mentioned, excluded from the scope of Article 1 of the 1952 Convention any offences against persons resulting in a hazardous situation that would require the coastal State's intervention – was consistently in line with the principles established in previous case law. The Court echoed in particular the distinction between internal and external effects of acts committed on board foreign ships (FRANCIONI, "Criminal Jurisdiction over Foreign Merchant Vessels: A New Analysis", IYIL, 1975, p. 27 ff., pp. 27-28; and MASTRONUZZI PELLECCHIA, "Sulla giurisdizione penale dello Stato costiero nel mare territorial", RDI, 1978, p. 258 ff., pp. 261-270), which, as is known, has been expressly taken into account in Article 27 UNCLOS (CATALDI, *Il passaggio delle navi straniere nel mare territoriale*, Milano, 1990, p. 300). Relying on its earlier jurisprudence concerning offences committed on board of foreign ships within the Italian territorial sea, it recalled that:

> "Flag State jurisdiction prevails where an offence committed on board the foreign ship in the territorial sea concerns activities and interests of the national community to which the ship belongs; whereas, instead, coastal State jurisdiction is established where the consequences of the offence have, or are likely to have, external repercussions affecting the territorial community's main interests. Such interests must be assessed not only with respect to the good protected by the breached norm, but also with respect to the genuine risk of prejudice to public peace and good order of territorial sea brought by the violation, such that coastal State's intervention would be needed" (para. 4, quoting *Corte di Cassazione (Sezioni Unite Penali), Criminal proceedings against Zaid Avraham*, 16 November 2011, No. 1002).

Further, the *Corte* went on to specify one peculiar aspect of such findings: "in order to assert the coastal State's jurisdiction, reference should be made both to the concept of 'actual disturbance' and of 'moral disturbance'. This latter relates to facts which have even only potential effects on public order and cause public alarm in the local community evidenced by the cooperation of the local security and health systems" (para. 4, quoting *Corte di Cassazione (Sez. I penale), Criminal proceedings against Tsvirinko*, 7 November 2007, No. 44306; on these two concepts, see JESSUP, *The Law of Territorial Waters and Maritime Jurisdiction*, New York, 1927, p. 191; and QUADRI, *Le navi private nel diritto internazionale*, Milano, 1939, p. 122).

Having underlined this, the *Corte* finally observed that if Italy had been the coastal State in this case, its jurisdiction would have undoubtedly been asserted given the "moral disturbance" caused by the event in question (for a critical appraisal of the "moral disturbance" approach, see MCDOUGAL and BURKE, *The Public Order of the Ocean: A Contemporary International Law of the Sea*, New Haven, 1962, p. 165 ff.).

Ultimately, with specific regard to the issue of the applicability of Article 27 UNCLOS to the present case, the Supreme Court agreed with the *Corte d'Appello* by considering this provision as not applicable since it covers only enforcement jurisdiction on board the foreign ship over internal acts. The *Cassazione* also gave weight to the content of Article 311(2) UNCLOS, pursuant to which UNCLOS "[...] shall not alter the rights and obligations of States Parties which arise from other agreements compatible with this Convention and which do not affect the enjoyment by other States Parties of their rights or the performance of their obligations under this Convention". In the Court's opinion, therefore, the UNCLOS would be in any case without prejudice to the application of the 1952 Convention.

To sum up, the reasoning of the Italian Supreme Court in the judgment under review appears to be twofold. First, since the UK has made a reservation pursuant to Article 4 of the 1952 Convention, this latter was not applicable to the case at hand. Second, and most importantly, had the UK not made any reservation to the above Convention, the case would not have fallen under the scope of Article 1 in any case. This is so because Article 1 cannot be interpreted in such an extensive way as to include also offences which determine dangerous situations calling for the coastal State's action.

It seems that the restrictive interpretation of Article 1 of the 1952 Convention adopted in the judgment under review, if isolated from the specific context of the case, overlooks any distinction among the maritime zones where criminal offences are committed. The *Corte* indeed excluded from the scope of Article 1 any offences against the person that urge coastal State's intervention. This appears to be quite striking since it potentially stretches the internal/external effects doctrine (and particularly the concept of "moral disturbance") to cover also events occurring on the high seas when consisting in offences against the person and, consequently, sets aside the question of the existence of any personal or territorial link for exercising criminal (adjudicative) jurisdiction. In other words, as the Court's interpretation objectively stands, criminal jurisdiction may be asserted by any coastal states whose intervention is required with respect to offences against the person occurring anywhere in the sea (the Italian text of the decision is published in Giur. It., 2015, p. 273 ff.).

LORIS MAROTTI

International maritime piracy – Articles 100-107 and 110 of the UN Convention on the Law of the Sea of 10 December 1982 – Prosecution of maritime piracy – Italian jurisdiction – Unconditional punishability – Articles 1135 and 1136 of the Italian Navigation Code – Italian criminal sanctions with specific reference to maritime piracy

Corte di Cassazione (Sez. V penale), 27 February 2015, No. 15977
Criminal proceedings against Abdi Abdullahi Ahmed, Gedi Aptidon Hassan, Mahamed Isse Karshi, Abdi Hassan Mahmoud, Abdillahi Alì Ahmed, Daley Mahamed Alì, Ahmaed Mahmed Alì and Hashi Abdi Hawiyke

In the case under review, the *Corte di Cassazione* addressed the question concerning the exercise of Italian jurisdiction on crimes connected to maritime piracy in line with Articles 1135 and 1136 of the Navigation Code, as well as on related crimes committed against Italy or against Italian citizens or goods on the high seas, or in the territorial waters of other States, in areas where specified types of multi-lateral counter-piracy operations are taking place, i.e. Operation Ocean Shield and Operation Atalanta.

On 10 October 2011, an Italian ship was attacked on the high seas. The crew, composed of about twenty people, including six Italians, was able to barricade it-self in the so-called *cittadella* – that is, the armoured part of the cockpit – and kept control of the ship, despite the attack having damaged equipment and instrumen-tation, and melted the electrical equipment. About twenty-four hours later, ships under the Ocean Shield Operation reached the hijacked Italian ship. In particular, after preliminary reconnaissance, British Royal Marines intervened operationally, arrested the hijackers, and freed the crew. The assailants were handed over to an Italian Navy cruiser, which was also participating in Ocean Shield Operation at the time. In the meantime, the so-called "mother ship", from which the smaller boats had operated the assault, was identified and the crew arrested.

Italian courts of first and second instances (respectively, *Corte di Assise di Roma* and *Corte di Assise d'Appello di Roma*) convicted the assailants for piracy, possession of stolen property and of weapons of war, and arson causing damage to equipment, the instrumentation, and ship equipment.

The *Corte di Cassazione* confirmed the first and second instances' judgments, while at the same time referring to the conclusions of a previous judgment related to international maritime piracy (*Corte di Cassazione (Sez. II penale)*, *Criminal proceedings against A.A.M. et al.* (*Montecristo* case), 4 February 2013, No. 26825, IYIL, 2013, p. 442 ff., with a comment by BEVILACQUA). The *Corte di Cassazione* restated the facts of the case at hand, including the *modus operandi* of the kidnap-pers, qualifying those acts and conducts as undoubtedly crimes of piracy, in line with the national jurisprudence by applying the Navigation Code. In particular, it took into consideration the most relevant evidence: i.e. the crew members and the security team being shot with their own weapons; people forced to take refuge in the *cittadella* (identifying the clear use of violence against people); the search for objects and people in the various rooms of the vessel; the actions taken to try to breach the *cittadella*; damage done to the onboard equipment and structures of the ship; the evidence of remote coordination and organization of the tasks; boarding the mother ship, where the leader was recognized (para. 2 of the conclusions on points of law).

At this point, after referring to the international and European legal framework for combating piracy, and this framework's implementation at Italian level (*ibid.*, paras. 3-9), the *Corte di Cassazione* highlighted the fact that the Italian normative system considers acts of piracy punishable under Italian law without limitation as regards the place in which they are carried out – i.e. regardless of whether an act occurred in national territorial waters, or on the high seas or in foreign territorial waters – when these acts are committed against Italian ships in any of the zones where the counter piracy missions in which Italy is taking part, e.g. Operation Ocean Shield (*ibid.*, para. 10), are operating. Therefore, the *Corte di Cassazione* confirmed that acts committed by the claimants, as was already upheld by the lower courts (*Corte di Assise* and *Corte di Assise di Appello*), must be unequivocally defined as acts of piracy carried out on board the Italian ship, and thus on Italian territory and to the detriment of Italian ships while operating in the operation zones of Ocean Shield (*ibid.* para. 11).

Consequently, the *Corte di Cassazione* confirmed the competence of *Corte d'Assise di Roma* to exercise Italian jurisdiction on piracy crimes and on those related to them, when actions are perpetrated against Italy or against Italian citizens or goods. As a final remark, it should be noted that the applicability of "unconditional punishability" by Italian courts in line with the aforementioned Italian norms for crimes committed abroad, including piracy, represents the application at the national level of criminal sanctions against pirates pursuant to international and European legal frameworks (the Italian text of the decision is available at: <http://www.italgiure.giustizia.it>).

CLAUDIA CINELLI

XI. TREATMENT OF ALIENS AND NATIONALITY

International protection – Obligation to provide information on access to and the procedures for international protection – Article 8 of EU Directive 2013/32 – Principle of consistent interpretation – Power of the judge to examine the legitimacy of the "detention" and "reception" measures

Corte di Cassazione (Sez. IV civile), 25 March 2015, No. 5926 (order)
Abraham Igberaese v. Ministero dell'Interno

The order of the *Corte di Cassazione* under review is indicative of a trend expressing the efforts and the difficulties of Italian courts to strengthen and align Italian asylum practices with international and European standards on human rights and international protection (on the Italian jurisprudence on this issue, see European Council on Refugees and Exiles, *Asylum Information Database, National Country Report: Italy*, December 2015, available at: <http://www.refworld.org/docid/568fd0384.html>), in a time of profound revisions at the EU level, intending to reconcile humanitarian concerns with the need to ensure security and external border controls (see Communication from the Commission to the European Parliament, the Council, the European Economic and Social Committee and the Committee of the Regions, *A European Agenda on Migration*, 13 May 2015, COM(2015) 240 final).

Before examining the reasoning of the Italian Supreme Court in the case at hand, let us summarize first the factual and procedural background of the decision.

The case arose from an appeal lodged before the *Corte di Cassazione* by a Nigerian national, rescued by the Italian Navy on 18 February 2014. Devoid of any identity document, he was identified as an irregular migrant. Consequently, the Police Commissioner of *Siracusa* issued, on the same day, two decrees: an expulsion order and an order to be conducted to an Immigration Detention Centre (*Centro di identificazione ed espulsione*, "CIE"), near Rome. During the judicial hearing before the *Giudice di Pace di Roma* responsible for the validation of the orders, the claimant expressed, on the one hand, his intention to apply for asylum and stated, on the other hand, that he had not been promptly informed about the possibility of access to international protection and that he had not received any interpreter's assistance before the Police Commissioner. Nevertheless, the *Giudice di Pace* confirmed the detention order (Order No. R.G. 7956/2014) without examining its proportionality or the merits of the expulsion order.

The claim against this decision was based on three main grounds: first, the violation of the right to be informed about the international protection procedures and the consequent inability to have access to the international protection procedures; second, the resulting violation of the right to be conducted to a Reception Center for Refugees and Asylum-seekers (*Centro di accoglienza per richiedenti asilo*, "CARA"), rather than to a CIE; and, third, the lack of any effective exam by the *Giudice di Pace* on the merits and proportionality of the measures established by the Police Commissioner.

The case under review raises the issue of the existence and the extension of the obligation to provide complete and clear information, in a general and systematic way, on the possibility and the modalities of lodging an application for international protection.

Notwithstanding some significant improvements, the Italian asylum system remains deficient in ensuring fast and safe access to procedures and therefore it raises some concerns of consistency with the reception, qualifications, and procedures standards, as well as the human rights obligations, established at the EU and international level (in this perspective, see UN High Commissioner for Refugees (UNHCR), *UNHCR Recommendations on Important Aspects of Refugee Protection in Italy*, July 2013, available at: http://www.refworld.org/docid/522f0efe4.html; European Court of Human Rights (Grand Chamber), *Tarakhel v. Switzerland*, Application No. 29217/12, Judgment of 4 November 2014).

Actually, such an explicit legal obligation to provide information on the possibility to submit an application for international protection is now contained in the new EU Asylum Procedures Directive 2013/32/EU of 26 June 2013 on Common Procedures for Granting and Withdrawing International Protection (OJ EU L180/60). Article 8 reads as follows:

> "Where there are indications that third-country nationals or stateless persons held in detention facilities or present at border crossing points, including transit zones, at external borders, may wish to make

> an application for international protection, Member States shall pro-
> vide them with information on the possibility to do so. [...] Member
> States shall make arrangements for interpretation to the extent neces-
> sary to facilitate access to the asylum procedure".

This statement implies the obligation to ensure effective access to legally safe and efficient asylum procedures. Accordingly, the Directive describes in detail the guarantees that Member States are required to provide to any person, even at border crossing points, potentially in need of international protection. Among these guarantees, a special relevance is granted to the individual right to be informed, in due time and in a language that is reasonable to assume the individual understands, if necessary with the assistance of an interpreter, about the procedures to be followed and rights and obligations during the entire proceedings. The possibility to communicate with the UNHCR and other territorial organizations is also to be provided for.

In its decision, the *Corte di Cassazione* began its reasoning by opportunely denying, on the one hand, the existence of national provisions expressly providing for a duty of information at border crossings. On the other hand, the Court observed, Directive 2013/32/UE had not yet come into force at the time of the event. As a consequence, the obligations arising from Article 8 of the Directive were not directly applicable in the case at hand. Regardless, the Court highlighted that the existence of an obligation to provide sufficient information on the procedures to follow in order to submit an application for international protection clearly emerges from the jurisprudence of the European Court of Human Rights (ECtHR). The Italian Supreme Court referred in particular to the judgment rendered in the case *M.S.S. v. Belgium and Greece* (Application No. 30696/09, Judgment of 21 January 2011), in which the ECtHR expressed the opinion that "the lack of access to information concerning the procedures to be followed is clearly a major obstacle in accessing asylum procedures" (para. 304). The ECtHR reiterated and clarified this statement in the case *Hirsi Jamaa and Others v. Italy* (Application No. 27765/09, Judgment of 23 February 2012), by emphasizing "the importance of guaranteeing anyone subject to a removal measure, the consequences of which are potentially irreversible, the right to obtain sufficient information to enable them to gain effective access to the relevant procedures and to substantiate their complaints" (para. 204).

After these general observations, the *Corte di Cassazione* established the existence of an obligation to provide sufficient information on the access and procedures to seek international protection *by way of interpretation*. In other words, the Court found the existence of an obligation to information by applying the generally recognized hermeneutical principles of accordance and consistency underlying the interpretation of domestic law in the light of international norms.

In this view, the decision of the Court firstly recalls the general duty of the national judges to ensure that any judicial decision is rendered in compliance with the provisions of EU Directives, even during the transposition process. Furthermore, the Italian Supreme Court evokes the application of the principle of interpretation constitutionally oriented to the respect of the provisions established by the European Convention on Human Rights, as interpreted by the jurisprudence of the ECtHR (on the principle of consistent interpretation of domestic law to the international obligations, see CANNIZZARO, "Interpretazione conforme fra tecniche ermeneutiche ed effetti normative", in BERNARDI (ed.), *L'interpretazione conforme al diritto dell'Unione europea*, Napoli, 2015, p. 3 ff).

As a further consequence on these statements, the order of the Italian Supreme Court revoked the expulsion and detention decisions issued with regard to the claimant because of the violation of the duty to provide information: even though the *Giudice di Pace* was not allowed to pursue any judicial review on the detention or expulsion measures, the *Corte di Cassazione* considered that this judge also had the power to detect the incidentally manifest unlawfulness of the detention and expulsion orders and to rule on it.

Based on the assumption that the lack of access to information concerning the procedures to be followed in order to seek international protection is clearly a major obstacle in accessing those procedures, the Court finally stated:

> "Whenever there are indications that third-country nationals or state-less persons, present at border crossing points, including transit zones, at external borders, may wish to make an application for international protection, the competent authorities of the Member States have the duty to provide them with information on the possibility to do so, ensuring the interpretation services to the extent necessary to facilitate access to the asylum procedure" (para. 3.2 of the Order).

Having acknowledged this, the decision under review is worth analyzing mainly because it offers an example of the practical impact and consequences of the application of the principle of the interpretation of the national law in accordance with the international obligations: indeed the application of the principle of consistent interpretation enables the Italian Supreme Court to reconstruct an obligation to provide information in the field of international protection. This obligation is in its turn the legal parameter employed by the Court to evaluate the validity of the judicial orders of detention and expulsion. The legal effects of this decision are therefore considerable.

The solution adopted by the Court in the order at hand appears largely inspired by the aim to remove inconsistencies arising from the Italian system and to ensure a substantial compliance with European and international standards on reception and treatment of migrant and asylum-seekers. At the same time, the line of reasoning of the Court arises in a perspective of continuity with the ongoing global reform of the Common European Asylum System, the main purpose of which is to grant an appropriate balance between different interests and values at stake (see, for further details, European Parliament, Directorate-General for Internal Policies, *Enhancing the Common European Asylum System and Alternatives to Dublin*, Study for the

LIBE Committee, 2015) (the Italian text of the decision is available at: <http://www.italgiure.giustizia.it>).

MAURA MARCHEGIANI

XII. HUMAN RIGHTS

Same-sex couples – Right to marry – Denial of same-sex marriage under the Italian legal system – Articles 8 and 12 of the European Convention on Human Rights – Need for a law creating an alternative form of protection of same-sex unions – Article 2 of the Italian Constitution

Corte di Cassazione (Sez. I civile), 9 February 2015, No. 2400
A.A. and D.S.P.G. v. Ministero dell'Interno – Sindaco del Comune di Roma

The case at hand concerns the refusal by the civil status officer to issue marriage banns to a same-sex couple who had so requested, as a preliminary step to celebrating marriage. The proceedings before the *Corte di Cassazione* constitute the last level of the judiciary review of the civil status officer's activity, both lower-level courts (the *Tribunale di Roma* and the *Corte di Appello di Roma*) having rejected the claimants' request. Specifically, the *Corte di Appello di Roma* upheld the refusal by the civil status officer to issue marriage banns, holding that the Italian legal framework regulating marriage clearly requires that the future spouses are of a different sex. Relying on the judgment of the *Corte Costituzionale* of 15 April 2010, No. 138, in the case *G.M. and others v. Presidenza del Consiglio dei Ministri*, which concerned a similar scenario to that of the claimants in the case under examination, the *Corte di Appello* found the Italian legislation not to be in contradiction with either the Italian Constitution or with the European Convention on Human Rights (ECHR) and the Charter of Fundamental Rights of the European Union (EU Charter).

In their appeal on points of law against the judgment of the *Corte di Appello di Roma*, the claimants requested a fresh referral of the Italian legislation regulating the institution of marriage (first of all, regarding issuance of marriage banns) to the *Corte Costituzionale*, arguing that, in the light of the more recent case law of the *Corte di Cassazione* (*Corte di Cassazione (Sez. I civile), A.G. and M.O v. Sindaco del Comune di Latina and procuratore della repubblica*, 15 March 2012, No. 4184), there were reasons to overrule the conclusions reached by the *Corte Costituzionale* in the judgment No. 138 of 2010 and to affirm their right to marry.

In rendering its judgment, the *Corte di Cassazione* began by recalling some of the conclusions reached by the *Corte Costituzionale* in its judgment No. 138. On that occasion, the *Corte Costituzionale* validated the constitutionality of the Italian legislation regulating marriage in the light of Article 29 of the Constitution, stating that this article "did not take account of homosexual unions, but rather intended to refer to marriage within the traditional meaning of that institution". With regard to the protection of fundamental rights enjoyed both as an individual and as part of a "social group", as guaranteed by Article 2 of the Constitution, the constitutional judge ruled that the concept of "social group" also applies to "homosexual unions, understood as the stable cohabitation of two individuals of the same sex, who are granted the fundamental right to live their situation freely as a couple and to obtain legal recognition thereof along with the associated rights and duties, according to the time-scales, procedures and limits specified by law". Nevertheless, "it is for the Parliament to determine – exercising its full discretion – the forms of guarantee and recognition for the aforementioned unions" (Judgment No. 138 of 2010, *cit. supra*, para. 8 of the conclusions on points of law). Finally, the *Corte Costituzionale* validated the conformity of the Italian legislation regulating marriage as regards the relevant provisions of international and supranational law, stating that both Article 12 ECHR and Article 9 EU Charter clearly reserve the detailed regulation of such matters to the discretion of national authorities.

This last conclusion of the *Corte Costituzionale* was confirmed by the latest judgments adopted by the European Court of Human Rights (ECtHR) on the subject, in particular *Schalk and Kopf v. Austria* (Application No. 30141/04, Judgment of 24 June 2010), *Gas and Dubois v. France* (Application No. 25951/07, Judgment of 15 March 2012), and *Hämäläinen v. Finland* (Application No. 37359/09, Judgment of 16 July 2014). With regard to this case law, the *Corte di Cassazione* concluded:

> "Article 12, although it formally refers to heterosexual marriage, does not exclude the possibility for Member States to extend this matrimonial model also to couples formed of same-sex persons, but in the same time, it does not include any kind of obligation in this sense. There is no doubt, however, that Article 8, which consecrates the right to respect for private and family life, includes the right to live a relationship as a same-sex couple which enjoys protection by law, but not necessarily under the form of making marriage available to such unions".

As concerns the need for a legislative intervention to create the legal form of protection of same-sex union rights, as affirmed by the *Corte Costituzionale* in its Judgment No. 138, the *Corte di Cassazione* reiterated the validity of this statement making reference also to a more recent judgment of the same Court (*Corte Costituzionale, B.A. and another v. Presidenza del Consiglio dei Ministri*, 11 June 2014, No. 170). This latter case concerned the automatic termination of the marriage originally celebrated between two persons of a different sex, by way of transcription in the civil status registry of the gender reassignment of one of the spouses. The *Corte Costituzionale* found the regulation to entail such an effect to be in contrast with Article 2 of the Constitution insofar as it does not provide that:

> "[T]he order reassigning the gender of one of the spouses, which causes the dissolution of the marriage, must in any case allow for the maintenance of a relationship regulated by law, if both spouses so wish, under another form of registered partnership that grants adequate protection to the rights and obligations of the couple, the regulation of which is reserved to the discretionary choice of the legislator" (Judgment No. 170/2014, para. 5.7. of the conclusions on points of law).

Finally, the *Corte di Cassazione* considered that, contrary to the complainants' allegation, the findings in its judgment No. 4184 of 2012 confirm that the same-sex marriage is an institution unknown to the Italian legal system: although not being in contrast with public order, same-sex marriages celebrated abroad cannot produce effects in the Italian legal system and, thus, cannot be regularly transcribed in the Italian civil status registries. The constitutional protection of same-sex unions is founded on Article 2 of the Italian Constitution, even though the lack of a specific regulation of such unions causes a breach of the rights arising from such relationships.

For the above-mentioned reasons, in the case under examination, the *Corte di Cassazione* held:

> "The constitutional and conventional legitimacy of the ordinary legislature with regard to the choice of forms and models by which to provide to unions between persons of the same sex a status of rights and obligations coherent at a constitutional level, leads to exclude the grounds for censorship requested by the claimants, not only from the perspective of the jurisprudential creation of marital unions between persons of the same sex – operation which would conduct to a result beyond the one allowed [...], consisting in the adjustment and homogenization of entitlements and exercise of rights – but also from the perspective of the claimed reasons of unconstitutionality" (p. 17).

In brief, faced with the negation of same-sex marriages in the Italian legal system and the lack of other specific regulation of same-sex unions, both the *Corte di Cassazione* and *Corte Costituzionale* pointed out the legal void, but could not establish through jurisprudence a general framework which would go beyond their competence.

Despite of the criticism one could bring to the approach of the *Corte Costituzionale* in its judgment No. 138 with regard to the interpretation of Article 29 of the Italian Constitution as limited to the initial will of its authors in 1946-1947 (see ROMBOLI, "Per la Corte costituzionale le coppie omosessuali sono formazioni sociali, ma non possono accedere al matrimonio", Foro it., 2010, p. 1367 ff.), it cannot be argued that this judgment and the one from the *Corte di Cassazione* under examination are in contrast with the international obligations of Italy in the field of same-sex marriage.

On the one hand, these judgments are not at variance with the interpretation of Article 12 ECHR offered by the Strasbourg Court. Namely, the progress made in *Schalk and Kopf v. Austria* as regards the extension of the right of same-sex couples to marry, Article 12 being considered for the first time applicable to same-sex marriage is actually just an open door to a potential future enhancement of States' obligations under Article 12, provided that an European consensus is reached on the matter (in similar terms, see PUSTORINO, "Same-Sex Couples Before the ECtHR: The Right to Marriage", in GALLO, PALADINI and PUSTORINO (eds.), *Same-Sex Couples Before National, Supranational and International Jurisdictions*, Berlin / Heidelberg, 2014, p. 399 ff., pp. 403-404). In other words, Article 12 ECHR is applicable, but it does not constitute a sufficient ground for the protection of same-sex marriage in the legal system of the contracting States: this is the position of the ECtHR, recently reaffirmed in *Oliari and others v. Italy* (Applications Nos. 18766/11 and 36030/11, Judgment of 21 July 2015, para. 192). In this regard, the judgment of the *Corte di Cassazione* of 15 March 2012, which relied largely on *Schalk and Kopf v. Austria*, and attempted to go further than the approach of *Corte Costituzionale* in the judgment No. 138 of 2010, does not reinforce the protection of same-sex marriage in the Italian legal system. According to this judgment a same-sex marriage celebrated abroad "exists", but still does not produce effects in the Italian legal system. Therefore, the reasoning of the *Corte di Cassazione* is correct as far as it considers that neither ECtHR case law, nor the judgment No. 4184 of 2012 of *Corte di Cassazione* bring any significant development justifying a fresh referral to the *Corte Costituzionale* of the denial of access to marriage for same-sex couples.

On the other hand, the position of Italian courts relating to same-sex marriage is not in contrast with Article 9 EU Charter, even though this provision asserts the right to marry without any specific reference to the sex of the future spouses. One cannot underestimate that Article 9 EU Charter refers to the national laws governing its exercise and that, according to the *Explanations relating to the Charter of Fundamental Rights* drawn up under the authority of the Praesidium of the Convention which drafted the Charter, "[t]his Article neither prohibits nor imposes the granting of the status of marriage to unions between people of the same sex". Therefore, in the absence of a national law awarding access to marriage to same-sex couples, Article 9 EU Charter does not apply – a limitation fully acknowledged by the *Corte di Cassazione* in its judgement No. 4184 of 2012.

However, the cautious approach of both the *Corte Costituzionale* and the *Corte di Cassazione* concerning same-sex marriage cannot be intended as a passive attitude as regards the protection of same-sex unions. After the recognition of same-sex couples as a "social group" – thus entitled, under Article 2 of the Constitution, to the fundamental right to obtain legal recognition of their relationship (Judgment No. 138, *cit. supra*) – in its more recent judgment No. 170 of 2014 (*cit. supra*), the *Corte Costituzionale* urged the legislator to promptly introduce a general regulation of same-sex unions, in order to avoid, as a result of gender reassignment of one of the spouses, the passage from a situation in which the spouses "enjoy the utmost legal protection" as a married couple, to a situation "in which protection is absolutely uncertain".

Subsequently, in the judgment of 21 April 2015 No. 8097, the *Corte di Cassazione* – ruling on the merits of the case at the origin of *Corte Costituzionale* judgment No. 170 of 2014 – took an unexpected stand and cancelled the annotation in the civil status registry of the marriage dissolution caused by the gender reassignment of one of the claimants. Therefore, the *Corte di Cassazione* maintained the recognition of the claimants' matrimonial rights and duties until such time as the Italian law provides an alternative regulation of their status as a same-sex couple, allowing for an appropriate protection of their mutual rights and duties. While at a first glance this judgement might seem as utterly incoherent with the position on same-sex marriage expressed in the judgment of 9 February 2015 No. 2400, upon closer examination – and noticing in particular that both judgments were adopted by the same section, with the participation of the same president and judge rapporteur – one has to conclude that the *Corte di Cassazione* is exerting the highest pressure on the Italian legislature to fill in the existing legal void in the protection of same-sex unions. Indeed, the contradiction in the Italian legal system to which the judgments of 9 February 2015 No. 2400 and of 21 April 2015 No. 8097 of the *Corte di Cassazione* may lead, can only be solved through the enactment of a law providing for the recognition and protection of same-sex unions. The need for a prompt intervention of the legislature was also highlighted by the Strasbourg Court in *Oliari and others v. Italy* (*cit. supra*, para. 185) (the Italian text of the decision is published in RDI, 2015, p. 660 ff.).

ANDREEA MARIA ROSU

XIII. INTERNATIONAL CRIMINAL LAW

Terrorist enlistment – Terrorist recruitment – Interpretation of domestic criminal law in accordance with international treaties – Council of Europe Convention on the Prevention of Terrorism – International Convention against the Recruitment, Use, Financing and Training of Mercenaries

Corte di Cassazione (Sez. I penale), 9 September 2015, No. 40699
Criminal proceedings against Elezi Elvis and Halili el Mahdi

With the judgment under review the *Corte di Cassazione* has for the first time provided important clarifications concerning the interpretation of Article 270 *quater* of the Italian Criminal Code and, more specifically, of the expression "*arruolamento con finalità di terrorismo*" ("enlistment for terrorist purposes") included therein.

The case concerns the attempt, allegedly undertaken by Elezi Elvis, an Albanian citizen living in Turin, to enlist Ben Ammar Mahmoud – a Moroccan national resident in Como (under-age at the time of the events) – in the terrorist group "Islamic State of Iraq and Levant" (ISIL or Daesh) with the aim of conducting acts of violence for terrorist purposes in the on-going armed conflict in Syria. Although it was undisputed that the minor never fled Italy for Syria, nor joined any military or paramilitary forces, Italian authorities in charge of the investigations concluded that consistent evidence existed to affirm the attempt made by Elezi Elvis, with the help of his uncle, Elezi Alban (an Albanian citizen and resident) to facilitate the arrival of Ben Ammar Mahmoud in Syria in order to join the ISIL ranks.

Investigative authorities relied, in particular, on several wiretaps to demonstrate the frequent contacts that occurred in the first half of 2014 between Elezi Elvis and Ben Ammar Mahmoud and the willingness of the latter to join the *jihad*. Based on wiretapping, investigators also concluded that a meeting presumably took place on 17 April 2014 in Turin between Elezi Elvis, the minor and two other individuals and that arrangements had been made for a second meeting involving Elezi Elvis, Elezi Alban, and Ben Ammar Mahmoud. Eventually, this second meeting, scheduled on 15 June 2014, was called off due to the minor's second thoughts over his decision to join ISIL. Investigators also focused on other elements as additional proofs of Elezi Elvis and Elezi Alban's links to ISIL, among which the active role allegedly played by them in the enlistment of another Moroccan citizen, El Abboubi Abbas, in 2013. Concerning Elezi Alban's role in facilitating the arrival of foreign fighters in Syria, they also adduced the assistance he provided to his brother-in-law, Balliu Idajet, in joining ISIL, as well as, more generally, some conversations hinting at his links with religious radicalism. According to the Public Prosecutor in charge of the investigations, these circumstances, considered together, amounted to tangible proof of the web of relations existing among ISIL members, Elezi Alban, and Elezi Envis, and allowed to "read" the conduct of the suspect with respect to Ben Ammar Mahamoud as an attempt to "enlistment for terroristic purposes".

On 26 February 2015, the *Giudice per le indagini preliminari* at the *Tribunale di Brescia* confirmed the charges formulated by the Public Prosecutor and ordered the provisional arrest of Elezi Elvis. On 24 April 2015, however, the *Tribunale del riesame di Brescia* annulled the pre-trial detention order against the accused based on the lack of sufficient evidence supporting the criminal charge. According to the *Tribunale*, in fact, the investigations had not adequately demonstrated that Elezi Elvis and his uncle had the authority to enlist anyone into the ISIL military or paramilitary ranks and/or had been directly in contact with any other individual having such a capacity. In addition, it was unlikely that the enlisting process could have actually occurred without the members of ISIL having verified the real intentions of the person interested in joining the organization. The *Tribunale* also found that evidence was lacking with respect to the decisive role allegedly played by Elezi Alban in the events leading to Balliu Idajet's decision to join ISIL. As to the applicable legal framework, the *Tribunale* further doubted the correctness of the charge of "attempt" with respect to the crime of enlistment for terrorism purposes, given that such an approach would excessively anticipate the threshold of criminal liability. Finally, it also declined to qualify Elezi Elvis's conduct in terms of "incitement", given that, at the time of the events – that is, before the amendments introduced by D.Lgs. No. 7 of 18 February 2015 – the act of joining military ranks for terrorism purposes did not amount to a crime.

The Public Prosecutor challenged the decision issued by the *Tribunale* before the *Corte di Cassazione* on the ground of the alleged mistakes in the application of the law and incorrect interpretation of the facts at stake.

In its judgment, which eventually upheld the Public Prosecutor's appeal, the Supreme Court focused on two main aspects: the meaning of the expression "enlistment for terrorism purposes", and the punishability of the related conduct in terms of "attempt" as per Article 56 of the Italian Criminal Code.

As to the first point, the Court endorsed the Public Prosecutor's view that Article 270 *quater* should be read and interpreted taking into account the broader and complex legal framework related to terrorist offences, including pertinent international rules. In particular, the Court made express reference to the Council of Europe Convention on the Prevention of Terrorism of 16 May 2005 (which has been signed – but not ratified – by Italy on 8 June 2005), which oriented the introduction of terrorist offences into the Italian legal system, made by DL No. 144 of 27 July 2005 (converted by Law No. 155 of 31 July 2005).

Pursuant to the *Cassazione*'s reasoning, whilst international rules – even when driving domestic legislative action – cannot suffice *per se* to interpret those criminal norms autonomously set by the national legislator, they can nonetheless provide a useful guide in identifying the *rationale* behind their adoption. Furthermore, the very transnational nature of international terrorism and the consequent need to ensure consistency between legal responses in different countries would also support the interpreter's need to take into due account international norms setting common standards.

Having established this, the *Corte di Cassazione* observed that both the 2005 Council of Europe Convention and other domestic provisions aimed at punishing terrorist offences reveal a general attitude to criminalize conducts which are preparatory to the commission of future offences, such as training and recruitment. The Supreme Court thus considered this "anticipative approach" as a general guiding principle, against which other interpretative criteria are to be applied (and tested), such as Articles 12 and 14 of the General Provisions on the Law (*Disposizioni sulla legge in generale*, Royal Decree No. 262 of 16 March 1942). The Supreme Court, in particular, excluded that the term "*arruolare*" ("enlisting") in Article 270 *quater* could be interpreted according to its textual meaning, which refers to the act of formally joining the armed forced. The purpose of this provision – i.e. to counter acts of violence for terrorist purposes, which, in practice, are often perpetrated by paramilitary groups or even cells composed of very few people – would indeed militate against such a reading. In the *Cassazione*'s view, moreover, the lack of references to the notion of "enlisting" in the 2005 Council of Europe Convention on Terrorism – although not providing binding guidance – would further strengthen this approach.

Once excluded that the term "enlistment" should be interpreted pursuant to its textual meaning, the Court further rejected the argument made by the Public Prosecutor, according to which the term "enlistment" would equate to that of "recruitment", as defined by Article 6 of the 2005 Council of Europe Convention. In reaching this conclusion, the Court paid particular attention to the fact that the Italian legislator has expressly used the term "recruitment" in Article 4 of the Law No. 210 of 12 May 1995 incorporating the 1989 International Convention against the Recruitment, Use, Financing and Training of Mercenaries into the domestic legal system. According to the said provision, the offence of "recruitment" would have an all-embracing and comprehensive meaning and would therefore include both the stage antecedent to the conclusion of the agreement between the recruiter and the potential member, and the subsequent act of joining a terrorist organization. Accordingly, the deliberate choice of the word "enlistment" in Article 270 *quater* would indicate the legislator's willingness to not excessively anticipate the threshold of criminal liability to include the mere proposal, especially in light of the need (strictly inherent to counter-terrorism measures) to distinguish the act of "enlistment" – amounting to a criminal offence – from mere proselytism.

Based on a sort of reasoning "by elimination", the Supreme Court thus concluded that the term "enlistment" in Article 270 *quater* should be interpreted to mean "engagement", that is the conclusion of a serious agreement between, on the one hand, the person making a proposal for participating in acts of violence or sabotage for terrorist purposes and, on the other hand, the person interested in joining the organization. Pursuant to the Court, in fact, the potential harm inherent to the conclusion of such a serious agreement would justify *per se* the criminalization of the relevant conduct. The *Cassazione* further specified that the conclusion of a "serious agreement", besides being characterized by the goal of conducting acts of violence or sabotage for terrorist purposes, necessarily requires both the proponent's actual capacity to enlist the person in the organization and the adherent's resolution to join it (thus, partially confirming in this last respect the reasoning of the *Tribunale del riesame*).

This interpretation would be supported, *inter alia*, by the recent amendment of Article 270 *quater* by means of D.Lgs. No. 7/2015 (*cit. supra*), thereby punishing the conduct of the person "enlisted" in the organization. Pursuant to the Court's reasoning, in fact, this legislative reform well illustrates the actual goal of the provision, that is, to prevent the increasing harmful potential of the group, which would result from the addition of a new "member".

The *Corte di Cassazione* relied on the aforementioned interpretation to conclude that the *Tribunale di Brescia* erroneously interpreted and applied Article 270 *quater* in the case concerning Elezi Elvis. Pursuant to the Supreme Court, the *Tribunale* should have established whether a "serious agreement" had been reached between the accused and Ben Ammar and, accordingly, whether the offence provided in Article 270 *quater* had been committed. To the contrary, the erroneous interpretation of said provision on the part of the *Tribunale del riesame* (which linked the commission of the crime to the occurrence of further events besides the conclusion of a serious agreement) had led it to undertake an "incomplete" assessment of the facts and evidence at stake.

The Supreme Court also disagreed with the *Tribunale*'s reluctant approach related to the punishment of the "mere attempt" of enlisting. Based on its interpretation of Article 270 *quater*, the Court upheld the possibility of punishing the mere "attempt" of enlisting a person for conducting acts of violence or sabotage for the purpose of terrorism. The potential harm inherent to the conclusion of a "serious agreement" for the aforementioned purposes would indeed allow for an anticipation of the threshold of punishment (i.e., so as to encompass also the mere attempt) any time a progression in the activity leading to the conclusion and realization of the said agreement can be identified.

The decision under review is noteworthy at least in two respects. On the one hand, within the Italian domestic legal order, the pronouncement under comment is praiseworthy insofar as it attempts to clarify for the first time the exact content of Article 270 *quater*, whose vagueness has been frequently challenged by commentators (see CAVALIERE, "Considerazioni critiche intorno al D.L. antiterrorismo n. 7 del 18 febbraio 2015", Diritto penale contemporaneo, 2015, p. 7 ff.). This "clarifying approach", moreover, comes at a time in which, due to the recent amendments introduced by D.Lgs. No. 7/2015, it is likely that this provision will be increasingly invoked in criminal proceedings at the domestic level. On the other, from an international law point of view, it may be argued that the decision in question could "contribute" to develop relevant subsequent practice, under Article 31(3)(b) of the 1969 Vienna Convention on the Law of Treaties (VCLT), with respect to the interpretation of those treaty norms orienting the adoption of the provisions at stake by the Italian legislator. This specific assumption, however, may be questioned based on the fact that the 2005 Council of Europe Convention on the Prevention of Terrorism merely refers to the conduct of "recruitment" and not "enlistment" and that the Italian Supreme Court expressly distinguished between these two conducts. Furthermore, it might be doubted whether acts of organs of a signatory State, which, however, has not ratified an international instrument, may have any "value" under Article 31(3)(b) VCLT. This provision seems to imply that, to be relevant, subsequent practice should be performed by the "parties to a treaty", that is, the States that, pursuant to Article 2(g) VCLT, have consented to be bound by a treaty and for which the treaty is in force (NOLTE, "First Report on Subsequent Agreements and Subsequent Practice in Relation to Treaty Interpretation", UN Doc. A/CN.4/660, 19 March 2013, para. 117).

That said, the reasoning of the Supreme Court still raises some criticism. First, the Court's reliance on existing international rules appears disjointed. Whilst the Court based its interpretation of the word "enlistment" on the "guiding principles" embodied in the Council of Europe Convention for the Prevention of Terrorism, it excluded that such Convention could provide further guidance for the interpretation of Article 270 *quater*, given its domestic "autonomous" nature. Secondly, the Supreme Court's distinction between "enlistment" and "recruitment", while fully consistent with the textual wording of Article 270 *quater*, ends up distancing the domestic legal framework from the international rules orienting its adoption (arguably, in apparent contrast with the Court's resort to these rules as relevant interpretative principles) and adding further complexity in a field – that of terrorist offences – which is *per se* characterized by the "nebulous" borders existing between distinct criminal offences. Moreover, the Supreme Court's use of the textual criterion of interpretation to distinguish between the conducts of "enlistment" and "recruitment" is also unconvincing: the Court's stance appears, in fact, hardly reconcilable, at least from a logical point of view, with its initial refusal to interpret the word "enlistment" pursuant to its literal meaning.

Some doubts may also be raised with respect to the interpretation given by the Supreme Court of the term "recruitment", as embodied in the International Convention against the Recruitment, Use, Financing and Training of Mercenaries. The Court directly relied on Article 4 of Law No. 210/1995 instead of interpreting the treaty itself in compliance with the rules on treaty interpretation as codified in Articles 31-32 VCLT. It may be argued that, if applied to the recalled conventional text, such interpretative criteria – which also require to take into account all pertinent rules of international law applicable between the parties, as well as subsequent State practice – could have lead the Supreme Court to a different conclusion.

Additionally, the *Corte di Cassazione*'s mere hint to the necessary respect for the fundamental principles embodied in the Constitution could have certainly benefited from a more thorough analysis. The "anticipative approach" that the Supreme Court has upheld also in light of relevant international law can in fact raise doubts concerning its compatibility with the principles of harm ("*offensività*") and legal certainty ("*determinatezza*"). The Court's quick reference to the risks underpinning the "anticipative" reading of Article 270 *quater* – especially in terms of distinguishability between the criminal offence of "enlistment" and mere proselytism – similarly lacked any thoughtful consideration. Rather, the Supreme Court seems to have relied, in practice, on the "anticipatory" approach undertaken at the international level as a sufficient ground to not further question its effective compatibility with domestic constitutional principles (as well as other international rules, to which Italy is bound, that enshrine or have been interpreted to embody similar principles). Moreover, the very interpretation of Article 270 *quater* upheld by the Court does not seem to foster legal certainty: one could wonder, for instance, what "serious agreement" should mean in practice. Therefore, the Supreme Court has lost an opportunity to better examine one of the most pressing issues arising out of the "emergency" approach which is increasingly driving law-making actions concerning terrorist offences (the Italian text of the decision is available at: <http://www.italgiure.giustizia.it>).

ELENA CARPANELLI

XV. INTERNATIONAL ECONOMIC LAW

Italy-Hungary Bilateral Investment Treaty of 7 February 1987 – Fair and equitable treatment of foreign investments – General principles of international investment law – Legitimate expectations of investors – Unilateral promises by States

Corte di Cassazione (Sez. III civile), 19 October 2015, No. 21085
San Marco Progetti Srl in liquidazione v. Magyar Nemzeti Vagyonkezelo, Republic of Hungary and Ministry of Finance of the Republic of Hungary

In the decision under review the *Corte di Cassazione* had the opportunity to examine whether unilateral declarations made by a State (and/or by State owned entities) may be considered capable of generating a legitimate expectation in a private foreign investor and, as a consequence, if such unilateral declarations could be the source of contractual and/or in tort liability for the State who made them.

In 1991, San Marco Progetti Srl ("Plaintiff" or "San Marco") undertook (jointly with the company Arrow Srl, which was not a party to the present dispute) to carry out two supplies of materials and services for the construction of plants for the production of airplane engines and aluminium cans in favour of the Hungarian company Elzett-Certa Zárgyárto Présöntô és Szerszámkésitô Vállalat (EC). EC was fully owned by the entity Allami Vagyonugynokseg, which – in turn – was 100% property of the Hungarian State. In order to be able to pay the price of the supplies, EC obtained a loan from the English Bank Morgan Grenfell & Co. Ltd. Such a loan was guaranteed, for 95% of its amount, by the Italian publicly owned company SACE and, for the remaining 5%, by San Marco itself.

In 1992, Hungary began a privatization process regarding State companies. Hungary further communicated to the Italian embassy in Budapest that it would guarantee the fulfilment of the obligations of the State entities that were being privatized. As a consequence, SACE withdrew its guarantee, Morgan Grenfell suspended the loan, and San Marco stopped the supply.

In order to obtain the re-activation of the supply, the Hungarian State – by means of certain declarations issued by its 100% owned newco Allami Vagyonkezelo Reszvenytarsasag (AVR), which, in turn, held 100% of the EC shares – stated that AVR "is responsible for all the debts of Elzett-Certa". Furthermore, the Hungarian Ministry for Privatizations, in a document directed to the Italian embassy in Budapest stated that "the Hungarian State will be ultimately responsible for the obligations of the Hungarian State Holding Company in the event of insolvency or liquidation of the same". Following these declarations SACE reinstated the guarantee, Morgan Grenfell issued the loan, and San Marco carried out the supply.

However, after the supply was completed but prior that the loan was reimbursed, EC was put in liquidation and AVR declared that it would not guarantee the debts of EC. As a consequence, Morgan Grenfell executed the guarantee issued by San Marco, which had to pay more than 6 million Euros to Morgan Grenfell. San

Marco, therefore, in 2005 filed a claim before the *Tribunale di Milano* in order to obtain: (i) a declaration of contractual liability of AVR, the Hungarian State, and the Ministry for Privatizations, or – alternatively – a declaration of in tort liability of them; and (ii) the reimbursement of the amount it had to pay to Morgan Greenfell. The *Tribunale*, after having affirmed its jurisdiction, rejected the claim and stated that each party was to pay its own expenses incurred in the litigation. The main reason why the claim was rejected was that the declarations by the Hungarian State (or State entities) were to be interpreted literally and therefore should be considered as mere information and not as a legal undertaking. All the parties appealed the decision before the *Corte d'Appello di Milano*. Magyar Nemzeti Vagyonkezelo (MNV, the successor of AVR), the Hungarian Ministry of Finance (which absorbed the Ministry of Privatizations), and the Hungarian State claimed that San Marco should bear all the expenses of the litigation. San Marco repeated the claims it made before the *Tribunale di Milano*. The *Corte d'Appello* rejected San Marco's claims (reaffirming the reasoning held by the Court of first instance) and stated that San Marco had also to pay the expenses of the litigation.

San Marco further appealed before the *Corte di Cassazione*. The *Corte di Cassazione* rejected the view expressed in the two preceding decisions. On the basis of the canons of contract interpretation provided by Italian law (Articles 1362 and 1363 of the Italian Civil Code, which are applicable also to unilateral declarations), the *Corte di Cassazione* stated that the characterization of the declarations made by Hungary (and/or Hungary's owned entities) to mere information was mistaken. Notably, the *Corte di Cassazione* recalled the rule of legitimate expectations in contract law (as well as the well-known principle of legal certainty) and stated that to qualify the declarations made by the Hungarian State (and entities) as mere information would constitute an "unacceptable twisting of the protection of third parties". Therefore, the unilateral declarations made by Hungary should not be construed in a literal way, but should take into account the context in which they were issued. In the *Corte*'s view, San Marco assumed the risks related to the performance of the supply only after having received certain reassurances by the Hungarian State (and/or State entities). The declarations by the Hungarian State had had the direct effect of persuading San Marco to carry out the supply and therefore could be not considered as having no legal value. This could give rise to both contractual and in tort liability. For the above reasons the *Corte di Cassazione* quashed the appeals judgment and referred again the dispute to the *Corte d'Appello di Milano*.

This decision deserves particular attention from the perspective of international investment law. In the present case, the *Corte di Cassazione* dealt with a dispute concerning a foreign investment according to Article 1 of the Italy-Hungary Bilateral Investment Treaty, signed on 7 February 1987, in force from 6 September 1989 to 10 January 2008 (and thus applicable to the case at hand *ratione temporis*), and implemented by Italy through Law No. 448 of 1989. Quite interestingly, this decision occurred in the uncommon circumstance of an investment dispute brought before a domestic judge having the same nationality as the investor. It is therefore worth verifying whether the solution reached by the *Corte di Cassazione* (which has been dealt with from a purely national perspective, i.e. only on the basis of the Italian rules on contractual interpretation, contractual liability and in tort liability) is in compliance with the relevant standards of international investment law.

Article 2(2) of the Italy-Hungary BIT states that each of the contracting parties will always provide foreign investors with fair and equitable treatment (FET). The source and content of this standard of treatment is highly controversial in international legal scholarship. As it has been convincingly argued, FET is best conceived of as a general principle of international investment law embodying certain other principles, such as due process of law, the protection of legitimate expectations and proportionality (see, also for the debate concerning the nature of the FET standard, PALOMBINO, *Il trattamento "giusto ed equo" degli investimenti stranieri*, Bologna, 2012, pp. 61-171).

For our purposes, it is necessary to focus on the principle of the protection of legitimate expectations. From such a general principle, international arbitral tribunals have derived concrete rules to be applied on a case-by-case basis (PALOMBINO, *cit. supra*, pp. 101-148), namely: (i) the obligation to protect legitimate expectations arising from a contract (*MTD Equity Sdn. Bhd and MTD Chile S.A. v. Chile*, ICSID Case No. ARB/01/7, Decision on Annulment of 21 March 2007, paras 160-167); (ii) the obligation to protect legitimate expectations arising from national laws (*Suez, Sociedad General de Aguas de Barcelona, S.A. and Vivendi Universal, S.A. v. Argentine Republic*, ICSID Case No. ARB/03/19, Decision on Liability of 30 July 2010, paras. 180-248); (iii) the obligation to protect legitimate expectations arising from a certain interpretation of a national law (*Duke Energy International Peru Investments No. 1 Ltd v. Republic of Peru*, ICSID Case No. ARB/03/28, Award and Partial Dissenting Opinions of 25 July 2008, para. 231); and (iv) the obligation to protect legitimate expectations arising from unilateral promises (*Total S.A. v. Argentina*, ICSID Case No. ARB/04/1, Decision on Liability, 27 December 2010, para. 128; PALOMBINO, *cit. supra*, pp. 108-132).

Remarkably enough, in the case at hand the *Corte di Cassazione* applied the latter rule. From a purely practical perspective, therefore, the judgment under comment is fully in compliance with international standards: by applying the provisions of the Italian Civil Code, the *Corte di Cassazione* was able to protect the legitimate expectations of the foreign investor (San Marco) against the host State (Hungary) in a way which is in all respect comparable to that required by international investment law.

From a theoretical point of view, however, the approach followed by the *Corte di Cassazione* may raise some concerns. Indeed, had the standards of protection offered by Italian law been lower than those set forth by international law, the *Corte di Cassazione*, by applying the former instead of the latter, would have deprived the plaintiff of the protection it enjoyed under international law (KOTUBY, "General Principles of Law, International Due Process, and the Modern Role of Private International Law", Duke Journal of Comparative & International Law, 2013, p.

411 ff., pp. 415 and 437). For this reason, in future disputes concerning foreign investments, Italian courts should pay greater attention to the relevant standards of international investment law. In this respect, it is worth recalling that the fact that the parties do not mention these standards in their pleadings should not be a decisive factor, as Italian judges are free to identify the rules applicable to the dispute at hand regardless of what has been pleaded by the parties under the well-known principle *iura novit curia* (Article 113 of the Italian Code of Civil Procedure) (the Italian text of the judgment is available at: <http://www.italgiure.giustizia.it>).

GIOVANNI ZARRA

XVII. RELATIONSHIP BETWEEN MUNICIPAL AND INTERNATIONAL LAW

Relationship between the Italian Constitution and the European Convention on Human Rights – Article 117(1) of the Italian Constitution – Consistent interpretation – Hierarchy of norms – Confiscation without conviction

Corte Costituzionale, 26 March 2015, No. 49

With decision No. 49 of 26 March 2015 the *Corte Costituzionale* clarified the relationship between the Italian Constitution, on the one hand, and the European Convention on Human Rights (ECHR) – and, thus, the case law of the European Court on Human Rights (ECtHR) – on the other.

The *Corte Costituzionale* was asked to take position on the constitutionality of Article 44(2) of DPR No. 380 of 6 June 2001, which states that "a final judgement of a criminal Court, that establishes that unlawful parcelling has occurred, shall order the confiscation of the land unlawfully parcelled and of the work unlawfully built". The rationale of this provision is to avoid that the unlawful parcelling of a land could bring an economic advantage to the author. In other words, if someone carries out an unlawful land development, such a violation implies the confiscation of the land. The measure must be adopted by the criminal court that has jurisdiction on the case. The Italian criminal courts' case law on the point is coherent in ordering a confiscation measure, either in case the author of the offence is found guilty, or the offence has been time-barred.

The ECtHR has been called to take position on the consistency of confiscation measures adopted on the ground of Article 44(2) of DPR No. 380/2001 with the ECHR, particularly with Article 7(1) ECHR and Article 1 of the First Additional Protocol to the ECHR. A comprehensive analysis of ECtHR case law falls outside the scope of the present paper. Notwithstanding, it is necessary to give some brief remarks on two key cases decided by the Strasbourg Court on the point: *Sud Fondi Srl and Others v. Italy*, Application No. 75909/01, Judgment of 20 January 2009; and *Varvara v. Italy*, Application No. 17475/09, Judgment of 29 October 2013. In the former case the European Court found a violation of Article 7(1) ECHR and Article 1 of the First Additional Protocol on the ground of the lack of clarity and foreseeability of the national statutory provision in question. Great relevance was given to the circumstance that the accused's error as to the legality of the building projects had been, in the Court of Cassation's view, inevitable. In the aftermath of the *Sud Fondi* case, and of judgement No. 239 of 16 July 2009 of the *Corte Costituzionale*, the *Corte di Cassazione* interpreted the provision at stake in the sense that the confiscation can be imposed on an accused person if the proceeding ends with a conviction or even without a prison sentence, insofar as the judge has ascertained the liability of the accused (*Corte di Cassazione (Sez. III penale), Criminal proceedings against Angelo Grova and others*, 16 February 2011, No. 5857). In the *Varvara* decision the ECtHR found a violation of the ECHR by Italian authorities for adopting a confiscation without conviction measure. More precisely, the Strasbourg Court "fail[ed] to see how punishing a defendant whose trial has not resulted in a conviction could be compatible with Article 7 of the Convention, which provision clearly sets out the principle of legality in criminal law" (para. 67).

The *Corte di Cassazione* addressed a referral order to the *Corte Costituzionale*, insofar as the confiscation of the plots had to be adopted "in parallel with the criminal judgement ruling that the offence was time-barred" (Judgment No. 49 of 2015, para. 1 of the conclusions on points of law). The *Corte di Cassazione* was convinced that the *Varvara* decision precluded the confiscation of property unless a conviction for the offence of unlawful parcelling is imposed. As a consequence, the *Corte di Cassazione* asked the *Corte Costituzionale* whether the substantial ban on confiscation without conviction, stemming from the ECtHR case law, was consistent with some constitutional provisions, particularly Articles 2, 9, 32, 41, 42 and 117. Such a referral aimed to a declaration of inconsistency of Article 44(2) DPR No. 380/2001, interpreted in the light of the *Varvara* judgement with the Constitution. In other words, the Italian Supreme Court challenged the norm in order to make the *Corte Costituzionale* declare a violation of the Constitution by Article 7 ECHR as interpreted by the ECtHR in *Varvara* case.

The second referral to the *Corte Costituzionale*, made by the *Tribunale di Teramo*, pursued a different, and to a certain extent opposite, purpose. The *Tribunale* asked the Court to take position on the consistency of Article 44(2) DPR No. 380/2001 with Article 117(1) of the Italian Constitution, as integrated by Article 7 ECHR. In this context, it is worth noting that Article 117(1) – after the reform of Title V of the Constitution – binds both national and regional legislatures, when drafting a law, to the respect of international obligations incumbent on Italy. Article 117(1) was interpreted by the *Corte Costituzionale* in the well-known twin decisions Nos. 348 and 349 of 22 October 2007 (see IYIL, 2007, p. 292 ff. with a comment by CATALDI) as requiring any judge, who has to apply a domestic norm conflicting with a ECHR (as interpreted by the ECtHR) to refer the case to the *Corte Costituzionale*. This should verify the consistency of the relevant conventional norm with the Constitution and, if this scrutiny is passed, should state the unconstitutionality of the domestic provision, as such a provision, violating the conventional norm, would violate Article 117(1).

The *Corte Costituzionale* decided to examine the two questions jointly and held that they were inadmissible. Notwithstanding, the Court took the chance to reconstruct and define the actual relationship between the ECHR and the Italian Constitution on the one hand, and the path that common judges have to follow when called to apply domestic provisions conflicting with conventional norms, on the other. A diachronic analysis of the *Corte Costituzionale* case law on the point could be helpful to assess whether the approach of the Court to the ECHR has changed (and in which direction).

As already mentioned, the twin decisions of 2007 drew up a precise and stringent link between European Convention and Constitution, based on hierarchy of norms arguments. The ECHR lies on a level which is lower than the Constitution, but higher than legislative measures. In other words, "Article 117(1) ultimately created a flexible reference to treaty provisions which may from time to time be relevant, giving life and substantive content to those international law obligations generically evoked and through them to the underlying principle, such as to be commonly classified as *interposed provisions*" (Judgment No. 349 of 2007, para. 6.2. of the conclusions on points of law; emphasis added). As a consequence, ordinary courts, in case of conflict between domestic law and the ECHR, should try to give an interpretation of the national provision in accordance with the conventional one, respecting the limits imposed by the literal wording of the provisions. If such an interpretation cannot fill the gap between national and international provisions, the courts cannot apply the ECHR norm directly, but they have to make a referral to the *Corte Costituzionale*.

Such a system, based on the aforesaid principle of consistent interpretation ("*interpretazione conforme*") implies that ordinary judges are obliged to give to the relevant provisions of the ECHR the same interpretation given by the Strasbourg Court, inasmuch as "definitive uniformity in application is guaranteed by the centralized interpretation of the [ECHR] attributed to the [ECtHR], which has the last word" (Judgment No. 349 of 2007, para. 6.2. of the conclusions on points of law). Only if the ECHR provision, as interpreted by the Strasbourg Court, is in direct contrast with the national relevant provision, must the ordinary judge refer the question to the *Corte Costituzionale* in order to solve such an antinomy.

It is worth noting that, in the decision under discussion, the *Corte Costituzionale* seems not to confirm such a system. This is true on two connected grounds: first, ordinary judges are not always bound by the interpretation given to the ECHR norms by the Strasbourg Court; and, second, the case law of the ECtHR can be relevant in domestic judgments only if some criteria are fulfilled.

Following the reasoning of the *Corte Costituzionale*, it is not "for the Strasbourg Court to determine the meaning of the national law, whereas, on the contrary, the European Court must assess whether the national law, as defined and applied by the national authorities, has led to violations of the higher provisions of the ECHR in the cases brought before it for examination" (Judgment No. 49 of 2015, para. 4 of the conclusions on points of law). Moreover, ordinary courts are obliged to interpret national law in a manner compatible with the ECHR only if such an interpretation is consistent with the Constitution. In the Court's wording, "this manner of proceeding reflects the *axiological predominance* of the Constitution over the ECHR" (*ibid.*; emphasis added).

Moving from a strictly dualistic perspective, the *Corte Costituzionale* conceives of international conventional law norms, binding Italy, as sub-constitutional in nature. As a consequence, any conflict between such provisions and the Constitution (or constitutional values) has to be solved on the ground of axiological arguments. The domestic legal system does not allow the entrance of conventional provisions inconsistent with constitutional norms (Article 117(1), similarly to Article 10(1) of the Constitution for general international law, should therefore contain an implicit safeguard clause of the constitutional legal system). Such a conclusion seems to be the only possible consequence of the above-mentioned axiological predominance of the Constitution. If such a reasoning is correct, it seems that the *Corte Costituzionale* switches from a hierarchy of norms argument to a values argument. This change of perspective obviously involves the whole question of the relationship between ECHR and the Constitution.

One may wonder whether the axiological approach adopted by the *Corte Costituzionale* creates a conflict with the European Convention system or not. It has to be observed that the Italian Constitution and the ECHR protect the same values – the fundamental rights of individuals – and that the conventional legal standards of human rights protection amount to minimum standards: "nothing in this Convention shall be construed as limiting or derogating from any of the human rights and fundamental freedoms which may be ensured under the laws of any High Contracting Party or under any other agreement to which it is a party" (Article 53 ECHR). As a consequence, from a theoretical point of view, no conflict of values arises from the relationship between conventional provisions and constitutional provisions, if the latter guarantee higher fundamental rights protection than those stemming from the Convention. On the contrary, if the Italian Constitution provides for lower standards, such an inconsistency could be envisaged. In practice, an antinomy between a constitutional provision and a conventional one – as interpreted by the ECtHR – could be at stake only when the Constitution imposes a balancing between different constitutional values, which results in a limitation of a fundamental right guaranteed by the ECHR. Such a situation was to some extent envisaged by the *Corte Costituzionale* in the decision *Ministro degli Interni v. Lorenzon Guido Luciano*, 19 November 2012, No. 264 (see IYIL, 2013, p. 454 ff., with a comment by PALOMBINO; and NESSI, ILDC 2062 (IT 2012)). As the Court observed, "the comparison between the protection provided for under the Convention and the constitutional protection of fundamental rights must be carried out whilst aiming to *achieve the broadest scope for guarantees*" (para. 4.1 of the conclusions on points of law; emphasis added). Such a concept "must be deemed to include the necessary balancing against other interests protected under constitutional law, that is, with other provisions of the Constitution which in turn guarantee fundamental rights liable to be affected by the expansion of individual protection" (*ibid.*). In the present case, and relying on the concept of broadest scope for guarantees, the Court could have reached the same result without introducing the critical concept of axiological predominance. It has to be considered that in the present case, the Court could have made a balancing between the relevant interests, insofar as the right to protection of property – as laid down in Article 1 of the First Additional of Protocol and in Article 42 of the Constitution – could have been put in balance with environment protection as well as with the right to health. In the broadest scope for guarantees perspective, the Court would have easily struck the balance between the aforesaid constitutional relevant rights and interests, without focusing on the axiological predominance of the Constitution over the ECHR (see RUGGERI, "Fissati nuovi paletti dalla Consulta a riguardo del rilievo della CEDU in ambito interno", Diritto Penale Contemporaneo, 2015, pp. 6-7).

It is very important to investigate the reasons of the above-mentioned *revirement*. Such reasons relate to the role of ordinary courts in the matter of application of ECHR norms, in the view of the *Corte Costituzionale*. From the twin decisions, the national judge – as already said – had to make a consistent interpretation of the domestic norm with the ECHR provision; only in the case where such an operation did not manage to solve the antinomy, the ordinary judge had to refer the question to the *Corte Costituzionale*. Instead, the present decision calls on ordinary courts to follow a more complicated procedure. National judges have to interpret national law in a manner compatible with the ECHR, but such an interpretation "is obviously subordinate to the priority task of reading the law in a manner compatible with the Constitution". In other words, ordinary courts have to make two different hermeneutical operations: on the one hand, they have to give a *conventionally* oriented interpretation of the domestic law and, on the other, they have to give a *constitutionally* oriented interpretation. The third point is matching the two different interpretations, and if the former is inconsistent with the latter, the national judge must refer the question of the constitutionality of the implementing law of the ECHR to the *Corte Costituzionale* (Law No. 848 of 4 August 1955), "as it is that law which permits the incorporation of such a rule into Italian law" (Judgment No. 49 of 2015, para. 5 of the conclusions on points of law).

In the view of the *Corte Costituzionale*, hermeneutical parameters stemming from the Constitution and from the ECHR must be applied "also to the judgments of the Strasbourg Court when it is not possible to infer directly from them [...] the effective principle of law which the Strasbourg Court sought to assert in order to resolve the specific case" (Judgment No. 49 of 2015, para. 6.1 of the conclusions on points of law). One might wonder whether the aim of the ECtHR, when called to assess the conventional consistency of a national measure, is to assert principles of law, taking into account the case-by-case approach followed by the Court. Moreover the use of interpretation criteria derived from domestic law (more precisely, the Constitution) seems not to be correct in relation to international conventional norms or case law based on such norms.

The *Corte Costituzionale*'s reasoning goes beyond such a statement, insofar as it asks the ordinary courts to situate "the individual ruling within *the continuous flow of case law* from the Strasbourg Court in order to infer a meaning from the ruling that can be reconciled with that case law, and which does not under any circumstances violate the Constitution" (para. 6.1 of the conclusions on points of law; emphasis added). In other words, in the Court's perspective, national judges should autonomously verify whether the relevant decision of the Strasbourg Court in the single case is coherent with (and therefore can be situated in) the *continuous flow* of the ECtHR case law. The above-described system, stemming from the decision under discussion, attributes a very complicated role to ordinary courts, when applying domestic law in matters object of decision by the Strasbourg Court. Moreover, the *Corte Costituzionale* has stated that ordinary courts cannot be considered as "passive recipients of an interpretative command issued elsewhere in the form of a court ruling, irrespective of the conditions that gave rise to it" (para. 7 of the conclusions on points of law). As a consequence, the national judge is necessarily bound by a European Court decision only if such a decision is adopted with regard to the proceeding of which the judge is subsequently apprised. In any other case, in fact, the ordinary courts have to comply exclusively with the "consolidated European case law concerning the relevant Convention provisions" (*ibid.*). In other words, ordinary courts are bound by Strasbourg Court interpretation of conventional provision, only insofar as such an interpretation arises from *consolidated law*.

Therefore, the notion of *consolidated law* has to be determined in the view of the *Corte Costituzionale*. For such a law to consolidate, a process based on the dialogue between the ECtHR and all the domestic courts called to apply the ECHR is necessary. In the reasoning of the Court, the correctness of this approach should be indirectly confirmed by the fact that Additional Protocol No. 16 to the ECHR (not yet in force), in providing for an advisory procedure in front of the Strasbourg Court, expressly states the non-binding nature of the opinions adopted. As a consequence, it can be confirmed that "an initial engagement based on argumentation within a perspective of cooperation between the courts rather than the hierarchical imposition of a particular interpretation concerning questions of principle which have not yet become established within case law" (*ibid.*).

Once again, the idea that the ECtHR case law is meant to solve questions of principle is not convincing. Neither does the reasoning of the Court seem to be persuasive, to the extent that it recalls Article 28 ECHR and the concept of well-established law used therein. Such a provision, in fact, is intended to define the competence of the three judges Committees, which are called to take position on the admissibility of individual applications. No indications can, thus, be found in such a provision on the concept of consolidated law, as well-established law in Article 28 perspective is considerably different from the concept of consolidated law in the *Corte Costituzionale* perspective. The same can be said about the idea of the Court that Grand Chamber judgments are the expression of consolidated law. If, on the one hand, it is true that Grand Chamber decisions are particularly authoritative, on the other it is not necessary that the Grand Chamber makes a decision on a certain question, to make the case law consolidated. Even Chamber decisions can be the expression of consolidated law, insofar as no intervention of the Grand Chamber on the point is asked in the conventional system.

The *Corte Costituzionale* itself recognizes the difficulty in affirming that a certain judicial interpretation of conventional norms has become consolidated. To this purpose, the Court indicates to ordinary courts some useful criteria to determine whether a particular decision of the Strasbourg Court is the expression of consolidated law or not. Such criteria are:

> "the creativity of the principle asserted, compared to the traditional approach of European case law; the potential for points of distinction or even contrast from other rulings of the Strasbourg Court; the existence of dissenting opinions, especially if fuelled by robust arguments; the fact that the decision made originates from an ordinary division and has not been endorsed by the Grand Chamber; the fact that, in the case before it, the European Court has not been able to assess the particular characteristics of the national legal system" (para. 7 of the conclusions on points of law).

Two problems arise from this statement: such criteria are mainly autonomous from the conventional system and do not give adequate relevance to the features of the system, and it is almost impossible for ordinary courts to verify the presence of such criteria in single cases. It has been argued, on the point, that the presence of dissenting opinions does not imply that the decision to which such opinions are attached cannot be considered the expression of consolidated law (see ZAGREBELSKY, "Corte Cost. n. 49/2015, giurisprudenza della Corte europea dei diritti umani, art. 117 Cost., obblighi derivanti dalla ratifica della Convenzione", available at: <www. associazionedeicostituzionalisti.it>, p. 4). As a consequence, except for the case of Grand Chamber decisions, it will be very difficult for national judges to find a consolidated case law. Nor does the reference made by the *Corte Costituzionale* to the pilot judgements seem to make sense, if one considers that a pilot judgement could be even the first decision on a certain question, insofar as it takes into account cases of structural violations that may derive from a particular domestic law or praxis (on the concept of pilot judgement, see WILDHABER, "Pilot Judgements in case of Structural or Systematic Problems at the National Level", in DEUTSCH and WOLFRUM (eds.), *The European Court of Human Rights Overwhelmed by Applications: Problems and Possible Solutions*, Berlin, 2009, p. 69 ff.).

Trying to resume the position of the *Corte Costituzionale* on the binding nature of European Court decisions for national judges, we can identify three different cases in which such judges must interpret domestic law in accordance with

Strasbourg case law: first, if the ECtHR decision refers to the specific case which has to be solved by the judge; second, if the ECtHR adopted a pilot judgment; and, thirdly, if the judge is convinced that the ECtHR decision is the expression of consolidated law. In all these cases, if the conventional interpretation of the domestic provision at stake leads to a conflict with any constitutional provision, ordinary courts cannot take into account the interpretation given by the Strasbourg Court.

From these brief remarks emerges a new and restrictive approach of the *Corte Costituzionale* to the ECHR and, consequently, to the case law of the ECtHR. One may wonder whether such an approach is pointed only to the ECHR or also to any "alien provisions" stemming from the international legal system. We would argue that an emerging trend can be envisaged, taking into account the decision under discussion and the judgment of the *Corte Costituzionale* on State immunity of 22 October 2014, No. 238 (on this judgment see the focus on the previous Volume of this Yearbook with contributions by FRANCIONI, PISILLO MAZZESCHI, BOTHE, CATALDI, and PALCHETTI). In such a decision the *Corte Costituzionale* underlined that international customary law cannot contrast with the fundamental principles of the Constitution or, rather, that Article 10(1) of the Constitution does not allow customary norms to find application in the domestic legal system, considering that the constitutional provision contains an implicit safeguard clause. In the present case, as already observed, the Court seems to trace a similar clause with a much more restrictive limitation in Article 117(1) of the Constitution. The crucial point is that the application of the interpretation developed by the *Corte Costituzionale* in judgment No. 238/2014 could bring national courts to ignore the European Court case law and, thus, the ECHR (the Italian text of the decision is published in RDI, 2015, p. 1022 ff.).

ALFREDO TERRASI

DIPLOMATIC AND PARLIAMENTARY PRACTICE

(edited by *Pietro Gargiulo* and *Marco Pertile*)[*]

III. STATES AND OTHER INTERNATIONAL LAW SUBJECTS

1. ON THE ESTABLISHMENT OF EGYPT'S EXCLUSIVE ECONOMIC ZONE AND THE ARREST OF TWO ITALIAN TRAWLERS

On 18 January 2015, two Italian trawlers (the *Jonathan* of Siracusa and the *Albachiara* of Cagliari) were arrested by the Egyptian coast guard about 36 nautical miles far from the coast of Egypt. The timely intervention of the Italian Government brought to the release of both the two vessels and their crews (except the catch) before a full day had passed since the incident. One month later, Mr. Lapo Pistelli, *Vice Ministro degli Affari esteri e della Cooperazione internazionale* (Deputy Minister of Foreign Affairs and International Cooperation) intervened at the 67th Meeting (XVII Legislature) of the *Terza Commissione Permanente – Affari esteri, Emigrazione* (3rd Permanent Commission – Foreign Affairs, Emigration) of the *Senato della Repubblica* (Senate of the Republic). Commenting upon these facts, Mr. Pistelli made a statement implicitly accepting the third-party effects of a bilateral treaty aimed at delimiting two Exclusive Economic Zones. In the words of the Deputy Minister:

> "As far as the legal questions are concerned […] it must, first of all, be clarified that the arrest of the two fishing vessels occurred due to their unauthorized fishing activity in a portion of the sea that the Arab Republic of Egypt claims to be its Exclusive Economic Zone (EEZ), on which it has its own functional jurisdiction as to the exploitation of fish resources in conformity with the Convention on the Law of the Sea signed in 1982 in Montego Bay (UNCLOS). In this regard, it must be remarked that the Arab Republic of Egypt has never formally established its own Exclusive Economic Zone by means of domestic legislation, which is, on the contrary, the usual procedure. This notwithstanding, on 17 February 2003 Egypt concluded an international agreement with Cyprus delimiting their respective Exclusive

[*] The materials compiled in this "Diplomatic and Parliamentary Practice" survey have been researched and translated by Chiara Tea Antoniazzi, Bianca Maganza, Julinda Beqiraj, Federica Cittadino, Michele Gagliardini, Alessio Gracis, Luca Poltronieri Rossetti, Alice Ruzza, Chiara Sisler, and Paolo Turrini.

Economic Zones. From this agreement, one can infer the willingness of Egypt to establish a sea zone subject to its own functional jurisdiction in fishing matters. On the basis of what is provided by UNCLOS, which broadly overlaps with international customary law, the coastal state may also subject fishing activities to its own laws and control, and thus seize foreign vessels carrying on unauthorized activities. At the same time, UNCLOS includes detailed provisions on the release of seized vessels".

He then recalled that "[a]s to the [...] possibility of concluding agreements granting fishing rights, [...] this subject matter falls within the exclusive competence of the European Union: this means, therefore, that member States may not autonomously negotiate bilateral agreements".

2. Two Parliamentary Motions on the Recognition of Palestine

On 27 February 2015, during its 383th Meeting (XVII Legislature), the *Camera dei Deputati* (Chamber of Deputies) was called upon to vote seven motions concerning initiatives for the recognition of the Palestinian State. Five of them were rejected (Motions nos. 1-00675, 1-00625, 1-00699, 1-00738 and 1-00747). Two were approved, but they do not seem to be fully consistent with each other. A full translation of the text of both motions is given hereunder. The text of Motion 1-00745 presented by MPs Speranza, Locatelli, Marazziti, Bossio, and Tidei reads as follows:

"The Chamber of Deputies, provided that:
the right of the Palestinian people to have their own State within recognized and internationally guaranteed boundaries and to peacefully coexist with the State of Israel, thus ensuring conditions of security and stability for both of them, has long been a well-established Italian and European position;
there is a widely shared belief at the international level that the actual achievement of this result may be brought about only through negotiations: on the mutual recognition of borders – starting from those of 1967 and including possible territorial exchanges between the parties – on a solution for the status of Jerusalem, and on the question of the right of return for Palestinian refugees;
at the international level, there is also a widely shared belief that this result cannot be pursued through the use of violence and terrorism, recalling in this regard the importance of respecting the three principles of the so-called quartet (USA, Russia, UN, and European Union), which requires, among other things, the right of the two peoples to live free from all violence and terrorist acts;

the stalemate of the negotiation process that risks fuelling violence and creating the conditions for bloody and tragic conflicts is worrying and deplorable;

as also confirmed by the resolution of the European Parliament – approved on 17 December 2014 by an overwhelming majority – it is necessary to avoid all actions that put into question the commitments taken in favor of a negotiated solution by inviting both parties to refrain from any action that might compromise the feasibility of, and prospects for, a solution based on the coexistence of two States, and by highlighting, among other things, that the expansion of the settlements is illegal, including from the point of view of international law; and that it is also necessary to promote the achievement of an agreement between all Palestinian political forces, which through the recognition of the State of Israel and the abandonment of violence may determine the conditions for a peaceful coexistence;

currently, the very high tension in the area, with a civil war going on in Syria, the alarming establishment of the self-styled Islamic State in an area between Iraq and, again, Syria, and the final phases of the nuclear talks with Iran, call for a greater political and diplomatic investment in the solution of the conflict, including through the greatest possible unity of purpose between Europe and the United States;

like other countries, Italy has already taken some important steps towards the recognition of Palestinian prerogatives, for instance through the vote in favor of the recognition of the status of Palestine as a 'UN non-member observer State', the attribution of full diplomatic status to the Palestinian representation in Italy, the continuing political support to Palestinian demands to become members of various international organizations;

Italy has repeatedly expressed its availability to formally recognize, at the right time and in the appropriate conditions, a Palestinian State alongside the State of Israel, peacefully coexisting;

the role of our country is already significant and it will be even more so in the future – also by working at the European and international levels – for development cooperation, for supporting stronger Palestinian institutions, as well as for strengthening cooperation and understanding in the wider Mediterranean and Middle-Eastern framework, on peace, security and human, social and economic development;

the international community must guarantee, in particular in Europe, the uncompromised opposition to any resurgence of violence and intolerance towards Jewish citizens and communities, who have already experienced, in the course of history, persecution and, in our Continent, real genocide; the recent episodes of anti-Semitism, racism and xenophobia call for a strong restatement that Judaism is an integral part of the European identity, and that Europe is also the home of Jews;

Pledges the Government:

to continue to support in every forum the goal of establishing a Palestinian State living in peace, security and prosperity side by side the State of Israel, on the basis of mutual recognition and the full undertaking of a reciprocal commitment to ensure citizens to live a secure life, safe from all violence and acts of terrorism;

to promote the recognition of Palestine as a democratic and sovereign State within the 1967 borders and with Jerusalem as a shared capital, taking fully into account the concerns and the legitimate interests of Israel;

to seek, to that end, coordinated action at the international level, and in particular in the framework of the European Union and the United Nations, with a view to finding a global and lasting solution for the peace process in the Middle East, based on the existence of two States, Palestinian and Israeli;

to take steps to support and promote the revival of the peace process by means of direct negotiations between the parties".

The text of Motion 1-00746, presented by MPs Alli, Rabino, De Girolamo, Mazziotti Di Celso, Cicchitto, Dorina Bianchi, Pizzolante, Scopelliti, Causin, and Sammarco, reads as follows:

"The Chamber of Deputies, provided that:

a comprehensive strategy is necessary to lead to a new situation in the Middle East, where there are conflicts partly unrelated to each other, like those erupted in Iraq and Syria, determined by the breakdown of both these States and the consequent affirmation of ISIS; the Libyan conflict that developed following the killing of Gaddafi before a new political balance could be achieved; the complex problems caused by the tragedy of a large number of immigrants oppressing countries like Jordan and Lebanon; the Israeli-Palestinian conflict;

in this framework, the Israeli-Palestinian conflict is currently under an armistice, which however does not rule out the risk of a resumption of hostilities and which still does not provide a stable and positive solution for this situation;

the dramatic humanitarian, political and social consequences of the Israeli-Palestinian conflict are a source of alarm and concern. The need for peace is made even more inevitable by the advance of Islamic fundamentalism, which operates particularly gruesome forms of terrorism in Syria and Iraq, and aims at exporting it to many other countries, simultaneously affecting the rest of the Islamic world, the Jews, Christians, and those who believe in other religions;

it is desirable that the international community, facing the stalled negotiations, gives its own contribution in the form of a constructive mediation between the parties, rather than by unilateral decisions that could possibly determine counterproductive outcomes;

the 'two peoples, two States' formula remains fully valid and is based on the parallel need to ensure the complete realization of the Palestinian State and the security of Israel;

it is a strategic interest of both Italy and Europe to contribute to the pacification of the Middle East, in view of the stabilization of the Mediterranean region and an intensification of the cooperation with the coastal States;

the State of Israel, even amid contradictions and errors, represents an outpost of real democracy in the Middle East; it is characterized by deep pluralism of ideas and stances, plays a very important role in the fight against any form of terrorism and is the expression of a history of Judaism that must be respected and protected against all forms of anti-Semitism. It is necessary that the State of Israel abstains from establishing new settlements;

the establishment of a Palestinian State is a worthy objective, also with a view to positively solving a long series of political conflicts and sufferings. Its actual accomplishment, however, requires an agreement between the two parties. Equally, necessary for a recognition of the Palestinian State is the achievement of a real political understanding between Al-Fatah and Hamas, one that entails the recognition of the State of Israel and the relinquishment of violence as a means of resolving the conflict; 'recognize to be recognized' is an inescapable equation;

a fair peace process goes through the free and genuine sharing of responsibilities between the parties, favored in every way by the European Union, the USA and Italy;

in this dramatic context the awareness demonstrated by the moderate Arab countries, from Egypt to Tunisia, from Jordan to Morocco, from Algeria to the United Arab Emirates, is worthy of praise. They are playing an essential role in contrasting the fundamentalist movements and pointing towards pacification. It is hoped that in the future the same role is played by other major States, such as Turkey and Saudi Arabia, and that reformist trends will prevail in Iran;

Pledges the Government:

to support both bilaterally and multilaterally in concert with European partners, the timely resumption of direct negotiations between

Israelis and Palestinians, as the highroad for the realization of the Oslo Accords;

to promote the achievement of a political understanding between Al-Fatah and Hamas, which, through the recognition of the State of Israel and the relinquishment of violence, creates the conditions for the recognition of a Palestinian State;

to promote within the European Union more resolute action on the Middle Eastern crisis, by restoring the special envoy for the peace process and, especially, by reminding to both parties the advantages of a special partnership with the Union, once the conflict will be over".

XI. TREATMENT OF ALIENS AND NATIONALITY

1. THE PURPOSES OF THE TRITON MISSION IN THE MEDITERRANEAN

On 21 January 2015, the *Ministro degli Interni* (Minister of Home Affairs), Mr. Angelino Alfano, intervened at the 112th meeting (XVII Legislature) of the *Quarta Commissione Permanente – Difesa* (4th Permanent Commission – Defence) of the *Senato della Repubblica* (Senate of the Republic). He answered a parliamentary question concerning, *inter alia*, the actual purposes of the *Triton* mission conducted on the European maritime boundaries in the Mediterranean Sea. Mr. Alfano recalled that "*Triton* is a surveillance mission on the maritime boundaries of the European Union, carried out by the Frontex agency together with many European states with the purpose of preventing irregular migration and the activities of those responsible for human trafficking, and coordinated in Italy by the Ministry of Home Affairs". He then stated:

> "It is absolutely evident that the ships involved in the *Triton* operation are under the obligation, whenever they have information about a craft carrying people at risk of their lives, to rescue them, irrespective of their nationality. Rescued migrants are conducted to Italy, except when they have been found in the territorial waters or the contiguous zone of Malta. Compliance with the principle of *non-refoulement*, however, is assured".

2. THE LEGAL STATUS OF CHILDREN BORN IN ITALY FROM PARENTS WHO BENEFIT FROM INTERNATIONAL PROTECTION

On 16 April 2015, the *Viceministro degli Interni* (Deputy Minister for Home Affairs), Mr. Filippo Bubbico intervened before the *Camera dei Deputati* (Chamber of Deputies, 432nd Meeting, XVII Legislature). He answered a parliamentary question concerning the legal status of children of people who benefit from international protection. At the outset, the Deputy Minister was asked to clarify whether it was true that, by means of a simple information circular, the Ministry of Home Affairs had intended to extend the acquisition of national citizenship on the basis of the *ius soli* principle to minors born in Italy from parents who benefit from international protection, similarly to what the law explicitly provides for minors born in Italy from stateless parents. Mr. Bubbico said:

> "[…] [T]he problem tackled by this administration is not the one mentioned in the parliamentary question, but is rather to avoid unreasonable discrimination in the treatment of minor children of a foreigner benefitting from international protection. According to the previous interpretation, as explicitly provided by law, the international protection afforded to a foreign citizen was automatically extended to their minor children who were in Italy at the time when the request was made, but not to the minor children who arrived in Italy at a later stage. The National Commission for the Right to Asylum intervened to revise this interpretation on the basis of some recent amendments in the law which further strengthened the principle of protection of family unity – upholding the interests of children being a matter of priority. In particular, this organ clarified, by means of an interpretative circular of 17 July [2014], that minors born in or arrived to Italy after the recognition of international protection for their parents also benefit from international protection until they reach majority […]".

3. THE GOVERNMENT'S VIEWS ON THE STRATEGY TO ADDRESS THE EMERGENCY MIGRATORY FLOWS FROM AFRICA

On 21 May 2015, the *Ministro della Difesa* (Minister of Defence), Ms. Roberta Pinotti, gave oral evidence before the *Senato della Repubblica* (Senate of the Republic, 456th Meeting, XVII Legislature) on the government's international security and defense strategy in the Euro-Mediterranean region. The Minister was asked questions concerning the proposed EU strategy to deal with the migratory flows from North Africa, focusing in particular on Libya. With specific reference to EUNAVFOR Med, the naval operation established by the European Council and lead by Rear Admiral Enrico Credendino of the Italian Navy, she reported that:

> "The first phase of the mission begins with the collection of information; moving on, the second and third phases involve direct intervention to stop the boats in order to avoid the transportation of migrants

and eventually proceed to the destruction of vessels – provided that the UN will adopt a resolution in that regard".

With regard to NATO's involvement, the Minister explained:

"Allow me to recall here an idea that Italy had previously announced to NATO through the Chief of Defense, that is, to make sure that the mission Active Endeavour, aimed at initiating counter-terrorism activities in the Eastern part of the Mediterranean, will also possibly support the control and safety of the sea; this is currently being considered by the EU".

The Minister also tackled the issue of the need of an authorization by the Libyan Government for actions on Libyan soil and the problems related to the existence of two rival governments in Tripoli and Tobruk. She affirmed:

"As regards the issue of Tobruk, which was addressed in two questions about Libya's reaction, we, alongside the whole international community, recognize the Parliament of Tobruk as legitimate. Apart from anticipations by the media in this sense, the Tobruk Parliament has not made any explicit and direct request for help on counterterrorism. However, things seem to be on the move, and if this is the case, there is maximum willingness to cooperate. To date, however, a mission on the Libyan soil or even on Libya's borders is not at issue".

And then she added:

"As regards possible requests that the Libyan Government might advance, those will be evaluated when made explicit. Meanwhile we are offering our full cooperation to the neighboring countries. In Tunisia, we work strenuously and cooperate in stopping terrorism and the tragedies (deaths and killings) caused by improvised explosive devices; we have provided the necessary night vision goggles to avoid this. We cooperate with Algeria – which has shown renewed interest – through joint teams and with maximum availability. We cooperate with Egypt, which has suffered major losses of military personnel, offering military cooperation in training and providing also the necessary devices for the training, as in the case of F-16 parts. This, in fact, was a request made by Egypt that we readily met because we think that Egypt is fundamental in the strategy to contain terrorism that, unfortunately, is also expanding into Libya".

4. THE DEBATE ON THE REVISION OF THE EUROPEAN ASYLUM POLICY

A. The Italian Proposal to Modify the European Asylum Policy

On 16 April 2015, the *Viceministro degli Interni* (Deputy Minister for Home Affairs), Mr. Filippo Bubbico intervened before the *Camera dei Deputati* (Chamber of Deputies, 432nd Meeting, XVII Legislature). He commented upon the current European asylum policy and the proposals advanced by Italy to modify it. He stated:

> "The government is working on a major revision of the European asylum policy, based on the principle that reception [of refugees] is a clear duty of Europe, as a political and institutional entity, and not of a single country alone. This principle can only be upheld by amending, or at least limiting the scope of the basic principle of the Dublin Regulation, according to which asylum seekers can only settle in the country in which they first entered. This principle is unfair for asylum seekers and refugees, deprived of their rights and expectations of family, social and work life; it is unfair also for the Member States that constitute the external border of the Union. During the semester of Italian Presidency [of the Union], aware of the strong opposition of the vast majority of the Member States to the complete elimination of this principle, we proposed a flexible application thereof taking into account, in the determination of the competent State, family aspects (in particular, family reunifications) and the interests of minors. Further, we put forward a proposal, previously elaborated by the European Commission, for the mutual recognition of decisions on asylum applications. Moreover, we are fostering the European and international acceptance of another solution, namely the possibility of anticipating the decision on asylum applications, which would be examined by outposts of the European Union in the countries of transit for migrants. These outposts, in cooperation with the United Nations High Commissioner for Refugees (UNHCR) and the International Organization for Migration, could also decide the destination of migrants, on the basis of previous arrangements between Member States".

B. On the Initiatives Aimed At Suspending the "Dublin III" Regulation

On 9 September 2015, at the *Camera dei Deputati* (Chamber of Deputies, 478th Meeting, XVII Legislature), the *Ministro degli Affari esteri e della Cooperazione internazionale* (Minister of Foreign Affairs and International Cooperation), Mr. Paolo Gentiloni Silveri, expressed the position of the government on the initiatives aimed at suspending the Dublin III Regulation. The interrogating Member of Parliament had asked if and when the Italian Government will formally propose the suspension or the overcoming of the Dublin Regulation thus establishing a European Right of Asylum. The Minister stated:

> "I agree […] on the need to overcome, to go beyond the current rules on the right to asylum in Europe. The reasons thereof are very simple. First of all, because those are rules of 25 years ago, a quarter of a century, and the phenomenon that we are facing, the phenomenon of migration, is surely not comparable to the situation of 25 years ago. In the second place, the everyday news and stories tell us that the pillar on which the regulation of Dublin is built, namely the fact that it is up to the country of first entry to take charge of the situation, is no longer sustainable. How is it possible to imagine that a country like Greece could bear the 400 thousand migrants who will arrive by the end of 2015? It is thus necessary to go beyond the Dublin rules and this position, which until some months ago was an isolated one, is now supported by several governments and is even included in the preamble of the proposal that the European Commission has described this morning at the European Parliament. Nevertheless, with the same frankness, I would like to say […] that the government does not fully agree, not on the idea but on the feasibility of a unilateral suspension of the Dublin regulation. The reason is very simple: you can do it in extremely urgent situations for some days – 15 days ago Germany, too, did it, although in a different manner – but the idea to unilaterally get out of the Dublin scheme, for a country as important as Italy, would mean *de facto* to undermine the whole system that we call the Schengen system, namely the one granting freedom of movement in Europe. We need to be brave enough to go beyond these old rules together".

C. Humanitarian Channels for Migratory Flows and Measures to Curb Human Trafficking

On 18 September 2015, during the 485th Meeting (XVII Legislature) of the *Camera dei Deputati* (*Chamber of Deputies*), *the Sottosegretario di Stato alla Presidenza del Consiglio dei Ministri* (Undersecretary of State to the Presidency of the Council of the Ministers), Mr. Gianclaudio Bressa, answered an urgent parliamentary question on the opening of humanitarian channels for migratory flows and on the possible measures to curb human trafficking. Mr. Bressa stressed the need to achieve a European right to asylum and described the measures adopted by the Italian Government. More precisely, he stated:

"Faced with this migration crisis, I believe we have contributed in a crucial way to raise awareness in Europe on the need to work first on reception, in order to achieve a European right of asylum that goes beyond the Dublin regulations – and at the same time to use in a better way, at the European level, the rules of repatriation. The increased awareness of the migration crisis also allowed widening the scope of the operation in the Mediterranean of the Frontex agency, namely the *Triton* operation. As regards the idea [...] of establishing hot spots in the countries where migrants leave from in order to identify those among them who are eligible for the refugee status, I note that this request is already included among the proposals made by the Italian Government during its semester of presidency of the European Union. The initiative, currently under examination in the Agenda on Migration presented by the European Commission, would imply an earlier decision on the applications for international protection, whose examination would be made by structures of the European Union established in transit countries. These structures, in cooperation with the UNHCR and the International Organization for Migration, could also decide the destination of the migrant, on the basis of previous agreements between member States. At the same time, the Italian Government has shown willingness to cooperate with the UNHCR and other humanitarian agencies to identify in countries particularly affected by the migratory flows those people who are eligible for the international protection – in particular, the most vulnerable of them – and could be resettled in Italy or other European Union countries. These initiatives, besides providing a better future to refugees, are a way to reduce the 'market place' of human traffickers. Furthermore, they represent a tangible manifestation of solidarity towards third countries that are on the frontline in the management of migratory flows in crisis areas. Since 2010, Italy has been engaged in the resettlement within its boundaries of hundreds of Afghan and Iraqi refugees. Moreover, thanks to the contribution of the European fund AMIF, procedures are being conducted in close cooperation with the UNHCR for the resettlement in Italy of 450 Syrian citizens from Lebanon and 50 Eritrean citizens from Sudan. Lastly, Italy has positively assessed the recommendation through which the European Commission proposed, in the framework of the European Agenda on Migration, to reinstall in Europe, over a period of two years, 20 thousand refugees located in third countries. But all these activities and figures tell us that the current tragedy is bigger than the commitments that we have taken, and that we must increase not only the awareness but also the determination that we have to do and can do more.

Still on the subject of resettlement, the Ministry of Interior has joined a project called EU-Frank, funded by FAMI and led by the Swedish Agency of Migration. The aim of the project is to develop tools and strategies to help the European Union member States and associated States implement national programs of resettlement. The project is expected to start next autumn and will last five years, until 2020".

He then addressed the problem of trafficking:

"It is important for us to work on transit countries, as we are doing, for example, in Niger. Definitely, this is not the solution of the problem but, still, it is a useful contribution to managing and, in part, also downsizing the migratory phenomenon. I agree, in conclusion, [...] [on] the importance of hindering the traffickers of human beings, a matter that is considered as a priority by the government, as witnessed by our participation in the EUNAVFOR Med operation. As I said before, this is the only way we can deter this heinous trade, stopping or at least limiting it".

XIV. CO-OPERATION IN JUDICIAL, LEGAL, SECURITY, AND SOCIO-ECONOMIC MATTERS

1. ITALY'S PARTICIPATION IN THE INTERNATIONAL COALITION AGAINST ISIL/DAESH AND ITS POSITION ON THE CONFLICTS IN SYRIA, IRAQ, AND LIBYA

A. The Aftermath of the Terrorist Attacks against the Satirical Magazine Charlie Hebdo

On 12 January 2015, in the aftermath of the terrorist attacks against the satirical magazine Charlie Hebdo in Paris, France, the *Ministro degli Affari esteri e della Cooperazione internazionale* (Minister for Foreign Affairs and International Cooperation), Mr. Paolo Gentiloni Silveri, reported before the *Senato della Repubblica* (Senate of the Republic, 372nd Meeting, XVII Legislature) on the position of Italy in the international fight against terrorism. Mr. Gentiloni illustrated, *inter alia*, Italy's efforts against ISIL/Daesh. He said:

"The battle against the Caliphate will be long and Italy is directly involved in it on the basis of Resolution 2170 of the United Nations Security Council, in particular with regard to the provision of arms and military trainers, both to Kurdish fighters and to

Iraqi forces. As you are aware, we have provided light weapons and anti-tank systems; we will have 290 trainers in the military base of Erbil collaborating with the forces that fight Daesh militias on the ground. Moreover, we have been undertaking several reconnaissance missions in Kuwait with our Tornados [jets] and Predators [drones]".

The Minister also hinted at the situation in Syria. He explained that "[w]e have been supporting the United Nations position in Syria. As you are aware, the United Nations is trying, also on the basis of a proposal of Italy, to obtain the 'freezing' of the situation in Aleppo. This model could be replicated in other parts of Syria". He then concluded that "[i]f a process of national reconciliation starts under the UN auspices, the government will propose to the Parliament to support it, including by means of a monitoring and peace-keeping intervention".

B. Italy's Position on the Need for a Political Transition in Syria

On 9 September 2015, during a question time taking place during the 478th Meeting (XVII Legislature) of the *Camera dei Deputati* (Chamber of Deputies), the *Ministro degli Affari esteri e della Cooperazione internazionale* (Minister of Foreign Affairs and International Cooperation), Mr. Paolo Gentiloni Silveri, took position on the need for a political transition in Syria. He stated the following:

"I have to say that the Italian position has been coherent since the very start of the acute phase of this crisis – that is, for two or three years now. We are convinced that, in addition to the containment of and military opposition to Daesh, a political transition is necessary. It is therefore our opinion that we have to overcome the current regime and the leadership of Mr. Bashar al-Assad through a transition avoiding the creation of another power and institutional vacuum. This already happened in other contexts – someone recalled Libya – and led to further tragedies. Some time ago, we were alone in holding such a view. Some said 'first of all, we kick Mr. Bashar al-Assad out through bombs', others said 'we stand by Mr. Bashar al-Assad to the last man'. As of today, the idea of a transition aimed at changing the dictatorship in a gradual and political way is spreading. As for other aspects, certainly the Italian Government participates in the anti-Daesh coalition. This is particularly true in Iraq where it supports the legitimate Iraqi Government and the Kurdish *Peshmerga* combatants, who are at the forefront in the fight against Daesh in the territory of the Iraqi Kurdistan".

C. The Italian Contribution to the Fight against ISIL/Daesh with reference to the Situation in Syria, Libya, Turkey, and Iraq

On 6 October 2015, the *Ministro degli Affari esteri e della Cooperazione internazionale* (Minister of Foreign Affairs and International Cooperation), Mr. Paolo Gentiloni Silveri, and the *Ministro della Difesa* (Minister of Defence), Ms. Roberta Pinotti, delivered two statements before the *Commissioni congiunte e riunite* (Joint Commissions) III and IV of the *Camera dei Deputati* (Chamber of Deputies) and 3rd and 4th of the *Senato della Repubblica* (Senate of Republic) (21ˢᵗ Meeting, XVII Legislature). Mr. Gentiloni started by illustrating the foreign policy of Italy with particular regard to the Mediterranean and Middle East areas. In this context, he recalled the role played by Italy in the fight against ISIL/Daesh. He stated:

> "Italy has always been part of the anti-Daesh coalition, where it plays a highly relevant role in all fields – not only in the military one, but also in the cultural, counter-information, and economic ones. From a military point of view, as you know, we are especially active [...] in Iraq, where we support a government that is trying to win back those parts of its territory that have been occupied by Daesh. We are urging the government to adopt a more inclusive policy towards the Sunnis, and to continue – notwithstanding economic difficulties (oil-related ones) – the dialogue initiated with the regional authorities of Kurdistan".

He then moved on to consider the situation in Syria:

> "The Russian intervention is a good thing, in some respects. [...] Unfortunately, this positive development subsequently resulted in very critical circumstances. Russian air strikes aimed at controversial targets: meaning that Russian fighter-bombers did not only hit some Daesh posts along the Euphrates, but also focused on a Northwestern area of Iraq where both the *Al-Nusra* Front (that is, terrorist qaedist/ jihadist groups), and certain constituents of the so-called Free Syrian Army operate extensively. The positions of this latter – as you know – have considerably weakened over the last two years. Therefore, we are dealing with controversial targets and very dangerous border violations [...] within the Turkish territory, which legitimately caused the reaction of the North Atlantic Council".

With respect to the obligation to defend the sovereignty of Turkey, he stated:

> "[...] There is no doubt that, since Turkey is a member of NATO, we all are under the obligation – whatever our judgment on cer-

tain aspects of the Turkish domestic and foreign policy – to defend the full sovereignty of our Allies. To sum up, the involvement of Russia is a good thing if [...] it takes place increasingly in coordination with the anti-Daesh coalition, and particularly with the United States. [...] Clearly, military coordination is vital to avoid not only ineffective interventions, but also risks of accidents. Therefore, we have an open position: we are firm in condemning the mistakes that have been made and in defending the sovereignty of NATO Members, but we also note the importance of the involvement of Russia [...]".

Then he addressed the situation in Libya and the need for a government of national unity:

"As far as Libya is concerned, as you know, the President of the Council of Ministers reiterated – in his statement before the General Assembly of the United Nations – that Italy is ready to take the lead in an international effort to stabilize Libya. We know that such an effort and such a potential role of Italy are linked to the achievement of a result – namely, that of a government of national unity [...]".

Subsequently, the *Ministro della Difesa* (Minister of Defence), Ms. Roberta Pinotti, took the floor and focused on the Italian contribution to the fight against ISIL/Daesh, particularly by means of training of local forces. She stated:

"Eighteen States are currently contributing to the training of Iraqi and Kurdish forces, and Italy is among those, having deployed one of the most substantial groups of trainers. In the last months, numerous training and specialization courses were conducted, involving both the Kurdish *Peshmerga* and the Iraqi forces. In August, the training carried out by our *Carabinieri* – deployed in the theatre of operations since June – has also started. As mentioned, we want to increase the number of *Carabinieri*, in order to intensify the training of those local forces that are meant to control the territories taken away from ISIS, thus avoiding the dangerous power vacuum that follows the fighting [...]".

Demand for clarifications by the members of the Parliamentary Commissions followed. In her reply, Ms. Pinotti excluded that Italy's support to the Kurdish *Peshmerga* was planned to be extended, in the present situation, to the Syrian *Peshmerga*. She stated:

"Italy is intervening in Iraq, as a member of the coalition, in agreement with the Iraqi Government. I know that we are talking about neighboring regions, and that the fight against Daesh is one, but the situation in Syria is different: at present, it would be complicated for Italy to intervene there, also in light of its constitutional constraints".

On 16 November 2015, during the 522nd Meeting (XVII Legislature) of the *Camera dei Deputati* (Chamber of Deputies) the *Ministro degli Affari esteri e della Cooperazione internazionale* (Minister of Foreign Affairs and International Cooperation), Mr. Paolo Gentiloni Silveri, made an urgent report on the terrorist attacks against the city of Paris in the night between 13 and 14 November 2015. He described again the role of Italy in the international coalition against ISIL/Daesh and stated:

> "In this context Italy plays its part, an important one within the anti-Daesh coalition: we have to state it proudly as we have hundreds of our soldiers engaged in such a task. We are, since the beginning, in the politico-military coalition fighting Daesh; we are part of the coordination group of 22 countries coordinating its activities; our Armed Forces have 280 units in Iraq, 200 of which train in Kurdistan those *Peshmerga* who, some days ago, liberated the city of Sinjar. We hereby recall the role of the *Peshmerga* and highlight with pride the fact that, at the moment, Italy is the *leading nation* in the military training of Kurdish forces, for I believe this to be very important in the context of what is happening in the area.
> Furthermore, our country plays a highly appreciated role in the training of the Iraqi police, involving around 100 *Carabinieri* trainers in Baghdad. We actually do much but, in light of what happened on Friday night in Paris, I think we should recognize that we have to do more and commit to each other to do more, as the situation in front of us deserves and requires that we do more as a country".

Then he addressed the situation in Syria as follows:

> "In Syria, we say two simple things: first of all, in order to dismiss Mr. Assad – the dictator, the responsible of the most dramatic humanitarian crisis of the last few years – without letting Daesh or Al Nusra filling the gap, we need a political transition; secondly, Russia can make a crucial contribution to this solution and to this political transition".

He added that "[a] transition that puts Mr. Bashar al-Assad out of the picture, without leaving a gap filled by terrorists. This is thus the path we aim to follow in Syria, while military activity and fighting against Daesh and terrorism goes on".

D. Italy's Position on the Involvement of the Russian Federation in the International Coalition against ISIL/Daesh

On 26 November 2015, the *Ministro degli Affari esteri e della Cooperazione internazionale* (Minister of Foreign Affairs and International Cooperation), Mr. Paolo Gentiloni Silveri, during a question time taking place at the *Camera dei Deputati* (Chamber of Deputies, 530th Meeting, XVII Legislature), took position on the possible involvement of the Russian Federation in the international coalition against ISIL/Daesh. He stated:

> "[…] the aim is to reinforce, to consolidate the action of the international coalition. We are first of all talking about a military issue: Italy is engaged in military terms on several fronts and in particular in Iraq, where – as you may know – it is the most engaged European country in the anti-Daesh coalition from a military point of view. Political aims are also crucial: the transition to be ensured in Syria, a more inclusive capacity towards the Sunni community in Iraq, a deal in Libya. I believe we should also add the need to – at least – try and further broaden the anti-Daesh coalition: we were among those trying to acknowledge both the problems and the opportunities related to the Russian presence in Syria, and we raised the issue of the possibility of extending this coalition to Russia, further involving Russia in it".

E. The Government's View on the Imposition of an Arms Embargo on Countries Allegedly Involved in Arms Trafficking with ISIL/Daesh

In the last quarter of 2015 the Italian Government reported twice before the *Camera dei Deputati* (Chamber of Deputies) on its arms sales policy to certain Middle East countries that are allegedly involved in illicit arms trafficking with ISIL/Daesh. The government also explained which measures and actions Italy has undertaken in the fight against ISIL and foreign terrorist fighters. On 26 November 2015 (530th Meeting – XVII Legislature), the *Ministro degli Affari esteri e della Cooperazione internazionale* (Minister of Foreign Affairs and International Cooperation), Mr. Paolo Gentiloni Silveri, explained:

> "It is important to reiterate that Italy, obviously, acts in accordance with domestic law and EU and international rules on embargoes and prohibited weapons systems. As concerns Saudi Arabia, which is a member of the anti-Daesh coalition, I must point out that it is not the first destination country of our exportations. According to the briefing report to the Parliament, the most recent available data on trade,

those for the year 2014, show that Saudi Arabia is the sixth country; according to the data for the previous year, which are the latest available providing a comparison with other big European countries, Italy is preceded in its exports to Riyadh by the UK, France, and Germany. That is, among the four big European countries, Italy is the one exporting less to Saudi Arabia. According to the latest data available, we have exported to Israel, a country friend of Italy, about three million Euros, compared to 260 from Germany, 36 from France, 28 from Romania and 12 from Great Britain. As far as countries such as Syria and Lebanon are concerned, the Italian Government, clearly, fully respects the embargo on the supply of arms to these countries, which in both cases was imposed at the international level in 2011".

Subsequently, on 4 December 2015 (536th Meeting, XVII Legislature), the *Sottosegretario di Stato per gli Affari esteri e la Cooperazione internazionale* (Undersecretary of State for Foreign Affairs and International Cooperation), Mr. Benedetto della Vedova, answered a parliamentary question concerning the appropriateness of the imposition of an arms embargo on Qatar and Turkey, by reason of their alleged responsibility in weapons transit and deliveries to ISIL/Daesh. He stated:

"First of all, on the issue of arms sales, I would like to remind that the government respects both national legislation, as it is obvious, and EU and international rules. Moreover, for the granting of authorizations, the Ministry of Foreign Affairs and International Cooperation rigorously applies the eight criteria set forth in the common position 2008/944/ PESC of the European Council of 8 December 2008 'common rules governing control of exports of military technology and equipment'. Such criteria establish a number of assessments to be made on the regional and domestic situation of those countries towards which the operations are to be conducted, including: the possible impact of exports and transit of technology and of military equipment on the recipient countries and on the regions nearby; the end use of the material; the possible risk of diversion or transfer to third parties; and the respect of international peace and human rights by the recipient governments. Furthermore, the government scrupulously respects embargos and other restrictive measures adopted at the international level".

And he added:

"In the context of the international coalition against ISIL and of the enhanced cooperation [by the] *small group,* created by the most active countries in the fights against Daesh, Italy co-chairs, along with the United States and Saudi Arabia, the Counter-ISIL Finance Group.

The aim of this group is to formulate and adopt concrete measures to drain Daesh financial resources, to jeopardize its ability to transfer and receive funds and, more generally, to undermine its economic sustainability. [...]

The working group, which consists of 28 countries and four multilateral institutions (the European Union, the Gulf Cooperation Council, the International Financial Action Task Force and the Egmont Group) can count on the support of partners in the Middle East and the Gulf, as well as Turkey and Qatar. Bahrain, Iraq, Jordan, Kuwait, Lebanon and the United Arab Emirates also actively participate in the works of the Counter-ISIL Finance Group. The direct involvement of these countries constitutes an important element in increasing the effectiveness of actions contrasting financial flows to Daesh and its affiliates and represents a useful tool fostering the harmonization of national legislations toward the highest international standards in the field of anti-money laundering and countering the financing of terrorism.

As to foreign terrorist fighters, the related countering actions are directly monitored by the same anti-ISIL coalition, as part of a specific working group coordinated by the Netherlands and Turkey. The working group also includes Qatar, which has approved an action plan setting out the necessary measures to be taken to contain this phenomenon. Among these, it is worth emphasizing the comprehensive sharing of intelligence – with regard to which every possible step must be taken to strengthen the coordination efforts at the European level –, the effective implementation of the UN Security Council resolution No. 2178 of 2014 and the urgent need to engage in *capacity building* measures in favor of least developed countries, designed at contrasting this phenomenon".

He then concluded:

"In this context, Italy has actively promoted a greater efficiency in the sharing of intelligence, in particular within the European framework. At the UN level, our country has promptly assured full enforcement of Security Council resolution No. 2178 of 2014 on foreign terrorist fighters through the antiterrorism decree and the international missions of last February".

2. THE WORK OF THE INTERNATIONAL LAW COMMISSION ON THE MOST FAVORED NATION CLAUSE

On 11 February 2015, during the debate in the Sixth Committee of the UN General Assembly (LXX Session) on the Report of the International Law

Commission on the Work of its Sixty-Sixth Session, the Italian delegate, Min. Plenipotentiary Andrea Tiriticco, submitted the comments of his delegation on a number of issues related to the Report, among which the Most Favored Nation (MFN) Clause. He expressed the appreciation of the Italian delegation for the report of the Study Group on the MFN Clause, which could "provide a useful contribution to a still complex and open debate in international law and assist in the interpretation and application of MFN clauses". Then he continued as follows:

> "Italy regards such a contribution as an important complement to the Draft Articles adopted in 1978 on the same topic. The latter remain a valuable term of reference, with special regard to the *eiusdem generis* principle, as a guardian for the appropriate interpretations of MFN clauses in full compliance with the principle of State consent as the main source of treaty rights and duties. My delegation shares the conclusions on the topic adopted by the Commission at its 3277th meeting on 23 July 2015, with special regard to the emphasis placed on the importance that the interpretation of MFN clauses be made consistently with the relevant provisions of the Vienna Convention on the Law of Treaties concerning treaty interpretation. As to the question whether in investment treaty arbitration MFN clauses should apply only to substantive obligations, or also to dispute settlement provisions, Italy subscribes to the conclusion of the Commission to the effect that it is a matter of interpretation of MFN clauses on a case-by-case basis, and that, accordingly, States are well advised to negotiate such clauses in explicit terms. In case where such clauses are not explicit on the matter, Italy believes that the application of MFN clauses to dispute settlement provisions should not be presumed".

3. THE WORK OF THE INTERNATIONAL LAW COMMISSION ON CRIMES AGAINST HUMANITY

On 11 February 2015, during the debate in the Sixth Committee of the UN General Assembly (LXX Session) on the Report of the International Law Commission on the Work of its Sixty-Sixth Session, the Italian delegate, Min. Plenipotentiary Andrea Tiriticco, submitted the comments of his delegation on a number of issues related to the Report, among which Chapter VII, on the topic of "Crimes against humanity". Mr. Tiriticco congratulated the special rapporteur, Mr. Sean Murphy, on the adoption of his first report and stated:

> "Italy is convinced of the potential benefits of developing a convention on crimes against humanity promoting the prevention, criminalization and cooperation among states. The positive attitude of the Italian del-

egation is based on the premises of the approach proposed and pursued by the Commission at the present stage of its work. Italy favors the decision to confine, for the time being, the scope of the draft articles to crimes against humanity. Most importantly, my delegation wishes to express its satisfaction for the approach clearly undertaken by the Commission to the effect that the draft articles are meant to avoid any conflicts with obligations arising from existing treaties relating to crimes against humanity, including those establishing international or 'hybrid' criminal courts, with special regard to the ICC.

As to the relationship with the latter, we fully subscribe to the point made by the Commission that the compatibility of the draft articles with the ICC Statute would lie on the fact that the draft articles will consist of obligations to adopt domestic legislation and to engage in inter-State cooperation, within the framework of a set of 'horizontal' legal relationships, whereas the Rome Statute governs legal relationships of a 'vertical' nature between the ICC and its States Parties. In the same vein, Italy supports the approach anticipated by the Commission whereby, not only would the draft articles be without prejudice to the Rome Statute in general, but, also, they should aim to enhance the principle of complementarity under the Statute in addressing inter-State cooperation on the prevention of the crimes in question and on the investigation, arrest, prosecution, extradition and punishment at the domestic level".

4. The Adoption of a Code of Conduct on Outer Space Activities

On 27 July 2015, within the context of the multilateral negotiations convened in New York by the European Union for the adoption of an International Code of Conduct for Outer Space Activities, Ambassador Inigo Lambertini, chargé d'affaires at the Permanent Mission of Italy to the United Nations, made the following statement:

"We support the comprehensive scope of the draft Code, which takes into consideration that outer space peaceful activities, by their very nature, serve both civil and military purposes. By this approach, the Code aims at setting up a framework where nations enhance mutual understanding and trust in outer space activities by peaceful means, thus preventing space from becoming an area of conflict. The consultative and information-sharing mechanisms designed in the draft Code would represent a crucial value added to the existing tools; likewise, the new substantive and procedural measures would help the preservation of the space environment in the interest of all States.

We also champion the view that provisions regulating the placement of weapons in outer space remain beyond the scope of the Code of Conduct, which is not meant to be an alternative to the initiatives dealing with the 'weaponization' of outer space.

Furthermore, Italy supports the fundamental principles on which the draft Code is based, namely: freedom for all states to use outer space for peaceful purposes, in accordance with international law and without harmful interference; preservation of the security, safety and integrity of space objects in orbit and space environment; promotion of the peaceful exploration and use of outer space for the benefit and in the interest of humankind; due consideration for the legitimate security concerns of States. We believe that those principles, being the core of the initiative, should remain unspoiled during the negotiations".

XVI. INTERNATIONAL ORGANIZATIONS

1. UNITED NATIONS SECURITY COUNCIL REFORM

On 30 October 2015, during the annual debate of the General Assembly (LXX Session) on Agenda item 121 entitled "Question of equitable representation on and increase in the membership of the Security Council and other matters related to the Security Council", Ambassador Stefano Cardi, Permanent Representative of Italy to the United Nations, made a statement on behalf of the Uniting for Consensus (UFC) Group.[1] At the outset of his statement, Mr. Cardi affirmed that the debate on the future of the Security Council should be more inclusive and transparent. He stated:

"The Inter-Governmental Negotiations are a membership-driven process, mandated by General Assembly decision 62/557. We need predictability through a clear agenda, not arbitrary guidance. Member States should be facilitated in their work, through timely information and extensive consultation. Each Member State, belonging to any negotiating group, has the right to be adequately informed about the procedure. The past has demonstrated that divisive approaches and initiatives complicate our process even further, distancing us from reaching our commonly shared goal of reform".

---

[1] The Uniting for Consensus (UFC) Group is an informal intergovernmental gathering, led by Italy, very active in the United Nations negotiations on the reform of the Security Council. In those negotiations in recent years the UFC Group positions have usually been in contrast with the G4 positions (Germany, Brazil, Japan, and India) whose main purpose is an enlargement in the permanent category of seats of the Security Council.

After having recalled Italy's and the UFC Group's support for the French/ Mexican initiative on the adoption of a Code of Conduct "aiming to limit the use of the veto and prevent the Council's inaction to make it more effective in the face of heinous international crimes", he expressed the UFC Group's position on how the Security Council should become more representative of present realities. Starting from the premise that the Security Council reform "should be reflective of the changes that have occurred in the last 70 years", he stated:

> "Let me summarize the three main changes that have taken place. Firstly, in these 70 years, not only has the number of UN Member States grown, but the relative weight of the different regional groups of the United Nations has also changed. This has led the membership to unanimously request an enlargement of the Council favoring areas that, to date, have been disadvantaged in the distribution of seats. The response of the UFC to this first trend is unequivocal: we support an enlargement of the Council up to 26 members, assigning the majority of added seats to Africa, the Asia-Pacific and Latin America. We also understand and heed the call of the Eastern European Group, and of cross-cutting groups of States – such as Small Island Developing States (SIDS), Small States and the Arab countries.
> Secondly, some Member States aspire to play a more prominent role in the Council. The UFC highly values the contribution that these States may offer to the maintenance of international peace and security. No one has asked them to forfeit their willingness to play a greater role in the Council. In fact, our proposal of longer-term seats with the possibility of an immediate re-election was conceived precisely to meet these expectations. Let me clarify: these seats would not be reserved to a select group of countries. All UN Member States willing to make a bigger contribution to the work of the Council would have the right to run for a longer-term seat. Our proposal is democratic in nature.
> Thirdly, over the past 70 years, we have experienced change at an incessantly faster pace in the international arena. The emergence of new regional actors and new global challenges imposes a modern vision for the Security Council, enhancing its flexibility not only in terms of operations, but also in terms of its very structure and representation. The reality of the XXI century is in continuous transformation, and a changing reality requires a Council able to adapt to it. We believe that regular elections are the best way to guarantee, not only a truly democratic and accountable Security Council, but also a Council able to continually adapt to the rapid changes of today and tomorrow. This is what we mean by inclusive Security Council. Let us offer to all Member States, especially Small States and Developing countries, which represent the majority of this membership, the opportunity to con-

tribute more to the Council's work. This goal can be achieved solely by ensuring a proper, fair and democratic system, through regular elections. This is what we mean by a Security Council in tune with the realities of the XXI century: a new, modern Council grounded on a profoundly democratic vision that carries within it inclusiveness and adaptability".

He then added:

"This is the path toward the early reform that our leaders called for more than 10 years ago. A reform that can be attained with no further delay, building on the many – already existing – convergences among Members States. A comprehensive reform of the Security Council that can be concretely achieved by enlarging the Council with new elected members, and by a more balanced and equitable representation of regional groups. An enhanced and closer relationship between the Security Council and the General Assembly, and improved working methods of the Council, including the question of the veto, are also areas that require our due attention".

Along the same lines, with specific relation to the enlargement of the Permanent Members of the Security Council, in a previous meeting, on 15 May 2015, within the context of the inter-governmental negotiations on the question of equitable representation on and increase in the membership of the Security Council, Ambassador Cardi had expressed the position of Italy and of the UFC Group as follows:

"We deserve a more democratic Council, based on merit and not privilege, that is accountable on a regular basis to the entire membership. We deserve a better representation of all groups, starting with those that are clearly under-represented in the Council, Africa first. We understand and heed the call from cross cutting categories of States, such as the Small Islands and Developing States, and from the many countries of the Eastern European group, which took advantage of the framework document to voice their request to be able to access the Council more frequently. In this respect, we are also in favor of considering the aspirations of the Arab countries.
Regional rotation is the solution, and elections are key. This is also true for countries aspiring to serve for longer periods in the Council. We have shown our readiness to cooperate with them to unlock the process by proposing the formula of longer-term re-electable seats. But we remain firm in our conviction that new permanent members, new veto powers, would not render the Council more transparent and effective, and we strongly believe in the general agreement on this very simple view".

XVIII. USE OF FORCE AND PEACE-KEEPING

1. ON BIOMETRIC DATA CAPTURE BY THE ITALIAN ARMED FORCES ABROAD: THE ITALIAN LEGISLATION ON DATA PROTECTION IS NOT APPLICABLE EXTRATERRITORIALLY

On 22 July 2015, the *Sottosegretario di Stato alla Difesa* (Undersecretary of State for Defense), Mr. Gioacchino Alfano, intervened before the *Terza Commissione permanente – Affari esteri, Emigrazione* (3rd Permanent Commission – Foreign Affairs, Emigration) of the *Senato della Repubblica* (Senate of the Republic) (141st Meeting – XVII Legislature). Mr. Alfano answered a parliamentary question on the constitution and deployment of an elite unit of the Armed Forces within the Task Force 45 (TF45) of the NATO-covered ISAF mission in Afghanistan. Being TF45 provided with biometric data capture equipment for its role of support to the Afghan security forces, Mr. Alfano dwelled on the legal basis for the collection of such data. He stated:

> "The capture of biometric data in Afghanistan has been carried out on the basis of operational regulations set forth by NATO military commands and established in accordance with specific directives adopted by NATO itself. Such documents represent the specific rules of the international organization leading the mission, to which the Italian Authority for the Protection of Personal Data (*Garante per la protezione dei dati personali*) referred to in its Opinion delivered in the meeting of 18 December 2014, which mentioned them as possible regulatory instruments for the processing of personal data captured on territories falling outside Italian jurisdiction. This is the case of international military operations, where the Code for the Protection of Personal Data, established under Legislative Decree No. 196 of 30 June 2003, is not applicable, as the Authority clarified".

XIX. ARMED CONFLICT, NEUTRALITY, AND DISARMAMENT

1. ITALY'S POSITION ON THE SITUATION IN UKRAINE AND ON SANCTIONS AGAINST THE RUSSIAN FEDERATION

A. The Minister of Foreign Affairs and International Cooperation on New Developments in the Conflict in Ukraine

On 13 February 2015, the *Ministro degli Affari esteri e della Cooperazione internazionale* (Minister of Foreign Affairs and International Cooperation), Mr. Paolo Gentiloni Silveri, participated in the 13th Meeting of the *Commissioni con-*

giunte (Joint Commissions) III of the *Camera dei Deputati* (Chamber of Deputies) and 3rd of the *Senato della Repubblica* (Senate of Republic) (XVII Legislature). The Minister examined some recent developments in the Ukrainian crisis and took position on the prospects of national reconstruction. He stated:

> "[T]he Italian Government positively takes note of the prospects for constitutional reform, mentioned among the Minsk points, regarding a special status for Ukrainian Eastern regions. Italy also positively looks at the fact that for the first time the Minsk agreement explicitly speaks about constitutional reforms, sets a specific time schedule on the adoption of a new text by the end of 2015, makes reference to a special status for concerned regions, and reiterates the importance of local elections".

He then addressed the thorny issue of the sanctions against the Russian Federation:

> "Italy has always taken the position that sanctions should be reversible, as well as proportional. Thus, in case of a de-escalation and of peace negotiations, it would be possible to think of a corresponding and gradual softening of sanctions. However, we must be aware that the opposite scenario is also possible so that, once some obligations are formally entered upon, should Russia fail to respect them, it would be inevitable not only to go on, but also to discuss a hardening of sanctions. This is not a prospect that Italy wants to materialize, but I am simply stating that it would be inevitable. We are still talking about, as you know, sanctions rather than providing weapons. The provision of weapons is a choice that we, just as many other European countries, do not deem appropriate. Therefore, the attitude that Europe and NATO will have in the coming months depends on to what extent Russia will keep up with the obligations it entered upon".

B. The Deputy Minister of Economic Development on Sanctions against Russia

In its 450th Meeting of 25 June 2015 (XVII Legislature) the *Camera dei Deputati* (Chamber of Deputies) was called upon to vote on several parliamentary motions concerning initiatives aimed at lifting the sanctions of the European Union against the Russian Federation and the achievement of a politico-diplomatic solution to the crisis in Ukraine. The *Viceministro dello sviluppo economico* (Deputy Minister of Economic Development), Mr. Carlo Calenda, illustrated to the Chamber the opinion of the government with regard to those motions. He stated:

"Italy carried out and will continue to carry out, in connection with its European and international partners, a constructive role in order to facilitate the resolution of the crisis and bring the relations with Moscow back to complete normality. However, this commitment cannot disregard the necessity to safeguard, above all, the principle of territorial integrity, which represents the reason behind the sanctions adopted against the Russian Federation. The government considers that when this principle is called into question at the gates of Europe, its safeguard is not only a duty towards the principles of international law and legality, but also, and above all, a necessary act in order to protect national interests that go well beyond those of trade".

The Chamber subsequently approved Motion no. 1-00920, presented by MPs Cicchitto, Amendola, Mazziotti Di Celso, Marazziti, Locatelli, and others, on which the government had previously expressed its favorable opinion. Hereunder are the most relevant parts of the Motion:

"The Chamber of Deputies, provided that:
in the affair concerning the sanctions against Russia we need to be aware that there are geo-political reasons that prevail over those of economic character, since [these sanctions] did constitute the most responsible and contained response to the politico-military initiatives taken by the Russian Government towards Ukraine;
Russia patently violated the sovereignty, territorial integrity, and independence of Ukraine, both by means of its unlawful annexation of Crimea, and the direct and indirect military assistance provided to separatist groups in Donbass, in open violation of international conventions;
lastly, actions of propaganda, forms of economic and financial pressure – also through the management of energy supplies – as well as episodes of military violation of the airspace and territorial waters fostering international tension, are repeated;
as regards the Ukrainian crisis, in order to avoid military solutions and, conversely, in the perspective of a negotiated solution at the diplomatic level, the Minsk agreements have been signed, which, however, are not ultimately being applied because of the persistence of frequent violations of the ceasefire, the failed completion of both the withdrawal of heavy weapons and the exchanges of prisoners, as well as the lack of developments with regard to the institutional reforms in Ukraine and the holding of local elections in Donbass;
the international community decided to put in place sanction mechanisms with respect to Russia, as the only instrument of pressure aimed

at deterring the Russian Government from its interferences and violations of international law;

within this framework, in July 2014 the European Union decided to
impose a package of sanctions against Russia that target the sectors of
defense and energy, as well as the Russian financial system, and that
Italy, as a member of the European Union, obviously applies;

the agreement between the European Governments established that
such measures should remain in force until the deadline set by the
Minsk peace agreements so that these are fully and completely implemented (31 December 2015). To this end the European Union decided to extend for additional six months, until January 2016, the
expiring sanctions;

[…] sanctions, although they represent an extra-ordinary instrument
and cannot be considered the optimal means for the solution of problems, in so far as they import sacrifices both for the populations subjected to them and the States enacting them, are nevertheless an inevitable solution, one agreed upon at the international level;

the effectiveness of sanctions against Russia is inseparable form the
maintenance of a unanimous consent on the part of the international community and their possible unilateral lifting on the part of our
country would constitute a grave and dangerous signal of weakening
of the western position and an implicit legitimation of the violations
committed by Russia in Ukraine;

Italy considers that the main way should be that of mediation. The
aim should be that of guaranteeing the sovereignty and territorial integrity of Ukraine with means that lead Russia to cease all those actions that provoked the imposition of sanctions;

it is desirable that all parties put an end to the violations of the Minsk
agreements and integrally implement their content by accomplishing
the requests of the international community and that, in the light of
this, it will be possible to re-establish, within a reasonably short period of time, a situation of normal relations with Russia,

Pledges the Government:

to intensify and strengthen its politico-diplomatic action towards
Russia, in order to urge the Russian Government to implement the
Minsk agreements, exercise its influence on the separatists and be
back in compliance with international law in Ukraine;

at the same time, to encourage the Ukrainian Government to fulfill
the institutional reforms required under the Minsk agreement, so that
a system assuring a degree of decentralization and a special status for
the Russian-speaking areas of Donbass could be implemented;

to support with strong conviction the action of the European Union
and any further effort of the international community going in the

same direction and, in this framework, to start a discussion at the European Union level on possible compensatory measures to support those businesses and supply-chain systems most affected by the Russian embargo;

[...] to act in conformity with the decisions of the international community as to the sanctions against Russia, keeping them in place until a different decision will be adopted by common deliberation on the basis of positive developments and a restored compliance with international law".

C. The Minister of Foreign Affairs and International Cooperation on the Decisions To Be Taken at the EU Level Regarding Sanctions against Russia

The issue of sanctions against Russia was dealt with also during the 530th Meeting (XVII Legislature) of the *Camera dei Deputati* (Chamber of Deputies) held on 26 November 2015. The *Ministro degli Affari esteri e della Cooperazione internazionale* (Minister of Foreign Affairs and International Cooperation), Mr. Paolo Gentiloni Silveri, answering a parliamentary question regarding the meeting of the G20 in Antalya, clarified the position of the government on sanctions against the Russian Federation and the future decisions to be adopted at the European level in that respect. He stated:

"[...] [O]bviously, at the G20 in Antalya no decision was taken as to sanctions, also because they were decided by the European Council and their possible prorogation must be decided by the European Council. [...] I would like to say two things on the Italian position: the first is that, even if it agreed on sanctions, during the last months Italy has always fought so that sanctions, which pertain to a very grave and specific act in Ukraine, would not entail a general severance of diplomatic relations with Russia, because it would have been a mistake, and we are proud of the fact that the necessity to keep a channel of dialogue open with Russia is no longer the Italian position only, but has become in the last months a widely shared one. What will be decided on sanctions at the meetings entitled to decide on them? Of course, it will be a common decision of 28 European countries, therefore not a simple one; and it will entirely depend on the reasons for which sanctions were put in place, namely the compliance with the Minsk Agreements. We should remember that these agreements are binding upon Russia, but are binding upon Ukraine as well".

He concluded by saying that "[...] [t]he assessment of this trend will be at the basis of a decision, which has by no means been adopted thus far".

2. The Government's Position on the EU Commission Legislative
    Proposal on Mandatory Traceability of Minerals from Armed
    Conflict Areas

On 12 June 2015, the *Viceministro degli Affari esteri e della Cooperazione
internazionale* (Deputy Minister of Foreign Affairs and International Cooperation),
Mr. Lapo Pistelli, participated in the 441st Meeting (XVII Legislature) of the
Camera dei Deputati (Chamber of Deputies). Mr. Pistelli answered a parliamentary
question on a legislative proposal of the European Commission on the traceability
of minerals from conflict areas. Before addressing the merits of the proposal, the
Deputy Minister specified: "I will answer, to some extent, on the basis of the information provided by the Ministry of Economic Development, which currently has
the primary responsibility for this matter, and being aware that [...] the complex
and sensitive issue of the traceability of minerals from conflict areas is still under
investigation at governmental level". He then added:

> "The European Parliament, meeting in plenary session on 20 May, vot-
> ed in favor of a legislative proposal the text of which is more stringent
> than both the original proposal of the European Commission, which is
> still under discussion in the Council, and the possible compromise solu-
> tion subsequently voted by the International Trade Committee of the
> European Parliament. The sensitivity of the issue, strongly expressed,
> within the government, by the Ministry of Economic Development, de-
> rives from the need to match mechanisms that can ensure the interrup-
> tion of the vicious circle fueled by illegally extracted resources with the
> rights and interests not only of industrial circles, but also of the work-
> force, at the European and, in particular, the Italian level. By extending
> the mandatory traceability to the entire production chain, notwithstand-
> ing – I add – the vagueness of its geographic scope, the Regulation, in the
> opinion of the government, risks being difficult to be applied by profes-
> sionals, especially if small- and medium-sized: basically, as maintained
> by trade associations, it is likely to penalize them, without any guarantee
> as to whether it will be able to effectively reach the target it sets for con-
> flict zones. For this reason, the European industry, not only in Italy but
> in all the relevant EU fora, has opposed the idea of introducing a man-
> datory regulation for the whole chain, irrespective of geographical areas
> and affecting the smallest traders as well as the biggest importers or the
> refineries. We have tried, during the semester of Italian Presidency, to
> advocate the need to give to the operators, first of all, new guidelines
> concerning geographical and product indications: this was the argument
> that we had recourse to, before demanding compliance with the rules. I
> must say that at this stage of dialogue and trialogue, an analysis, together
> with other ministries, is still ongoing, about the economic, legal and

commercial aspects of the Commission proposal in the Council, and also – I must say – a better detailed assessment of the substantive impact of this legislative initiative on the European and national economy and in particular on small- and medium-sized enterprises".

He then concluded as follows:

"This is a pretty classic case of policy consistency; we can question and assess its importance, but the legitimate demands of industry and the productive world – concerning the need not to increase the burden on small- and medium-sized enterprises and to introduce rules that are understandable and allowing compliance, with a clear time horizon and geographically localized with specific reference to products – are a genuine need; on the other hand, we must avoid incurring in a black-and-white evaluation, which leads us to only consider the needs of the productive world […]. [In that respect] I want to remind you of the Kimberley Process, concerning the issue of diamonds, and to mention a situation recalled few days ago in Milan, by a high representative of the FAO, in the presence of Amartya Sen: the situation of a famous and important African country, which, despite being one of the leading gold producers, sees that national budget heading to be loss-making, since the extraction of gold is entrusted to foreign companies subsidized by the government – I will not tell which one – and which do not produce any revenue for the country. This is evidence of how much this matter is politically delicate and complex and requires us, therefore, to consider not only the reasons of producers, extractors and users of materials, but also the need for a greater consistency of development policies".

3. THE GOVERNMENT'S POSITION ON THE EU INTERPRETATIVE NOTICE ON GOODS ORIGINATING FROM THE TERRITORIES OCCUPIED BY ISRAEL

On 27 November 2015, at the *Camera dei Deputati* (Chamber of Deputies, 531st Meeting, XVII Legislature) the *Sottosegretario di Stato per lo sviluppo economico* (Undersecretary of State for Economic Development), Ms. Simona Vicari answered a parliamentary question on the European Commission interpretative notice on the indication of origin of goods from the territories occupied by Israel. Ms. Vicari stated:

"[…] On 11 November the European Commission adopted an interpretative notice on the indication of origin of goods from the territories occupied by Israel since June 1967, which was published in the EU Official Journal in Section C, i.e. the section concerning non-binding acts. This document, prepared by the Directorate General TAXUD, does not entail any regulatory change as regards the commercial agreement in force between the European Union and Israel. It constitutes a technical clarification from the European Commission to the benefit of Member States, in particular their customs authorities, for correct information of consumers and the application of tariff differentiation between the goods produced in Israel and those produced in the West Bank".

She then added:

"In December 2004, the EU-Israel Customs Cooperation Committee adopted a technical agreement under which Israel is obliged to specify, in each certificate of origin of a product, the place of production, identified through the use of postal codes; based on this system, products made in Israel benefit from a preferential tariff scheme, as provided by the Association Agreement between the European Union and Israel, while no preference can be accorded to goods produced in the settlements of the West Bank and the Golan Heights, which are not recognized as territories belonging to Israel under international law. The United Kingdom since 2009, Denmark since 2013 and Belgium since 2014 have been applying in their domestic legal systems similar guidelines, which put in different categories food produced in Israel, in the settlements and in the West Bank. In terms of trade flows, the guidelines for the indication of origin will have little practical effect, since they will only affect two percent of the total amount of Israeli exports to the European Union. In Europe, Italy is the third supplier of Israel, after Germany and Belgium, the latter's data being, however, strongly influenced by the trade in worked diamonds. Italy imports from Israel, mainly, basic chemicals, fertilizers, plastic and rubber materials and optical instruments: these are products that do not fall under the categories covered by the measures on the indication of origin".

Ms. Vicari then noted how "[u]nsurprisingly, the publication of the notice has triggered an almost unanimous condemnation by Israeli institutions and political forces". And she finally added:

"Basically, Israel treats the question of the indication of origin as a boycott and connects it to the campaign 'Boycott, Divestment and Sanctions' carried out by some European lobbies and that, on the contrary, the European Union and Italy strongly oppose. In this regard, it should be noted that the adoption of measures for the correct indication of origin will, conversely, be useful in limiting the scope and harmfulness of open-ended boycotts against Israeli products. The government is committed to continue to closely monitor this matter and its future developments".

4. THE PURSUIT OF NUCLEAR DISARMAMENT

On 13 October 2015, during the general debate at the First Committee of the General Assembly of the United Nations (LXX Session), Ambassador Vinicio Mati, Permanent Representative of Italy to the Conference on Disarmament, made the following statement on the pursuit of nuclear disarmament and the Nuclear Non-Proliferation Treaty (NPT). He stated:

> "In the nuclear field, the NPT remains the cornerstone of the global non-proliferation regime and the essential foundation for the pursuit of nuclear disarmament. We call for its universalization and for the full implementation of its three mutually reinforcing pillars. We also underscore the indispensable role of the IAEA and support its strengthening, including through universal adherence to Comprehensive Safeguards Agreements and Additional Protocols. We deeply regret that consensus could not be reached at the 9th Review Conference of the NPT, but we trust that the efforts made to bridge different positions will not be in vain. We must continue to work to achieve the objectives of the Treaty, including through the full implementation of the 2010 Action Plan".

He then continued as follows:

> "Further major reductions in nuclear arsenals and their eventual elimination require our cooperation in addressing the security and humanitarian dimensions of nuclear weapons. Concern over the devastating impact of nuclear weapon explosions on human beings and on the environment underpins our actions on disarmament and non-proliferation. The hard practical work necessary to bring us closer to a world free of nuclear weapons must be further carried on and be centered not only on humanitarian but also on security considerations. We are convinced that such action should focus on practical and effective measures. We must simultaneously advance non-proliferation and disarmament as mutually reinforcing processes and create a more peaceful world. In this prospect, the entry into force of the Comprehensive Test-Ban Treaty (CTBT) remains a top priority. We urge all States whose ratification is essential for its entry into force to

sign and/or ratify it. Pending this, we support a comprehensive moratorium on nuclear weapons tests".

On a previous occasion, on 6 May 2015, within the context of the Review Conference of the Parties to the NPT (Main Committee II), Mr. Mati had dwelled on the specific issue of the compatibility of NATO's nuclear basing arrangements with the NPT itself. He had stated:

> "[…] I would like to reiterate – as already underlined by other delegations and ours – that these arrangements were already in place when the NPT entered into force in 1970. They were made clear to the NPT negotiating delegations and were made public. The abovementioned arrangements are fully compatible with the NPT obligations of NATO Allies".

AGREEMENTS TO WHICH ITALY IS A PARTY AND AGREEMENTS AND UNDERSTANDINGS TO WHICH ITALIAN REGIONS AND AUTONOMOUS PROVINCES ARE PARTIES

(edited by *Chiara Altafin* and *Marina Mancini*)

This section is divided into two sub-sections. Sub-section I includes agreements concluded by Italy, while sub-section II comprises agreements and understandings to which the Italian Regions and Autonomous Provinces of Trento and Bolzano are parties.

I
AGREEMENTS TO WHICH ITALY IS A PARTY

This sub-section is divided into two parts. Part A) contains the list of agreements signed by Italy and published in the *Gazzetta Ufficiale* in 2015. Part B) lists the agreements signed by Italy and published before 2015, of which the entry into force was announced in the *Gazzetta Ufficiale* in 2015.

In both parts the agreements are listed by subject matter and, within the same subject matter, multilateral agreements are placed before bilateral ones. Multilateral agreements are in chronological order, while bilateral agreements are listed in alphabetical order according to the international subject with which they were signed. In the case of more than one bilateral agreement with the same international subject, they are in chronological order.

If an agreement has entered into force, the date of entry into force is indicated. For those agreements requiring a law authorising ratification, the date of entry into force is deduced – as a rule – from the schedules published periodically by the *Ministero degli affari esteri* (Ministry of Foreign Affairs) in the *Supplemento Ordinario* (Suppl.) to the *Gazzetta Ufficiale* (GU).

A)
AGREEMENTS SIGNED BY ITALY,
PUBLISHED IN THE *GAZZETTA UFFICIALE* IN 2015

IV. DIPLOMATIC AND CONSULAR RELATIONS

Bilateral Agreements

Agreement between Italy and *Argentina* on the Employment of the Family Members of the Diplomatic, Consular, Administrative, and Technical Staff, done at Rome on 17 July 2003, with Interpretative Exchange of Letters, done at Rome on 25 June and 3 September 2012, implemented by Law No. 49 of 23 April 2015 (GU No. 102 of 5 May 2015), entered into force on 1 August 2015 (GU Suppl. to No. 164 of 17 July 2015);

Agreement between Italy and *Brazil* on the Employment of the Family Members of the Diplomatic, Consular, Administrative, and Technical Staff, done at Rome on 11 November 2008, with Interpretative Exchange of Letters, done at Rome on 28 August and 12 October 2012, implemented by Law No. 15 of 10 February 2015 (GU No. 51 of 3 March 2015);

Agreement between Italy and *Chile* on the Employment Authorization of the Family Members of the Diplomatic, Consular, Administrative, and Technical Staff of the Diplomatic Missions and Consular Representations, done at Rome on 13 December 2013, implemented by Law No. 166 of 29 September 2015 (GU No. 245 of 21 October 2015);

Agreement between Italy and *Mongolia* on the Exemption of Visa Requirements for Holders of Diplomatic Passports, done at Rome on 14 July 2014, entered into force on 18 November 2014 (GU Suppl. to No. 21 of 27 January 2015).

VII.   LAW OF THE SEA

Bilateral Agreements

Agreement between Italy and *Algeria* on Search and Rescue at Sea, done at Algiers on 14 November 2012, entered into force on 18 December 2014 (GU Suppl. to No. 21 of 27 January 2015).

IX. CULTURAL HERITAGE

Multilateral Agreements

European Convention on the Protection of the Archaeological Heritage (Revised), done at Valletta on 16 January 1992, implemented by Law No. 57 of 29 April 2015 (GU No. 108 of 12 May 2015).

X. AIR AND SPACE LAW

Bilateral Agreements

Framework Agreement between Italy and the *United States of America* for Co-operation in the Exploration and Use of Outer Space for Peaceful Purposes, done at Washington on 19 March 2013, implemented by Law No. 197 of 16 November 2015 (GU No. 292 of 16 December 2015).

XI. TREATMENT OF ALIENS AND NATIONALITY

Multilateral Agreements

Convention on the Reduction of Statelessness, done at New York on 30 August 1961, implemented by Law No. 162 of 29 September 2015 (GU No. 237 of 12 October 2015).

Bilateral Agreements

Agreement between Italy and *Kosovo* on Readmission of Persons Residing without Authorization, done at Rome on 15 April 2014, entered into force on 26 March 2015 (GU Suppl. to No. 116 of 21 May 2015).

XII. HUMAN RIGHTS

Multilateral Agreements

Convention on Jurisdiction, Applicable Law, Recognition, Enforcement, and Co-operation in Respect of Parental Responsibility and Measures for the Protection of Children, done at The Hague on 19 October 1996, implemented by Law No. 101 of 18 June 2015 (GU No. 157 of 9 July 2015);

International Convention for the Protection of All Persons from Enforced Disappearance, adopted by the General Assembly of the United Nations on 20 December 2006, implemented by Law No. 131 of 29 July 2015 (GU No. 192 of 20 August 2015);

Optional Protocol to the Convention on the Rights of the Child on a Communications Procedure, adopted by the General Assembly of the United Nations on 19 December 2011, implemented by Law No. 199 of 16 November 2015 (GU No. 293 of 17 December 2015).

XIV. CO-OPERATION IN JUDICIAL, LEGAL, SECURITY, AND SOCIO-ECONOMIC MATTERS

1. LEGAL AND JUDICIAL CO-OPERATION

Bilateral Agreements

Co-operation Agreement between Italy and *Afghanistan* on Preventing and Combating Illicit Trafficking in Narcotic Drugs, Psychotropic Substances and Their Precursors, done at Rome on 2 June 2011, implemented by Law No. 13 of 10 February 2015 (GU No. 50 of 2 March 2015);

Treaty between Italy and *Brazil* on the Transfer of Sentenced Persons, done at Brasilia on 27 March 2008, implemented by Law No. 17 of 10 February 2015 (GU No. 52 of 4 March 2015);

Agreement between Italy and *Kazakhstan* on Co-operation in Combating Organized Crime, Illicit Traffic in Narcotic Drugs, Psychotropic Substances, Precursors, and Chemicals Used for Their Production, Terrorism, and Other Forms of Crime, done at Rome on 5 November 2009, implemented by Law No. 216 of 7 December 2015 (GU No. 5 of 8 January 2016);

Treaty between Italy and *Kazakhstan* on the Transfer of Sentenced Persons, done at Astana on 8 November 2013, implemented by Law No. 79 of 16 June 2015 (GU No. 143 of 23 June 2015);

Treaty between Italy and *Mexico* on Extradition, done at Rome on 28 July 2011, implemented by Law No. 89 of 15 June 2015 (GU No. 152 of 3 July 2015);

Treaty between Italy and *Mexico* on Legal Assistance in Criminal Matters, done at Rome on 28 July 2011, implemented by Law No. 90 of 15 June 2015 (GU No. 152 of 3 July 2015);

Additional Bilateral Agreement between Italy and *Montenegro* to the European Convention on Extradition of 13 December 1957 Aimed at Facilitating Its Application, done at Podgorica on 25 July 2013, implemented by Law No. 63 of 6 May 2015 (GU No. 113 of 18 May 2015);

Additional Bilateral Agreement between Italy and *Montenegro* to the European Convention on Mutual Assistance in Criminal Matters of 20 April 1959 Aimed at Facilitating Its Application, done at Podgorica on 25 July 2013, implemented by Law No. 63 of 6 May 2015 (GU No. 113 of 18 May 2015);

Treaty between Italy and the *People's Republic of China* on Mutual Legal Assistance in Criminal Matters, done at Rome on 7 October 2010, implemented by Law No. 64 of 29 April 2015 (GU No. 114 of 19 May 2015), entered into force on 16 August 2015 (GU Suppl. to No. 253 of 30 October 2015);

Treaty between Italy and the *People's Republic of China* on Extradition, done at Rome on 7 October 2010, implemented by Law No. 161 of 24 September 2015 (GU No. 235 of 9 October 2015);

Co-operation Agreement between Italy and *Turkey* on Combating Serious Crime in particular Terrorism and Organized Crime, done at Rome on 8 May 2012, implemented by Law No. 5 of 12 January 2015 (GU No. 23 of 29 January 2015).

2.   MILITARY AND SECURITY MATTERS

Multilateral Agreements

Amendment to the Convention on the Physical Protection of Nuclear Material, done at Vienna on 8 July 2005, implemented by Law No. 58 of 28 April 2015 (GU No. 109 of 13 May 2015).

Bilateral Agreements

Agreement between Italy and *Albania* on Mutual Protection of Classified Information, done at Tirana on 9 December 2014, entered into force on 29 April 2015 (GU Suppl. to No. 164 of 17 July 2015);

Agreement between Italy and *Chile* on Defence Co-operation, done at Rome on 25 July 2014, implemented by Law No. 200 of 16 November 2015 (GU No. 294 of 18 December 2015);

Agreement between Italy and *Kazakhstan* on Military Co-operation, done at Rome on 7 June 2012, implemented by Law No. 94 of 16 June 2015 (GU No. 154 of 6 July 2015);

Agreement between Italy and *Ukraine* on Transit of Military Cargo and Personnel through the Territory of Ukraine in connection with the Participation of the Italian Armed Forces in the Afghanistan International Security Assistance Force, done at Kiev on 21 February 2013, entered into force on 25 May 2015 (GU Suppl. to No. 164 of 17 July 2015);

Exchange of Notes on the Agreement between Italy and *United Arab Emirates* Concerning Co-operation in the Field of Defence of 13 December 2003, done at Abu Dhabi on 13 and 23 March 2015, entered into force on 16 March 2015 (GU Suppl. to No. 253 of 30 October 2015).

3. Cultural, Educational, Scientific and Technological Co-operation

Bilateral Agreements

Co-operation Agreement between Italy and *Bosnia and Herzegovina* in the Fields of Culture, Education and Sport, done at Mostar on 19 July 2004, implemented by Law No. 14 of 10 February 2015 (GU No. 51 of 3 March 2015);

Agreement between Italy and *Chile* on Scientific and Technological Co-operation, done at Rome on 16 October 2007, implemented by Law No. 165 of 29 September 2015 (GU No. 244 of 20 October 2015);

Agreement between Italy and *San Marino* on Radio-Television Co-operation, with Annex, done at Rome on 5 March 2008, implemented by Law No. 164 of 29 September 2015 (GU No. 243 of 19 October 2015).

4. Neighbourly Relations

Bilateral Agreements

Agreement between Italy and *France* relating to the Cross-Border Transfer of Waste Resulting from the Construction of the Tenda Road Tunnel, done at Ajaccio on 26 October 2013, entered into force on 1 September 2015 (GU Suppl. to No. 253 of 30 October 2015);

Agreement between Italy and *Sovereign Order of Malta* on Postal Services, done at Rome on 18 December 2014, entered into force on 26 March 2015 (GU Suppl. to No. 164 of 17 July 2015).

5. TRANSPORT

Bilateral Agreements

Amendment to the Air Transport Agreement between Italy and *Mexico* of 23 December 1965, as subsequently amended, done at Mexico City on 13 January 2014, entered into force on 18 August 2015 (GU Suppl. to No. 253 of 30 October 2015);

Agreement between Italy and *Switzerland* for the Development of Railway Infrastructures, done at Berna on 28 January 2014, entered into force on 1 May 2015 (GU Suppl. to No. 164 of 17 July 2015);

Agreement between Italy and *Uruguay* for the Mutual Recognition of Driving Licences, done at Montevideo on 5 November 2014, entered into force on 17 May 2015 (GU Suppl. to No. 164 of 17 July 2015).

6. SOCIAL SECURITY

Bilateral Agreements

Agreement between Italy and *Canada* on Social Security, done at Rome on 22 May 1995, with Additional Protocol, done at Rome on 22 May 2003 (GU No. 154 of 6 July 2015);

Agreement between Italy and *Japan* on Social Security, done at Rome on 6 February 2009, implemented by Law No. 97 of 18 June 2015 (GU No. 156 of 8 July 2015);

Agreement between Italy and *Israel* on Social Security, done at Jerusalem on 2 February 2010, implemented by Law No. 98 of 18 June 2015 (GU No. 156 of 8 July 2015);

Agreement between Italy and *Turkey* on Social Security, done at Rome on 8 May 2012, implemented by Law No. 35 of 11 March 2015 (GU No. 74 of 30 March 2015).

XV. INTERNATIONAL ECONOMIC LAW

1. GENERAL ECONOMIC AND FINANCIAL CO-OPERATION

Bilateral Agreements

Agreement between Italy and *Montenegro* on Strategic Co-operation, done at Rome on 6 February 2010, implemented by Law No. 50 of 28 April 2015 (GU No. 102 of 5 May 2015), entered into force on 20 May 2015 (GU Suppl. to No. 164 of 17 July 2015);

Agreement between Italy and *San Marino* on Economic Co-operation, done at San Marino on 31 March 2009, entered into force on 26 January 2015 (GU Suppl. to No. 116 of 21 May 2015).

2. TAXATION

Bilateral Agreements

Agreement between Italy and the *Cayman Islands* on the Exchange of Information Relating to Tax Matters, done at London on 3 December 2012, implemented by Law No. 100 of 18 June 2015 (GU No. 157 of 9 July 2015), entered into force on 13 August 2015 (GU Suppl. to No. 253 of 30 October 2015);

Agreement between Italy and the *Hong Kong Special Administrative Region of the People's Republic of China* for the Avoidance of Double Taxation with respect to Taxes on Income and the Prevention of Fiscal Evasion, with Protocol, done at Hong Kong on 14 January 2013, implemented by Law No. 96 of 18 June 2015 (GU No. 155 of 7 July 2015), entered into force on 10 August 2015 (GU Suppl. to No. 253 of 30 October 2015);

Agreement between Italy and the *Isle of Man* for the Exchange of Information Relating to Tax Matters, done at London on 16 September 2013, implemented by Law No. 12 of 10 February 2015 (GU No. 50 of 2 March 2015);

Protocol of Amendment to the Convention between Italy and *Mexico* of 8 July 1991 for the Avoidance of Double Taxation with respect to Taxes on Income and the Prevention of Fiscal Evasion, done at Mexico City on 23 June 2011, implemented by Law No. 203 of 29 December 2014 (GU No. 22 of 28 January 2015);

Agreement between Italy and the *States of Guernsey* on the Exchange of Information Relating to Tax Matters, done at London on 5 September 2012 (GU No. 52 of 4 March 2015);

Agreement between Italy and the *United States of America* to Improve International Tax Compliance and to Implement FATCA (Foreign Account Tax Compliance Act), with Annexes, done at Rome on 10 January 2014, implemented by Law No. 95 of 18 June 2015 (GU No. 155 of 7 July 2015).

3.   ECONOMIC DEVELOPMENT AND DEVELOPMENT CO-OPERATION

Bilateral Agreements

Agreement between Italy and *Afghanistan* on a Soft Loan Awarding for "Enhancing the Civil Aviation Sector through the Upgrade of the Herat Airport to International Standards", done at Kabul on 11 February 2014, entered into force on 4 December 2014 (GU Suppl. to No. 21 of 27 January 2015);

Agreement between Italy and *Egypt* on a Soft Loan Awarding for the "Sustainable Agricultural Mechanization System Improvement in Minia and Fayoum Governorates", done at Sharm el-Sheikh on 14 March 2015, entered into force on 20 July 2015 (GU Suppl. to No. 253 of 30 October 2015);

Agreement between Italy and *El Salvador* for the Implementation of the Project "Expansion of Higher Education Provision to Improve Productivity in Twelve Departments of the Country", done at Antiguo Cuscatlán on 18 February 2014, entered into force on 6 January 2015 (GU Suppl. to No. 116 of 21 May 2015);

Agreement between Italy and *El Salvador* for the Implementation of the Project "Program on Prevention and Rehabilitation of Young People at Risk and in Conflict with the Law", done at Antiguo Cuscatlán on 2 June 2014, entered into force on 12 August 2015 (GU Suppl. to No. 253 of 30 October 2015);

Agreement between Italy and *Ethiopia* for the Implementation of the Programme: Financing of the Initiative "Italian Contribution to the Promotion of Basic Services Programme Phase III (PBS 3)", done at Addis Ababa on 5 September 2014, entered into force on 18 May 2015 (GU Suppl. to No. 164 of 17 July 2015);

Agreement between Italy and the Principality of *Monaco* in the Field of Development Co-operation, done at Monaco on 31 March 2015, entered into force on 13 July 2015 (GU Suppl. to No. 253 of 30 October 2015);

Memorandum of Understanding between Italy and *Palestine*, done at Ramallah on 5 March 2015, entered into force on 4 August 2015 (GU Suppl. to No. 253 of 30 October 2015);

Exchange of Notes on the Amendment to the Agreement between Italy and *People's Republic of China* on the Financing of the "Vocational Training Programme" of 11 October 2001, done at Beijing on 3 October and 3 December 2014, entered into force on 30 July 2015 (GU Suppl. to No. 253 of 30 October 2015);

Exchange of Notes on the Amendment to the Memorandum of Understanding between Italy and *People's Republic of China* on the Financing of the "Support to the Chinese County and District Hospital of Western and Middle Provinces Program" of 6 December 2004, done at Beijing on 3 October and 3 December 2014, entered into force on 30 July 2015 (GU Suppl. to No. 253 of 30 October 2015);

Exchange of Notes on the Amendment to the Memorandum of Understanding between Italy and *People's Republic of China* on the Financing of the "Environmental Programme" of 18 September 2006, done at Beijing on 3 October and 3 December 2014, entered into force on 30 July 2015 (GU Suppl. to No. 253 of 30 October 2015).

XVI. INTERNATIONAL ORGANIZATIONS

1. HEADQUARTERS AGREEMENTS AND LEGAL STATUS

Bilateral Agreements

Memorandum of Agreement between Italy and the *World Health Organization – Regional Office for Europe* Concerning the WHO European Office for Investment for Health and Development, located in Venice, Italy, with Amendment and Annexes, done at Rome on 23 November 2012, implemented by Law No. 205 of 7 December 2015 (GU No. 298 of 23 December 2015).

2. EUROPEAN UNION

Multilateral Agreements

Agreement on the Transfer and Mutualisation of Contributions to the Single Resolution Fund, with Annexes, done at Brussels on 21 May 2014, implemented by Law No. 188 of 26 November 2015 (GU No. 277 of 27 November 2015).

Bilateral Agreements

Free Trade Agreement between the European Union and its Member States, of the one part, and the *Republic of Korea*, of the other part, with Annexes, done at Brussels on 6 October 2010, implemented by Law No. 138 of 4 August 2015 (GU Suppl. to No. 204 of 3 September 2015);

Trade Agreement between the European Union and its Member States, of the one part, and *Colombia* and *Peru*, of the other part, done at Brussels on 26 June 2012, implemented by Law No. 120 of 24 July 2015 (GU Suppl. to No. 184 of 10 August 2015);

Association Agreement between the European Union and the European Atomic Energy Community and their Member States, of the one part, and *Georgia*, of the other part, done at Brussels on 27 June 2014, implemented by Law No. 218 of 7 December 2015 (GU No. 6 of 9 January 2016);

Association Agreement between the European Union and the European Atomic Energy Community and their Member States, of the one part, and *Moldova*, of the other part, done at Brussels on 27 June 2014, implemented by Law No. 217 of 7 December 2015 (GU No. 6 of 9 January 2016);

Association Agreement between the European Union and the European Atomic Energy Community and their Member States, of the one part, and *Ukraine*, of the other part, done at Brussels on 27 June 2014, implemented by Law No. 169 of 29 September 2015 (GU No. 247 of 23 October 2015).

B)
AGREEMENTS SIGNED BY ITALY, PUBLISHED BEFORE 2014, THE ENTRY INTO FORCE OF WHICH WAS ANNOUNCED IN THE *GAZZETTA UFFICIALE* IN 2015

XIV. CO-OPERATION IN JUDICIAL, LEGAL, SECURITY, AND SOCIO-ECONOMIC MATTERS

1. LEGAL AND JUDICIAL CO-OPERATION

Agreement between Italy and *San Marino* on Co-operation for Preventing and Suppressing Criminality, done at Rome on 29 February 2012, implemented by Law No. 167 of 17 October 2014 (GU No. 265 of 14 November 2014), entered into force on 4 February 2015 (GU Suppl. to No. 164 of 17 July 2015);

Agreement between Italy and *United States of America* on Enhancing Co-operation in Preventing and Combating Serious Crime, done at Rome on 28 May 2009, implemented by Law No. 99 of 3 July 2014 (GU No. 163 of 16 July 2014), entered into force on 3 October 2014 (GU Suppl. to No. 116 of 21 May 2015).

2. MILITARY AND SECURITY MATTERS

Multilateral Agreements

Arms Trade Treaty, done at New York on 2 April 2013, implemented by Law No. 118 of 4 October 2013 (GU No. 242 of 15 October 2013), entered into force on 24 December 2014 (GU Suppl. to No. 21 of 27 January 2015).

XV. INTERNATIONAL ECONOMIC LAW

1. GENERAL ECONOMIC AND FINANCIAL CO-OPERATION

Bilateral Agreements

Agreement between Italy and *San Marino* on Financial Co-operation, done at San Marino on 26 February 2009, implemented by Law No. 149 of 3 October 2014 (GU No. 247 of 23 October 2014), entered into force on 26 January 2015 (GU Suppl. to No. 116 of 21 May 2015).

2. TAXATION

Bilateral Agreements

Additional Protocol to the Convention between Italy and the *Republic of Korea* for the Avoidance of Double Taxation and the Prevention of Fiscal Evasion with Respect to Taxes on Income, done at Seoul on 3 April 2012, implemented by Law No. 156 of 17 October 2014 (GU No. 252 of 29 October 2014), entered into force on 23 January 2015 (GU Suppl. to No. 116 of 21 May 2015);

Agreement between Italy and *Jersey* on the Exchange of Information relating to Tax Matters, done at London on 13 March 2012, implemented by Law No. 158 of 17 October 2014 (GU No. 253 of 30 October 2014), entered into force on 26 January 2015 (GU Suppl. to No. 116 of 21 May 2015);

Additional Protocol Amending the Convention between Italy and *Luxembourg* for the Avoidance of Double Taxation, done at Luxembourg on 21 June 2012, implemented by Law No. 150 of 3 October 2014 (GU No. 248 of 24 January 2014), entered into force on 20 January 2015 (GU Suppl. to No. 116 of 21 May 2015).

3. LABOUR

Multilateral Agreements

Maritime Labour Convention, done at Geneva on 23 February 2006, implemented by Law No. 113 of 23 September 2013 (GU No. 237 of 9 October 2013), entered into force on 19 November 2014 (GU Suppl. to No. 21 of 27 January 2015).

XVI. INTERNATIONAL ORGANIZATIONS

1. HEADQUARTERS AGREEMENTS AND LEGAL STATUS

Bilateral Agreements

Exchange of Notes Amending Article 1 of the Headquarters Agreement between Italy and the *International Institute for the Unification of Private Law (UNIDROIT)* of 25 July 1967, as Amended with Exchange of Notes of 5 and 9 June 1995, done at Rome on 21 December 2012, implemented by Law No. 143 of 23 September 2014 (GU No. 236 of 10 October 2014), entered into force on 5 November 2014 (GU Suppl. to No. 21 of 27 January 2015).

2. EUROPEAN UNION

Multilateral Agreements

Protocol on the Concerns of the Irish People on the Treaty of Lisbon, done at Brussels on 13 June 2012, implemented by Law No. 149 of 3 October 2014 (GU No. 247 of 23 October 2014), entered into force on 2 December 2014 (GU Suppl. to No. 21 of 27 January 2015).

II

AGREEMENTS AND UNDERSTANDINGS TO WHICH ITALIAN REGIONS
AND AUTONOMOUS PROVINCES ARE PARTIES

Italy is composed of twenty Regions: Abruzzo; Basilicata; Calabria; Campania; Emilia-Romagna; Friuli-Venezia Giulia; Lazio; Liguria; Lombardia; Marche; Molise; Piemonte; Puglia; Sardegna; Sicilia; Toscana; Trentino-Alto Adige; Umbria; Valle d'Aosta; and Veneto. Each Region comprises two or more Provinces, except Valle d'Aosta. Trentino-Alto Adige comprises the Autonomous Provinces of Trento and Bolzano.

The Regions and the aforementioned Autonomous Provinces are entitled to conclude agreements with foreign States and understandings with territorial entities of foreign States in conformity with Law No. 131 of 5 June 2003 (published in the *Gazzetta Ufficiale* No. 132 of 10 June 2003). This Law contains provisions necessary to implement Constitutional Law No. 3 of 18 October 2001 reforming Title V of the Constitution. It provides, *inter alia*, for the implementation of amendments to Article 117 of the Constitution concerning the "treaty-making power" of Regions. Article 6, paragraph 3, gives the Regions and the Autonomous Provinces the power to enter into international agreements with foreign States on matters falling within their legislative competence, when receiving full powers from the Ministry of Foreign Affairs as provided for by customary international law and the Vienna Convention on the Law of Treaties of 1969. On the other hand, Article 6, paragraph 2, vests the Regions and the Autonomous Provinces with the power to conclude understandings with territorial entities of foreign States on the same matters, upon notice to the Presidency of the Council of Ministers and the Ministry of Foreign Affairs. These understandings do not have any effect on Italian foreign policy nor entail financial burdens for the State. They do not constitute international agreements *stricto sensu*.

The Regions and the Autonomous Provinces of Trento and Bolzano are also entitled to enter into understandings with territorial entities of neighbouring States on trans-frontier co-operation, in conformity with Law No. 948 of 19 November 1984 (published in the *Supplemento Ordinario* to *Gazzetta Ufficiale* No. 18 of 22 January 1985). This Law implements the European Outline Convention on Transfrontier Co-operation between Territorial Communities or Authorities, drawn up by the Council of Europe and done at Madrid on 21 May 1980. Article 3 enables Regions, Provinces and Municipalities to conclude understandings with neighbouring foreign territorial communities or authorities, subject to the adoption of a bilateral agreement between Italy and the neighbouring State. These understandings do not constitute international agreements *stricto sensu*. However, the Regions and the Autonomous Provinces of Trento and Bolzano can also enter into understandings with territorial entities of neighbouring States on trans-frontier co-operation, in order to implement European Union regulations in the field of regional policy. The Madrid Convention and Law No. 948/1984 do not apply to these understandings, according to Constitutional Court Judgment No. 258 of 22 July 2004 (available at: <http://www.cortecostituzionale.it/>).

This sub-section is divided into two parts. Part A) lists the international agreements that the Italian Regions and Autonomous Provinces of Trento and Bolzano signed with foreign States in 2015. Part B) contains a list of understandings that the Italian Regions and Autonomous Provinces of Trento and Bolzano signed with territorial entities of foreign States in the same year. Both the international agreements and the understandings are listed by Region or Province. They are in alphabetical order by reference to the foreign State or the territorial entity with which they were signed. Their subject matter is specified whenever it is not evident from the title.

A)
AGREEMENTS SIGNED BY ITALIAN REGIONS AND AUTONOMOUS PROVINCES IN 2015

LOMBARDIA

Bilateral Agreements

Co-operation Agreement between Lombardia and *San Marino*, done at Milan on 21 October 2015. Subject matter: co-operation in the fields of economic relations, trade and tourism.

MARCHE

Bilateral Agreements

Understanding between Marche and the Health Human Resources Development Center of the *People's Republic of China* on the Development of Human Resources in the Health Sector, done at Ancona on 2 July 2015, entered into force on the same day.

B)
UNDERSTANDINGS SIGNED BY ITALIAN REGIONS
AND AUTONOMOUS PROVINCES IN 2015

AUTONOMOUS PROVINCE OF BOLZANO

Multilateral Understandings

Understanding on Co-operation between the Autonomous Province of Bolzano, the Autonomous Province of Trento and the State of Tyrol (Austria) on the Management of the Common Representation in Brussels of the Autonomous Provinces of Bolzano and Trento and the State of Tyrol, done on 28 May 2015, entered into force on the same day.

AUTONOMOUS PROVINCE OF TRENTO

Multilateral Understandings

Understanding on Co-operation between the Autonomous Province of Bolzano, the Autonomous Province of Trento and the State of Tyrol (Austria) on the Management of the Common Representation in Brussels of the Autonomous Provinces of Bolzano and Trento and the State of Tyrol, done on 28 May 2015, entered into force on the same day.

EMILIA-ROMAGNA

Bilateral Understandings

Protocol of Understanding between Emilia-Romagna and the *Province of Guangdong (People's Republic of China)* for the Establishment of a Partnership, done at Guangzhou on 11 May 2015, entered into force on the same day.

FRIULI-VENEZIA GIULIA

Bilateral Understandings

Letter of Intent between Friuli-Venezia Giulia and the *Shizuoka Prefecture (Japan)*, done at Trieste on October 27, 2015, entered into force on the same day. Subject matter: co-operation in the fields of sports and tourism.

LOMBARDIA

Bilateral Understandings

Protocol of Understanding between Lombardia and the *Autonomous Community of the Basque Country (Spain)* for the Promotion of Competitiveness in the Agrifood Sector, done at Milan on 22 October 2015;

Understanding between Lombardia and the *Republic and Canton of Ticino (Switzerland)*, done at Como on 16 June 2015. Subject matter: co-operation in the fields of trade, tourism, energy, transport, education, culture, environment, health, sports and youth.

VENETO

Bilateral Understandings

Understanding for Friendship and Co-operation between Veneto and the *County of Berat (Albania)*, done at Venice and Berat on 24 February and 6 March 2015, entered into force on 6 March 2015;

Understanding for Friendship and Co-operation between Veneto and the *County of Tirana (Albania)*, done at Venice and Tirana on 24 February and 4 March 2015, entered into force on 4 March 2015;

Understanding for Friendship and Co-operation between Veneto and the *Region of Minsk (Belarus)*, done at Venice on 14 October 2015, entered into force on the same day;

Understanding for Friendship and Co-operation between Veneto and the *State of Espirito Santo (Brazil)*, done at Venice on 18 November 2015, entered into force on the same day.

UMBRIA

Bilateral Understandings

Memorandum of Understanding between Umbria and the *Province of Sichuan (People's Republic of China)* for Co-operation in the Field of Education, done at Chengdu on 20 November 2015, entered into force on the same day;

Protocol of Understanding between Umbria and the *Province of Yunnan (People's Republic of China)* on the Development of Friendly Relations of Co-operation, done at Milan on 4 July 2015.

LEGISLATION

(edited by *Pia Acconci*)

VIII. ENVIRONMENT

Law No. 194 of 1 December 2015 (GU No. 288 of 11 December 2015)
Provisions for the establishment of a national system for the protection and enhancement of biodiversity of agricultural and food products, through the prevention of depopulation, genetic erosion, and extinction, as well as the protection of rural land. This Law has been adopted in conformity with the 1992 Convention on Biological Diversity and the 2001 International Treaty on Plant Genetic Resources for Food and Agriculture.

Law No. 221 of 28 December 2015 (GU No. 13 of 18 January 2016)
Provisions for the promotion of measures for the "green economy" and the control of the excessive usage of natural resources of the sea and land. Law No. 221/2015 aims to introduce best practices for waste management, such as differentiated collection and recycling, to promote the sustainable production of energy, and ensure "universal" access to water in terms of drinkable water and sanitation systems. This Law also regulates green public procurement and administrative procedures for health and environmental impact assessment.

PIA ACCONCI

XI. TREATMENT OF ALIENS AND NATIONALITY

DPCM of 2 April 2015 (GU No. 104 of 7 May 2015)
Temporary planning of the flows of non-EU seasonal workers for the year 2015.

This Decree has been adopted pursuant to Italian law on immigration (see Law No. 189 of 30 July 2002, IYIL, 2002, p. 346 ff.) in order to specify the number of non-EU seasonal workers to enter the Italian territory for the year 2015.

Article 1 of the Decree establishes a quota of 13,000 persons, which confirms the downward trend of the past four years (60,000 in 2011; 35,000 in 2012; 30,000 in 2013, and 15,000 in 2014). Such a dramatic decrease results from a reduced need for the traditional seasonal activities, such as tourism, hospitality and agriculture, in which foreign labour has found employment, as evidenced from the declining number of applications received in the previous year.

The quota is to be allocated to the regions and autonomous provinces by the Ministry of Welfare, and it concerns seasonal workers from twenty-four non-

EU Member States, namely: Albania; Algeria; Bosnia-Herzegovina; Republic of Korea; Egypt; Former Yugoslav Republic of Macedonia; the Republic of the Philippines; Gambia; Ghana; Japan; India; Kosovo; Morocco; Mauritius; Moldova; Montenegro; Niger; Nigeria; Pakistan; Senegal; Serbia; Sri Lanka; Ukraine; and Tunisia.

Part of this quota is reserved for those non-EU workers (1,500) who have entered the territory of Italy for at least two consecutive years to provide their seasonal work, and for whom the employer has requested a multi-year permit. This provision clearly aims at facilitating the use of multi-year permits for seasonal work, which can simplify the procedure and optimize the time required to hire manpower.

DPCM of 14 December 2015 (GU No. 26 of 2 February 2016)
Temporary planning of the flows of non-EU workers for the year 2016.

This Decree, adopted pursuant to Italian law on immigration (see Law No. 189 of 30 July 2002, IYIL, 2002, p. 346 ff.), establishes the maximum quota for non-EU workers, both seasonal and non-seasonal, who can enter the territory of Italy for the year 2016. This quota of 17,850 non-seasonal workers, both employed and self-employed, has been kept at the same level as in the past years, and refers to different categories of non-EU citizens, notably: 1,000 non-EU citizens who have completed specific programs of training and education in their States of origin, according to Article 23 of Law 286/98 (Article 2.1); 2,400 self-employed workers who are professionals, or businessmen operating in sectors of interest to the Italian economy, investing their own resources in a significant manner (not less than 500,000 Euros) in Italy, thus creating at least three new positions in the labour market; internationally-renowned artists; self-employed workers who intend to establish "innovative start-ups" in Italy (Article 2.2); 100 self-employed or non-seasonal employed workers of Italian origin, residing in Argentina, Uruguay, Venezuela, and Brazil (Article 2.3); 100 non-EU workers, coming from States that took part in the Universal Exhibition Milan 2015 (Article 2.4); a series of conversions into permits of stay for employed work in favour of specific categories of non-EU citizens (Article 3.1), namely 4,600 holders of seasonal work permit, 6,500 holders of permits for study, internship or vocational training, and 1,300 holders of EU long-stay permits that have been issued to third-State citizens by another EU Member State; a series of conversions into permits of stay for self-employed work in favour of 1,500 holders of permits for study, internship or vocational training, and 350 holders of EU long-stay permits that have been issued to third-country citizens by another EU Member State.

These various quotas will be allocated by the Ministry of Welfare, taking into account the actual needs of the labour market, to the Italian Regions and autonomous Provinces.

Article 4 of this Decree is finally devoted to the planning of non-EU seasonal workers for the year 2016, establishing the same quota of 13,000 as Article 1 of DPCM of 2 April 2015 (cf. *supra*). The total number of States whose citizens can benefit from this provision rises to twenty-seven: twenty-four States included in DPCM of 2 April 2015, plus Ivory Coast, Ethiopia, and Sudan.

GIANLUCA RUBAGOTTI

XVIII. USE OF FORCE AND PEACE-KEEPING

Law No. 43 of 17 April 2015 (GU No. 91 of 20 April 2015)
Enactment as a Law, with amendments, of Decree Law No. 7 of 18 February 2015 concerning urgent measures to fight terrorism, including international terrorism, as well as the extension of international missions of the Armed and Police Forces, development cooperation initiatives and support to reconstruction processes, and participation in initiatives by international organizations to consolidate peace and stabilization processes.

Law No. 117 of 4 August 2015 (GU No. 181 of 6 August 2015)
Enactment as a Law of Decree Law No. 99 of 8 July 2015 concerning urgent measures for the participation of military personnel in the EU military operation EUNAVFOR MED.

Law No. 198 of 11 December 2015 (GU No. 292 of 16 December 2015)
Enactment as a Law, with amendments, of Decree Law No. 174 of 30 October 2015, concerning the extension of international missions of the Armed and Police Forces, development cooperation initiatives and support to reconstruction processes, and participation in initiatives by international organizations to consolidate peace and stabilization processes.

These laws concern the Italian participation, for the year 2015, to different international missions: humanitarian missions, development cooperation, peace and stabilization, some of which involving armed or police forces. Law No. 43/2015 covers the period from 1 January to 30 September, while Law No. 198/2015 provides for a further extension until 31 December 2015.

The first part of both laws, in particular, authorizes the necessary expenses in order to support the participation of the Italian armed and police forces in the following international missions and other activities:

Europe – (a) Military personnel: Multinational Specialized Unit (MSU), Security Force Training Plan in Kosovo, European Union Rule of Law Mission in Kosovo (EULEX Kosovo); Joint Enterprise, in the Balkan region; EUFOR ALTHEA, the EU mission in Bosnia-Herzegovina, which includes the Integrated Police Unit (IPU) mission; NATO operation Baltic Air Policing (until 31 August);

United Nations Peacekeeping Force in Cyprus (UNFICYP); Active Endeavour, in the Mediterranean Sea; EUNAVFOR MED, EU military operation in central and southern Mediterranean Sea.

Europe – (b) Police Forces: Cooperation activities carried out by Italian police forces in Albania and in the Balkan area; European Union Rule of Law Mission in Kosovo (EULEX Kosovo), and United Nations Mission in Kosovo (UNMIK).

Asia – Military personnel in NATO Resolute Support Mission (RSM), in compliance with UN Security Council Resolution No. 2189 of 2014, and EUPOL in Afghanistan; Military personnel in the UAE, Bahrein, Qatar and Tampa in connection with the missions in the Middle East and Asia; Various staff of the Italian Red Cross for sanitary support of the international missions in the Middle East and Asia; Military personnel in United Nations Interim Force in Lebanon (UNIFIL), including the deployment of naval units in UNIFIL Maritime Task Force; Military personnel in Temporary International Presence in Hebron (TIPH 2), as well as in training activities in favour of the Palestinian Security Forces; Military personnel in European Union Border Assistance Mission in Rafah (EUBAM Rafah); Police forces in European Union Police Mission for the Palestinian Territories (EUPOL COPPS); Military personnel in EUMM Georgia, the EU mission in Georgia; Military personnel in the activities of the International coalition to fight the terroristic threat of the Islamic state in Iraq and the Levant (ISIL).

Africa – Military personnel in European Union Border Assistance Mission in Lybia (EUBAM Lybia) as well as for activities of assistance, support and training in favor of Libyan security forces (only until 30 September); Finance Police personnel for training activities in favor of the Libyan Coastal Guard, in implementation of cooperation agreements between the Italian and Libyan Governments to face the phenomenon of illegal migration and human trafficking (until 30 September); Military personnel in Atalanta, the EU operation against international piracy; Military personnel in the EU missions EUTM Somalia and EUCAP Nestor, as well as in the EU initiatives for Regional Maritime Capacity Building in Eastern Africa and Western Indian Ocean; Military personnel for activities of training in favor of Somali and Djibouti police forces; Military personnel in United Nations Multidimensional Integrated Stabilization Mission in Mali (MINUSMA), as well as European Union EUCAP Missions in Sahel Niger and Sahel Mali and EUTM Mali; Military personnel in the EU mission in the Central African Republic (EUFOR RCA) (until 30 September); Military personnel in the military group of international observers of the end of military conflict in the Republic of Mozambique (EMOCHM) (only until 30 September).

The second part of both laws focuses on different initiatives, with a broad scope both thematically and geographically. A series of development cooperation initiatives are envisaged throughout the year, with a view to improving life conditions of civilians and refugees, as well as to supporting reconstruction efforts in States such as Afghanistan, Ethiopia, Central African Republic, Guinea, Iraq, Liberia, Libya, Mali, Myanmar, Niger, Pakistan, Palestine, Sierra Leone, Syria, Somalia, Sudan,

South Sudan, Yemen and, as far as refugees are concerned, their neighboring States. These initiatives are to take into account the primary objectives, the directives and the principles of Law No. 141/2014 (cf. IYIL, 2014, p. 536 ff.).

Finally, a series of initiatives are envisaged to support reconstruction processes of States in conflict or post-conflict situations, such as financial support for the Afghan security and police forces, support of peace processes in Sub-Sahara Africa, Latin America and the Caribbean, operational interventions to protect Italian citizens and interests abroad.

Law No. 43/2015 furthermore establishes a series of urgent measures to face the threat of terrorism, also at the international level. In particular, the procedures for the police forces to treat personal data have been simplified, in full compliance with the rights recognised to the persons involved; the activities of the system of information for the security of the Italian Republic have been enhanced; the framework provided by criminal law has been made more stringent, notably by introducing the offense of organising, financing or propagandizing travels abroad with a view to committing terrorist activities; the provisions concerning the use of explosives, as well as the expulsion of foreigners, have been tightened up; the use of military personnel has been increased; the new "National Anti-mafia and Antiterrorism Directorate" has been created within the General Prosecutor's Office.

GIANLUCA RUBAGOTTI

BIBLIOGRAPHIES

ITALIAN BIBLIOGRAPHICAL INDEX
OF INTERNATIONAL LAW 2015

(edited by *Giulio Bartolini* and *Alessandro Chechi*)

This bibliography includes books and articles published during the year 2015, with some exceptions going back to 2014.

Items are listed only once, under their most appropriate heading. Headings correspond to the Classification Scheme adopted for the Italian practice relating to international law.

Unless otherwise specified, texts are in the same language as corresponding entries in the bibliography.

When available, translations of titles have been reproduced from the original source.

The bibliography includes only works on public international law. Works considered as belonging to European Union law and to private international law are generally omitted.

Any indication of items inadvertently omitted will be appreciated with a view to publication in the next volume of the *Yearbook*.

I. INTERNATIONAL LAW IN GENERAL

ARCARI M. and SCOVAZZI T., *Corso di diritto internazionale* (International Law Course), Milano, 2015, pp. 402.

BARTOLINI G., "Le leggi razziali e la dottrina italiana di diritto internazionale" (Racial Laws and Italian Scholars of International Law), in RESTA G. and ZENO-ZENCOVICH V. (eds.), *Leggi razziali. Passato/Presente*, Roma, 2015, p. 55 ff.

CECCHINI G.L., "Ricordo di Tito Ballarino" (*In memoriam* of Tito Ballarino), RCGI, 2015, p. 7 ff.

CONFORTI B. and FOCARELLI C., *Le Nazioni Unite* (The United Nations), 10th ed., Padova, 2015, pp. 551.

FOCARELLI C., *Diritto internazionale* (International Law), 3rd ed., Padova, 2015, pp. 548.

FOCARELLI C., *Trattato di diritto internazionale* (Treatise on International Law), Torino, 2015, pp. 2552.

GIOIA A., *Manuale di diritto internazionale* (Manual on International Law), 5th ed., Milano, 2015, pp. 542.

GUARINO G., "Alla base del diritto internazionale: Spunti critici preliminari per una analisi del diritto internazionale come sistema" (At the Foundations of

International Law: Remarks for an Analysis of International Law as a System), OIDU, 2015, p. 1193 ff.

LUZZATTO R., "Ricordo di Piero Ziccardi" (*In memoriam* of Piero Ziccardi), RDI, 2015, p. 546 ff.

NESI G. and GARGIULO P. (eds.), *Luigi Ferrari Bravo. Il diritto internazionale come professione* (Luigi Ferrari Bravo. International Law as a Profession), Napoli, 2015, pp. 308.

PANEBIANCO M., "Ricordo di Piero Ziccardi" (*In memoriam* of Piero Ziccardi), RCGI, 2015, p. 15 ff.

ZICCARDI CAPALDO G., "From International Constitutionalism to Global Constitutionalism: Vision and Modernity of the Thought of Rolando Quadri", The Global Community, 2014, p. 957 ff.

II. INTERNATIONAL CUSTOM, LAW OF TREATIES AND OTHER SOURCES OF INTERNATIONAL LAW

CREMA L., "Subsequent Practice in *Hassan v. United Kingdom*: When Things Seem To Go Wrong in the Life of a Living Instrument", QIL, Zoom-in 15, 2015, p. 3 ff.

DISTEFANO G., "L'accord tacite ou l'univers parallèle du droit des traités", QIL, Zoom-in 18, 2015, p. 17 ff.

SCISO E., "La regola sulla immunità giurisdizionale dello Stato davanti alla Corte costituzionale" (The Customary Rule on State Immunity Before the Italian Constitutional Court), DUDI, 2015, p. 61 ff.

STARITA M., "L'interpretazione dei trattati che determinano frontiere" (The Interpretation of Boundary Treaties), RDI, 2015, p. 337 ff.

TANZI A., "Le forme della codificazione e sviluppo progressivo del diritto internazionale" (Codification and Progressive Development of International Law), in NESI G. and GARGIULO P. (eds.), *Luigi Ferrari Bravo. Il diritto internazionale come professione*, Napoli, 2015, p. 151 ff.

VILLANI U., "La rilevazione della consuetudine internazionale: una lezione ancora attuale" (The Identification of International Customary Law), in NESI G. and GARGIULO P. (eds.), *Luigi Ferrari Bravo. Il diritto internazionale come professione*, Napoli, 2015, p. 67 ff.

III. STATES AND OTHER INTERNATIONAL ENTITIES

MILANO E., "La Bosnia-Erzegovina a venti anni da Dayton: un sintetico bilancio" (Bosnia-Herzegovina Twenty Years after Dayton: An Assessment), CI, 2015, p. 509 ff.

PANELLA L., "La Somalia: dagli accordi di Kampala alla Costituzione della Repubblica Federale Parlamentare. La rinascita di uno 'Stato fallito'?" (Somalia: From the Kampala Agreements to the Constitution of the Parlamentary Federal Republic. The Rebirth of a "Failed State"?), OIDU, 2015, p. 818 ff.

PASCALE G., "Sulla posizione dell'individuo nel diritto internazionale: il caso *Campbell* e le vicende successive nell'Africa australe" (The Status of Individuals in International Law: The Campbell Case and Its Follow-Up in Austral Africa), RDI, 2015, p. 852 ff.

SINAGRA A., "Sovranità dello Stato e divieto di ingerenza nei suoi affari interni" (State Sovereignty and the Prohibition of Intervention in Domestic Matters), RCGI, 2015, p. 37 ff.

TREVISANUT S., "Is There Something Wrong with the Increasing Role of Private Actors?", in RYNGAERT C., MOLENAAR E.J. and NOUWEN S.M.H. (eds.), *What's Wrong with International Law? Liber Amicorum A.H.A. Soons*, Leiden, 2015, p. 63 ff.

TREVISANUT S., "The Role of Private Actors in Offshore Energy: Shifting Models of Participation", in TREVISANUT S. and BANKES N. (eds.), *Energy from the Sea. An International Law Perspective on Ocean Energy*, Leiden, 2015, p. 85 ff.

IV. DIPLOMATIC AND CONSULAR RELATIONS

BALDI S. and NESI G. (eds.), *Diplomatici in azione. Aspetti giuridici e politici della prassi diplomatica nel mondo contemporaneo* (Diplomats in Action. Legal and Political Issues of Contemporary Diplomatic Practice), Napoli, 2015, pp. 174.

CARPANELLI E., "On the Inviolability of Diplomatic Archives and Documents: The 1961 Vienna Convention on Diplomatic Relations to the Test of *WikiLeaks*", RDI, 2015, p. 834 ff.

CURTI GIALDINO C., *Lineamenti di diritto diplomatico e consolare* (Elements of Diplomatic and Consular Law), Torino, 2015, pp. 572.

PALCHETTI P., "Can State Action on Behalf of Victims Be an Alternative to Individual Access to Justice in Case of Grave Breaches of Human Rights?", IYIL, 2014, p. 53 ff.

V. IMMUNITIES

CATALDI G., "Jurisdictional Immunities of Foreign States and Human Rights: Which Balance between Domestic Order's Fundamental Values and International Customary Law?", in MAIORESCU T. (ed.), *Law between Modernization and Tradition – Implications for the Legal, Political, Administrative and Public Order Organization*, Bucarest, 2015, p. 560 ff.

CHECHI A., "Introductory Note to Judgment No. 238-2014", ILM, 2015, p. 471 ff.

CONFORTI B., "A Few Remarks on the Functional Immunity of the Organs of Foreign States", QIL, Zoom-out 17, 2015, p. 69 ff.

CONFORTI B., "Il legislatore torna indietro di circa novant'anni: la nuova norma sull'esecuzione sui conti correnti di Stati stranieri" (The Italian Legislator Goes Ninety Years Back: The New Rule Concerning Enforcement on Bank Accounts of Foreign States), RDI, 2015, p. 558 ff.

FARNELLI G.M., "A Controversial Dialogue between International and Domestic Courts on Functional Immunity", The Law & Practice of International Courts and Tribunals, 2015, p. 255 ff.

GIUFFRIDA R., "L'immunità dei beni degli Stati dalla giurisdizione esecutiva e cautelare nel diritto internazionale e italiano" (State Immunity in the International and Italian Legal Orders), OIDU, 2015, p. 237 ff.

INSOLIA A., "The *Haiti Cholera* Case and UN's Immunity from Civil Jurisdiction: Nothing New Under the Sun", CI, 2015, p. 419 ff.

PAVONI R., "Choleric Notes on the *Haiti Cholera Case*", QIL, Zoom-in 19, 2015, p. 19 ff.

PAVONI R., "*Simoncioni v. Germany*: Italian Constitutional Court Decision on Law Implementing Immunity of Foreign States from War Crimes Compensation Claims in Accordance with 2012 ICJ Judgment", AJIL, 2015, p. 400 ff.

PISILLO MAZZESCHI R., "The Functional Immunity of State Officials from Foreign Jurisdiction: A Critique of the Traditional Theories", QIL, Zoom out 17, 2015, p. 3 ff.

RONZITTI N., "La Cour constitutionnelle italienne et l'immunité juridictionnelle des États", AFDI, 2014, p. 3 ff.

RONZITTI N., "The Immunity of State Organs – A Reply to Pisillo Mazzeschi", QIL, Zoom-out 17, 2015), p. 59 ff.

SCISO E., "L'immunità giurisdizionale dello Stato tra diritto interno e diritto internazionale" (The Jurisdictional Immunity of the State between National and International Law), in NESI G. and GARGIULO P. (eds.), *Luigi Ferrari Bravo. Il diritto internazionale come professione*, Napoli, 2015, p. 109 ff.

VEZZANI S., "Immunità dello Stato estero dalla giurisdizione e diritto di accesso al giudice alla luce della Carta dei diritti fondamentali: riflessioni in margine al caso *Benkharbouche e Janah*" (Jurisdictional Immunities of Foreign States and the Right of Access to Court under the Charter of Fundamental Rights: A Comment on the *Benkharbouche and Janah* Case), RDI, 2015, p. 904 ff.

VII. LAW OF THE SEA

BO M., "The Interplay between International Law and National Law in the First Italian Prosecution of Piracy: The *M/V Montecristo* Case", IYIL, 2014, p. 289 ff.

CANNONE A., "L'ordinanza del Tribunale internazionale del diritto del mare sulla vicenda della Enrica Lexie" (The Order of the International Tribunal for the Law of the Sea in the Enrica Lexie Case), RDI, 2015, p. 1144 ff.

FARNELLI G.M., "Vessel Protection Detachments and Maritime Security: An Evaluation of Four Years of Italian Practice", Maritime Safety and Security Law Journal, 2015, p. 16 ff.

LANDO M., "Establishing the Existence of a 'Dispute' under UNCLOS at the Provisional Measures Stage: The Enrica Lexie Case", QIL, Zoom-in 22, 2015, p. 3 ff.

MAROTTI L., "Sulla funzione consultiva del Tribunale internazionale del diritto del mare" (On the Advisory Function of the International Tribunal for the Law of the Sea), RDI, 2015, p. 1171 ff.

MENEGAZZI S., "Military Exercises in the Exclusive Economic Zones: The Chinese Perspective", Maritime Safety and Security Law Journal, 2015, p. 56 ff.

NOTO M.C., "Atti di protesta violenta in mare: pirateria, terrorismo o fattispecie autonoma?" (Acts of Violent Protest at Sea: Are They Piracy, Terrorism or a Separate Offence?), RDI, 2015, p. 1198 ff.

PAPANICOLOPULU I., "Considerations of Humanity in the Enrica Lexie Case", QIL, Zoom-in 22, 2015, p. 25 ff.

RONZITTI N., "Il regime giuridico delle navi da guerra affondate" (The Legal Regime for War Sunken Wessels), Rivista marittima, 2015, p. 34 ff.

VIII. ENVIRONMENT

BEQIRAJ J., "Water Resources' Exploitation and Trade Flows: The Impact of International Trade Law", in ROMANIN JACUR F., BONFANTI A. and SEATZU F. (eds.), *Natural Resources Grabbing: An International Law Perspective*, Leiden, 2015, p. 338 ff.

BERNARDINI F., "The Normative and Institutional Evolution of the Convention", in TANZI A., MCINTYRE O., KOLLIOPOULOS A., RIEU-CLARKE A. and KINNA R. (eds.), *The UNECE Convention on the Protection and Use of Transboundary Watercourses and International Lakes. Its Contribution to International Water Cooperation*, Leiden, 2015, p. 32 ff.

BONFANTI A. and ROMANIN JACUR F., "Energy from the Sea and the Protection of the Marine Environment: Treaty-Based Regimes and Ocean Corporate Social Responsibility", in TREVISANUT S. and BANKES N. (eds.), *Energy from the Sea. An International Law Perspective on Ocean Energy*, Leiden, 2015, p. 62 ff.

BONFANTI A., "The WTO Members' Right to Protect Animals in International Trade: A TBT Perspective", in ROMANIN JACUR F., BONFANTI A. and SEATZU F. (eds.), *Natural Resources Grabbing: An International Law Perspective*, Leiden, 2015, p. 317 ff.

CINELLI C., "Protection and Preservation of the Arctic Marine Environment", IYIL, 2014, p. 159 ff.

CITTADINO F., "Public Interest to Environmental Protection and Indigenous Peoples' Rights: Procedural Rights to Participation and Substantive Guarantees", in POTO M. and LOHSE E.J. (eds.), *Participatory Rights in the Environmental Decision-Making Process and the Implementation of the Aarhus Convention: A Comparative Perspective*, Berlin, 2015, p. 75 ff.

ESPA I., "Energy Export Restrictions in the WTO between Resources Nationalism and Sustainable Development", in ROMANIN JACUR F., BONFANTI A. and SEATZU F. (eds.), *Natural Resources Grabbing: An International Law Perspective*, Leiden, 2015, p. 361 ff.

FASOLI E., "The German Criteria for Access to Justice under the Scrutiny of the Aarhus Convention Compliance Committee and of the Court of Justice of the European Union: Is There Room for Similar Proceedings against Italy?", in POTO M. and LOHSE E.J. (eds.), *Participatory Rights in the Environmental Decision-Making Process and the Implementation of the Aarhus Convention: A Comparative Perspective*, Berlin, 2015, p. 189 ff.

FERRI N., *Conflicts over the Conservation of Marine Living Resources: Third States, Governance, Fragmentation and other Recurring Issues in International Law*, Torino, 2015, pp. 266.

FRANCIONI F., "Principle 1: Human Beings and the Environment", in VIÑUALES E.J. (ed.), *The Rio Declaration on Environment and Development. A Commentary*, Oxford, 2015, p. 93 ff.

FRANCIONI F., "The Preamble of the Rio Declaration", in VIÑUALES E.J. (ed.), *The Rio Declaration on Environment and Development. A Commentary*, Oxford, 2015, p. 85 ff.

FRANCIONI F., "The Private Sector and the Challenge of Implementation", in DUPUY P.-M. and VIÑUALES J.E. (eds.), *Harnessing Foreign Investment to Promote Environmental Protection. Incentives and Safeguards*, Cambridge, 2015, p. 24 ff.

MOLASCHI V., "The Implementation of the Aarhus Convention in Italy: A Strong 'Vision' and a Weak 'Voice'", in POTO M. and LOHSE E.J. (eds.), *Participatory Rights in the Environmental Decision-Making Process and the Implementation of the Aarhus Convention: A Comparative Perspective*, Berlin, 2015, p. 105 ff.

MONTINI M., "The Rise of 'Internal Environmental Conflicts' within the Green Economy", IYIL, 2014, p. 95 ff.

MORGERA E., "Benefit-sharing as a Bridge between the Environmental and Human Rights Accountability of Multinational Corporations", in BOER B. (ed.), *Environmental Law Dimensions of Human Rights*, Oxford, 2015, p. 37 ff.

MORGERA E., "From Corporate Social Responsibility to Accountability Mechanisms", in DUPUY P.-M. and VIÑUALES J.E. (eds.), *Harnessing Foreign Investment to Promote Environmental Protection. Incentives and Safeguards*, Cambridge, 2015, p. 321 ff.

MORGERA E., "Justice, Equity and Benefit-Sharing under the Nagoya Protocol to the Convention on Biological Diversity", IYIL, 2014, p. 113 ff.

PAROLA G., "Ecological Interest as a Leading Rationale for Participation: Ecological Duties of the Citizens and the Authorities", in POTO M. and LOHSE E.J. (eds.), *Participatory Rights in the Environmental Decision-Making Process and the Implementation of the Aarhus Convention: A Comparative Perspective*, Berlin, 2015, p. 15 ff.

PAVONI R., "Channelling Investment into Biodiversity Conservation: ABS and PES Schemes", in DUPUY P.-M. and VIÑUALES J.E. (eds.), *Harnessing Foreign Investment to Promote Environmental Protection. Incentives and Safeguards*, Cambridge, 2015, p. 206 ff.

PAVONI R., "Environmental Jurisprudence of the European and Inter-American Courts of Human Rights: Comparative Insights", in BOER B. (ed.), *Environmental Law Dimensions of Human Rights*, Oxford, 2015, p. 69 ff.

POTO M. and LOHSE E.J. (eds.), *Participatory Rights in the Environmental Decision-Making Process and the Implementation of the Aarhus Convention: A Comparative Perspective*, Berlin, 2015, pp. 260.

POTO M., "Strenghts and Weaknesses of Environmental Participation under the Aarhus Convention: What Lies beyond Rhetorical Proceduralisation?", in POTO M. and LOHSE E.J. (eds.), *Participatory Rights in the Environmental Decision-Making Process and the Implementation of the Aarhus Convention: A Comparative Perspective*, Berlin, 2015, p. 93 ff.

ROMANIN JACUR F., "Lights and Shadows in the Relationship between International Law and Sustainable Investments: The Challenges of 'Natural Resources Grabbing' and Their Effects on State Sovereignty", QIL, Zoom-in 21, 2015, p. 3 ff.

ROMANIN JACUR F., "Tackling the Grabbing of Genetic Resources and of Associated Traditional Knowledge Trough the Nagoya Protocol", in ROMANIN JACUR F., BONFANTI A. and SEATZU F. (eds.), *Natural Resources Grabbing: An International Law Perspective*, Leiden, 2015, p. 139 ff.

SARTORETTI C., "The Aarhus Convention between Protection of Human Rights and Protection of the Environment", in POTO M. and LOHSE E.J. (eds.), *Participatory Rights in the Environmental Decision-Making Process and the Implementation of the Aarhus Convention: A Comparative Perspective*, Berlin, 2015, p. 45 ff.

SAVARESI A., "Natural Resources Grabbing: The Case of Tropical Forests and REDD+", in ROMANIN JACUR F., BONFANTI A. and SEATZU F. (eds.), *Natural Resources Grabbing: An International Law Perspective*, Leiden, 2015, p. 159 ff.

SCOVAZZI T., "Negotiating Conservation and Sustainable Use of Marine Biological Diversity in Areas beyond National Jurisdiction: Prospects and Challenges", IYIL, 2014, p. 63 ff.

SCOVAZZI T., "The Exploitation of Resources of the Deep Seabed and the Protection of the Environment", GYIL, 2014, p. 181 ff.

TANZI A. and KOLLIOPOULOS A., "The International Water Law Process and Transboundary Groundwater: Supplementing the Water Convention with the 2012 UNECE Model Provisions", in TANZI A., MCINTYRE O., KOLLIOPOULOS A., RIEU-CLARKE A. and KINNA R. (eds.), *The UNECE Convention on the Protection and Use of Transboundary Watercourses and International Lakes. Its Contribution to International Water Cooperation*, Leiden, 2015, p. 408 ff.

TANZI A. and KOLLIOPOULOS A., "The No-Harm Rule", in TANZI A., MCINTYRE O., KOLLIOPOULOS A., RIEU-CLARKE A. and KINNA R. (eds.), *The UNECE Convention on the Protection and Use of Transboundary Watercourses and International Lakes. Its Contribution to International Water Cooperation*, Leiden, 2015, p. 131 ff.

TANZI A. and MCINTYRE O., "The Principle of Equitable and Reasonable Utilisation", in TANZI A., MCINTYRE O., KOLLIOPOULOS A., RIEU-CLARKE A. and KINNA R. (eds.), *The UNECE Convention on the Protection and Use of Transboundary Watercourses and International Lakes. Its Contribution to International Water Cooperation*, Leiden, 2015, p. 146 ff.

TANZI A., KOLLIOPOULOS A. and NIKIFOROVA N., "Normative Features of the UNECE Water Convention", in TANZI A., MCINTYRE O., KOLLIOPOULOS A., RIEU-CLARKE A. and KINNA R. (eds.), *The UNECE Convention on the Protection and Use of Transboundary Watercourses and International Lakes. Its Contribution to International Water Cooperation*, Leiden, 2015, p. 116 ff.

TANZI A., MCINTYRE O. and KOLLIOPOULOS A., "The Contribution of the UNECE Water Convention to International Water Law", in TANZI A., MCINTYRE O., KOLLIOPOULOS A., RIEU-CLARKE A. and KINNA R. (eds.), *The UNECE Convention on the Protection and Use of Transboundary Watercourses and International Lakes. Its Contribution to International Water Cooperation*, Leiden, 2015, p. 531 ff.

TANZI A., MCINTYRE O., KOLLIOPOULOS A., RIEU-CLARKE A. and KINNA R. (eds.), *The UNECE Convention on the Protection and Use of Transboundary Watercourses and International Lakes. Its Contribution to International Water Cooperation*, Leiden, 2015, pp. 547.

TIGNINO M., "Principle 23: The Environment of Oppressed Peoples", in VIÑUALES E.J. (ed.), *The Rio Declaration on Environment and Development. A Commentary*, Oxford, 2015, p. 557 ff.

TIGNINO M., BOISSON DE CHARZOURNES L. and LEB C., "The UNECE Water Convention and Multilateral Environmental Agreements", in TANZI A., MCINTYRE O., KOLLIOPOULOS A., RIEU-CLARKE A. and KINNA R. (eds.), *The UNECE Convention on the Protection and Use of Transboundary Watercourses and International Lakes. Its Contribution to International Water Cooperation*, Leiden, 2015, p. 60 ff.

TURRINI P., "Participatory Rights and the Notion of Interest in Environmental Decision-Making: A Theoretical Sketch and Some International Legal Considerations", in POTO M. and LOHSE E.J. (eds.), *Participatory Rights in the Environmental Decision-Making Process and the Implementation of the Aarhus Convention: A Comparative Perspective*, Berlin, 2015, p. 59 ff.

IX. CULTURAL HERITAGE

BERSANI L., "La dimensione umana del patrimonio culturale nel diritto internazionale: identità e diritti culturali" (The Human Dimension of Cultural Heritage under International Law: Cultural Identity and Cultural Rights), CI, 2015, p. 37 ff.

CHECHI A., "Non-State Actors and Cultural Heritage: Friends or Foes?", Anuario de la Facultad de Derecho de la Universidad Autónoma de Madrid, Vol. 19, 2015, p. 457 ff.

CHECHI A., "Rescuing Cultural Heritage from War and Terrorism: A View from Switzerland", Santander Art and Culture Law Review, 2/2015, 83-100.

CHECHI A., "State Immunity, Property Rights, and Cultural Objects on Loan", IJCP, 2015, p. 279 ff.

XI. TREATMENT OF ALIENS AND NATIONALITY

AMADEO S. and SPITALERI F. (eds.), *Le garanzie fondamentali dell'immigrato in Europa* (Migrants' Fundamental Guarantees in Europe), Torino, 2015, pp. 432.

BOLOGNESE S., "Il ricorso a garanzie individuali nell'ambito dei c.d. 'trasferimenti Dublino': ancora sul caso *Tarakhel*" (Individual Assurances in the Context of Dublin Transfers. A Comment to the Tarakhel Case), DUDI, 2015, p. 233 ff.

CATALDI G., "Immigrazione e diritto alla cittadinanza nell'ordinamento internazionale: aspetti generali" (Immigration and Right to Nationality in International Law), in CATALDI G. et al. (eds.), *Immigrazione e diritto alla cittadinanza*, Napoli, 2015, p. 225 ff.

CATALDI G., "Migranti 'economici' e rifugiati: emergenze (vere o presunte) e diritto del mare" ("Economic" Migrants and Refugees: (Real or Alleged) Emergencies and Law of the Sea), La Rivista delle politiche sociali, 2015, No. 2-3, p. 27 ff.

CATALDI G., "Traffico dei migranti nel Mediterraneo" (Migrant Trafficking in the Mediterranean), Giur It., 2015, p. 1498 ff.

GUARINO G., "Sovranità dello Stato, diritti fondamentali e migrazioni: gli elementi di una contraddizione" (State Sovereignty, Fundamental Rights and Migrations: Contradictory Elements), OIDU, 2015, p. 46 ff.

MATERA C., "Another Parochial Decision? The Common European Asylum System at the Crossroad between IHL and Refugee Law in Diakité", QIL, Zoom-in 12, 2015, p. 3 ff.

PALLADINO R., "La 'derogabilità' del 'sistema Dublino' dell'UE nella sentenza *Tarakhel* della Corte europea: dalle 'deficienze sistemiche' ai 'seri dubbi sulle attuali capacità del sistema' italiano di accoglienza" (The 'Derogation' of the EU 'Dublin System' in the *Tarakhel* Judgment of the European Court: From 'Systemic Deficiencies' to 'Serious Doubts as to the Current Capacities' of the Italian Reception System), DUDI, 2015, p. 226 ff.

XII. HUMAN RIGHTS

BEQIRAJ J., "Economic and Social Rights of Children Migrant Workers: The Case of Domestic Work", in GOODWIN-GILL G.S. and WECKEL P. (eds.), *Migration and Refugee Protection in the 21st Century: International Legal Aspects*, Leiden, 2015, p. 349 ff.

BEQIRAJ J., "Indigenous Peoples' Cultural Identity under EU Law and the ECHR: A Non-Trade Interest or a Human Right?", in IPPOLITO F. and IGLESIAS SÁNCHEZ S. (eds.), *Protecting Vulnerable Groups: The European Human Rights Framework*, Oxford, 2015, p. 159 ff.

BORGNA G., "Il genocidio armeno (non) passa in giudicato: in margine al caso *Perinçek*" (The Armenian Genocide Is (Not) Final. The Grand Chamber of the European Court Puts a Stop to Criminalization of Genocide Denial), DUDI, 2015, p. 697 ff.

BORGNA G., "La prassi delle decisioni di inammissibilità della Corte europea al vaglio del Comitato ONU dei diritti umani: rischio di un 'cortocircuito' fra i due sistemi di protezione?" (Inadmissibility Decisions of the European Court Under the Lens of the UN Human Rights Committee: A Possible Short Circuit Between the Two Protection Mechanisms?), DUDI, 2015, p. 135 ff.

BORRACCETTI M., "The Right to Water and Access to Water Resources in the European Development Policy", in ROMANIN JACUR F., BONFANTI A. and SEATZU F. (eds.), *Natural Resources Grabbing: An International Law Perspective*, Leiden, 2015, p. 116 ff.

CALIGIURI A., "Il contributo della giurisprudenza della Corte interamericana dei diritti umani in tema di tutela dei diritti territoriali dei popoli indigeni" (The Contribution of the Jurisprudence of the Inter-American Court of Human Rights to the Protection of the Territorial Rights of Indigenous Peoples), DUDI, 2015, p. 435 ff.

CATALDI G., "Il problema della 'sanabilità' del contrasto e il rinvio alla Corte costituzionale alla luce del caso *Staibano c. Italia*" (The Problem of Remedying the Contrast and the Referral to the Constitutional Court in the Light of the Case *Staibano c. Italy*), I diritti dell'uomo, cronache e battaglie, 2015, p. 93 ff.

CHIUSSI L., "Food for Thought on the Right to Food", CI, 2015, p. 355 ff.

CITTADINO F., "The Balance between Indigenous Rights and the Protection of Nature: Some Remnants of the Colonial Past", African Yearbook of International Law, 2015, p. 223 ff.

CONFORTI B. and DE DOMINICIS M., "La giurisprudenza della Corte di Strasburgo in tema di obblighi positivi" (The Jurisprudence of the Strasbourg Court in matters of Positive Obligations), in NESI G. and GARGIULO P. (eds.), *Luigi Ferrari Bravo. Il diritto internazionale come professione*, Napoli, 2015, p. 295 ff.

CONFORTI B., "La Cour constitutionnelle italienne et les droits de l'homme meconnus sur le plan international", RGDIP, 2015, p. 353 ff.

COSTATO L., "Il 'male minore': Guantanamo o cibo?" (The "Lesser Evil": Guantanamo or Food?), in GESTRI M. (ed.), *Cibo e Diritto. Dalla Dichiarazione Universale alla Carta di Milano*, Modena, 2015, p. 33 ff.

DEL GUERCIO A., "Il riconoscimento giuridico dell'identità di genere delle persone transgender, tra sterilizzazione imposta e diritto all'autodeterminazione. Il caso *Y.Y. c. Turchia* e le cautele della Corte europea" (The Legal Recognition of Gender Identity of Transgender People Between Enforced Sterilization and the Right to Self-Determination. The case *Y.Y. v. Turkey* and the Cautiousness of the European Court), DUDI, 2015, p. 441 ff.

DI BENEDETTO S., "Il caso *Yukos*: un quadro d'insieme" (The *Yukos* Case: An Overview), DUDI, 2015, p. 327 ff.

DI TURI C., "Conflitto armato internazionale, diserzione e nozione di 'persecuzione': quali prospettive per l'obiezione di coscienza dopo il caso *Shepherd?*" (International Armed Conflict, Desertion and the Concept of Persecution: Which Prospects for Conscientious Objectors After the *Shepherd* Case?), RDI, 2015, p. 1263 ff.

FASCIGLIONE M., "Towards a Human Rights Treaty on Transnational Corporations and Other Business Enterprises: The First Session of the UN Openended Intergovernmental Working Group", DUDI, 2015, p. 673 ff.

FAVUZZA F., "Recenti sviluppi in materia di diritto alla libertà e alla sicurezza personale: il General Comment No. 35 del Comitato dei diritti umani" (Recent Developments with Regard to the Right to Liberty and Security of Persons: The Human Rights Committee General Comment No. 35), DUDI, 2015, p. 181 ff.

FERACI O., "La tutela 'indiretta' dell'art. 6, par. 1, CEDU in tema di processo contumaciale civile con riguardo all'efficacia delle decisioni straniere rese da giudici di Stati membri dell'Unione europea" (The 'Indirect' Protection of Article 6, para. 1, of the ECHR with Regard to Civil Trial in Absentia Concerning the Enforcement of EU Member States' Judgments), DUDI, 2015, p. 188 ff.

GAJA G., "Una mancata disconnessione relativamente alla Convenzione europea dei diritti dell'uomo?" (A Failed Disconnection Relating to the European Convention on Human Rights?), RDI, 2015, p. 148 ff.

GESTRI M. (ed.), *Cibo e Diritto. Dalla Dichiarazione Universale alla Carta di Milano* (Food and Law: From the Universal Declaration to the Milan Charter), Modena, 2015, pp. 135.

GESTRI M., "Il diritto fondamentale al cibo: quale il contributo della Carta di Milano?" (The Fundamental Right to Food: What Is the Role of the Milan Charter?), in GESTRI M. (ed.), *Cibo e Diritto. Dalla Dichiarazione Universale alla Carta di Milano*, Modena, 2015, p. 7 ff.

LEOTTA S.E., "L'esposizione in pubblico dei simboli religiosi individuali: la pronuncia sul caso S.A.S. v. France, ennesima chance persa per Strasburgo?" (The Public Display of Individual Religious Symbols: The S.A.S. v. France Case: A Missed Opportunity for Strasbourg?), CI, 2015, p. 389 ff.

LONGOBARDO M., "Sull'imparzialità dei membri delle Commissioni di inchiesta istituite dal Consiglio dei diritti umani" (Remarks on the Impartiality of the Members of the Human Rights Council Fact-Finding Missions), DUDI, 2015, p. 465 ff.

MAGI L., "Gli obblighi incompatibili derivanti dalla CEDU e dalla Carta delle Nazioni Unite, nella giurisprudenza della Corte europea dei diritti umani: riflessioni critico-ricostruttive" (Conflicting Obligations Arising from the ECHR and the UN Charter: Some Reflections on the ECtHR Case Law), DUDI, 2015, p. 519 ff.

MALAGUTI M.C., "The Taking of Property by the State: 'Expropriation by Litigation' under International Investment Law Versus Protection of Property under the ECHR in the Yukos Saga", DUDI, 2015, p. 337 ff.

MANCA L., "Il relatore speciale delle Nazioni Unite sul diritto all'alimentazione" (The UN Special Rapporteur on the Right to Food), OIDU, 2015, p. 630 ff.

NIGRO R., "La responsabilità degli Internet Service Providers e la Convenzione europea dei diritti umani: il caso *Delfi AS*" (The Internet Service Provider's Liability and the European Convention on Human Rights: The *Delfi AS* Case), DUDI, 2015, p. 681 ff.

OLIVITO E. (ed.), *Gender and Migration in Italy. A Multilayered Perspective*, Farnham, 2015, pp. 244.

PACE M., "'Mercificazione' dell'istruzione e salvaguardia del diritto all'educazione nei recenti Rapporti del Relatore speciale sul diritto all'istruzione" (The 'Commercialization' of Education and the Protection of the Right to Education in the Recent Reports of the Special Rapporteur on the Right to Education), DUDI, 2015, p. 455 ff.

PANELLA L., "La revoca della cittadinanza nel quadro della lotta al terrorismo internazionale" (The Revocation of Citizenship in the Fight against International Terrorism), OIDU, 2015, p. 457 ff.

PAROLARI P., "Velo integrale e rispetto per le differenze nella giurisprudenza della Corte europea dei diritti umani: il caso *S.A.S. c. Francia*" (Full-Face Veil and Respect for Differences in the Case Law of the European Court of Human Rights: The Case *S.A.S. v. France*), DUDI, 2015, p. 85 ff.

PINESCHI L., *La tutela internazionale dei diritti umani* (The International Protection of Human Rights), 2nd ed., Milano, 2015, pp. 899.

PITEA C., "Azioni di contrasto alla pirateria e Convenzione europea dei diritti umani: questioni di attribuzione e di applicazione extraterritoriale" (Counter-Piracy Operations and the European Convention on Human Rights: Issues of Attribution and Extra-Territorial Application), DUDI, 2015, p. 489 ff.

RANDAZZO B., "Sussidiarietà della tutela convenzionale e nuove prove di dialogo tra le Corti. *Parrillo c. Italia*: novità in tema di accessibilità del giudizio costituzionale dopo le 'sentenze gemelle' (e la sentenza n. 49 del 2015)" (Subsidiarity of Conventional Defense and Attempts of Dialogue Among the Courts. *Parrillo v. Italy*: New Developments on Accessibility of the Constitutional Review After the 'Twin Judgments' (and the Judgment No. 49 of 2015)), DUDI, 2015, p. 67 ff.

RUOZZI E., "Land Grabbing and International Human Rights: The Jurisprudence of the Inter-American Court of Human Rights on the Rights of Indigenous Peoples", in ROMANIN JACUR F., BONFANTI A. and SEATZU F. (eds.), *Natural Resources Grabbing: An International Law Perspective*, Leiden, 2015, p. 75 ff.

SAVARESE E., "In margine al caso *Oliari*: ovvero di come il limbo italiano delle coppie omosessuali abbia violato gli obblighi positivi dell'art. 8 CEDU" (On the Border of the Case *Oliari*: That Is How the Italian Limbo Has Violated the Positive Obligations Under ECHR Art. 8), DUDI, 2015, p. 655 ff.

SCHILLACI A., "'Enjoy Liberty as We Learn Its Meaning'. *Obergefell v. Hodges* tra libertà, uguaglianza e pari dignità ("Enjoy Liberty as We Learn Its Meaning". Liberty, Equality and Equal Dignity in *Obergefell v. Hodges*), DUDI, 2015, p. 639 ff.

SEATZU F., "Reshaping EU Old Age Law in the Light of the Normative Standards in International Human Rights Law in Relation to Older Persons", in IPPOLITO F. and IGLESIAS SÁNCHEZ S. (eds.), *Protecting Vulnerable Groups: The European Human Rights Framework*, Oxford, 2015, p. 49 ff.

SONELLI S., "Convenzione europea dei diritti dell'uomo e giudici nazionali nella giurisprudenza 'trial and error' della Corte costituzionale" (The European Convention on Human Rights and National Courts in the 'Trial and Error' Case Law of the Constitutional Court), RDI, 2015, p. 1155 ff.

STARITA M., "La sentenza della Grande Camera della Corte europea dei diritti umani nel caso *S.A.S. c. Francia*: una 'sentenza-monito', ma di che tipo?" (The Judgment of the Grand Chamber of the European Court of Human Rights in *S.A.S. v. France*: Assessing the Problem of the Legal Value of the Court's Warnings), DUDI, 2015, p. 101 ff.

TONOLO S., "Identità personale, maternità surrogata e superiore interesse del minore nella più recente giurisprudenza della Corte europea dei diritti dell'uomo" (Surrogacy and the Right to Personal Identity Before the European Court of Human Rights: The Compatibility of the Public Policy Exception with the Requirements of the Article 8 of the ECHR), DUDI, 2015, p. 202 ff.

VANNUCCINI S., "Significant Issues of Juvenile Justice in the Americas with a Special Focus on the Use of the Penalty of Life in Prison against Adolescent Offenders", CI, 2015, p. 549 ff.

VITUCCI M.C., "La sentenza della Corte suprema degli Stati Uniti sul matrimonio omosessuale nella prospettiva di una internazionalista" (United States Supreme Court Decision on Same-Sex Marriage in the Perspective of International Law), DUDI, 2015, p. 625 ff.

ZAGREBELSKY V., "*Parrillo c. Italia.* Il destino degli embrioni congelati tra Convenzione europea dei diritti umani e Costituzione" (*Parrillo v. Italy.* The Cryopreserved Embryos' Destiny Between the European Court of Human Rights and the Italian Constitution), DUDI, 2015, p. 609 ff.

XIII. INTERNATIONAL CRIMINAL LAW

ALÌ A., "La risposta della Comunità internazionale al fenomeno dei Foreign Terrorist Fighters" (The Reaction of the International Community to the Phenomenon of Foreign Terrorist Fighters), CI, 2015, p. 181 ff.

BENVENUTO F., "Sulla centralità del procedimento di riparazione in favore delle vittime nel sistema della Corte penale internazionale: la sentenza della Camera d'Appello del 3 marzo 2015" (The Centrality of the Reparation Proceeding in the International Criminal Court: The Appeals Chamber Decision of 3 March 2015), DUDI, 2015, p. 470 ff.

BOSCHIERO N., "The ICC Judicial Finding on Non-Cooperation Against the DRC and No Immunity for Al-Bashir Based on UNSC Resolution 1593", JICJ, 2015, p. 625 ff.

CALIGIURI A., "La Commissione verità e riconciliazione del Canada e la riscoperta del concetto di 'genocidio culturale'" (The Truth and Reconciliation Commission of Canada and the Rediscovery of the Concept of 'Cultural Genocide'), DUDI, 2015, p. 705 ff.

CIAMPI A., "Il meccanismo di cooperazione della Corte penale internazionale alla prova dei fatti: che cosa, e perché, non ha funzionato" (What Is Not Working in the Functioning of the Cooperation Regime of the International Criminal Court and Why), DUDI, 2015, p. 151 ff.

CIMIOTTA E., "The First Steps of the Extraordinary African Chambers: A New Mixed Criminal Tribunal?", JICJ, 2015, p. 177 ff.

COSTANTINI B., "I processi per crimini di guerra davanti ai tribunali militari" (The Proceedings for War Crimes before Military Tribunals), in WENIN R., FORNASARI G. and FRONZA E. (eds.), *La persecuzione dei crimini internazionali. Una riflessione sui diversi meccanismi di risposta*, Napoli, 2015, p. 147 ff.

FARNELLI G.M., *Contrasto e repressione della violenza marittima nel diritto internazionale contemporaneo* (The Fight against Maritime Violence in Contemporary International Law), Napoli, 2015, pp. 384.

FOCARELLI C., "International Criminal Justice (2014)", IYIL, 2014, p. 365 ff.

FORNASARI G. and WENIN R., "La giustizia di transizione" (Transitional Justice), in WENIN R., FORNASARI G. and FRONZA E. (eds.), *La persecuzione dei crimi-*

ni internazionali. Una riflessione sui diversi meccanismi di risposta, Napoli, 2015, p. 47 ff.

FORNASARI G., FRONZA E. and WENIN R., (eds.), *La persecuzione dei crimini internazionali. Una riflessione sui diversi meccanismi di risposta* (The Prosecution of International Crimes. A Reflection on the Different Response Mechanisms), Napoli, 2015, pp. 230.

LATTANZI F., "I tribunali penali internazionali creati ad hoc dal Consiglio di sicurezza" (The Ad Hoc International Criminal Tribunals Created by the Security Council), in WENIN R., FORNASARI G. and FRONZA E. (eds.), *La persecuzione dei crimini internazionali. Una riflessione sui diversi meccanismi di risposta*, Napoli, 2015, p. 67 ff.

MAGI L., "Criminal Conduct on the High Seas: Is a General Rule on Jurisdiction to Prosecute still Missing?", RDI, 2015, p. 79 ff.

MANCINI M., "Adesione della Palestina allo Statuto di Roma e dichiarazione di accettazione della giurisdizione della Corte penale internazionale" (Palestine's Accession to the Rome Statute and Declaration Accepting the Jurisdiction of the International Criminal Court), OIDU, 2015, p. 358 ff.

MARCHESI A., "Il caso *Reverberi* e gli attuali limiti della collaborazione italiana alla punizione di crimini internazionali" (The *Reverberi* Case and the Current Limits of Italian Cooperation in the Punishment of International Crimes), DUDI, 2015, p. 218 ff.

MELONI C., "I nodi della responsabilità per genocidio nel diritto penale internazionale: tra dimensione collettiva e imputazione individuale, precetto internazionale e accertamento nazionale" (Conundrums of the Responsibility for Genocide in International Criminal Law: Between Collective Dimension and Individual Attribution, International Norm and Domestic Implementation), DUDI, 2015, p. 589 ff.

NAPOLETANO N., "Non-State Entity's 'Ability to Lodge' a Declaration Pursuant to Article 12(3) of the ICC Statute", QIL, Zoom-in 20, 2015, p. 17 ff.

NESI G., "La repressione dei crimini internazionali tra diritto di autodeterminazione dei popoli e affermazione della statualità" (The Repression of International Crimes between the Right to Self-Determination and Statehood), in WENIN R., FORNASARI G. and FRONZA E. (eds.), *La persecuzione dei crimini internazionali. Una riflessione sui diversi meccanismi di risposta*, Napoli, 2015, p. 23 ff.

PONTI C., "The Crime of Indiscriminate Attack and Unlawful Conventional Weapons: The Legacy of the ICTY Jurisprudence", Journal of International Humanitarian Legal Studies, 2015, p. 118 ff.

PROSPERI L., "Ricevibilità ed efficacia giuridica della dichiarazione di accettazione della giurisdizione della Corte penale internazionale da parte della Palestina" (The Declaration of Jurisdiction of the ICC by Palestine), OIDU, 2015, p. 337 ff.

SALVADEGO L., "L'obbligo di cooperazione per la protezione dei testimoni nella giustizia penale internazionale e il 'giusto processo costituzionale'" (States'

Obligations to Cooperate for the Protection of Witnesses in International Criminal Justice and the Principle of 'Due Process'), DUDI, 2015, p. 411 ff.

XIV. CO-OPERATION IN JUDICIAL, LEGAL, SECURITY, AND SOCIO-ECONOMIC MATTERS

BARTOLINI G., "La definizione di disastro nel progetto di articoli della Commissione del diritto internazionale" (The Definition of Disaster in the Draft Articles of the International Law Commission), RDI, 2015, p. 155 ff.

XV. INTERNATIONAL ECONOMIC LAW

BASSAN F., *Research Handbook on Sovereign Wealth Funds and International Investment Law*, Cheltenham, 2015, pp. 435.

BORDIGNON M., GRECO R. and LEPORE G., "Water Grabbing and Water Rights: Indigenous 'Sovereignty' v. State Sovereignty?", in ROMANIN JACUR F., BONFANTI A. and SEATZU F. (eds.), *Natural Resources Grabbing: An International Law Perspective*, Leiden, 2015, p. 93 ff.

BORLINI L., "The Reform of the Fight against Money Laundering and Terrorism Financing: From the 2012 FATF Recommendations to the New EU Legislation", DCI, 2015, p. 737 ff.

COSTAMAGNA F., "Accordi commerciali regionali e diritto dell'OMC" (Regional Trade Agreements and WTO Law), in VENTURINI G. (ed.), *L'Organizzazione Mondiale del Commercio*, 3rd ed., Milano, 2015, p. 275 ff.

DI BENEDETTO S., "The Double Relevance of the 'Corporate Veil' in the Yukos PCA Case and the Doctrine of the Abuse of Rights", DUDI, 2015, p. 387 ff.

DORDI C., "L'Accordo generale sul commercio dei servizi" (General Agreement on Trade in Services), in VENTURINI G. (ed.), *L'Organizzazione Mondiale del Commercio*, 3rd ed., Milano, 2015, p. 151 ff.

GULOTTA C., *Il sostegno alle esportazioni nel diritto internazionale* (Support to Exportations in International Law), Milano, 2015, pp. 222.

LENZERINI F., "Investment Projects Affecting Indigenous Heritage", in VADI V. and DE WITTE B. (eds.), *Culture and International Economic Law*, Abingdon/New York, 2015, p. 72 ff.

LUPONE A., "Proprietà intellettuale e scambi internazionali" (Intellectual Property and International Trade), in VENTURINI G. (ed.), *L'Organizzazione Mondiale del Commercio*, 3rd ed., Milano, 2015, p. 199 ff.

MAURO M.R., "Sovereign Default and Litigation: *NML Capital, Ltd. v. Argentina*", IYIL, 2014, p. 249 ff.

PAVONI R. and FOCARELLI C., "Accordo generale sulle tariffe e il commercio (GATT) e altri accordi sugli scambi di merci" (The General Agreement on

Tariffs and Trade and other Agreements on the Trade in Goods), in FOCARELLI C., *Trattato di diritto internazionale*, Torino, 2015, p. 1314 ff.

PAVONI R. and FOCARELLI C., "Accordo sugli aspetti dei diritti di proprietà intellettuale attinenti al commercio (TRIPs) e Organizzazione Mondiale della Proprietà Intellettuale" (Agreement on Trade-Related Aspects of Intellectual Property Rights (TRIPs) and World Intellectual Property Organization), in FOCARELLI C., *Trattato di diritto internazionale*, Torino, 2015, p. 1435 ff.

ROMANIN JACUR F., BONFANTI A. and SEATZU F. (eds.), *Natural Resources Grabbing: An International Law Perspective*, Leiden, 2015, pp. 462.

RUOZZI E., "La disciplina delle misure non tariffarie" (The Regulation of Non-Tariff Measures), in VENTURINI G. (ed.), *L'Organizzazione Mondiale del Commercio*, 3rd ed., Milano, 2015, p. 95 ff.

SACERDOTI G. and RECANATI M., "Approaches to Investment Protection Outside of Specific International Investment Agreements and Investor-State Settlement", in BUNGENBERG J.M. et al. (eds.), *International Investment Law*, Oxford, 2015, p. 1839 ff.

SANNA S., "Il GATT 1994 e gli accordi in materia doganale" (The GATT 1994 and the Agreements in Customs Matters), in VENTURINI G. (ed.), *L'Organizzazione Mondiale del Commercio*, 3rd ed., Milano, 2015, p. 23 ff.

SILIGARDI S., "La disciplina delle misure di difesa commerciale" (The Regulation of Trade Defense Measures), in VENTURINI G. (ed.), *L'Organizzazione Mondiale del Commercio*, 3rd ed., Milano, 2015, p. 63 ff.

TREVISANUT S. and BANKES N. (eds.), *Energy from the Sea. An International Law Perspective on Ocean Energy*, Leiden, 2015, pp. 182.

TREVISANUT S. and BANKES N., "Introduction: Energy from the Sea", in TREVISANUT S. and BANKES N. (eds.), *Energy from the Sea. An International Law Perspective on Ocean Energy*, Leiden, 2015, p. 1 ff.

VADI V. and DE WITTE B. (eds.), *Culture and International Economic Law*, London/New York, 2015, pp. 270.

VADI V., "Cultural Heritage in International Economic Law", in VADI V. and DE WITTE B. (eds.) *Culture and International Economic Law*, London/New York, 2015, p. 53 ff.

VADI V., "Introducing Culture and International Economic Law", in VADI V. and DE WITTE B. (eds.), *Culture and International Economic Law*, London/New York, 2015, p. 1 ff.

VADI V., "Towards a New Dialectics – Pharmaceutical Patents, Public Health and Foreign Direct Investments", New York Journal of Intellectual Property and Entertainment Law, 2015, p. 1 ff.

VENTURINI G. (ed.), *L'Organizzazione Mondiale del Commercio* (The World Trade Organization), 3rd ed., Milano, 2015, pp. 541.

VENTURINI G., "La struttura istituzionale dell'OMC" (The WTO Institutional Structure), in VENTURINI G. (ed.), *L'Organizzazione Mondiale del Commercio*, 3rd ed., Milano, 2015, p. 3 ff.

VIOLI F., "The Practice of Land Grabbing and Its Compatibility with the Exercise of Territorial Sovereignty", in ROMANIN JACUR F., BONFANTI A. and SEATZU F. (eds.), *Natural Resources Grabbing: An International Law Perspective*, Leiden, 2015, p. 17 ff.

XVI. INTERNATIONAL ORGANIZATIONS

ACCONCI P., "The Reaction to the Ebola Epidemic within the United Nations Framework: What Next for the World Health Organization?", Max Planck UNYB, 2014, p. 405 ff.

ARCARI M., "Coordinamento e concorrenza tra organi politici delle organizzazioni internazionali e istanze giurisdizionali internazionali" (Coordination and Competition between the Political Organs of International Organizations and International Judicial Bodies), in VELLANO M. (ed.), *Il futuro delle organizzazioni internazionali. Prospettive giuridiche, XIX Convegno SIDI Courmayeur 2015*, Napoli, 2015, p. 167 ff.

CAFARO S., "Elementi per la costruzione di una teoria della democraticità delle organizzazioni internazionali" (On the Development of a Theory on Democracy within International Organizations), in VELLANO M. (ed.), *Il futuro delle organizzazioni internazionali. Prospettive giuridiche, XIX Convegno SIDI Courmayeur 2015*, Napoli, 2015, p. 293 ff.

CAFARO S., "The International Financial Crisis and the Evolution of the Bretton Woods Institutions", in VIRZO R. and INGRAVALLO I. (eds.), *Evolutions in the Law of International Organizations*, Leiden, 2015, p. 192 ff.

CELLAMARE G., "The Activities for the Maintenance of International Peace in the Relationship between the United Nations and Regional Organizations", in VIRZO R. and INGRAVALLO I. (eds.), *Evolutions in the Law of International Organizations*, Leiden, 2015, p. 132 ff.

DI BLASE A., "Il sistema di voto nel Consiglio di sicurezza e il ruolo dell'Assemblea generale" (The Voting System of the Security Council and the Role of the General Assembly), in VELLANO M. (ed.), *Il futuro delle organizzazioni internazionali. Prospettive giuridiche, XIX Convegno SIDI Courmayeur 2015*, Napoli, 2015, p. 83 ff.

DI STASI A., "About Soft International Organizations", in VIRZO R. and INGRAVALLO I. (eds.), *Evolutions in the Law of International Organizations*, Leiden, 2015, p. 44 ff.

GALLO D., "The Right of Access to Justice for the Staff of International Organizations: The Need for a Reform in the Light of the ICJ Advisory Opinion of 1 February 2012", in VIRZO R. and INGRAVALLO I. (eds.), *Evolutions in the Law of International Organizations*, Leiden, 2015, p. 509 ff.

GASBARRI L., "Responsabilità di un'organizzazione internazionale in materie di competenza esclusiva: imputazione e obbligo di risultato secondo il

Tribunale internazionale del diritto del mare" (Responsibility of International Organizations in Matters of Exclusive Competence: Attribution and Obligations of Results According to the International Tribunal of the Law of the Sea), RDI, 2015, p. 911 ff.

GRADONI L., "La spettacolarizzazione della lotta alla fame ovvero l'impotenza delle organizzazioni internazionali di fronte alla sfida della sicurezza alimentare mondiale" (The Spectacularization of the Fight against Hunger, or rather the Helplessness of International Organizations with respect to the Challenge of Global Food Security), in VELLANO M. (ed.), *Il futuro delle organizzazioni internazionali. Prospettive giuridiche, XIX Convegno SIDI Courmayeur 2015*, Napoli, 2015, p. 237 ff.

INGRAVALLO I., "Handle with Care! The Succession between International Organizations", in VIRZO R. and INGRAVALLO I. (eds.), *Evolutions in the Law of International Organizations*, Leiden, 2015, p. 451 ff.

MAINETTI V., "The League of Nations and the Emergence of Privileges and Immunities of International Organizations", in VIRZO R. and INGRAVALLO I. (eds.), *Evolutions in the Law of International Organizations*, Leiden, 2015, p. 324 ff.

MARCHISIO S., "Possibili strumenti per coordinare le organizzazioni internazionali" (Possible Instruments to Coordinate International Organizations), in VELLANO M. (ed.), *Il futuro delle organizzazioni internazionali. Prospettive giuridiche, XIX Convegno SIDI Courmayeur 2015*, Napoli, 2015, p. 125 ff.

MAURO M.R., "The Protection of Non-Economic Values and the Evolution of International Economic Organizations: The Case of the World Bank", in VIRZO R. and INGRAVALLO I. (eds.), *Evolutions in the Law of International Organizations*, Leiden, 2015, p. 244 ff.

NESI G., "Brevi note su diritto e politica all'ONU. Ammissione, accreditamento, rappresentanza e status di osservatore in Assemblea Generale" (Remarks on UN Law and Practice. Admission, Accreditation, Representation and Observer Status at the General Assembly), in VELLANO M. (ed.), *Il futuro delle organizzazioni internazionali. Prospettive giuridiche, XIX Convegno SIDI Courmayeur 2015*, Napoli, 2015, p. 601 ff.

ODELLO M. and SEATZU F. (eds.), *Latin American and Caribbean International Institutional Law*, The Hague, 2015, pp. 259.

ODELLO M., "The Andean Community of Nations", in ODELLO M. and SEATZU F. (eds.), *Latin American and Caribbean International Institutional Law*, The Hague, 2015, p. 117 ff.

ORZAN M.F., "International Organizations and Immunity from Legal Process: An Uncertain Evolution", in VIRZO R. and INGRAVALLO I. (eds.), *Evolutions in the Law of International Organizations*, Leiden, 2015, p. 364 ff.

PENNETTA P., "Brevi note su alcune nuove espressioni del regionalismo africano" (Remarks on New Developments in African Regionalism), CI, 2015, p. 577 ff.

PENNETTA P., "International Regional Organizations: Problems and Issues", in VIRZO R. and INGRAVALLO I. (eds.), *Evolutions in the Law of International Organizations*, Leiden, 2015, p. 70 ff.

POLI L., "La risoluzione n. 2177 (2014) del Consiglio di sicurezza delle Nazioni Unite e la qualificazione dell'epidemia di ebola come minaccia alla pace ed alla sicurezza internazionale" (UN Security Council Resolution No. 2177 (2014) and the Qualification of the Ebola Outbreak as a Threat to International Peace and Security), DUDI, 2015, p. 238 ff.

POLSI A., "Universalism and Regionalism in the History of the United Nations and of Specialized Agencies", in VIRZO R. and INGRAVALLO I. (eds.), *Evolutions in the Law of International Organizations*, Leiden, 2015, p. 116 ff.

PUSTORINO P., "Coordinamento e conflitto fra norme internazionali e regole di organizzazioni internazionali nella giurisprudenza nazionale" (Coordination and Conflict between International Norms and Rules of International Organizations in Domestic Jurisprudence), in VELLANO M. (ed.), *Il futuro delle organizzazioni internazionali. Prospettive giuridiche, XIX Convegno SIDI Courmayeur 2015*, Napoli, 2015, p. 197 ff.

RONZITTI N., "Foreign Terrorist Fighters e legge antiterrorismo" (Foreign Terrorist Fighters and the Italian Anti-Terrorism Law), RDI, 2015, p. 881 ff.

SEATZU F., "Economic Integration in the Caribbean Region: Re-Discussing the Capacity of the CARICOM", The Global Community, 2014, p. 171 ff.

SEATZU F., "Latin American Subregional Development Institutions", in ODELLO M. and SEATZU F. (eds.), *Latin American and Caribbean International Institutional Law*, The Hague, 2015, p. 65 ff.

SEATZU F., "On the World Bank's Efforts in Defence of the Human Right to Land", in ROMANIN JACUR F., BONFANTI A. and SEATZU F. (eds.), *Natural Resources Grabbing: An International Law Perspective*, Leiden, 2015, p. 294 ff.

SEATZU F., "The Alliance of the Pacific: A New Instrument of Latin American and Caribbean Economic Integration?", in ODELLO M. and SEATZU F. (eds.), *Latin American and Caribbean International Institutional Law*, The Hague, 2015, p. 193 ff.

SEATZU F., "The Caribbean Community (CARICOM)", in ODELLO M. and SEATZU F. (eds.), *Latin American and Caribbean International Institutional Law*, The Hague, 2015, p. 219 ff.

SEATZU F., "The Southern Common Market (Mercosur)", in ODELLO M. and SEATZU F. (eds.), *Latin American and Caribbean International Institutional Law*, The Hague, 2015, p. 159 ff.

TANCREDI A., "L'ibridazione pubblico-privata di alcune organizzazioni internazionali" (The Public-Private Hybridization of Some International Organizations), in VELLANO M. (ed.), *Il futuro delle organizzazioni internazionali. Prospettive giuridiche, XIX Convegno SIDI Courmayeur 2015*, Napoli, 2015, p. 331 ff.

VELLANO M. (ed.), *Il futuro delle organizzazioni internazionali. Prospettive giuridiche, XIX Convegno SIDI Courmayeur 2015* (The Future of International

Organizations. Legal Perspectives, XIX SIDI Conference Courmayer 2015), Napoli, 2015, pp. 637.

VILLANI U., "Aspetti problematici della democrazia nelle organizzazioni internazionali" (Problematic Aspects of Democracy within International Organizations), in VELLANO M. (ed.), *Il futuro delle organizzazioni internazionali. Prospettive giuridiche, XIX Convegno SIDI Courmayeur 2015*, Napoli, 2015, p. 283 ff.

VIRZO R. and INGRAVALLO I. (eds.), *Evolutions in the Law of International Organizations*, Leiden, 2015, pp. 547.

VIRZO R., "The Proliferation of Institutional Acts of International Organizations: A Proposal for Their Classification", in VIRZO R. and INGRAVALLO I. (eds.), *Evolutions in the Law of International Organizations*, Leiden, 2015, p. 291 ff.

XVII. RELATIONSHIP BETWEEN MUNICIPAL AND INTERNATIONAL LAW

AMOROSO D., "Judicial Abdication in Foreign Affairs and the Effectiveness of International Law", Chinese Journal of International Law, 2015, p. 99 ff.

CANNIZZARO E., "Jurisdictional Immunities and Judicial Protection: The Decision of the Italian Constitutional Court No. 238 of 2014", RDI, 2015, p. 126 ff.

CATALDI G., "A Historic Decision of the Italian Constitutional Court on the Balance Between the Italian Legal Order's Fundamental Values and Customary International Law", IYIL, 2014, p. 37 ff.

CATALDI G., "La Corte costituzionale e il ricorso ai 'contro-limiti' nel rapporto tra consuetudini internazionali e diritti fondamentali: *oportet ut scandala eveniant*" (The Constitutional Court and the Use of 'Counter-Limits' in the Relationship Between International Customs and Fundamental Rights: *Oportet ut Scandala Eveniant*), DUDI, 2015, p. 41 ff.

FRANCIONI F., "From Deference to Disobedience: The Uncertain Fate of Constitutional Court Decision No. 238/2014", IYIL, 2014, p. 1 ff.

PALOMBINO F.M., "Quale futuro per i giudizi di costituzionalità delle norme internazionali generali? Il modello rivisitato della sentenza interpretativa di rigetto" (Which Future for Decisions of the Constitutional Court Concerning the Constitutionality of General International Law? The Revised Model of an Interpretive Decision Rejecting a Question Addressed to the Court), RDI, 2015, p. 151 ff.

PANEBIANCO M., "La costituzione internazionale degli 'Arab Gulf States'" (The International Constitution of "Arab Gulf States"), RCGI, 2015, p. 17 ff.

PISILLO MAZZESCHI R., "Access to Justice in Constitutional and International Law: The Recent Judgment of the Italian Constitutional Court", IYIL, 2014, p. 25 ff.

PISILLO MAZZESCHI R., "La sentenza n. 238 del 2014 della Corte costituzionale ed i suoi possibili effetti sul diritto internazionale" (The Judgment No. 238/2014 of the Constitutional Court and Its Possible Effects on International Law), DUDI, 2015, p. 23 ff.

PUSTORINO P., "La sentenza n. 238 del 2014 della Corte costituzionale: limiti e prospettive nell'ottica della giurisprudenza italiana" (The Judgment No. 238/2014 of the Constitutional Court: Limits and Perspectives in the Framework of the Italian Jurisprudence), DUDI, 2015, p. 51 ff.

SCISO E., "Brevi considerazioni sui primi seguiti della sentenza della Corte costituzionale 238/2014" (Remarks on the First Follow-Up to Judgment No. 238 of 2014 of the Italian Constitutional Court), RDI, 2015, p. 887 ff.

STAIANO F., "The Italian Implementation of the Council of Europe Convention on Violence against Women and Victims' Rights to Reparations", IYIL, 2014, p. 269 ff.

TANZI A., "Un difficile dialogo tra Corte internazionale di giustizia e Corte costituzionale" (A Difficult Dialogue between the International Court of Justice and the Italian Constitutional Court), CI, 2015, p. 13 ff.

ZANGHÌ C., "Une nouvelle limitation à l'immunité de juridiction des Etats dans l'arrêt 238 de 2014 de la Cour Constitutionnelle italienne?", OIDU, 2015, p. 1 ff.

XVIII. USE OF FORCE AND PEACE-KEEPING

BERNARDINI A., "Dall'Iraq e Jugoslavia all'Ucraina: contro la sovranità statale e l'autodeterminazione dei popoli" (From Iraq and Yugoslavia to Ukraine: Against State Sovereignity and Self-Determination), OIDU, 2015, p. 752 ff.

BIANCHI A., "The International Regulation of the Use of Force: The Politics of Interpretative Method", in VAN DEN HERIK L. and SCHRIJVER N. (eds.), *Counter-Terrorism Strategies in a Fragmented International Legal Order. Meeting the Challenges*, Cambridge, 2015, p. 283 ff.

CARCANO A., *The Transformation of Occupied Territory in International Law*, Leiden, 2015, pp. 540.

CELLAMARE G., *Le operazioni di peacekeeping delle organizzazioni regionali* (The Peacekeeping Operations of Regional Organizations), Bari, 2015, pp. 164.

COLACINO N., "From Just War to Permanent Self-Defence: The Use of Drones in Counterterrorism and Its Questionable Consistency with International Law Standards", OIDU, 2015, p. 607 ff.

LONGOBARDO M. And VIOLI F., *"Quo vadis peace-keeping?* La compatibilità dell'Intervention Brigade in Congo con i principi regolanti le operazioni di pace" (*Quo Vadis* Peace-Keeping? The Compatibility of the Intervention Brigade Deployed in the Congo with he Principles of Peace Operations in Light of Its Recent Practice), CI, 2015, p. 245 ff.

MANCINI M., "The Effects of a State of War or Armed Conflict", in WELLER M. (ed.), *The Oxford Handbook of the Use of Force in International Law*, Oxford, 2015, p. 988 ff.

PALCHETTI P., "Consequences for Third States as a Result of an Unlawful Use of Force", in WELLER M. (ed.), *The Oxford Handbook of the Use of Force in International Law*, Oxford, 2015, p. 1224 ff.

PAVONE I.R., "The Crisis of the 'Responsibility to Protect' Doctrine in the Light of the Syrian Civil War", The Global Community, 2014, p. 103 ff.

PERTILE M., "The Changing Environment and Emerging Resource Conflicts", in WELLER M. and SOLOMOU A. (eds.), *The Oxford Handbook on the Use of Force*, Oxford, 2015, p. 1077 ff.

PICONE P., "Unilateralismo e guerra contro l'ISIS" (Unilateralism and War Against ISIS), RDI, 2015, p. 5 ff.

ZICCARDI CAPALDO G., "'Tutelary' Intervention to Counter the New Unlawful Territorial Situations: A *Tertium Genus* of Military Intervention in International Law?", The Global Community, 2014, p. 3 ff.

XIX. ARMED CONFLICT, NEUTRALITY, AND DISARMAMENT

ARCHIBUGI D., CROCE M. and SALVATORE A., "Law of Nations or Perpetual Peace? Two Early International Theories on the Use of Force", in WELLER M. (ed.), *The Oxford Handbook of the Use of Force in International Law*, Oxford, 2015, p. 56 ff.

BENVENUTI P., "Relationship with Prior and Subsequent Treaties and Conventions", in GAETA P., CLAPHAM A. and SASSÒLI M. (eds.), *The 1949 Geneva Conventions. A Commentary*, Oxford, 2015, p. 689 ff.

BORELLI S., "*Jaloud v Netherlands* and *Hassan v United Kingdom*: Time for a Principled Approach in the Application of the ECHR to Military Action Abroad", QIL, Zoom-in 16, 2015, p. 25 ff.

BUFALINI A., "An Autonomous Notion of Non-International Armed Conflict in EU Asylum Law: Is There Any Role for International Humanitarian Law?", QIL, Zoom-in 12, 2015, p. 21 ff.

GAETA P., "Grave Breaches of the Geneva Conventions", in GAETA P., CLAPHAM A. and SASSÒLI M. (eds.), *The 1949 Geneva Conventions. A Commentary*, Oxford, 2015, p. 615 ff.

GAETA P., "The Interplay between the Geneva Conventions and International Criminal Law", in GAETA P., CLAPHAM A. and SASSÒLI M. (eds.), *The 1949 Geneva Conventions. A Commentary*, Oxford, 2015, p. 737 ff.

GAETA P., CLAPHAM A. and SASSÒLI M. (eds.), *The 1949 Geneva Conventions. A Commentary*, Oxford, 2015, pp. 1760.

LATTANZI F., "Humanitarian Assistance", in GAETA P., CLAPHAM A. and SASSÒLI M. (eds.), *The 1949 Geneva Conventions. A Commentary*, Oxford, 2015, p. 231 ff.

LEANZA U., "Conflitti armati interni e regionalizzazione delle guerre civili" (Internal Armed Conflicts and Regionalization of Civil Wars), CI, 2015, p. 349 ff.

PERTILE M., "On the Financing of Civil Wars through Natural Resources: Is there a Duty of Vigilance for Third States on the Activities of Trans-National Corporations?", in ROMANIN JACUR F., BONFANTI A. and SEATZU F. (eds.), *Natural Resources Grabbing: An International Law Perspective*, Leiden, 2015, p. 381 ff.

RANALDI V., "Nuclear Weapons: The International Regulation of Their Use and Possession and the Current Case of Iran's Disarmament", RCGI, 2015, p. 97 ff.

RONZITTI N., "Protected Areas", in GAETA P., CLAPHAM A. and SASSÒLI M. (eds.), *The 1949 Geneva Conventions. A Commentary*, Oxford, 2015, p. 369 ff.

SANNA S., "Treatment of Prisoners of War", in GAETA P., CLAPHAM A. and SASSÒLI M. (eds.), *The 1949 Geneva Conventions. A Commentary*, Oxford, 2015, p. 977 ff.

SOMMARIO E., "Sull'applicazione concorrente della Convenzione europea per i diritti umani e del diritto internazionale umanitario: il caso *Hassan*" (On the Concurrent Application of the ECHR and International Humanitarian Law: The *Hassan* Case), DUDI, 2015, p. 210 ff.

VENTURINI G., "The Temporal Scope of Application of the Conventions", in GAETA P., CLAPHAM A. and SASSÒLI M. (eds.), *The 1949 Geneva Conventions. A Commentary*, Oxford, 2015, p. 51 ff.

VIERUCCI L., "Applicability of the Conventions by Means of Ad Hoc Agreements", in GAETA P., CLAPHAM A. and SASSÒLI M. (eds.), *The 1949 Geneva Conventions. A Commentary*, Oxford, 2015, p. 509 ff.

XX.   INTERNATIONAL RESPONSIBILITY

BARTOLINI G., "Attribution of Conduct and Liability Issues Arising From International Disaster Relief Missions: Theoretical and Pragmatic Approaches to Guaranteeing Accountability", Vanderbilt Journal of Transnational Law, 2015, p. 1029 ff.

BUFALINI A., "La responsabilità internazionale dello Stato per atti di genocidio: un regime in cerca di autonomia" (The Legal Regime of State Responsibility for Genocide and Its Quest for Autonomy), DUDI, 2015, p. 571 ff.

LIGUORI A., "*Shared responsibility* per violazioni di diritti umani nel corso di *peacekeeping operations* delle Nazioni Unite: quale ruolo per la Corte europea dei diritti umani?" (Shared Responsibility for Breaches of Human Rights in United Nations Peacekeeping Operations: Which Role for the European Court of Human Rights?), RDI, 2015, p. 517 ff.

PALCHETTI P., "Attributing the Conduct of the Dutchbat in Srebrenica: The 2014 Judgment of the District Court in the *Mothers of Srebrenica* Case", NILR, 2015, p. 279 ff.

PALCHETTI P., "Unità, pluralità o inutilità dei regimi di responsabilità internazionale applicabili alle organizzazioni" (Unity, Plurality, or Uselessness of the Regimes of International Responsibility Applicable to International Organizations), in VELLANO M. (ed.), *Il futuro delle organizzazioni internazionali. Prospettive giuridiche*, Napoli, 2015, p. 43 ff.

PICONE P., "Gli obblighi *erga omnes* tra passato e futuro" (Obligations *Erga Omnes* Between Past and Future), RDI, 2015, p. 1081 ff.

PUSTORINO P., "The Control Criterion between Responsibility of States and Responsibility of International Organizations", in VIRZO R. and INGRAVALLO I. (eds.), *Evolutions in the Law of International Organizations*, Leiden, 2015, p. 406 ff.

SPAGNOLO A., "Attribuzione delle condotte e accertamento della giurisdizione in casi di violazioni di massa dei diritti fondamentali: sulla recente giurisprudenza della Corte europea" (Attribution of Conduct and Jurisdiction in Cases of Mass Violations of Fundamental Rights: The Recent Jurisprudence of the European Court of Human Rights), DUDI, 2015, p. 690 ff.

XXI. INTERNATIONAL DISPUTE SETTLEMENT

ADINOLFI G., "La soluzione delle controversie" (Dispute Settlement), in VENTURINI G. (ed.), *L'Organizzazione Mondiale del Commercio*, 3rd ed., Milano, 2015, p. 303 ff.

AMOROSO D., "The Judicial Activity of the International Court of Justice in 2014", IYIL, 2014, p. 317 ff.

ARCARI M., MILANO E. and TANZI A., "Introduction: The Contribution of Courts and Tribunals to the Development of International Law", The Law & Practice of International Courts and Tribunals, 2015, p. 7 ff.

BUFALINI A., "The Principle of Legality and the Role of Customary International Law in the Interpretation of the ICC Statute", The Law & Practice of International Courts and Tribunals, 2015, p. 233 ff.

DEL VECCHIO A., *I Tribunali internazionali tra globalizzazione e localismi* (International Tribunals between Globalization and Localisms), 2nd ed., Bari, 2015, pp. 376.

FORLATI S., "Il potere della Corte internazionale di giustizia di modificare misure cautelari precedentemente adottate: quali limiti all'esercizio della funzione giudiziaria internazionale?" (The Power of the International Court of Justice to Modify Its Provisional Measures: Are There Limitations to the Exercise of the International Judicial Function?), RDI, 2015, p. 897 ff.

FRULLI M., "The Contribution of International Criminal Tribunals to the Development of International Law: The Prominence of *Opinio Juris* and the Moralization of Customary Law", The Law & Practice of International Courts and Tribunals, 2015, p. 80 ff.

GAJA G., "Requesting the ICJ to Revoke or Modify Provisional Measures", The Law & Practice of International Courts and Tribunals, 2015, p. 1 ff.

GATTINI A. and CORTESI G., "Some New Evidence on the ICJ's Treatment of Evidence: The Second Genocide Case", Leiden JIL, 2015, p. 899 ff.

GIORGETTI C. (ed.), *Challenges and Recusals of Judges and Arbitrators in International Courts and Tribunals*, Leiden, 2015, pp. 428.

GIORGETTI C., "The Challenges and Recusals at the International Court of Justice", in GIORGETTI C. (ed.), *Challenges and Recusals of Judges and Arbitrators in International Courts and Tribunals*, Leiden, 2015, p. 3 ff.

GRECO R., "The Impact of the Human Right to Water on Investment Disputes", RDI, 2015, p. 444 ff.

MALINTOPPI L. and CARLEVARIS A., "Challenges of Arbitrators, Lessons from the ICC", in GIORGETTI C. (ed.), *Challenges and Recusals of Judges and Arbitrators in International Courts and Tribunals*, Leiden, 2015, p. 140 ff.

PALCHETTI P., "*'A Key Institution for Interpreting International Law and Guaranteeing Global Compliance with Its Provisions'*: la dichiarazione italiana di accettazione della competenza della Corte internazionale di giustizia" ("A Key Institution for Interpreting International Law and Guaranteeing Global Compliance with Its Provisions": The Italian Declaration Accepting the Jurisdiction of the International Court of Justice), RDI, 2015, p. 114 ff.

RAIMONDI G., "Il giudice della Corte europea dei diritti dell'uomo" (The Judge of the European Court of Human Rights), in NESI G. and GARGIULO P. (eds.), *Luigi Ferrari Bravo. Il diritto internazionale come professione*, Napoli, 2015, p. 19 ff.

RUSSO D., "Sull'uso della ragionevolezza da parte della Corte internazionale di giustizia nel controllo sull'esercizio dei poteri discrezionali degli Stati" (On the Use of the Criterion of Reasonableness by the International Court of Justice in the Review of the Exercise by States of their Discretionary Powers), RDI, 2015, p. 487 ff.

SACERDOTI G. (ed.), "The WTO Dispute Settlement System in 2014", IYIL, 2014, p. 395 ff.

SACERDOTI G., "From Law Professor to International Adjudicator: The WTO Appellate Body and ICSID Arbitration Compared, A Personal Account", in CARON D. et al. (eds.), *Practising Virtue – Inside International Arbitration*, Oxford, 2015, p. 204 ff.

SACERDOTI G., "Il ruolo delle organizzazioni internazionali nella soluzione delle controversie" (International Organizations and the Settlement of Disputes), in VELLANO M. (ed.), *Il futuro delle organizzazioni internazionali. Prospettive giuridiche, XIX Convegno SIDI Courmayeur 2015*, Napoli, 2015, p. 19 ff.

SACERDOTI G., "Settling International Economic Disputes: The WTO and other Models. Trade and Investments", in ROVINE A. (ed.), *Contemporary Issues in International Arbitration and Mediation: The Fordham Papers 2014*, Leiden, 2015, p. 309 ff.

SAVARESE E., "The Arbitral Practice of the International Centre for Settlement of Investment Disputes (ICSID) in 2014", IYIL, 2014, p. 431 ff.

SCOVAZZI T., "Between Law and Science: Some Considerations Inspired by the *Whaling in the Antarctic* Judgment", QIL, Zoom-in 14, 2015, p. 13 ff.

SEATZU F. "The Treatment of International Law in the Jurisprudence of the World Bank Administrative Tribunal", The Law & Practice of International Courts and Tribunals, 2015, p. 130 ff.

TANCREDI A., "Accordi post-giudiziali e natura del sistema di soluzione delle controversie dell'OMC" (Post-Judicial Agreements and the Nature of the WTO Dispute Settlement System), in NESI G. and GARGIULO P. (eds.), *Luigi Ferrari Bravo. Il diritto internazionale come professione*, Napoli, 2015, p. 249 ff.

TANZI A. and CONTARTESE C., "Dispute Prevention, Dispute Settlement and Implementation Facilitation in International Water Law: The Added Value of the Establishment of an Implementation Mechanism under the Water Convention", in TANZI A., MCINTYRE O., KOLLIOPOULOS A., RIEU-CLARKE A. and KINNA R. (eds.), *The UNECE Convention on the Protection and Use of Transboundary Watercourses and International Lakes. Its Contribution to International Water Cooperation*, Leiden, 2015, p. 317 ff.

TINO E., "Settlement of Disputes by International Courts and Tribunals of Regional International Organizations", in VIRZO R. and INGRAVALLO I. (eds.), *Evolutions in the Law of International Organizations*, Leiden, 2015, p. 468 ff.

TREVES T., "The International Tribunal for the Law of the Sea and Other Law of the Sea Jurisdictions (2014)", IYIL, 2014, p. 341 ff.

VADI V., "Beyond Known Worlds: Climate Change Governance by Arbitral Tribunals?", Vanderbilt Journal of Transnational Law, 2015, p. 1285 ff.

VADI V., "Crossed Destinies: International Economic Courts and the Protection of Cultural Heritage", JIEL, 2015, p. 51 ff.

VADI V., "Global Cultural Governance by Arbitral Tribunals: The Making of a *Lex Administrativa Culturalis*", Boston University International Law Journal, 2015, p. 101 ff.

VADI V., "Proportionality, Reasonableness and Standards of Review in Investment Treaty Arbitration", Yearbook of International Investment Law and Policy, 2013/2014, p. 201 ff.

VADI V., "The Migration of Constitutional Ideas: The Strange Case of Proportionality in International Investment Law and Arbitration", Yearbook of International Investment Law and Policy, 2013/2014, p. 337 ff.

VADI V., *Analogies in International Investment Law and Arbitration*, Cambridge, 2015, pp. 320.

REVIEW OF BOOKS

(edited by *Marco Gestri*)

MARC WELLER (ed.), *The Oxford Handbook of the Use of Force in International Law*, Oxford, Oxford University Press, 2015, pp. lxxxix-1280.

Writing handbooks on the most important subjects of international law has become very popular and the Handbook edited by Marc Weller follows this trend dealing with one of the most controversial topics in international relations: the use of force. A band of scholars has been employed to contribute, coming from several geographical areas stretching from Japan to Australia, US, Latin America, and Western Europe. This means that the Handbook mainly represents the Western vision, since no Russian or Chinese scholars took part in this ambitious endeavour.

The Handbook is divided into seven Parts: Introduction (I); Collective Security and the Non-Use of Force (II); The Prohibition of the Use of Force, Self-Defence, and Other Concepts (III); Action on Behalf of Peoples and Populations (IV); Revival of Classical Concepts? (V); Emerging Areas? (VI); General Problems (VII).

The present reviewer prefers to focus on a number of general issues that are dealt with across the whole volume instead of examining each section in turn. This does not mean that individual topics worthy of attention are not considered.

Marc Weller, in his long introduction, explains why a Handbook on use of force is needed and the main features of the volume. Weller's introduction functions also as a kind of conclusion: the Handbook lacks a final Chapter and it is difficult to construe a unitary vision since the contributors do not always share the same doctrinal opinions.

The prohibition of the threat or use of force is now an undisputed rule of international law. Michael Glennon is one of the few (or only?) scholars who still contends the relevance and cogency of the rule. His arguments, that were formulated some years ago and gained currency at the time of Bush's US presidency and intervention in Iraq, are again offered to the sceptics and then criticized. This time the critiques are authored by James Crawford and Rowan Nicholson, who use sound arguments of positive law to demonstrate the inconsistency of Glennon's reasoning.

The reader is surprised to find a Chapter on "Feminist Perspectives on the Law on the Use of Force", written by Gina Heathcote. A feminist approach has relevance for *jus in bello* and issues related to the protection of women against rape and other forms of sexual violence and the status of women as members of armed forces during hostilities. But what of *jus ad bellum*? Are women better equipped for a pacifist reading of the UN Charter provisions on use of force than men? As State practice and "the teaching of the most highly qualified publicists" show, women are not neglected. Several of them are or have been protagonists in the field either as members or heads of government (suffice to quote Margaret Thatcher and the Falkland/ Malvinas war) or as authors of articles and books on *jus ad bellum* issues.

The Handbook through its Chapters takes into consideration the major problems relating to the use of force, dealing not only with *jus ad bellum* but also with *jus in bello*.

One of the most debated theoretical problems regards the nature of the provision banning the use of force. It is accepted doctrine that it belongs to customary international law. But what about *jus cogens*? The question is dealt with mainly by Alexander Orakhelashvili and André de Hoogh. The *jus cogens* nature of the prohibition on the use of force brings Orakhelashvili to conclude that only self-defence, traditionally interpreted, and the *ad hoc* consent given by a constitutionally legitimate government are lawful exceptions, whereas other alleged exceptions – such as intervention for protecting nationals abroad, humanitarian intervention, self-defence against non- State actors, etc. – are labelled violations of international law. Better articulated is the line of reasoning of de Hoogh, who takes into account in critical terms the thesis according to which not all violations of the use of force are covered by a peremptory norm of international law, but only those that substantiate the notion of aggression. One of the problems raised by considering all violations of the prohibition of the use of force to be an infringement of *jus cogens* is the impossibility of *ex post facto* justification of an illegal action, even when the justification is given by the Security Council.

The content of the prohibition embodied in Article 2(4) is obviously central to the Handbook and is dealt with by Nico Schrijver, while the question of the meaning of threat of force, a topic often difficult to decipher, is considered by François Dubuisson and Anne Lagerwall who point out the symmetry between threat and use of force.

Self-defence against non-State actors is considered by a number of contributors. The most conservative view is given by Orakhelashvili who adheres to the jurisprudence of the International Court of Justice (*Palestinian Wall* and *DRC v. Uganda*). The majority of contributors have a different view. For instance, Jordan Paust correctly notes that nothing in Article 51 of the UN Charter restricts the right of self-defence to armed attacks by a State. The same line of reasoning is taken by Kimberley Trapp. In wondering whether non-State actors can mount an armed attack, she rebuts the negative theories and gives a reading of relevant ICJ jurisprudence different from that adopted by those that have a restrictive view of Article 51. A specific contribution on the subject is given by Lindsay Moir in his contribution on "Action against Host States and Terrorist Groups", dealing specifically with a response to an armed attack by terrorist groups whose action cannot be attributed to the territorial State. He quotes extensive State practice, which is supported by the operations by the US and other countries against ISIL in Syria. In effect, as Jorg Kammerhofer points out in his Chapter on "The Resilience of the Restrictive Rules on Self-defence", the view that self-defence is admissible even against a non-State actor armed attack is theoretically sustainable without the need to appeal to a change in State practice to demonstrate an evolution of the law of self-defence.

Sanctions and countermeasures are briefly debated. Jean d'Aspremont observes how smart and targeted sanctions have resolved issues in this area and discusses mechanisms put in place to protect the rights of individuals; countermeasures are examined in connection with cyber operations in the excellent Chapter by Michael Schmitt who gives a concise and complete view on the use of cyber force and international law, while countermeasures by third States are explored by Paolo Palchetti. For Ramesh Thakur, sanctions are counterproductive since they end by inflicting suffering to citizens while the ruling class may make profit by controlling illicit traffic of forbidden goods. Thakur is also sceptical of the efficacy of smart sanctions.

A large part of the Handbook is dedicated to permissible uses of force, both uncontroversial and mooted. Self-defence is uncontroversial. However scholars are divided on the conditions that allow its exercise. Orakhelashvili espouses the traditional (continental) view: self-defence may be resorted to only after an armed attack has occurred. This old fashioned doctrine cannot continue to be upheld in the face of modern weaponry and the danger of being attacked in such a way as to be unable to react, as shown by Ashley Deeks, in her Chapter on "Taming the Doctrine of Pre-emption" and by other contributors (Claus Kress, Noam Lubell, and Daniel Joyner).

Collective self-defence and its distinction from actions in collective security is thoroughly examined by Michael Wood, while Terry Gill tries to shed light on the rule requiring termination of action in self-defence once the Security Council has taken proper enforcement measures.

The other traditional lawful exercise of use of force is the consent by the territorial State in which the intervention takes place. This subject is dealt with not only in the context of intervention by invitation, but also by those who are dealing with the use of force by regional organisations. In his Chapter on "Intervention by Invitation" Gregory Fox revisits the doctrine of the lawfulness of intervention with the consent of the constituted government and takes into consideration the new practice inaugurated by intervention in Libya at the request of insurgents recognised as the "legitimate representative" of the people of the country – a practice continued with the Syrian opposition groups. A new variation is that of a new government, different from an ousted one or from an insurgent entity, which has the blessing of the Security Council but is devoid of effectiveness. The example is the Libyan Government of National Accord as envisaged by UN Security Council Resolution 2259 (2016). The legitimacy of a government requesting intervention is also a central issue in the Chapter by David Wippman on "Pro-Democratic Intervention". As far as regional organisations are concerned, the main question is whether they need to be authorised by the Security Council in order to take enforcement action. This topic is taken into consideration in a number of Chapters, which deal with it either fully or partially (Ian Johnstone, Erika de Wet, and Jen Michel Arrighi).

In addition to self-defence, States are allowed to use force if authorised by the Security Council. The topic is discussed by a number of contributors to the Handbook and it is specifically considered in the Part on Collective Security, since the operations are viewed under the perspective of collective action, even though carried out by States individually or under the aegis of a regional organisation. Niels Blokker counts 80 operations authorised by the Security Council between 2000 and 2012. The main problem with authorised operations lies in the control by the Security Council of the conduct of States carrying out the operation and the individuation of the subject responsible, should a wrongful act occur. Time limits and operation reporting are among the tools recommended in order to stay away from blank cheque authorisations. Another problem is the lack of clarity and imprecision of the resolution authorising the use of force and the temptation to rely on an "implied authorisation" to justify the recourse to armed action. According to Ian Johnstone a categorical refusal of the doctrine of implied authorisation is too formalistic, since it does not delve into the real meaning of a resolution, which must be understood by using all interpretational tools offered by international law.

The Handbook also deals with armed actions whose legality is mooted and are the object of controversy: rescuing nationals abroad, humanitarian intervention and intervention for facilitating self-determination. The first category of armed actions is examined by Matthias Forteau, who concludes that the issue of legality of using force for rescuing nationals abroad "remains largely undecided" because of the division between those supporting a right of intervention (the West) and those contrary to it, as is shown by the firm opposition of the Latin-American countries in the General Assembly Sixth Committee. For Nigel Rodley humanitarian intervention carried out with forcible action cannot be considered lawful; however a genuine humanitarian intervention may result in a mitigation of wrongful conduct of the intervening State/States.

Elizabeth Chadwick deals with the interesting topic of national liberation wars after the end of colonialism. It is a rather confusing Chapter, which does not take due account of the distinction between peoples and minorities that it is the foundation of modern theory on national liberation wars. Moreover, struggles for democracy, inequality or high unemployment cannot be assembled under the label of national liberation wars if we want to preserve the technical meaning of the concept.

Armed reprisals are forbidden as Shane Darcy reminds us, quoting UN documents and doctrinal opinions. I would add also the Helsinki CSCE principles, that the author neglects to cite.

The review by Claus Kress of the jurisprudence of the ICJ on the use of force is extremely useful and unravels the myth that controversies dealing with the *jus ad bellum* are non-justiciable.

The system of collective security centred on actions taken directly by the Security Council, including peace-keeping, and quite apart from actions taken by the individual State, is the object of a number of Chapters, commencing with Ramesh Thakur, who reviews the main features of collective security, including peace operations and the main proposals for their amelioration. Nigel White's interesting Chapter takes into account the relationship between the Security Council and General Assembly in matters of international peace and security. He tries to save the spirit of the Uniting for Peace resolution which may compensate for the inaction of the Security Council, which still persists on many occasions notwithstanding the end of cold war. The practice of peacekeeping operations, with specific emphasis on the protection of civilians, is reviewed by Haidi Willmot and Ralph Mamiya. Nicholas Tsagourias assesses the applicability of the "responsibility to protect" doctrine to UN operations and its distinction from the use of force to protect civilians. Of interest is the Chapter by Scott Sheeran on the use of force in UN operations: the author points out how the concept has been changed over time from the original use of force in self-defence only of the members of the mission to the wider concept of self-defence for protecting the mandate of the mission and civilians. There is – he concludes – "a need for an update and reconceptualization of the theory of use of force by UN peacekeepers under international law". André Nollkaemper has written an important Chapter on "'Failure to Protect' in International Law" assessing, *inter alia*, the question of "bystander States", examining whether they can be held responsible for not intervening and putting to an end atrocities.

A number of Chapters are dedicated to the *jus in bello*. Keiichiro Okimoto tries to clarify the relationship between *jus ad bellum* and *jus in bello*. The principle of equality of belligerents is considered and the author quotes a number of authorities and international judgments restating the validity of this principle. A more critical approach is however needed. If the Democratic Republic of North Vietnam is the leading case in which the principle has overtly been challenged, it is to be remembered that the Soviet Union has been always critical and the reservation appended to Article 85 of the Third Geneva Convention is in some way reminiscent of the fact that the principle of equality of belligerents is not easily palatable for a number of countries. Other contributions relevant for *jus in bello* (and partly for *jus ad bellum*) are those of Martin Wahlisch, who offers a panoply of examples of cease-fire, truces, peace agreements, and peace treaties, and of Marina Mancini who, in her contribution on "The Effects of a State of War or Armed Conflict", gives an insight into an issue difficult to systemise after the entry into force of the UN Charter. The contribution of Marco Pertile is also relevant in this context, since he tries to shed new light on the problem of exploitation of natural resources in occupied territories, the unlawful territorial situations, and the duty of non-recognition. Jean Christophe Martin deals with the theatre of operations in land, sea and air warfare, including a short remark on cyberwarfare.

The other contributions are devoted to specific fields that are dealt with under the perspective of *jus ad bellum*, *jus in bello* or both. Daniel Joyner indicates the proliferation of Weapons of Mass Destruction (WMD) as the major factor that has generated the gap between the current interpretation of the law prohibiting the use of force and the dynamics of armaments and geopolitical change. He proposes new rules to fill the gap or the reinterpretation of the existing ones, such as the expansion of the law of self-defence allowing a counterproliferation-oriented pre-emptive use of force. The proliferation of WMD is also the subject of the Chapter by Vasco Becker-Weinberg and Guglielmo Verdirame seen from the point of view of shipping interdiction. Private Military Companies (PMC) are also a relatively new phenomenon. They raise problems of *jus in bello* as proven by the attempts to regulate them with new conventional law or with soft law instruments such as the Montreux Document. The Chapter by Ian Ralby focuses on PMCs and *jus ad bellum*, an inquiry that has no real relevance since PMCs operate on the side of State or non-State actors and only raise problems of State responsibility or of the law of insurgency when they act on the side of rebels.

The law of the sea also has its own place in the Handbook. Wolff Heintschel von Heinegg deals with blockades under *jus ad bellum* and *jus in bello* and interdiction operations. A question mark is raised concerning interdiction operations against foreign flags taken as a countermeasure for a wrongful act of the flag State. Bill Gilmore examines hot pursuit, a classical concept of the law of the sea, including its controversial application on land or air. The use of force against pirates is dealt with by Douglas Guilfoyle, who has written extensively on security at sea. His findings are generally to be shared. However, his commentary on the *Enrica Lexie* incident and on the two Italian marines posted on board to protect the ship from pirate attacks and accused of having shot dead Indian fishermen is not correct. Italy not only invoked Article 97 of the UN Convention on the Law of the Sea, but also the doctrine of functional immunity to exclude Indian jurisdiction, contrary to what Guilfoyle affirms (he says that Italy failed to invoke State immunity).

In conclusion, the Handbook contains well-documented and complete research on the problems raised by the prohibition of the threat and use of force in international law and its exceptions. It also contains incursions on related topics such as the law of the sea. Issues of *jus in bello* are also considered. The Handbook is not a Manual of International Law, but a kind of florilegium where the most important subjects of *jus ad bellum* are considered. For this reason one can find opposite views and a variety of doctrinal opinions, from the most conservative to the most modern that are in keeping with the evolution of international law. A conclusion pointing out the different interpretations on major questions would have been desirable.

Having said that, Weller's Handbook should be praised for the richness of the contributions, which stimulate the attention of the reader. The Handbook is to be recommended to those who want to deepen their understanding of the topic of use of force in international relations and are interested in having a global outlook on such an important subject of international law.

NATALINO RONZITTI[*]

---

[*] Of the Board of Editors.

ROBERTO VIRZO and IVAN INGRAVALLO (eds.), *Evolutions in the Law of International Organizations*, Leiden/Boston, Brill Nijhoff, 2015, pp. xxvi-547.

The volume *Evolutions in the Law of International Organizations*, edited by Ivan Ingravallo and Roberto Virzo (Associate Professors of International Law at the Universities of Bari and Sannio, respectively), is a valuable example of Italian scholars' ongoing interest in the phenomenon of international institutional law and offers an overview of some crucial elements regarding the development of international organisations. The book constitutes volume 54 of the prestigious series "Evolutions in the Law of International Organizations" coordinated by Niels Blokker, Professor of International Institutional Law at the University of Leiden.

The edited volume consists of twenty Chapters written by Italian and other scholars, with an appropriate mix between professors who have shown a dedicated interest in such issues over the past decades and emerging voices capable of providing fitting contributions due to their specific interest in these subjects.

An opportune feature of this volume, which could also be replicated in other contexts, is the inclusion of contributions by non-legal scholars, who are able to offer different perspectives on the subjects addressed. This is the case, first, of the contribution by Alessandro Polsi, Full Professor of the History of Political Institutions at the University of Pisa. Testimony to Polsi's long-standing interest in the history of international organisations, Chapter 4 (pp. 116-131) is devoted to the issue of "Universalism and Regionalism in the History of the United Nations and of Specialized Agencies", placing these phenomena under a historian's lens. Second, Chapter 8 on "The Evolution of the Banking Supervision Architecture in Europe" (pp. 224-243), by Concetta Brescia Morra, analyses this never-ending saga from the point of view of a Professor of Economic Law. Such "contaminations" are more than welcome, especially in areas such as that of international organisations. Indeed, a perspective strictly limited to legal elements can hardly hope to paint a comprehensive picture of the whole framework of analysis: this is emphasised by the constant interest in the topic demonstrated by scholars from other disciplines, and international relations experts in particular (see recently, among others, HURD, *International Organizations. Politics, Law, Practice*, 2nd ed., Cambridge, 2013; and ARCHER, *International Organizations*, 4th ed., London, 2015).

"Evolutions" is the *leitmotif* that characterises both the title of the volume and the content of the majority of its Chapters. This pertinently reflects the ever-changing nature of international organisations, their proliferation and the different characteristics they need to adopt in order to fulfil the basic necessity of their existence: providing for structured and appropriate cooperation in areas that can no longer be managed by single States. The "evolution" paradigm has also implied the need for international organisations, like any living entity, to adapt to sometimes hostile and challenging (political and legal) environments. As exemplified by several Chapters in this volume, this has implied the need for international organisations to partly reshape their features and address certain challenges posed by competing interests within the international community in order to be more fit for such purposes (e.g., the human rights discourse, accountability issues, etc.). Living, furthermore, in a period characterised by "Euphoria and Criticism" towards international organisations, as identified by Niels Blokker in his periodisation of this legal phenomenon within his "General Introduction" (p. 1 ff.), this volume provides timely insights into the evolutionary trends of international institutional law.

Apart from the abovementioned introduction, the volume is divided into two sections: Part 1 is devoted to "Evolutions in the Models of International Organizations – Recent Developments", while Part 2 focuses on "Evolution in the Institutional Law of International Organizations – Selected Issues". It is however difficult to draw a clear dividing line between the sections as some contributions are relevant to both.

Several Chapters in Part 1 seek to reappraise models of international institutional law and emphasise their ductile nature. In this regard reference can be made to the contributions of Marie-Clotide Runavot (Chapter 1, "The Intergovernmental Organization and the Institutionalization of International Relations", pp. 17-43), Angela Di Stasi (Chapter 2, "About Soft International Organizations: An Open Question", pp. 44-69), and Piero Pennetta ("International Regional Organizations: Problems and Issues", pp. 70-115).

Ruvanot focuses her analysis on the challenges faced by the "archetypal" model of intergovernmental organisations, nowadays probably better qualified as a mere "prototype". In this regard the increasing relevance of the role of other international organisations and non-governmental organisations, as well as private individuals within the framework of activities and in the membership of international organisations, as well as new typologies of law-making processes, are qualified as significant elements, capable of placing the "prototype" model in jeopardy.

Such remarks are reinforced when the parallel trend towards more flexible methods for the institutionalisation of international relations is taken into account. This latter element is addressed in particular by Angela Di Stasi, through her analysis of "informal" international organisations, which are still intended to implement the goals and values of States but largely lack the structural characteristics typical of "traditional" intergovernmental organisations. Di Stasi's Chapter illustrates the key elements of this additional phenomenon, which characterises the current development of international cooperation. While "soft" international organisations can hardly correspond to a single model, due to the variety in their elements and their interaction with more structured forms of cooperation, they nowadays constitute a significant part of this branch of law and are capable of creating potential challenges to traditional legal categories.

Finally, the long essay by Pennetta offers an in-depth reconstruction of the peculiarities characterising regional models of international cooperation, which are particularly relevant for their quantitative and qualitative growth. A partly related exemplification of this latter phenomenon can be found in Giovanni Cellamare's specific focus on "The Activities for the Maintenance of International Peace in the Relationship between the United Nations and Regional Organizations" (pp. 132-170). In Chapter 5 Cellamare, on the basis of his previous extensive analysis of this subject, provides a critical overview of regional organisations' increased tendency to assume responsibility for the maintenance of peace and security. This significant trend will certainly demand greater attention from scholars in the near future, also taking into account the necessity to properly identify other elements in the complex legal puzzle that characterises the activities of regional organisations in this area. Mention could be made, for instance, of the recent pledge submitted by NATO in front of the 32nd International Conference of Red Cross and Red Crescent Movements held in December 2015, whereby NATO expressed its commitment "to abide by the rules and principles of International Humanitarian Law" (see pledge No. SP320061). This pledge, which constitutes a novelty in such international conferences, obviously raises the related issue of the identification of pertinent *jus in bello* rules of relevance to this entity while involved in maintaining peace and security.

A sort of sub-section of Part 1 is devoted to the evolution of institutional law pertaining to international financial and economic organisations. In addition to the abovementioned essay by Morra, Susanna Cafaro focuses on "The International Financial Crisis and the Evolution of the Bretton Woods Institutions" (Chapter 7, pp. 192-223), providing a critical analysis as well as suggestions on reforms to the global economic governance aimed at increasing its legitimacy and efficiency; also on the basis of lessons learned through the (unfortunately enduring) financial crisis that began in 2008. Similarly, Maria Rosaria Mauro ("The Protection of Non-Economic Values and the Evolution of International Economic Organizations: The Case of the World Bank", Chapter 9, pp. 244-274) provides an overview of this topic, with a particular emphasis on mechanisms aimed at evaluating the impact on human rights of policies developed by such organisations.

Finally, this section offers two further relevant Chapters. Jacob Katz Cogan, one of the emerging leading voices in the area of international institutional law (see his forthcoming volume as co-editor *The Oxford Handbook of International Organizations*, Oxford University Press) provides a very interesting analysis of a topic to which scholars have not yet granted the specific attention it deserves: i.e. decisions by the International Law Commission (ILC) on the final form of its work and its recommendation to the UN General Assembly on what action the latter should take on its completed text. Having had the personal privilege to provide assistance to one of the Special Rapporteurs of the ILC involved in the realisation of a set of draft articles, and having witnessed the fascinating approach with which the Rapporteurs and the Commission assess the form to be provided to "their creatures", it is a real pleasure to find in Cogan's Chapter a very careful and fair assessment of some of the dynamics concerning the form of the ILC's work and its changing and flexible nature. Finally, Chapter 6 by Víctor Luis Gutiérrez Castillo and Jonatán Cruz Ángeles on "Islam and International Organizations: The Organization of Islamic Cooperation" (pp. 171-191) allows the reader to appreciate the pivotal role played by the Organisation of Islamic Cooperation in several contexts and some difficulties related to the common trend of overlapping activities and memberships among different organisations, exemplified, in this case, with regard to the League of Arab States.

Part 2 focuses on the "Evolution in the Institutional Law of International Organizations – Selected Issues". The selection of topics is obviously based on the sole preference of the editors and authors, as several other issues could also have been addressed. Nonetheless, the choice also appears to be based on the need to deal with some of the most topical challenges, both in terms of the relevance of topics and their legal complexity.

A substantial portion of this Part is centred around some partly-related sub-themes: the accountability and responsibility of international organisations; immunities of organisations and their staff; and the human rights paradigm. Such topics undeniably represent some of the most challenging issues currently faced by international organisations (and consequently by scholars too). In this regard this Part offers helpful insights into some critical issues.

First, concerning the immunities of international organisations, in Chapter 12 on "The League of Nations and the Emergence of Privileges and Immunities of International Organizations" (pp. 324-363), Vittorio Mainetti offers a very accurate reconstruction of one of the first provisions ever adopted referring to the immunity and inviolability of an international organisation: namely Article 7 of the 1919 Covenant of the League of Nations. This Chapter allows the reader to appreciate both the relevance of this provision for subsequent rules in this area and the actual interpretation and implementation of Article 7, especially with regard to host States. Such a rich analysis on the League of Nations can easily be explained by this scholar's involvement in one of the most fascinating volumes recently published in the area of international institutional law: KOLB (ed.), *Commentaire sur le Pacte de la Société des Nations*, Bruxelles, 2014. Mainetti also contributed to the latter text with a Chapter devoted to Article 7 of the Covenant, which largely differs in content from the one examined here. Regarding the current challenges related to the immunities of international organisations, the volume provides an overview in Chapter 13 (pp. 364-380) on "International Organizations and Immunity from Legal Process: An Uncertain Evolution" by Massimo Francesco Orzan. This Chapter focuses specifically on the nature and legal basis of international organisations' immunities before national courts, taking into account the fragmented scenario inferred from domestic practice.

Part 2 dedicates a series of Chapters to the relevance of the human rights discourse and accountability/responsibility issues raised by the activities of international organisations, with regard to both their internal and external dimensions.

First, Guillaume Le Floch offers a comprehensive analysis of the problematic issues raised by the "external" dimension of international organisations' activities, with respect to the position of third parties, in Chapter 14 on the "Responsibility for Human Rights Violations by International Organizations" (pp. 381-406). Le Floch considers both the nebulous framework of potential human rights obligations binding such entities, especially in the light of relevant novelties in this regard, such as the possibility of some recent human rights treaties also being ratified by international organisations, as well as the consequences arising from the violation of such rules. Not unsurprisingly, the author maintains that the mechanisms developed to date to provide remedies to potential victims remain both embryonic and largely unsatisfactory. The possibility of holding an international organisation and/or its Member States responsible under international law for the violation of rules pertaining to this legal order is obviously based on the settlement of attribution criteria. This issue is analysed in depth by Pietro Pustorino in Chapter 15 (pp. 407-422) on "The Control Criterion between Responsibility of States and Responsibility of International Organizations", which includes a comparison of relevant solutions provided by the ILC in its draft articles on the responsibility of States and international organisations. Pustorino remains unpersuaded by the solution adopted by the ILC in Article 7 of the draft articles on the responsibility of international organisations, a provision qualified as not reflecting customary international law.

As for the relevance of the human rights debate in the "internal" dimension of international organisations, reference could be made to Chapter 16 (pp. 423-450) by Berta Esperanza Hernández-Truyol on "International Organizations and Gender Discrimination: Supersexing Gender Mainstreaming", where the author claims that international organisations need to place sex equality among their goals, using the UN system as a paradigm to emphasise failures in this regard, and Chapter 19 by Daniele Gallo (pp. 509-532) on "The Right of Access to Justice for the Staff of International Organizations", which mainly provides a review of the ICJ Advisory Opinion of 1 February 2012 on a judgment in this area by the Administrative Tribunal of the International Labour Organisation.

Finally, other Chapters focus on basic issues concerning the law of international organisations, seeking to evaluate the developments related to recent trends in this area. In this regard Chapter 11 by Roberto Virzo on "The Proliferation of Institutional Acts of International Organizations: A Proposal for Their Classification" (pp. 293-323) provides a reappraisal of this traditional topic with some innovative elements of analysis. Taking into account the complex decision-making process characterising such entities, Virzo emphasises how, through a multifaceted series of unilateral acts, international organisations aim to both deal with the challenges posed by the international community in order to properly absolve their functions and to override the inherent rigidity of their constituent instruments in relation to acts to be adopted. Particular attention is paid to authorisations provided to Member States. While legal analyses have traditionally circumscribed this latter phenomenon to a review of the practice of the UN Security Council, the author is convincingly able to demonstrate how a similar trend can also be identified in relation to other international organisations, thus clarifying the role of such acts in international institutional law. Chapter 17 by Ivan Ingravallo focuses on a highly controversial topic: "Handle with Care! The Succession between International Organizations" (pp. 451-467). Ingravallo's analysis focuses on the relatively common phenomenon of changes in the institutions performing a specific task related to international cooperation, a situation not comparable to the similar phenomenon experienced by States. The variety of situations occurring in such cases (e.g., the involvement in succession of a Conference of States or a soft organisation, rather than a proper international organisation; cases of the mere transformation of an international organisation, where no succession occurs; inconsistent international practice) are analysed thoroughly in this contribution, in which the author maintains the need to pay attention to substantive elements (e.g., functions performed) rather than formal ones (e.g., international subjectivity) as the primary point of reference for legal analysis. Finally, Elisa Tino in Chapter 18 on the "Settlement of Disputes by International Courts and Tribunals of Regional International Organizations" (pp. 468-508) provides a comparative assessment of the trend of "judicialisation" which has involved several international organisations in this area.

In general terms this volume is valuable as it provides a sound reassessment and further analysis of some of the main elements of interest in current debate concerning international institutional law. This area appropriately continues to be the subject of academic interest, due to the changing nature of the phenomenon of international cooperation in relation to various causes, which have clearly impacted both the models and structures of international organisations "at large", as well as solutions on specific issues.

The volume would probably have benefitted from a specific introduction by the editors themselves, explaining their rationale as well as the choice of topics addressed, which has led to a sort of pick-and-mix approach in relation to some issues. Similarly, more coherent organisation of some Chapters would have been beneficial: for instance, several papers lack proper conclusions, which might have helped readers to better appreciate and evaluate the "evolutions" in the topics examined. Nonetheless, as maintained in the review of individual Chapters, this volume clearly merits attention by scholars with a specific interest in the area of the law of international organisations.

GIULIO BARTOLINI[*]

ANDREA DE GUTTRY, FRANCESCA CAPONE and CHRISTOPHE PAULUSSEN (eds.), *Foreign Fighters under International Law and Beyond*, The Hague, Asser Press/Springer, 2016, pp. xxiii-533.

Since the outbreak of the conflicts in Syria and Iraq international lawyers have started showing a keen interest in the current responses by the international community to the old – but certainly today more challenging than ever – phenomenon

---

[*] Associate Professor of International Law, University of Roma Tre.

of foreign fighters. In this respect, one can safely assert that, among the recent scholarly work on the subject (see notably KRÄHENMANN, *Foreign Fighters under International Law*, Geneva Academy of International Humanitarian Law and Human Rights, Academy Briefing No. 7, Geneva, 2014; and, among the relevant Italian contributions, SOSSAI, "*Foreign terrorist fighters*: una nozione ai confini del diritto internazionale", Federalismi.it, 25 September 2015; and ALÌ, "La risposta della comunità internazionale al fenomeno dei *foreign terrorist fighters*", CI, 2015, p. 181 ff.), the book under review is to date the most complete and comprehensive study.

Drawing from a multidisciplinary approach – as the title itself suggests – the aim of the book, in the editors' words, is "[…] to offer academics, policy makers and the public at large various observations on how the foreign fighters problem, not necessarily the foreign *terrorist* fighters problem, can be somewhat contained […] in an effective and long term way" (Chapter 1, "Introduction", p. 3). The need to depart from an exclusively counter-terrorism narrative in tackling the problem of foreign fighters is indeed also reflected in the same definition of foreign fighters provided by the editors in their introduction. Foreign fighters are, in their definition, "[…] individuals, driven mainly by ideology, religion and/or kinship, who leave their country of origin or their country of habitual residence to join a party engaged in an armed conflict" (p. 2). Such a definition, as the editors admit, is even broader than that employed by scholars (notably KRÄHENMANN, *cit. supra*) who also share, on the one hand, the not necessarily counter-terrorism terminology, but, on the other hand, still limit the definition to individuals joining a non-State armed group. Admittedly, the choice to give such an extensive definition, also inclusive of foreigners fighting alongside the established government, is due to the fact that there is no "ascertained legal meaning under the existing legal framework" of the phenomenon (p. 2). But this vast definition, as we shall see, also best fits with the multidisciplinary and cross-cutting character of the analysis carried out throughout the book.

The volume is divided into four Parts and consists of 25 Chapters. Part I of the book (Chapters 2 to 8) is the "beyond" part of the research and is entitled "Foreign Fighters: A Multidisciplinary Overview of New Challenges for an Old Phenomenon".

Chapter 1, by Edwin Bakker and Mark Singleton, is a general overview of the phenomenon of foreign fighters with a specific focus on the conflict in Syria and Iraq ("Foreign Fighters in the Syria and Iraq Conflict: Statistics and Characteristics of a Rapidly Growing Phenomenon"). Besides critically investigating the historical background, the reasons for this phenomenon and the current reactions at the national level (which, in the authors' view, "[…] focus largely on short-term, mainly 'hard end', repressive actions, addressing symptoms rather than root causes", p. 22), the Chapter usefully provides the latest statistical data – mainly based on empirical research by the International Centre for the Study of Radicalisation and Political Violence (ICSR) – about the growing number of foreign fighters in Syria and Iraq. Arriving at estimate a number of more than 30,000 foreign fighters "of all sorts" for the entire conflicts in Syria and Iraq, the authors interestingly include in their survey the impressive numbers of foreign fighters joining the side of governments (in Syria and Iraq) and Kurdish groups (pp. 16-18).

The contribution by Marcello Flores (Chapter 2) is purely based on a historical analysis of the phenomenon of "volunteers" ("Foreign Fighters Involvement in National and International War: A Historical Survey"), a term which, as the author explains, addresses better, under the historical lens, individuals joining "[...] a threatened government, a non State actor, a minority group seeking to come to power or national or diverse ethnic groups seeking their independence" (p. 28). Flores' historical survey – which, albeit briefer, appears to be more comprehensive than that included in a recently published book (MALET, *Foreign Fighters. Transnational Identity in Civil Conflicts*, Oxford, 2013) – covers events starting from the numerous wars of independence during the so-called Age of Revolutions, with a focus on the American Revolution and the Latin American and Greek wars of independence, to the new and "global" wars of the 20th and 21st century, passing through the 19th century revolutions in Europe (with an original analysis of the Italian *Risorgimento*) and the two World Wars. Such a stimulating historical investigation is essentially aimed at showing how the difficulty in defining and categorising "to a few immutable patterns" (p. 46) the experiences of volunteers is due to their multifaceted character which, in turn, "[...] lies mainly in the changing structure of institutional powers, State structures and kinds of governments, and more so historically than it does today" (p. 45).

Quite interesting reflections on the phenomenon of foreign fighters under the International Relations (IR) theory are offered by Francesco Strazzari in Chapter 4 ("Foreign Fighters as a Challenge for International Relations Theory"). After highlighting the difficulties – largely shared, as seen thus far, by scholars in different areas – in defining and conceiving foreign fighters as a "discrete actor category distinct from insurgents and terrorists" (p. 52), the author sketches the reasons why an IR theoretical framework needs to go beyond the traditional "Westphalian thinking" and the "orthodoxy of State-centric militarism" (p. 55). An IR theory under which the phenomenon might be evaluated should not underestimate, in the author's view, the fundamental changes in international relations, especially in terms of enhanced transnational communications, and their impact upon the concept of sovereignty. Only by bearing in mind that foreign fighters "inhabit a world where [...] hybrid spaces are regions and sub-regions where different control logics compete, overlap and often connive – and where the foundations of State legitimacy are questioned" (p. 61), will IR theory really be able to tackle the issue and critically dismantle any form of nationalistic and State-centric reactions to it.

As to the motivations that drive an individual to become a foreign fighter, some light is shed in Chapter 5 by Ross Frenett and Tanya Silverman ("Foreign Fighters: Motivations for Travel to Foreign Conflicts"). While admitting that these are "deeply personal reasons which are specific to that individual" (p. 74), the authors base their empirical research on a series of interviews carried out with individuals directly or indirectly involved in the phenomenon. In sum, they identify three constantly recurring motivational factors: "(1) outrage at what is alleged to be happening in the country where the conflict is taking place and empathy with the people being affected; (2) adherence to the ideology of the group an individual wishes to join and (3) a search for identity and belonging" (p. 65).

Chapter 6, by Gabriel Weimann, deals with the role of social media in the recruitment process of foreign fighters ("The Emerging Role of Social Media in the Recruitment of Foreign Fighters"). The author provides interesting data on the employment by the Islamic State of online platforms and analyses the different stages of online recruitment (conceived as a multi-step process). He also focuses on the emerging practice of "narrowcasting", where the recruitment efforts target specific and most sensible groups (such as Muslim youth and women), and on the use of social networks and media (Twitter, Facebook, YouTube) in the ISIS recruitment strategy. Lastly, Weimann reflects on the well-known challenges of countermeasures against online recruitment (including "soft" measures such as online counterterrorism narrative campaigns) which, as he appropriately points out, "should involve a careful examination of the prices in terms of civil liberties" (p. 94).

In the recruitment process and use of foreign fighters by the Islamic State, a key role is also often played by gendered dynamics, motivations and strategies. The Chapter by Dallin Van Leuven, Dyan Mazurana and Rachel Gordon (Chapter 7, "Analysing the Recruitment and Use of Foreign Men and Women in ISIL through a Gender Perspective") consists of an original and detailed inquiry on how ISIS' gender ideology affects actions towards men and women before and after joining the group, including the practice of sexual and gender-based violence. It offers a broader understanding of the phenomenon through an often overlooked perspective which, in the case of foreign fighters joining ISIS, appears instead more appropriate than ever.

Chapter 8, by Fabrizio Coticchia, deals with the "pure military dimension" of the phenomenon of foreign fighters ("The Military Impact of Foreign Fighters on the Battlefield: The Case of the ISIL", p. 124) and concludes Part I of the book. In particular, the author tries to identify some patterns relating to the military impact of foreign fighters on civil wars – that is to say how they are "exploited" by local insurgents (p. 129) – with a specific focus on the Islamic State tactics. He analyses foreign fighters' influence on the battlefield by considering the four dimensions of training, conventional tactics, military emulation, and suicide attacks, as well as the potential negative impact of foreign fighters on the unity of local groups, which often makes them most suitable for suicide attacks.

Parts II, III and IV of the book are specifically devoted to the phenomenon of foreign fighters seen under a strict (international) legal perspective.

Part II (Chapters 9 to 12) is entitled "The Legal Dimension: The Status of Foreign Fighters" and opens with an interesting essay by Emanuele Sommario on "The Status of Foreign Fighters under International Humanitarian Law" (Chapter

9). Sommario brings foreign fighters to the legal frameworks of both international and non-international armed conflicts. In the first case, he analyses the situation in which they could obtain the status of combatant and, as a consequence, that of prisoner of war in case of capture, both under Article 4 of the third Geneva Convention (as fully-fledged members of the armed forces of one of the party to the conflict or, most unlikely, as "members of other militias and members of other volunteer corps") and the first Additional Protocol. As to non-international armed conflicts he considers the cases in which foreign fighters could join the State's armed forces or the rebelling non-State actors. He concludes his analysis by taking into account the differences between mercenaries and foreign fighters – admitting that "[…] the risks of overlap between the two categories is extremely limited" (p. 157).

The question of whether international criminal responsibility might be attached to foreign fighters is dealt with by Robert Heinsch in Chapter 10 ("Foreign Fighters and International Criminal Law"). The author rightly observes that being a foreign fighter as such does not automatically trigger an international criminal responsibility: "[w]hat remains decisive are concrete *actions* these foreign fighters take" (p. 163), which often consist in committing core crimes of international criminal law and/or acts of terrorism when provided by a relevant legal instrument (such as the war crime regime). Difficulties might however be encountered when assessing the subjective elements of the alleged crimes as well as the modes of liability, especially with respect to the superior responsibility. Heinsch's Chapter ends with a survey of the possible judicial *fora* where foreign fighters can be prosecuted.

Chapter 11, by Francesca Capone ("Child Soldiers: The Expanding Practice of Minors Recruited to Become Foreign Fighters"), highlights several inadequacies of the existing legal framework concerning the recruitment and use of child soldiers especially when faced with the case of children in the ranks of foreign fighters. Interestingly, the author lingers on the international criminalisation (in the statutes of the Special Court for Sierra Leone and of the International Criminal Court) of conscription, enlistment or use of children under the age of 15 to participate actively in hostilities and criticises both the age limit and the uncertain scope of the "active participation" requirement. A hypothetical intervention of the ICC in Syria and Iraq, the author observes, would certainly be affected by these factors since the question of "whether sexual violence and enslavement, the main crimes committed against girls by ISIS, can be regarded as a type of offence covered by the prohibition on recruiting and using child soldiers is not trivial" (p. 199).

Daniele Amoroso's contribution (Chapter 12) deals with "Armed Opposition Groups' (and Foreign Fighters') Abidance by International Human Rights Law: The Issue of Compliance in Syria and Iraq". His praiseworthy analysis offers some answers to the following issues: "(i) to what extent [International human rights law] binds the parties to an internal conflict; (ii) under which conditions human rights violations committed by foreign fighters are attributable to them; and (iii) what legal consequences ensue from such violations" (p. 206). By confining his investigation to foreign fighters alongside the armed opposition group and by employing a "progressive model" according to which human rights obligations bind in principle all armed opposition groups (p. 210), the author admits that, as to the first question, the degree of "abidingness" should be assessed on a case-by-case basis. Quite convincingly, Amoroso maintains that, saving certain customary norms (such as the right not to be tortured or enslaved), "whose violation is triggered even by isolated incidents" (p. 213), a functional perspective rightly suggests that "the scope of human rights obligations incumbent on armed groups would be a 'function' of the authority they exert: the more authority they wield, the wider and more intense their obligations will be" (p. 212). As to the second question, there is more uncertainty given the rather scarce practice concerning the secondary obligations (cessation, reparation, and guarantee of non-repetition) following human rights breaches. Lastly, the third question, relating to the (legal?) reactions by the international community to such violations, raises several thought-provoking issues. The author in fact concludes by leaving the door half open to possible consolidation of customary rules allowing humanitarian intervention and the supply of arms to rebel groups fighting against ISIS.

Part III of the book ("Tackling the Problem of Foreign Fighters at the Supranational Level", Chapters 13 to 19) collects essays specifically addressing the international reactions to the phenomenon.

Chapter 13, by Sandra Krähenmann, focusing on "The Obligations under International Law of the Foreign Fighter's State of Nationality or Habitual Residence, State of Transit and State of Destination", provides a critical overview of a series of international law obligations incumbent on all States involved in foreign fighters' mobilisation (State of origin, State of transit, and State of destination) aimed at preventing their departure, their arrival and their return. Krähenmann – who also authored one of the first detailed studies entirely devoted to foreign fighters (cit. supra) – traces in a very refined way the content of such obligations and the interplay among them especially in the light of the most recent Security Council Resolutions (notably Res. 2178 (2014)), which, as indeed remarked by most of the authors contributing to Part III of the book, raises several concerns for it carries "a great potential for abuse" (p. 257).

In this latter regard, a specific and critical assessment of the approach adopted by the UN, and notably by the Security Council, towards the phenomenon at hand is made by Andrea de Guttry in Chapter 14 ("The Role Played by the UN in Countering the Phenomenon of Foreign Terrorist Fighters"). After generally illustrating the UN counter-terrorism strategy and the relevant UN actors, de Guttry analyses in a very attentive manner all aspects of the two abovementioned Security Council resolutions of 2014. Besides critically evaluating the "inescapable" correlation between foreign fighters and terrorists in the UN approach, the author sees a "contradiction in terms" between the trend of the Security Council to act as a "global legislator" and lack of adequate monitoring mechanisms of States' implementation (p. 278). The author also stresses the need for a more appropriate balance between counter-terrorism and human rights which is still far from being achieved especially in national practice. He finally welcomes what he defines as the "holistic approach" adopted by the Security Council in countering foreign terrorist fighters, according to which "terrorism will not be defeated by military force, law enforcement measures, and intelligence operations alone" (preamble of Res. 2178), but needs to be thwarted using "all available means" and "in line with [the specific] context's legal, cultural, sociological and economic background" (p. 280).

The complex and crucial question of the balance between counter-terrorism and human rights, in the light of the impact that international responses to the phenomenon of foreign fighters have on international human rights obligations of States, is addressed in much more detail by Alex Conte (Chapter 15, "States' Prevention and Responses to the Phenomenon of Foreign Fighters against the Backdrop of Human Rights Obligations"). Conte's analysis confirms that counter-terrorism measures must comply with human rights obligations even when adopted in implementation of Security Council resolutions. In reviewing the UN Global Counter-Terrorism Strategy and the relevant Security Council resolutions, the author concludes by pointing out that complementarity and mutual reinforcement between security and human rights "is a natural consequence of State's legal obligations under customary international human rights law and human rights treaties, and reflects the flexibility of human rights to accommodate security and public order objectives" (p. 297).

Chapter 16, by Gilles de Kerchove and Christiane Höhn, carefully illustrates the European Union (EU) strategy in addressing the phenomenon of foreign fighters ("The Regional Answers and Governance Structure for Dealing with Foreign Fighters: The Case of the EU"). According to the authors, the EU is "pioneering a regional approach to foreign fighters", even if its role remains "supportive" as the Member States are "the key actors in counter-terrorism" (p. 301). The wide range of measures and policies included in the EU strategy – which can be dated back to the 22 measures found by the Justice and Home Affair Council in 2013 and is constantly challenged by new threats – is also serving, the authors observe, as a model for the global response in broader contexts, such as the UN.

Still focusing on the EU level, the contribution by Matteo E. Bonfanti addresses limitations and opportunities that existing tools for sharing intelligence on foreign fighters present (Chapter 17, "Collecting and Sharing Intelligence on Foreign Fighters in the EU and its Member States: Existing Tools, Limitations and Opportunities"). Bonfanti contends that such existing tools appear to be sufficient and adequate to pursue concrete actions of prevention, even if, at the end of the day, their effective implementation depends on Member States' willingness to cooperate in this delicate field. This should call for policies aimed at reducing States' "endemic reluctance" in sharing intelligence (p. 351).

The Chapter by Annalisa Creta analyses OSCE strategy towards the phenomenon of foreign fighters (Chapter 18, "Towards Effective Regional Responses to the Phenomenon of Foreign Fighters: The OSCE Toolbox"). Interestingly, after describing all the initiatives and measures taken by the organisation in relation to other measures taken at global and regional level, the author concludes that this strategy actually consists of a "rule of law-based set of 'ready-made' responses that is flexible enough to be *adapted* to new threats posed by terrorism and their evolving and multifaceted shapes". However, she warns against an all-encompassing "blanket approach" which "might run the risk of generating unfocused solutions if not tailored to the specific phenomenon" (p. 369). In this regard, indeed, the above-mentioned "holistic approach" to which the Security Council appears to be oriented seems the most effective one.

In concluding Part III of the book, Linda Darkwa's essay gives an accurate analysis on the role of the African Union with respect to the phenomenon of foreign fighters in Africa (Chapter 19, "The African Union and the Phenomenon of Foreign Fighters in Africa"). Notwithstanding the particular vulnerability of the continent to the problem of foreign fighters, the African Union is still silent on the phenomenon. In particular, the author highlights the lack of legal instruments and tools within the organisation specifically addressing the foreign fighters issue and critically wonders whether existing instruments on peace and security are really sufficient for this. By urging for the Union to have "a robust and dispassionate conversation on the issue to guarantee the development of the most appropriate interventions" (p. 385), Darkwa concludes with several suggestions on how to stimulate a lucid discourse on foreign fighters in Africa.

The fourth and last Part of the book (Chapters 20 to 25) is entitled "Tackling the Phenomenon of Foreign Fighters at the National Level" and looks at the different domestic reactions to the phenomenon.

Chapter 20, by Christophe Paulussen and Eva Entenmann, investigates "National Responses in Select Western European Countries to the Foreign Fighter Phenomenon". The selected countries are Belgium, France, Germany, the Netherlands, and the United Kingdom, namely the countries with highest number of foreign fighters who have joined armed groups in the Syria and Iraq conflicts. The Chapter is focused mainly on legislative (several laws have in fact been passed in response of the relevant Security Council resolutions) and judicial developments concerning foreign fighters in these countries. Of particular interest is the survey of the (otherwise not easily to come by) criminal prosecution practice in these States and the relating case law which shows, among other things, how many evidentiary hurdles are in fact shared by most of the judiciary when dealing with the phenomenon.

The practice by selected Western "non-EU" countries is analysed by Aaron Y. Zelin and Jonathan Prohov in Chapter 21 ("How Western Non-EU States Are Responding to Foreign Fighters: A Glance at the USA, Canada, Australia and New Zealand's Laws and Policies"). As the Chapter's title indicates, the authors mostly address law and policy practice of these countries, leaving aside the judicial practice. The comparative perspective adopted by the authors reveals that counterterrorism strategies are in fact progressively converging, and this of course also involves foreign fighters' responses. In this context, a leading and "inspiring" role has been, and still is, played by the United States, which is after all the most experienced in this field.

Chapter 22, by Daveed Gartenstein-Ross and Bridget Moreng, provides five very well-structured case studies on policies adopted within the Middle East and North Africa region ("MENA Countries' Responses to the Foreign Fighter Phenomenon"). The authors focus in particular on policies and strategies both to stem the flow of foreign fighters and for dealing with returnees employed by Tunisia, Saudi Arabia, Morocco, Jordan, and Lebanon, which are a "particularly large source of fighters" (p. 446).

The Chapter by Laura Van Waas deals with a very captivating topic, namely the practice of depriving nationality as a policy instrument in reacting to the phenomenon of foreign fighters (Chapter 23 "Foreign Fighters and the Deprivation of Nationality: National Practices and International Law Implications"). Such practice – which has recently attracted the attention of several scholars (a recent Italian contribution is offered by CIPOLLETTI, "La privazione della cittadinanza nel contrasto ai *foreign terrorist fighters* e il diritto internazionale", RDI, 2016, p. 117 ff.) – is spreading among States facing the threat of foreign terrorist fighters and raises many prickly issues to be addressed from an international legal standpoint. After a rather quick review of national practice and motivations for such measures invoked by commentators, the author efficaciously traces the international law implications of denationalisation stemming from international human rights (notably from the prohibition of arbitrary deprivation of nationality), from the need to avoid statelessness and from the principle of non-discrimination. Given the number of international legal constraints, she concludes by wondering whether such a measure "can truly be deemed to serve the aim of safeguarding national security". Apparently the answer is "no": "[e]ven in a relatively permissive form, such as in the UK, [deprivation of nationality] remains a very marginal policy instrument" (p. 485).

Chapter 24, by Francesca Vietti and Mike Bisi, analyses the impact of foreign fighters on particular categories of individuals, namely internally displaced persons, asylum seekers and refugees ("Caught in the Crossfire: The Impact of Foreign Fighters on Internally Displaced Persons, Asylum Seekers and Refugees from Syria and Iraq"). As the authors carefully demonstrate, the fact that these people mostly use the same routes of foreign fighters can negatively affect their international protection. Indeed, both the risks of associating foreign fighters with them and the negative impact of States' measure to contrast foreign fighters are concrete. A series of recommendations to contain such negative effects are finally provided by the authors.

In the concluding Chapter (Chapter 25, "Concluding Remarks") the editors mainly summarise the key issues addressed, the answers given and the questions raised throughout the book. The final observations simply call for more investment by all stakeholders involved in the four key factors for discouraging and countering the phenomenon of foreign fighters, namely capacity building, prevention, education, and reintegration.

Some final observations by the present reviewer are also in order. As has been shown in discussing each Chapter, the volume is dense with useful information and references and offers much food for thought both from legal and non-legal perspectives. The complexities of the phenomenon of foreign fighters and the "perplexities" that arise when looking at the current national and international responses are all discussed in a truly original and high-quality way. There is no doubt that all scholars approaching this topic in the future cannot refrain from taking into account this contribution which is likely to become the scientific cornerstone in the field.

Having said this, we cannot but highlight one feature of the book. Whilst reading, one sometimes has the impression that a real coordination or "unity" among the contributions is lacking. The volume collects a number of essays which, instead of being grounded on a common research hypothesis, come across as "self-contained" (even if they address the same, though multifaceted, phenomenon). This might explain, for example, why, even though there is no overlapping among the contributions, there is some repetition in the Chapters' introductory parts, as to the description of current events and the general characteristics of the phenomenon. Admittedly, however, this lack of interconnection among the contributions is a natural and inevitable consequence of the ultimate aim of the book, which is to provide the "academics, policy makers and the public at large" (p. 3) with "a deeper and broader understanding" (p. 518) of a phenomenon that, given this goal, could not be reduced to a single and uniform perspective. In this respect, one cannot deny that this goal has been successfully accomplished.

LORIS MAROTTI*

SAVERIO DI BENEDETTO, *International Investment Law and the Environment*, Cheltenham/Northampton, Edward Elgar, 2013, pp. xxii-250.

The book under review deals with the implementation of environmental concerns within international investment law. Starting from the assumption that "[t]he sharp and sudden growth of foreign investments in the last two decades has contributed to pollution and environmental degradation, mainly in developing countries" (p. ix), the author has examined whether it is possible to reconcile foreign investor rights and environmental protection and whether – if a State takes some actions due to the necessity to protect its environment – such actions can be considered as exempted from paying damages (and/or compensation) to foreign investors, even if they are in violation of one or more standards of treatment of foreign investors.

This topic has already been the subject of a monograph (VIÑUALES, *Foreign Investment and the Environment in International Law*, Cambridge, 2012) and several articles (see, *inter alia*, FAUCHALD, "International Investment Law and Environmental Protection", YIEL, 2007, pp. 3-47; and PAVONI, "Environmental Rights, Sustainable Development, and Investor-State Case Law: A Critical

---

* Ph.D. in International Law and European Union Law, University of Macerata.

Appraisal", in DUPUY, PETERSMANN AND FRANCIONI (eds.), *Human Rights in International Investment Law and Arbitration*, Oxford, 2009, pp. 525-556), but has been dealt with in a very original and ambitious way by the author of this book. Indeed, by starting from an analysis of the possibility of integrating environmental concerns within the framework of investment arbitration, the book aims at understanding whether *all* non-commercial concerns may find a place within international investment law and arbitration. As noted by Di Benedetto, his "inquiry into the integration of environmental issues into the context of international investment law may provide a paradigmatic model for the broader theme of integrating non-economic matters into the tissue of rules that protect foreign investment" (p. x).

This attempt to integrate, within international investment law, values which, at first glance, seem completely detached from this area of law (mainly aimed at attracting investment by granting rights, and not obligations, to investors) has required the author to carry out a prior analysis of the alleged orderliness of international investment law and the possible role of international investment law within the bigger framework of international law. Di Benedetto, as will be better explained below, starts from the assumption that non-commercial concerns may be integrated into international investment law only if this area of law is not seen as an isolated self-contained regime but as a sub-system of international law to be integrated with all the other sub-systems.

Having assumed this perspective, "the book outlines a possible method for reconciling investor rights and environmental concerns, which is centred around the model of legal exception and highlights the role of legal principles" (p. x). By proposing a hermeneutical path that moves from internal to systemic arguments, the book finally tries to offer a unitary solution to the issue of integration of non-commercial values within international investment law by applying the model of legal exception, the paradigm of which is Article XX of the GATT.

The book is divided into two Parts, each of them composed of four Chapters. The first Part of the work (Chapters 1 to 4) is more general in its scope and is aimed at providing readers with the legal framework in which to place the subsequent discussion. The second Part of the book (Chapters 5 to 8) is more specific and analyses the various ways in which non-commercial concerns may be integrated within international investment law.

Chapter 1 is aimed at introducing the work and at providing the readers with the reasons why international investment law actors can no longer ignore environmental concerns. Indeed, historically, according to the author, enterprises have been "incentivized, through relaxed national rules, to move or establish production sectors abroad with the aim of reducing, *inter alia*, the costs involved in protecting the environment" (pp. 5-6). This has generated what Di Benedetto defines a "race to the bottom" (p. 8) as a result of the fact that States, willing to improve the commerce within their borders, have renounced the protection of their environment to some extent. States have let international law aimed at incentivising foreign investment prevail over national rules aimed at protecting the environment and, due to the circumstance that "local fears about pollution and nature degradation [...] are in practice rarely dealt with at an international level" (p. 6) this has generated a lack of protection for environmental concerns.

Chapter 2 sets forth the goal of the book. It explains that, within the framework of international law, a clash of values emerges: on the one side, the necessity to improve commerce and incentivise foreign investment by way of liberalising internal and international rules regarding the setting up of investments; on the other side, the necessity to avoid risks for human health (and the environment in general) created by conduct negatively affecting the environment. According to Di Benedetto, at the stage of negotiations of treaties for the promotion and protection of foreign investment, the balancing factor in this axiological contrast is the role of State sovereignty. If States are willing to attract more investments they could consider renouncing environmental protection and vice versa. However, once the treaty exists and a dispute arises, "the environmental aim of challenged measures may constitute a possible argument in the host [S]tate's defence in international investment arbitration. Most of the main principles of international investment law conceal potential contrasts or conflicts with the host State measures that are aimed at protecting fundamental interests such as human health and natural ecosystems" (p. 14). The question that Chapter 2 poses therefore, that is answered within the rest of the book, is whether – if a dispute on a State measure aimed at protecting the environment arises – the aim of the measure may play a role in avoiding (or at least mitigating) the State's responsibility. This question directly involves a need to search for the legal tools that may allow environmental concerns to play a role in international investment disputes.

Chapter 3 starts from the assumption that, in order for environmental concerns to be involved in international investment disputes, it is necessary to understand the relationships (if any) of international investment law within the bigger framework of public international law. According to Di Benedetto, at first glance, "[t]he concept of fragmentation is well suited to international investment law. The image which best synthesizes it is that of a patchwork, given its fragmentation into a multiplicity of autonomous legal instruments and, by the same token, the settlement of investment disputes by independent investment tribunals" (p. 22). However according to the author, with closer analysis, it is possible to understand that "this fragmented picture of investment treaty regimes could be overcome by following a systemic approach that looks at the overall experience of arbitral tribunals, or even at the unifying role of general international law" (p. 23). Di Benedetto carries out a careful analysis of scholarly opinion regarding the alleged orderliness of international investment law and its role within international law, i.e. those that consider international investment law as a self-contained regime and those that consider international investment law as a *de facto* multilateral sub-system of public international law. According to Di Benedetto the non-applicability of the notion of self-contained regime to international investment law is confirmed both by case law and scholarly opinion. It is indeed necessary to consider international investment law as a part of general international law that has developed its own principles; however, it is always necessary to avoid the "risk of conceiving international investment law as detached from the rest of international law" (p. 41), thus giving prevalence to an integrative approach within the various areas of public international law. Only this approach can allow arbitrators to give relevance to non-commercial concerns (and in particular environmental concerns) within international investment law.

Chapter 4, closing the first Part of the book, looks at the law applicable in international investment disputes. According to Di Benedetto, while "[t]he integration of values such as those concerning the environment and human health into international investment law by way of choosing the applicable law appears to be of limited feasibility because of the existing rules and practice governing investment treaty arbitration" (p. 54), non-commercial concerns might find a place in international investment disputes by way of interpretation of the applicable law. In this regard, arbitrators should find a balance between "the Scylla of a literal or teleological interpretation biased towards investors and the Charybdis of excessively systemic interpretations that lead to unrealistic legal arguments" (p. 54). In the author's view "the contextual and, above all, the teleological canon may, in several international legal contexts, support an interpretation of rules that allows for a consideration of concurring legal principles and current social beliefs that are not implied in the rationale of the applied rule" (p. 77). Furthermore, as will be seen when discussing Chapter 6, Di Benedetto strongly believes that the systemic interpretation set forth by Article 31(3)(c) of the 1969 Vienna Convention on the Law of Treaties (VCLT) may offer a valuable tool for integrating non-commercial concerns within international investment law.

Chapter 5, opening Part 2, looks at rules of international investment law and at the interpretative techniques that may be used in order to let arbitrators take non-commercial values into account when interpreting international investment law. In Di Benedetto's view, it is essential that arbitrators have somehow "acknowledged that these values have a direct relevance to the process of determining the meaning of applicable investment rules" (p. 85). The author analyses the various standards of treatment of foreign investments and, by analysing the case law in depth, strikes a balance between such standards and the necessity of protecting the environment. First of all Di Benedetto explains that if a violation of the most favoured nation or national treatment clauses is motivated by environmental concerns, this may be a basis for considering such a violation "unlike" a violation which is not aimed at protecting the environment. Secondly, he demonstrates that it is also possible to interpret the fair and equitable treatment standard, and in particular its sub-category of legitimate expectations, in order to take environmental concerns into account. Indeed, Di Benedetto puts forward the existence of an "evolutionary trend" in arbitral case law according to which the expectations of foreign investors would not be legitimate if they do not take the right of a State to regulate domestic matters in order to protect the environment into account (pp. 116-117). Finally, with regard to expropriation, after having recalled the differences between direct and indirect expropriation, the author endorses the approach of some tribunals which have acknowledged that there could be an exception to the rule which requires a State to pay compensation, in cases of measures tantamount to expropriation, if these measures do not have a discriminatory character, respect due process of law *and fulfil a public purpose* (p. 124 and ff.). Indeed, according to Di Benedetto, these tribunals have applied "the legal model of derogation, or exception. The justification of [S]tate measures by the tribunals does not actually rely on the explicit interpretation of one or other of the constituting elements of investment principles, but is affirmed in and of itself and results in the non-application of the abovementioned rule, when the elements for derogation [i.e. the presence of an environmental concern] established by the tribunals recur". (p. 125). In conclusion, the author sees "a degree of coherence among the vast majority of arguments" related to the integration of environmental concerns into international investment law "which add a justificatory element to the applicable rule and might be linked to the model of legal exception" (p. 132). This model is examined by the author in depth in Chapter 7.

Chapter 6 analyses the possible systemic approaches for addressing interactions and conflicts between foreign investor rights and environmental concerns. The first of them, in the author's opinion, could be offered by Article 31(3)(c) VCLT. In this regard, Di Benedetto states that "this canon requires the consideration of normative elements that are distinct from the applicable treaty in question and its context, and which belong to the body of international law" (pp. 135-136). In the author's view this rule might therefore allow for the consideration of values that are external to international investment law, such as environmental concerns. The author however shows his awareness of the fact that "[s]ystemic interpretation is not commonly used by investment tribunals to integrate external values into investment regimes" (p. 137). Furthermore, the author recognises another limit to the application of Article 31(3)(c), given the fact that this rule allows for systemic interpretation only in light of international rules applicable between the parties (in this regard, it is worth noting that customary international law does not involve rules on the protection of the environment). A second route for systemic integration of non-commercial values within international investment law is found by Di Benedetto in some modern treaties on the promotion and protection of foreign investments, which are not only guided by property and commercial purposes. The author shows, in this regard, that several recently drafted treaties (such as Canada, USA and Norway's Model BITs) involve environmental concerns in their preambles. The problem with this approach is that the majority of BITs still do not set forth any rule providing for environmental protection. The third, and in the author's view most important, approach to systemic integration of non-commercial values within international investment law may be provided by the assumption that "the entire body of the rules, principles and purposes of international law should be taken into account when interpreting regime rules" (p. 156). However, even in this regard, the author recognises that it would be "truly problematic to generalize this kind of interpretation into a formal systemic canon to interpret international (investment) rules" (p. 156).

Chapter 7 analyses the legal model of exception as a possible way to integrate non-commercial values into international investment law. According to Di Benedetto, the "idea that legal exceptions may connect autonomous systems of law is indeed appropriate" (p. 162) in order to integrate various areas of international law. After having analysed the concept of legal exception (i.e. a factor internal to a rule which identifies cases of both partial and complete non application of such rule) (p. 160), the author provides the readers with an analysis of the application of the legal model of exception both in general international law (e.g., in case of a state of necessity) and in WTO law (by analysing the rule of Article XX GATT in depth, which expressly recognises the protection of the environment as an exception to the other GATT rules). In Di Benedetto's opinion, this latter rule has inspired several other treaty provisions, including several provisions of international investment treaties (e.g., Article 17 of the 2009 ASEAN Comprehensive Investment Agreement, and Article 10.1 of the Canada Model BIT), which are strongly welcomed by the author. Furthermore, Di Benedetto finds the application of the legal model of exception also in certain investment arbitral awards, one of which (*S.D. Myers Inc. v. Canada*, UNCITRAL, Partial Award of 11 November 2000, par. 22) expressly recognises that a "[S]tate's right to protect the environment according to its own standards partly informs the core of sovereignty. Here, the tribunal affirms the [S]tate right to determine its own levels of environmental protection, which counters NAFTA economic obligations" (p. 194). This award is considered by Di Benedetto as the one which "to a certain extent opens and concludes the hermeneutical path proposed by this book, moving from internal to systemic arguments, and finally defines an exceptional model by offering a unitary solution to the integrative issue" (p. 196). In conclusion, the author states that "exceptions, in their various forms, may be a key legal tool to reconcile foreign investment rules and environmental concerns" (p. 208), even if he shows his awareness of the fact that "there is, however, a real difficulty in the transposition of general exceptions into investment regimes, which directly derives from the structural differences between the WTO legal system and international investment law" (p. 199).

Chapter 8, which concludes the work, gives an overview of the proposed solution and is aimed at providing the reader with a view of the concrete application of the proposed approach. The author explains that the issue of the integration of non-commercial values within international investment law is far from being settled but strongly argues that the model of exception is the approach that could actually foster the integration of these conflicting values. Di Benedetto argues that it is not possible to "categorically define the subset of situations that justify the non-application" of international investment law standards (p. 217). He therefore seems to endorse a case-by-case approach in which tribunals strike a balance between the conflicting values of investment protection (the rule) and the safeguard of the environment (the exception) and, on the basis of the concrete circumstances, lets the rule or the exception prevail.

From the perspective of international investment law scholarship, Di Benedetto's effort to try to integrate values not related to the promotion and protection of investments within the framework of international investment arbitration is laudable and really adds something to the debate. Furthermore, the author's opinion can be shared also from a substantive point of view, due to the fact that it has been scientifically established that the aforementioned "race to the bottom" is determining several problems both in relation to human health and to the environment in general.

However, the actual concern related to the integration of these values in international investment law is the fact that the existence, as well as the content, of general international law obligations related to the environment is far from being settled (CONFORTI, *Diritto internazionale*, 10th ed., Napoli, 2015, pp. 235-243). As a consequence, it is not easy for a State to argue, in investment disputes, that, when it negotiated a treaty for the promotion and protection of investments, it was not aware of the necessity to balance such promotion and protection with the necessity to expressly provide for clauses aimed at ensuring the protection of its environment. Moreover, as of today, the case law is too limited to understand whether environmental concerns (and non-commercial values in general) will find a place in the interpretative processes of arbitral tribunals, notably by means of a broad systemic interpretation such as the one endorsed by the author. Similarly, the case law is not yet sufficient to easily affirm that concepts born in WTO law, such as the model of legal exceptions and the concept of "likeness", can be easily applied in international investment law. Di Benedetto, however, appears perfectly conscious of these circumstances.

A final remark is related to the circumstance that the book is limited to the analysis of arguments arising either in international investment law or, more generally, in public international law. What the book does not consider is that today many BITs set forth that foreign investments shall comply with the law of the host State (see KNAHR, "Investment 'in accordance with host State law'", Transnational Dispute Management, 2007, pp. 1-28; and MOLOO AND KHACHATURIAN, "The Compliance with the Law Requirement in International Investment Law", Fordham International Investment Law Journal, 2011, pp. 1473-1501). On the basis of this assumption, it could be said that, when the investment must comply with the host State's law, it should comply also with national regulations on the protection of the environment (and of other non-commercial values). This circumstance could let national law play a major role in investment arbitration and could improve the level of environmental protection and protect it from the phenomenon of the "race to the bottom".

In conclusion, despite these minor remarks, the book under review merits praise, because it draws necessary attention to an important issue of international investment law. Indeed, this book could, *de jure condendo*, play a significant role in giving future tribunals a theoretical framework for integrating non-commercial values into international investment law.

GIOVANNI ZARRA*

* J.D., University of Napoli "Federico II"; LL.M., Queen Mary University of London; Ph.D., University of Napoli "Federico II".

INDEX*

---

* This Index has been compiled by Daniele Amoroso. The most significant judicial cases and legal instruments cited throughout the volume have also been included.

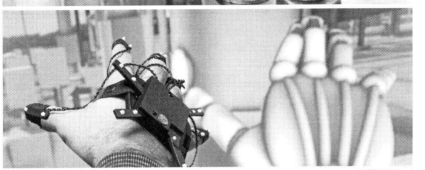

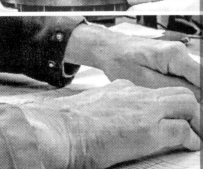

Printed in the United States
By Bookmasters